D1344241

*Jim Murray's*

# WHISKY BIBLE
## 2007

**This 2007 edition of Jim Murray's Whisky Bible is dedicated to
Mike and Barbara Smith whose friendship,
kindness and support has made so much possible. Thank you.**

This edition published 2006

10 9 8 7 6 5 4 3 2 1

The "Jim Murray's" logo and the "Whisky Bible" logo are trade marks of Jim Murray
and are used under licence.

A CIP catalogue record for this book is available from the British Library

ISBN 10: 1-84442-147-3
ISBN 13: 978-1-84442-147-3

Printed in England

Written and Edited by: Jim Murray
Design: Jim Murray, Darren Jordan
Maps: James Murray
Production team: James Murray, Dani Dal Molin, Mike Leaman, Howard Buchanan
Sample Research: Dani Dal Molin, David Rankin, Edna Mycawka

**Author's Note**
I have used the spelling "whiskey" or "whisky" depending on how the individual
distillers prefer. All Scotch is "whisky". So is Canadian. All Irish, these days, is
"whiskey", though that was not always the case. In Kentucky, bourbon and rye
are spelt "whiskey", with the exception of the produce of the early Times/Old
Forester Distillery and Maker's Mark which they bottle as "whisky". In Tennessee,
it is a 50-50 split: Dickel is "whisky", while Daniel's is "whiskey".

# Jim Murray's

# WHISKY BIBLE
## 2007

*The world's leading whisky guide from
the world's foremost whisky authority*

**CARLTON**
**BOOKS**

# Contents

# Introduction

**W**ell, this Bible is nothing if not up-to-date. Usually, I am sitting shirt-sleeved on the veranda of the cricket pavilion in my beloved Ockley in Surrey, the sun setting towards Godalming, plunging nearby Leith Hill into a purple-hued twilight. Or I am in the leafy haven of Borat's Glade with the summer sun lazering a path through the Sycamore and Elderflower trees to try and disrupt the clarity of my laptop. Wherever I am, it is high summer and I am constructing the Introduction to my latest Whisky Bible, another 750 or so new whiskies and whiskeys tasted and another best-selling book about to be put to bed. A glass of the JMWB Whisky of the Year is close to hand.

As I write the Introduction for the 2007 edition I sit in my tasting lab, more or less my home, day and night, for the last six months. Outside chill winds hurl wintery rains into brick and wood and although it has just gone nine in the morning, light has been with us for less than two hours. Because it is mid-November and tomorrow, hopefully, Jim Murray's Whisky Bible 2007 will at last be printed for the Christmas rush. No exotic printing locations this time of Singapore, Peru or Italy. Just good old Northamptonshire in England to save time. But being a bit – well, a lot – later it means that scores, possibly hundreds, of extra whiskies have been included: late bottlings that normally would miss the deadline. So there are well over 1,000 whiskies fresh to market included in this 2007 Bible, plus nearly 300 re-tastes. Even stripping the book of obsolete bottlings, that takes the number of whiskies included this year to a staggering 3,600, requiring an extra 24 pages to accommodate them. And still no extra cost to the cover price.

But why so late? I hear you chorus. Unfortunately, some non-stop travelling early in the year meant I was perhaps overly susceptible to picking up the odd germ or a million on planes. And, on cue, I went down with a chest infection. Now, for a whisky writer, there's not much worse than a chest infection, other than maybe two chest infections. And that is exactly what I got. One a few weeks after the other. Knocking me out for about six weeks in total. And no matter how good your nose and palate may be, that's a bit of an unequal struggle. Now, I suppose I could have bluffed it. Just written the tasting notes on memory and instinct alone. But that is not how I work. I tell it as I find. And if I can't find it, then I don't tell it. That was not all. Weaks later I came home from Chicago to find someone standing in my living room at 2am helping himself to my property. Police retrieved one of my computers - mangled, sadly - and the other has never been found. That didn't exactly speed things up, either.

But there was some good news to this adventure. While in San Francisco an horticulturalist and reader of my books, a Dr Neal De Vos, very kindly presented to me a sealed bottle of 8-y-o Old Overholt rye...the real McCoy distilled in Pennsylvania. It was a magnificent gesture. Sadly, before I had the chance to taste it, it vanished along with my computers, complete with Dr De Vos' card. A couple of months back the police returned the rye to me, too...intact. And when the 2007 Bible is finally printed I shall crack it open after its 60-year wait and toast the success of the fastest selling whisky book in the world. And the kindness of Dr De Vos, of course. So enjoy the world's whiskies...and this Bible.

Jim Murray
The Tasting Room
Wellingborough (November 2006)

# How to Read
# The Bible

**T**he whole point of this book is for the whisky lover – be he or she an experienced connoisseur or, better fun still, simply starting out on the long and joyous path of discovery – to have ready access to easy-to-understand information about as many whiskies is possible. And I mean a lot. Thousands.

This book does not quite include every whisky on the market ... just by far and away the vast majority. And those that have been missed this time round – either through accident, logistics or design – will appear in later editions once we can source a sample.

## Whisky Scoring

The marking for this book is tailored to the consumer and scores run out just a little higher than I use for my own personal references. But such is the way it has been devised it has not affected my order of preference.

Each whisky is given a rating out of 100. Twenty-five marks are given to each of four factors: nose (**n**), taste (**t**), finish (**f**), balance and overall complexity (**b**). That means that 50% of the marks are given for flavour alone and 25% for the nose, often an overlooked part of the whisky equation. The area of balance and complexity covers all three previous factors and a usually hidden one besides:

**Nose:** this is simply the aroma. Often requires more than one inspection as hidden aromas can sometimes reveal themselves after time in the glass and increased contact with air. The nose very often tells much about a whisky, but – as we shall see – equally can be quite misleading.

**Taste:** this is the immediate arrival on the palate and involves the flavour profile up to, and including, the time it reaches maximum intensity and complexity.

**Finish:** often the least understood part of a tasting. This is the tail and flourish of the whisky's signature, often revealing the effects of ageing. The better whiskies tend to finish well and longer without too much oak excess.

**Balance:** This is the part it takes a little experience to appreciate but it can be mastered by anyone. For a whisky to work well on the nose and palate, it should not be too one-sided in its character. If you are looking for an older whisky, it should have evidence of oak, but not so much that all other flavours and aromas are drowned out. Likewise, a whisky matured or finished in a sherry butt must offer a lot more than just wine alone and the greatest Islay malts, for instance, revel in depth and complexity beyond the smoky effects of peat.

Each whisky has been analysed by me without adding water or ice. I have taken each whisky as it was poured from the bottle and used no more than warming in an identical glass to extract and discover the character of the whisky. To have added water would have been pointless: it would have been an inconsistent factor as people, when pouring water, add different amounts at varying temperatures. The only constant with the whisky you and I taste will be when it has been poured directly from the bottle.

Even if you and I taste the same whiskies at the same temperature and from identical glasses – and even share the same values in whisky – our scores may still be different. Because a factor that is built into my evaluation is drawn from expectation and experience. When I sample a whisky from a certain distillery at such-and-such an age or from this type of barrel or that, I would expect it to offer me certain qualities. It has taken me 30 years to acquire this knowledge (which I try to add to day by day!) and an enthusiast cannot be expected to learn it overnight. But, hopefully, Jim Murray's Whisky Bible will help...!

### Score chart
Within the parentheses () is the overall score out of 100.
**0–50** Nothing short of absolutely diabolical.
**51–64** Nasty and well worth avoiding.
**65–69** Very unimpressive indeed.
**70–74** Usually drinkable but don't expect the earth to move.
**75–79** Average and usually pleasant though sometimes flawed.
**80–84** Good whisky worth trying.
**85–89** Very good to excellent whiskies definitely worth buying.
**90–93** Brilliant.
**94–97** Superstar whiskies that give us all a reason to live.
**98–100** Better than anything I've ever tasted!

### Key to Abbreviations & Symbols
**%** Percentage strength of whisky measured as alcohol by volume. **b** Overall balance and complexity. **bott** Date of bottling. **db** Distillery bottling. In other words, an expression brought out by the owners of the distillery. **dist** Date of distillation or spirit first put into cask. **f** Finish. **n** Nose. **nc** Non-coloured. **ncf** Non-chill-filtered. **sc** Single cask. **t** Taste. ❊ New entry for 2007. ⊙ Retasted – no change. ⊙⊙ Retasted and re-evaluated.

### Finding Your Whisky
**Worldwide Malts:** Whiskies are listed alphabetically throughout the book. In the case of single malts, the distilleries run A–Z style with distillery bottlings appearing at the top of the list in order of age, starting with youngest first. After age comes vintage. After all the "official" distillery bottlings are listed, next come other bottlings, again in alphabetical order. Single malts without a distillery named (or perhaps named after a dead one) are given their own section, as are vatted malts.
**Worldwide Blends:** These are simply listed alphabetically, irrespective of which company produce them. So "Black Bottle" appears ahead of "White Horse" and Japanese blends begin with "Amber" and ends with "Za". In the case of brands being named after companies or individuals the first letter of the brand will dictate where it is listed. So William Grant, for instance, will be found under "W" for William rather "G" for Grant.
**Bourbon/Rye:** One of the most confusing types of whiskey to list because often the name of the brand bears no relation to the name of the distillery that made it. Also, brands may be sold from one company to another, or shortfalls in stock may see companies buying bourbons from another. For that reason all the brands have been listed alphabetically with the name of the bottling distiller being added at the end.
**Irish Whiskey:** There are four types of Irish whiskey: (i) pure pot still; (ii) single malt, (iii) single grain and (iv) blended. Some whiskies may have "pure pot still" on the label, but are actually single malts. So check both sections.
### Bottle Information
As no labels are included in this book I have tried to include all the relevant information you will find on the label to make identification of the brand straightforward. Where known I have included date of distillation and bottling. Also the cask number for further recognition. At the end of the tasting notes I have included the strength and, if known, number of bottles (sometimes abbreviated to btls) released and in which markets.

# Bible Thumping
# Who Can Bear a
# Wounded Spirit?

**I**had so hoped it would never come to this. But malt whisky – Scotch in
particular – will soon be coming face to face with the White Stilton
Question.

Not many people are aware of the White Stilton Question. Not least
because few know what real White Stilton actually is. Blue Stilton: now
that's another matter. That mouldy old green'n'cream cheese is a world-
renowned delicacy. And rightly so.

But go into the average Cheese Shop anywhere in Britain, ask for a White Stilton
and there is a 99.9% chance of a Monty Python moment. "Not today, governor." Or
"Sorry, fresh out of it." And a gentle enquiry as to when some might arrive will be
met with pursed lips, a furrowed brow and "Well, not this week. Or probably
month. Year, even. Not much demand for it 'round 'ere. Tell you what, though, I can
get you a nice bit of White Stilton and Apricot. Or Walnut. Nice texture, White Stilton
and Walnut. Apricot's a bit sweeter, though."

These were depressing conversations. To the extent that I have long given up in
my quest for unmolested White Stilton and now buy it only in a wonderful, tucked-
away Cheese Shop in Melton Mowbray, the quaint market town in Leicestershire
where this most shy and misunderstood of cheeses is made.

Very interesting. But what the hell has all this to do with whisky, you might
understandably be thinking. Well, it's this. I was in a whisky shop (surprise,
surprise) a few months back and a guy – admitting he was a bit of a whisky
novice - came in asking for the malt from a particular distillery. He was offered two
choices and each had been finished in some exotic cask or other. He bought one
and left the shop apparently happy and excited with his purchase. However, I
knew the bottling. It wasn't exactly good. And, of course, I knew the distillery, which
was a particularly fine if little-known one. And I felt sad that this chap would be
getting an entirely false impression of what the distillery was all about. Melton
Mowbray and its beautifully crumbly, mildly salty, astonishingly delicate and brain-
explodingly complex white cheese came swiftly to mind. This guy had been
palmed off with apricots and walnuts and he was missing out on the real deal.

So I cannot tell a lie and say that my heart didn't sink from time to time whilst
tasting for the 2007 edition of Jim Murray's Whisky Bible. Because of the 1,000 new
whiskies fresh to market, some 100 of them were cask finishes of one sort or
another. Which may not sound like much, but, when you throw in the hype factor
often surrounding them, it offers a distorted picture of a nation's whisky.

I can take you to the moment it all started. It was back in 1994 that I penned a
world exclusive about Glenmorangie developing and launching their Port Wood
finish for my Sunday Telegraph drinks slot. I loved it and predicted success. I had
also guessed that there would be copycat bottlings but I cannot remember
thinking it would reach today's astonishing and alarming levels.

As it happens, Glenmorangie didn't invent the category. That honour fell some
years before to J&B. They owned a new distillery called Auchroisk and when their
first distillates had matured through sufficiently, wanted to market it as a single

malt – The Singleton. However, J&B's then long-serving and highly respected blender, Jim Milne, spotted a problem as the spirit matured: it wasn't all that good as a straight malt. Fine for blending, but far too light to hold any great presence in a whisky glass. A sign that things were not quite as they should be was when the oak from the bourbon casks began dominating at a relatively young age. So Jim fell back on the old trick of rounding the malt off in sherry for some months to paper over the cracks. By no means the first blender to do this, but The Singleton of Auchroisk was the first to make a virtue of it on their label and extensive marketing.

However, Glenmorangie was the first, using Port and then Madeira, actually to set out a programme of producing, for marketing purposes, specific cask finishes. The rest, as they say, is history. Or rather it isn't. It is very much the present which, frankly, worries me.

In the early days I embraced all new bottlings, good or bad. My reasoning was that it was great for whisky drinkers to have choice. And the opportunity to learn more about whisky; plus, in the case of 'Morangie, there was always the standard 10-year-old to fall back on as the benchmark. A part of me still feels that to be true.

But as independents and the big boys alike started wading into the category it wasn't long before the novelty wore off, especially after some were distinctly lacking in grace, balance and – for one blend finished in an Islay cask – logic or common sense. One of the big problems with cask finishes is that you never know if spirit and cask have reached peak harmony. Or even if they are able to reach any form of balance and harmonisation at all. This is simply because each cask is different and there is insufficient data and experience to know what will happen next. Put a malt in a second fill bourbon barrel and, depending which part of the warehouse it will live in, you can pretty much plot its course in advance. Not so individual cask finishes, and the number of scrambled, imbalanced malts I have found on whisky shelves was beginning to ring alarm bells.

Those bells are still ringing. Louder than ever. And not least because of the White Stilton Question. Years ago there were only two types of Stilton: Blue and White. But supermarkets initially turned their backs on White Stilton, preferring to stock better known British crumbly whites such as Wensleydale, Cheshire and Caerphilly. To fight back, the Stilton industry started producing what, ironically, they call "blends". It was – and they would probably be the first to admit - purely an exercise in cosmetics. They wanted the product to look good and sound sexy. So now, as well as the ubiquitous White Stilton and Apricot, you can also get it with Strawberry and Peach, Raspberry, Blueberry, Ginger, Mango and Ginger, Lemon, Pear and Apple, Tropical Fruit, Fruit Mix and even Pear and Caramel. The result is that for every slice of traditional White Stilton sold, five slices of blended cross the counter. And a nation imperceptibly loses sight of one of its great traditions.

Although travelling the globe for half the year, visiting some of the finest restaurants and trying almost every delicacy known to man, if I could take someone anywhere in the world for a great meal, it would be to Melton Mowbray. There I would sit them down to slice open a one pound pork pie made in Nottingham Street at Dickinson and Morris (not at their satellite factory near Leicester), accompanied by a Long Clawson Dairy White Stilton, moist and fresh and devoid of any mould aroma....or bloody apricot. All washed down with a pint of stupendously traditional 3.6% Cooking Bitter from the Grainstore Brewery in nearby Oakham. That, ladies and gentleman, is, in traditional culinary terms and in my most humble opinion, about as good as it gets. But how many people from these fair isles would be able to argue for or against that proposition? Fewer and fewer every year.

And aren't these cask finishes also often a matter of cosmetics, born out of a company's fear that its cask will just be one of many fighting the same battleground? So, to sex it up, a pretty French or mysterious Hungarian name can be splattered all over the label? Irrespective of what happens to the quality of the whisky? Perhaps not always so, but I'll take some convincing that this isn't more than occasionally the case.

Doubtless, there are those also who are doing this out of fun. To see what they can conjure up. It is part of man's nature and spirit to test boundaries. But why bottle it if the end product is inferior? Or riddled and ruined with sulphur, as so often seems to be the case when Spanish and French wines are involved? How many priceless malts from lost distilleries have I tasted over the years wrecked by the injudicious finishing in casks that should never be let anywhere near a whisky warehouse? Too many, that's how many.

It would be irresponsible to dismiss all finishes out of hand. Some can even be exceptional. Whiskies matured or carefully finished in rum casks certainly have a tendency to thrive; and oak-infused drams like the extraordinary Glenmorangie Truffle Oak, Famous Grouse Scottish oak, and the now bizarrely outlawed Compass Box Spice Tree, underline that grain and oak tend to be the best mix of all.

Meanwhile, wine-influenced malts like Penderyn, because of their lightness of body, have the ability to blossom in a controlled Madeira environment. But there the Madeira has been built into the maturation process to form the house style because balance has been enhanced rather than compromised. That was the result of research and knowledge. Not hit- and- hope and the promise of a fancy label. Some independents, like Murray McDavid, have – surprisingly – gone into Finishing overdrive. And though a number of their bottlings don't come even close to working, others, like their Macallan Sauternes finish, give even the most experienced of whisky tasters one of the most joyful rides on the palate ever.

So I am not calling for a blanket ban on cask finishing. But, certainly, it would be the balm of hurt minds if companies showed greater bravery in discrimination. A fearless adage must be adopted: if it doesn't work, don't bottle it. It's an expensive route to take, but one that will work in favour of both the bottler and distillery.

Instead, surely, greater effort ought to be made to extract the best out of the cask by showing whisky lovers just what the distillery is capable of. With distillers, that means spending greater time selecting and vatting casks to create a specific style from that distillery. I did that, for instance, in the early days of the Knappogue Castle brands by selecting various weeks' distillations from Cooley and then vatting the differing styles together to create the desired effect. When production shifted to Bushmills, where there was negligible difference in the weekly distillates, I selected types of bourbon cask (either first, second or third fill) and played about with the percentages until I again came up with a recipe which spelled elegance. It takes time and hard work. But, then, has there ever been any other way of producing excellent whisky?

The independents will rightly say they can't do that as they don't have sufficient stocks. Or manpower. But rather than tipping a decent cask into a wine one for something different, they should either leave alone or conduct experiments to vat it with a cask from one or more other distilleries to produce vattings of unique textures and taste. Another superb way for whisky lovers to learn about the ways malt interact. And for independents to avoid the sulphur trap.

In the meantime, help yourself to malts finished in, amongst others, Bordeaux, Rousanne, Syrah, Medoc, Cru Bourgogne, Muscatel, Manzanilla, Calvados, Grenache, White Rioja, the appalling Tokay, Armagnac and Uncle Tom Cobley. One bottler proudly told me that when the cask was filled, there was still a little wine sloshing around the bottom. Great.

But, as I pointed out in my tasting notes on one particular finish, how would a wine lover like it if I poured a dollop of Highland Park into their bottle of 1970 Chateau Latour? Might then not quite be the Latour he wanted or loved. But never mind: it'd go well with the White Stilton and Apricot...

# Review of the Whisky Year

**Z**zzzzzz....what? Was that it? Is that another whisky year gone? No major takeovers? No multi-billion-pound deals with one enormous company swallowing another whole and spitting out the bits....?

Thank the Friar John Corr for that, then...

What the industry needs right now is a bit of stability. Executives having the confidence to get on with their job; distillery managers remembering what their head office telephone number is. We need a year or two of quiet. In the boardrooms, anyway. And, well, maybe not too quiet. After all, it's the small changes that can make whisky so fascinating. And there have been some small changes over the last year: mainly aftershocks following the massive quake caused by Pernod's absorption of Allied just prior my writing of the review for the 2006 edition of Jim Murray's Whisky Bible. And some of these small aftershocks have been, well, errr...large.

Like, for instance, Jim Beam getting government regulatory approval to take on a third working Kentucky distillery, **Maker's Mark** in Loretto no less. And confirming the purchase of probably one of the world's top three most under-rated distilleries, **Ardmore** in Scotland, the key malt to their newly acquired Teacher's blend, both deals setting the seal on the entire $5.2 billion investment parent company Fortune Brands made into Allied's goodies.

And like the sale of **Glen Grant**. A beautiful Speysider – equally in the glass and to visit - making a quite unique style of flinty malt which works a treat both as a singleton and blend. Pernod was duty-bound to offload it on account of its strength on the export markets. So as it excels in Italy in particular – as a five-year-old – little surprise it was Milan-based Campari who splashed the cash just a few days before Christmas. In this case the little matter of 115 million Euros (£77 million) bringing with it, for a further 15 million Euros, two established blends, including **Old Smuggler**.

One of my own personal highlights of the year was when I drove, out of curiosity, into the distillery's car park on a bleak Speyside winter's day just to find out how things were going a few months after the deal had been completed... and saw Dennis Malcolm stepping out of the manager's door. Nearly two decades had passed since I first met Dennis standing by that very same door. Hand outstretched, he announced: "Great timing, Jim. This is my first day back!" This was a shock, not least because I thought he was still manager of **Balmenach**. But his garden still backed on to Glen Grant, most of his windows still looked directly down onto the granite-clad, turreted distillery and neither his heart nor soul had ever really left the place. Enjoying the first dram with him by the old safe since the days when there was barely a single grey hair in my beard was truly touching. Passing time may have diminished us both slightly physically, but it was quickly apparent that his passion and enthusiasm remained unquenched. For a couple of hours everything seemed right with the whisky world. And moments like that are special. Especially when so much experience and talent has leaked out of the industry in recent years.

And on the subject of crashing into old friends, what a delight to see former **Laphroaig** distillery manager Iain Henderson the other day. After a short spell at **Edradour** he has decided to make his swansong at England's first purpose-built whisky distillery for over a century, **St George's** near Thetford in Norfolk. Now this is a useful distillery for me, being just 85 miles away – an hour and a half by road –

rather than the normal 500 or 5,000 or 12,000 miles I normally traverse to see a pot still hiss. And being in the relative flatlands of Norfolk, it is not exactly the first location that would have sprung to mind to plant a malt distillery. But I have to say the setting is near perfect. A railway line with crossing is nearby and closer still what looks like an old mill. It's all beautifully backwater. The lands attached to the distillery are extensive and lead to the ambling river Thet. The area is soft and pleasing on the eye; the distillery, a hybrid of a kind of Elizabethan E-shape and Romano-British manor, is no less sympathetic and will look better still when the pagoda is placed slap bang in the middle of it all.

As it is, the two brand new Forsyth pot stills – both to a **Macallan** design but the tiny size of **Edradour's** – as well as the mashtun and three small stainless steel fermenting vessels are all in place. I can't deny it was a thrill to be told I was the first outsider to see the plant up and about to run: mashing was beginning the following week, using local Norfolk barley. The speed in which the whole place has taken shape has been mind-blowing. Usually I check on the progress of distilleries in terms of half-yearly calls. Here from planning permission to distilling has taken ten months. It has helped that the people behind the Norfolk Whisky Co are a father and son team, James and Andrew Nelstrop, who have funded the million pound project privately. It is also useful that Andrew happens to be a builder. So, considering planning was not granted by a bemused local council until January 2006 and it was November 11th (eight days before the first spirit ran) when Iain and Andrew showed me round, this has to be the fastest bit of distillery building to this scale – possibly anywhere in the world – since Victorian times. And we could be in for some fun times. Andrew is aware there is another **St George** distillery – in California. "We are not going to call our whisky St George's," he assures me. "We are just going to call it English. English Whisky. That way people will ask for an English the same way they'll ask for a Scotch." I'd like to see how the Trademark people view that one...

But St. George's is not the only addition to the world's whisky distilling firmament. Since July 2006 South Africa has boasted a second malt whisky distillery, the latest being in Silverton, Pretoria, at Moritz **Kallmeyer's** Drayman's Brewery. Moritz is calling his malt a Scotch style, though until the spirit is ready in three years time he won't know if he is nearer some European types. And although, with genuine deference, he humbly says he won't be able to match the quality of a typical malt found in Scotland, I think when I pop in to see him, hopefully during 2007, I might bring with me some **Swissky** from Switzerland and **McCarthy's** from Oregon, USA, to show that, if you put your mind to it, you can often make something even better....

With China heading towards a top ten nation in whisky consumption, no surprises to hear that Taiwan has entered the list of whisky distilling islands with a plant at **Yuan-shan** in I-Lan county. Taiwan is on my programme of tasting venues during 2007, so that's something I'll check out and report on later. Meanwhile, on sleepy and beautiful Victoria Island, British Columbia, Canada, the race is on to make the first regular malt whisky in BC since **Okanagen** fell silent. Wine maker Ken Winchester has his German pot still in place at his Winchester Cellars winery – soon to be distillery – at Saamich on the outskirts of Victoria. And is almost certain to pip to the post Andrew Currie's Shelter Point project, which has its distilling licence but may not be up and running until Spring 2007 at the earliest. Ken is on course to distil for the first time in January 2007 and hopefully I'll be able to report on the website (yes, really!!) – and in next year's edition – the new make's character as I'll be visiting him just a few days later. The beer will be made at one of the micro breweries in town. And the still, he tells me, will also from time to time be producing a grappa to use up the 30 tons of waste from his winery and pay off the investment in the equipment. While in Victoria I'll also be fully investigating the rumour that one of the genuinely decent guys of whisky, Andrew Currie, is officially re-naming himself Andrew Currie the Second after also seeing his advanced plan of opening the first purpose-built whisky distillery in England scuppered in improbable time and so comprehensively by the Norfolk Whisky Co.

The Lowlands of Scotland now boast four working distilleries (along with Bladnoch, Auchentoshan and Glenkinchie) thanks to the opening of the charming and most traditional of farmhouse distilleries: Daftmill. Brothers Ian and Francis Cuthbert set in motion the building of the distillery near Auchermuchty in Fife back in 2003, but it was in December 2005 that malt spirit was produced for the first time. So far 77 bourbon barrels of unpeated malt have been filled with a target to reach 100 by the year's end; and a programme to fill 150 more casks during 2007 as well as take on full time distilling staff. And whilst in the Lowlands, the internal industry rumour mill has been grinding out stories of Bladnoch being for sale. It is owned by another pair of brothers, Northern Irish property developers Raymond and Colin Armstrong, although it has been Raymond who has had the hands-on passion to get distilling back to at least a cottage industry size in order to satisfy the 25,000 tourists who visit each year. With Raymond approaching his 60s and looking for later security he is planning on exchanging land in Northern Ireland for his brother's shares in the distillery. Raymond Armstrong's fondness for the distillery has not waned since he took it off Diageo's hands after they closed it in 1993 and has enjoyed running it as what even he admits is a "hobby", bringing back production in January 2000. But while not actively seeking a buyer, and keen to develop the distillery from a part-time to a full time operational one, he has also admitted to me that if anyone comes in with a bid in excess of £3 million, he will have to listen. Interesting. Even more interesting is a covenant, if I remember correctly, that he cannot distil above a certain amount. With the way things are in Scotland it may be a clause Diageo may be relieved to turn a very blind eye to, or even ditch.

Because there is a bit of a whisky shortage around the world. We know all about the bourbon and rye problems. But it is Scotland where things have taken on a quite dramatic turn with the big players now holding back younger whiskies that once they would have released onto the open market. The reason is China. Diageo are miffed that they are playing second fiddle there to Pernod and want to change that. Pernod want things to remain the same. So as both gear up for a major assault, stocks are being kept to feed the anticipated growth. The losers are the Europeans in particular – including Britain – used to seeing ultra cheap own label brands of reasonable quality in supermarkets. I have already detected at least one brand dropping in quality markedly: a coincidence? This is also likely to have a knock-on effect with independent bottlers further down the line. For the small, independent distiller times have rarely looked so good.

Especially new distilleries who offer something different. And in the last year we have seen two very different types of whisky hit the shelves for the first time. The most significant in Europe, is Mackmyra – one of the most magical distilleries I have ever visited – which has unleashed Swedish whisky to the world, the third of its three bottlings picking up my European Mainland Whisky of the Year Award. And there is now, in additon, a Colorado malt whiskey. Made in Denver, like Mackmyra it is released young and no less big, using virgin oak. And, like Mackmyra, it has a tendency to sell out a matter of weeks after being released. What they also have in common is that their whiskies, while high class, don't have anything similar in style by comparison. So 2006 was a classic year for broadening whisky's spectrum.

So, it's been good news all the way. Well, not quite. Whisky shortage or no, the world's biggest whisky (or at least alcohol) distillery, the Pernod Ricard Seagram Distillery in Lawrenceburg, Indiana, has been told that its days are numbered. Initially there was hope and joy when Pernod took over the plant and quickly set up a new line of fruit-flavoured Martinis. But not now. Its eventual closure will mean that (with distilling in Georgia also gone) bourbon for the first time since the days when it was first invented or discovered, depending on your point of view, is now made exclusively in Kentucky. Genuinely sad news, this. Because although Lawrenceburg wasn't exactly the most beautiful plant I have spent time at, it certainly made extremely high grade bourbon and rye (considerably better, I thought, than its former sister distillery, **Four Roses**) and I will be gathering up as many bottles of Cougar as I can get my hands on.

Also we have said goodbye to Stuart Thompson's tenure as **Ardbeg** distillery manager, where he made many friends. And another island distillery manager who will be parting shortly is **Isle of Arran's** Gordon Mitchell. Gordon had been at the distillery since it was no more than mud and blueprints and recently saw his spirit mature into a graceful and top-ranking 10-year-old. Job brilliantly done, he is making way but will stay on until his successor is firmly established. Gordon and I spent many happy hours together at Arran, most of them during historic moments concerning the distillery. But perhaps my abiding memory will be the look on his face as he sat next to me at Wembley Stadium when Paul Gascoigne scored his wonder goal against his beloved Scotland in the 1996 European Championships. Priceless.

And did I say there had been no take-overs? Well, not exactly true. Inver House, whose gems include **Knockdhu** (aka **An Cnoc**), **Balblair** and **Pulteney** are in new hands. But the owners remain in Thailand with Pacific Spirits being bought out by the much larger Thai Beverages. So no discernable change, except a gateway into larger markets. Also, **Whyte and Mackay** is again the centre of speculation regarding a takeover. This time the party showing keen interest is the giant Indian concern, United Breweries. United, although having last year bought out rivals Shaw Wallace, still found their hunger for growth less than assuaged and turned their attention to Scotland. The figure discussed is £400 million and one Indian paper actually printed a story saying the sale had gone through — much to the consternation and bemusement of the Whyte and Mackay board. They privately feel their company is worth something nearer 50% more. So no deal. Yet....

Heavy stuff. So back to the good news. Apparently, drinking whisky is as good for your health as red wine. We'll, we all knew that. Except this time it was announced to the public by whisky consultant Dr Jim Swan (no, not a medical doc) during a conference on biochemistry where he told delighted (and probably a few relieved) delegates that there is a greater amount of the cancer preventative antioxidant ellagic acid in a glass of single malt than there is in a similar measure of red wine. Typically, some bod from a cancer organisation pooh-poohed Dr Swan's helpful information and suggested people instead turned their attention to fruit, which has greater levels of this antioxidant than both wine and whisky. Well, being someone who has spent more hours than I should admit nosing and tasting every type of fruit known to man in the interests of whisky research, I can assure this person that malt is far more of a fun option to stay healthy. But, just to be on the on the safe side, I'll continue to drink both red wine and whisky. And up my morning melon intake.

Now, has anyone found themselves getting high on **Highland Park** lately? No? Well, you might in future. Because the **Orkney** distillery has had their livery painted all over the aircraft flown by Loganair, the airline which operates flights to and from the islands making this almost certainly the first whisky brand to reach for the skies in such a way. The question now is: will sales really begin to take off?

And finally...is your name Robbo? Then maybe fame, though probably not fortune, could await you. During 2006 Edrington's esoteric (and I have to say pretty good) small batch brand, **Jon Mark and Robbo** became Robbo-less. The three mentioned and displayed to the world in cartoon form are employees of Edrington. Or should I say, in one case, were. Because Robbo, in real life former Macallan man David Robertson, has left Edrington ("looking for a fresh challenge," as he put it to me) to join Whyte and Mackay. It's rare enough to find a Scotch whisky with the name of a company employee all over it. Rarer still when that employee actually works for a rival. So it will be interesting to see how Edrington tackle this tricky one. I have no idea if they really are looking for another Robbo. Unlikely, I suppose. Perhaps one option is to re-name the brand Jon, Mark...and Matthew. Or Luke. How can it then fail not to get a good rating in the Bible...?

# Jim Murray's Whisky Bible Award Winners 2007

**N**ow that was tough.

**It's OK you lot saying: "Wow, drinking over a 1,000 whiskies in a few months. Hard work, but someone's got to do it." Well, you're not wrong. And when you have to pick the very best out of the very best of the new bottlings and measure them against the old ones, then, believe me, the brain cells take as much a battering as the tastebuds.**

Especially when, like this year, it has easily been the best crop of whiskies I've ever inspected. And many of the re-tastes had moved on significantly from their last inspection. Which is why perhaps, for the first time, Scotch has triumphed over bourbon. For the last three years George T Stagg has laid siege to Jim Murray Whisky Bible's Whisky of the Year Award. Now its vice-like grip has been loosened. In fact, despite an astonishing second bottling, it didn't even get best bourbon, being narrowly pipped by its stablemate, the boundary-pushing and quite stunning Buffalo Trace Twice Barrelled. But carrying off the Award, and with it my heart, was Old Parr Superior 18 Years Old, which, like the great old man, just seems to get better year on year.

Curiously, of the five whiskies short-listed and re-tasted against each other as potential winners, two didn't get any kind of award, so high has the calibre been, so close the scoring. Missing out was the Stagg. And the honey-jewelled Johnnie Walker Gold Label, which came in a short distance behind the earthier Old Parr Superior. This, in turn, had to see off the Buffalo Trace and the sublime Brora 30.

Now, I know that The Award will put a cat amongst the pigeons. I mean, it's just not the done thing, is it? Giving a mere blend an award higher than a single malt. But I have always argued that a blended whisky should, by its very nature, offer a more complex and more beautifully defined dram. And here is one that has. Not only that, but actually displaying some of the elements being found in all the other whiskies vying for the highest honour.

The awards decision-making process took ten days of re-tasting, on top of tasting all the whiskies for the Bible over six months. Yet by the end of that process I have no doubts whatsoever, despite the closeness. And I have to say that in Old Parr Superior, here we have a whisky old enough to show a slight bourbony sub-strata, but confident enough to allow the smoke full weight, the lighter malts and fruits a succulence to excite every tastebud, and just enough grain bite to remind you this is a blend. So suave, silky complexity balances with an occasionally rougher edge with just the right sprinkling of stardust. In other words, a whisky that has a near perfect degree of everything. Be it malt, blend, bourbon, Irish, Japanese, whatever, you just can't ask for more than that!

# Award Winners

### 2007 World Whisky of the Year
**Old Parr Superior 18 Years Old**

### 2007 World Whisky of the Year Runner Up
**Buffalo Trace Experimental Collection Twice Barreled**

### Scotch Single Malt of the Year
**Brora 30 Years Old Fourth Release 56.4%**

### Best New Scotch Whisky of the Year (single cask)
**Tullibardine 1966 cask 2312**

### Best New Scotch Whisky of the Year (multiple casks)
**Ardbeg Young Uigeadail**

### Best Single Malt of the Year 12 Years and Under
**Glenmorangie Truffle Oak 1993**

### Best Single Malt of the Year 13 to 21 Years
**BenRiach 1975 cask 7007**

### Best Single Malt of the Year 21 Years and Over
**Brora 30 Years old 56.4%**

### Scotch Vatted Malt of the Year
**Compass Box Spice Tree (2nd bottling)**

### Scotch Blended Whisky of the Year
**Old Parr Superior 18 Years Old**

### Scotch Blended Whisky of the Year (Over 12 Years)
**Old Parr Superior 18 Years Old**

### Scotch Blended Whisky of the Year (8-12 Years)
**White Horse Aged 12 Years**

### Scotch Premium Blended Whisky of the Year (No age statement)
**Dewar's Signature**

### Scotch Standard Blended Whisky of the Year (No age statement)
**William Grant's Family Reserve**

### Best New Scotch Blended Whisky
**Famous Grouse Scottish Oak Finish**

### Bourbon of the Year
**Buffalo Trace Experimental Collection Twice Barreled**

### Best Bourbon Aged Over 13 Years
**Buffalo Trace Experimental Collection Twice Barreled**

### Best Bourbon Aged 10-12 Years
**Elijah Craig 12**

### Best Bourbon Aged Under 10 Years
**Labrot and Graham Woodford Reserve Four Grain**

### Rye Whiskey of the Year
**Rittenhouse Rye 21 Years old Barrel No 28**

### Rye Whiskey of the Year Aged 12 Years or Under
**Old Potrero Hotaling's Whiskey Aged 11 Years Essay MCMVI - MMVI**

### Irish Whiskey of the Year
**Redbreast 15 Years Old**

### Japanese Whisky of the Year
**Nikka Single Cask Coffee Grain 1992**

### Japanese Single Malt of the Year
**The Hakushu Single Malt Aged 18 Years**

### Japanese Blended Whisky of the Year
**Nikka Single Cask Coffee Grain 1992**

### Canadian Whisky of the Year
**Alberta Premium 25 Years Old**

### Best Small Batch Distillery Whisky of the Year
**McCarthy's Oregon Single Malt**

### European Mainland Whisky of the Year
**Mackmyra Preludium 03 Svensk Single Malt Whisky**

# The Rankings (97–94)

## 97

### Scotch Single Malts
Ardbeg Ping No 1 Single Cask
Brora 30 Years Old 56.4%
Old Malt Cask Ardbeg 1975 Aged 25
### Blended Scotch
Old Parr Superior 18 Years Old
### Bourbon
George T Stagg (64.5%)
George T Stagg (68.8%)
George T Stagg Spring 2005 Release

## 96

### Scotch Single Malts
Ardbeg 1976 Single Cask No. 2390
Ardbeg 1977
Ardbeg Kildalton 1980
Ardbeg Provenance 1974
Ardbeg Young Uigeadail
Old Malt Cask Ardbeg 25 Years Old
Scotch Malt Whisky Society Cask No.
  66.16 Aged 20 Years (Ardmore)
BenRiach 1984 Limited Release
  Cask Bottling
Norse Cask Selection Bowmore 1993
Brora 30 Years Old 56.6%
Port Charlotte 4 Years Old
Member's Legacy Caperdonich 1967
  Aged 36 Years (Cask 4947)
Platinum Old and Rare Caperdonich 36
Platinum Clynelish 23 Years Old
Glenfarclas 1954 Aged 46 Years
Glenmorangie Truffle Oak
Glen Moray 1986 Commem Bottling
Highland Park 25 Years Old
Isle of Jura Aged 36 Years
Duncan Taylor Longmorn 1978
Murray McDavid Mission Macallan 1985
Aberdeen Distillers Rosebank 12 Y O
The Bottlers Teaninich 1982 21 Years
Tullibardine 1966 World Cup Edition
### Scotch Vatted Malts
Serendipity
### Blended Scotch
Ballantine's 17 Years Old
Johnnie Walker Gold Label
The Centenary Blend 18 Years Old
William Lawson's Founder's Reserve
  Aged 18 Years
### Irish Single Malt
Bushmills Rare Aged 21
### American Single Malt
McCarthy's Aged 3 Years

### Bourbon
Buffalo Trace Experimental Collection
  Twice Barrelled
Elijah Craig 12 Years Old
Evan Williams 12 Years
George T. Stagg (70.3%)
Wild Turkey Russell's Reserve Aged 10
  Years 101 Proof
### Single Malt Rye
Old Potrero Single Malt Hotaling's
  Whiskey Aged 11 Years
### Straight Rye
Rittenhouse 21 Years Old Barrel no.28
Sazerac Rye 18 Years Old
### Japanese Single Malt
The Cask of Hakushu 1989
Yoichi 12 Years Old 70th Anniversary

## 95

### Scotch Single Malts
Aberlour a'bunadh Batch No. 8
Ardbeg 1965
Ardbeg 1974 Single Cask No. 2751
Ardbeg 1975 Single Cask No. 4704
Ardbeg Airigh Nam Beist 1990
Cadenhead's Authentic Collection
  Ardbeg Aged 11 Years (57.4%)
Cadenhead's Ardbeg Aged 12 Years
Cadenhead's Authentic Collection
  Ardbeg Aged 13 Years 1993
Old Malt Cask Ardbeg 12 Years Old
Cadenhead's AC Balvenie 25 Years
The BenRiach Curiositas Aged 10
  Years Single Peated Malt
BenRiach Authenticus Over 21 Years
BenRiach Fine Wood Finishes
  Aged 15 Years Madeira Barrel
The BenRiach 1975 Limited Release
Duncan Taylor Bowmore 1966
Bruichladdich "Islands" Aged 20 Years
  Third Edition
Dun Bheagan Caol Ila Aged 14 Years
Old Malt Cask Caol Ila 25 Years Old
Member's Legacy Caperdonich 1967
  Aged 36 Years (Cask 4945)
Mackillop's Choice Clynelish 1989
Murray McDavid Clynelish 1994
Old Malt Cask Clynelish Aged 13Years
The Whisky Fair Clynelish 32 Years
The Dalmore 62 Years Old
Dalwhinnie 15 Years Old
Gordon & MacPhail Glencadam 1974
Glendronach Aged 33 Years

Glenfarclas 15 Years Old

Glenfiddich 15 Years Old

Glenglassaugh 1973 Family Silver

Dewar Rattray Glen Grant 1985

Duncan Taylor Special Selection No 2 Glen Grant 1970

Private Collection Glen Grant 1953

Cadenhead's Chairman's Stock Glenlivet (Minmore) Aged 30 Years

Glen Ord 25 Years Old

The Glenrothes 1979

Highland Park Aged 18 Years

Dewar RattrayHighland Park 1981

Mac Y 10th Anniversary Isle of Arran Aged 10 Years

Lagavulin Aged 16 Years

The Whisky Fair "Vanilla Sky" Aged 13 Years (Lagavulin)

Laphroaig 1/4 Cask

Cadenhead's Authentic Collection Laphroaig Aged 13 Years

Cadenhead's Authentic Collection Lochside Aged 23 Years

The Queen of the Moorlands Rare Cask Longmorn 12 Years Old

Macallan 18 Years Old

The Macallan 1949 (53 Years Old)

The Macallan 1970 (32 Years Old)

The Macallan Fine Oak 15 Years Old

Cadenhead's Macallan-Glenlivet 16

Cadenhead's Authentic Collection Mannochmore Aged 14 Years

Port Ellen 4th Release Aged 25 Years

Old Malt Cask Port Ellen Aged 25 Years

Old Malt Cask Port Ellen 25 Years Old (bott Apr 06)

Rosebank Aged 12 Years

Cask Strength Rosebank 1990

Longrow 10 Years Old 1994

Coopers Choice Strathisla 1969

Talisker Aged 20 Years

Tullibardine 1973

Tullibardine 1986 John Black Selection

**Unspecified Single Malts (Islay)**

Auld Reekie Islay Malt

**Scotch Vatted Malts**

Compass Box Juveniles

Wild Scotsman Aged 15 Years

**Blended Scotch**

Antiquary 21 Years Old

Dewar's Signature

The Famous Grouse Scottish Oak Fin

The Royal & Ancient 28 Years

Royal Salute 50 Years Old

William Grant's 25 Years Old

**Irish Pure Pot Still**

Midleton 1973 Pure Pot Still

**Irish Single Malt**

Bushmills Select Casks Aged 12 Years

Knappogue Castle 1994

**Irish Blended**

Jameson

**American Single Malt**

McCarthy's Oregon Single Malt

**Bourbon**

Daniel Stewart Aged 12 Years

Evan Williams 15 Years

Old Bardstown Aged 10 Years Estate Bottled

Old Rip Van Winkle 15 Years Old

Wild Turkey Rare Breed

Woodford Reserve Master's Collection Four Grain

**Straight Rye**

Rittenhouse 21 Y O Barrel no. 8

Sazerac 6 Years Old

**Canadian**

Alberta Premium

Alberta Premium 25 Years Old

Crown Royal Limited Edition

**Japanese Single Malt**

Hakushu 1984

Yoichi Key Malt Aged 12 Years "Peaty & Salty"

Yoichi 20 Years Old

Yoichi Nikka Single Cask Malt Whisky 1991

**Japanese Vatted Malt**

Pure Malt Black

**Japanese Single Grain**

Nikka Single Cask Coffey Grain 1992

**Swedish Single Malt**

Mackmyra Preludium 03 Svensk

**Welsh Single Malt**

Penderyn Welsh Rugby Union 125th Anniversary Edition

**Australian Single Malt**

Sullivans Cove 6 Years Old

## 94

**Scottish Single Malts**

Aberlour a'bunadh Batch 14

Aberlour Warehouse No. 1 Hand Filled (cask1714)

Aberlour Warehouse No. 1 Hand Filled (cask 6524)

Ardbeg 10 Years Old

Ardbeg 1974 Single Cask No. 2743

Ardbeg 1974 Single Cask No. 2749

Ardbeg 1975 Single Cask No. 4720

Cadenhead's Authentic Collection Ardbeg Aged 11 Years (59.5%)

Connoisseurs Choice Ardbeg 1976

Platinum Old and Rare Ardbeg Aged 29 Years

Ardmore 100th Anniversary 12 Years

Cask Ardmore 1990

Cadenhead's Authentic Collection Balblair Aged 16 Years

The Balvenie Roasted Malt 14

The Balvenie Merry Christmas 2005

The BenRiach 1984 Limited Release Cask Bottling

Duncan Taylor Collection Benriach 1968 Aged 36 Years

Harris Whisky Co. Benrinnes Aged 13

Benromach 1968

Benromach Cask Strength 1980

Bladnoch Aged 10 Years

Chieftain's Bladnoch Aged 14 Years Rum Barrel Finish

Bowmore Dawn

Cadenhead's Authentic Collection Bowmore Aged 14 Years 1992

Bruichladdich XVII Year Old

Bruichladdich Infinity

Bruichladdich Links "Turnberry 10th Limited Edition" 14 Years Old

Bruichladdich 3D

Berry's' Own Selection Bruichladdich 1991 Aged 15 Years

Cadenhead's Authentic Collection Bruichladdich Aged 18 Years

Duncan Taylor Collection Bruichladdich 1966 Aged 39 Years

Old Malt Cask Bruichladdich Aged 13 Years

Bunnahabhain 1971 Aged 35 Years 125th Anniversary

Berry's' Own Selection Caol Ila 1996 Aged 10 Years

Cadenhead's Authentic Collection Caol Ila Aged 15 Years

Private Collection Caol Ila Vintage Rum Finish 1990

Duncan Taylor Caperdonich 1970 Aged 33 Years

Cask Strength Clynelish 1990

Cadenhead's AC Cragganmore 16 Y O

Duncan Taylor Collection Dallas Dhu 1975 Aged 29 Years

Duncan Taylor Collection Dallas Dhu 1981 Aged 14 Years

Cadenhead's Authentic Collection Glen Elgin-Glenlivet Aged 13 Years

Glenfiddich 1937

Glenfiddich 1973 Vintage

The Spirit Safe & Cask Glen Garioch 1988 Aged 18 Years

Berrys' Own Selection Glen Grant 1972 31 Years Old

The Glenlivet Nadurra 16 Years Old

The Queen of the Moorlands Rare Cask Glenlivet 30 Years Old "The Chairman's Bottling" Edition XVI

Glenkeir Treasures Glen Mhor 30 Y O

Glenmorangie 10 Years Old

Glenmorangie Golden Rum Cask Fin.

Glen Moray 1962 Very Rare Vintage

Glen Moray Mountain Oak

The Glenrothes 1974

Glenrothes 1979 Single Cask

Old Masters Glenrothes 1988 Aged 17

Rare Old Glenugie 1968

Cask Strength Highland Park 1994

Gordon & MacPhail Cask Strength Highland Park 1991

Cadenhead's Dumbarton (Inverleven Stills) 18 Years Old

The Arran Malt Single Sherry Cask

Knockdhu 23 Years Old

Laphroaig Aged 30 Years

Laphroaig Aged 40 Years

Premier Barrel Laphroaig 7 Years Old

Murray McDavid Mission Linkwood 1983 Aged 23 Years

Old Malt Cask Lochside Aged 14 Years

James MacArthur Longmorn 1990

Norse Cask Selection Longmorn 1990

Macallan 10 Years Old (cask strength)

The Macallan 1989

The Macallan Cask Strength

The Macallan Easter Elchies 14 Years

The Macallan Fine Oak 25 Years Old

Cadenhead's Authentic Collection Macallan-Glenlivet Aged 17 Years

Duncan Taylor Coll Macallan 1969

Duncan Taylor Collection Macallan 1986 Aged 18 Years

Gordon & MacPhail Speymalt Macallan 1938

Platinum Selection Macallan 26 Years Old Rum Finish

Scott's Selection Macallan 1985

Harris Whisky Co. Macduff Aged 14

Dun Bheagan Port Ellen 23 Years Old

Provenance Port Ellen 21 Years Old

Old Malt Cask Rosebank 23 Years Old

Provenance Lochnagar 12 Years Old

Duncan Taylor Collection Scapa 1977

Chieftain's Springbank Aged 31 Years
Dun Bheagan Springbank 1969 Aged
  35 Years
Strathisla Distillery Edition 15 Years
Cadenhead's Authentic Collection
  Strathisla-Glenlivet Aged 18 Years
Cask Strength Strathisla 1985
Dewar Rattray Individual Cask
  Bottling Strathmill 1989
Talisker Aged 18 Years
Talisker 25 Years Old
Dun Bheagan Teaninich 1984 Aged 18
Blackadder Raw Cask Ledaig 13 Y O
Chieftain's Ledaig 31 Years Old
Dun Bheagan Leidaig Aged 29 Years
Murray McDavid Tomintoul 1973
Mission IV Aged 31 Years
Tullibardine 1993 Sherry Wood Finish
Connoisseurs Choice Tullibardine 1994

**Unspecified Single Malts (Islay)**
Finlaggen Old Reserve Islay
The Ileach Peaty Islay

**Scotch Vatted Malts**
Century of Malts
Clan Denny
Compass Box Oak Cross Malt Scotch
  Whisky
Compass Box The Spice Tree
The Famous Grouse 30 Years Old Malt
The Six Isles Pure Island Malt Uisge
  Beatha

**Single Grain Scotch**
Clan Denny Grain Caledonian 40 Y O
Duncan Taylor Cameronbridge 1979

**Blended Scotch**
Ballantine's Original Character
Chivas Brothers Oldest and Finest
Tanner's Peaty Creag Aged 8 Years
White Horse Aged 12 Years
William Grant's Family Reserve

**Irish Pure Pot Still**
Redbreast 15 Years Old

**Irish Single Malt**
Connemara Cask Strength
Knappogue Castle 1992
Clontarf Single Malt

**Irish Blended**
Jameson 12 Years Old
Jameson 1780 Matured 12 Years
Jameson Gold

**Bourbon**
Buffalo Trace
Eagle Rare Single Barrel 10 Years
Evan Williams Vintage 1995 Single
  Barrel Vintage

George T. Stagg (70.6%)
Jefferson's Reserve 15 Year Old
Old Forester Birthday Bourbon
  Distilled Spring 1993 Bottled 2005
Old Forester Birthday Bourbon 1995
Old Taylor Aged 6 Years
Virgin Bourbon 15 Years Old 101 Proof

**Single Malt Rye**
Old Potrero Essay 8-RW-ARM-8-A
Old Potrero Essay 10-SRW-ARM-E

**Straight Rye**
Rittenhouse 21 Y O Barrel no.14
Rittenhouse 21 Y O Barrel no.21
Rittenhouse 21 Y O Barrel no.23
Rittenhouse 21 Y O Barrel no.27
Sazerac Kentucky Straight Rye 18
  Years Old 90 Proof

**Japanese Single Malt**
Suntory Pure Malt Hakushu 20 Years
Karuizawa 1979 Aged 24 Years
Karuizawa 1986 Aged 17 Years
Shirakawa 32 Years Old Single Malt
Yoichi 15 Years Old (code 10|44 green
  back label)

**Japanese Blended**
Nikka Master Blend Blended Whisky
  12 Years Old 70th Anniversary
Special Reserve 10 Years Old

**Austrian Oat Whisky**
Waldviertler Hafer Whisky 2000

**French Single Malt**
Taol Esa 1999

**Swiss Malt Whisky**
Swissky Exklusiv Abfüllung
Zurcher Single Lakeland Malt Whisky
  3 Years Old

**Australian Malt Whisky**
Bakery Hill Classic Malt Cask Strength
Bakery Hill Peated Malt Cask Strength

**Indian Single Malt**
Amrut Cask Strength
Stillman's Dram Single Malt Whisky
  Limited Edition

# Scottish Malts

**F**or those of you deciding to take the plunge and head off into the labyrinthine world of Scotch malt whisky, a piece of advice. And that is, be careful who you take your advice from. Because, too often, I hear that you should leave the Islays until you have tackled the featherlight Speysiders and the bolder, weightier Highlanders. This is just complete, patronising nonsense. The only time that rings true is if you are tasting a number of whiskies in one day. Then leave the smoky ones to last, so the lighter chaps get a fair hearing.

I know many people who didn't like whisky until they got a Talisker from Skye inside them, or a Lagavulin to swamp their tastebuds with oily iodine. The fact is, you can take your map of malt whisky, start at any point and head in any direction you feel. There are no hard and fast rules. Certainly with over 2,000 tasting notes for Scottish malts here you should have some help in picking where this journey of a lifetime begins.

It is also worth remembering not to be seduced by age. It is true that some of the highest scores are given to big-aged whiskies. But they are the exception rather than the rule: the truth is that the majority of malts, once they have lived beyond 20 years or so, suffer from oak influence rather than benefit. Part of the fun of discovering whiskies is to see how malts from different distilleries to perform to age and type of cask. Happy discovering.

SKY

Talisker

Tobermo

## Islay

Bunnahabhain

Caol Ila

Kilchoman

Bruichladdich

Bowmore

ISLAY

Port Ellen          Ardbeg

Laphroaig          Lagavulin

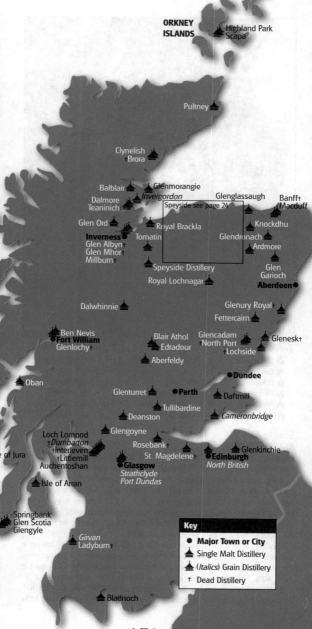

ORKNEY
ISLANDS

Highland Park
Scapa

Pultney

Clynelish
†Brora

Balblair
Dalmore
Teaninich
*Invergordon*

Glenmorangie
Glenglassaugh
Banff†
Macduff

Speyside see page 24

Glen Ord
Royal Brackla
Knockdhu

Inverness●
Tomatin
Glendronach
Ardmore

Glen Albyn†
Glen Mhor†
Millburn†

Speyside Distillery
Glen
Garioch

Royal Lochnagar
Aberdeen●

Dalwhinnie
Glenury Royal†
Fettercairn

Ben Nevis
Fort William
Glenlochy†

Blair Athol
Edradour
Aberfeldy

Glencadam
†North Port
†Lochside
Glenesk†

●Dundee

Oban
Glenturret
●Perth
Daftmill

Tullibardine
*Cameronbridge*

Deanston

Glengoyne

Loch Lomond
†Dumbarton
†Inverleven
†Littlemill
Auchentoshan

Rosebank
St. Magdelene†
●Edinburgh
Glenkinchie

Isle of Jura
●Glasgow
*Strathclyde
Port Dundas*
*North British*

Isle of Arran

Springbank
Glen Scotia
Glengyle

*Girvan*
Ladyburn†

Bladnoch

**Key**

● **Major Town or City**
▲ Single Malt Distillery
▲ (*Italics*) Grain Distillery
† Dead Distillery

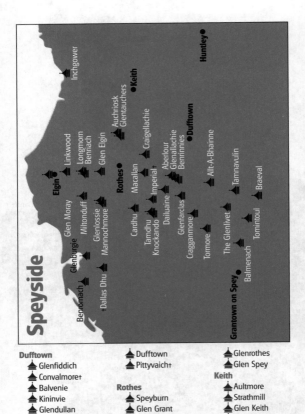

**Speyside**

**Dufftown**
- Glenfiddich
- Convalmore†
- Balvenie
- Kininvie
- Glendullan
- Mortlach

- Dufftown
- Pittyvaich†

**Rothes**
- Speyburn
- Glen Grant
- Caperdonich†

- Glenrothes
- Glen Spey

**Keith**
- Aultmore
- Strathmill
- Glen Keith
- Strathisla

## Single Malts
### ABERFELDY
**Highlands (Perthshire), 1898. John Dewar & Sons. Working.**

Aberfeldy Aged 12 Years db **(89) n**22 softly honied, rich and clean; **t**23 lighter in body than the nose suggests, a prick of first smoke, then spice, but the honey develops; **f**22 pretty long with developing vanilla and soft oils and very late honey again; **b**22 I have long loved this malt and it shows to good effect here although I'm not sure if the strength does it any favours. **40%**

⋰ Aberfeldy Aged 21 Years db **(86) n**24 **t**22 **f**19 **b**21. Never quite lives up to the blood orange and vaguely smoky nose. **40%**

Aberfeldy Age d 25 Years db **(85) n**24 **t**21 **f**19 **b**21. Just doesn't live up to the nose. When Tommy Dewar wrote, "We have a great regard for old age when it is bottled," as quoted on the label, I'm not sure he had as many as 25 years in mind. **40%**. *150 bottles to mark opening of Dewar's World of Whisky.*

⋰ Connoisseurs Choice Glen Aberfeldy 1988 **(83) n**20 **t**22 **f**20 **b**21. Attractively nutty with a big digestive biscuit, mildly salty kick and dry finale. **43%**.

⋅⋅⋅ **Connoisseurs Choice Aberfeldy 1991** bott 13/06/06 **(91) n**23 seaweedy, but without any tangible peat; **t**23 mouthwatering yet, like the nose, displaying the most extraordinary and inexplicable coastal tendencies; **f**22 the saltiness continues though some wonderful barley does re-emerge for a sweetish finish; **b**23 Aberfeldy is one of those distilleries just screaming to be discovered. Surprisingly few great casks get out there, but here is one. Though its impersonation of an old school Bunnahabhain is as impressive as it is bizarre. **46%**. *Gordon & MacPhail, US Market.*

**Coopers Choice Aberfeldy 1974 Aged 29 Years** bott 03 **(88) n**22 **t**22 **f**22 **b**22. A bitter-sweet delight that does the reputation of this excellent di stillery no harm. **46%**. *The Vintage Malt Whisky Co.*

## ABERLOUR
**Speyside, 1826. Chivas Bros. Working.**

**Aberlour 10 Years Old** db **(87) n**22 different nose to how it's been for the last decade: much more grapey-style fruit and lavender to the trademark mint: genuinely deep and brooding with a soft marzipan sweetness; **t**22 dry in parts with the oak really hitting home; the spread of delicate honey is teasing; **f**21 toffee and spice; **b**22 big stuff: a whole lot older than ten years. **43%**

**Aberlour a'bunadh Batch No. 7** db **(87) n**23 **t**20 **f**23 **b**21. Can you have too much of a good thing? Possibly. The intensity of this sherry cask is almost unbearable, but it has to be said that the cask itself is faultless and of rare quality. In some ways, it is too good... **59.9%. ncf.**

⋅⋅⋅ **Aberlour a'bunadh Batch No. 8** db **(95) n**23 it's the old honeycomb and teasing spices one-two. Irresistible; **t**24 stunningly intense malty shockwaves are met by seismic sherry. Imagine the results: better still, taste them...; **f**24 beautifully nutty with hints of praline and marzipan: lasts seemingly forever; **b**24 another a'bunadh that sends this distillery into the stratosphere. The best I've encountered yet. **60.2%**

**Aberlour a'bunadh Batch 13** db **(88) n**23 very similar in style to the 15-y-o Sherry Wood Finish; **t**23 lively, fresh fruit and mouthwatering malt: not for the squeamish; **f**21 thin-ish; cream toffee; **b**22 the dull-ish finish apart, this is sheer entertainment and one for late, cold nights. **59.8%**

**Aberlour a'bunadh Batch 14** db **(94) n**23 slightly earthy but the grape is genuinely clean, intense and spicy; **t**25 truly glorious, actually quite perfect, delivery of balance between the unimpeachable grape and malt concentrate that gathers on the palate and bores into the tastebuds like a tornado into a Midwest town. One of the great moments of Speyside whisky drinking; **f**22 relatively short, but the shock waves continue amid some toffee; **b**24 it would be easy to pass this off as just another whisky from first time of trying, probably because of the relative ordinariness of the finish. But instinct should tell you to try again and watch. Try and find if there is a fault in the quality of the distillate or cask; find a winner between bitter and sweet. You will be amazed! **59.5%**

⋅⋅⋅ **Aberlour A'bunadh Batch 15** db **(84) n**20 **t**20 **f**23 **b**21. A rogue lightly sulphured cask has taken the edge of this one. A shame. No: bloody annoying!! **59.6%. ncf.**

⋅⋅⋅ **Aberlour a'bunadh Batch 16** db **(87) n**21 I don't believe it: sulphur again. Someone is becoming a bit careless here. Fortunately, the blinding brilliance of some of the other sherry butts have helped limit the damage; **t**23 the intense kumquat/orange tang to the sherry-trifle grape is pure joy and helps take the mind off the furry-interference of that single sulphur cask. Chewy...and so could have been a champion; **f**22 the odd, telling off-note remains but you can't entirely suppress the fruit; **b**21 for this to happen once is bad for a world-great dram. Twice in a row is close to being the stuff of nightmares. The real shame is that this could so easily have been 2007 Whisky Bible Whisky of the Year, because some of the other casks still bear the hallmark of greatness...I could weep. **59.6%. ncf.**

**Aberlour 12 Years Old Sherry Matured** db **(90) n**24 few latter-day sherry butts come through this clean and complete; just the right degree of spiciness; **t**23 silky, decisive oloroso again showing an uncanny excellence in spice: not a single off note; f21 flattens out slightly; b22 another vastly improved, beautiful expression displaying genuine class. **40%**

⫶ **Aberlour 13 Years Old** Sherry cask, hand fill db **(84)** n21 t22 f20 b21. Skimps on the complexity. **58.8%**

**Aberlour 15 Year Old Double Cask Matured** db **(84)** n23 t22 f19 b20. Brilliant nose full of vibrant apples and spiced sultana, but then, after a complex, chewy, malt-enriched kick-off, falls surprisingly flat on its face. **40%**

**Aberlour 15 Years Cuvee Marie d'Ecosse** db **(91)** n22 fresh sherry trace with kumquats and lime for extra zest; t24 beautifully ethereal with the malt drifting in all directions while the fruit offers no weight at all; f22 light vanilla apologetically drifts into the picture. The smoke of old has gone; b23 this always was a deceptive lightweight, and it's got lighter still. It is sold primarily in France, and one can assume only that this is God's way of making amends for that pretentious, over-rated, caramel-ridden rubbish called Cognac they've had to endure. **43%** ⊙⊙

**Aberlour 15 Year Old Sherry Finish** db **(91)** n24 exceptionally clever use of oak to add a drier element to the sharper boiled cooking apple. And a whiff of the fermenting vessel, too. Love it! t22 the sharp fruit of the nose is magnified here ten times for one of the strangest mouth arrivals I've ever come across: the roof of the mouth won't know what's hit it; f23 wave upon wave of malt concentrate; b22 quite unique: freaky, even. Really a whisky to be discovered and ridden. Once you acclimatize, you'll adore it. **43%**

**Aberlour 16 Year Old Double Cask Matured** db **(81)** n19 t21 f20 b21. Pleasant, but marred by an imbalanced nose and a dreary finish. **43%**

⫶ **Aberlour 1975** cask no. 4579, bott 11 Apr 05 db **(82)** n21 t21 f20 b20. A little hot and cramped. **48.5%**

**Aberlour 100 Proof** db **(91)** n23 beneath this sherried, volcanic start there is something rather sweet and honied. One of the most two-toned noses you'll find in a long while; t23 sweet to begin and honied, too. The maltiness keeps its shape for some time. Between the middle and end an ebulliient spiciness takes hold  f22 massively long and fruity; b23 stunning, sensational whisky, the most extraordinary Speysider of them all ...which it was when I wrote those official notes for the bottling back in '97, I think. Other malts have superseded it now, but on re-tasting I stand by those original notes, though I disassociate myself entirely with  the rubbish: "In order to savour Aberlour 100 at its best add 1/3 to 1/2 pure water. **57.1%**

⫶ **Aberlour Warehouse No. 1 Aged 13 Years** Sherry cask no. 1947, filled Mar 93 db **(91)** n23 splash-it-on-oloroso with heavy roast Brazilian; t23 the tastebuds vanish under a tidal wave of ultra-fresh sherry; spices abound as mocha meets the middle; f23 those Exocet-style spices continue for a while before fizzing out under the oloroso; b22 if you are into sherry-influenced whisky, it's multiple orgasm time. My money, though, is on the malt being better still when the butt is used for a second time... **57.6%. sc ncf.**

⫶ **Aberlour Warehouse No. 1 Hand Filled** First fill Bourbon cask no. 1296, filled into cask Sept 93, bott 11 Apr 06 db **(94)** n24 mega intense malt with acacia honey and golden syrup dominating; t23 more of the same with an early oak tang; f24 settles beautifully and a coppery richness propagates the honey; b23 there are many excellent reasons for visiting Speyside. Encountering magnificent casks like this is one of them. **61.5%.** *From the distillery only.*

⫶ **Aberlour Warehouse No. 1 Hand Filled** Sherry cask 1st fill 1714, filled Nov 92, bott 11 Apr 06 db **(93)** n24 blind, this could easily pass for Demerara rum (a70/30 blend of AWM and REV, to be precise); t23 the uncanny rum theme continues on delivery; eventually some rich sherry and lighter barley begin to restore sanity; f23 back to Demerara. Fabulous: but what the hell is happening??? Softening caramel finishes the journey; b23 when I first tasted this at the distillery, it reminded me of Jamaican rum. Back in my lab, I thought

Demerara. And all this from a sherry butt. This game never fails to amaze you... **57.6%.** *From the distillery only.*

⁙ **Aberlour Warehouse No. 1 Hand Filled** Sherry cask 6524, filled 26 May 89, bott April 05 db **(94) n**24 classic ultra clean and fresh Oloroso; **t**24 chewy. Mouthwatering and spicy. The grape/barley balance just about 60/40. 100% superb; **f**23 lingering and elastic; **b**23 if lessons are given in exactly how a 15-year-old Speyside malt matured in a sherry butt should be, then here is the demonstration model. *From the distillery only.*

**Berrys' Own Selection Aberlour 1989 14 Years Old** bott 04 **(92) n**23 newly mown grass on a cricket square; a squeeze of lemon and lime; **t**24 ohhhhh! This just gets the tastebuds salivating: absolutely brilliantly distilled malt that has embraced the oak with natural grace; **f**22 soft gingery spices and delicate traces of malt; **b**23 you can't help thinking that the distillery are missing out big time on a trick or two by not bottling at least one of their range in this wonderfully fresh bourbon form. Just so mouth-puckeringly refreshing. **46%.**

⁙ **Berry's Own Selection Aberlour 1994 Aged 11 Years** casks 8847/ 8850, dist 94, bott 05 **(75) n**19 **t**19 **f**18 **b**19. Refreshing, malty, almost new-make. But I'm not sure someone got the cuts quite right on this one. **46%.**

**Blackadder Raw Cask Aberlour 14 Years Old** cask no. 3322, dist 7 May 90, bott Nov 04 **(85) n**23 **t**23 **f**19 **b**20. The black tinge to the whisky looks a bit dodgy from the start: the mayhem on the palate comes as no great surprise. A malt which, technically, fails on several levels, yet, frankly, is fun! **59.9%**

⁙ **Duncan Taylor Collection Aberlour 1995** cask no. 5249, dist Sept 95, bott Mar 06 **(85) n**22 **t**21 **f**21 **b**21. Jammy dodgers and treacle tart. **43.1%.** *406 bottles.*

**Cadenhead's Aberlour-Glenlivet 13 Years Old** dist 89, bott 03/03 **(86) n**21 **t**22 **f**22 **b**21. If you ever wanted to know what a blender looks for in 12-ishyear- old Speyside from a cask that is on its second or third filling, this is just about the perfect example. **46%**

**Cadenhead's Authentic Collection Aberlour – Glenlivet Aged 15 Years** dist 89, bott May 05 **(80) n**21 **t**21 **f**19 **b**19. Massive ultra-sweet gristy kick to start, but the esters seem slightly out of alignment. Big enjoyable stuff, though. **58.6%.** *288 bottles.*

**Old Malt Cask Aberlour Aged 14 Years** dist Nov 89, bott Feb 04 **(80) n**20 **t**21 **f**20 **b**19. Malty and mouthwatering, but a little on the hot side. **50%. nc ncf sc.**

**Old Master's Aberlour 1989** cask no. 12198 bott 04 **(73) n**18 **t**19 **f**19 **b**17. Unyielding and fiery it never quite settles into a comfort zone. **56.8%.**

**Scotts Selection Aberlour 1989** bott 05 **(83) n**20 **t**21 **f**22 **b**20. An attractive, if conservative, expression, though the hint of strawberry on the finish is as intriguing as it is delicious. **53.8%.** *Speyside Distillers.*

# ALLT-A-BHAINNE
## Speyside, 1975. Chivas Bros. Working.

**Cadenhead's Authentic Collection Allt-A-Bhainne Aged 12 Years** dist 92, bott Feb 05 **(88) n**21 pleasing malty-oaky simplicity; **t**23 a quite beautiful development of sweet barley-sugar allowing in just enough oak for extra depth; **f**22 a gentle landing with the oak and a touch of white pepper mingling with the steady barley; **b**22 an above average offering from this distillery thanks to a degree of softening oiliness that helps intensify the rich malty middle. **57.6%**

**Connoisseurs Choice Allt A Bhainne 1991 (83) n**20 **t**22 **f**20 **b**21. Clean, sexy and simpering, the honeyed thread makes up for bulimic body. **43%.** *G&M*

⁙ **Dun Bheagan Allt-A-Bhainne Aged 28 Years (87) n**23 young, busy and charming; a big fruity edge to this though soft oak thrives amid the barley; **t**24 explosive stuff with malty fireworks popping around the palate. The barley is much, much younger than its age – there is almost a new- makey freshness. Some clean sherry has also made its presence felt: the overall picture is fussy, but strikingly attractive; **f**20 lets the side down slightly with some very odd sherry-led incursions. Long, but confused; **b**20 a decent malt bowling along beautifully until it hits some very weird sherry buffers. **60.2%.** *Ian Macleod.*

**Old Malt Cask Allt-A-Bhainne Aged 15 Years** dist 14 Nov 89, bott 23 Mar 05 **(74) n**17 **t**20 **f**18 **b**19. The poor nose and unimpressive finish point towards a not very well made spirit. **50%.** *Douglas Laing & Co.*

⋰ **Old Masters Allt-A-Bhainne 1995 Aged 10 Years** cask no. 140864, dist 95, bott 06 **(89) n**21 green and fresh; new make beefed up with a dash of manuka honey; **t**23 the delivery is very, very young, but the thrust of the barley is wonderful. Clean, fabulously textured and gently oiled, the deft barley-sugar sweetness delights; **f**22 long, thanks to that youthful, oily coating. No more than trace oak involvement, but just so chewy and lip-smacking with excellent late cocoa; **b**23 a pretty well- used cask means that this whisky could pass for six or seven. But it is clean, fascinating and genuinely delicious fare. **58.9%.** *James MacArthur.*

## ANCNOC ( see Knockdhu)

## ARDBEG
### Islay, 1815. Glenmorangie Plc. Working.

**Ardbeg 10 Years Old** db **(94) n**24 oily, slapped-on-all-over-with-a-trowelpeat that leaves nothing uncoated. A lovely salty tang gives an extra tweak; **t**24 amazing, grassy, salivating sweetness of the malt on one level; lip-smacking, chewy, gently oiled peat on another; soft traces of cocoa where they meet; **f**23 more moderate, thoughtful spices than of old, with a gentle fruitiness in the ascendancy as the fade begins, massaged, of course, by the most subtle of smoke; **b**23 close your eyes and enjoy. **46%**

**Ardbeg 17 Years Old** (earlier bottlings) db **(92) n**23 **t**22 **f**23 **b**24. OK, I admit I had a big hand in this, creating it with the help of Glenmorangie Plc's John Smith. It was designed to take the weight off the better vintages of Ardbeg whilst ensuring a constant supply around the world. Certainly one of the more subtle expressions you are likely to find, though criticised by some for not being peaty enough. As the whisky's creator, all I can say is they are missing the point. **40%**

**Ardbeg 17 Years Old** (present bottlings) db **(90) n**22 **t**23 **f**22 **b**23. The peat has all but vanished and cannot really be compared to the original 17-year-old: it's a bit like tasting a Macallan without the sherry: fascinating to see the naked body underneath, and certainly more of a turn on. Peat or no peat, great whisky by any standards. **40%**

**Ardbeg Guaranteed 30 Years Old** db **(91) n**24 **t**23 **f**21 **b**23. An unsual beast, one of the last ever bottled by Allied. The charm and complexity early on is enormous, but the fade rate is surprising. That said, still a dram of considerable magnificence. **40%**

**Ardbeg 1965** db **(95) n**24 how does it do it? How can an Ardbeg manage to hang together all such vivid classic Ardbegian riches after some 40 years in the cask? The earthiness of the smoke coupled with those orangey citrus notes means this can only be pre '78 Ardbeg. No other distillery can put this character together; **t**23 early, light arrival of citrus, then sweetening malt staving off a big surge of smoky sap; the body, so delicate to start, begins to groan under the weight, but it's all melt-in-the-mouth and improbably gentle; **f**24 goes back into classic Ardbeg overdrive with gentle, lapping waves of peat reek over the vanilla and cocoa oakiness; **b**24 it seems unreasonable to hope that one of the oldest Ardbegs ever bottled will be a classic. But prayers are answered...and with interest. A note for Ardbeg lovers of a nervous disposition: I didn't spit a drop.... **42%** *Bottled 2005 – not for release until July 2006.*

⋰ **Ardbeg 1972 Single Cask No. 2738** db **(92) n**23 anyone who has experienced the darting, wispy warmth of passing peat-reek in a storm-lashed Scottish coastal village will recognize this immediately, made all the more vivid by the slight coke-smoke, too; citrus and vanilla back up attractively; **t**23 immediate spice attack but it's the gristy, vanilla-clad peat that stars; again some orangey-citrus lightens the load; **f**23 the peats gather more heavily now, but grape thins it and helps see off any over-active oak; **b**23 charming, evocative but enough lightning and thunder to show this is still alive and kicking. **53.1%**

··⊱ **Ardbeg 1974 Single Cask No. 2741** bott 20.9.05 db **(81) n**19 **t**21 **f**21 **b**20. Gin!!! Juniper, orange peel, coriander, the lot!!! What the hell is all that about? Fabulous nose for a gin, but for an Ardbeg.... Even the delivery says much the same thing. After tasting this, I retired to my lab and blended a tiny amount of high quality gin with a standard ancient Ardbeg...and got a very similar result. A bottling hall fault? Or a freak? For the record, quality-wise, if I wasn't marking it as an Ardbeg and simply gave it a score for flavour etc, it'd get 93!!! **51.9%.** *122 bottles.*

··⊱ **Ardbeg 1974 Single Cask No. 2742** bott 20.9.05 db **(92) n**22 cooing vanilla and citrus; the peats are dry and dainty; **t**24 lush, beautifully textured barley, juicy sultana and a slow evolving of peat: a seduction of the highest order; **f**23 how can something so gentle last so long; the cocoa- sprinkled peats carry with them that lush fruitiness; **b**23 for a whisky of this antiquity the freshness is astounding; the peat has faded, though. But not enough for it not to plot the course. **42.7%.** *36 bottles.*

··⊱ **Ardbeg 1974 Single Cask No. 2743** bott 20.9.05 db **(94) n**23 a robust delivery of Seville orange and peat reek; a touch of chocolate-covered marzipan, too; **t**24 big esters and fruit, almost rum-like in its delivery. Then spices and peat bloom and abound; **f**23 jaffa cakes and dark chocolate again; the spice buzz and barley are beautiful; **b**24 just one of those casks that makes you hold your glass in awe. **51.7%.** *106 bottles.*

··⊱ **Ardbeg 1974 Single Cask No. 2749** bott 20.9.05 db **(94) n**24 a touch of the farm yards mixing in with rockpools and open peat fires. Wonderful...; **t**23 an unusually firm, brittle start with the barley offering a flinty yet fruity edge; the smoke is refined and delicate; **f**23 a touch oilier now with those peats showing increasing weight. Again a lovely fruity, slightly juicy edge; **b**24 this is, quite simply, great whisky. **51%.** *120 bottles.*

··⊱ **Ardbeg 1974 Single Cask No. 2751** bott 05 db **(95) n**24 a crisp nose with tight, Fishermen's Friend bite and the most extraordinary coastal tang: almost a blueprint for how old Ardbegs should be...; **t**24 firm, pulsing barley and smoky and an eking out of something citrussy. This lasts only a second as a second, more emphatic wave of peat re-emerges; **f**23 a surprisingly fast drop off of action but the emerging soft oils take the mocha, toasty vanilla to its drawn out conclusion; **b**24 just stunning whisky that can be only Ardbeg. **51.8%.** *141 bottles.*

··⊱ **Ardbeg 1974 Single Cask No. 2752** bott 20.9.05 db **(91) n**22 marauding fruit has done its best to dull the nose slightly: some achievement...; **t**23 astonishingly fruity with a vague hint of lychee amid the chunky smoke; **f**23 it's more of the same, only with the peat drying slightly and a lovely gristy freshness emerging; **b**23 a very different Ardbeg: just one cask along but this sibling looks nothing like the others. **52.1%.** *133 bottles.*

··⊱ **Ardbeg 1975 Single Cask No. 4699** db **(92) n**23 the weightlessness of the fine and moderate smoke helps amplify the oak, but the balance remains excellent; **t**23 again, soufflé light and then a slow, growling peat presence. Detectable barley sweetness sees off any oak; **f**23 perhaps a shade tired with some dryness accentuated by cocoa and spices but the freshness of the delicate grape is wonderful; **b**23 I had to come back to this cask three times, as the palate has to be spot- on to get the story here. At first I thought it was over-oaked; on second tasting got a different reading. These third and fourth times my palate has been free of a slight blocked nose etc and the patience has paid dividends. Yes, it is on the aged side, but the shades of subtlety astound. **40.9%.** *121 bottles.*

**Ardbeg 1975 Single Cask No. 4701** db **(87) n**22 **t**22 **f**21 **b**22. Unusual mouthfeel for an Ardbeg: hard and relatively unyielding for this distillery. **46.4%**

**Ardbeg 1975 Single Cask No. 4703** db **(91) n**22 **t**23 **f**23 **b**23. A lovely Ardbeg that is quite lethargic despite its obvious riches. **47.7%**

**Ardbeg 1975 Single Cask No. 4704** ex oloroso db **(95) n**24 I have been flung back into a warehouse by the lapping shores and I have my nose stuck in a butt: coastal, salty, fresh yet ancient, barley-sweet yet oaky-dry, smoke laden yet curiously light, firm traces of bourbon despite being unmistakably Scotch: Ardbeg at its most typically paradoxical; **t**24 dissolving malt leaves the way for a rampant, raisiny-grapey depth to battle it out with the smoke; towards the middle the malt re-emerges unscathed and sweet; **f**23 layer upon layer of barley which defies the years and then a crushed-sultana sweetness adding fruit to the fun; **b**24 genius will out.... **47.2%**

**Ardbeg 1975 Single Cask No. 4716** db **(86) n**21 **t**22 **f**22 **b**21. Doesn't quite take off and develop like the average Ardbeg of this era. Still a little gem, though. **45%**

٭ **Ardbeg 1975 Single Cask No. 4717** bott 8 May 06 db **(90) n**22 excellent peats try to paper over the worrying oaky cracks; **t**22 oak-starched start but saved by improbably intense and mouthwatering barley which appears almost from nowhere; **f**23 the recovery continues with soft fruits adding to the dazzling peats; long and actually softens and juices up as it keeps stretching the horizon; **b**23 perhaps no other distillery in the world could have got away with this: there is enough evidence in both nose and delivery for those of us who have been around a bit to fear the worst. Yet, somehow, this not only comes back from life support but begins to sing and dance on its deathbed. Astonishing...and mildly frightening! **46.3%**. *165 bottles.*

**Ardbeg 1975 Single Cask No. 4718** db **(83) n**20 **t**22 **f**20 **b**21. The least inspiring of the individual casks, revealing that Ardbeg is mortal after all. Still amasses a complexity other whiskies dream about but the finish, like the nose, is bitter and less than perfect. **46.7%**

٭ **Ardbeg 1975 Single Cask No 4719** bott 29 Apr 05 db **(87) n**20 battered, peaty but failing; **t**23 worrying oak, then an avalanche of juicy malt. The sweetness levels are rising by the second, as it the peat; **f**22 long with some wonderful light roast coffee (kind of Kenyan-Indian mix), allowing the spices and roaming peats to flourish, but still enough oak just to remind you of its age; **b**22 tries the same trick as its sibling, 4717, but doesn't quite make it. Or so you think until you taste it a third and final time before signing the death certificate. And then... **44.7%**. *188 bottles.*

٭ **Ardbeg 1975 Single Cask No. 4720** bott 16.2.06 db **(94) n**23 crushed toffee apple; the smoke no more than toys with the nose; **t**23 silky, fruity grape and barley unite for a mouthwatering entry, then soft thrusts of peat from the rear; **f**24 the two styles meet for the most erotic finale, with every single tastebuds being toyed with at different levels of intensity. Complex and sheer genius; **b**24 this must have been one hell of a sherry butt in its day: come to think of it, it was its day right up until 16th February 2006. A genuine great whisky, and for those who love both sherry and peat, well life has just got even better... **41.4%**. *207 bottles.*

**Ardbeg 1976 Single Cask No. 2390** Sherry butt filled 24 Nov 76, hand bott at dist 27 Apr 02 db **(96) n**24 **t**25 **f**23 **b**24. When you die, have a bottle of this put beside you in the coffin to take to the afterworld: this is just one of those drams of a lifetime. **53.1%**. *494 bottles. Sold only at distillery.*

**Ardbeg 1976 Single Cask No. 2395** db **(93) n**24 **t**23 **f**22 **b**24. Supremely weighted malt with more oak than it needs but enough charisma to see it off. **54.4%**

**Ardbeg 1976 Single Cask No. 2396** db **(91) n**24 **t**23 **f**21 **b**23. This was marked in the mid-80s. Then I tasted again ... and again ... and again.... Superb. **53.5%**

**Ardbeg 1976 Single Cask No. 2398** db **(89) n**23 nose-twitching stuff: the oak and peat are sharp-edged and bold; sandalwood, marshmallow and damp leather football boots add to the bitter-sweet enigma; **t**22 equally punchy on the palate with a fizzing oak dryness perfectly countered by a peaty-Demerara sweetness; **f**22 much drier now but the malt digs deep for some weighty barley; **b**22 old and noble. **52.3%**

**Ardbeg 1976 Single Cask No. 3275** db **(85) n**22 **t**21 **f**21 **b**21. A quite different, light dram highlighting the scope of the peating levels in those ownmade malt days. Those who thought the lightly peated 17-year-old vatting a recent un-Ardbegian invention and vociferously decried it are in for a reality check and a large slice of humble pie. **44.6%**

**Ardbeg 1977** db **(96)** n25 t24 f23 b24. When working through the Ardbeg stocks, I earmarked '77 a special vintage, the sweetest of them all. So it has proved. Only the '74 absorbed that extra oak that gave greater all-round complexity. Either way, the quality of the distillate is beyond measure: simply one of the greatest experiences – whisky or otherwise – of your life. **46%**

**Ardbeg 1978** db **(91)** n23 t24 f22 b22. An Ardbeg on the edge of losing it because of encroaching oak, hence the decision made by John Smith and I to bottle this vintage early alongside the 17-year-old version. Nearly ten years on, still looks a pretty decent bottling, though slightly under strength! **43%**

⁙ **Ardbeg Airigh Nam Beist Limited 1990 Release** bott 06 db **(95)** n24 dark and deep yet sensuous and gentle; there is a distinctive organic quality to this (not in the health drink sense...); lots of clues to location, with a rich salty texture to the aroma; t24 big, thick with flavour, yet not oils. Huge peat, yet always allowing the sweet barley strands to filter through; f23 those coastal, salty notes at last arrive as does a dusting of cocoa; b24 there is only one distillery on earth that could make something so gigantic, yet so delicate. And mind-blowingly complex. Smoky sophistication. **46%. ncf.**

**Ardbeg Kildalton 1980** bott 04 db **(96)** n23 t24 f24 b25. Many years back, when I helped get Ardbeg back on the road, I selected certain years as vintages and created the 17-year-old by using this unpeated version as the heart, with some overly old but highly peated casks to ensure the Ardbeg style flourished and equilibrium was maintained. The one and only recommendation I made that was not carried out, though, was to launch Kildalton as a malt in its own right, showing – uniquely – the inner working of Ardbeg in much the same way as a bourbon cask version does to Macallan. Now, at very long last, they have got around to it. This is better now than when it was 17 years old, and a degree of unbalanced freshness remained (to confirm my suspicions, I have tasted it against the samples I took then). It has developed extra fruit and complexity, making it a breathtaking treat – a masterpiece map of Ardbeg – that no true whisky connoisseur can afford to miss... and proof positive that Ardbeg doesn't need peat to bring complexity, balance and Scotch whisky to their highest peaks.... **57.6%**

**Ardbeg Lord of the Isles** db **(87)** n23 as if two peat types are working in tandem: one soft, toffeed and lilting, the other firmer, drier; t23 big peat kick at first then a more sombre maltiness; f20 slightly flat and disappointing; b21 a dram that starts well enough but complexity becomes scarcer as a cream-toffee effect mingles with the peat. **46%**

⁙ **Ardbeg Ping No 1 Single Cask** cask 2780, dist 27 Oct 72, bott 14 Oct 04 db **(97)** n24 we are back to model steam locomotives with the most beguiling array of sensuous peats since the legendary OMC '75; slightly farm-yardy., a dab here and there of grape and citrus. Words never do justice, because this is all about nuance and timing: ladies and gentlemen, only Ardbeg can give you this; t24 sweet peats dissolve immediately into the palate; the barley adds a juicy layer or eight; vanilla is present, as is mocha and muscovado sugar; f24 just so long, and the sweetness that evolves towards the middle refusing to die; the peat is so fragile yet powering enough to shape and re-shape the structure and direction of the dram. This is lithe and living whisky, showing shape and form from nose to the longest of finishes; b25 there'll be another scramble to Copenhagen when the world gets word of this one...sadly I didn't get this until just after the last Bible went to press: as an October 04 bottling this might have won Whisky of the Year, but we'll never know! **51.4%.** *245 bottles for Juuls Vinhandel, Denmark.*

**Ardbeg Provenance 1974** bott 99 db **(96)** n24 t25 f23 b24. This is an exercise in subtlety and charisma, the beauty and the beast drawn into one. Until I came across the 25-year-old OMC verson during a thunderstorm in Denmark, this was arguably the finest whisky I had ever tasted: I opened this and drank from it to see in the year 2000. When I went through the Ardbeg warehouse stocks in 1997 I earmarked the '74 and '77 vintages as something special. This bottling has done me proud. **55.6%**

**Ardbeg Single Cask 2740** db **(83)** n21 t21 f20 b21. A bit hot with lots of oak to chew on. **52.3%**. *Belgium only.*

**Ardbeg Single Cask 2782** db **(87)** n22 t22 f21 b22. Positively schizophrenic. **52.3%**. *Italy only.*

⋰ **Ardbeg Still Young** dist 98, 2nd release bott 06 db **(93)** n24 still the sizzling smoky bacon, with perhaps a salty-buttered Arbroath Smoky for company; even a touch of the dentists...; t24 if this was any more delicate or highly strung, my tastebuds would have a breakdown. The peats are enormous, but simply hover and then land like butterflies; the barley offers moisture; f22 even at this age the oak begin to have an input, drying and adding a vanilla pod to the sweeter peats. Lengthy and lip-smacking; b23 a couple of generations back – maybe even less – this would not have been so much "Still Young" as "Getting on a Bit." This is a very good natural age for an Ardbeg as the oak is making a speech, which refuses to let it go on too long. Stylish – as one might expect. And, in my books, should be a regular feature. Go on. Be bold. Be proud say it: Ardbeg Aged 8 Years. Get away from the marketing straightjacket of old age... **56.2%. ncf.**

**Ardbeg Uigeadail** db **(89)** n25 awesome package of intense peat reek amid complex fruitcake and leather notes. Everything about this nose is broadside-big yet the massive oak never once oversteps its mark. A whiff of engine oil compliments the kippers. Perfection; t22 begins with a mind-blowing array of bitter-sweet oaky notes and then a strangely fruity peat entry; real scattergun whisky; f20 very odd finish with an off-key fruit element that flattens the usual Ardbeg grand finale; b22 a curious Ardbeg with a nose to die for. Some tinkering regarding the finish may lift this to being a true classic **54.1%**

**Ardbeg Very Young** db **(91)** n22 cured bacon on rye bread; a seasoning saltiness compliments the firmer peat while a second, lighter, level floats around. Complex stuff; t24 the initial strike is sweet malt followed by spicy peat; cocoa arrival on middle; f22 a tad oily which carries sweet, smoky malt all the way; b23 this bottling helps demonstrate the true genius of Ardbeg's versatility. **58.9%**

**Ardbeg Very Young For Discussion 1997** bott 03 db **(82)** n19 t22 f21 b21 Some Ardbeg greatness here, even with a phenols on the low side. Just that a poor, soapy bourbon cask has damaged proceedings somewhat. **58.9%**

⋰ **Ardbeg Young Uigeadail** db **(96)** n23 a touch of fruit, a little detracting soap, serious barley sugar and prickly peat. That's just the first layer...; t25 sumptuous, near perfectly weighted delivery with mollassed peat dried with some real toasty oak. Big and bordering on bruising, though the smoke does hold back slightly even if the spices don't; light oil keeps the wheels turning. The star turn in the late middle is the Quality Street candy hazelnut caramel – watch out for it; f24 layers of mocha and peat...as far as the tastebuds' detection abilities stretch; b24 forget the slight off-key nose: what really takes the breath away here is the ability to give so much yet at no stage ever be sweet or dry, just a mind-blowing mixture of both. Don't expect instant results here. Your taste buds need to learn and adapt. But by the fourth or fifth mouthful you will start getting the barely believable picture. **59.9%**

**Benedict XVI "Habemus Cerevisiam Destillatum!"** Commemorative Bottling to Honour the Pontificate **(91)** n22 t23 f24 b22. If Ardbeg wasn't blessed before, it probably has been now...this Ardbeg (though the distillery isn't mentioned on the label for some obscure legal reason) has been matured for a while in oak grown near the village of Gewekin, close to the Pope's home town of Regensburg, Germany. I take my funny hat off to the members of the local whisky club. You have excelled tourselves, herrs and fräuleins. **50%**. *Regensburger Whisky Club.*

**Cadenhead's Authentic Collection Ardbeg Aged 11 Years** Bourbon Hogshead, dist 93, bott May 05 **(95)** n24 my late old dad's allotment in Surrey: bonfires, freshly cut sticks of rhubarb, a hint of compost, freshly dug earth; t24 bitter-sweet malt that becomes more barley-sugar sweet as it progresses; the way the malt dissolves in the mouth is natural poetry; f23 a gradual build-up of fruit as the smoke delves and delivers then disappears. Long and enormously intricate; b24 touchingly evocative and beautiful; from a whisky standpoint...well, nothing short of mesmerically brilliant. **57.4%**. *270 bottles.*

**Cadenhead's Authentic Collection Ardbeg Aged 11 Years** Bourbon Hogshead, dist 93, bott May 05 **(94)** n23 rich, rugged peat with Surrey bonfires again, but fractionally less weighty and complex than its sister cask; t24 dry and intense with the malt, peat and oak arriving in one enormous tidal wave. Soft fruits eventually show. Stunning: some of the best post-maltings complexity delivered in bottle; f23 lovely cocoa and coffee notes survive with distant hints of citrus enlivening the growing dryness; b24 Ardbeg at its most unpredictable and enduring. A must for any collector. **59.5%**. *312 bottles.*

⋯ **Cadenhead's Ardbeg Aged 12 Years** dist 94, bott Sept 06 **(95)** n25 stick your head in a silent maltings kiln and you aren't too far away; the intensity appears to be on varying levels and the phenol level's high even for an Ardbeg. The grassy, citrussy sub plot adds just the right relief. Of its type, quite perfect; t24 how many peated malts do you find this crisp and mouth-watering? This is sensational because the palate is serenaded by smoke and barley in almost equal measures. Salivating and chewy; f23 now the smoke intensifies as the barley vanishes. This is all about variations of peat, being dry and clingy on one hand, and sweeter and lighter on another; b23 a second – maybe even third – fill bourbon cask allows for a warts and all look at a magnificent malt. Considering the lack of oaky input, the complexity astonishes. Ardbeg will be kicking themselves it was left to an independent to bottle something quite so revealing, sublime and different. **46%**. *396 bottles.*

⋯ **Cadenhead's Ardbeg Aged 12 Years (93)** n23 lively, gristy, farm-yardy; t23 puckering barley and then a wonderful wave of spice along with a plummy fruitiness; about as salivating as Ardbeg of this age gets; f23 back to soft grists again with loping layers of peat; b24 another Ardbeg that took over half an hour to get to truly appreciate. This really is complicated stuff. **58.2%**

⋯ **Cadenhead's Authentic Collection Ardbeg Aged 12 Years** Bourbon Hogshead, dist 93, bott Feb 06 **(93)** n22 dull, oily and hard to pick the structure. Some beautiful peats, though; t24 thumping smoke riding on a barley-gristy ticket and no shortage of cocoa; a real firecracker of an opening with brilliant juxtaposition between exploding spices and very sweet barley; f24 the vanillas and cocoa help overcome the oils and now we have some serious complexity. b23 an oily creature and early on it appears some Ardbeg magic is lost because of it. But on third and fourth inspection, that is clearly not the case: it's cranked up the finish and is never less than sheer bliss!! **59.3%**. *318 bottles.*

⋯ **Cadenhead's Authentic Collection Ardbeg Aged 13 Years 1993** Bourbon hogshead, dist 93, bott Nov 06 **(95)** n22 peppery edge to smoke t25 massive: almost pure Talisker in its spiced up delivery; the barley sweetens and juices the palate and smoke rumbles beautifully as those peppers bombard the roof of the mouth: TNT in a bottle; f24 more white pepper as the barley melts towards cocoa and coffee; the peat rumbles forever; b24 the spiciest Ardbeg I've ever come across: blind this is Talisker, though the peat depth is a giveaway. Once tasted never forgotten. **61.1%**. *246 bottles.*

**Connoiseurs Choice Ardbeg 1975 (91)** n24 t22 f23 b22 a seemingly demure dram that sends all kinds of hidden, delicious messages. **43%**. *G&M.*

**Connoisseurs Choice Ardbeg 1976 (94)** n24 Old Ardbeg in all its glory: there is a depth to the peat unique to the distillery and its fusion with the oak is pure textbook stuff. Quite awesome...; t24 fruit melts in the mouth and takes with it improbably juicy malt and an astonishing peat signature that is thick in phenols but somehow pliable enough to allow every other character to shine; f23 extremely soft with more fruit salad and punchy, slightly nipping and biting peat; b23 a wonderful Ardbeg of the old, original school that spellbindingly defies its years. Well done G&M for giving us some classic Ardbeg. But next time can we have it at 46%, please...!! **43%**. *Gordon & MacPhail.*

**Connoisseurs Choice Ardbeg 1995 (90)** n22 intricate and bitty; mildly yeasty and oaty; the peat is shy and demure; t22 young barley and diced apples give a youthful feel to the proceedings; f24 the late arrival of soft oak gives something for the malt to play against, and now the complexity rapidly develops. Playful spices and teasing smoke makes embodies the beauty; b22 Ardbeg at its most lethargic, and made at a time of enormous uncertainty at the distillery. But the finish alone projects this into Premier League status. **40%**. *G&M.*

⚬ **Connoisseurs Choice Ardbeg 1996 (88)** n21 eerily light and quiet both in terms of peat and strength: a bit like going to see Pink Floyd and the only thing unplugged are the amplifiers...; t22 light, gristy, juicy barley; the peat arrives at first as an afterthought but soon gathers momentum – and then vanishes again; f22 such a well behaved finale with soft vanilla here, a wisp of peat and heather there; b23 such a strange experience to find Ardbeg at 40%: I can hardly remember the last time I did. Hopefully, it will be the last....!! **40%**. *G&M.*

**La Reserve Ardbeg 9 Years Old (83)** n20 t22 f20 b21. Exceptionally clean, big peat but the complexity has not fully developed. **60.9%**

**Mackillop's Choice Ardbeg 1991** dist Oct 91 **(92)** n22 deftly smoked with oak and oranges in equal measure; wonderfully relaxed; t23 as delicate on the palate as the nose, with the smoke again refusing to force the issue and happy to play along with the malt-vanilla theme; f23 a fabulous interplay between dry vanilla and juicy malt; b24 nothing particularly exceptional about this cask. And it gets 92. Need I say more...? **43%**. *Angus Dundee.*

⚬ **Murray McDavid Ardbeg Aged 14 Years** Matured in Bourbon casks, dist 91, bott 05 **(91)** n23 three star turn with that trademark multi-dimensional peat and citrus character; t23 a delightful marriage of citrus and grist; refreshing yet enormously deep; f22 caramel wafer with praline and, of course, sweet peats; b23 can this distillery do no wrong? **46%. nc ncf**. *360 bottles.*

**Old Malt Cask Ardbeg 1993 Aged 10 Years** dist Mar 93, bott Jan 04 **(85)** n22 t21 f21 b21. Was on its way to becoming a top grade cask. **50%. nc ncf.**

**Old Malt Cask Ardbeg 1993 Aged 10 Years** dist Mar 93, bottApr 04 **(80)** n19 t20 f21 b20. Recovers from below par nose for an attractive, flinty-peat finish. **50%. nc ncf.** *Douglas Laing. 634 bottles.*

**Old Malt Cask Ardbeg 1975 Aged 25 Years** dist Oct 75, bott Oct 00 **(97)** n25 t24 f23 b25. Is this the best independent bottling of whisky of all time? I would say yes. And it would be a hard job to find a better single cask throughout Ardbeg's warehouses. I have tasted more individual casks of Ardbeg than any other whisky critic living, but never have I found one that so captures the brilliance of the world's greatest distillery – even my mark of 97 is me just nitpicking and being mean! Just one single glass at bottle strength – don't you dare add a single drop of water to this one – a quiet room, and you will be lost in the labyrinth of this great whisky for hours if not days. Will you ever get to the bottom of it? I very much doubt it. **50%**. *Douglas Laing. 702 bottles.*

**Old Malt Cask Ardbeg 10 Years Old** dist Oct 94, bott May 05 **(91)** n22 one of the firmest noses I've come across in bottled form for a while, with the malt showing little give despite the softness of the smoke; t23 the firmness transports to the palate but works wonderfully in chipping away at the oak; wonderful bitter-sweet character with pulse smoke; f23 long, becoming more salivating as it progresses with some late salt; b23 a quality little number. **50%.**

**Old Malt Cask Ardbeg 12 Years Old** Rum finish, dist 1 Oct 92, bott 14 Oct 04 **(95)** n24 dry, with the peat showing signs of pre-78 depth and complexity. Toasty and alluring; t24 quite fabulous arrival of what would be ultradry oak and peat were it not for the mouthwatering, saliva-gushing input of the barley; lovely fruits and even nut in the form of semi-dry Danish marzipan; f22 long, pulsing peat of a once-lost style with so many enormous sub-plots of bittersweet, fruity complexity; b25 those lucky buggers in downtown Manhattan! If Park Avenue have any bottles left, beat a path to their shelves as soon as you read this and get as many as you can afford. **50%.** *Douglas Laing & Co. For Park Avenue Liquor, NY, USA.*

**Old Malt Cask Ardbeg 14 Years Old** dist 28 Mar 91, bott 5 Apr 05 **(93)** n24 floral and perfumed with a touch of lavender; herby and earthy. And smoky...the complexity takes some unravelling; t22 very sharp on the palate; almost a bite to the malt with some vanilla flooding in but kept at bay by undulating smoke; f23 salty and fruity with a decidedly citrussy slant. The smoke heads off in a milky-coffee direction; b24 a busy, slightly directionless Ardbeg that keeps you guessing..and intrigued. **50%.** *Douglas Laing & Co.*

⌁⌁ **Old Malt Cask Ardbeg 14 Years Old** dist Mar 91, bott Aug 05 **(92)** n23 gossamer-light peat couched in some of the thick stuff, quite mossy and north-facing garden-ish; t23 gosh! Just how juicy can Ardbeg become? Swirling smoke but really it is the ripeness of the barley that impresses; f23 at last the peats form some kind of shape and structure, ushering the vanillas along the longish path; b23 Ardbeg coming off a slightly different tack, but still no less beautiful. **50%.**

⌁⌁ **Old Malt Cask Ardbeg 15 Years Old** dist Mar 91, bott Mar 06 **(92)** n23 heady, pungent peats battle orange peel, sultanas and even a touch of liquorice head on. The thing is, just how many layers are there?; t23 big and rich, the grapey theme continues until unseated by a hickory/peat stand; well spiced early but fades; f23 long, more hickory and Fishermen's Friend cough sweet with the sweetness holding sway throughout and the return of spice is perfect; b23 a dram that threatens to run amok but a sweet malty theme pervades. **50%.** *341 bottles.*

⌁⌁ **Old Malt Cask Ardbeg 15 Years Old** Rum finish, dist Mar 91, bott July 06 **(82)** n20 t22 f20 b20. Austere and lacking in the usual Ardbegian grace and elegance: I'm not sure this has been bottled at a time when the Ardbeg and rum were on the best speaking terms. **50%.** *Douglas Laing. 378 bottles.*

**Platinum Old and Rare Cask Ardbeg Aged 29 Years** dist 75, bott 04 **(94)** n24 some marmalade and nuts freshens the delicate peat reek: classic old Ardbeg that embraces the oak; t24 immediately the mouth is cluttered by peat of varying enormity; just the odd flake of toasted honeycomb can be found; f23 beautiful mocha just so compliments the vanilla and smoke; some soft toffee leaves a gentle trail and controls the mounting oak; b23 holds back from going full frontal. **58.3%.** *Douglas Laing.*

**Silver Seal Ardbeg 26 Years Old (79)** n20 t21 f19 b19. Spiced, sweet but flattened by caramel base line. **46%**

**Spirit of Scotland Ardbeg 1974 (86)** n22 t22 f20 b21. Oddball Ardbeg with everything in black and white and with complexity at a minimum. **40%**

**Spirit of Scotland Ardbeg 1993** cask 1091, bott Jul 03 db **(88)** n23 salty, farmyardy and bracing; t22 slow start then a steady development of vanilla and peat; pretty salty and puckering throughout; f21 dry toast while the peat rolls in; b21 one to be taken in large mouthfuls for full eye-watering effect. **52.3%.** *Potstill, Vienna. 295 bottles.*

# ARDMORE
### Speyside, 1899. Fortune Brands. Working.

**Ardmore 100th Anniversary 12 Years Old** dist 86, bott 99 db**(94)** n24 t23 f23 b24. This was to be one of the great whiskies of 1999. As this didn't get Allied switched on to what a truly great malt this is, nothing will. Quite fantastic.

**Ardmore 100th Anniversary 21 Years Old** db **(91)** n24 t22 f22 b23. A malt which simply caresses the tastebuds. The fruit influence is important but the malt and smoke are intriguingly subtle. It just gets better each time you taste it. **43%**

**Cask Ardmore 1990 (94)** n24 the peat arrives in a gristy, powdered form; the barley remains fresh and young with hints of orange; t23 mouthfilling, gently oiled, the peat fills around the palate at leisure while the oak offers the dryer chalky backdrop; f23 the mouthwatering, fresh properties continue, and the peat gently caresses whatever its contacts. Sweet and beguiling; b24 for late-coming Islayphiles, this loquacious, Lothario of a malt is closest you will ever get to seeing Port Ellen at its long-lost peak. **55.8%.** *G&M.*

⋯ **Gordon & MacPhail Ardmore Aged 16 Years** dist 90, bott 06 **(87)** n23 clean but seriously above average peat even by Ardmore standards; t22 pretty gristy for its age with an even radiation of smoke and spice; f20 smoky custard; b22 enjoyable; just perhaps lacking the usual complexity. **43%**

**Provenance Ardmore 12 Years Old** dist 18 Mar 92, bott 03 Dec 04 **(86)** n22 t21 f22 b21. The closest I have ever seen Ardmore come to being an Islay: tasting blind I'd have sworn this was Caol Ila. Attractive, but nothing like as complex and sophisticated as your average Ardmore. **46%.** *Douglas Laing & Co.*

⋯ **Provenance Ardmore Aged 12 Years** casks DMG 1328 & 1329, dist Spring 92, bott Summer 04 **(89)** n22 firm malt gives full scope to the soft but gently penetrating peat; t23 relaxed, with the barley coating the mouth beautifully; no oaky cracks and really understated sweet smoke; f22 oily style continues, ensuring excellent length. Intense barley pulses to the finish line; b22 much less peaty delivery than the nose suggests; the oils are exquisite. **46%.** *McGibbon's.*

⋯ **Provenance Ardmore 12 Years Old** dist Oct 93, bott Summer 06 **(93)** n24 perhaps only Ardmore can offer this style of smokiness: light, but because of the delicate, intricate nature of the other aromas appears smokier than it actually is. Cream rice pudding with a splodge of raspberry jam; vanilla wafer; t23 apologetic oils offer a thin layer of peat around the palate; elsewhere a degree of gristiness yields a juicy sweetness; f23 oaks and spices play are equal to any smoke; b23 great to see the distillery bottled at arguably its optimum age from second fill. Charming, absorbing and complex whisky that craves time to discover. **46%.**

**Scotch Malt Whisky Society Cask No. 66.16 Aged 20 Years (96)** n25 t24 f23 b24. Best whisky not to win an award in 2006 Bible. **54.8%**

**Scott's Selection Ardmore 1977 Sherry Wood** bott 03 **(86)** n22 t22 f21 b21. Another summer or two in cask and the balance would have been lost. **58.1%**

⋯ **The Single Malt of Scotland Ardmore Aged 11 Years Vintage 1994** cask no. 121011 **(82)** n20 t21 f21 b20. very strange Ardmore: hot in part and also from a cask which is not entirely at ease with itself. That said, the oily peat positively throbs and many excellent moments are to be had. **60.8%.** *The Whisky Exchange. 789 bottles.*

**The Un-chillfiltered Collection Ardmore Aged 12 Years** casks 4862 & 4863, dist 23 Jun 92, bott 10 Dec 04 **(84)** n22 t20 f22 b20. Strangely subdued, though the richness of the exotic fruit pleases immensely. **46%. nc ncf.** *Signatory, 540 bottles.*

⋯ **Whisky Magazine France Ardmore 1990** bott 2006 **(93)** n23 lean and clean, the peats are profound yet luxuriating in a gristy lightness; t24 divine delivery with that grist to the fore and helping to intensify the smoke; f23 hardens again with crisp barley pounding with confidence and class; b23 curses! The French have got their hands on the best bottling of Ardmore this year. **60.2%.** *400 bottles.*

## ARRAN (see Isle of Arran)

## AUCHENTOSHAN
**Lowlands, 1800. Morrison Bowmore. Working.**

**Auchentoshan 10 Years Old** db **(87)** n21 slightly soapy but redeemed by a mixture of boiled ginger and malt; t23 really delightful barley-sugar thrust and a dusting of vanilla; f22 rich esters and delicious sweet, malty chewability to the end: almost a touch of Jamaica pot still rum about it; b21 the most enjoyable bottling of Auchentoshan 10 for the last decade. **40%**

**Auchentoshan 12 years Old** db **(93) n**22 lilting malt and figs with, amazingly, some smoke: a real teasing surprise-package; **t**23 that curious smokiness hits the palate early, and then the sweetness heads in a Demerara direction; f24 medium roast Java combines with the sweet smoke for a spellbinding finale of extraordinary length; **b**24 this is legendary stuff. It could be a freak, smoky one-off. If so, here's a tip: get a bottle...NOW!! **43%**

·※· **Auchentoshan Aged 17 Years Bordeaux Wine Finish** db **(82) n**21 **t**21 **f**20 **b**20. Very oily early on by 'Toshan standards with the grape dominating throughout. Intriguingly tart and sharp, but perhaps overly so. Lovely ironic bourbon thrust to nose, though. **51%**. *3600 bottles.*

**Auchentoshan 18 Years Old** Limited Edition Selection of first and second fill oloroso sherry butts db **(89) n**22 clean and majorly complex grape; attractively dry; **t**23 brilliant fruit/barley delivery in excellent harmony. Salivating and mildly spicy; f22 bitter orange and vanilla; **b**22 a quite beautifully orchestrated Lowlander. **55.8%**. *4800 bottles.* ☉ ☉

**Auchentoshan 21 Years Old** db **(89) n**20 thin, clean but unpromising and surprisingly citrussy for its age; **t**24 really stunning mouth arrival with that deliciously estered, sweet maltiness that appears to be becoming an Auchentoshan trait; f23 soft, sultry malt with a thoughtful sprinkling of oak; **b**22 this was once a hot little number, worth avoiding. Now a Lowland treasure. **43%**

**Auchentoshan 1962** db **(88) n**21 cedar and mint; also a highly unusual, acidy hint of a big red wine that has been left in the glass; **t**22 silky and mouth-filling with more winey notes, but really it is the steady, intense malt that stars; f22 about as soft a fade as can be imagined with Jamaican Blue mountain coffee fitting in with the digestive biscuity follow-through; **b**23 a genuinely different malt. One to get to know. **40%**

·※· **Auchentoshan 1973** Sherry, dist 14 Mar 73, bott 08 July 05 db **(74) n**20 moist date but a big winey toffee-apple note tries to muscle in and send off −key; **t**19 the very first moment is a nano-second of barley-wine bliss − then it goes a bit frantic with a metallic bite sending everything out of kilter. Some dates try to return, but it's too little, too late; f17 hard and harsh; **b**18 just doesn't work. **55.5%**. *480 bottles.*

**Auchentoshan 1978** (*see* Auchentoshan 18 Years Old)

**Auchentoshan Select** db **(85) n**21 **t**22 **f**21 **b**21. Vastly improved and a gentle, refreshing and untaxing treat. **40%**

**Auchentoshan Three Wood** db **(84) n**22 **t**21 **f**21 **b**20. Still can't help thinking that the spirit from this distillery is simply too delicate for this type of treatment and the actual character vanishes under the welter of wood. **43%**

**Aberdeen Distillers Auchentoshan 1992** cask 6196 dist Oct 92, bott Nov 03 **(82) n**20 **t**21 **f**21 **b**20. They don't come much more youthful or sweeter than this. **43%**.

**Berrys' Own Selection Auchentoshan 1983 21 Years Old** bott 04 **(77) n**17 **t**20 f19 **b**20. Estery, malty and sweet, but not up to the usual very high standards of Berrys' Own. **46%**. *Berry Bros & Rudd.*

·※· **Berry's' Own Selection Auchentoshan 1983 Aged 22 Years (71) n**19 t18 f17 **b**17. Almost a Japanese buckwheat style. But a rare off-cask from this bottler: by 'eck it's grim. **46%**. *Berry Bros & Rudd..*

**Cadenhead's Authentic Collection Auchentoshan Aged 12 Years** dist 92, bott May 05 **(82) n**19 **t**22 **f**21 **b**19. Some seriously chewy moments, but has that old-fashioned Auchentoashan off-target feel. **57.2%**. *294 bottles.*

·※· **Dewar Rattray Individual Cask Bottling Auchentoshan 1991 Aged 15 Years** cask no. 478, dist Feb 91, bott May 06 **(83) n**19 **t**22 **f**21 **b**21. It's not often you get a slightly feinty triple distilled whisky... but you have one here. On the plus side there is enough body here for you to get your tongue around... **59%**. *390 bottles.*

⋅⋅⋅ **Duncan Taylor Collection Auchentoshan 1999** cask no. 800003, dist Mar 99, bott Mar 06 **(73) n**21 **t**21 **f**15 **b**16. After textbook nose and delivery, falls apart alarmingly and bitterly as the balance with oak is lost. **43%**. *430 bottles.*

**MacLeod's Lowland Single Malt Aged 8 Years (74) n**17 **t**20 **f**18 **b**19. Thin, malty and cream-toffee sweet. **40%**. *Ian MacLeod (Auchentoshan, though not stated).*

⋅⋅⋅ **Murray McDavid Auchentoshan 1992 (77) n**19 **t**20 **f**19 **b**19. Creamy, fruity...but somehow not on the ball. **46%**.

⋅⋅⋅ **Murray McDavid Mission Auchentoshan 1981 Aged 25 Years** Bourbon/ Mourvedre, bott 06 **(85) n**22 **t**22 **f**20 **b**21. The calm nose gives no warning of the grapey, mouthwatering turbulence ahead. **55.7%. nc ncf**. *350 bottles.*

**Old Malt Cask Auchentoshan Aged 25 Years** dist Oct 78, bott Oct 03 **(93) n**24 **t**23 **f**22 **b**24. Not what I expected ... in fact, an entirely unique fingerprint to any Lowlander (indeed perhaps any malt) I have tasted before, and that is saying something. For any Lowland fans, you miss this at your peril. For others, find a good half hour to simply sit back, drink, close eyes, and be truly entertained and amazed. **50%. nc ncf sc**. *Douglas Laing.*

⋅⋅⋅ **Provenance Auchentoshan Aged 10 Years** dist Apr 95, bott Nov 05 (83) n20 t22 f21 b20. An attractive interplay of solid and soft barley. Refreshing and more-ish. **46%**. *McGibbon's.*

⋅⋅⋅ **Secret Stills Auchentoshan Aged 17 Years** Distillery no.3, sherry hogshead casks 5746/7, dist 8.12.89, bott Jun 06 **(83) n**21 **t**22 **f**19 **b**21. Pleasant, undemanding though perhaps thwarted rather than enriched by the sherry. **45%**. *G&M. 500 bottles.*

**The Un-Chillfiltered Collection Auchentoshan Aged 12 Years** Bourbon Barrels 7336/7337, dist 25 Nov 92, bott 23 Feb 05 **(79) n**19 **t**22 **f**18 **b**20. Curiously perfumed, some powering oaky punches lay into the thick malt. **46%. nc ncf**. *Signatory. 509 bottles.*

**Vom Fass Auchentoshan 12 Years Old (88) n**22 clean and green; **t**23 startlingly early cocoa kick: not unlike a chocolate lime. Wonderfully refreshing; **f**22 soft, lazy, yet lingering. Any lighter and it would float out of the glass; **b**21 great to see the distillery living up to its regional style so eloquently. Twelve by name, six by nature! **40%**. *Austria.*

**Whisky Galore Auchentoshan 1990 Aged 12 Years (78) n**19 **t**20 **f**19 **b**20. Young, thin, sharp and tangy. **46%**

# AUCHROISK
## Speyside, 1974. Diageo. Working.

**Auchroisk Aged 10 Years** db **(84) n**20 **t**22 **f**21 **b**21. Tangy orange on the nose, the malt amplified by a curious saltiness on the palate. **43%**. *Flora and Fauna.*

**Blackadder Raw Cask Auchroisk 1989** cask no 30264 dist Jun 89, bott Nov 03 **(84) n**22 **t**21 **f**21 **b**20. The distillers were surprised how light their malt was then the distillery began operation – hence the use of sherry finishing in The Singleton. Here we have confirmation: a Speysider that tastes like a very good young bourbon, or an old grain whisky. Delicious it may be, but I've marked it down slightly as I like my Speysiders to taste of malt. **61.9%. nc ncf sc**.

**Cadenhead's Authentic Collection Auchroisk Aged 15 Years** Sherry Butt, dist 89, bott May 05 **(69) n**15 **t**20 **f**16 **b**18. Sulphur tainted; shame because the honey delivery is a noble waste. **59.5%**. *636 bottles.*

⋅⋅⋅ **Cadenhead's Authentic Collection Auchroisk Aged 16 Years** Butt, dist 89, bott Sept 06 **(71) n**17 **t**18 **f**18 **b**18. Sulphur-clobbered. A tragedy, as there are some great moments here – if you are able to isolate them. **58.8%**. *666 bottles.*

⋅⋅⋅ **Chieftain's Auchroisk Aged 11 Years Medoc Finish (79) n**20 **t**22 **f**18 **b**19. Salivating but thin. **43%**. *Ian Macleod.*

⋅⋅⋅ **Connoisseurs Choice Auchroisk 1993 (78) n**19 **t**21 **f**19 **b**19. Simplistic malt essay of few words. **43%**. *Gordon & MacPhail.*

⋅⋅⋅ **Kingsbury's New Celtic Auchroisk 15 Years Old** cask no. 3653, dist 90 **(86) n**22 t22 f20 b22 this distillery produces blending malt. Casks worthy of bottling are few and far between: this, with its intense barley, is one. **62.8%.** *Japan Import System.*

⋆ **Maverick Auchroisk Aged 12 Years Port Finish** dist 93, bott 04 **(87) n**20 poppy seeds and pepper; **t**23 beautiful delivery of warming fruit and juicy barley; **f**22 medium length, and a gentle burn of soft spice in oil; **b**22 maverick right enough...an Auchroisk at last that can get the pulse racing! Now this is a good example of justified cask finishing. **46%. nc ncf.** *Murray McDavid.*

⋆ **Old Malt Cask Auchroisk Aged 16 Years (81) n**21 **t**20 **f**20 **b**20. Pear drops and barley. **50%.** *Douglas Laing.*

⋆ **Old Malt Cask Auchroisk Aged 30 Years** dist Apr 75, bott Nov 05 **(77) n**21 **t**19 **f**18 **b**19. A 30-y-o Auchroisk....!! I must be getting old. I remember standing outside my spirit merchants in Cross Street, Manchester, waiting for the delivery of the first-ever bottling – a distillery bottled 12 year old. But what a disappointment most bottlings have been since, and this is typically thin and lacklustre. **48.9%. nc ncf.** *Douglas Laing.* 239 bottles.

**Private Cellars Selection Auchroisk 1989** bott 04 **(88) n**23 wonderful fruit, beautifully clean and precise. The malt adds a relaxed second layer; **t**21 juicy but showing sings of tiredness; **f**22 recovers for a spectacular spice explosion balanced by sweet barley; **b**22 Auchroisk and spice in the same sentence: doesn't happen very often. A real charmer. **43%.** *Speyside Distillers.*

**Scotts Selection Auchroisk 1989** bott 05 **(77) n**19 **t**21 **f**18 **b**19. Decent malt surge; otherwise dry and nondescript. **63.9%.** *Speyside Distillers.*

## AULTMORE
### Speyside, 1896. John Dewar & Son. Working.

**Aultmore 12 Years Old** db **(86) n**22 **t**22 **f**20 **b**22. Do any of you remember the old DCL distillery bottling of this from, what, 25 years ago? Well, this is nothing like it. **40%** *John Dewar & Sons.*

**Connoisseurs Choice Aultmore 1989 (87) n**21 freshly sandpapered floors plus some honey and under-ripe fig. A distant hint of peat-smoke; **t**22 excellent clarity to the clean barley; intelligent sparring between barley and vanilla-oak; **f**22 a delightful smoke-fade returns ensuring excellent bitter-sweet character; **b**22 clean, impressive whisky that perfectly captures the distillery fingerprint: about time, too, for this usually an ill-served Speysider. **43%**

⋆ **Dun Bheagan Aultmore Aged 15 Years (76) n**19 **t**19 **f**19 **b**19. A bit dense, monosyllabic and bitter. **43%.** *Ian Macleod.*

⋆ **Norse Cask Selection Aultmore 1989 Aged 15 Years (83) n**18 **t**23 **f**21 **b**21. Tricky vintage at this distillery, '89. Usually the nose sucks and this one's no exception. However, the intensity of the barley delivery is mind-blowingly beautiful. **55.8%.** *Quality World, Denmark.*

⋆ **Old Malt Cask Aultmore 16 Years Old** dist June 1989, bott Dec 05 **(66) n**17 **t**17 **f**16 **b**16. One for the mother-in-law. **50%.** *Douglas Laing.* 270 bottles.

**Old Master's Aultmore 1989** cask 2454 bott 03 **(86) n**21 **t**22 **f**22 **b**21. A welcome return to the old, effective and big style of 25 years ago. **60.5%**

**Old Masters Aultmore 1989 15 Year Old** cask no. 726, bott Feb 05 **(89) n**20 pretty confused; **t**23 wonderful, dank Jamaican ginger cake – with extra ginger. A bit of a spot the malt competition; **f**23 perhaps only Talisker at full throttle can match this for sheer spice wooomph!! **b**23 delicious gingery spice and busy throughout and though a fraction out of alignment it hardly seems to matter. For those who like their whisky hot! **54.9%.** *James MacArthur.*

**Private Cellars Selection Aultmore 1987** bott 04 **(84) n**21 **t**20 **f**22 **b**21. Wonderful honeycomb flows through the finale. **43%.** *Speyside Distillers.*

**Provenance Aultmore 12 Years Old** dist Spring 92, bott Autumn 04 **(81) n**22 **t**19 **f**20 **b**20. Fabulous early interaction between soft smoke, honied malt and citrus and clattering oak. But the oak just has too much sway. **46%.** *Douglas Laing*

⋄ The Single Malt of Scotland Aultmore Aged 13 Years Vintage 1992 cask 3852 **(90)** n23 high octane barley: as intense as it gets; t23 beautiful gloss to the ultra-intense barley shuts out any telling oak interference; f22 well integrated with vanilla forming beautiful patterns on the single-minded malt; b22 simplistic but one of the best Aultmores of the last five or six years. **57.6%**. *The Whisky Exchange.*

Whisky Galore Aultmore 1987 Aged 15 Years **(85)** n22 t21 f21 b21. The clean, uncluttered stuff blenders crave for. **46%**

Whisky Galore Aultmore 1989 Aged 14 Years **(78)** n20 t20 f19 b19. A pleasantish dram, but the sherry is indistinct. **46%**

## BALBLAIR
### Highlands (Northern), 1872. Inver House. Working.

Balblair 10 Years Old db **(86)** n21 t22 f22 b21. Such an improved dram away from the clutches of caramel. **40%** ⊙

Balblair Aged 16 Years db **(84)** n22 t22 f20 b20. Definitely gone up a notch in the last year. The lime on the nose has been replaced by dim Seville oranges; the once boring finish reveals elements of fruit and spice. It's the barley- rich middle that shines, though, and some more work will belt this up into the high 90s where this great distillery belongs. **40%** ⊙ ⊙

Balblair Aged 24 Years Limited Edition dist 1979, bott Oct 03 db **(90)** n23 t22 f22 b23 absolutely spot-on whisky from a truly great distillery. The absence of colouring on this underlines my assertion that this is a distillery that is far too good to be tampered with at any age. **46%**. *3150 bottles.*

Balblair 35 Years Old Limited Edition db **(91)** n23 debonair and regal, there is wonderful confidence to the elegant ginger and citrus lead while the oak offers grey around the temples; t23 more slivers of caramelised ginger as the intense malt spices up and the oak forms almost a cloudy haze on the palate; f22 gentle and sweet, a touch of cocoa offers excellent balance, though its age really shows at the death; b23 textured and weighted almost to perfection, the malt really does display enormous depth. **45.4%**

Balblair 38 Years Old Limited Edition db **(93)** n23 tangerines on the turn; lavender guarding the wardrobe; t23 massive oak injection suggests that it's past its sell-by date, but a magnificent infusion of ripe fruit ranging from juiceleaking plums to grapefruit brings this back to life; f23 a pulsating finish with soft spices amid the juice and barley; b24 what a treat of a dram, always teetering at the edge of the cliff but being brought back to safety by some extraordinary fruit. **44%**

Balblair 1989 Limited Edition db **(82)** n21 t21 f20 b20. Good honey in places. **46%**

⋄ Balblair Peaty 1992 cask 2932 **(88)** n21 a vague smoky buzz; youthful for its age; t22 sweet and biting at first then a wave of soft peat; f23 quite classy at the death as varying waves of bitter-sweet malt and oak delve into the light smoke; b22 Very good distillate, but don't expect an Ardbeg or even an Ardmore here. **58.8%**

⋄ Balblair Peaty 1992 cask 3026 **(81)** n20 t20 f21 b20. Re-defines the term "peaty". The delicate smoke hides behind firm malt; takes a little time to get going though there is no doubting the overall quality. Just comes up a bit short on the complexity stakes. **61.5%**

Balblair Elements db **(84)** n20 t20 f23 b21. Just like the Scottish elements, this seems to change dramatically from bottling to bottling. This one starts indifferently but the finish is an essay in luxurious honey. **40%**

⋄ Cadenhead's Authentic Collection Balblair Aged 16 Years dist 90, bott Sept 06 **(94)** n23 pithy, fruit stones. Take your time here: this is very complex; t24 astonishing exhibition of sweet-dry harmonization; a wonderful early fruit edge which is then met full on by a dry, oakier blast. Pure complexity and indulgence; f23 massive cocoa arrival in tidal waves; b24 One of those stunning casks which reveals little on first meeting, but after getting to know you offers nothing but sheer elegance: a malt just oozing class. **58.8%**. *174 bottles.*

∴ **Dewar Rattray Individual cask Bottling Balblair 1990 Aged 15 Years** cask no. 1145, dist Apr 90, bott Sept 05 **(89) n**23 exemplary balance considering the crispness of the barley; **t**22 juicy barley dripping off firm but unobtrusive oak; **f**22 softens with slices of toast and vanilla; **b**22 just one of those whiskies that works brilliantly, though hard to say exactly why. **62.9%.** *680 bottles.*

**Harrods Balnagown Balblair (88) n**22 sharp malt, a little green and raw: the fresh-mown grass is irresistible; **t**23 citrussy fruit notes; **f**20 vanilla, caramel; **b**22 lovely, but a tad duller on the caramel finish than I remember. **40%** ☉ ☉

∴ **Private Collection Balblair 1973 (90) n**22 not quite impenetrable sherry, but close; **t**24 chewy and spicy with moist and dry malts. Just so stunningly juicy for its age; **f**22 big dry mocha finish, getting roasty late on; **b**22 what an excellent sherry cask this whisky has been housed in. Bottled just in time, though. **45%.** *G&M.*

∴ **The Single Malt of Scotland Balblair Aged 40 Years Anniversary Selection** Hogshead cask no. 1346 **(89) n**22 enticing, fruity nose that is exotic yet traditional. There is the most delicate puff of peat, but four decades of oak offers us mango with a dash of passion fruit. Over-ripe, but lovely; **t**22 as silky as one would expect from this type of oak development; there is a puckering element, too. But holds together against the odds; **f**23 loads of cocoa but just enough barley sweetness – and again that charming little smoke injection - to balance things out; **b**22 another cliff-hanger, with the oak threatening to get away from things, but remains stylishly impressive to the last. **42.8%. nc ncf.** *The Whisky Exchange. 152 bottles.*

# BALMENACH
## Speyside, 1824. Inver House. Working.

**Balmenach Aged 25 Years Golden Jubilee** db **(89) n**21 **t**23 **f**22 **b**23. What a glorious old charmer this is! An essay in balance despite the bludgeoning nature of the beast early on. Takes a little time to get to know and appreciate: persevere with this belter because it is classic stuff for its age. **58%.** *Around 800 decanters.*

**Blackadder Aberdeen Distillery Balmenach 14 Years Old** cask no. 2500, dist Apr 90, bott Nov 04 **(86) n**20 **t**23 **f**22 **b**21. Never quite hits a comfortable pitch or rhythm yet still has enough charisma to entertain. **46%**

∴ **The Bottlers Balmenach 21 Years Old** Spanish oak, refill sherry, cask no. 3056, dist Dec 84, bott Dec 05 **(82) n**19 **t**22 **f**21 **b**20. Lots to chew on, clever use of distant smoke and at times attractively spiced. But we have come to expect rather more from this particular bottler. **57.8%**

∴ **Cadenhead's Authentic Collection Balmenach-Glenlivet Aged 17 Years** Bourbon Hogshead, dist 89, bott Sept 06 **(90) n**23 sexily soft: wafer-thin oak, sultry barley and a dab of something vaguely fruity all in perfect proportions; **t**22 short, muddled delivery and then a spreading of finely-tuned, trim malt; **f**22 bigger oak say, the light bitterness balancing the juicier barley; **b**23 in many ways simplistic, but has that certain something that picks it out above the norm. **53.1%.** *312 bottles.*

∴ **Chieftain's Balmenach 15 Years Old** Hogshead **(77) n**19 **t**21 **f**18 **b**19. Fruity and pleasant, but a fraction too over-oaked. **43%.** *Ian MacLeod.*

**Deerstalker Balmenach Aged 12 Years (82) n**20 **t**21 **f**20 **b**21. Surprisingly and disappointingly dull, with just enough sweet malt in there to see off the worst of the big oak thanks to this being the new, natural-coloured bottling. Even so, this seems a lot older than twelve. **40%.** *Aberko.*

**Deerstalker Balmenach Aged 18 Years (89) n**23 near faultless sherry butt influence gives a zesty, mocha-tinged frame to the heavyweight malt; **t**23 superb arrival of spicy, Christmas puddingy fruit that zips around the palate leaving a delicious trail of sweet barley; **f**21 the oak kicks in reluctantly, but its arrival is welcome and balancing; **b**22 perhaps the more distant hint of sulphur, but it really is acceptable here: this naturally coloured update is amazingly fresh and mouthwatering for all its age and sherry influence; a massive improvement on the old, caramel-enhanced bottlings. **46%. ncf.** *Aberko.*

Old Malt Cask Balmenach 20 Years Old dist Jan 84, bott Sep 04 (91) n23 butterscotch and apricot; astonishingly crisp for its age; t23 intense, ultra-concentrated malt sweetened further by a dash of sugar cane; oak adds a touch of calming vanilla towards the middle; f23 layers of malt ensure a long finale with the faintest hint of smoke at the death; b22 a charmer for the sweettoothed. 50%.

Private Cellars Selection Balmenach 1979 bott 03 (77) n19 t20 f19 b19. Caramelised and nondescript: I've seen witches offering a hillier terrain. 43%.

## THE BALVENIE
### Speyside, 1892. William Grant & Sons. Working.

The Balvenie Aged 10 Years Founders Reserve db (90) n23 astonishing complexity: the fruit is relaxed, sultanas and malty suet. A sliver of smoke and no more: everything is hinted and nudged at rather than stated. Superb; t24 here we go again: threads of malt binding together barely detectable nuances. Thin liquorice here, grape there, smoke and vanilla somewhere else; f20 Light muscovado-toffee flattens out the earlier complexity. The bitter-sweet balance remains brilliant to the end; b23 just one of those all-time-great standard 10-year-olds from a great distillery – pity they've decided to kill it off. 40% ⊙

The Balvenie Double Wood Aged 12 Years db (77) n22 t20 f17 b18. I had hoped to report an improvement on this expression from one of the world's greatest distilleries. But, sadly, no can do. Over the top with the sherry, then later the caramel (either added or natural), this just never gets going and Balvenie's legendary complexity is buried far too deep to find. 40%

⠸ Balvenie Rum Wood Aged 14 Years db (88) n22 excitable malt; lively almost piercing sugars; t23 incredible spice delivery, seriously warming and increasingly sensual as the malt fights back; f21 lots of toffee-barley; b22 tasted blind I would never have recognized the distillery: I'm not sure if that's a good thing. 47.1%

⠸ The Balvenie Roasted Malt Aged 14 Years dist 92 db (94) n23 thick, sweet, intense, vaguely floral, even more vaguely bourbony but very, very different; t25 salivating for all the enormity. The fruitiness is in barley concentrate form and offers a delivery as memorable as it is unique; the barley juice appears to seep into the palate in equal spurts. Breathtaking and nigh-on perfect; f23 warming spices develop while the oak tries to gain a foothold into the silky barley; a tad thin towards the end; b23 having beaten the drum for this distillery longer than any independent observer breathing, it is so rewarding to find a bottling that so encapsulates Balvenie's brilliance. To do so, though, they have used a percentage of malt briefly germinated before being massively roasted in the style of a stout beer. The result is not unlike some European mainland malt whisky styles but fortified with the usual Balvenie complexity and weight. For the first 25 seconds on the palate it is, quite frankly, probably as good as anything you are likely to taste for many years and only the quick-ish finish robs it of a certain Bible Award. 47.1%. ncf.

The Balvenie Aged 15 Years Single Barrel db (93) n23 cracking vanilla-malt split. Complex, intriguing, something to really get your nose into. Quite maltings-floorish; t24 massive malt surge is invigorating and mouthwatering. Glorious; f22 keeps clean and relatively oak-free; b24 just one of those drams that should be within touching distance at strategic points around the house. 50.4%. *Being single barrel the bottlings do change quite regularly: fortunately the magnificence of the quality rarely does.*

⠸ Balvenie New Wood Aged 17 Years db (85) n23 t22 f19 b21. A naturally good age for Balvenie: the nose is lucid and exciting, the early delivery is thick with rich malt. This, though, has sucked out lots of caramel from the wood to leave an annoyingly flat finish. 40%

The Balvenie Aged 21 Years Port Wood db (87) n23 clean, mouthwatering evidence of fresh port pipes; t22 the wine swamps the malt for a while, but being Balvenie the complexity returns and sweet maltiness leads the way; f21 vanilla and toffee; **b**21 using port pipes like this can backfire on a malt as complex as Balvenie, but this one comes through with flying Scottish and Portuguese colours. **40%** ⊙⊙

**The Balvenie Thirty Aged 30 Years** db **(92) n**24 a fusion of fruits from grape to pears, all topped off with smoke and a hint of tiring oak; **t**23 stand-your-spoon-in-the-stuff proportions and seasoned with a hint of spice; **f**22 the oak which threatens on the nose erupts slightly on the finish, but still the malt offers an intensity that softens the blow; **b**23 Balvenie is a rare Speysider that by and large manages to handle encroaching age with ease up to this type of vintage. **47.3%**

**The Balvenie Aged 50 Years** cask 191 db **(87) n**23 coffee and biscuits alongside the ultra-ripe, thick sherry, not unlike moist cherry fruitcake. Smoke remains after the sherry is burnt out; **t**23 some suppressed oak does its best to escape, but has a major battle to fight its way through the layers of big grape. Lovely spices point in the direction of some peat; **f**19 pretty shattered oak offers a bitter finale, but the fruit does all it can to soften things and lengthen out matters; **b**22 a noble dram battered by oak but comes through with a degree of nobility. *Natural strength.*

**The Balvenie 1967 Vintage Cask** db **(89) n**24 **t**22 **f**21 **b**22. Dry and complex.

**The Balvenie 1968 Vintage Cask** db **(86) n**23 **t**22 **f**20 **b**21. The delicate sweetness accentuates the dry finale. Pretty delicious. **50.8%**

**The Balvenie 1971 Vintage Cask** cask no. 8919 db **(78) n**21 **t**20 **f**18 **b**19. Wonderfully exotic fruit (often a sign of advanced age) on the nose, and for all the undoubted complexity on show the oak has defeated even a Balvenie here. **46.8%**

**The Balvenie 1971 Vintage Cask** cask no. 8921 db **(79) n**20 **t**21 **f**19 **b**19. The barley tries its complex best, but it's an unequal struggle against the oak. **46.9%**

**The Balvenie 1971 Vintage Cask** cask 8935 db **(90) n**23 a slight Canadian whisky/bourbony element here thanks to the sweet influence of the grain against the firm oakiness. Attractive and quite complex; **t**22 beautiful malt develops in both intensity and sweetness; soft natural caramel and vanillas begin to fill the middle; **f**22 pulsing barley and lashings of vanilla: freeze it and you could make an ice cream from this! **b**23 of the three, this was the only one worth bottling in the sainted name of Balvenie thanks to the malty sweetness seeing off the oak and in a way that offers style and enormity. This really is a beauty! And such can sometimes be the thin line between something that works (in this case wonderfully) and something that doesn't. **47.3%**

**The Balvenie 1972 Vintage Cask** db **(88) n**22 **t**23 **f**21 **b**22. A superb, lightly smoked Balvenie that shows some age but wears it well. *Natural strength.*

⸞⸞⸞ **Balvenie 1972 Vintage** cask no. 14811 db **(82) n**20 **t**22 **f**20 **b**20. A tiring, exotic fruited effort which glows rather than shines. **47.3%**

**The Balvenie 1973 Vintage Cask** db **(92) n**22 distinctly bourbony with sweet leathery tones sitting beside vanilla and a trickle of honey. Just a distant waft of peat brings us back to Scotland; **t**24 this is the acceptable face of oak: delicate bourbony notes gush at you, then a honey spice middle with vanilla ice cream; **f**22 natural caramel slows it all down but still waves of bourbony sweetness both rattle and caress the tastebuds; **b**24 some purists will find too many stars and stripes to the character if this malt. Even I thought I was in a Wild Turkey warehouse for a moment or two. But sheer quality cannot be denied. **49.7%**

**The Balvenie 1989 Port Wood** db **(83) n**20 **t**22 **f**21 **b**20. The nose is remarkably undemonstrative, all the fruity action arriving up front early on the tastebuds. Good follow-through. **40%**

**The Balvenie 1991 Port Wood** db **(91) n**23 darting barley and fruit gives a feather-light alternative to the much thicker, duskier malty oak beneath; **t**23 enormous weight and depth offered by the chewing malt; the fruit is a peripheral, spice-wielding addition to complexity; **f**22 a few strands of caramel (natural, I hope) add to the weight of the rich malt finale; **b**23 I have long argued that two of the most complex noses in the world belong to Glenmorangie and Balvenie. So, a decade after Morangie began the trend, it was interesting to see how

Balvenie coped with port pipes. Well, Balvenie's bigger body means that it is a little more heavy-handed. But as for complexity, Balvenie may even shade it by continuing to head down the malt rather than fruit path, using the port only to season rather than dominate. **40%**

⁓ **The Balvenie Merry Christmas 2005** cask 749, dist 91, bott 25/10/05 db **(94) n**24 the type of cask isn't stated. But this is like almost pure Demerara rum hob-nobbing with top-of-the-table rich Balvenie malt. The result is uniquely brilliant; **t**24 more Demerara-style kick with all kinds of tangent sugary, mollased notes heading off in every conceivable direction. Again the malt holds firm and digs in with some big oak notes; **f**23 roasty, hickory, toasty and some boiled fruit sweets; **b**23 Balvenie as you've never seen it before. But will definitely want to see again. **58.4%.** *60 bottles.*

**Cadenhead's Authentic Collection Balvenie - Glenlivet Aged 25 Years** Bourbon Hogshead, dist 79, bott May 05 **(95) n**24 dank, north-facing gardens, earthy and rich; some zesty barley adds a telling counterpunch. Such wonderful complexity; **t**24 perhaps the most intense malt you will find on the market today: everything flawless and in concentrate. Wow!! **f**23 some natural caramels escape to flattens things down slightly, but still the malt continues its enormous way. Memorable and truly beautiful; **b**24 Cadenhead's have bravely named Balvenie as the distillery here: how apposite in the year Deep Throat revealed his own identity. I'm sure this dram will be enjoyed by those able to spot a work of art in the offices of solicitors and barristers around the UK... Quite an exhibit in anyone's living-room. **52.7%.** *234 bottles.*

⁓ **Cadenhead's Chairman's Stock Balvenie-Glenlivet Aged 27 Years** dist 79, bott May 06 **(93) n**24 such depth: you need a mini-sub to get to the bottom of the complex barley-oak interplay, rounded off with a swirl of peat smoke and apple; **t**24 sweet, almost gristy intensity to the malt; the layering of the barley-sugar and oak is mind-blowing; **f**22 a slight hint of sweet apple, just like the nose; deft vanilla brings things to a close; **b**23 although from a bourbon cask, Balvenie shown in a fruit-candy hue. Gorgeous. **52.5%.** *264 bottles.*

# BANFF
## Speyside, 1863–1983. Demolished.

**Banff Rare Malts 21 Year Old** 2004 db **(90) n**22 tangy, salty oak with citrus and distant lavender and smoke; **t**24 sensational arrival of pulsing malt and fruit enriched by wonderful smoky spices and the most delicate oiliness; **f**22 reverts to a more docile barley and vanilla merchant; **b**22 a quietly complex but brilliantly impressive addition to the Rare Malts range. **57.1%**

**Berrys' Own Selection Banff 1975 Aged 28 Years** bott 04 **(79) n**21 **t**20 **f**19 **b**19. Attractive apples, but feeling its age. **46%.** *Berry Bros & Rudd.*

⁓ **Cadenhead's Banff 29 Years Old (73) n**19 **t**19 **f**18 **b**17. Too heavily oaked: should have been bottled at **25. 52%**

⁓ **Rarest of the Rare Banff 1975** cask 3421, dist Nov 75, bott Apr 06 **(78) n**22 **t**20 **f**18 **b**18. Lovely nose and early malt delivery. But oak, sadly, has won the battle. **43.5%.** *Duncan Taylor. 179 bottles.*

⁓ **Rarest of the Rare Banff 1980** cask 2912, dist Nov 80, bott Apr 06 **(91) n**24 like entering a cake shop; **t**23 the prominent honey on nose is immediately transferred to the palate; an oaky buzz gives way to big barley; **f**22 milky-coffee; **b**22 some Banff bottlings can be supreme and here is one. Even the oaky threat retreats with good grace. **53.1%.** *Duncan Taylor. 181 bottles.*

# BEN NEVIS
## Highland (Western), 1825. Nikka. Working.

**Ben Nevis 10 Years Old** db **(88) n**21 enormously chunky and weighty: for a 10-y-o the oak is thick, but sweetened medley of ripe fruits; **t**22 an almost syrupy mouth feel: a tad cloying but the malt is something you can so get your teeth into;

f23 long with traces of liquorice and hickory; b22 a massive malt that has steadied itself in recent bottlings, but keep those knives and forks to hand! **46%** ☉ ☉

**Ben Nevis Ten Years Old** bott 03 db **(88)** n21 t24 f20 b23. Bottled for the Japanese market, this expression shows Ben Nevis at its most colourful, characterful and complex: no shrinking violet, this. The mouth arrival is spellbinding. The definitive 10-year-old Ben Nevis for whisky clubs to chase. **43%**. *Japan only.*

**Ben Nevis 30 Years Old** cask 2519 db **(86)** n22 t22 f20 b22. A malt living on the edge: just about over the top oak but there is enough sweetness around not only too see it through but to make for a fascinating cocoa and coffee dram. **56.9%**

**Ben Nevis 1990 Port Wood Finish** bott 04 db **(92)** n21 nutty and fruity, there is some freshly ground coffee – and smoke – lurking, too. Marked down only by a slight sulphur-ish blemish; t24 bloody hell!! Few whiskies have quite so many flavour profiles landing simultaneously on the palate. There is a distinct metallic note that seems to explode in harmony with rich honey and about the most intense barley you will ever find. Oily, and coats the mouth with a fruity, suety layer. The fruitiness just disappears off the scale; f23 a very slight peat smoke drifts out towards the sweet barley while the oak offers a drier level; b24 pouring into the glass is a startling experience: it is like a Beaujolais. In 30 years of nosing my way around whisky warehouses and labs, never have I come across something as entirely unique as this: distillery manager Colin Ross deserves a medal struck for producing something so extraordinary. Collectors around the world will eventually trade their spouse for bottles of this. **61.6%**

**Cadenhead's Authentic Collection Ben Nevis 14 Year Old** dist 90, bott May 05 **(87)** n22 marauding sherry of decent standard if, distantly, a trifle flawed; t22 perhaps a slight overdose on the oloroso, but then pans out to reveal much sharper malty tones: quite green on the palate, almost of unripe grape; f21 long, green grape-fruity with developing cocoa and toast; b22 borderline sherry butts where the cracks show but are repaired by the enormity of the rich malt. **66.1%**.

⋙ **Duncan Taylor Collection Ben Nevis 1996** cask 25, dist Feb 96, bott Mar 06 **(86)** n22 t21 f22 b21. A lovely, second used cask allowing the malt to sing to the heavens. **46%**. *386 bottles.*

⋙ **Murray McDavid Ben Nevis Aged 6 Years** Bourbon/Vintage Port, dist 99, bott 05 **(69)** n16 t18 f18 b17. Disproves the saying: "Any port in a storm." Sinks my boat. **46%. nc ncf.** *6000 bottles.*

**Platinum Ben Nevis 1963** cask 03/08/07 **(75)** n21 t19 f17 b18. Crushing, eyewatering oak saved only by a sweet, bourbony element. **45.8%.** *Douglas Laing.*

⋙ **Platinum Ben Nevis Aged 36 Years** dist Oct 68, bott Aug 05 **(75)** n20 t19 f18 b18. A semi-butyric plot doesn't help the cause here. At first it looks as though it might be a tasty bourbon-style number but falls apart in the glass. **49.1%**. *155 bottles.*

⋙ **Provenance Ben Nevis Aged 9 Years** dist July 96, bott Nov 05 **(77)** n21 t19 f18 b19. Pulls up a bit short, even allowing for its tender years. **46%**. *McGibbon's.*

⋙ **Provenance Ben Nevis Aged 10 Years** **(87)** n23 rich, strands of coconut in sugar syrup balanced by chalky oak: beautiful; t22 feather-light barley delivery beefed up by a big body surge; f20 thins out towards the finale; b22 tails off surprisingly fast after such a wonderfully confident start. **46%**. *Douglas Laing.*

⋙ **Whisky Galore Ben Nevis Aged 8 Years** dist 96, bott 05 **(82)** n21 t20 f21 b20. Complexity hovers around the zero mark, but there is no denying the fresh, malty deliciousness. **46%. nc ncf.** *Duncan Taylor.*

# BENRIACH
**Speyside, 1898. The BenRiach Distillery Co. Working.**

**Benriach 10 Years Old** db **(77)** n18 t22 f18 b19. Thankfully this caramelinfested disaster from the old Seagram days (an essay in how to screw up a decent malt if ever there was one) is being withdrawn. If you find any, either get it as a collector's item or simply (and preferably) ignore. **43%**

**The BenRiach Curiositas Aged 10 Years Single Peated Malt** db **(95)** n24 Arbroath smokies that have spent longer than usual in the reek; beautiful citrus and crystal clear malt underpin the chunkiness; t24 mesmerising, succulent malt that simply melts on the tastebuds: enormously sweet, yet the balance is contained by deft oak, mouthwatering barley and a swift volley of peppering spices; f23 long, and keeps its shape: just so clean, with vanilla and a hint of cocoa adding singing in harmony to the peaty tune with near perfect bitter-sweetness for good measure; b24 there are much lauded Islay whiskies that would dream of this kind of clarity and complexity: absolutely top-of-the-range single malt that should be on every connoisseur's must-have list **46%** ☉

⠂⠒ **The BenRiach Aged 12 Years** (L06046) db **(83)** n21 t22 f20 b20. Very pleasant, but just not quite there by comparison with the previous bottling. A touch of soap on the nose, some stunning honey development on the palate but it's just a touch too flat. **40%**

**The BenRiach Aged 12 Years** (L4230BB, bott 17 Aug 04) db **(89)** n23 just so clean and mouthwatering: has Speyside character ever been so succinctly nutshelled? t23 brilliant sharpness to the sweet barley-sugar malt, nipping at the tastebuds like a playful lover; f21 much more subdued, but in the quick, clean, style of this distillery; b22 enchanting. **40%**

⠂⠒ **The BenRiach Aged 16 Years** (L05040) db **(93)** n23 playful smoke gives a phenolic haze to the striking malt and mounting oak; t24 sensational mouth-arrival: the degree of barley sweetness is perfect as are the soft oils and harmony between smoke and spice. Stunningly beautiful; f23 starchy vanilla at the death with the oak making some form of controlled impact; b23 just one of those whiskies that makes you contemplate the bottle in awe. **43%**

**The BenRiach Aged 16 Years** (L4230BB – bott 17 Aug 04) db **(93)** n23 a wonderfully intricate tale of ground hazelnut, thinly spread manuka honey, Lubek marzipan and malt, all set on toasted bread; t24 silky malt and delicate honey enlivened by soft spices; a sub-stratum of fruit weaves gently through the malty maze; f22 a touch of smoke offers a little weight to the developing vanilla; b24 for many this will be a revelation. Because I learnt some of my trade at this distillery, I long wondered when I would see it at its best. Those who tasted the original Seagram travesty of a malt would hardly look twice, which was a crying shame, because this bottling confirms BenRiach as one of the most delicate and complex Speysiders on the market. It can only beg the question: why, with all the previous owner's resources, was this never available in this form before? **43%**

**The BenRiach Aged 20 Years** (L4231BB – bott 18 Aug 04) db **(88)** n23 Milkybar Kid meets the Man Who Likes to Say Yes: white chocolate with a touch of ripe pineapple and sweet peat. Quite lovely and wonderfully intricate as it oxidises; t23 early, sharp, almost acidic malt (is that the pineapple again?), then a waxy sheen as the spicy oak and a touch of honey appear; f21 has thinned out in time-honoured BenRiach (and Benriach) tradition, but remains clean and gentle; b21 never quite lives up to the nose or early mouth arrival but at this age for a light Speysider it would have been a miracle if it had. Even so, a barnstorming beaut! **43%**

**Benriach Peated Authenticus Peated Malt Aged 21 Years** db **(95)** n24 nosing blind, this has to be Laphroaig. Maybe with a dash of salty Ardbeg (thanks to the oranges). Yet it's pure Benriach; t24 a stupendous fruit-juiciness moistens the much drier smoke; the peat is chunky yet manageable, the spices warming but controlled with a slight Bowmore-style sweetness; the malt, free of smoke, chips in with some honey; f23 classic peaty sweetness that fades almost imperceptibly slowly. Almost endless; b24 still can't get my head around Seagram sitting on this little lot and doing absolutely nothing about it. It's beyond mind-boggling. The most south-east Islay of all Speysiders (except for that dash of Bowmore), including a generous pinch of salt...! This is a previously unknown masterpiece pulled not from an attic but a warehouse where it lay forgotten and unloved and one that connoisseurs around the world are going to spend hours and days getting to know, and perhaps even longer on websites discussing! **46%. nc ncf.** ⊙⊙

**BenRiach Origine Over 12 Years** db **(90) n**23 oranges and barley sugar; fresh cut sweet grass; **t**23 the controlled intensity is spellbinding: the slight nuttiness mingles with firm barley, which blends with the shards of citrus, which incorporates beautifully the evolving spice; **f**21 slightly duller but the spices persist and the late, fudge-barley sees off any oak intrusion; **b**23 another little classic from Benriach, though this one feels as though it is operating within its own limits. Could there have been more? **40%.** USA.

⠶ **The BenRiach Fine Wood Finishes Age Over 12 Years Dark Rum Jamaican Barrel** Richly Peated (Pre-bottled TN) db **(90) n**22 smouldering peat cut from the deep; **t**23 a sugary coating to the smoke gives way to blossoming barley; **f**22 remains rich and beautifully textured as the soft oak also absorbs the gentle sweetness; **b**23 some experiments I have carried out in my own lab, and having tasted some similarly treated Caol Ila, reveal that certain rum and peat were made for each other. This is enormous stuff. **46%. nc ncf.**

⠶ **The BenRiach Fine Wood Finishes Age Over 12 Years Pedro Ximenez Butt** Richly Peated (Pre-bottled TN) db **(93) n**23 a biting peat that is chunky, hard and bristling with personality; **t**23 soft oils help soften the peaty blows, early on hickory and camp coffee come into play; **f**24 barley-sugar and vanilla. The dryness is controlled and soft; rarely does the aging process work quite so well. The waves are large and go on for ever. Genuine class. Wonderful; **b**23 forget about the Pedro Ximenez finish: it has made little discernible difference and is a distraction. This is all about absolutely brilliant whisky. Embrace. **46%. nc ncf.**

⠶ **The BenRiach Fine Wood Finishes Age Over 12 Years Tawny Port Hogshead** Richly Peated (Pre-bottled TN) db **(85) n**18 **t**22 **f**23 **b**22 the nose is awkward, but the Port influence on the palate is telling and so refreshing. **46%. nc ncf.**

⠶ **The BenRiach Fine Wood Finishes Age Over 15 Years Henriques Madeira Barrel** (Pre-bottled TN) db **(95) n**24 such is the clarity of the wine, that you can just about spot the House; things are enlivened by the kind of soft spices you pray for and an injection of oaky vanilla that appears to be measured to the last atom. The big question here is: does it get 24 or 25...?; **t**24 dense fruit: you can almost chew the grape and spit out the pips. Especially beautiful are the peaks and troughs of the countering sweetness and dryness – two extremes yet somehow in complete harmony. Ting...; **f**22 dry oak but still the palate drips with concentrated barley and grape. Wow! **b**25 This is an essay in subtlety. And further proof that Madeira casks are giving malt something that sherry so often fails to do these days. If bottled in the same form as I have sampled it here, we have one of the recent truly great Speysiders on our hands! **46%. nc ncf.**

⠶ **The BenRiach Fine Wood Finishes Age Over 15 Years Pedro Ximenez Butt** (Pre-bottled TN) db **(86) n**24 **t**23 **f**19 **b**20. A disappointing end to a spellbinding story. With its inlay of sweeteded carrot juice, probably the most complex new aroma on Sepyside, though **46%. nc ncf.**

⠶ **The BenRiach Fine Wood Finishes Age Over 15 Years Dark Rum Jamaican Barrel** (Pre-bottled TN) db **(86) n**21 **t**23 **f**21 **b**21. A bit of a hotchpotch, even Canadian in style, but those with a sweet tooth will walk the plank for this one. **46%. nc ncf.**

⠶ **The BenRiach Fine Wood Finishes Aged Over 15 Years Tawny Port Hogshead** (Pre-bottled TN) db **(92) n**24 unlike the disastrous 12-y-o, this is exactly how a port pipe should influence a malt: rose petals and Turkish delight sprinkled with baked brown sugar and oozing soft grape. Add to that a sultry bourbon influence, and you have one hell of an aroma; **t**23 perfect weight; the barley parcelled up in gentle natural caramels and juicy wine. Soft sugars lighten the mood while spices threaten. Some over-enthusiastic oak in the middle; **f**22 long and becomes rather too intense; **b**23 another quite wondrous malt from this new range of BenRiach. I can usually take or leave cask finishes. I cannot remember ever having been faced with a succession of awesome whiskies. **46%. nc ncf.**

⋅⋅⋅ **The BenRiach Limited Edition Bottlings Age Over 25 Years** bott 06 db **(79)** n19 t21 f20 b19. A thread of golden syrup helps control the slightly over attentive oak. **50%. nc ncf.**

⋅⋅⋅ **The BenRiach Limited Edition Bottlings Age Over 30 Years** bott 06 db **(88)** n20 not entirely happy with itself; thin and gluey with just a touch of barley to compensate; t22 lush and fruity: ultra-ripe sultanas and then a spicy injection of barley-come-oak; f24 absolutely wonderful denouement with some liquorish notes intertwining brilliantly with the Blue Mountain coffee, grist and honeycomb in near enough perfect proportions and weight. If only all life's finishes could be this good...; b22 a finish of legend. **50%. nc ncf.**

⋅⋅⋅ **BenRiach Limited Release Single Cask Bottling Aged 16 Years** cask 802, dist 88, bott Sept 05 db **(85)** n22 t21 f21 b21. Excellent barley-sugar. Spiced-up oak and natural caramels make for a relatively short-haul flight. **54.7%. sc.** *675 bottles.*

⋅⋅⋅ **BenRiach Limited Release Single Cask Bottling Aged 25 Years** Hogshead cask 10985, dist 79, bott Sept 05 db **(89)** n22 intriguing fanfare of mildly smoked bourbon; t23 hallmark gorgeous delivery; here the oaky intrusion is contained to an off-beat wave that falls between the early mouthwatering, honey-brushed malt and a middle of delightful cocoa; f22 spicy yet mouthwatering to the death; b22 isolates the one moment of over-eager oak brilliantly and enchants us with a succession of delicate tones. **57.5%. sc.** *228 bottles.*

⋅⋅⋅ **BenRiach Limited Release Single Cask Bottling Aged 29 Years** hogshead cask 7211, dist 75, bott Sept 05 db **(87)** n20 bit of a gluepot; t22 muscular and malty, there is a wonderful sheen to the barley; f23 the finale radiates pure cocoa; b22 aggressive and forceful, the oak just about stays in line. **59.1%. sc.** *216 botles.*

⋅⋅⋅ **BenRiach Limited Release Single Cask Bottling Aged 33 Years** hogshead cask 4043, dist 72, bott Sept 05 db **(88)** n22 a delicate dusting of peat does little to dull the apple and barley freshness; t23 lush, intensely malty, wonderful barley-sugar and the lightest of peat. Tender and terrific; f21 soft, semi-exotic fruit soothes the oak; b22 a charming, if slightly tired, malt with a sprinkling of something for everyone – sherry apart. **49%. sc.** *261 bottles.*

**The BenRiach 1966 Limited Release Cask Bottling,** hogshead cask 2382, bott Dec 04 db **(90)** n23 kumquats and honeydew melon; the oaky tones mingle with gristy malt and the faintest whiff of smoke; t21 early oak dissipates as the intense, sweet malt fights back; warming and lively; f23 goes into complexity overdrive as the early battles are settled and now there is wave upon wave of vaguely smoked, vanilla-edged malt that is enriched further by a sliver of Jaffa cake and dark chocolate; b23 an eloquent and truly majestic early contribution to Scotland's 40th anniversary celebrations of England winning the 1966 World Cup. **50%**

⋅⋅⋅ **The BenRiach 1968 Limited Release Cask Bottling** hogshead cask 2712, bott Jun 06 db **(89)** n22 the usual oak-led nose but here softened by a light drizzle of guava and Asian pear; t23 wonderful, lush malt delivery; just brimming with warming – almost slightly hot – barley; f22 lots of vanilla and even a touch of banana. The oak makes for a forceful farewell; b22 subtle fruits abound despite – in fact probably because of – the oak. **52%. nc ncf.** *155 bottles.*

**The BenRiach 1970 Limited Release Cask Bottling** cask 4005, bott Dec 04, db **(88)** n23 t23 f20 b22 chewy and charming, but a season or three beyond its prime. Even so, there is no mistaking a class act when you see one. **51.2%**

⋅⋅⋅ **The BenRiach 1972 Limited Release Cask Bottling** Re-racked sherry butt cask 1733, bott Jun 06 db **(77)** n21 t20 f18 b18. Too oaked. **45%. nc ncf.**

⋅⋅⋅ **The BenRiach 1975 Limited Release Cask Bottling** Gomez cask 7007, bott Jun 06 db **(95)** n24 toffee apple dipped in exceptionally fine, dry sherry; coal smoke, various spices and vanilla play their part, as does moist cherry cake and slightly burned raisins; t24 just so fresh and mouthwatering: there are a few waves of puckering oak, but they are seen off by fruitcake and sherry. Beautifully spiced and cleverly sweet; f23 long with lashing of vanilla and custard and sprinkled with cocoa

. That coal smoke returns to add further length; **b**24 if I'm not mistaken, I happened upon a sample from this cask when I paid the distillery a visit early in 2006. It tasted sensational then and no worse in my sample room. An entirely faultless sherry butt of a style very rarely encountered today. A classic. **55%. nc ncf.**

⁘ **The BenRiach 1976 Limited Release Cask Bottling** Hogshead cask no. 8084, bott Jun 06 db **(84) n**20 **t**22 **f**21 **b**21. A real spicefest with the dominant oak shades at time by the excellent, though short-lived traces of manuka honey. For those who chew sweetened toothpicks. **56%. nc ncf**. *192 bottles.*

**The BenRiach 1978 Limited Release Cask Bottling** hogshead cask 1589, bott Dec 04 db **(90) n**20 heavy oak; mildly spiced; **t**23 wow! The nose gives no indication of the rich honeyfest to follow. Beautifully sweet, soft fruit and a hint of burnt fudge and cocoa; **f**23 long, with more honeycomb and chocolate and pulsing spices; **b**24 ignore the nose. And to descend its astonishing depths, allow it to breathe in the glass for a little while and get to body temperature. **54.4%**

⁘ **The BenRiach 1978 Limited Release Cask Bottling** hogshead cask 1596, bott Jun 06 db **(93) n**22 slightly thin, chalky and wallpaper-gluey. But enough malt abounds to ensure attractiveness; **t**24 sublime delivery. If you want to know just what a near perfection of beautifully layered, vanilla-led oak and mouthwatering, maple-syrup sweetened barley looks like, here you go; **f**23 charming, multilayered and very long finish with more of the same, but becoming gradually drier; some late spice and even the most distant puff of smoke finish things with a flourish; **b**24 the kind of cask you want at the bottom of your bed, so you can get up in the middle of the night and pray to it. **52%. nc ncf**. *199 bottles.*

⁘ **The BenRiach 1980 Limited Release Cask Bottling** Virgin oak cask 2535, bott Jun 06 db **(88) n**24 that waxy honey and armchair leather effect one associates with bourbon; **t**23 usual near-perfect BenRiach delivery (how many of the world's distilleries have such a just-so degree of oiliness to the body?) with a sliver of Demerara of honeycomb coating the barley, then the oak grabs hold; **f**20 toasty, roasty, massive oak; **b**21 the nose is the stuff of dreams, the mouth arrival is the most classic of drams, then some real problems fending off the tannins. But some moments of genius here. **52%. nc ncf**. *236 bottles.*

⁘ **The BenRiach 1984 Limited Release Cask Bottling** cask 594, bott Jun 06 db **(96) n**25 mainland Scottish peat gets no more delicate or sublime than this: a truly faultless aroma, this is a nose that repays 20 to 30 minutes study. The shift in shape and form of the peat-reek is beguiling yet for all its hypnotic power its seems fragile enough to collapse into peat dust at any minute. A world-great aroma; **t**24 as the nose suggests, the malts dissolves in the mouth; the peaty deposits offer varying depth and intensity, from a sweet cough lozenge to kippers. The bitter-sweet balance is beyond reproach; **f**23 long, seductively layered and excellent oaky strands to soak up the lingering smoke; remains chewable and lip-smacking for many, many minutes dying out to strains of medium roast Old Brown Java coffee; **b**24 it is malts like this that turn whisky into an art form. An unforgettable and very rare experience: easily one of the whiskies of the year. **54%. nc ncf**. *240 bottles.*

⁘ **The BenRiach 1984 Limited Release Cask Bottling** hogshead cask 627, bott Dec 04 db **(94) n**24 kipperish quality to the peat on display, complete with a lump of melting butter. Take time over this stunning nose before finally drinking; **t**24 for all the strength, sweet malt and soft vanilla make the first impact, followed swiftly by that delicate yet confident smoke; **f**22 lingering peat remains sweet, gentle but persistent; the malty vanilla flutters around charmingly, and there is even a nip of something citrussy to lighten things; **b**24 even those who think they don't like peat might be won over by this, fresh from Speyside's charm school. **55%**

⁘ **The BenRiach 1984 Limited Release Cask Bottling** Re-racked sherry butt cask no. 1438, bott Jun 06 db **(85) n**22 **t**22 **f**20 **b**21. Some lovely, kippery moments but the oak breaks the spell. **54%. nc ncf.** *656 bottles.*

⟶ **The BenRiach 1986 Limited Release Cask Bottling** Original Gomez cask 9632, bott Jun 06 db **(77)** n18 t21 f19 b19. Hugely disappointing: not even the tidal wave of fresh barley can save this one from its undesired and off-key sherried-shackles. **55%. nc ncf.** *661 bottles.*

⟶ **The BenRiach 1988 Limited Release Cask Bottling** Butt cask no. 802, re-racked into oloroso sherry 26 Oct 04, bott Sept 05 db **(87)** n22 light, punchy sherry offering pure white grape; t23 charismatic delivery brimming with beautifully married fruit and barley; the confident spices tickle and tease while soft oils coat the palate; f20 drier, toasty oak notes, though watch out for that grape-juice effect very late on; b22 big whisky with fabulous early presence but too much dryness on the finish. **54.7%. nc ncf.** *675 bottles.*

**The BenRiach Heart of Speyside** (L4230BB – bott 17 Aug 04) db **(79)** n19 t22 f19 b19. Decent, fizzing, mildly spiced malt, but could do with being a whole lot brighter. **40%**

⟶ **Chieftain's Benriach 13 Years Old** Fino sherry **(79)** n20 t21 f19 b19. Lovely fruitcake, marzipan and delicate smoke but the feeling that something is vaguely amiss on the nose is born out on the finish. **43%.** *Ian MacLeod.*

⟶ **Craigellachie Hotel Benriach 1976** cask 8079, bott 05 **(88)** n23 profound oak of top quality; a sandalwood/barley marriage made in heaven; t24 just enormous: for all its age and oak influence, still the barley bubbles to the surface causing salivation and joy in equals measures; beautiful spices buzz about a bit; f19 on the oak-stew side, but just enough exotic fruit for it to get away with it; b22 thanks to the mouthwatering barley, a dram still to be reckoned with. **57.6%.** *UK.*

⟶ **D&M Connoisseurs' Club Bottling Aged 18 Years** cask 5112, dist Apr 87 **(87)** n20 traces of butterscotch, but a bit dull; t23 probing malt is supported by waves of intensifying fruit; f22 excellent delivery of very soft oil and rich mocha; b22 takes its time to find its range, but a second or third glass should do the trick. **55.7%.** *D&M Wines and Liquors USA.*

⟶ **Dun Bheagan BenRiach Aged 10 Years** **(86)** n21 t22 f21 b22. A delicate, delicious and youthful Benriach in full blending colours. **43%.** *Ian Macleod.*

**Duncan Taylor Collection Benriach 1968 Aged 36 Years** cask no. 2595, dist Nov 68, bott Mar 05 **(94)** n24 freshly diced apples in new-mown hay; t24 astonishingly delicate semi-molassed sweetness that caresses and tones the booming malt and hickory-enriched oak; f22 relatively quiet and retiring with the dependence of vanilla; b24 one of nature's treasures. **50.7%**

⟶ **Mac Y 10th Anniversary BenRiach Aged 12 Years** cask no 807, dist 94, bott 06 **(89)** n22 intense, farmyardy, playfully teasing peats given extra weight thanks to sherry. That said, maybe not the best oloroso butt of all time but the smoke deals with any inadequacies comfortably; t23 multi-structured with an early thinnish, off-key edge to the burgeoning smoke. Develops into a massive mouthful with the barley and peats back on track and the oak pitching in beautifully; f22 soft spices and a youthfulness now to the peat. The grape is a bit over eager and wayward. But long, fascinating and very tasty stuff; b22 massive whisky offering rough and tumble. Lurches all over the palate with virtually no direction. But, my word, it's one hell of a ride!! **56%. nc ncf.** *Denmark. 700 bottles.*

**Old Malt Cask Benriach 15 Years Old** dist 27 Mar 90, bott 11 May 05 **(76)** n17 t21 f19 b20. For all the creamy toffee and wonderfully intense barley on delivery, the soapy oak has gone through the top. **50%.** *Douglas Laing & Co.*

⟶ **The Whisky Fair Benriach 1986 Aged 19 Years** Bourbon Hogshead 2972, dist 86, bott 06 **(79)** n21 t21 f18 b19. Unpeated or unsherried Benriach at this age often fails to comfortably see off the oak. Like now. **54.7%.** *Germany. 297 bottles*

# BENRINNES
**Speyside, 1826. Diageo. Working.**

**Benrinnes Aged 15 Years** db **(70)** n16 t19 f17 b18. What a shame that in the year the independent bottlers at last get it right for Benrinnes, the actual owners of the distillery make such a pig's ear of it. Sulphured and sicklysweet, this bottling has little to do with the very good whisky made there day in day out by its talented team. Depressing. **43%.** *Flora and Fauna.*

**The Bottlers Benrinnes 1985 Aged 17 Years Old** cask 1852 **(82) n**22 **t**19 **f**21 **b**20. Great nose, but disintegrates to a degree on the palate and never quite finds a rhythm; adore the lingering spices, though. **60.2%.** *Raeborn Fine Wines.*

❖ **Cadenhead's Authentic Collection Benrinnes Aged 18 Years** Bourbon Hogshead, dist 88, bott Sept 06 **(92) n**23 a citrussy element sharpens the spices; **t**24 salivating from the first moment; stunning barley layering; **f**22 lightens dramatically with a vanilla blast; **b**23 a magnificent Speysider. This distillery is, at last, coming out of the shadows. **55.9%.** *246 bottles.*

❖ **Connoisseurs Choice Benrinnes 1991 (84) n**22 **t**21 **f**21 **b**20. One of the new breed of Benrinnes, showing a degree of promise but still hampered by some ordinary casks. **43%.** *Gordon & MacPhail.*

❖ **Dewar Rattray Individual Cask Bottling Benrinnes 1989 Aged 14 Years** cask 6835, dist Nov 90, bott Nov 04 **(79) n**18 **t**22 **f**19 **b**20. The fish, chip and vinegar nose, though novel, doesn't bode well, but the bubble gum and malt reply is pretty tasty. Very high esters here. **59.3%.** *524 bottles.*

❖ **D&M Connoisseurs' Club Bottling Benrinnes Aged 17 Years** cask 913, dist Mar 89 **(91) n**23 light with a sexy barley texture on several levels. Outstanding complexity; **t**23 fresh, bitter-sweet barley. Grain and oak have locked horns but the battle is refined and mildly salivating; **f**22 lots of vanilla and sweetening barley sugar; **b**23 a rare example of Benrinnes in stunning and most complex form. Bloody well done D&M!! **43%. nc ncf.** *US by Angus Dundee.*

**Dun Bheagan Benrinnes Aged 11 years** cask 8259, dist 92, bott 04 **(85) n**20 **t**23 **f**21 **b**21. A Benrinnes actually worthy of the name: most bottlings from this distillery have been so disappointing in recent years, though I have long suspected that the casks supplied have been wanting. This is a reasonable cask and the honeycombed malt responds accordingly. **43%. nc ncf.** *396 bottles.*

❖ **Gordon MacPhail Reserve Benrinnes 1974** cask 3870, bott 10 Apr 04 **(85) n**23 **t**22 **f**20 **b**20. A distillery which always draws the short straw when it comes to casks. Despite wallowing in real full-bodied and – for once – exceptionally clean sherry, it's too much. Balance has been not so much lost as obliterated. But enjoyably drinkable? Oh, yes... **46%.** *For Juuls Vinhandel, Denmark. 234 bottles.*

❖ **Harris Whisky Co. Benrinnes Aged 13 Years** cask 7014, dist Sept 92, bott Jan 06 **(94) n**23 light, grassy barley sprinkled with custard powder. Just so delicate and inviting; **t**24 an equally delicate sweetness combined with a soft yet more pronounced oil than you might expect from a 3D malt; the timbre of the barley is divine; **f**23 long with luxurious and slow fade of glorious barley; **b**24 proof that the skilled distillers of Benrinnes have not often been well served by those supplying the casks. This is decent wood and the result is a delicate, clean, complex, salivating and fascinating malt of the highest grade sprinkled with star quality throughout. **55%. nc ncf.** *The Harris Whisky Co.*

**Luvians Bottle Shop Commemorative Bottling 1983–2004 Benrinnes 21 Years Old (81) n**19 **t**22 **f**20 **b**20. A shade too much oak on the sappy nose, and the finish also has a few wrinkles, but the freshness of the malt on delivery is highly attractive. **40%.** *Luvians, Cupar, Scotland.*

**Mackillop's Choice Benrinnes Cask Strength** cask no. 912, dist Mar 89 **(88) n**22 suety, gristy, doughy and delicious! **t**23 bleeding hell!! You are blasted back against the wall as a fearsome delivery of malt concentrate explodes on arrival on the palate. The sweetness becomes almost too intense, but a dose of oaky vanilla helps calm it a little. Not what one normally expects from this distillery; **f**21 soft malt and spice; **b**22 I was wondering when I'd see this distillery's make in a half decent cask and able to express itself properly. Well done, Lorn!! **58.8%.** *Angus Dundee.*

❖ **Old Malt Cask Benrinnes Aged 14 Years** dist Nov 90, bott Nov 04 **(77) n**19 **t**20 **f**20 **b**18. Barley-rich and buttery if a little banal. **50%.** *Douglas Laing. 655 bottles.*

**Scotts Selection Benrinnes 1979** bott 04 **(89) n**23 just the vaguest hint of smoke adds an almost disproportionate degree of weight. Probably the best Benrinnes nose I've found outside a lab; **t**22 the mouth is awash with sweet, deliciously chewy malt; **f**22 lingers with a developing spiciness balanced by figs and vanilla; **b**22 just great to see the distillery represented, as I know how good it can sometimes be. Superb. **53.5%.** *Speyside Distillers.*

# BENROMACH
**Speyside, 1898. Gordon & MacPhail. Working.**

⸭ **Benromach 22 Years Old Finished in Port Pipes** db **(86) n**22 **t**23 **f**20 **b**21. Slightly Jekyll and Hyde. **45%.** *3500 bottles.*

⸭ **Benromach 25 Years Old** db **(92) n**24 seriously sexy with spices interplaying with tactile malt: the bitter-sweet balance is just so.There is even the faintest flicker of peat-smoke to underscore the pedigree; **t**22 an early, surprising, delivery of caramel amongst the juicy barley; **f**23 lots of gentle spices warm the enriched barley and ice-creamy vanilla; **b**23 a classic old-age Speysider, showing all the quality you'd hope for. **43%**

⸭ **Benromach Classic 55 Years Old** dist 49, bott 04 db **(93) n**24 sheer brinkmanship: the first signs of a perhaps too much bitter oak, until it softens and smiles in the glass as gentle Canadian-style corny-caramel notes gather intensity and bulk. The countering sweetness is charming. Next a soft delivery of clementines lightens things further. And even the strains of vanishing peat A 23.5 if ever there was one... what the hell, let's round it up...; **t**23 the citrus arrives first, then increasingly large waves of salivating, highly intense barley. A big oaky storm brews, but keeps a distance but the vibrancy is astonishing; **f**22 maltesers and latte, remains silky soft and when the oak does break the bitterness adds rather than subtracts; **b**24 only distillery owners G&M could come up with something like this. Scotland had a King in those far off days. In fact, so did the British Empire – and there was still an Empire (just) in 1949. And this has to be a king of aged whiskies because it bears virtually no scars of time. Charlie Hewitt was back as manager of recently relegated Millwall; my parents were in their first year of marriage; Surrey were on the cusp of forming a cricket team to dominate the English game for the next decade and some guy in Scotland, possibly long dead and his name lost to history, laid down one cask that a generation and a half on would delight and astound a lucky few. That's whisky for you. **42.4%.** *83 bottles.*

⸭ **Benromach 1968** db **(94) n**25 hands up all those who would mark this as just about the perfect sherry butt? Apples, liquorice, orange peel – all the usual suspects. Clean, no off-notes, and just the right degree of oak. Pheeew!!; **t**24 no spitting here as the intense barley links seamlessly with the fat fruit. The oak is more upfront, but it's chalky challenge is restrained enough; **f**22 honeycomb arrives like thunder after a hot spell; bitters up as the oak demands a final say; **b**23 an absolutely stunning cask which just cracks under the oak at the end. But the build up until then is unforgettable. **41.8%**

**Benromach Cask Strength 1980** db **(94) n**23 almost Highland Parkesque in its clever, not to mention delicious, honey-gentle smoke overture. Just missing the heather; **t**24 bloody hell!! If you have a sweet tooth then don't bother with a bottle: buy a case! The intensity of the honey is shocking, but once you have acclimatized, then wallow in its hidden, spicy depths. As enormous as any Speysider gets; **f**23 wonderful delivery of oak; and then that soft waft of smoke returns: some surprising hints of citrus amid the powering malt; **b**24 they were probably led to the cask by the bees: clazzzzic! **58.6%**

⸭ **Benromach Organic** db **(91) n**23 massive oak input and the freshest oak imaginable. But sits comfortably with the young pulsing malts. Wow!!; **t**23 oak arrives first again, but has enough deftness of touch to allow the rich, mouthwatering malts to prosper; **f**22 plenty of vanillins and natural, sweet toffee;

**b**23 young and matured in possibly first fill bourbon or, more likely, European (even Scottish) oak; you cannot do other than sit up and take notice of this guns-blazing big 'un. An absolute treat! **43%. nc ncf.**

**Benromach Traditional** db **(88) n**23 young, lively but very clean peat smoke; **t**22 a natural harmony between smoke, barley and light vanillins; **f**22 the gristy sweetness fades for more bitter oak; **b**21 a much more comfortable and complete malt than it was a couple of years back with the peating level upped slightly but, vitally, finding much better balance. **40%** ☉ ☉

**Benromach Vintage 1969** db **(73) n**19 **t**19 **f**17 **b**18. They were dancing on the Moon when they made this: sadly, nothing out of this world about it now. **43%**

**Benromach Tokaji Wood Finish Aged 21 Years** db **(69) n**17 **t**16 **f**17 **b**16. An interesting experiment: one, let's hope, never to be repeated. **45%** ☉

**Cask Benromach 1980** db **(86) n**19 **t**22 **f**23 **b**22. Salivating barley and spice: one hell of a delicious mouthful. **58.1%**

## BEN WYVIS
### Highland (Northern) 1965–1977. Demolished.

**Ben Wyvis Aged 27 Years** cask 1061, dist 72 db **(78) n**21 vanilla, soft oak with a sweet structure and the malt is intact – amazing for a light whisky for this age – with some softening caramel; **t**20 big malt, toffee presence then becoming gradually hotter, not peppery, simply from the way it has been distilled; **f**18 very thin, surprisingly little oak, meagre malt and more bite: the finale is sweet and coated with late oil; **b**19 this is by no means great whisky, but it is certainly among the most rare you will ever locate. There are hints here of why the distillery closed: certainly even after all these years the oak cannot paper over the cracks. That said, you are drinking history and romance and it should be enjoyed with due reverence. **43.1%**. *146 bottles.*

## BLADNOCH
### Lowland, 1817. Working.

**Bladnoch Aged 10 Years** db **(94) n**23 lemon and lime, marmalade on fresh-sliced flour-topped crusty bread; **t**24 immensely fruity and chewy, lush and mouthwatering and then the most beguiling build-up of spices: the mouthfeel is full and faultless; **f**23 long, remains mildly peppery and then a dryer advance of oak. The line between bitter and sweet is not once crossed; **b**24 this is probably the ultimate Bladnoch, certainly the best I have tasted in over 25 years. This Flora and Fauna bottling by then owners United Distillers should be regarded as the must-get-at-all-costs Bladnoch. If the new owner can create something even to hang on to this one's coat-tails then he has excelled himself. For those few of us lucky enough to experience this, this dram is nothing short of a piece of Lowland legend and folklore. **43%.** *For those of you with a nervous disposition, the author would like to point out that not a single drop of this whisky was spat out during the creation of these tasting notes.*

**Bladnoch 13 Years Old** dist July 91 db **(84) n**20 **t**20 **f**22 **b**22. A refined dram that celebrates the gentleness of the malt with a pleasing bitter-sweet melody. A hint of citrus and honey on the excellent finish but the oak plays slightly too enthusiastic a part early on. **40%. nc.**

**Bladnoch Aged 13 Years** (Distillery View) db **(81) n**19 **t**21 **f**20 **b**21. The malt and oaky-chewiness make the right sounds, but it's all a little muffled. **40%. ncf**

**Bladnoch Aged 13 Years** (Beltie) db **(89) n**21 confident, striding vanilla but the oak is enlivened by an intriguing malt-citrus mix; **t**23 brilliant! The arrival is immediately enveloped in fresh, grassy malt weighted by an estery oiliness and simple oak; **f**23 wave upon wave of soft malt turning into pure cocoa; **b**22 by no means a complex dram, just one that works if anything because of its faultless, vigorous simplicity. **55%. ncf sc.**

⠶ **Bladnoch 15 Years Old** db **(88)** n21 barely ripe pears; t23 mouthwatering, fresh barley and virtually no oak; f22 bitters out slightly as some vague vestiges of oak get amongst the barley, apples and pears; b22 this distillery's whisky is unquestionably as good now as at any time in living memory. The liberal use of second fill casks here has accentuated the lively fruitiness. **40%**

**Bladnoch 15 Years Old** dist Sep 88 db **(86)** n22 t22 f21 b21. With its ciderbrandy and apple effect, deeply unusual and delicious. **46%. nc ncf.**

**Bladnoch 15 Years Old (The Sheep)** db **(88)** n22 much thinner nose than of old but the barley is lovely; t22 the barley imposes itself in a different manner from previous bottling, being a drier style adorned with peppers; f22 quality oak frames the malt beautifully; b22 strikingly attractive whisky, but lost some of its estery sheen and charisma since I tasted an early bottling of this. **55%** ☉ ☉

⠶ **Bladnoch 15 Years Old Rum Finish** cask no. 5144 db **(76)** n23 t20 f16 b17. The hugely complex nose is misleading as to regard the rest of the whisky. This has spent 18 months rounding off in rum cask: it should have been either a shorter time, or more, because it has hit a stage in its development where it has entirely lost balance, especially on the viciously bitter finish. **55%**

⠶ **Berry's Own Selection Bladnoch 1992 Aged 13 Years (84)** n21 t22 f20 b21. This is a very strange Bladnoch. There are certain richly-malted aspects which are wonderful. But I cannot help wondering if this was bottled after a gin run. Because there are definite elements of juniper on the nose and finish. **46%.**

⠶ **Cadenhead's Authentic Collection Bladnoch Aged 16 Years** dist 89, bott Sep 05 **(89)** n22 greengages and custard, sprinkled with gristy malt; t22 lip-smacking, mouthwatering honey-roast barley, waves and waves of the stuff; f21 roasty, dry and finely spiced; b23 a quality cask of Lowland with some serious guts and attitude. **54.9%.** 276 bottles.

**Cask Strength Bladnoch 1991 (82)** n19 t22 f21 b20. A thuggish, bullying nose compensated by a mouth arrival of the most intense, unambiguous malt imaginable. **54.8%.** G&M

**Chieftan's Bladnoch Aged 14 Years Rum Barrel Finish** casks nos. 2073 & 2077, dist May 90, bott Jun 04 **(94)** n23 some may remember a candy in Britain (and the Empire) called Black Jacks. I can even remember when they were a farthing each...groan. Sniff this to recall your early childhood. Fabulous! t24 the malt remains absolutely resolute and unruffled as a sweet Demerara thread weaves intricate patterns; the middle is an explosion of complexities as all oaky-maltyrummy factions meet; f23 soft and chewy with a touch of milky-liquorice and we are back to Black Jacks once again; b24 I have a sneaking suspicion I may have unwittingly contributed to this while I blended Sea Wynde Rum. I'm not letting those casks go so easily next time...!! **46%. nc nc.** Ian Macleod. 318 bottles.

**Connoisseurs Choice Bladnoch 1991 (83)** n20 t22 f21 b20. Unusually oily for Bladnoch; grassy, green, mouthwatering, but complexity at a premium. **40%.**

**Coopers Choice Bladnoch 1990 Sherry Finish 12 Years Old** bott 03 **(84)** n20 t22 f21 b20. Begins promisingly with a delicious doughy, biscuity malt arrival and finishes simply if a little meekly. **46%. nc ncf.** The Vintage Malt Whisky Co Ltd.

**James MacArthur Bladnoch 1992 12 Year Old** bott Mar 05 **(81)** n20 t22 f19 b20. Rich malt, not unlike an old Lincoln biscuit. Shards of Demerara for good measure. **43%**

⠶ **John McDougall's Selection Bladnoch Aged 14 Years** cask no. 3317 **(93)** n23 varying levels of chalky oak sweetened by barley sugar; t24 a stunning and malt-encrusted riot of apricot, butterscotch and raspberry jam; f23 stays on the sublimely sweetened theme, though the oak plays a delicate anchoring role; b23 I can just imagine John McDougall wandering around the warehouse on the banks of the eponymous river and happening across this cask: a secretly chalked x on a stave and the owners wouldn't have stood a chance... **55.8%.** 250 bottles.

⠶ **Old Malt Cask Bladnoch 15 Years Old** dist Nov 90, bott May 06 **(86)** n22 t22 f21 b21. Steady as a rock: eschews complexity for sheer malty delight. **50%.** 333 btls.

**Old Malt Cask Bladnoch 21 Years Old** dist 31 Dec 83, bott 22 Mar 05 **(88) n**21 mildly salty, crushed Digestive biscuits you put out for the birds – after nicking some yourself; **t**23 fabulous rich malt, and really not much else to report; **f**22 malt and developing, slightly brittle, oaky dryness; **b**22 relentless and remorseless, the jaw-achingly chewy malt goes on and on and on! **50%.** *Douglas Laing & Co.*

**Old Masters Bladnoch 1992 12 Years Old** cask no. 744, bott May 04 **(87) n**21 **t**23 **f**22 **b**21. Clean and refreshing early on. **56.1%.** *James MacArthur.*

**Old Masters Bladnoch 1992 13 Years Old** cask 752, bott 05 **(87) n**21 dozing vanilla and malt, relaxed further by a touch of lavender; **t**23 beautiful, near faultless intensity to the salivating malt; fresh and firm; **f**21 maybe a touch of coriander to the vanilla. Still the malt pulses; **b**22 shimmering. **56.9%.**

**Private Cellars Selection Bladnoch 1987** bott 04 **(78) n**21 **t**20 **f**18 **b**19. The body is curiously flat, though the nose is very sharp, vaguely farmyardy and strangely compelling **43%.** *Speyside Distillers*

**Provenance 13 Years Old** dist Sum 91, bott Aut 04 **(84) n**21 **t**21 **f**21 **b**21. Charming little softie, showing good oak but refusing to stray off the path. **46%**

❖ **Provenance Bladnoch 14 Years Old** dist Nov 90, bott July 05 **(79) n**22 **t**20 **f**18 **b**19. Pleasant and malt-fresh to start, but soon runs out of steam and collapses at the finish. **46%.** *McGibbon's.*

**Scott's Selection Bladnoch 1984** bott 03 **(83) n**20 **t**22 **f**20 **b**21. Candy store aroma and a beautiful mouthwatering grassy attack on the palate. **58%**

**Scotts Selection Bladnoch 1990** bott 04 **(86) n**20 shy if a little rural; **t**22 comes alive wonderfully with wave after wave of crisp barley; **f**22 stunning cocoa amid spicey barley; **b**23 forget the non-committal nose, what arrives on the palate is just so full of vivid shapes and contours. **53.4%.** *Speyside Distillers.*

## BLAIR ATHOL
**Highlands (Perthshire), 1798. Diageo. Working.**

**Blair Athol Aged 12 Years** db **(77) n**18 **t**19 **f**21 **b**19. Thick, fruity, syrupy and a little sulphury and heavy. The finish has some attractive complexity among the chunkyness. **43%.** *Flora and Fauna range.*

**Cadenhead's Authentic Collection Blair Athol Aged 15 Years** dist 89, bott Feb 05 **(84) n**21 **t**22 **f**20 **b**21. No shrinking violet, but the barley sugar start sets the dram up well. **55.6%.** *198 bottles.*

**Cadenhead's Authentic Collection Blair Athol Aged 16 Years** Bourbon Hogshead, dist 89, bott May 05 **(75) n**18 **t**20 **f**18 **b**19. High esters, dubious oak but oversweet and ungainly. **56.2%.** *312 bottles.*

❖ **Connoisseurs Choice Blair Athol 1993 (89) n**23 refreshing, new-mown straw and citrus; **t**23 gorgeous clarity to the barley despite the early intensity. Refreshing, excellently balanced sweetness; **f**21 gets a bit bitter and furry towards the end; **b**22 I remember then distillery manager Mike Nicholson telling me he had cleaned up this distillery's act. Now living in western Canada, I know he'll be reading this. So, what can I say? Well done, Mike. Absolutely great job: this – even taking the untidy finish into account - is very good whisky. And well done, G&M for selecting a sympathetic cask and giving the malt a chance. **43%.** *Gordon & MacPhail.*

**Old Malt Cask Blair Athol Aged 13 Years** dist May 90, bott Oct 03 **(85) n**21 **t**22 **f**20 **b**22. Not often you find a younger Blair Athol charming you, but this is one. **50%. nc ncf sc.** *Douglas Laing. 300 bottles.*

❖ **Old Malt Cask Blair Athol Aged 21 Years** dist Feb 84, bott Aug 05 **(79) n**22 **t**20 **f**18 **b**19. The flat delivery doesn't match the attractive nose. **50%.** *271 bottles.*

**Platinum Old and Rare Blair Athol 37 Years Old** dist Jan 66 **(85) n**22 **t**21 **f**21 **b**21. Unusual and unyielding, few malts come quite so thick-set and viscous. **41.8%**

❖ **Premier Barrel Blair Athol 11 Years Old** Sherry, dist Nov 94, bott Feb 06 **(85) n**21 **t**22 **f**21 **b**21. A neat and tidy malt with grist 'n' grape. One of the cleaner, juicier examples I've come across. **46%.** *Douglas Laing. 867 bottles.*

**Provenance Blair Athol Aged 12 Years** dist 1 Feb 93, bott 5 May 05 **(75) n**18 **t**20 **f**18 **b**19. Silk purses. Sows ears. **46%**. *Douglas Laing & Co.*

⚬ **Provenance Blair Athol 12 Years Old** Sherry, dist Dec 93, bott Feb 06 **(77) n**19 **t**19 **f**20 **b**19. Underwhelming. But a little bit of smoke sneaks in from somewhere. **46%**. *McGibbon's.*

⚬ **Provenance Blair Athol 12 Years Old** Sherry, dist May 94, bott Aug 06 **(70) n**16 **t**18 **f**18 **b**18. Gosh! How this takes me back to the sulphurous old days at the distillery. **46%**. *McGibbon's.*

# BOWMORE
**Islay, 1779. Suntory. Working.**

**Bowmore 12 Years Old** db **(85) n**21 **t**22 **f**21 **b**21. Revealing greater peaty youth than of old. **40%**

⚬ **Bowmore Aged 16 Years Limited Edition** dist 89, bott 05 db **(90) n**21 a youthful aroma with smoking peat embers; **t**23 dazzling, multi-layered peat offers varying degrees of intensity and sweetness, from Fishermen's Friends cough candy to Tyrolean smoked cheese; **f**23 long with excellent vanilla involvement and a dash of buttery kipper; **b**23 the nose promises little but the complexity and sure-footedness of this malt is truly wonderful. **51.8%. ncf.**

⚬ **Bowmore Aged 16 Years Limited Edition** Oloroso sherry, dist 90, bott 06 db **(89) n**24 if you stick your head in the malt kiln, this – exactly - is what you get. When it's not alight, I mean...; **t**22 a surprising degree of fruit takes the lead but that incredibly pungent peat does all it can to resist and gain control. Enormous, though hardly structured; **f**21 semi-sweetened hickory; **b**22 It has peat. And fruit. And never the two do meet. But the battle for supremacy is engrossing. **53.8%. ncf.**

**Bowmore 17 Years Old** db **(93) n**23 the peat could be made from helium, so light is it. Even so, it remains the dominant feature in a complex aroma; **t**23 sweat peat at first, then juicy malt; **f**23 long, fragile with the peat lingering but refusing to undermine the complexity; **b**24 remains Bowmore at its most complex, but it has lightened considerably of late and its mesmeric skills lie in its ability to simply flutter over the tastebuds. Fabulous. **43%**

**Bowmore 25 Years Old** db **(86) n**22 **t**22 **f**21 **b**21. Not the big, chunky guy of yore: the age would surprise you if tasted blind. **43%**

⚬ **Bowmore Aged 37 Years 1968 Limited Edition** db **(90) n**22 you can hardly see the peat for the exotic fruit, which means only one thing...; **t**23 so juicy and non-specific fruity, except maybe some mango. The peat finally arrives like the 7th Cavalry; **f**22 long and subtle with vanilla stratas of varying intensity; **b**23 one of those casks that's past its sell-by date, yet somehow works to glorious effect. Most of the peat has been kicked out, but it's as gentle a ride as you'll find. **43.4%.**

**Bowmore 1957** db **(91) n**23 **t**23 **f**22 **b**23. Nothing from 1957 has the right to be this well preserved and sophisticated. It appears I have a challenger... **40.1%**

**Bowmore 1964 Vintage Bourbon Cask** db **(86) n**23 **t**21 **f**21 **b**21. Just about holds together for a very enjoyable dram. The peat has been absorbed to create an unusual rye effect. **43.2%**

**Bowmore 1964 Vintage Fino Cask** db **(90) n**21 **t**23 **f**23 **b**23. Sheer quality. Curiously, much more Bushmills in style than Bowmore. Exquisite stuff. **49.6%**

⚬ **Bowmore 1971 Vintage 34 Years Old** Sherry cask db **(86) n**23 **t**22 **f**20 **b**21. Loses it on the finish. But one for those who like their whisky big and with splinters aplenty. **51%**. *960 bottles.*

**Bowmore Claret Bordeaux Wine Cask** db **(62) n**16 **t**16 **f**17 **b**13. When this first came out the then distillery boss Jim McEwan and I fell out (temporarily, of course!): he loved it, I loathed it. For the sake of this book (and it needed a good reason) I re-visited this whisky. And I still loathe it. The whisky has been swamped by the wine, is raw and the character of a distillery I love has been obliterated with all balance sacrificed. Oh dear, oh dear. **56%**

**Bowmore Darkest** db **(68)** n17 t18 f16 b17. I had hoped it might have changed since my last review: it has – it's got worse! Entirely out of sync, shapeless and at times frankly awful. **43%**

**Bowmore Dawn** db **(94)** n23 young, raw, yet complete peat in a style unique to Bowmore; t24 the arrival on the palate is momentous: it is sweet yet the intensity of the peat and oak crashing wave upon giant wave upon the palate acts as the perfect foil; f23 much drier with that excellent and highly distinctive chocolate swiss roll (unique to Bowmore) kicking in. Still room for lots of malt and a sliver of fruit; b24 none other of the distillery-bottled range quite nutshells Bowmore as well as this. Fabulous and markedly improved in recent years, this is a must-have malt for any true Islayophile. Overtaken the 17-y-o as the flagship brand. **51.5%** ⊙

**Bowmore Dusk** db **(80)** n18 t19 f23 b20. Another youngster, almost a mirror image to the Oddbins exclusive bottling of Bowmore or Islay (can't remember) of about 15 or 16 years ago. Memorable for the astonishing finish.. Love it!! **50%** ⊙

**Bowmore Legend** db **(80)** n21 t21 f18 b20. Refreshing, clean malt and raw, young-ish smoke. **40%**

**Bowmore Mariner** db **(89)** n21 uncultured and tattooed, the peat on this is asking for a punch-up; t24 I've worked out the Mariner: it's the Fisherman's Friend cough sweet: warming, biting, fizzing with lashings of raw peat and barley sugar; f22 apologetic oak and its smoke all the way; b22 less abrasive than of old, it is still a roughneck, and enormous and delicious fun all the way. **43%**

**Bowmore Surf** db **(82)** n23 t21 f18 b20. Not too impressed with this, once: called it more of a ripple. The finish still lacks quality and graft and the suspicion here falls on caramel. That said, the astonishing nose is all about recently used malt kilns and is worth buying just to sniff alone. **43%** ⊙⊙

⠶ **Berry's Own Selection Bowmore Aged 11 Years (84)** n20 t23 f21 b20. To see Bowmore like this from a second- (or even third) - filled bourbon cask makes for interesting tasting: such is the mouthwatering malt intensity, and so retiring is the peat, this could almost pass for lightly smoked Speyside. **56.2%**. *Berry Bros & Rudd.*

**Blackadder Raw Cask Bowmore 1989** Bourbon barrel no. 22535, dist 21 Sep 89, bott Mar 03 **(79)** n20 t19 f20 b20. As cask 22533 above. **62.9%. nc ncf sc.**

**Blackadder Raw Cask Bowmore 1989** cask 22536 dist Sep 89, bott Nov 03 **(85)** n23 t20 f21 b21. Despite being a hot-head there is enough complexity to search for. **60.2%**

**Blackadder Raw Cask Bowmore 1991** cask no. 10597 dist Sep 91, bott Nov 03 **(81)** n22 t19 f20 b20. Great nose but just a fraction unwieldy on the palate. **60.3%**

**Cadenhead's Authentic Collection Bowmore Aged 13 Years** Bourbon Hogshead, dist 91, bott May 05 **(81)** n23 t21 f18 b19. Quite hot and peppery but the complexity of peat on the nose is exceptional. **60%**. *300 bottles.*

⠶ **Cadenhead's Authentic Collection Bowmore 14 Years** dist 91, bott Sep 05 **(87)** n21 firm and closed; t22 lovely oils help develop the sweet peat; f21 good length with smoke attached to the cocoa; b23 understated and impressive, it overcomes a lazy nose to offer excellent Islay. **59.1%**. *288 bottles.*

⠶ **Cadenhead's Authentic Collection Bowmore Aged 14 Years** Bourbon Hogshead, dist 91, bott Feb 06 **(84)** n22 t23 f19 b20. Nose and delivery exquisite with outstanding peating level. But the finish is too dry and dusty. **56.1%**. *294 bottles.*

⠶ **Cadenhead's Authentic Collection Bowmore Aged 14 Years 1992** Bourbon hogshead, dist 92, bott Nov 06 **(94)** n23 unusual, almost uncharted style: Fisherman's Friends have gone, replaced by drier, more refined smoke; t24 the best Bowmore delivery for a year or two: juicy barley fits like a glove with the crunchy peat; f23 long, spiced, so clean and charismatic; b24 a charmer with sweet barley a perfect foil for the smoke. Bowmore at its very best. **54.4%**. *294 bottles.*

**Coopers Choice Bowmore 1990** bott 03 (12 Years Old) **(88)** n21 t22 f23 b22. As impressive an example of Bowmore of this age as you could hope for. **43%**.

**Dewar Rattray Individual Cask Bottling Bowmore Aged 14 Years** Sherry butt cask no. 2054, dist 15.7.91, bott 28.9.05 **(86)** n21 t22 f21 b22. Some 20-30 years ago Bowmore was famed for its high quality sherry casks. This is not quite up with the legendary stuff especially with the peat being a little shy. **59.6%.** *575 bottles.*

**Dewar Rattray Cask Collection Bowmore 14 Years Old** cask 2056, dist 15 July 91, bott 15 May 06 **(87)** n22 chunky and a bit of a thug. The unstable peats lash out at everything; t20 rough and ready; hot, peppery stuff with Fishermen's Friends abounding; f23 a zillion waves keep the tastebuds busy; the peat is pretty loud and screams long into the distance; b22 For those wanting a bit of rough. **57.8%.**

**Dewar Rattray Individual Cask Bottling Bowmore 1989 Aged 17 Years** Sherry cask 1095, dist Feb 89, bott May 06 **(66)** n15 t18 f16 b17. From a sherry cask, apparently. But the nose and finish suggests something metallic got into that cask and given it a strange, seriously flawed personality. A shame. **49.6%.** *180 bottles.*

**Duncan Taylor Collection Bowmore 1966** cask no 3312, dist May 66, bott May 06 **(93)** n24 coal dust, distant peat reek and mango chutney in near perfect proportions. Stunning; t24 a velvet delivery of something vaguely bourbony then a steady procession of soft peat and delicate fruit; the level of sweetness could not be better; f22 the oak is a friend here as it tops off proceeding with wonderful, semi-sweet vanilla; b23 just one of those wonder casks. The line is so very fine between greatness and plain ordinary when you get to exotic fruit time. Here it has kept both feet in greatness. **43.2%.** *130 bottles.*

**Duncan Taylor Collection Bowmore 1966** cask no. 3317, dist May 66, bott May 06 **(95)** n23 well aged, very high quality bourbon. The peat is no more than a foil to the leather and ripe cherries; t25 yes... yes... yes... yesssss! Meg Ryan wouldn't have to fake this one as soft, pulsing waves of pleasure build up in intensity. It starts sweet and slightly peaty, then various degrees of fruit surf in. All the time the barley is simply melting on every taste bud on the palate and warming spices are added to the intensity that guarantees glory; f23 tires very slightly; ample compensation with those playful spices digging deep under the sugary skin and receding as the light cocoa notes arrive. From first to very long last, this is the type of whisky we pray we will one day find. It just makes tender love to you from the moment it caresses your nose; b24 my last whisky of the day, and what a colossus; what an all-time memorable dram to take to bed with me. No cleaning of the teeth tonight. A Whisky of the Year contender? We'll see. Curiously Duncan Taylor had another high quality 66 (distilled especially by the Scots to commemorate the impending victory by England in the World Cup Finals, a few weeks later – thanks guys!) which came out at exactly the same strength. That, after 40 years, is very weird. However, this is the darker of the two and suggests it comes from a better bourbon cask, hence less fruit and more balance. I was going to savour this after England lifted the World Cup again in Germany. Only my hopes were Swede-bashed. Still, I can toast 40 years of supporting Millwall, instead. Anyway, there are pitifully few bottles of this. Are you in your mother-in-law's will...? **43.2%.** *171 bottles.*

**Duncan Taylor 1968 Aged 35 Years** cask 1424 **(88)** t22 playful, sweat peat amid toasty vanilla; t22 clean barley with some leathery, waxy honey neobourbony notes; f22 the peat returns – just – to add a modicum of weight to the clean, fruity finish; b22 classy, but one of the most lightweight 35 y-o of all time: and probably the lightest from a medium to heavyweight Islay. There must have been a peat shortage that year... **42.05%**

**Duncan Taylor Collection Bowmore 1968** cask 1429, dist Feb 68, bott July 05 **(80)** n20 t21 f19 b20. Like the other DC 68 Bowmore, this has been divested of its peaty status thanks to time: regard this as very lightly smoked. **42.8%.** *182 bottles.*

**Duncan Taylor Collection Bowmore 1968** cask 3826, dist Oct 68, bott May 06 **(83)** n21 t22 f20 b20. We are again firmly into exotic fruit territory here, which reveals a degree of over-aging. Occasionally, if the Whisky Gods are smiling, that can turn into a true superstar – as it did with the Bowmore 66 (see above). Not this time, though it has its moments. **41%.** *150 bottles.*

**Duncan Taylor Collection Bowmore 1969 Aged 35 Years** cask 6089, dist Nov 69, bott Jan 05 **(77) n**20 **t**20 **f**18 **b**19. The nose hints at the soapy oak having gone through the top and the finish confirms it. Very mild. Japan only. **42.7%**

⸬ **Duncan Taylor Collection Bowmore 1969** cask 6089, dist Nov 69, bott Nov 05 **(89) n**22 perky peat, fruit candy; **t**23 rounded with the smoke forming guard of honour for the starring pomegranate and vanilla; **f**21 oak thunders on, but some underlying barley sweetness maintains the balance; **b**23 does exceptionally well to hold its line in the face of a full oaky charge. Great stuff. **42.7%**. *226 btls.*

**Duncan Taylor Collection Bowmore 1982** cask 89545, dist Oct 82, bott Mar 05 **(87) n**22 curious: like a bourbon make from peated corn! **t**22 oily sweetness still has that corn effect and then the malt arrives; **f**21 vanilla and malt; **b**22 very sweet, malty and only moderately peated. **62.6%**

⸬ **Duncan Taylor Collection Bowmore 1982** cask no. 89545, dist Oct 82, bott Mar 05 **(74) n**19 **t**20 **f**17 **b**18. Like its sister bottling (above) there is bourbon on the nose, and displays the same lack of rhythm and elegance. Only here it has lost shape and direction, as well. Not a whisky happy with itself. **62.2%**. *157 bottles.*

⸬ **Duncan Taylor Collection Bowmore 1982** cask 85014, dist Oct 82, bott 15 Mar 06 **(79) n**21 **t**19 **f**20 **b**19. Jam and cream Swiss role amid the ungainly peat. An awkward customer. **58%**

**Duncan Taylor Collection Bowmore 1987 Aged 17 Years** cask no. 18020, dist Oct 87, bott Mar 05 **(86) n**21 **t**22 **f**23 **b**20. At Bowmore's optimum age, but this one falls all over the palate like it was drunk. Take the figure one away from the 17, and you might have the age of the style. **57.9%**

⸬ **Duncan Taylor Collection Bowmore 1987** cask 18027, dist Oct 87, bott Apr 06 **(81) n**21 **t**22 **f**18 **b**20. Distinctly pungent and peppery in that uniquely and un-unnervingly fresh Bowmore style; just runs out of legs at the finish. **58.4%**. *252 bottles.*

⸬ **Dun Eideann Bowmore 10 Years Old** cask 4250 **(91) n**22 good sweet/dry balance to the smoke; **t**22 a light, citrussy flourish to the gathering peat; heads towards hickory near the middle; **f**24 molassed and sweetening, the finish gathers weight, cocoa and delicate oils impressively; **b**23 a charming, well-mannered Bowmore benefiting from a sensible upbringing in a good home. **46%**. *Signatory.*

**Hart Brothers Bowmore Aged 12 Years** dist 91 **(87) n**21 **t**23 **f**22 **b**21. A thirst-quenching Islay of few frills. **46%**

**Jim McEwan's Celtic Heartlands Bowmore 1968 (86) n**22 **t**21 **f**22 **b**21. Unusual Bowmore (though not for a '68) where the peat has almost drifted out of the equation to be replaced by soft stewed fruit and bourbon. **40.6%**

⸬ **Kingsbury's Single Cask Bowmore 17 Years Old** cask 2849, dist 87 **(89) n**22 The youthfulness of this nose is more like a classic Bowmore at 7 rather than a present-day 17. Only with a Bowmore from this era are you likely to find this phenomenon. Lovely, though! **t**22 here we go again: everything I would expect from a youthful version of the malt. The sweetness offers pure barley; the smoke is Fishermen's Friend at its warmest. That can come from one distillery only; **f**23 multiple layers of teasing peat, each at varying intensity. The oak plays a relaxed, tempering part; **b**22 the youngest 17 year old you'll ever see. Until you find another Bowmore... **46%**. *Japan Import System.*

**Mackillop's Choice Bowmore** dist Apr 90 **(92) n**22 oily, full and prisoner-dispatching; **t**24 one of the best Islay deliveries of the year (and I admit I had to swallow here!!). Perfect degree of sweetness balancing out a drier, seaweedy sub-plot; **f**23 layer upon layer of dissolving malt with the peat restrained and distinctly coastal. Wonderful...; **b**23 on the nose, I'd have sworn this was Caol Ila. But rarely does that distillery quite hit this level of sweet complexity. **43%**. *Angus Dundee.*

⸬ **Murray McDavid Bowmore Aged 9 Years** Matured in Bourbon/Syrah casks enhanced in Guigal Hermitage Rouge casks, dist 96, bott 05 **(91) n**22 sprightly only tells the half of it; so pink is this stuff you half expect essence of panther, or even paraffin. Instead you get clipped barley and even more sharply clipped peat. The grape is bristling, too, but seems under-ripe. Very, very different;

**t**24 the peat goes AWOL for the first five seconds, entirely incapable of getting through the barley-fruit mix; then the smoke surges through, taking few prisoners en-route before intermingling gloriously and adding to the beautiful confusion on the palate; **f**22 relaxes for the first time and at last the youthfulness of the malt begins to reveal itself, especially as the oak just about entirely gagged; **b**23 wow! Now that was different – and there aren't that many whiskies in Scotland I can call a first! **46%. nc ncf.** *1,500 bottles.*

⇒ **Norse Cask Selection Bowmore 1993 Aged 11 Years (96) n**24 a picnic by the sea: plenty of ozone and salt, the most beautiful peat-reek with clear iodine form rock pools. Man, this is soooo Islay...!!!; **t**24 a meal in itself: thick, intense layering of 90% cocoa chocolate with sludgy peat and gorgeously sweet barley, all sprinkled with a little sea salt; the degree of oiliness just about hits perfection; **f**24 long and sweetens as the gristiness to the barley comes through, shuddering layers of more cocoa and peat that go on ad-infinitum. **b**24 why do we so rarely see casks of this distillery's malt exactly the way I remember it some 25-years ago? This is a true classic destined to be one of the talked-about all-lifetime greats. Sod the sample: I'm off to find a bottle...!! **65.5%.** *Quality World, Denmark.*

**Old Malt Cask Bowmore Aged 12 Years** dist Apr 91, bott Feb 04 **(84) n**23 **t**20 **f**21 **b**20. The brilliant, ultra delicate nose isn't quite fully backed up on the palate. **50%.**

⇒ **Old Masters Bowmore Aged 12 Years** cask no. 20100, dist 94, bott 06 **(83) n**20 **t**21 **f**22 **b**20. Decent, delicate whisky for those who prefer their peat toned down a little. **57.8%.** *James MacArthur.*

**Old Malt Cask Bowmore 13 Years Old** dist April 91, bott Dec 04 **(84) n**19 **t**22 **f**23 **b**20. Chunky and chewy, the malt dominates throughout. The late chocolate swiss roll finale is pretty delicious. **50%.** *Douglas Laing & Co. 254 bottles.*

**Old Malt Cask Bowmore Aged 14 Years** dist Feb 89, bott Aug 03 **(80) n**19 **t**21 **f**20 **b**20. One of the more lightly peated bottlings of recent times displaying lots of natural caramel. **50%.** *Douglas Laing.*

**Old Malt Cask Bowmore Aged 15 Years** dist Apr 88, bott Mar 04 **(84) n**22 **t**21 **f**21 **b**20. More hot whisky from a time when those stills were obviously getting a bit of stick. A sweet malty complexity battles hard to make itself heard. **50%**

⇒ **Old Masters Bowmore 1990 Aged 15 Years** cask no. 1168, bott 05 **(84) n**21 **t**22 **f**21 **b**20. A sugary sweetness glazes the soft peat but for all its charm complexity is at a minimum. **51.1%.** *James MacArthur.*

**Old Malt Cask Bowmore 20 Years Old** dist Mar 84, bott Jun 04 **(86) n**21 **t**22 **f**21 **b**22. Distinctly unusual, quirky even. Not quite one for the purists and even maybe slightly out of kilter, but there is no denying the fun. **50%.** *Douglas Laing.*

⇒ **Old Malt Cask Bowmore 21 Years Old Sherry Finish** dist Oct 84, bott Sept 06 **(86) n**21 **t**22 **f**22 **b**21. With its molassed Fisherman's Friend and Ovaltine, this is such a direct ancestor of the 6-years-old bottled in 1992 for Oddbins that's it's almost scary. You would never believe its age otherwise. **50%.** *309 bottles.*

**Old Masters Bowmore 1989** bott 03 **(83) n**21 **t**20 **f**22 **b**20. A fruity, attractive expression that is as sweet and oily as this distillery ever gets. **57.3%.**

**Provenance Bowmore Over 12 Years** dist Spring 91, bott Winter 04 **(90) n**22 **t**23 **f**22 **b**23. A really sexy, elegant shape to this one; younger than its years and caresses the senses expertly. **46%.** *Douglas McGibbon for Premium Spirits, Belgium.*

**Provenance Bowmore 13 Years Old** dist 10 Apr, bott 21 Mar 05 **(86) n**20 **t**22 **f**22 **b**22. Untaxing and unsophisticated, it's one for simple pleasures. **46%.**

⇒ **The Queen of the Moorlands Rare Cask Bowmore 1995** cask 271035 **(90) n**22 Bowmore at its most bonfiresque; **t**22 young, sweet and well smoked with the body an attractive dual personality of softness and extreme rigidity; **f**23 goes into overdrive here with the intensity of the peat now building up above the Bowmore norm and the accompanying spices letting rip; **b**23 a rock solid and above average version of this distillery at 10. **57.2%. ncf sc.** *The Wine Shop, Leek. 108 btls.*

**Royal Mile Whiskies Bowmore Young Peaty Islay** cask 20022, dist 17 Feb 99, bott Mar 05 **(84)** n21 t22 f22 b19. Brilliant to see Bowmore in this Bambi-like state. So sweet, the peat goes in every direction. Fond memories of the old Oddbins bottlings of 15 years ago, when they still knew how to have fun... **61.5%**. *322 btls.*

⋙ **Secret Stills Bowmore Aged 17 Years** Distillery no.4, release no. 1, casks 7049/7050, dist 19 Aug 89, bott Jun 06 **(92)** n24 dogged peat whimpers and snarls with a bi-polar display of softness and aggression. Lovely salt attaches to the gristier element; t23 perfect sweetness in having dry oak assuring a cut-off point to the developing demerara-laced peat; f22 bitter-sweet; some coffee with the smoke **b**23 not too much secret about Bowmore, being one of the more eponymous Islays. Great, though, to see it at arguably its best age. And in such great nick. **45%**. *Gordon & MacPhail. 650 btls.*

⋙ **The Spirit Safe & Cask Bowmore 1990 Aged 15 Years** Hogshead, dist 90, bott May 06 **(83)** n20 t22 f21 b20. Lethargic peat and honey dependent. Clean but oaky towards the finish. **53.1%. nc ncf.** *Celtic Whisky Compagnie, France.*

**The Un-Chillfiltered Collection Bowmore Aged 12 Years** Hogsheads 2234 and 2235, dist 6 May 92, bott 8 Dec 04 **(83)** n19 t22 f21 b21. Someone must have forgotten to put some peat in the kiln. **46%. nc ncf.** *Signatory. 731 bottles.*

**The Vintage House Bowmore 20 Years Old (91)** n22 t23 f23 b23. Another brinkman's malt with the oak going as far as is safe. Enormous depth and complex peat that, beyond the spice, has to be sought. **52.7%. ncf.** *Vintage House, London.*

**Vom Fass Bowmore 12 Years Old (85)** n20 t21 f22 b21. For those who prefer their peat to whisper rather than shout. **40%**. *Austria.*

**Duncan Taylor & Co. Wilson & Morgan Barrel Selection Bowmore 1993** bott 04 **(86)** n21 t22 f22 b21. A standard, clean, sweet and attractive expression. **50%**

## BRAES OF GLENLIVET (see Braeval)

## BRAEVAL
### Speyside, 1974. Chivas. Silent.
**Deerstalker Braeval Aged 10 Years (91)** n23 ripe gooseberries and fat watermelon balance beautifully with the no less refreshing malt; t23 just so stunningly clean and uncluttered, giving the malt a clear, mouthwatering path to dazzle and shimmer; f23 gloriously long and chewy for a malt so light, with a slow procession of oak adding spice at the death; b22 can hardly be called complex, but the allure is its simple, honest, delicate, mouth-cleansing intensity. The secret, though, is its near perfect degree of sweetness. The youngest of the Deerstalker range, but the best by a long way – and another reminder of what we are missing from this very good distillery. **40%**

⋙ **Old Malt Cask Braes of Glenlivet Aged 13 Years** Refill Hogshead 1498, dist Nov 90, bott Oct 04 **(83)** n21 t22 f20 b20. Some very decent barley-oak combinations, but a bit fierce in part. **50%. nc ncf.** *Douglas Laing.*

⋙ **Old Malt Cask Braeval 16 Years Old Wine Finish** dist May 90, bott Sept 06 **(84)** n20 t21 f22 b21. Pretty closed on nose and arrival but finally opens up to let loose some firm barley and oak. **50%**. *Douglas Laing. 327 bottles.*

**Provenance Braes o' Glenlivet Aged 13 Years** dist Nov 90, bott Oct 04 **(84)** n20 t22 f21 b21. Attractive, but rather simplistically sweet for a Braes with an enormous natural caramel surge. Pure Speyside, though! **46%. nc ncf.**

⋙ **Provenance Braeval Aged 8 Years** dist Nov 96, bott Nov 04 **(87)** n22 beefed up barley as you might expect, but the oak thrust is a surprise; t23 what wonderful barley intensity. Youthful, but showing greater age than the norm; f21 slightly off-key with the oak offering a bitter finale; b21 unmissable youth, but probably a first fill cask has helped here. **46%**. *McGibbon's.*

## BRECHIN (see North Port)

# BRORA
## Highland (northern), 1819–1983. Diageo. Closed.

**Brora 30 Years Old** db **(92) n**23 supremely balanced and intact after all these years. The full-on smoke offers a sweet counter to the well-behaved oak. An apologetic hint of pine reveals some of the age. Majestic, nonetheless; **t**22 the full strength plays into the hands of the beguiling oak-peat character. Despite the wood chippings, the sweetness of the barley keeps the tastebuds panting: this is sexy stuff; **f**23 good breeding here as the oak backs off to offer nibbling vanilla and marmalade and just the right percentages of smoke-fuelled spice; **b**24 oh, it does the heart such good to find aged malts like this. Near sublime. **55.7%**

**Brora 30 Years Old** db **(96) n**25 near enough faultless smoke, less seaweed than farmyard. But there are countless layers here with malt and oak visible, so to speak. Perfect harmony; **t**24 the sweetness of the malt defies time: you could be running your finger along the mill at the old Broro distillery in the days when it was probably Scotland's prettiest working distillery; **f**24 just so long and relaxed. Try and count the layers of smoked malt, then lightly smoked oak as one by one they strike against the tastebuds. You can't: there's too many. For good measure, there is a very late surge of fresh, mouthwatering malt as well; **b**23 I'll dock it a mark as it doesn't quite have that extraordinary (almost immeasurable but profound) extra depth, complexity and balance that all the top Ardbegs possess. I'm a heartless bugger, me. But being purely analytical, I think that's a fair call. Scotch of the year? It's up there. Just a Rosebank and maybe a fluke vatting to battle with. I understand they are getting very low on Brora now. The lab has done the distillery proud with this one: nothing like its age and then best I've seen it since it was in its prime at 12. Sensational and a lifetime must-have. **56.6%**

-:- **Brora 30 Years Old** db **(97) n**24 that stunning Brora farmyard again, perhaps with a touch of extra fruit this time round. Beautiful structure, layering and harmony; **t**25 Gosh! Perfect or what? How can something be this old yet offer such a gristy sweetness? Chewy, smoky, barely oaky but 100 okay-dokey; **f**24 some late peat spice buzz adds a bit of bite to the smoke-fuelled serenity of this dram. A touch of something citrus helps thin out the layers; **b**24 here we go again! Just like last year's bottling, we have something of near unbelievable beauty with the weight perfectly pitched and the barley-oak interaction the stuff of dreams. And as for the peat: an entirely unique species, a giant that is so gentle. Last year's bottling was one of the whiskies of the year. This even better version is the perfect follow-up. **56.4%**

**Chieftain's Brora Aged 23 Years Pedro Ximenez** Sherry butt cask 1510, dist Nov 81, bott Mar 05 **n**23 lovely sweetness to offset the drier oak; fruit, smoke and vanilla abound; **t**24 sweet grape and soft smoke in almost equal proportions; oak also makes an early impact; **f**22 slightly drier with singed raisins and late cocoa; **b**24 the sherry is profound but doesn't overwhelm the intricate character of the malt. **46%. nc ncf.**

-:- **Dun Bheagan Brora Aged 23 Years** Sherry butt **(86) n**22 **t**23 **f**20 **b**21. Some uncommonly good sherry influence at work here. **48%.** *Ian Macleod.*

**Dun Bheagan Brora 1980 Aged 23 Years** bott 29 Jan 04 **(84) n**21 **t**22 **f**21 **b**20. Freaky Brora: a blast of peat early on, but lurches around the palate as if drunk. Some odd (as in strange) fruit notes, but enjoyable in an eccentric kind of way. **50%.**

**Dun Bheagan Brora Aged 23 Years, Vintage Bottling Butt** cask 1513, dist 81, bott 04 **(86) n**22 **t**22 **f**21 **b**21. The peatiness of the Brora is dimming with age; there is just enough sparkle left to make this rather lovely. **48.6%. nc ncf.** *336 btls.*

**Old Malt Cask Brora Aged 21 Years** dist Jun 82, bott Apr 04 **(75) n**19 **t**19 **f**18 **b**19. Cowsheds: tail-swishing livestock. And that's just the nose ... **50%.** *708 btls.*

-:- **Old Malt Cask Brora Aged 22 Years** dist Mar 83, bott Sept 05 **(84) n**21 **t**22 **f**20 **b**21. Intense oaked-barley-toffee apple but the peat is notable for its absence, though a coal-dusty smokiness is apparent. **50%.** *Douglas Laing. 224 bottles.*

-:- **Old Malt Cask Brora Aged 22 Years** dist 17 Mar 83, bott May 05 **(78) n**19 **t**21 **f**19 **b**19. Another curiously smokeless expression. **50%.** *Douglas Laing. 421 bottles.*

# BRUICHLADDICH
## Islay, 1881. Bruichladdich Ltd, Working.

**Bruichladdich 10 Years Old** db **(90)** n22 beautifully clean and zesty, the malt is almost juvenile; t23 sweet, fruity then malty charge along the tastebuds that geets the mouth salivating; f23 the usual soft vanilla and custard but a bigger barley kick in the latter stages; b22 more oomph than previous bottlings, yet still retaining its fragile personality. Truly great stuff for a standard bottling. **46%** ☺ ☺

**Bruichladdich 12 Years Old** db **(87)** n21 salivatingly sharp Seville oranges with some sub strata of grape juice and unusually firm malt; t22 a big, almost riotous arrival of fruit and grain: about as mouthwatering an Islay as you'll find; f22 a bevvy of delicate spices and vanilla; b22 a busy Laddie full of juicy fun. **46%. nc ncf.**

⟨ **Bruichladdich 12 Years Old 2nd Edition** db **(88)** n23 big barrage of fruit; crisp barley beautifully integrates with oak; t22 an uneven, mildly uncertain, delivery due to the grape being out of sync with the big barley; give it about eight-ten seconds and they have found a delicious degree of harmony; f22 long with the intense, chiselled flavours still slightly at odds, but calming down with some oils; b21 a similar type of wine involvement to "Waves", but this is oilier in the old-fashioned 'Laddie style and lacks a little of the sparkle. The fruit on the finish is outstanding, though, and I don't think you or I would turn down a third glass... **46%**

**Bruichladdich Aged 15 Years** db **(89)** n22 t22 f22 b23. A coastal, laid-back dram where complexity is spotted by the tastebuds in the same way eyes become accustomed to the dark. **46%**

⟨ **Bruichladdich 15 Years Old 2nd Edition** db **(86)** n22 t23 f20 b21. Delicious, as usual, but something, possibly fruity, appears to be holding back the show. **46%**

**Bruichladdich XVII Year Old** db **(94)** n23 gentle citrus-led fruit caresses the nose; soft malt counters the spice; t23 mild malt offers both a sharp barley thrust and a much softer gristy sweetness; f24 the mouthwatering richness continues to the very end with some spices suggesting oak but the malt remaining in control; b24 there has been a quite enormous jump in quality between "official" tastings of this malt. Where once it was just delicate, it is now delicate and raucous: soft and rough lovemaking to the palate. A dram dedicated to Laddie blender Jim McEwan's sex life, one assumes! Lucky bugger! **46%** ☺

**Bruichladdich Flirtation 20 Year Old** db **(88)** n23 ripe sultanas and dough; t22 juicy fruit; a drier, vanilla-dominated maltiness; f21 more vanilla topped with grape; b22 all the fun is in the chase with this one.... **46%**

⟨ **Bruichladdich Flirtation Aged 20 Years Second Edition** db **(86)** n21 t22 f22 b21. Hi sugar! A Laddie for those with a sweet tooth. **46%**

**Bruichladdich Full Strength 1989** db **(89)** n21 t21 f24 b23. A dram built for a shitty day: first it thumps you back to life with its high alcohol barley and then spends the next two minutes making love to your tastebuds. Aaaaahhhhh... **57.1%**

⟨ **Bruichladdich Infinity** db **(94)** n24 lazy smoke slowly disengages itself from the thick barley. Seriously sexy; t24 enormously viscous as the honeycombed barley grips to the roof of the mouth while sweet peat thuds around the palate; f22 some timid vanillins shove their head above the peaty parapet; b24 from a distillery that has been known to distil more than twice, here's something that might have been in the pot only once, such in the enormity and intensity of the malt. Knife, fork and spoon needed for this one...and you could stand them up in it. To infinity, indeed...and beyond...!! **55.5%**

⟨ **Bruichladdich "Islands" Aged 20 Years Third Edition** Aged in Madeira db **(95)** n23 sublime balance between keen grape and drier vanilla. A light-heavyweight; or is it a heavy-lightweight; t24 immediate buzz to the mouth and then, on secondary impact, the most luscious fruity delivery which entirely cleanses the palate; sweet but some lovely spices counter perfectly; f24 long, lithe and light, again its that soft pepper and barley which sits so happily with the grape; b24 just perfect for those looking to spice up their whisky lives. **46%**

⟶ **Bunnahabhain Islay Festival Bottling 2006 14 Years Old** Pedro Ximenez Finish db **(78)** n18 t19 f21 b20. Call me an old misery guts. But only trace elements of the distillery style survive – a salty blast about three quarters in. Has some good moments, but not enough. And too many fault lines. **52.6%.** *761 bottles.*

**Bruichladdich Legacy 1965** db **(90)** n22 floral and muscular: a bit like a men's changing room after the talc has been thrown about; t23 improbably slick on the palate with a degree of bourbony sweet liquorish and natural caramel but the malt remains intact; f22 dries attractively with some spices as an extra; b23 well, I don't now how it did it, but a malt as gentle as Bruichladdich has survived nearly 40 years in the cask with barely a wrinkle. Not a single off note! **41.8%.** *1500 btls.*

**Bruichladdich Legacy 1966** db **(92)** n23 t23 f23 b23. No sappiness or bitterness here, just grace, charm, melting malt: that's my laddie! **40.6%**

**Bruichladdich "Links" Royal Troon 14 Years Old** db **(89)** n23 t23 f21. Almost b22 a very different sort of 'Laddie that eschews its usual malty softness for a hard-edged charisma. **46%. nc ncf.** *12000 bottles.*

⟶ **Bruichladdich Links "Royal Liverpool Hoylake" 14 Years Old** db **(89)** n23 another wonderful compendium of varying fruit nuances...and barley; t23 astonishing freshness to the delivery massages every single taste bud; f21 oily, gentle fruits, but a little flat; b22 a conservative malt by 'Laddie's recent standards: should go down in the Clubhouse well... **46%**

⟶ **Bruichladdich Links "Turnberry 10th Limited Edition" 14 Years Old** db **(94)** n24 as soft, tantalizing and teasing as fingernails down the spine. And just as fruity...; t24 oh yes....the softness of delivery, the valuation of the fruit, only to be attacked and overcome by the voluminous and unstriated barley... words simply fail me...; f22 a sombre finish with a more bitter edge to the complex fruit and cocoa; b24 at first I thought this was the first scotch whisky to be named after roads of British housing estates for the nouveau riche...then I realised they were golf courses....Majorly complex malt; I could nose and taste there was some Port in there somewhere, but something else was happening. Research reveals that something is Pedro Ximenez. Talented bloke is Pedro... **46%**

⟶ **Bruichladdich Rocks** db **(82)** n19 t22 f20 b21. Perhaps softer than you'd imagine something called "rocks"! Beautiful little malty charge on entry. **46%**

**Bruichladdich 3D** db **(94)** n24 t24 f22 b24. Absolute quality distillate displaying almost mind-boggling complexity and a wonderful degree of spontaneity. **46%.**

**Bruichladdich 3D 2nd Edition Moine Mhor** db **(91)** n22 bigger age and the peat comes chunkier rather than the soft wafts of the 1st edition; t23 almost in-your-face delivery of smoke-encrusted fruit: this is enormous and the intensity is furthered by the delicious cocoa towards the middle and a burst of spice; f23 softer than the 1st edition with the smoke making a soft landing for the vanilla and; the sweetness at the death reminds me of the raspberry jam in a Swiss role...yummy! b23 The re-creation kind of underlines that the 1st edition was, perhaps, a one-off. This is top-rate whisky and no mistake. But falls short of the 1st edition's near genius. This will be an interesting set to collect over the years. **50%**

**Bruichladdich Vintage 1970** db **(87)** n23 t23 f20 b21. Utter bliss. Before the oak kicks in. **44.2%**

⟶ **Bruichladdich 1970** db **(79)** n21 t20 f19 b19. Plucked from the warehouse just in time; lovely fruits on the nose and delivery, but becomes a bit sappy as the finish works overtime to regain lost ground. **40.2%.** *Taiwan.*

**Bruichladdich Vintage 1973** db **(88)** n22 t22 f21 b23. First sight suggests that the oak is too intrusive; give it time and instead you get a genuinely delicious bourbony strata to a fabulously complex whisky. **40.2%. nc ncf.** *4200 bottles.*

**Bruichladdich Vintage 1984** db **(86)** n22 t22 f21 b21. Surprising amount of age present considering the richness of the malt. **46%**

⟶ **Bruichladdich Waves Aged 7 Years** db **(90)** n21 young, with clipped fruit and smoke; t23 mouthwatering barley at first, soon swamped in light grape; f23 stylish finale with the gathering smoke really feeling at home with the Madeira. Seriously classy despite the obvious youth; **b**23 compact, tasty little fruitfest lengthened by evidence of soft smoke and extra clean grape. Proof absolute that whisky at 7 years old can offer just as must delight as something twice or three times its age. **46%**

⋰ **Bruichladdich WMD II - The Yellow Submarine 1991** db **(75) n**20 **t**19 **f**18 **b**18. Sorry guys. But by this distillery's normally orbital standards, while quite drinkable, this one just doesn't have the balance and sinks. **46%**

**Berry's Own Selection Bruichladdich 1991 13 Year Old** bott 04 **(87) n**20 soft citrus; **t**22 sparkling, malt-intense; **f**23 more citrus and wonderful spices as the malt takes off stunningly; **b**22 slow starter becomes radiant as it awakes. **53.6%.**

⋰ **Berry's' Own Selection Bruichladdich 1991 Aged 15 Years (94) n**24 greengages, honey, salt and a vague smokiness combine for something rather wonderful; **t**24 a stunning honey thread weaves through the crystal-clear barley; threatens to be mouthwatering, but prevented at the last minute by drier vanilla. The weight and delicacy of the sweetness defy the odds. 'Laddie, you feel, unplugged...; **f**23 raspberry jam raps itself around that renegade peat; **b**23 unexpected little gems like this make you feel so lucky to do this job... **46%.**

⋰ **Cadenhead's Authentic Collection Bruichladdich 12 Years** Bourbon Hogshead, dist 93, bott Sep 05 **(85) n**20 **t**22 **f**22 **b**21. Oily, hugely barley-intense, straight-down-the-line 'Laddie. Not even the hint of a deviation. **55.8%.** *312 bottles.*

**Cadenhead's Authentic Collection Bruichladdich Aged 18 Years** Bourbon Hogshead, dist 86, bott May 05 **(94) n**24 peat reek? A soft wisp of it here and there? Surely not. It is, though. But that is not all: wonderful saltiness and grandstanding oak. Fabulous; **t**23 succulent wave upon wave of mouthwatering barley sugar and treacle. Vanilla gathers towards the middle, as does cocoa – surprisingly early on; **f**23 that hint of smoke on the nose is confirmed at the smouldering death; **b**24 what a glass of class... **55.8%.** *270 bottles.*

⋰ **Cask Strength Bruichladdich 1990 (83) n**20 **t**21 **f**21 **b**21. Oaky and salt encrusted; a lovely honey edge, too. But forget the strength: this is hot whisky; a wave of glistening barley cools it – to a degree. **54.9%.** *Gordon & MacPhail.*

**Coopers Choice Bruichladdich 1991 Port Wood Finish 12 Years Old** bott 03 **(85) n**22 **t**23 **f**19 **b**21. Loses it towards the finish, but the mouth arrival would turn on any tastebud. **46%.** *Vintage Malt Whisky Co.*

⋰ **The Coopers Choice Bruichladdich 1991 Matured for 14 Years** bott 06 **(82) n**22 **t**21 **f**19 **b**20. The oily richness to the early barley is stunning. **46%.**

⋰ **Dewar Rattray Individual Cask Bottling Bruichladdich 1993 Aged 12 Years** cask no. 1558, dist Apr 93, bott Sept 05 **(86) n**21 **t**23 **f**21 **b**21. An enjoyable if straightforward expression. **55.1%.** *329 bottles.*

**Duncan Taylor Collection Bruichladdich 1966 Aged 39 Years** bott Jan 05 **(94) n**23 the oak is in place but is nearly too subtle to be true. Delicious (seemingly improbable) stewed and buttered potato melts into the malt; **t**24 the gentle intensity of the malt is heightened by the bitter-sweet enormity. Layers of vanilla but a touch of marmalade and natural caramel add a soft confusion; **f**23 no spice or anything suggesting big oak. The malt recedes, the vanilla gathers, but it's a timeless experience; **b**24 an awesome cask that has withstood the test of time with barely a blemish. A quite mesmerizing and near unbelievable malt. **41.4%**

⋰ **Duncan Taylor Collection Bruichladdich 1990** dist Jun 90, bott Sept 05 **(90) n**22 enormously hard barley with a rummy-liquorice-hickory depth to the fruit. All prisoners slaughtered; **t**23 rock-hard, vivid barley yet salivating and sharp; **f**22 the undulating sweetness pans out to something nutty, almost marzipan in style; **b**23 blind-tasted, I'd never have recognized this as a 'Laddie in a 100 years. In fact, I'd have no idea what the hell this was. In some eyes, possibly a faulty cask. But what faults...!!! Very different, and rather excellent to boot. **54.7%.** *736 bottles.*

⋰ **Dun Eideann Bruichladdich 10 Years Old** cask 3036 **(89) n**22 a squeeze of lemon and a shake of salt on the transparent barley; **t**23 simplistic, softly oiled and salivating young barley pans out into something much more complex; f22 lovely vanilla tints as it dries; b22 an honest, delightfully complex cask. **46%.** *Signatory*.

⸫ **James MacAthur's Bruichladdich Aged 14 Years** dist 91, bott 05 **(90)** n22 lively citrus thins out the intense barley; t23 deft, playful barley offers a grassy lightness which allows in some early, excellent vanilla and spice; f22 long, multi-layered barley of just the right weight; b23 a honey of a cask. **43%.**

**Murray McDavid Bruichladdich 1986** cask MM514, bott 03 db **(80)** n21 t20 f20 b19. Good oak and gooseberries on the nose and malty-salt on the body. **46%**

**Murray McDavid Bruichladdich 1989 (89)** n23 eggy batter, vanilla and sultana; t23 clean, uncluttered barley; attractively oily with a drier, sawdusty middle and excellent spice counterblast; f21 medium length, soft vanilla and fading barley; b22 little wonder MM can pick a spot-on Laddie! **46%**

**Old Malt Cask Bruichladdich Aged 13 Years** dist Mar 90, bott Oct 03 **(94)** n24 t24 f22 b24. One of those rare occasions where you would love to hug the cask this matured in. This is near faultless whisky that simply beguiles you with each understated, tastebud-teasing mouthful. **50%. nc ncf sc.** *Douglas Laing. 330 bottles.*

⸫ **Old Malt Cask Bruichladdich 15 Years Old** Bourbon finish, dist Dec 90, bott July 06 **(88)** n21 curious vanilla/suet pudding/sultana, yet lacking balance; t23 busy with mouthwatering spices and gathering barley intensity; f22 soft oils guide the gentle oak to calmer waters and onto cocoa; b22 lurches drunkenly all over the palate but the main thrust really is beautiful and big. Very different. **50%.**

**Old Malt Cask Bruichladdich Aged 17 Years** dist Nov 86, bott Dec 03 **(87)** n20 t23 f22 b22. A punchy, heavyweight that eschews subtlety for effect. **50%. nc ncf.**

**Old Master's Bruichladdich 1991** cask 2295, bott 04 **(90)** n20 t24 f23 b23. After an average nose the arrival on the palate is a celebration of exceptionally well made, complex malt. **58.7%.** *James MacArthur.*

⸫ **Port Charlotte 4 Years Old** dist 12th Jun 01, bott 25th Nov 05 **(96)** n25 quite possibly the most coastal whisky I have ever nosed: it is as if the peat has been diluted only by seawater. This smells of rotting distilleries and malt kilns. It is unique and unquestionably the most evocative thing I have ever sniffed. I close my eyes and I am on undiscovered Islay, before I ever wrote about the place; when I could wander around barely-known distilleries alone. No matter how it tastes, it cannot paint a picture so vividly, or bring back such a lost joy as the nose, or even a sense of loss of how things used to be. ...I don't know if you believe this or not, but it has actually brought a lump to my throat and a slightly moistened eye. I think I should pause before tasting...; t24 salty, fruity, even – eventually – wild raspberries and banging on the door all the time, massive peat wanting to be let in; f23 dry despite its age though enough mollased mocha to keep the rumbling peat sweet and company; b24 so stupendous – and moving – is the nose that it takes time to focus on what happens palate-wise. Not quite so good, as one might suspect. But still a unique and astonishingly pleasurable take on Islay. **61.4%.** *The Whisky Shop, Gordon Homer's Private Stock. 39 bottles.*

**Private Cellars Selection Bruichladdich 1989** bott 03 **(83)** n20 t21 f21 b20. Sweet-ish and pleasant. **43%.** *Speyside Distillers.*

**Provenance Bruichladdich 11 Year Old** dist 25 Nov 93, bott 23 Feb 05 **(87)** n22 citrus and kiwi fruit; t22 mouthwatering malt with zero oak interference; f21 barley; b22 at its cleanest and unpeatiest. Unusual but fun. **46%.** *Douglas Laing.*

**Provenance Bruichladdich Aged 11 Years** dist 2 Dec 93, bott 21 Apr 05 **(87)** n22 apples and grass: light and clean even by Bruichladdich's old standards; t22 simplistic malt with a faint degree of salt; a hint of tinned peaches does for the fruit interest; f21 dry-ish with no shortage of vanilla; b22 An enjoyable Laddie with less oil than usually found from this era. **46%.** *Douglas Laing & Co.*

**Provenance Bruichladdich Over 13 Years** dist Spring 90, bott Autumn 03 **(88)** n21 t22 f22 b23. A really excellent cask – probably second fill bourbon – give a perfect insight into the depth of this distillery. Tremendous stuff. **46%.** *Douglas McGibbon.*

**Scott's Selection Bruichladdich 1986** bott 03 **(88) n**21 **t**22 **f**23 **b**22. One of those high-quality whiskies that offers a bit of everything ... except peat. **60%**

**Scott's Selection Bruichladdich 1990** bott 05 **(91) n**22 sharp and tangy with excellent fruit bite; **t**24 mouthwatering malt concentrate. The salty seasoning raises the flavour intensity to mouth-puckering levels. Wonderful! **f**22 levels off with salt and vanilla; **b**23 a wonderful cask with not a single blemish or off note. Very true to the distillery. And with a touch of attitude, too. **56.5%**. *Speyside Distillers.*

**Spirit of the Isles Bruichladdich 1991 Rum Cask Finish** bott 03 **(85) n**22 **t**23 **f**19 **b**21. Was doing well until the rum arrived: worth trying just for the mouth arrival alone. **46%**. Liquid Gold/John MacDougall.

**Vom Fass Bruichladdich 14 Years Old (84) n**19 **t**22 **f**21 **b**22. A hint of soap on the nose, but the stewed apples and malt concentrate compensate wonderfully. Pleasantly oiled and spiced. The odd hint of smoke, too! **46%**. Austria.

**Whisky Galore Bruichladdich 1991 Aged 12 Years (87) n**22 **t**22 **f**21 **b**22. Unusual to find Laddie in a second (ot third) fill cask: the distillery's output in its most natural, naked state. **46%**

**Wilson & Morgan Barrel Selection Bruichladdich 1993** bott 04 **(90) n**21 salty, punchy, nipping, malty, charismatic; **t**23 beautifully rich malt with lots of bounce and shape to the intense barley; **f**23 even hints of honey to this one, then milk chocolate; long and intense to the deliciously juicy dregs; **b**23 exemplary bitter-sweet balance. A minor classic. Beware: Jim McEwen will be chasing you for every last bottle. **50%**

## BUNNAHABHAIN
### Islay, 1881. Burn Stewart. Working.

**Bunnahabhain Aged 12 Years** db **(89) n**23 very sharp malt, almost nosepinchingwith a distinctly salty, softly sherried bite; **t**23 tangy fruit, then a wave of salted oak and crisp barley. Busy and bracing and teasingly sweet in places; **f**21 soft malt and salted vanilla; **b**22 much back to its old, eye-watering self: less emphasis on sherry and more on its coastal roots. Brilliantly evocative and very true to the distillery. One sad note: this is from a new bottling that has been re-designed. It is elegant and attractive, keeping close to the original. But I must say that the label which served the Bunna for the last quarter century always reminded me of when I used to holiday at the distillery in the early 80s, with the bottle waiting on the table by a peat fire as the rain relentlessly lashed the cottage. I loved the fact that the label never changed and the reference to "Westering Home" which we would sing, Bunna in hand, once safely inside and away from the gale. There was a permanency about the label, as there is the distillery. Little things...but at least the whisky is almost back to top form. **40%**

-:⊱- **Bunnahabhain XVIII Aged 18 Years** db **(86) n**20 **t**23 **f**22 **b**21. The nose puts you on the back foot but by the third mouthful it is easier to pick up the nuances of this decently weighted dram. **43%**

-:⊱- **Bunnahabhain XXV Aged 25 Years** db **(93) n**22 some serious coastal saltiness here...and grape; **t**24 big saline kick as the oak offers some early latte; mouthwatering barley also impresses, topped off with brown sugar and damson tart; **f**23 more milky coffee with an oatcake side dish; **b**24 a fruity Bunna, but jam-packed with all the big barley-salt notes which set this distillery apart. One of the few bottlings around at the moment that us Bunna Old Timers can hold up and say: "Yeah, this is the business." Quite superb. **43%**

-:⊱- **Bunnahabhain 1971 Aged 35 Years 125th Anniversary** bott Oct 06 db **(94) n**25 close your eyes and you can breath in the warehouses in the shadow of the Paps of Jura: a stunning combination of sea-salt and the cleanest, most high quality sherry butts imaginable. Smokeless Bunna just exactly as it should be and faultless; **t**24 near spot-on delivery of juicy, mouth-watering grape again sprinkled liberally with sea-salt and dried with lightly pulsing oak yet enough barley escapes the intensity for balancing lightness while deft spices abound; f22 dries, but never too much, though there is a spicy rumble amid the gathering oak; b23 when I stayed at the distillery on holiday in both 1983 and 1984 – long before I let on the secret of it being a must-experience whisky destination – the 12 year-old Bunna that sat on my table before the peat fire came from sister casks of what we are tasting here. Previous owners Highland lost the plot with Bunna when they strangled it with sherry, often sulphured, and though the grape shapes the malt here, there is enough of the old clean signature to take me back to those wonderful days. Frankly, it is doubtful if this great distillery's anniversary could have been celebrated in finer style. **44.9%. ncf.** *750 bottles.*

⬩⬩⬩ **Berry's' Own Selection Bunnahabhain 1974 Aged 31 Years (77)** n19 t20 f19 b19. Entirely drinkable and fruitily enjoyable. But just the wrong side of the oaky line to be a great. **46%.** *Berry Bros & Rudd.*

**Cadenhead's Authentic Collection Bunnahabhain Aged 26 Years** Bourbon Hogshead, dist 79, bott May 05 **(71)** n19 t18 f17 b17. Tangy and off-key. **49%.** *216 bottles.*

**Celtic Heartlands Bunnahabhain 1966** bott 25 Apr 05 **(80)** n19 t20 f21 b20. A fascinating dram: almost an experiment to see how long a whisky can remain just that in cask. And discover its state just before it dips below 40%. Here we have, as suspected, a degree too much oak, especially on the nose and very early mouth delivery. But you cannot but be impressed by the finish which somehow conjures essences of a sweet, estery, Jamaican-style rum from stills sitting on the Sound of Islay. **40.1%.** *McEwan/Bruichladdich.*

⬩⬩⬩ **Chieftain's Bunnahabhain Aged 10 Years Sherry Finish (79)** n20 t21 f19 b19. Bit of a half-way house with the sherry seemingly scrubbing out much of the bourbon complexity, but not quite imparted enough of its own character. **46%.**

⬩⬩⬩ **Dun Bheagan Bunnahabhain Aged 10 Years Manzanilla Finish (86)** n22 t22 f20 b22. Distinctive fruity bite to this. **46%.** *Ian Macleod.*

⬩⬩⬩ **Dun Bheagan Bunnahabhain Aged 10 Years Rum Finish (88)** n22 cleansed barley; t23 lush, sugar-coated malt retaining some mouthwatering moments; f22 remains sweet, gristy, clean and easy going; b21 hardly complex but the rum has impacted with an agreeable sweetness. **46%.** *Ian Macleod.*

**Duncan Taylor Bannahabhain 1966 Aged 36 Years** cask 4874 **(77)** n23 t19 f17 b18. The nose is outstandingly complex but age catches up with it. **40.7%**

**Duncan Taylor Bunnahabhain 1967 Aged 35 Years** cask 3325 **(86)** n22 t23 f20 b21. Starts brilliantly but fades. **40.2%**

⬩⬩⬩ **Duncan Taylor Collection Bunnahabhain 1967** cask no. 3328, dist Mar 67, bott Nov 05 **(89)** n23 rich bourbon backbone; waxy barley sugar; t22 slightly eye-watering where the oak has got through, but the mouthwatering coffee-barley qualities are sublime; f22 a whole pack of caramelized biscuits and late, gristy barley; b22 big, refined and has stayed honest. **40.8%.** *209 bottles.*

⬩⬩⬩ **Murray McDavid Mission Bunnahabhain 1966** Oloroso sherry **(86)** n21 t23 f20 b22. Creaks a fair bit, but never goes snap... **40.3%.** *500 bottles.*

⬩⬩⬩ **Old Malt Cask Bunnahabhain Aged 12 Years** Hogshead cask 2132, dist Nov 92, bott Sept 05 **(93)** n23 beautiful oak-salt interaction; the barley as clear and crisp as the Paps on a sunny January morning; t24 stunning delivery with perfect sharp-sweet tones getting the juices flowing big time; great oak-spice buzz at back of the tongue; f23 pretty long with that gentle vanillas taking control; b23 so good to see the distillery at probably its best age and away from sherry butts...the way it used to be..!! **50%. nc ncf.** *Douglas Laing.*

**Old Malt Cask Bunnahabhain Aged 14 Years** dist Mar 89, bott Nov 03 **(76)** n19 t20 f17 b18. A rather mouthwatering yet strangely off-balance Bunna with a bitter finish. **50%. nc ncf sc.** *Douglas Laing. 282 bottles.*

⬩⬩⬩ **Old Malt Cask Bunnahabhain Aged 15 Years** cask 1056, dist. Mar 89, bott May 04 **(79)** n19 t21 f20 b19. Clean but tame fare. **50%.** *Douglas Laing. 159 bottles.*

**Peerless Bunnahabhain 1966** cask 4872, dist Jun 66 **(89)** n22 t23 f21 b23.

This is a stupendous Bunna, the best at this age I have ever found. And bottled in the nick of time if the strength is anything to go by ... **40.1%**. *Duncan Taylor.*

**Peerless Bunnahabhain 1967** (*see* Duncan Taylor Bunna 67)

⁂ **Provenance Bunnahabhain Aged 12 Years** dist Nov 92, bott Aug 05 **(84)** n22 t21 f20 b21. Gristy and soft, but lacking some of the distillery's more bracing qualities. **46%**. *McGibbon's.*

**Royal Mile Whiskies Bunnahabhain 1971** cask 6249 **(87)** n22 distinctly salty, with diced apple in the drying oak; t21 big, chewy, natural toffee; f23 good sweetness to see off the warming oak, and the very late, exotic fruit is quite a classy surprise; b21 a tad too much age but the finish is memorable. **46%. ncf.**

**Scott's Selection Bunnahabhain 1984** bott 04 **(86)** n22 t21 f22 b21 Bunna has always peaked at between 8 and 12 for me; this one has just made it through. **57.5%**. *Speyside Distillers.*

**Scott's Selection Bunnahabhain 1977** bott 05 **(84)** n21 t22 f20 b21. Predictably salty and perhaps a touch tart. **49.6%**. *Speyside Distillers.*

**Signatory Bunnahabhain 1978 Aged 26 Years** cask 2539, dist 30 Mar 78, bott 11 Mar 05 **(90)** n22 fruitcake liberally sprinkled with salt; t23 big fruity stuff you could stick a fork in, with some zesty, orangey notes amid the burnt raisins; the malt arrives reluctantly; f22 fades slowly and slightly tartly but always enough malt around to even up the sweetness; some late cocoa towards the end tops things off perfectly; b23 melts the heart to see a non-sulphured sherry-casked Bunna. One performing somersaults on the tastebuds, too! **54.6%**. *468 bottles.*

**Spirit of the Isles Bunnahabhain 1982** bott 03 **(93)** n24 t23 f23 b24. The guy who chose this cask and I have known each other for over 20 years: I have never known him to use his life-long insight into whisky with more telling effect. Bunna in aspic. **46%**. *Liquid Gold/John MacDougall.*

**Vom Fass Bunnahabhain 9 Years Old (83)** n20 t23 f21 b19. Curiously lightly peated with the odd thread of honey. Wonderfully mouthwatering throughout, struggles to find a balance. An elegant and delicate rarity. **40%**. *Austria.*

## CAOL ILA
### Islay, 1846. Diageo. Working.

**Caol Ila Aged 12 Years** db **(89)** n23 a coastal, salty biting tang (please don't tell me this has been matured on the mainland!) with hints of rockpools and visions of rock pipits and oystercatchers among the seaweed; t23 enormously oily, coating the palate with a mildly subdued smokiness and then a burst of gristy malt; f21 caramel and oil; b22 a telling improvement on the old 12-y-o with much greater expression and width. **43%**

**Caol Ila Aged 18 Years** db **(80)** n21 t20 f19 b20. Another improvement on the last bottling, especially with the comfortable integration of citrus. But still too much oil spoils the dram, particularly at the death. **43%**

**Caol Ila 25 Years Old** dist 78 db **(90)** n24 one of the best CI noses in many a year thanks to an oaky platform to reach those higher phenolic notes. Wonderful tangerine notes thin out the aroma beautifully; t23 at first light, deft fruit, again to a degree on the citrussy side, then a rumbling, oily procession of peat; f21 long but disappointingly oily and flat by comparison; b22 a wonderful Caol Ila in so many respects: truly great. Yet another, like most it has to be said, that noses better than it tastes because of the massive oiliness. Still some genuine quality here, make no mistake. **59.4%**

⁂ **Caol Ila 1979** db **(74)** n20 t19 f17 b18. Hugely disappointing. I could go on about tropical fruit yada, yada, yada. Truth is, it just conks out under the weight of the oak. Too old. Simple as that. **58.6%**

⁂ **Caol Ila 1996** Refill AM 406 db **(92)** n24 spot-on bourbon casks have allowed full reign to the complexity here. None of the usual attendant oils, and an enticing degree of gist to some fruity barley; some wonderful farm-yardy stuff; **t**23 great body with just enough oil to lightly coat the palate; peat is slightly bolder than usual for this distillery and also two-toned with variation on weight; **f**22 long, lacking in complexity but the sugared peat fade is very attractive; **b**23 Oh!! If only all Caol Ila's could be quite so light on their feet and sophisticated... **43%**. *For Juuls Vinhandel, Denmark. 445 bottles.*

**Caol Ila Cask Strength** bott 21 Jun 04 db **(87) n**23 a brilliant Caol Ila nose with real attitude on the iodine and magnitude on the malt; **t**22 for a few seconds the malt hits the palate with abandon before an all-consuming oiliness crashes the life out of it. The peatiness offers additional, much required, spice; **f**21 slightly simplistic smoke; **b**21 quite wonderful in parts, but that accursed oil...!! **55%**

**Aberdeen Distillers Caol Ila 10 Years Old** cask 6978, dist 10 May 93, bott Oct 03 **(91) n**24 **t**23 **f**22 **b**22. Really clean, soft and decisive without that clinging oil, this is Caol Ila as so very rarely seen these days. **43%**. *Blackadder.*

**Aberdeen Distillers Caol Ila 1993** dist May 93, bott Oct 03 **(83) n**21 **t**20 **f**22 **b**20. Light but chewy peat within a vanilla frame. **43%**

**Adelphi Caol Ila 1988 Aged 15 Years** cask 4247 **(84) n**20 **t**21 **f**22 **b**21. Tart, citrus-dominated, sweet barley but at times violently assertive. **59.3%**

**Adelphi Caol Ila 1990 Aged 13 Years** cask 4842 **(79) n**22 **t**19 **f**20 **b**18. Estery, mildly rummy, hot and sweet in part. **59.6%**

**Adelphi Caol Ila 1991 Aged 12 Years** cask 13374 **(92) n**24 **t**23 **f**22 **b**23. Exceptional Caol Ilas are getting harder to find: this is one. **57.5%**

⋅⋅⋅ **Berry's' Own Selection Caol Ila 1996 Aged 10 Years (94) n**23 with its hints of apple and celery, this pretty subtle by Caol Ila standards; even a touch of the gristy Port Ellens about it. Spooky; **t**24 beautifully delivered peat on a base of sugared black pepper. This is so big for this distillery, but also just so mercurial; **f**23 long, remains lush and the slow development of the cocoa is pure tease; **b**24 so often the malt from this distillery passes my heart by. Excellent blending malt, usually, but a bit of a plodder in the glass. Here Dougie McIvor has pulled a stunner out of the hat. A must have collector's item for those who want to wallow in ultra delicate and complex Islays. **57%**. *Berry Bros & Rudd.*

**Blackadder Raw Cask Caol Ila 1990** cask 4161 dist Apr 90, bott Nov 03 **(76) n**20 **t**19 **f**18 **b**19. Hot and just doesn't sit comfortably. **57.7%**

**Blackadder Raw Cask Caol Ila 25 Years Old** cask no. 5334, dist 02 May 79, bott Jun 04 **(87) n**22 **t**20 **f**23 **b**22. After so long in the cask anything can happen, but the denouement comes as a pleasant surprise. **61.2%**

⋅⋅⋅ **Cadenhead's Authentic Collection Caol Ila Aged 11 Years** Bourbon Hogshead, dist 95, bott Feb 06 **(86) n**20 **t**22 **f**23 **b**21. A particularly oily expression that rewards patience. **60.5%**. *330 bottles.*

**Cadenhead's Caol Ila Aged 12 Years** dist 93, bott Feb 05 **(92) n**24 one of the great Caol Ila noses of recent years: the peat is big but arrives in almost apologetic waves, hardly wanting to intrude on the sweet malt and diced apple and figs. It is to your nose what gentle fingers can be to your spine... **t**23 the softest of landings as at first barely detectable peat increases in magnitude but never enough to disturb the soft rhythm of the pulsing malt; **f**22 just a shade too gentle and oily for its own good; **b**23 drips with quality and finesse. **46%**. *390 bottles.*

⋅⋅⋅ **Cadenhead's Authentic Collection Caol Ila Aged 15 Years** Bourbon Hogshead, dist 91, bott Sept 06 **(94) n**23 chunky with some serious peat embers; above average phenol levels and excellent clarity; **t**23 juicy barley and stunning spices. But it's the richness to the honeycomb sweetness that really impresses, allowing the oak to integrate charmingly; **f**24 long and pulsing with grace and balance. Some toasty notes absorbed by the lingering sweetness of the barley while the peat continues to fill every crevice it can find; **b**24 oh, if only all Caol Ilas could be this gloriously structured. The distillery at it's best. **56.3%**. *318 bottles.*

**Cadenhead's Caol Ila Bond Reserve Aged 25 Years (93) n**24 an almost improbable degree of ripe citrus in perfect harmony with the most thoughtful of peats. Oak pulses gently but with enormous manners; t24 silky peat dissolves on the plate as again wave upon wave of citrus adds a mouthwatering dimension. Oils begin to gather but fail to dampen the complexity; f22 controlled, oily vanilla and smoke; b23 good ol' Cadenhead! They've turned up trumps again!! **53.4%.**

**Cask Caol Ila 1991 (93) n**23 Tally ho! Melton Hunt fruit cake comes to Islay; **t**23 sultana and raisin in a peaty sauce; **f**23 delicate for all its obvious enormity as some late malt and oaky-vanilla try to take centre stage, only to be outflanked by the rising spice; **b**24 unusual, drier, fruitier, spicier, quite memorable Caol Ila. Good old G&M: they certainly know how to pick a belter! **57.4%.** *G&M.*

**Cask Caol Ila 1993 (80) n**19 t21 f20 b20. Rock-hard, sweet, metallic and unforgiving. **57.8%.** *Gordon & MacPhail.*

⋅⋅⋅ **Cask Strength Caol Ila 1994 (90) n**23 profound fruity nose: plums and some hidden citrus balancing out the dull peat; **t**22 quality arrival with soft barley forced ahead of massive spice; liquorice and natural caramel softens the oak delivery; **f**22 a long, fruity finale cannot disguise the medium roast Java and toast; **b**23 a lovely cask with a few surprises up its sleeve; refuses to take the normal Caol Ila route. **58.2%.**

**Chieftain's Caol Ila Aged 9 Years Medoc Finish** casks 90441/90444, dist Jun 95, bott Feb 05 **(86) n**20 t22 f22 b22. Hardly one for the purists. **50%. nc ncf.** *1674 btls.*

⋅⋅⋅ **Chieftain's Caol Ila 10 Years Old Hogshead (78) n**20 t20 f19 b19. A hard-as-nails nose and delivery: I have seen more give from a taxman. **43%.**

⋅⋅⋅ **Chieftain's Caol Ila Aged 11 Years Hogshead (89) n**23 an unlikely and quite delicious combination of violets and diffused peat reek; **t**22 excellent barley sweetness allows the peat to drop in gently and confidently; **f**22 some hickory dryness but remains gentle and discreet; **b**22 a wonderful cask of Caol Ila which accentuates the understatement. **43%.** *Ian Macleod.*

**Chieftain's Caol Ila 1993 Aged 11 Years Rum Finish** bott 26 Mar 04 **(84) n**23 t22 f19 b20. The nose is at its industrial best but despite a bright, animated start on the palate the balance is lost towards the bitter end. **46%.** *Ian Macleod.*

⋅⋅⋅ **Chieftain's Caol Ila Aged 12 Years** Hogshead **(77) n**19 t20 f19 b19. Pleasant and plodding in its own way, but has little to say. **43%.** *Ian Macleod.*

⋅⋅⋅ **Chieftain's Caol Ila 12 Years Old Rum Finish (83) n**22 t20 f20 b21. Slightly too oily and thick to fully take advantage of the proffered rum influence. But the peat is more polished than it might be. **46%.** *Ian Macleod.*

⋅⋅⋅ **Connoisseurs Choice Caol Ila 1993 (81) n**21 t20 f21 b19. The nip and bite to the nose is hardly matched by the supine, oily delivery to the palate. **40%.**

⋅⋅⋅ **Connoisseurs Choice Caol Ila 1994 (72) n**17 t19 f18 b18. Misses the target: just never feels right either on nose or palate. **40%.** *Gordon & MacPhail.*

⋅⋅⋅ **Connoisseurs Choice Caol Ila 1995** bott 18 Apr 06 **(91) n**23 soft oils, but the peats are of varying depth; **t**23 excellent weight and richness to the malt; the smoke refuses to take the sweet route; **f**22 plenty of vanilla and coffee; **b**23 now that's a Caol Ila on song and balanced. **46%.** *G&M. US Market.*

⋅⋅⋅ **The Coopers Choice Caol Ila 1984 Years 21 Old** bott 06 **(84) n**22 t22 f20 b20. An interesting bottle for those with a literary bent. Especially George Orwell fans. He wrote his novel "1984" on Jura, and it is almost inconceivable that he spent time on the island without looking out onto the Caol Ila distillery, across from him and the Sound of Islay. The whisky then was made in different stills and would have been a lot weightier than this. But for all its oaky flaws, not too a bad dram to keep the book company. The spices, in particular, are a page turner. **46%.**

**Coopers Choice Coal Ila 1990 14 Years Old**, Single Cask Range, bott 05 **(76) n**18 t20 f18 b18. Harsh and disappointing. **46%. ncf.** *Vintage Malt Whisky Co.*

**Coopers Choice Caol Ila 1991** bott 03 (11 Years old) **(83) n**20 t21 f20 b22. So, now you have it – the UNPEATED! Caol Ila. From a cask that could sit undetected a mile or two along the coast at Bunna, this bottling ranks alongside the latter Ardbeg 17-y-o and the bourbon cask Macallans. Not the first time I have tasted Caol Ila in this form, but the first time I can ever remember seeing it bottled. **43%.**

**Coopers Choice Caol Ila 1991 12 Years Old** bott 04 **(78)** n19 t19 f20 **b**20. Fuggy and not quite on song. **46%**. *The Vintage Malt Whisky Co Ltd.*

**Distillery No. 2 Caol Ila 1989** cask no 4655 **(78)** n20 t19 f20 **b**19. Bitumen, newly tarred road on the nose, slightly off course on the palate. **56.2%**. *Denmark.*

**Dun Bheagan Caol Ila 1993 Aged 10 Years** bott 15 Mar 04 **(87)** n22 t22 f21 **b**22. Slightly plodding but above average Caol Ila these days. **43%**. *William Maxwell.*

⋙ **Dun Bheagan Caol Ila Aged 11 Years (82)** n21 t21 f20 **b**20. The tastebuds get a good peaty buffeting, but plenty of oil on hand to soften the blows. **43%**.

⋙ **Dun Bheagan Caol Ila Aged 12 Years** Hogshead **(85)** n20 t23 f21 **b**21. Some delicious coffee notes crystallise at the finale as the peat calms down. A pleasant, if sometimes bumpy, ride. **43%**. *Ian Macleod.*

⋙ **Dun Bheagan Caol Ila Aged 14 Years** Hogshead **(95)** n24 a much drier nose than the norm, yet allowing the barley and peat to surface. Also a lack of oil – thankfully!! What remains is custard powder and dry banana. Easily one of the most complex and confident noses from this distillery for many a year; t23 just enough oil to ensure a gentle landing for the marauding, juicy barley and enough oomph for the peat to race full throttle into each and every taste bud; f24 fabulous complexity to the finish here because – so rarely with this distillery – the oiliness has gone and we are left behind with varying, complex layers of encrusted phenols, rock salt and freshly ground peppers. Yet the barley remains fresh and salivating; **b**24 sheer quality all the way. Easily one of the finest Caol Ilas I have tasted in over 25 years... **53.8%**. *Ian Macleod.*

⋙ **Dun Bheagan Caol Ila 16 Years Old** Hogshead **(83)** n21 t22 f20 **b**20. Astonishingly sweet for its age; the odd touch of marzipan on the smoke apart, hardly taxes the tastebuds. **46%**. *Ian Macleod.*

**Gordon & MacPhail Reserve Caol Ila 1995 Aged 8 Years (81)** n20 t21 f20 **b**20. Punchy, biting big peat; needs a dose of complexity. **55.5%**. *Scoma Germany.*

**Hart Brothers Caol Ila Aged 10 Years** dist May 93 bott Nov 03 **(87)** n22 t21 f22 **b**22. For once a Caol Ila not swamped in exaggerated oil. **57.3%**

**Mackillop's Choice Caol Ila** dist Feb 90 **(91)** n23 attractively dry oak against a slightly fruity but intensely smoky maltiness. Quite sophisticated; t22 dissolving gristy malt but dissolves into rich oil; f23 very sweet and chewy but the oil dissipates to leave a charming oakiness; **b**23 such a relief to see a Caol Ila stripped mainly of its oily vineer. What lies behind is high class and of considerable depth. **43%**. *Angus Dundee.*

⋙ **Murray McDavid Caol Ila 1991 Aged 15 Years** Bourbon/Mourvedre/Syrah **(88)** n24 freshly cracked oysters by a peat fire and glass of heavy, opened-too-early red; t22 big juicy start with the peat pushed far into the background, bizarrely thirst-quenching; f21 as the smoke finds its feet some balance is lost; remarkably light finish, if slightly too bitter; **b**21 you get the feeling that no whisky can live up to that extraordinary and quite unique nose; and this one doesn't quite make it. The freshness of the grape is wonderful, but it never quite finds a way of entirely gelling with the smoke. That said, it's worth the experience as this is something very different and offers many plusses. **46%. nc ncf.** *2600 bottles.*

⋙ **Murray McDavid Caol Ila 1993 Aged 12 Years** Bourbon/Chenin Blanc **(89)** n23 rock pools: about as salty as Caol Ila gets; t22 major spat between fruit and smoke with some delicious arm-wrestling; f22 smoke wins, and celebrates by calling up vanilla and a touch of spice; **b**22 charming and unusual. **46%**. *2700 btls.*

⋙ **Old Malt Cask Caol Ila Aged 10 Years For A Fine Cigar's Pleasure** Bourbon Hogshead **(88)** n22 "Earthy, oily with smoke and pepper" says the label. Correct; t23 "round and spicy with peaty smoke." That only tells the half of it: spices get in early as the barley really cranks up the sweetness and there's a saline kick from the digestive biscuit. The peat rumbles deliciously with malcontent; f21 "salty, coastal and coffee'd" Perhaps: I'd certainly go with the coffee. But for me just fizzles out under an oily avalanche – as this distillery's whisky is so often apt to do; **b**22 I don't smoke, so can't vouch for its ability to keep a cigar good company. But as Caol Ila casks go, this is a cut above. **50%. nc ncf.** *Douglas Laing.*

**Old Malt Cask Caol Ila Aged 12 Years** dist Nov 90, bott Aug 03 **(87)** n23 t23 f22 b22. Much better than the tight nose suggests: in fact it's a joy. **50%. nc ncf.**

**Old Malt Cask Caol Ila 12 Years Old** dist Aug 91, bott Aug 04 **(92)** n23 great nose: really firm and holds the peat brilliantly; t23 big, yet very gentle in its slightly gristy smokiness: the waves of sweet, malty smoke keep relentlessly pounding the tastebuds; f22 thins out very slightly as the oak has a bigger say; a trace of ginger on the finale; b24 honest, steady as a Pap, unmistakable Caol Ila. **50%.**

**Old Malt Cask Caol Ila Aged 12 Years Sherry Finish** dist Sep 91, bott Feb 04 **(78)** n23 t19 f18 b18. Classic nose, hard as nails, loses balance somewhat on the palate. The label gives a possible reason why. **50%. nc ncf sc.** *360 btls.*

⁙ **Old Malt Cask Caol Ila 12 Years Old** Wine finish, dist Mar 94, bott July 06 **(92)** n23 firm barley and peat: this could almost go snap; t24 is this really Caol Ila? The fruit is a shrinking violet to the massive peat attack which is crisp and lean; f22 usually the palate is by now swamped in oil; instead there is smoke-flavoured cocoa and a sprinkle of mollased sugar; b23 is it the wine at work here? Something appears to have removed the usual gushing oil and this crisper Caol Ila is a charmer, a real class act. **50%.** *Douglas Laing.*

**Old Malt Cask Caol Ila Aged 14 Years** dist Jan 90, bott Feb 04 **(92)** n24 t23 f22 b23. A Caol Ila that any Islay-phile will recognise every time. A sexy little charmer. **50%. nc ncf sc.** *Douglas Laing.*

⁙ **Old Malt Cask Caol Ila 15 Years Old** dist 10 Jan 90, bott 14 Jun 05 **(84)** n22 t21 f21 b20. A bit of a spitfire: hot stuff but unquestionably entertaining. **50%.**

**Old Malt Cask Caol Ila 25 Year Old** dist 2 May 79, bott 13 Apr 05 **(88)** n21 flint and peat in equal measures; t22 softening, citrussy malt but the peat hovers and hands clumsily; f23 thankfully the oil is scarce and allows a wonderful delivery of spices sweet malt to counter the developing vanilla; b22 a very curious, mildly out of tune Caol Ila that thrives on the lack of oil. **50%.** *Douglas Laing & Co.*

⁙ **Old Malt Cask Caol Ila Aged 25 Years** dist Nov 79, bott Aug 05 **(75)** n20 t19 f18 b18. Strangled by the oak. **50%.** *Douglas Laing. 271 bottles.*

⁙ **Old Malt Cask Caol Ila 25 Years Old** dist Apr 80, bott Jan 06 **(95)** n24 firm and lucid, the peat-oak symbiosis is about as much as you could ask for at this age. Very few Caol Ilas offer this type of grace and nutty beauty; t22 decent body and jumbled messages. Takes time to get going; f25 it is all about the unbelievably long finale. It is all there: fresh barley, the most playful fruity notes under honeyed almonds. And all bathed in cocoa-dusted peat. Take your time with this one: about three hours should do the trick; b24 it is impossible not to become besotted with this one. **50%.** *Douglas Laing. 327 bottles.*

⁙ **Premier Barrel Caol Ila 10 Years Old** dist Jan 95, bott Dec 05 **(92)** n23 brilliant! Parcels of peat waft effortlessly around; there is a sweet mocha element and all softened by well oiled barley; spotted dick abounds...; t23 melt-in-the-mouth stuff: both barley and peat home in on the tastebuds relentlessly but both caress rather than smother. The waves are countless; f23 a wonderfully orchestrated finale: somewhere some vague hints of lime dovetail in with the banana and vanilla. But it all relative: the smokey barley continues to pull the strings; b23 a premier barrel by name and nature. **46%.** *Douglas Laing. 401 bottles.*

⁙ **Private Collection Caol Ila Demerara Rum Finish 1990** casks 99/103 2,3, dist 31 Jan 90, bott June 05 **(86)** n20 t23 f22 b21. Lots to chew on but never quite finds its length. **45%.** *Gordon & MacPhail. 650 bottles.*

⁙ **Private Collection Caol Ila Vintage Rum Finish 1990** casks 99/103 1, dist 31 Jan 90, bott June 05 **(94)** n24 such is the enormity of the nose, so well does the rum and peat combine that, for reasons I can't even begin to understand or explain, the first punches of the aroma are very similar to a freshly opened First Growth Bordeaux prior to oxidization. The riches are near unfathomable; t23 the sweetness of the peat forms glorious layers amply supported by barley and an unusual element – probably rum; f23 there is very little house cooking oil to this, so the more complex oaks and barley have a chance to shine; b24 Works a treat but, curiously, has more Demerara character than an actual Demerara!! **45%.** *G&M. 865 bottles.*

⋙ **Private Collection Caol Ila Cognac 1991** bott 02 Feb 06 **(86) n**22 **t**22 **f**20 **b**22. Brittle and sweet: probably the least oily Caol Ila on the market and not easily recognisable from this distillery at all. **46%.** *Gordon & MacPhail US Market.*

⋙ **Private Collection Caol Ila Marsala Wood 1995 (88) n**23 floral and fruity; oily peat reek; **t**22 excellent bitter-sweet delivery – edging on the sweet side as it always should; **f**21 pretty oaky and oily. Just a tad too bitter; **b**22 always a touch nervous when encountering such wine finishes, as they have a propensity to end in tears. But, the dull finish apart, this is a real entertainer. **45%.** *G&M.*

**Provenance Caol Ila 10 Years Old** dist Winter 94, bott Summer 04 **(89) n**23 beautifully gristy and fresh: a touch of citrus apart, the ghost of Port Ellen, perhaps; **t**23 dissolves on the palate first with excellent malt then soft vanilla; the sweetness is controlled and remains on the gristy side; **f**21 fades a fraction too quickly in the oiliness; **b**22 a little peach. **46%.** *Douglas Laing & Co.*

⋙ **Provenance Caol Ila Aged Over 10 Years** hogshead DMG 1714-1715, dist Aut 94, bott Wint 05 **(89) n**22 teasingly layered peat operates off both sweet and drier levels; **t**23 hallmark oiliness works so much better when not hauling oak around: it's peat and barley all the way; **f**22 vaguely toasty yet sweet...and long thanks to those oils. The shortage of oak really does give this a lift; **b**22 a dream of a Caol Ila – about as uncluttered a bottling you'll ever find. **46%. nc ncf.**

⋙ **Provenance Caol Ila 10 Years Old** dist Feb 96, bott Autumn 06 **(84) n**21 **t**21 **f**21 **b**21. Ultra clean Caol Ila with firm smoke and a decent barley development from the late middle. **46%.** *McGibbon's.*

**Provenance Caol Ila 12 Years Old** dist 1 Oct 91, bott 30 Apr 04 **(87) n**23 **t**20 **f**22 **b**22. Delicate, complex, well structured. Just lacks that touch of wine. **46%.**

**Provenance Caol Ila 13 Years Old** dist Autumn 91, bott Spring 04 **(82) n**21 **t**21 **f**20 **b**20. A medium peated, easy going Islay. **46%**

⋙ **The Queen of the Moorlands Rare Cask Caol Ila 10 Years Old** dist 6 Jun 95, bott 16 Jun 05 **(88) n**22 sweet and oily. Oh, and peaty...; **t**23 lush delivery and a fine development of fresh barley and the deeper smoky tones; **f**21 tails off as the oak gives it a bitter tweak; **b**22 does what it says on the tin. **46%. sc.** *The Wine Shop Leek, UK. 318 bottles.*

⋙ **Scott's Selection Caol Ila** dist 84, bott 06 **(85) n**20 **t**23 **f**21 **b**21. The mintiness to the nose is a pretty useful air sock. Pretty major oak interference throughout, but there is enough juice remaining in the gristiness to ensure some delicious, quality moments. **53.5%.** *Speyside Distillers.*

⋙ **Signatory Un-Chill Filtered Collection Caol Ila Aged 14 Years** dist 15 Jul 90, bott 2 Mar 05 **(86) n**23 **t**21 **f**21 **b**21. Oily smoked Rupp; attractively inert. **46%.**

**The Wee Dram Caol Ila Aged 12 Years (93) n**23 attractive mixture of peat reek and burning coal: a free Scottish fireplace in winter with every sniff; **t**24 a shade estery with the clean, faultless, mildly grassy malt leading the way; the peat arrives first as an afterthought and, once established, builds by degree; the sensational middle even displays some brave honey; **f**23 some oak arrives to slightly lighten the peat intensity. But it is never less than very big; **b**23 so many Caol Ila bottlings of recents years have been dull and workmanlike. For once we have a cask that shows life and elegance despite the enormous weight: Caol Ila as it should be – except the strength! **40%.** *The Wee Dram, Derbyshire, UK.*

**The Whisky Fair Caol Ila Aged 13 Years** Bourbon Hogshead 4734, dist Mar 91, bott Feb 05 **(84) n**21 **t**21 **f**22 **b**20. Oily and mildly on the hot side. **54.2%. nc ncf.** *359 bottles.*

⋙ **The Whisky Fair Caol Ila 26 Year Old** Bourbon Hogshead, dist May 79 **(88) n**22 the oaky onslaught is soft and full of bourbon character: the peat hardly gets a look in ...!; **t**23 buzzing spices impact immediately, showing the oak really is alive. Again the peat has to take a back seat as, finally, some barley sweetens things out **f**22 lots of liquorice and chocolate hazelnut; **b**21 a remarkable malt: my guess is that you have a barely used first-fill bourbon barrel at work here. The results are near unique. **57.2%**. *Germany. 212 bottles.*

**Whisky Galore Caol Ila 1990 Aged 12 Years** (83) **n**20 **t**22 **f**21 **b**20. Another clean and delicious Caol Ila that is just missing out on the complexity. **46%.**

**Whisky Galore Caol Ila 1992 Aged 12 Years** cask 1273, dist Jan 92, bott 04 **(78)** **n**20 **t**20 **f**19 **b**19. Fat, sweet and sluggish. **46%.** *Duncan Taylor & Co Ltd.*

⠿ **Whisky Galore Caol Ila 1992** dist Mar 92, bott 23 Mar 06 **(90)** **n**23 busy, structured and gristy: not your typical Caol Ila; **t**23 again waves of mounting intensity and, though oily, the sweetness is kept in check; **f**22 back to smoke and vanilla; also a trace of attractive coffee; **b**22 as with most Caol Ilas, the thick oil forms a gravity field that lets little really take off. But look closely enough and distinct charm and complexity can be found close to the surface. **46%.** *471 btls.*

**Wilson & Morgan Barrel Selection Caol Ila 1992** bott 04 **(87)** **n**22 **t**22 **f**21 **b**22. One of the most delicate Caol Ila expressions for a while. **46%**

**Wilson & Morgan Barrel Selection Caol Ila 1994** bott 04 **(85)** **n**21 **t**23 **f**20 **b**21. Competent, clean and chewy. **50%**

# CAPERDONICH
## Speyside, 1898. Chivas. Silent.

**Caperdonich 16 Years Old Cask Strength Edition** dist 88, bott 05 db **(88)** **n**23 a bourbony weight can't contain the bubbling, ultra-clean malt; **t**21 hot as Hades on arrival; settles for the most stunning honey follow-through; **f**23 continues in an intense malty vain and the honey follows like Mary's lamb. Really impressive, truth be told! **b**22 the first actual distillery bottling I can remember from this distillery in my drinking lifetime – some 30 years. And this isn't half bad, though the early heat on the palate gives some indication as to why we have been waiting so long. I'd not be surprised if it surprised one or two in the Chivas lab! **55.8%. ncf.**

**The Bottlers Caperdonich 1976 Aged 27 Years** cask 8965 **(89)** **n**22 slighly over-developed oak but the malt remains graceful and intact; **t**22 juicy, shimmering malt that explodes on impact; the oak offers pleasing spice. Excellent bitter-sweet signature; **f**23 buttery with hints of butterscotch; the oak adds a gentle waxiness; **b**22 another outstanding Caperdonich that has come alive in old age. **54.3%.**

**Connoisseurs Choice Caperdonich 1968** **(84)** **n**21 **t**22 **f**20 **b**21. A lovely golden, mildly honied malt is spoilt slightly by a degree of over-enthusiastic oak. Having said that, it's a real charmer. **46%.** *Gordon & MacPhail.*

**Connoisseurs Choice Caperdonich 1980** **(74)** **n**19 **t**19 **f**18 **b**18. Typical of the distillery: thin and hot, though there is a decent early malt surge. **46%.**

**Duncan Taylor Caperdonich 1968 Aged 34 Years** cask 3568 **(85)** **n**22 **t**22 **f**20 **b**21 Caper being its usual confusing self. **41.8%**

⠿ **Duncan Taylor Collection Caperdonich 1968** bott 5 Apr 06 **(81)** **n**21 **t**20 **f**21 **b**19. Oaky-dokey. Enough barley hangs on to make interesting. **40.3%**

**Duncan Taylor Caperdonich 1970 Aged 33 Years** cask 4380 **(94)** **n**23 unusually coastal and saline with white-wine sharpness by no means in keeping with its age; a hint of smoke? **t**24 angels sing as the most salivating barley imaginable forms a juicy alliance with understated grape; some peat makes a halfhearted attempt to reach the middle; **f**23 long, a touch of smoke and cocoa, but still the barley fizzes; **b**24 another masterpiece from the slowest-maturing whisky distillery on earth. **50.7%**

⠿ **Lonach Caperdonich 33 Years Old** **(86)** **n**20 **t**22 **f**22 **b**22. Kept itself in good shape. **42.3%.** *Duncan Taylor.*

⠿ **Lonach Caperdonich 37 Years Old** **(90)** **n**21 sponge pudding with a dab of maple syrup; **t**23 fills the mouth superbly with the golden/maple syrup continuing to evolve; wonderful spices are then unleashed; **f**23 varying degrees of oak pan out into a wonderful Jamaican Blue mountain finale; **b**23 on first taste, seems to be doddering. On third and fourth the true character emerges. Give it time...and it'll give you 37 years. **41.5%.** *Duncan Taylor.*

⫶⫶ **Lonach Caperdonich 1972** cask vx2, dist Oct 72, bott Mar 06 **(86) n**22 **t**22 **f**21 **b**21. An enjoyable but ultimately tired imitation of the great '67 casks. **41.9%.**

**Member's Legacy Caperdonich 1967 Aged 36 Years** cask 4945 **(95) n**24 Sensational aroma: blind tasted we've a bourbon-old fashioned Canadian on our hands. Also cream toffee with faintest dab of smoke; **t**24 big, big, big: prisoner-slaughtering stuff, with at first a golden thread of barley, then runs through several layers of gathering oak; **f**23 dries with liquorice as the oak that has given us that big bourbon arrival digs in; **b**24 one of four consecutive spell-binding casks. **57.2%**

**Member's Legacy Caperdonich 1967 Aged 36 Years** cask 4947 **(96) n**24 this sister aroma of cask 4945 and the all-conquering Platinum Old and Rare has a very different dimension: this is coastal, with a salty, seaweedy tang to it, maybe through some covert peat. Mazy, complex, confusing and perhaps scored down in the end only by a splinter of oak too many; **t**24 a pea from the same pod as the platinum old with a sexy, silky, see-through marmalady fruitiness that coats the very back of the roof of the mouth whilst that astonishing briny bourbon character kicks open the doors and makes a swaggering entrance; this is all high-octane, rather hot stuff where the oak is taken to its ultimate level without ruining the fun; **f**24 just, so long you could read the first part of War and Peace whilst its still deciding just what its going to do....in the end it settles of a bourbn theme of startling honeycomb sweetness tempered wonderfully by those drier, saltier oaky notes. All topped with wondrous chocolate; **b**24 alongside its sister cask, above, and last year's all-conquering cask, this represents one of the most extraordinary batches of malt of all time. **57.6%**

⫶⫶ **Murray McDavid Mission Caperdonich 1968** Sherry/Madeira **(85) n**23 **t**20 **f**21 **b**21. A wondrous, sniffed-to-be-believed nose; then real fruity fireworks with probably the spiciest dram of all time and big malty finish. Some people may rate this one as a lifetime best. Others will hate it. I'm somewhere in between, although I suspect, given time, I could become hooked... **46.2%.** *500 btls.*

**Murray MacDavid Mission 2 Caperdonich 1968 (82) n**21 **t**21 **f**20 **b**20. Some oily butter follows on from the oaked barley; lots of nip. **46%. nc ncf.**

⫶⫶ **Old Malt Cask Caperdonich 32 Years Old Wine Finish** dist Dec 73, bott Sept 06 **(89) n**22 some punchy oak filtering through the grapey (though not customary exotic!) fruit; **t**23 manic delivery of intense but delicious oak with barley-fruit. Dense and chewy; **f**22 tongue-tingling spices and, at last, a thickening of the barley; **b**22 rather map-less with some gung-ho oak and bruising barley. Great fun in its tired but rebellious way. **50%.** *Douglas Laing. 272 bottles.*

**Peerless Caperdonich 1968** (*see* Duncan Taylor Caperdonich 1968)

**Peerless Caperdonich 1970** (*see* Duncan Taylor Caperdonich 1970)

**Platinum Old and Rare Caperdonich Aged 36 Years** dist Nov 67 **(96) n**24 **t**24 **f**24 **b**24. So there we have it. A distillery that can't live day to day because its general spirit is so average can, in the right conditions, offer one of the greatest whisky experiences on Earth. Such is the beauty – and tragedy – of whisky. **57.9%.**

⫶⫶ **Platinum Caperdonich 37 Years Old** Rum finish, dist Nov 67, bott Oct 05 **(75) n**20 **t**19 **f**18 **b**18. Big, unforgiving oak. **56.4%.** *Douglas Laing. 133 bottles.*

# CARDHU
## Speyside, 1824. Diageo. Working.

**Cardhu 12 Years Old** db **(90) n**23 just about the cleanest, most uncluttered, pure, sweet malt you will ever find, a touch of apple, perhaps, giving an extra dimension; **t**24 again the malt is pure and rich, just a thread of oak adding some dryness and depth; **f**21 vanilla and malt; **b**22 a classic: welcome back! **40%** *(see also Cardhu Pure Malt)* ☉

# CLYNELISH
### Highlands (Northern), 1968. Diageo. Working.

**Clynelish 14 Years Old** (old Flora and Fauna label) db **(86)** n22 f22 b22. A lovely dram with a sweet malt dependency rather than the usual Clynelish complexity. **43%**

**Clynelish 14 Years Old** (new "Coastal Highland" label) bott lott no. L4316 db **(79)** n18 t21 f20 b20. How bloody annoying! Just this week I write in a top-selling American magazine what a consistent dram this is (and have just spotted, bizarrely, that the label claims the very same thing) when a few days later I taste this... Just a miniscule sulphur blemish, but enough to drop this down a few points despite the lovely depth to the delicate smoke. A one-off, I'm sure. **46%**

⫶⫶⫶ **Adelphi Clynelish 1995 Aged 10 Years** Sherry butt cask 12783, bott Jun 06 **(85)** n22 t21 f22 b20. A curious Clynelish offering boldness and thrust though harmonization is a bit awry due, mainly, to a soft sulphur buzz. **59.3%.** *698 btls.*

**Blackadder Raw Cask Clynelish 1990** cask 3593, one year sherry finish, dist 11 May 90, bott Nov 03 **(78)** n20 t20 f20 b18. A decent mouthfiller but the sherry and malt aren't on speaking terms **59.3%** *258 bottles.*

**The Bottlers Clynelish 1984 16 Years Old** cask 4016 **(91)** n23 spiced orange with custard and pears; t23 muscovado sugar sprinkled over 8-y-o bourbon, all wrapped in developing fruitcake and grape; f23 long, a hint of smoke the vanilla; becomes quite oily and fat; b22 not the normal guise for Clynelish, but looks in its pomp in this powerful sherry-spice romp. **58.5%.** *Raeborn Fine Wines.*

⫶⫶⫶ **Cadenhead's Authentic Collection Clynelish Aged 12 Years** dist 93, bott Feb 06 **(91)** n21 brusque barley, lazy oak and teasing snatch of something vaguely smoky; t24 velvety entrance for all the strength with intensity of the lush barley quite startling; subtle hints of white pepper and citrus ride on a slightly viscous wave: exuberant and quite brilliant; f23 at last some serious complexity as cocoa-oak weaves deliciously through firm two-toned barley; b23 charming barley-rich and proud: underlines the beauty of a simple bourbon refill. **60%.** *630 btls.*

⫶⫶⫶ **Cadenhead's Authentic Collection Clynelish Aged 13 Years** Bourbon Hogshead, dist 92, bott Sept 06 **(91)** n22 citrus and vague bubble gum clings to the rich barley; t23 intense with a non-specific fruitiness dovetailing with the mammoth barley; f23 long with touches of mocha; b23 charming Clynelish that works the oak so beautifully you almost wouldn't notice. **57.2%.** *294 bottles.*

**Cadenhead's Authentic Collection Clynelish Aged 15 Years** Bourbon Barrel, dist 90, bott May 05 **(90)** n22 a touch soapy, but the lemon-lime fruitiness adds fizz to the malt; t23 just stunning arrival of early spice and malt concentrate; f22 lovely interplay between the sweet malt, butterscotch and oak; b23 just one of those genuinely complex and sexy casks that thrill you to the core. **56%.** *162 bottles.*

**Cadenhead's Authentic Collection Clynelish Aged 15 Years** Bourbon Barrel, dist 90, bott May 05 **(84)** n23 t22 f19 b20. Wonderful, bourbontouched nose, but over-egged on the oak all round. **56.1%.** *144 bottles.*

**Cask Strength Clynelish 1990 (94)** n23 an oloroso butt of the very highest magnitude does a reasonable job of drowning out the malt, but fails...just. When it's this good, though, you can forgive it! t23 majestically intense, a point dropped for maybe the sherry just overpowering the malt slightly on entry, but the honey-spice barley fights back supremely; f24 enormously long and complex: the balance now is absolutely spot on, especially with the big spice kick towards the finale; b24 I had no idea sherry butts like this still existed. **57.6%**

⫶⫶⫶ **Chieftain's Clynelish 12 Years Old** Sherry wood **(84)** n19 t22 f22 b21. Recovers well from the less than impressive nose and benefits from an attractive viscosity and decent sweetness. Quite charming. **43%.** *Ian Macleod.*

**Chieftain's Clynelish 1989 Aged 18 Years** Sherry cask, bott 10 Feb 04 **(84)** n19 t21 f22 b22. Starts poorly on the nose and then blossoms on the palate with a sweet, fruit-invigorated barley surge. **46%.** *William Maxwell for South Africa.*

**Connoisseurs Choice Clynelish 1993 (89) n**22 beautifully delicate with a waft of dry marzipan on the crisp barley; **t**23 initially every bit as clean, mouthwatering and refreshing as the nose suggests, then a shard of soft peat can be chewed towards the middle; **f**22 dies at the death but with some late strands of oak and peat offering belated and surprising weight; **b**22 feigns to fade after a glorious start and middle but carries on to a wonderful conclusion. **43%.** *G&M.*

**Distillery No 5 Clynelish 1990 (86) n**21 **t**21 **f**22 **b**22. What a pleasure to find Clynelish in its most naked, blendable state. Mesmerising malt intensity. **46%**

**Dun Bheagan Clynelish 13 Years Old** Hogshead **(79) n**20 **t**21 **f**19 **b**19. Some pleasant shards of honey and butterscotch cannot disguise the relatively hot nature of this one. **46%.** *Ian Macleod.*

**Mackillop's Choice Clynelish 1989** cask 1140, dist Feb 89 **(95) n**24 brilliant. On the nose this is not only pure Clynelish, but the distillery nutshelled better than I have ever seen it in bottle. Wonderful honey buttress against the developing oak; **t**25 yikes! What can you say? The fabulous honey is found on several levels: there is both acacia and manuca in there; but it's sexily spiced up. The malt runs through with a refreshing clarity that could be easily missed. Just so close to getting full marks here...oh what the hell...!! **f**22 gentle honeycomb and spice with soft vanilla oak; **b**24 just such wonderful honey structure to this, but there is much more to it than that. Better than sex: sorry, ladies, but it's true! **56.7%.** *Angus Dundee.*

**Murray McDavid Clynelish 1994 Aged 11 Years** Bourbon/Viognier, bott 05 **(95) n**23 driest Clynelish on record, until you look beyond the oak and find shy sultana. Talk about intrigue...; **t**23 aloof sophistication: everything controlled and firm but the barley does show the most tantalizing sweetness amid the martini-dry lead and there is just enough mouth-watering character to offer contrast; **f**24 the denouement is a furthering of this sophistication, with a gin-like quality to the spices and tart fruits. Mesmerising ...; **b**25 the most subtle of drams offering ever-increasing body and spices; the usual Clynelish sweetness is kept in check and the fruit has accentuated the drier oak. Makes for a decent aperitif. Though I may not be the world's greatest advocate for cask finishes and I continue my call for restraint, but when something this complex, intriguing and so thoroughly enjoyable turns up in the glass, I can only stand, applaud and say "bravo"... **46.2%. nc ncf.** *1800 btls.*

**Murray McDavid Mission III Clynelish 1983 (79) n**20 **t**21 **f**19 **b**19. Tired and unemotional. **46%**

**Murray McDavid Mission IV Clynelish 1976 Aged 28 Years** drawn 25 Apr 05 **(93) n**23 waxy, strawberry tarts and butterscotch; **t**24 more fruit salad, with strawberries still on top. Soft vanilla offers dryness to the sweet malt; **f**23 peaches and cream: implausibly soft for a malt so old; **b**23 a peach in every sense. **46%**

**Old Malt Cask Clynelish Aged 13 Years** Refill hogshead 1499, dist Jan 91, bott Oct 04 **(90) n**22 a hint of smoke on the sherry; **t**23 delicate oils and bracing malts with a salty, vaguely smoky tang; **f**22 gentle spices are in keeping with an unusually measured production; **b**23 beautifully soothing: this is all about grace and elegance. **50%. nc ncf.** *Douglas Laing.*

**Old Malt Cask Clynelish Aged Over 13 Years** Rum Finish, dist July 89, bott Feb 03 **(95) n**25 sexy and delicate with infused poppy seed and rose petal. The dynamics of the spiced barley/wood are nigh-on perfect. Something to stick your nose in and keep there; **t**23 the rum is wonderfully understated but there is unquestionably something of unusual origin latching onto the intense barley; the barley-oak layers are numerous and of astounding subtlety; **f**23 only at the very death does the rum come into its own, with a vague hint of non-coloured Demerara, though such is the integrity of the crisp barley, it is just about impossible to be sure of the rum's origin; **b**24 This is a masterpiece! Damn it, why didn't Douglas Laing send this to me when they bottled it? It could well have been an award winner. My thanks to Duncan Chisholm for sending me something very special. Should you see this around anywhere, rip the shop owner's arm off. **50%. sc nc ncf.**

**Old Malt Cask Clynelish Aged 14 Years** dist Jan 90, bott Feb 04 **(84) n**23 **t**22 **f**19 **b**20. As mouthwatering as the barley may be it is the fabulous covertly smoked aroma that impresses most. **50%. nc ncf sc.** *Douglas Laing.*

**Old Malt Cask Clynelish Aged 14 Years** Rum Finish cask 3850, dist June 89, bott Sep 03 **(85) n**22 **t**23 **f**19 **b**21. Despite the untidy unravelling at the finish, there are many mouth-puckering moments. Great fun. **50%. nc ncf.** *312 bottles.*

⠿ **Platinum Clynelish 23 Years Old** Rum finish, dist Apr 83, bott Aug 06 **(96) n**23 a strange, early off-ish note is encircled and over-run by an increased delivery of kumquat and barley. Leave in the glass for a good five minutes before nosing: the improvement is astonishing; **t**25 a quite perfect delivery of intense fruit coupled with sparkling barley; the freshness belies the great age and the development of spices is faultless; **f**24 long with not a single blemish. Only now does something on the rum side make itself known, but is so delicate it is impossible to declare exactly the extent of its influence, or even what rum it may be; **b**24 it seems like rum finishes are working pretty well this year. What a treat! This is a classic. **55.3%.** *Douglas Laing. 254 bottles.*

⠿ **Platinum Selection Clynelish Aged 32 Years** dist Mar 73, bott Aug 05 **(80) n**19 **t**23 **f**19 **b**19. Gone through the top slightly on the nose, though it does have its exotic, fruity moments. It's the arrival on the palate that really thrills with a stunning array of spiced tropical fruits nailed down by oak. The finish though, shows its age, and it ain't always pretty. There is a fine line in whisky between success and failure and this malt is standing right astride it. **55.1%.** *232 bottles.*

⠿ **Private Collection Clynelish 1969 (82) n**20 **t**21 **f**21 **b**20. Just hangs onto its integrity by the width of an oak's bark; enough mocha-themed fruit and spicy complexity and charm to see it through some dodgy moments. **45%.** *G&M.*

**Provenance Clynelish 13 Years Old** dist Spring 91, bott Autumn 04 **(85) n**21 **t**22 **f**22 **b**21. Not for one second complex, the grassy, bitter-sweet style of the malt is delicious. **46%.** *Douglas Laing & Co.*

**Provenance Clynelish 14 Years Old** dist 26 Feb 90, bott 1 Feb 05 **(83) n**20 **t**22 **f**20 **b**21. Gentle, undemanding malt with the spotlight on clean, uncluttered barley. **46%.** *Douglas Laing & Co.*

**Provenance Clynelish 15 Year Old** dist 18 May 89, bott 14 Apr 05 **(83) n**22 **t**21 **f**20 **b**20. Marmamlade on thick buttered bread. **46%.** *Douglas Laing.*

**Scotch Single Malt Circle Clynelish 1990** cask 3963, dist May 90, bott Oct 04 **(86) n**21 **t**22 **f**21 **b**21. A bitter-sweet dram that leans more closely to bitter. **57.4%.**

**Signatory Clynelish Vintage 1983** cask 2695, dist 11May 83, bott 3 Oct 03 **(84) n**22 **t**22 **f**20 **b**20. Brilliant nose offering just a touch of honey, but fades after the promisingly malty start. **43% nc.** *343 bottles.*

⠿ **The Single Malt of Scotland Clynelish Aged 11 Years Vintage 1994** Sherry butt **(79) n**19 **t**22 **f**19 **b**19. Blood oranges and magnificent spice but the butt is a big but... **58.9%.** *The Whisky Exchange. 367 bottles.*

⠿ **The Single Malt of Scotland Clynelish Aged 13 Years Vintage 1992** cask 7156 **(90) n**22 delightfully bourbony, though the malt projects a 3D sharpness and strands of honey; **t**23 brittle, mouthwatering malt impact, mega salivating and never distracted despite the slow arrival of custard tart; **f**22 lovely spices abound; **b**23 a fabulous bottling which shows this great distillery at its malty best. **58%.** *The Whisky Exchange.*

⠿ **The Single Malt of Scotland Clynelish Aged 32 Years Vintage 1972** Hogshead cask 15619, dist 13 Dec 72, bott 02 Nov 05 **(88) n**22 exotic fruit underscores the big age on this; **t**23 the delivery is a triumph with truly salivating malt coursing through the oak; **f**21 tires as the nose suggests it might but still holds together attractively. Teasing smoke and cocoa add ballast; **b**22 a cask that has just – but only just – held together and any oak flaws are enormously outweighed by the brilliance of the barley. **49.9%. nc ncf.** *The Whisky Exchange. 226 bottles.*

⊹ **Tanner's Clynelish 10 Year Old 1992 (90) n**23 oakier, spicier, altogether punchier than the age suggests. Intriguing layers of peat and orange entertain; **t**22 enormous attitude as it hits the palate slogging. The taste-buds barely stand a chance against repeated blows from the frenzied oak-studded barley; the spices fizz leaving a distant trail of something smoky; **f**22 good length; pleasing and surprising depth to the bitter chocolate and mildly over-aged citrus. You can chew your jaw off; **b**23 good grief! I didn't expect this – not from a ten-year-old! The evidence is weighed towards a first-filled bourbon cask. Having said that. It probably isn't a 10-y-o: it was distilled in 1992, not '95 or '96. A corking Clynelish at its most belligerent and revealing a depth some insist it doesn't possess. Oh yeah? Well try this – if you're man enough. **45%**. *Tanners Wine Merchants, UK.*

**The Whisky Exchange Clynelish 1972 Aged 32 Years (89) n**20 tired; mildly soaped; **t**22 mango and freshly squeezed barley sugar: the intensity of the malt surprises; **f**24 long, eloquently spiced and strands of deliciously muted honeycomb; **b**23 the nose suggests little of the sheer brilliance that is to follow. **49.4%.**

⊹ **The Whisky Fair Clynelish Aged 32 Years** dist Feb 74, bott Apr 06 **(95) n**24 probably the optimum aroma for a malt of this age and style: the oak is big and rules the roost, but the richness and range and the barley-spice combination is something to marvel at; **t**24 three different types of honey, starting with acacia, moving towards honeycomb but getting into full throttle manuka. Strands of toffee apple and then soft smoke offer both lightness and depth; **f**23 enormous length and depth; complexity continues unmolested; **b**24 just one of those malts that it is a rare privilege to come across in life. Whoever found the cask should be given the Freedom of Germany. **58.6%. nc ncf.** *Germany. 266 btls.*

**Whisky Galore Clynelish 1990 Aged 13 Years (78) n**20 **t**19 **f**20 **b**19. Some tobacco notes amid the barley. **46%**

**Whisky Galore Clynelish 1992 Aged 11 Years (84) n**22 **t**22 **f**20 **b**20. Gristy, beautifully clean malt with a slight peat accent; lacks development. **46%**

**Wilson & Morgan Barrel Selection Clynelish 1989** Marsala Finish bott 03 **(91) n**21 **t**22 **f**24 **b**24. Dusty nose but a real spicefest on the juicy palate. A sensual sensation. **46%**

## COLEBURN
**Speyside, 1897–1985. Diageo. Closed.**

**Connoisseurs Choice Coleburn 1972 (72) n**17 **t**20 **f**18 **b**17. A strange, off-balanced, rather sweet malt. One for collectors rather than purists.**40%.** *G & M.*

⊹ **Connoisseurs Choice Coleburn 1981 (81) n**21 **t**21 **f**19 **b**20. Usual thin, hot stuff from Coleburn but benefits from a big malt kick. Way above the norm. **43%**

⊹ **Old Malt Cask Coleburn Aged 25 Years** dist Feb 80, bott Aug 05 **(68) n**20 **t**17 **f**15 **b**16. Best Coleburn nose in years, but spectacularly disintegrates on the palate as is its wont. **50%.** *Douglas Laing. 661 bottles.*

## CONVALMORE
**Speyside, 1894–1985. Closed.**

⊹ **Convalmore 1977** bott 05 db **(91) n**23 wonderfully layered barley offering many hues of intensity and tartness, embracing fruit gums, bourbon and even very gentle peat; **t**23 mouth-puckering barley is sharp and intense, then a softening sweetness radiates out as both soft- and hard-edged oaks home in; **f**22 mildly out of sync for the first time, but settles as some soft butterscotch and liquorice arrives; **b**23 must be blended with Botox, as there is no detrimental ageing to either nose or delivery. A quite lovely and charming whisky to remember this lost – and extremely rare - distillery by. **57.9%.** *3900 bottles.*

**Convalmore Rare Malt 24 Years Old** dist 78, db **(88) n**23 Peaches and cream ... and pretty juicy peach at that. One of the fruitiest noses on the market; **t**23 not even a straffing of searing spices can reduce the peachy onslaught. About as juicy and salivating as it gets for a malt so old; **f**20 an abrupt entry of cocoadusted oak plus some lingering barley; **b**22 another stunning version of a muchmissed distillery, begging the question as to why it was ever closed. **59.4%**

**Rare Old Convalmore 1960 (86) n**22 **t**22 **f**21 **b**21. Takes some studying to get to the bottom of this one: take your time. **40%**. *Gordon & MacPhail.*

**Scott's Selection Convalmore 1975** bott 04 **(93) n**23 herbal, especially lavender and Alpine flowers (honest, gov'!); **t**24 absolutely immaculate balance on the palate between lush malt and a herbal, peppery attack; **f**22 tires somewhat as the oak gains a bitter foothold. But the taste of crushed Alpine violets remains, as does a late bitter-marmalade note; **b**24 not for the first time a distillery that had problems cutting the mustard when alive produces something of authentic beauty when dead. **49.5%**. *Speyside Distillers.*

# CRAGGANMORE
**Speyside, 1870. Diageo. Working.**

**Cragganmore 10 Year Old** dist 93 db **(84) n**20 **t**23 **f**20 **b**21. The sheer beauty of the softly fruited malt on the mouth arrival is glorious. But the oak hasdone the whisky few other favours. **60.1%**

**Cragganmore 12 years old** db **(89) n**23 a weirdly coastal, salty slant to this, with ripe sultanas; **t**23 beautiful banana delivery, custard and malt but with lush, grapey undertones; **f**21 thins out with some vanilla at the death; **b**22 the best Cragganmore 12 I've come across for a while, though the original Cragganmore of a dozen or so years ago was so much better. And still could be: much more bourbon-cask oriented. "The most complex aroma of any malt," boasts the label. As wonderful as it is, I really don't think so. Obviously no-one at Diageo has stuck their nose in a glass of Glenmorangie. Or Ardmore. Or Glen Elgin.... **40%**

**Blackadder Raw Cask Cragganmore 14 Years Old** cask 1969, dist 13 Sep 89, bott Jun 04 **(92) n**22 massively firm malt; a mild sprinkle of salt; **t**24 stunningly intact arrival of rich, slightly salty, mouthwatering malt: few Speysiders possess this kind of concentrated intensity, or exemplary balance; **f**22 some chalky malt drifts into the malty clutter; **b**24 one or two old blenders I know, long retired, used to come over all unnecessary when Cragganmore was mentioned. "Wonderful blending malt," they would purr. No slouch as a single either on this form. **56.6%**

**Blackadder Raw Cask Cragganmore 15 Years Old** cask 1970, dist 13 Sep 89, bott Dec 04 **(87) n**21 sizeable oak; **t**22 intensely sweet barley; **f**22 more rumbling, mouthwatering malt and a soft infusion of vanilla-oak; **b**21 much sweeter than its sister cask, with more natural toffee dumbing down the complexity. **57.9%**

**Cadenhead's Cragganmore-Glenlivet Aged 15 Years** dist 89, bott Feb 05 **(91) n**24 this is how I remember it from when I first inspected a whole range of samples in the late 80s: quite brilliant citrus notes enlivening the rich malt. Clean, gently complex and not a single off note; **t**23 soft, lilting, grassy malt that carries just enough oak for ballast; **f**21 gentle vanilla tones; **b**23 deft, relaxing and quite classic, most probably second-fill Cragganmore from outstanding distillate. **46%**. *306 btls.*

**Cadenhead's Authentic Collection Cragganmore-Glenlivet Aged 15 Years** dist 89, bott Feb 05 **(89) n**21 malty with some drying oak; **t**22 again the oak arrives early to add a touch of spice to the unwavering malt; **f**23 firm malt again with a vanilla and dry flaked coconut finish and a surprising residual touch of citrus and smoke; **b**23 bold oak strokes on the malty canvas. **57.8%**. *606 bottles.*

⌐≈ **Cadenhead's Authentic Collection Cragganmore-Glenlivet Aged 16 Years** dist 89, bott Sep 05 **(94) n**24 fabulous: the most delicate fruit imaginable adds pith to a sweet and salty barley base; the range of the oak is mind-boggling; **t**23 fantastic spice buzz pitches in harmony with the waxy barley and burnt honeycomb; **f**23 lots, lots more of the same, except the honey sweetens slightly as the oak grip lessens; **b**24 a sublime cask has extracted every last ultra-complex nuance it can find. **58.6%**. *678 bottles.*

⁘ **Individual Cask Bottling 1993 Aged 12 Years** cask 1911, dist Apr 93, bott Jan 06 **(86)** n20 t22 f22 b22. A pretty standard version of a high-class Speysider. The complexity does shine through eventually. **59.3%.** *311 bottles.*

⁘ **Murray McDavid Cragganmore Aged 12 Years** Bourboun/Syrah enhanced in Guigal Cotes Rotie, dist 93, bott 05 **(89)** n23 crisp barley encased in clipped fruit and spice; t23 firm and clean, the barley-grape act really does show delicious harmony; f21 bitters down slightly as the oak ups the pace; b22 charming and sophisticated: the near perfect aperitif. **46%. nc ncf.** *2100 bottles.*

⁘ **Murray McDavid Mission Cragganmore 1985 Aged 21 Years** Guigal Côte Rôtie. Bourbon/Syrah **(82)** n23 t21 f19 b19. When they say bourbon, they aren't kidding: parts of this is pure Kentucky, especially on the glorious nose. But the truth is that it's gone through the wood and after the brain-blowing entry, things slip downhill. **56.5%. nc ncf.** *665 bottles.*

⁘ **Old Masters Cragganmore 1993 Aged 13 Years** cask 1905, dist 93, bott 06 **(79)** n19 t20 f21 b19. Decent, but overly sweet and one might expect a bit more from this distillery. **61%.** *James MacArthur.*

# CRAIGELLACHIE
**Speyside, 1891. Dewar's. Working.**

**Craigellachie 14 Years Old** db **(82)** n21 t22 f19 b21. Complex nose and battles deliciously and maltily before the indifferent finish; quite a bit of bite. **40%**

**Connoisseurs Choice Craigellachie 1988 (90)** n21 grassy, citrussy and crisp, but just enough honey to promise age; t24 really beautiful malt, sweet and mouthwatering and aided by a lovely puff of smoke; f22 dries slightly but there is depth and some tangy blood orange; b23 a shimmering beauty: probably the best bottled expression from this distillery at this age I have ever tasted. **43%.** *G & M.*

⁘ **Connoisseurs Choice Craigellachie 1989 (87)** n21 indulgent oak plays brinkmanship. It's foot slips over the edge a few times but there is just enough coal-smoked barley to pull it back; t21 a delivery of pure silk also heads quickly to oak; f23 at last harmony is found as kumquats, passion fruit and spice surf on the tides of gentle oils. Some late smoke wraps things up well; b22 the developing exotic fruit suggests a whisky almost twice its age. Quite a surprise package. A cheapskate could shove on a fake label claiming to be a 30-year-old and who the hell would know ...??? **43%.** *Gordon & MacPhail.*

**The Craigellachie Hotel Craigellachie Single Cask Bottling 2003** cask 1416, dist 3 Mar 82, bott 28 Oct 03 **(77)** n19 t20 f18 b19. A disappointing bottling that despite an early malt surge on the palate falls victim to a less than glorious cask.

⁘ **Dewar Rattray Individual Cask Bottling Craigellachie 1989 Aged 15 Years** cask 3882, dist Oct 90, bott Sept 05 **(79)** n20 t22 f18 b19. A furry, bitter finale points towards a lacking cask. A shame, as the delivery offers barley at its most eye-watering. **54.2%.** *315 bottles.*

⁘ **Murray McDavid Mission Craigellachie 1970** Sherry/Rousanne **(89)** n22 an early form of tired oak, but it is swept under a tide of sultanas and cucumber; t23 mouthwatering and increasingly fruity. The depth of complexity appears to increase with each intense wave; f22 some oaky bitterness, but soothed by a dusting of heavy roast Java; b22 one of the few '06 crop of Craigellachies not creaking under the weight of oak. This unusual wine combination appears to have an empathy with the malt. Something to take your time over. **40.5%.** *110 bottles.*

**Murray McDavid Mission III Craigellachie 1970** Refill sherry **(93)** n23 oaky spice off-set by damson plums in custard; t24 stunning!!! The arrival simply glimmers with fabulous barley in that sweet custardy setting; an usual form of sweetness, this, fruity and refined, though not in a sugary way; f22 natural caramel blunts the richer tones but there is soft sherry back-up; b24 when I tell people that Craigellachie can be a God, I'm looked upon with incredulity. Well, get your lips around this! Also rare to find this distillery in any form of sherry. **46%**

⟍⟋ **Old Malt Cask Craigellachie Aged 13 Years** Hogshead 1613, dist Aug 91, bott Jan 05 **(86)** n21 t22 f22 b21. A simple malt. **50%. nc ncf.** *Douglas Laing.*

⟍⟋ **Old Malt Cask Craigellachie Aged 14 Years** cask 1037, dist Oct 89, bott Oct 03 **(80)** n19 t21 f20 b20. Soft, delicate oils, which always used to be a feature of this distillery, have returned to lay the citrus sweetness on with a trowel. **50%.** *318 btls.*

⟍⟋ **Platinum Selection Craigellachie Aged 32 Years** dist May 73, bott Aug 05 **(84)** n20 t23 f21 b20. Almost a relative of the Connoisseur's Choice '89, except the fruit here – and we are talking market places of the stuff – has just a little too much oak on the finish for this to be up there with the stars. For a few glorious seconds, though... **42.7%.** *Douglas Laing. 181 bottles.*

⟍⟋ **Provenance Craigellachie 10 Years Old** dist Feb 96, bott Jan 06 **(83)** n22 t21 f20 b20. Gristy, grassy and pure Speyside. **46%.** *McGibbon's.*

**Provenance Craigellachie 13 Years Old** dist 21 Aug 91, bott 20 Jan 05 **(83)** n21 t22 f21 b20. Intensely malty and slightly oily fare from an oft-used bourbon cask that is beginning to creak a bit. **46%.** *Douglas Laing & Co.*

**The Wee Dram Craigellachie 15 Years Old** db **(89)** n23 fascinating meeting of ultra-lazy smoke and slightly less lazy grapey fruit. Rounded off with a layer of intense malt and shyer citrus; t21 chewy, big and increasingly fatty; f22 breaks down into more complex characters, with fruit at the fore and cocoaoak towards the finale; b23 takes its time to get into gear on the palate, but once it does it backs up the nose in proclaiming a beaut! **43%.** *The Wee Dram, Bakewell, UK.*

## CROFTENGEA (see Loch Lomond)

## DAILUAINE
### Speyside, 1854. Diageo. Working.

**Dailuaine Aged 16 Years** bott lot no. L4334 db **(79)** n19 t21 f20 b19. Syrupy, almost grotesquely heavy at times; the lighter, more considered notes of previous bottlings have been lost under an avalanche of sugary, over-ripe tomatoes. Definitely one for those who want a massive dram. **43%**

⟍⟋ **Berry's' Own Selection Dailuaine 1974 Aged 31 Years (83)** n23 t21 f19 b20. Sparkling, salivating bitter-sweet barley at first then a heavy oak portcullis shuts off the fun. **46%.** *Berry Bros & Rudd.*

**Blackadder Raw Cask Dailuaine 30 Years Old** cask 15956 dist 14 Dec 73, bott Mar 04 **(84)** n20 t22 f22 b20. A bit over-tired but enough riches to make for a chewy middle. **59.9%**

**Blackadder Raw Cask Dailuaine 30 Years Old** cask 15957 dist 14 Dec 73, bott Mar 04 **(79)** n21 t19 f20 b19. Becoming oak saturated. **57.7%**

⟍⟋ **Chieftain's Dailuaine Aged 10 Years (88)** n21 the barley and oak barely gel; t23 rock-solid malt: no compromising at all!; f22 barley sugar and mallows; b22 hard-nosed malt, takes time to unravel. Ignore the occasional flat bit. **43%.**

⟍⟋ **Connoisseurs Choice Dailuaine 1991 (78)** n21 t20 f18 b19. Another Dailuaine felled by oak. **43%.** *Gordon & MacPhail.*

⟍⟋ **Norse Cask Selection Dailuaine 1989 Aged 14 Years (79)** n20 t19 f21 b19. Diamond-hard and revealing exactly why this is such good blending malt. **60.4%.** *Quality World, Denmark.*

**Old Master's Dailuaine 1976** cask 5967, bott 04 **(84)** n21 t22 f21 b20. A strapping malt abounding in spices and fruit; a sweetie with no shortage of oak and punch. **57.1%.** *James MacArthur.*

## DALLAS DHU
### Speyside, 1899–1983. Closed. Now a museum.

**Dallas Dhu 21 Years Old Rare Malts Selection (83)** n21 t21 f20 b21. An uncompromising barley-rich effort as one might expect, but otherwise a bit thin and lacking that usual extra depth. **61.9%.** *United Distillers/Diageo.*

Chieftan's Dallas Dhu Aged 25 Years cask 1380 dist Jun 79, bott Sep 04 **(88)** n20 showing weariness; t24 defies the nose to explode with ultra-chewy, clean honied malt: similar to the better casks at half its age; f22 sympathetic drying oak; **b**22 forget the forbidding oakiness of the nose: this is sheer class. **55%. nc ncf.** *498 btls.*

⋰ **Duncan Taylor Collection Dallas Dhu 1975** cask no. 2481, dist Dec 75, bott Apr 06 **(85)** n18 t22 f23 **b**22. Avoid the nose of a clapped-out cask: the unperturbed grace of an unsophisticated but beautiful malt is there to be chewed. **51%.**

**Duncan Taylor Collection Dallas Dhu 1975 Aged 29 Years** cask 2484, dist Dec 75, bott Feb 05 **(94)** n23 earthy and honied, the flaky, sawdusty oak really is beginning to dig deep; t23 melt-in-the-mouth malt and honey makes for a sprightly old-timer; f24 some really lovely and quite unexpected smoke regenerates what appears to be a tiring dram, though the honey hangs on to the end...which is a long time in coming; **b**24 you have to be impressed with this. Dallas Dhu wasn't built to make whisky of this age, but sheer quality has persevered. We have a minor classic here: a must-have whisky, though one to taste and revere rather than let sit and gather dust. **47.1%.**

⋰ **Duncan Taylor Collection Dallas Dhu 1981 Aged 14 Years** Sherry cask 387, dist Apr 81 **(94)** n23 concentrated barley with well-matured farmhouse cake thrown in; **t**24 a delivery to die for: faultless, concentrated barley – again with that peculiar tart citrus kick that appears to attack the fillings! – and then oak ushering in a hint of Jameson chocolate truffle; f23 almost too long for belief: wave upon wave, layer upon layer of increasingly intense barley and burnt fudge; **b**24 could this be one of the last bottlings that – at cask strength and not tampered with by cask finishing – shows this great distillery in its full glory...? **58.3%.** *523 btls.*

⋰ **Gordon & MacPhail Dallas Dhu 1982 (89)** n22 almost mash-tun barley clean and sweet; t23 intense barley with a peculiar and attractive citrus tartness; f22 lengthy for something so soft, and unremittingly malty; **b**22 it's a sombre and sobering thought that whisky from the penultimate year of distillation at this distillery is now close on 25 years old. **40%.** *Gordon & MacPhail.*

**Murray McDavid Mission III Dallas Dhu 1974 (91)** n22 sliced cucumber beside a glass of sweet sherry; t24 does sherry come any cleaner or cleverly covert than this? Boiled fruit sweets and Fishermen's Friends make a warming, mouthwatering combination; f22 a hint of Jenever and natural caramel rounds it off beautifully; **b**23 are they sure they can't re-open this distillery...? **46%.**

⋰ **Murray McDavid Mission Dallas Dhu 1979** Bourbon/Marsanne, bott 06 **(73)** n19 t18 f18 **b**18. Off-key and unforgiving. Not the way a lost treasure like Dallas Dhu should be remembered. **57.8%. nc ncf.** *240 bottles.*

**Old Malt Cask Dallas Dhu 32 Years Old** dist Mar 72, bott Oct 04 **(84)** n20 t22 f22 **b**20. Loads of toast and burned honeycomb; showing age but the bourbony character is quite delicious. **50%.** *Douglas Laing & Co.*

**The Whisky Fair Dallas Dhu 23 Years Old Bourbon Hogshead** dist May 81 **(90)** n23 whole-hearted kippery peat dovetailing with lemon and lime; t22 massively oily and rich, the peat clings to every crevice. Some citrus tries to thin it out; f23 lychees and white grape juice weighted down with youthful peat; **b**22 last year I raised my eyebrows at this smoked-up version. They have sent me another sample...and yes, it really is the kippery brute I described. What a fabulous find by the boys from the Whisky Fair!!! Well done, chaps! **53.5%.** *Germany. 164 bottles.* ⊙ ⊙

# DALMORE
**Highland (northern), 1839. Whyte and Mackay. Working.**

⋰ **Cadenhead's Authentic Collection Dalmore Aged 14 Years** Bourbon Hogshead, dist 92, bott May 06 **(88)** n23 delightfully structured with barley holding sway; t22 firm oak adds backbone to the juicy barley; f22 remains firm; **b**21 exceptionally malty. **62%.** *306 bottles.*

⠿ **Cadenhead's Authentic Collection Dalmore Aged 16 Years** dist 89, bott Sep 05 **(91)** n22 moist malt cookies; t24 superb delivery of high- octane barley: fresh, lively and clean; f22 long, relying on vanilla; b23 pretty simple. But pretty superb, too... **56.7%**. *216 bottles.*

⠿ **Chieftain's Dalmore Aged 10 Years** Hogshead **(78)** n19 t21 f19 b19. A bit of a sweaty armpit nose and the malt meanders aimlessly, if sweetly and fruitily, around the palate. **58%**. *Ian Macleod.*

⠿ **Chieftain's Dalmore Aged 10 Years Medoc Finish** casks 90431 & 90434, dist Nov 94, bott Feb 05 **(80)** n19 t21 f20 b20. Seriously lethargic. **43%. nc ncf.**

**Dalmore 12 Years Old** db **(91)** n22 big, fruity, firm, a threat of smoke, weighty; t24 well-muscled malt surge followed by clean fruity tones, immaculate mouth-presence and bitter-sweet balance; f22 long, tapering fruit-malt residue, some brown sugar coating and uncomplicated oak; b23 simply one of the great Highland malt whiskies at just about the perfect age: what I would do to see this unplugged at 46% minimum and no bottling hall interference. **40%**

**The Dalmore 21 Years Old** db **(87)** n22 just how many citrus notes can we find here? Answers on a postcard ... on second thoughts, don't. Just beautifully light and effervescent for its age: a genuine delight; t23 again, wonderfully fruity though this time the malt pushes through confidently to create its own chewy island: fabulous texture; f20 simplifies towards toffee slightly too much in the interests of great balance. A lovely coffee flourish late on; b22 bottled elegance. **43%**

**The Dalmore 30 Years Old Stillman's Dram (89)** n23 nuts, oranges in a rich fruitcake; lime marmalade adds to the fruit cocktail: seductive; t22 enormous fruit explosion, silky malt then an injection of bitter oak; f22 medium length; the emphasis is on the malt as the oakiness burns off. Complexity levels rise as the fruit recedes and spices arrive late; b22 in some ways the ultimate bitter-sweet dram, with the burnt-toast oak fighting against the sweet fruit and malt. **45%**

**The Dalmore 50 Years Old** db **(88)** n21 buxom and bourbony, the oak makes no secret of the antiquity; t19 oak again arrives first and without apology, some salty malt creaking in later. Ripe cherries offer a mouthwatering backdrop; f25 comes into its own as harmony is achieved as the oak quietens to allow a beautiful malt-cherry interplay. Spices arrive for good measure in an absolutely has-it-all, faultless finish: really as much a privilege to taste as a delight; b23 takes a while to warm up, but when it does becomes a genuinely classy and memorable dram befitting one of the world's great and undervalued distilleries. **52%**

**The Dalmore 62 Years Old** db **(95)** n23 PM or REV marked demerara potstill rum, surely? Massive coffee presence, clean and enormous, stunning, topdrawer peat just to round things off; t25 this is brilliant: pure silk wrapping fabulous moist fruitcake soaked in finest oloroso sherry and then weighed with peat which somehow has defied nature and survived in cask all these years. I really cannot fault this: I sit here stunned and in awe; f24 perfect spices with flecks of ginger and lemon rind; b24 if I am just half as beautiful, elegant and fascinating as this by the time I reach 62, I'll be a happy man. Somehow I doubt it. A once-in-a-lifetime whisky – something that comes around every 62 years, in fact. Forget Dalmore Cigar Malt – even I might be tempted to start smoking just to get a full bottle of this. **40.5%**

**The Dalmore 1966** db **(86)** n23 t22 f20 b21. A remakable dram for the years that it has kept its fruity integrity despite the big age. **44.6%**

**The Dalmore 1973 Gonzalez Byass Sherry Cask Finish** db **(93)** n24 t23 f22 b24. What happens when you get one of Scotland's greatest – if entirely undervalued – drams and fill it into what what was obviously a special, handpicked, clean and flawless sherry butt? You get this this ultra-complex gem **52.3%**

**The Dalmore Black Isle** db **(77)** n19 t20 f19 b19. Very little of the complexity I automatically associate with Dalmore; slightly furry and a little drab. **40%**

The Dalmore Cigar Malt db **(71)** n17 t20 f16 b18. For me, flat and un-Dalmore-like. But there again I have never smoked as much as a cigarette in all my life. **43%**

Cadenhead's Authentic Collection Dalmore Aged 15 Years dist 89, bott Feb 05 **(91)** n22 salty crisps and rock hard Glen Grant-esque gristy malt. Striking and attractively austere; t23 brittle malt cracks to allow in a kumquatcitrus fruitiness; never less than mouthwatering; f22 just fades as some natural caramel and vanilla dumb it down a little; b23 Dalmore at its most deliciously devilish. **57.5%**. *198 bottles.*

Old Malt Cask Dalmore Aged 10 Years dist Oct 93, bott Feb 04 **(82)** n22 t23 f18 b19. Cracklingly beautiful nose and early mouth development; the finish is bitter and dry. **50%. nc ncf sc.** *Douglas Laing. 395 bottles.*

∴ Old Malt Cask Dalmore Aged 14 Years dist Feb 91, bott Aug 05 **(78)** n20 t19 f20 b19. A touch of tiring, fizzy oak kicks it out of orbit. **50%.** *Douglas Laing. 340 bottles.*

∴ Old Malt Cask Dalmore Aged 14 Years Refill Hogshead 2094, dist Feb 91, bott Sept 05 **(88)** n23 gooseberries and custard; t22 sublimely clean and soft malt; f21 crème brulee; b22 excellent body and charisma. **50%. nc ncf.** *340 btls.*

Provenance Dalmore Over 12 Years dist Summer 92, bott Summer 04 **(86)** n21 t22 f22 b21. A rare Dalmore in this second or even third-fill cask form: just so deliciously clean and delicate. **46%**

Provenance Dalmore 14 Years Old dist 25 Feb 91, bott 24 Mar 05 **(86)** n21 t22 f21 b22. Very decent second-fill bourbon Dalmore. **46%.**

Provenance Dalmore Over 14 Years dist Spring 89, bott Autumn 03 **(86)** n21 t22 f21 b22. A charming, faultless, unspectacular yet rewarding bottling. **46%.**

## DALWHINNIE
### Highlands (central), 1898. Diageo. Working.

Dalwhinnie 15 Years Old db **(95)** n24 sublime stuff: a curious mixture of coke smoke and peat-reek wafts teasingly over the gently honied malt. A hint of melon offers some fruit but the caressing malt stars; t24 that rarest of combinations: at once silky and malt intense, yet at the same time peppery and tin-hat time for the tastebuds, but the silk wins out and a sheen of barley sugar coats everything, soft peat included; f23 some cocoa and coffee notes, yet the pervading slightly honied sweetness means that there is no bitterness that cannot be controlled; b24 a malt it is hard to decide whether to drink or bath in: I suggest you do both. One of the most complete mainland malts of them all. Know anyone who reckons they don't like whisky? Give them a glass of this – that's them cured. Oh, if only the average masterpiece could be this good. **43%**

Dalwhinnie 29 Years Old dist 73 db **(85)** n21 t20 f23 b21. Fighting whisky; an old bruiser for its age with plenty of tongue-pulverising oomph; one for those hunting the atypical. **57.8%**

## DEANSTON
### Highlands (Perthshire), 1966. Burn Stewart. Working.

Deanston 6 Years Old db **(83)** n20 t21 f22 b20. Great news for those of us who remember how good Deanston was a decade or two ago: it's on its way back. A delightfully clean dram with its trademark honey character restored. A little beauty slightly undermined by caramel. **40%**

Deanston 12 Years Old db **(78)** n19 t21 f19 b19. A fabulous transformation has taken this from one of the worst distillery bottled malts in Scotland to a dram that can hold it's head up with something approaching pride. Still some distance to go to reach the quality levels of a decade ago: there remains a thinness to the nose and finish, but some of the old honey and lustre has returned. **40%** ⊙ ⊙

Deanston 17 Year Old db **(68)** n17 t17 f17 b17. A 17-year-old anorexic with agoraphobia: painfully thin and goes nowhere. **40%**

Deanston 1967 casks 1051-2, filled Friday 31st Mar 67 db **(90)** n23 the very faintest hint of peat rubs shoulders with high fluting honey and polished pine floors; **t**23 the loud oak influence is perfectly tempered by rich barley concentrate. Sweet towards the middle with hints of honey and peat; **f**21 spiced and softening towards vanilla; **b**23 the oak is full on but there is so much class around that cannot gain control. A Perthshire beauty. **50.7%. nc.**

**Lombard Deanston 1977 (89)** **n**23 honey and salted butter on toast; a hint of vague sap but the sweetness is balanced; **t**22 excellent translation onto the palate: an immediate sweetness arrives with some of the most intense barley you can imagine; **f**22 the dry, oaky tones are controlled and offer hickory and spice; **b**22 a Perthshire thoroughbred just champing at the bit with honey. **49.6%. ncf nc.**

**The Whisky Shop Deanston 12 Year Old Oloroso Finish (71)** **n**18 t18 f17 **b**18. I wonder if I'll ever drink an enjoyable Deanston again... **40%**

## DUFFTOWN
**Speyside, 1898. Diageo. Silent.**

**Dufftown Aged 15 Years** db **(69)** **n**16 t19 f17 b17. Rubbery, syrupy and sickly sweet: Dufftown in a nutshell. **43%.** *Flora and Fauna range.*

**Dufftown Rare Malts Aged 21 Years** dist 1975 db **(59)** **n**14 t17 f14 b14. Not rare enough. **54.8%**

**Berrys' Own Selection Dufftown 1979 25 Year Old (83)** **n**21 t23 f19 b20. The bitter, flaky finish lets down the crisp, confident start. The sweet, roast-malt mouth arrival is as good as this dreadful distillery ever gets. **46%.** *Berry Bros & Rudd.*

⋅∷⋅ **Connoisseurs Choice Dufftown 1993 (80)** **n**19 t21 f20 b20. Sweet, malty and stylish, this is a very pleasant dram. Simplistic, maybe. But infinitely better than the dirty, rubbery stuff hurled at us for the last 20-30 years... **43%.** *Gordon & MacPhail.*

⋅∷⋅ **Murray McDavid Maverick Dufftown Aged Over 10 Years** Bourbon cask W0405, Syrah finish from Languedoc region, dist 93, bott 04 **(79)** **n**20 t21 f19 b19. Pretty good. And probably the fruitiest expression I've ever come across. Falls out of sync towards the finish, but trying to guide a Dufftown is like attempting to stop a 100mph train by holding your hand out and closing your eyes. **46%. nc ncf.**

**Old Malt Cask Dufftown Aged 12 Years** dist Dec 91, bott Feb 04 **(83)** **n**21 t22 f20 **b**20. Easily one of the most pleasant bottlings from this distillery; unusually clean, untroubled by complexity. **50%. nc ncf sc.** *Douglas Laing.*

**Old Malt Cask Dufftown Aged 14 Years** dist Sep 88, bott Aug 03 **(73)** **n**20 t19 f16 **b**18. Typically unbalanced, it lurches all over the palate with a mildly cloying mouthfeel. Enjoy the ride! **50%. nc ncf sc.** *Douglas Laing.*

**Private Cellars Selection Dufftown 1985** bott 04 **(74)** **n**20 t21 f16 b17. Syrup and rubber. **43%.** *Speyside Distillers.*

**Scott's Selection Dufftown 1985** bott 04 **(81)** **n**21 t21 f19 **b**20. Starts attractively with a big, bourbony kick but unravels untidily at the death. **57.1%.**

**Vom Fass Dufftown 11 Years Old (73)** **n**18 t20 f18 b17. Mildly soapy cask redeemed by a big bourbon kick and some curiously raisiny malt. Typical, unwieldy Dufftown scruffbag. **59.4%.** *Austria.*

**Wilson & Morgan Barrel Selection Dufftown 15 Years Old** dist 85 **(73)** **n**18 t19 f18 **b**18. Oaky spice attack loses battle against the cloying, dirty-ish intensity. Big and brawny. **56.8%**

**Wilson & Morgan Barrel Selection Dufftown 1989** Marsala Finish bott 03 **(85)** **n**19 t21 f23 **b**22. A distinctly better-class dram from a consistently poor distillery. The fruity-spice is genuinely delicious. **46%**

## DUNGLASS ( see Littlemill)

## EDRADOUR
**Highland (Perthshire), 1837. Signatory. Working.**

**Edradour 10 Years Old** db **(86)** **n**21 t22 f22 **b**21. A better version of one of the most inconsistent drams in the world. **40%**

··· **Edradour 'Straight from the Cask' Aged 10 Years Sauternes Finish** cask 04/457/5, dist 20 Apr 94, bott 22 Feb 05 db **(77)** n19 t21 f18 b19. This does have its moment of sheer brilliance, about five seconds in, but it is gone in a trice. The whole secret to great whisky is that it must have balance and if this malt were a trapeze artist it'd be dead by the time it reached half way across. **56.2%.**

**Edradour Signatory Aged 10 Years** cask 361, dist Oct 93, bott 24 Feb 04, db **(89)** n22 firm sherry; ample rich fruitcake; t23 youthful, rich barley; then wave upon wave of faultlessly clean grape; f21 remains young in character; b23 a very unusual but entertaining marriage between young barley and big sherry. **46%.**

# FETTERCAIRN
### Highland (Eastern), 1824. Whyte and Mackay. Working.

**Fettercairn 12 Year Old** db **(66)** n14 t19 f16 b17. If the nose doesn't get you, what follows probably will...Grim doesn't quite cover it. **40%**

**Fettercairn 1824** db **(69)** n17 t19 f16 b17. By Fettercairn standards, not a bad offering. Relatively free from its inherent sulphury and rubbery qualities, this displays a sweet nutty character not altogether unattractive – though caramel plays a calming role here. Need my arm twisting for a second glass, though. **40%**

**Connoisseurs Choice Fettercairn 1992 (61)** n13 t17 f16 b15. Sulphury, burning car tyres on the nose and cloying sweetness on the palate with a dirty finish. Business as usual at Fettercairn, then. **46%.** *Gordon & MacPhail.*

**Old Malt Cask Fettercairn 13 Years Old** dist Mar 91, bott Aug 04 **(80)** n18 t20 f22 b20. Somewhat cloying and lacking direction, though the finish is rather distinguished. What we have here that rarest of beasts: a drinkable, enjoyable and relatively clean Fettercairn... **50%.** *Douglas Laing & Co.*

**Part Nan Angelen Fettercairn 25 Years Old (79)** n19 t20 f20 b20. Decent sherry influence, but rather thick and muddled. **40%**

**Private Cellars Selection Fettercairn 1989** bott 04 **(64)** n18 t17 f14 b15. I have no idea what this is about. It doesn't really taste of anything. And is there a finish...? **43%.**

**Scott's Selection Fettercairn 1989** bott 05 **(76)** n18 t20 f19 b19. Big barley sugar kick; cumbersome, awkward and cloying; could well appeal to liqueur lovers. **55.9%.**

# GLEN ALBYN
### Highland (Northern) 1846–1983. Demolished.

**Gordon & MacPhail Rare Vintage Glen Albyn 1966 (87)** n19 a touch soapy and gentle smoke; t23 wonderful sweet malt lead works perfectly with drier herby, fruity notes; f22 waves of smoke crash against the firm malt and toasty oak; b23 not sure this malt was ever built for this kind of age, but a sophisticated degree of exotic fruit and smoke-induced spice defies the odds for a delicious trip down Memory Lane. **43%**

**Gordon & MacPhail Rare Vintage Glen Albyn 1975 (78)** n19 t20 f19 b20. Too much soapy age, though the sweet malt and soft smoke linger. **46%**

··· **Old Malt Cask Glen Albyn 35 Years Old** dist 26 Sept 69, bott Jul 05 **(90)** n24 a star-studded aroma for something this ancient: the oak weaves delicate vanilla patterns around the apple-honey-barley lead. As aromas go, a veritable gold nugget for its age; t23 early barley absolutely rips through the tastebuds helped along the way by a glossy sweetness and a puff of smoke and cocoa; f21 the drying oak lays claim with tolerable force; b22 understandable signs of longevity, but overall this is simply wonderful. **50%.** *Douglas Laing. 229 bottles.*

··· **Rarest of the Rare Glen Albyn 1979** cask 3960, dist Dec 79, bott Mar 06 **(91)** n23 melon and barley play host to a clever, nose-nipping spiciness. So relaxed: supreme confidence here; t23 the incredibly fresh, salivating barley intertwines with glorious vanilla to give a drier tier to the delicately sweet malt; f22 some chalky vanilla and mocha but the barley holds true; b23 of Scotland's disappearing malts, this is going with flourish. **57.3%.** *Duncan Taylor. 244 bottles.*

## GLENALLACHIE
### Speyside, 1968. Chivas. Working.

   Glenallachie 15 Years Old Distillery Edition db **(81)** n20 t21 f19 **b**19. Real battle between nature and nurture: an exceptional sherry butt has silk gloves and honied marzipan, while a hot-tempered bruiser lurks beneath. **58%**

   Glenallachie Cask Strength Edition 15 Years Old dist 89, bott 05 db **(86)** n21 under rock-hard sherry lurks rock-hard malt; **t**23 surprisingly attractive malt tones chisel their way through the grape. Tough, but great fun! **f**20 furry and slightly off-key; **b**21 you should never expect too much from this distillery, but this is an unusual expression this does little to impress but much to entertain. **58%. ncf.**

   ⁘ **Connoisseurs Choice Glenallachie 1992 (67)** n18 t17 f16 b16. Sweaty armpits: this really isn't Scotland's finest distillery, is it. **46%.** *Gordon & MacPhail.*

   **Dun Bheagan Glenallachie 1991 Aged 12 Years** bourbon barrel bott 11 Sept 03 **(86)** n21 t22 f21 **b**22. The raging fire that normally accompanies Glenallachie has been doused. **43%.** *William Maxwell.*

   ⁘ **Dun Bheagan Glenallachie Aged 13 Years** Sherry finish **(68)** n19 t18 f15 **b**16. Just dreadful. Further confirmation, hardly that it's needed, that here is a distillery which should rarely be bottled. **43%.** *Ian Macleod.*

   ⁘ **Provenance Glenallachie Aged 12 Years** Refill Hogshead DMG 1879, dist Spring 93, bott Winter 06 **(83)** n19 t21 f22 **b**21. A rare beast: an attractive and drinkable Glenallachie. Vindaloo-esque but the barley is clean, crisp and precise with a sexy little sweetening of the malt. A really enjoyable experience...and it's not often I've said that about one of these Johnnies. **46%.**

   **Scotch Single Malt Circle Glenallachie 1981** cask 600, dist 18 May 81, bott 4 Nov 03 **(79)** n21 t20 f19 **b**19. A malty, fudgy sweetness negates the burning undercurrent. By no means the worst Glenallachie I've tasted. **55.9%** *Germany.*

## GLENBURGIE
### Speyside, 1810. Chivas. Working.

   ⁘ **Glenburgie Aged 15 Years** Bott code L00/129 db **(84)** n22 t23 f19 **b**20. Doing so well until the spectacularly flat, bitter finish. Orangey citrus and liquorice had abounded. **46%**

   **Douglas Taylor Glenburgie 1969 Aged 34 Years** cask 6753 **(78)** n21 t20 f18 **b**19. Begins maltily, but later a fraction too resinous. **45.7%**

   **Gordon and MacPhail Glenburgie 1964 (91)** n22 blood oranges and putty; quite attractive, really; **t**22 dense barley-oak body but the sweetness from the malt really is excellent; **f**24 serious amounts of very dark chocolate dissipate as an oily maltfest returns with some late citrus and spice; almost too well orchestrated and beautifully behaved to be true; **b**23 this is one of those really old numbers that defy age and belief. Just so, so beautiful. **40%**

   ⁘ **Gordon & MacPhail Reserve Glenburgie 1990** bott 09 Aug 05 **(91)** n24 stupendous! Classic aroma of over-ripe dates and mellow spices. Just so rare these days...; **t**23 big, bitter-sweet with loads of toffee-apple and a sub-plot of oily malt. A real chewathon; **f**22 relatively flat, but a soft retreat with caramel lingering about; **b**22 for those looking for big, nutty in-your-face chestnut-coloured sherry, time to use up a few air miles to the USA. **40%.** *US Market.*

   **Old Malt Cask Glenburgie Aged 13 Years** dist Nov 90, bott Nov 03 **(91)** n23 t23 f22 **b**23. A sophisticated malt offering a fabulous coastal tang. The complexity goes through the roof. **50%. nc ncf sc.** *Douglas Laing. 240 bottles.*

## GLENCADAM
### Highland (Eastern), 1825. Angus Dundee. Working.

   **Glencadam Aged 15 Years** db **(84)** n19 t22 f22 **b**21. The first distillery-bottled Glencadam I can remember thanks to new owners and the brakes are never taken off. The middle and early finale are really quite sublime with that glorious malt-intense signature that offers the kind of irresistible drive and style to the tastebuds that Frank Lampard gives to Chelsea...and it's worth getting just for that. But something, a roasty caramel maybe, is holding back on the start and finish: oh, what might have been! Delicious all the same! **40%**

**Berrys' Own Selection 1991 Glencadam, 12 Years Old**, bott 04 **(87)** n20 lazy malt, sawdusty oak: quite gristy; t23 a peach of an arrival with a mouthwatering, barley-sugar sweetness gathering in intensity before a gripping outbreak of spices; f22 labours slightly under the gathering oak but the spices continue to fizz; **b**22 a real treat, showing the distillery to its best advantage. **46%.**

**Cadenhead's Authentic Collection Glencadam Aged 15 Years** dist 89, bott Feb 05 **(85)** n21 t22 f20 b22. A clean, deliciously intense malt with no great pretensions to complexity and all the emphasis on the barley. **58.3%.** *222 bottles.*

·⊹· **Cadenhead's Authentic Collection Glencadam Aged 17 Years** Bourbon, dist 89, bott May 06 **(81)** n20 t21 f20 b20. A pulsing, pounding malt that's big on barley but wants for development **57.8%.** *234 bottles.*

·⊹· **D&M Aficionados' Club Bottling Glencadam Aged 31 Years** cask 2, dist Dec 74 **(86)** n22 t23 f20 b21. Holds together despite the splinters; the bourbon theme is never less than attractive. **43%. nc ncf.** *US by Angus Dundee .*

·⊹· **Dun Bheagan Glencadam 20 Years Old** Hogshead **(80)** n20 t19 f21 b20. For all its age it remains hot stuff. The honey influence will win friends, though. **48%**

·⊹· **Gordon & MacPhail Reserve Glencadam 1974** dist 2 Sep 74, bott 28 Oct.05 **(95)** n24 high calibre honey-oak dovetailing; Battenburg cake; t23 wonderful firmness to both the barley and oak with hints of acacia honey and so much more, including the orangey bit in a Jaffa Cake; f24 long, exceptionally rich with marzipan – Danish, one presumes – and dark chocolate; b24 Copenhagen has become even more wonderful with the best Glencadam I've ever come across. This is a masterpiece malt. **46%.** *Gordon & MacPhail. 182 btls.*

·⊹· **Platinum Glencadam 1985** dist Jun 85, bott Nov 05 **(84)** n19 t22 f21 b22. A typically curious malt, as one expects from this distillery from this time. The heat in the whisky suggests hard-pressed stills, but there is a sheen to the honey-barley intensity that is quite beautiful. **54.2%.** *Douglas Laing. 306 bottles.*

**Vom Fass Glencadam 13 Years Old (83)** n21 t21 f20 b21. Charmingly fruity and light with emphasis on citrus and barley sugar. **40%.**

·⊹· **The Whisky Fair Artist Edition Glencadam Aged 32 Years** Bourbon Hogshead, dist Apr 1973, bott Feb 06 **(81)** n19 t21 f20 b21. Some chewy chocolate pudding for desert but the main course is a feisty, oaky affair. **46.4%. nc ncf.** *Germany. 87 bottles.*

**Whisky Galore Glencadam 1991 Aged 12 Years (83)** n20 t22 f21 b20. What we are talking here is clean, simple, uncomplicated and pretty delicious malt – with the emphasis on malt. **46%.** *Douglas Taylor & Co.*

# GLENCRAIG
**Speyside, 1958. Allied. Two Lomond stills operating within the Glenburgie plant. Now silent.**

**Connoisseurs Choice Glencraig 1970 (90)** n22 oily, malty notes of considerable weight and brilliant bitter-sweet balance. The fruit is ripe and salivating; t22 big malt, with deft oiliness gives weight to the body. Silky and sits perfectly on the palate. A touch of smoke is an added bonus; f22 vanilla and sweet malt; b24 absolutely brilliant malt: why it was discontinued I'll never know. Few Speysiders achieve such harmony in weight and balance. If you ever see a bottle, grab it. And heartfelt congrats to G&M for preserving posterity: and priceless posterity at that. A company way ahead of its time. **40%.** *G&M.*

**Connoisseurs Choice Glencraig 1975 (85)** n21 t22 f21 b21. A once great whisky that has seen better days and trying for all its worth to maintain dignity. It suceeds this time, but for how much longer only later bottlings will reveal. **40%.**

# GLENDRONACH

**Speyside, 1826. Chivas. Working.**

**Glendronach Original Aged 12 Years Double Matured** db **(88) n**23 dense, ripe plummy fruit: serious touches of fruitcake, complete with brown sugars. Oak does give a vanilla topping but barley also punches through. Some coal smoke buzzes around, too. Needs some time to get the full story; **t**21 some serious infighting here, some of it off-key, between grape and grain. The grape wins but is not entirely unbloodied as the mouthwatering barley has some juicy moments; **f**22 the lull after the storm; much more measured doses of bitter marmalade and vanilla, softening towards a gentle spice within the cocoa. Very different; **b**22 vastly improved from the sulphur-tainted bottling of last year. In fact, their most enjoyable standard distillery bottling I've had for many years. But forget about the whisky: the blurb on the back is among the most interesting you likely to find anywhere. And I quote: "Founder James Allardice called the original Glendronach, 'The Guid Glendronach'. But there's no need to imitate his marketing methods. The first converts to his malt were the 'ladies of the night' in Edinburgh's Canongate!" Fascinating. And as a professional whisky taster I am left wondering: did they swallow or spit... **40%** ☉ ☉

**Glendronach 15 Years Old** db **(83) n**20 **t**22 **f**20 **b**21. Chocolate fudge and grape juice to start then tails off towards a slightly bitter, dry finish. **40%**

**Glendronach Aged 33 Years** db Oloroso Sherry **(95) n**24 it's as if your head is stuck in a sherry butt still in the bodega; be transported back in time to when soft, very gently smoked malt still had the wherewithal to link with the grape and offer something teasing yet profound, ripe yet beautifully fresh. Majestic...; **t**24 sublime sherry arrival with a wonderful toffee-apple, honeycomb and leather (almost very old bourbon) theme; the malt is almost thick enough to cut, and the softest smoke imaginable combines to add extra weight to the fruit; **f**23 the oak now arrives, but offering layers of vanilla to complement the fruit; still the smoke drifts and this adds further to the near bitter-sweet perfection; **b**24 want to know what sherry should really nose like: invest in a bottle of this. This is a vivid malt boasting spellbinding clarity and charm. A golden nugget of a dram, which would have been better still at 46%. **40%**

**The Glendronach 1968** db **(92) n**23 nuts, clean sherry of the highest order; **t**22 exceptionally together with the most vibrant oloroso: not a single off note; **f**23 astonishing depth, with more than a touch of pot still Demerara (PM mark to be precise); **b**24 an almost extinct style of sherry that is faultless in its firmness and clarity. This was bottled in 1993 – I remember it well. Astonishingly, some bottles have just turned up in Whisky of the World Duty Free in UK and this is how it tastes now. Grab while you can. **43%**

**Blackadder Raw Cask Glendronach 28 Years Old** cask 3407 dist Dec 74, bott Nov 03 **(85) n**19 **t**22 **f**22 **b**22. Limps its way to an attractive conclusion. **48.6%**

**Murray McDavid Mission IV Glendronach 1976 Aged 27 Years (87) n**21 coal dust and grist; **t**23 hard-as-nails malt pings around the palate; a degree of barley sugar sweetens things while a wisp of smoke offers weight; **f**21 spicy and warming; **b**22 a curiously attractive dram from an enigmatic distillery. **46%**

⠾ **Murray McDavid Glendronach 1990 Aged 16 Years** Bourbon/Port, bott 06 **(84) n**22 **t**22 **f**19 **b**21. I admit this is a distillery I have long failed to get my head round in its normal state. But when confronted by something that looks like paraffin and surely from Pipes on express delivery from Oporto, then my horizons are widened again. If anything the Port is too good, as the malt is lost without trace towards the finish. But the juicy arrival to that point is a delight, as are the soft spices that offer needed ballast. **46%. nc ncf.** *3500 bottles*

**Old Malt Cask Glendronach 20 Years Old** dist 2 Feb 85, bott 18 Apr 05 **(88) n**23 distinct character of pre-caramelised Demerara; **t**22 more rich, estery caramel and fruit; **f**21 sweetens as some malt at last arrives; **b**22 a rum cove. **50%.**

Whisky Galore Glendronach 1990 Aged 13 Years **(86) n**21 **t**22 **f**21 **b**22. Outwardly simple, but a little more classy and complex than it first appears.

Wilson & Morgan Barrel Selection Glendronach 1990 Port Finish bott 04 **(86) n**18 **t**23 **f**23 **b**22. This fruit and custard offering must have come from a fresh port pipe after years in a second fill bourbon. The result looks like distilled flamingo, but a lot more mouthwatering. **46%**

## GLENDULLAN (see also below)
### Speyside, 1898–1985. Closed.
⋅⋅⋅ **Murray McDavid Glendullan 1996** Bourbon/Grenache, bott 05 **(81) n**20 **t**21 **f**20 **b**20. Curious, salted celery to the nose; the behaviour on the palate is no less singular. Clean, spicy and confused – and that's just the guy writing these notes. **46%. nc ncf.** *3600 bottles.*

⋅⋅⋅ **Old Malt Cask Glendullan Aged 14 Years** Refill Hogshead 2131, dist Aug 91, bott Sept 05 **(86) n**22 **t**23 **f**20 **b**21. An oily expression. **50%. nc ncf.**

**Platinum Old and Rare Glendullan Aged 34 Years** dist Mar 72, bott Jan 03 **(78) n**20 **t**22 **f**18 **b**18. Big malty mouth arrival but the balance suffers later. **46.8%**

**Platinum Old and Rare Glendullan 36 Years Old (89) n**20 the oak is in the vanguard followed by a train of marginally sweeter elements. Malt and vanilla intertwine plus spice and sultanas. A dash of peat adds extra weight; **t**23 outstanding arrival of beautifully textured and sweetened malt – almost gristy in the way it dissolves in the mouth. Oak is much less pronounced than on the nose except for the very initial impact. Wonderfully spiced; **f**23 long, very subtly smoked: a bombardment of peppers gives way to cocoa; **b**23 a whiff of brilliance from the original old stills of this little-known but reliable Speysider. **55.1%.**

⋅⋅⋅ **Provenance Glendullan Aged 10 Years** Sherry finish, dist Nov 94, bott Dec 04 **(80) n**22 **t**21 **f**18 **b**19. Finishing in sherry has bigged-up the nose, but at what cost to the delivery and finish on the palate? **46 %.** *McGibbon's.*

⋅⋅⋅ **Provenance Glendullan 14 Years** dist Aug 91, bott Aug 05 **(89) n**22 light, clean barley; **t**23 a salivating freshness that pulses ripe barley; **f**22 soft oils help sweeten and lengthen the finale with a touch of cocoa at the death; **b**22 impeccably behaved and makes all the right noises. **46%.** *McGibbon's.*

## GLENDULLAN (see also above)
### Speyside, 1972. Diageo. Working.
**Glendullan Aged 8 Years** db **(89) n**20 fresh, gingery, zesty; **t**22 distinctly mealy and malty. **f**24 brilliant – really stunning grassy malt powers through. Speyside in a glass – and a nutshell; **b**23 this is just how I like my Speysiders: young fresh and uplifting. A charming malt.

**Glendullan Aged 12 Years** (new stock circa 03, bottling mark – on reverse of label – L19R01457997, dark green print) db **(77) n**19 **t**20 **f**19 **b**19. Oily, flat and bitter towards the finish. Really disappointing. **43%.** *Flora and Fauna range.*

**Glendullan Aged 12 Years** batch no. 00195262 db **(85) n**22 **t**22 **f**20 **b**21. Intriguing and a good example of where oak starts to lop points off what had recently been excellent stuff. **43%**

⋅⋅⋅ **Glendullan 1978 Rare Malt** db **(88) n**23 exceptional piquancy to this with the quietness of the oak shattered by a lemon-citrus shrill. Genuinely wonderful; **t**22 a lovely, tart start with that citrus making a crashing entry but the oak barges in soon after and coffee is soon on the menu; **f**21 more coffee and lemon cake, though it by now a very small slice; **b**22 Sherlock Holmes would have loved this one: he would have found it lemon-entry. **56.8%**

## GLEN ELGIN
### Speyside, 1900. Diageo. Working.
**Glen Elgin Aged 12 Years** db **(89) n**23 blistering, mouthwatering fruit of

unspecified origin. The intensity of the malt is breathtaking; t24 stunning fresh malt arrival, salivating barley that is both crisp and lush: then a big round of spice amid some squashed, over-ripe plums. Faultless mouthfeel; f20 the spice continues as does the intense malt but is devalued dramatically by a bitter-toffee effect; b22 absolutely murders Cragganmore as Diageo's top dog bottled Speysider. The marks would be several points further north if one – rightly or wrongly – didn't get the feeling that some caramel was weaving a derogatory spell. Brilliant stuff nonetheless. States Pot Still on label – not to be confused with Irish Pot Still. This is 100% malt... and it shows! **43%**

**Glen Elgin Aged 32 Years** db **(68)** n15 t19 f17 b17. Unacceptably soapy and sappy, even for its age. Really disappointing. **42.3%**

**Berrys' Own Selection Glen Elgin 1975 28 Years Old** bott 04 **(89)** n21 hot crossed buns, complete with a sliver of salted butter; t23 excellent fruitmalt balance; quite sweet at first, almost a glazed cherry, fruitcake delivery; f23 complex development of honey and spices; b22 rare to find a Glen Elgin in this excellent sherry guise without caramel interfering. For those of us with access to regular blending samples, this distillery makes astonishingly good malt: easily one of the unsung heroes of scotch. At last a chance to see just why. **46%**

**Cadenhead's Authentic Collection Glen Elgin-Glenlivet Aged 13 Years (94)** n24 probably a second-fill bourbon cask allows unfettered insight into the green apple fruitiness that mingles with grist and coal dust. Complex and seductive; t24 much younger than its 13 years, and that's great news for Glen Elgin which peaks earlier than most. Salivating and green, some watered honey sweetens the juicy, sharp grass; f23 layers of chewability and even the oak-flaked vanilla cannot dampen the freshness; b23 when asked what is my favourite Speysider, I often consider Glen Elgin before plumping for Balvenie. If more truly genius casks like this were around, the answer might be different. **59.5%**. *672 bottles*.

**Connoisseurs Choice Glen Elgin 1968 (84)** n23 t21 f20 b20. Expressive nose full of diced pineapple and suet: loses it in the telling of the tale. **46%**. *G&M*.

**Mackillop's Choice Glen Elgin** cask 3542, dist Jul 76 **(88)** n22 such a wonderful fruit overture, all ripe if slightly tinned; t23 enormous body to the malt, with the fruit again quick off the blocks and delightful late delivery of soft smoke: stylish stuff; f22 very long, chewy and spicy, with even more late smoke arriving; b22 gloriously textured whisky: reminds me of a fruit trifle of the mid '70s! **42.6%**.

⋅⋅⋅ **Old Malt Cask Glen Elgin Aged 20 Years** dist Apr 85, bott Oct 05 **(83)** n21 t21 f21 b20. Surprisingly salty for an Elgin; an oaky tang has also got in to disrupt the high quality malt harmony. **50%**. *Douglas Laing. 302 bottles*.

**Scott's Selection Glen Elgin 1980** bott 04 **(81)** n21 t22 f18 b20. Moments of high elegance at the beginning, but a tad too much oak for comfort. **43.3%**

**Whisky Galore Glen Elgin 1991 Aged 12 Years (71)** n17 t19 f17 b18. No shortage of bitter orange; at time teeth-tingling sweet but the odd off note too many. **46%**

# GLENESK
### Highland (Eastern), 1897–1985. Closed.

**Connoisseurs Choice Glenesk 1984 (78)** n19 t21 f19 b19. Still too syrupy for its own good, but so much better than other G&M bottlings from this less than distinguished late distillery. **43%**. *Gordon & MacPhail*.

**Old Malt Cask Glenesk 30 Years Old** dist Feb 74, bott Aug 04 **(79)** n20 t21 f18 b19. A bright barley-sugar and coal dust start then reverts to sickly, sugar and cod-liver type. **50%**. *Douglas Laing & Co*.

# GLENFARCLAS
### Speyside, 1836. J&G Grant. Working.

**Glenfarclas 8 Years Old** db **(89)** n23 soft, intense malt under a gentle layer of clean grape and blood oranges; the most distant and surprising hint of freshly grilled kipper; **t**22 luxurious and gentle, the sweetness is Demerara oriented; **f**22 much more oak than one might expect from a youngster; some quite excellent fruit follow-through; **b**22 just such a much more together, harmonious and confident dram than the old bottling: an absolute little cracker. A taste of their final bottling under the old label shows all the above except the kipper on the nose. **40%** ⊙⊙

⋯ **Glenfarclas 8 Years Old** db **(86) n**21 **t**22 **f**22 **b**21. Less intense sherry allows the youth of this malt to stand out. Mildly quirky as a Glenfarclas and enormous entertainment. **40%**

**Glenfardas 10 Years Old** db **(80) n**19 **t**20 **f**22 **b**19. Always an enjoyable malt, but for some reason this version never seems to fire on all cylinders. There is a vague honey sheen which works well with the barley, but struggles for balance and the nose is a bit sweaty. Still has distinctly impressive elements but an odd fish. **40%** ⊙⊙

**Glenfarclas 12 Years Old** db **(89) n**22 oops! Nothing like its usual near brilliant self early on, but some golden strands of honey compensate handsomely; **t**23 recovers superbly to offer lashings of the trademark honeycomb amid a riot of gentle oaky spice; the light sprinkling of muscovado sugar is sublime, as is the crushed raisins; **f**22 more burned honeycomb and some subtle extra oak offers dry vanilla; **b**23 from this sample just the odd cask has tarnished the usual brilliance, but it's still good enough to offer moments of Speyside most glorious. **43%** ⊙

**Glenfarclas 15 Years Old** db **(95) n**23 such is the intensity of the fruit and sugar-rich barley, there is an element of medium ester Jamaican pot still rum to this, a feeling intensified by an orangey-oak influence that seems greater than 15 years. The top-shelf sherry, though, is of a classical type rarely found these days, though common 30 years ago; **t**24 succulent and stupendous. Barley sugar shows first then a sherry input that borders on intense but dissipates as the spicy oak digs in; **f**24 long, chewy, a tad oily and fades with a wonderful coffee-vanilla combination and a late surge of something bourbony; **b**24 Eureka!!! The 15-y-o back to how I can remember it in the past. Some of you may have been scared away by some less than impressive recent bottlings. It's safe to come back because now it has been returned to its position as one of Scotland's most sublime malts. The quality of the sherry is astonishing; its interaction with the barley is a wondrous joy. Go find and get... **46%** ⊙⊙

⋯ **Glenfarclas 17 Years Old** db **(93) n**23 just so light and playful: custard powder lightens and sweetens, sultana softens, barley moistens, spice threatens...; **t**23 the relaxed sherry influence really lets the honey deliver; delightfully roasty and well spiced towards the middle; **f**23 when I was a kid there was a candy – pretend tobacco, no less! – made from strands of coconut and sweetened with a Demerara syrup. My, this takes me back...; **b**24 an excellent age for this distillery, allowing just enough oak in to stir up the complexity. A stupendous addition to the range. **40%**

**Glenfarclas 21 Years Old** db **(83) n**20 **t**23 **f**19 **b**21. A chorus of sweet, honied malt and mildly spiced, teasing fruit on the fabulous mouth arrival and middle compensates for the blips. **43%**. ⊙

**Glenfarclas 25 Years Old** db **(88) n**22 a heavy, impervious nose with the sherry and oak providing a cleanly-built wall; **t**23 much softer with an immediate mouthwatering delivery full of prime, sweet barley and then toasted raisins; **f**21 soft vanilla; fruitcake and cream; **b**22 an distinct improvement on previous bottlings with the finish here having much more to say. **43%** ⊙⊙

**Glenfarclas 30 Years Old** db **(85) n**20 **t**22 **f**21 **b**22. Flawed yet juicy. **43%** ⊙⊙

**Glenfarclas 40 Years Old Millennium Edition** db **(92) n**23 **t**23 **f**23 **b**23 an almost immaculate portrayal of an old-fashioned, high-quality malt with unblemished sherry freshness and depth. The hallmark of quality is the sherry's refusal to dominate the spicy, softly peated malt. The oak offers a bourbony sweetness but ensures a rich depth throughout. Quite outstanding for its age. **nc ncf.**

⁘ **Glenfarclas 50 Years Old** db **(92)** n24 Unique. Almost a marriage between 20-y-o bourbon and intense, old-fashioned sherry. Earthy, weighty stuff that repays time in the glass and oxidization because only then does the subtlety become apparent and a soft peat-reek reveal itself; t23 an unexpected sweet – even mouthwatering - arrival, again with a touch of peat to add counter ballast to the intense richness of the sherry. The oak is intense from the middle onwards, but of such high quality that it merely accompanies rather then dominates; f22 warming black peppers ping around the palate; some lovely cocoa oils coat the mouth for a bitter-sweet, warming and very long finish; b23 Most whiskies cannot survive such great age. This one really does bloom in the glass and the earthy, peaty aspect makes it all the more memorable. It has taken 50 years to reach this state. Give a glass of this at least an hour's inquisition, as I have. Your patience will be rewarded many times over. **44.4%**

**Glenfarclas 105 Cask Strength 10 Years Old** db **(91)** n22 perfect fresh sherry influence; clean, intense, charismatic, fruity and precise; t23 rather confusing as the might of the malt and sherry battle for supremacy: takes time to settle and the drier oak helps enormously to accentuate the honied qualities of the malt; f23 a fine, layered oak seeing off the sweeter honeycomb theme for a distinguished finale; b23 this, for various reasons, has been a regular dram of mine for over 20 years. It has been at its very best in recent bottlings, though the nose here doesn't quite hit the heights. **60%** ⊙ ⊙

⁘ **Glenfarclas 1954 Aged 46 Years** dist 16 Jun 54, bott 27 Jul 00 db **(96)** n24 the clarity of the sherry defies belief; just a fraction too much oak for perfection but the kumquats and most subtle coriander give this such a delightful lift. A squirt of soft peat balances it out gloriously; t25 Faultless. Absolute perfect harmonisation on the palate as the dissolving oloroso integrates seamlessly with the rich barley and developing spices. The chewiness is provided by German-style caramelized biscuit, the elegance by a clever mixture and intriguing of Muscovado and Demerara sugars; f23 edges towards oak-fuelled bitterness, but some soft peats generate an excellent sweet, earthy repost; the oak is big and slightly bitter towards the end; b24 sincere apologies for missing out on this in earlier editions of the Bible. Apparently, though, this can still be found. Buy two: one to drink, the other to be buried with. **43%**. *1193 bottles.*

**Glenfarclas Vintage 1968** db **(92)** n23 t23 f23 b23. Just one of those sherry casks that was destined for greatness in Scotland. **43%**. *USA.*

**Glenfarclas 1969** cask 2895, dist 16 May 69, bott 02 Sep 03 db **(85)** n21 t21 f22 b21. An unbelievably relaxed malt for one so old. **40.1%**. *205 bottles.*

**Glenfarclas 1969** cask 2898 dist 16 May 69, bott 02 Sep 03 db **(89)** n23 t24 f21 b21. If it had been able to continue at the pace achieved on mouth arrival we would have had a major classic. **41.7%**. *197 bottles.*

**Glenfarclas 1969** cask 2899, dist 16 May 69, bott 02 Sep 03 db **(92)** n23 t22 f24 b23. Sophisticated and full of honeycomb/Demerara depth. **41.1%**.

**Glenfarclas 1970** db **(83)** n20 t20 f22 b21. Rich and spicy. **50.1%. nc ncf.**

**Glenfarclas 1972** db **(92)** n23 t23 f23 b23. A steady-as-a-rock malt that never alters course from its deliciously clean-sherried path; some real sophistication here. **43%**

**Glenfarclas Vintage 1973** db **(89)** n24 t21 f22 b22. A deceptively delicate malt where some complexity is over-ridden by oil. **46%**. *Germany.*

⁘ **Glenfarclas 1974** bott 12 Dec 05 db **(89)** n22 heavy duty sherry, and the oak is no less imposing; t23 beautiful, spiced up delivery of intense oloroso leaving space enough for some demerara sweetness to filter through; f22 soft, vanilla wafers with sweetened mocha; b22 almost too indulgent in sherry, but the stunning dark sugar balance offers the perfect counter to the big oak. A real late night dram of substance. **57.4%**. *USA Market.*

**Glenfarclas 1974 Single Cask**, cask no. 6042, dist 11 Jul 74, bott 26 Oct 04 db **(90)** n22 a curious, unique and highly attractive intertwining of soft sherry and asparagus! **t**22 asparagus-free development of warming grape that edges towards the Glenfarclas trademark of honeycomb; **f**23 very long and increasingly roasty: the honeycomb remains a constant and some almondy nuttiness furthers the complexity; **b**23 one of those beautiful malts that repays careful study. **53.3%.** *288 bottles.*

**Glenfarclas 1978** db **(83) n**22 **t**21 **f**20 **b**20. Sweet chestnuts and malt to nose; hot, sweet and malty to taste. **53.3%.nc ncf.** *J&G Grant.*

**Glenfarclas 1979** db **(89) n**22 big, sweet, chocolate pudding and fruit; **t**23 spicy from the off and a lovely fanning out of chewy malt and burnt fudge; **f**22 very long with some toasted honeycomb in there; **b**22 a big, bruising, fullflavoured malt that takes no prisoners. **51.8%. nc ncf.** *J&G Grant.*

**Glenfarclas 1980** db **(69) n**16 **t**19 **f**17 **b**17 . Rich but sulphur-stained. **55%.** *J&G Grant.*

∵ **Glenfarclas 1982 Vintage** db **(90) n**22 fat sultanas and fresh-cut grass; **t**22 immensely sweet by Glenfarclas standards with a big barley rush; **f**23 stunningly layered with delicate vanilla found with varying levels of toastiness; **b**23 a good choice for the market as there is extraordinary youth for a malt so old. Just so clean and quietly sophisticated. **43%.** *Spain Market.*

**Glenfarclas 1985 18 Years Old** Refill Sherry Hogshead cask no. 2823, dist Sept 85, bott Oct 03 db **(83) n**21 **t**19 **f**23 **b**20. Hot whisky: a strange choice for a single cask, though the fabulous honey theme that tries to develop may be a clue. The finish is outstanding. **48.5%.** *308 bottles.*

**Glenfarclas 1986 Fino Sherry Cask** db **(90) n**22 **t**22 **f**23 **b**23. An eye-closing, think-about-it dram. A laid-back classic. **43%.** *J&G Grant.*

**Glenfarclas Vintage 1987 Refill Oloroso Cask** db **(93) n**23 **t**23 **f**23 **b**24. Sherry bottlings of this integrity and class are appallingly thin on the ground. I have come all the way to Europe to track it down: and worth every mile travelled, too. **46%.** *Imported by Mahler-Besse, Bordeaux.*

**Glenfarclas 1989 14 Years Old**, Plain Oak Hogshead cask no. 505, dist 89, bott Oct 03 db **(92) n**23 **t**24 **f**22 **b**23. Exceptionally well-made whisky where the malt positively glows. **58.7%.** *307 bottles.*

**Glenfarclas 1989 Oloroso Sherry Cask 1st Fill** db **(90) n**24 cream toffee, mocha, brown sugar – and not an off-note in sight; **t**23 mouthwatering sweet malt despite the forming dry notes. The oak is chunky for its age, but the malt and sherry are wonderfully sure-footed. Not dissimilar to a demerara pot-still rum in mouthfeel; **f**21 the oak gathers pace to offer liquorice and soft oils; **b**22 it says "1st fill Sherry" on the label. A waste of ink. Just one sniff will tell you! **43%**

**Glenfarclas Vintage 1990** db **(88) n**23 flawless sherry, thick barley refusing to be outdone; **t**22 dry sherry leads the way before a grapey sweeting and spicy richness intervenes; **f**21 a bit sluggish towards the finale with a sherry-toffee simplicity; **b**22 just refuses to go that extra mile for complexity. **46%.** *Germany.*

∵ **Glenfarclas 1994 Aged 12 Years** cask no. 3847 db **(92) n**23 fabulous mix of oloroso sherry and Demerara rum. Heady, fruity and vibrant; **t**24 the big strength is lost in the velvet body; again a rummy theme continues. Pulsing and mouth-watering, the barley battles through; **f**22 spices and liquorish; **b**23 a wonderful, unspoiled oloroso cask at its clean, nutty best. **58.3%. sc.** *Germany.*

∵ **Glenfarclas Heritage** db **(91) n**22 an unusually clipped nose with firm and precise malt though the oak does give a suety backdrop; **t**22 surprisingly mouthwatering despite the dull fruitiness at first then ups the barley voltage; **f**23 a really classy follow through natural toffee offering a creamy late surge; vanilla and barley intermingles beautifully, as does that understated fruitiness that has been shyly apparent throughout; **b**24 a real treat of a malt offering stylish intensity. Lucky French! **40%.** *The Heritage Malt Collection, France.*

**Adelphi The Whisky That Cannot Be Named 1953** cask 1668 dist 53 **(89) n**23 defies the years with a cushioned impact of natural caramel, vanilla and grape; lovely bourbony sub-plot; **t**23 confident nuggets of oak but the intense, slightly honeyed, barley-grape counter delights; f20 runs slightly out of steam towards the softly oaked finale, but after 50 years, who wouldn't; b22 they won't say which distillery this comes from but, to me, Glenfarclas is written all over this: few can display such sherried countenance after so many years. The perfect birthday dram for all those born in that year. **54.3%**

**Blackadder Blairfindy Aged 23 Years** cask 2003/BF/01 dist Jun 80, bott Nov 03 **(77)** n19 t20 f19 b19. Heavily oaked. **57.5%**

**Blackadder Raw Cask Blairfindy 24 Years Old,** cask no. 5984, dist 6 Jun 80, bott Jun 04 **(86)** n21 t22 f21 b22. A comfortable cask working well within its range. **55.8%**

**Blackadder Raw Cask Blairfindy 40 Years Old,** Sherry butt cask no. 4710, dist Dec 64, bott Dec 04, **(71)** n17 t20 f16 b18. I'm getting sulphur on a 40-y-o whisky. Puzzling – and hugely disappointing. Maybe I'm wrong, but perhaps they put this into a "fresh" sherry butt just prior to bottling. I don't know. Just a guess. But it would explain a lot. **55.3%**

**Blairfindy Raw Cask 39 Year Old** Sherry butt cask no. 4552, dist 65, bott May 05 **(89)** n23 lightly honied and teasingly complex; t21 spicy, lightly oaked beginning with the malt jogging into position followed by caressing oils; f22 beautiful strands of soft Demerera and golden syrup; b23 an intriguing sherry butt with very little colour – or fruit. **55.6%.** *Taiwan.*

**Blairfindy Raw Cask 39 Year Old** Sherry butt cask no. 4003 dist 66, bott June 05 **(88)** n24 a sheer joy, a total dream: sherry as it should be. Untarnished, bold with spice and liquorice, hints of sherry trifle; t22 a big, riproaring, grapey, pithy start, but then closes quickly to more chocolatey notes; f21 thumping, sweetened oak; b21 a haphazard beast full of fun. **46.6%.** *Taiwan.*

**Blairfindy Raw Cask 40 Year Old** Sherry butt cask 4711, dist 64, bott May 05 **(86)** n22 t21 f21 b22. Phew! A malt bristling with age and chunky intent. **55%.**

✧ **Cadenhead's Authentic Collection Glenfarclas Aged 17 Years** Bourbon Hogshead, dist 88, bott May 05 **(90)** n23 waxy wooden floors, pepper, diced apple and spiced pears: quite superb; t23 shimmering malt of profound intensity; wonderful esters propel the barley-sugar sweetness to every corner of the palate; f22 enormously long with the gristy barley freshness actually upping in tempo; b22 so rare to see Glenfarclas in ex-bourbon form, and on this evidence we are being denied a Speyside classic. Beautifully made and matured, not a blemish to be found. **57%.** *288 bottles.*

✧ **Cadenhead's Authentic Collection Glenfarclas Aged 18 Years** Bourbon Hogshead, dist 88, bott May 06 **(87)** n20 not entirely happy with itself: some farmyardy notes confuse the rich barley; t23 big, semi-thuggish malt offers countless waves of salivating complexity; the oak plays a clever, restrained and spicy part; f22 oak to the fore; the barley refuses to secede; b22 firebrand malt that for all its rawness delivers intense quality by the mouthful... **55.2%.** *276 btls.*

✧ **Cadenhead's Chairman's Stock Glenfarclas Aged 33 Years** Bourbon Hogshead, dist 72, bott Sep 05 **(78)** n20 t21 f18 b19. The oak has too great a say and isn't really worth listening to. **43.4%.** *132 bottles.*

✧ **Cadenhead's Chairman's Stock Glenfarclas Aged 33 Years** Bourbon Hogshead, dist 73, bott Sept 06 **(93)** n23 zesty, Seville orange with a squeeze of kiwi fruit and blackberry. Yum! t24 for all the fruit nose, it's unmolested barley which arrives first. Soon the fruits are lining up again, not least pithy grape and blackberry; spices abound and astound; f22 oak has a big say after all this time but the cocoa-vanilla dryness counters the earlier fruit with aplomb; b24 as you might expect, a malt of such antiquity takes time to settle and is helped by oxidization. But when it hits its stride becomes a class act of the first order. **42.6%.** *120 btls.*

**Distillery No 3 Glenfarclas 1990** cask no 1106 **(88)** n18 t23 f24 b23 the honey that surges through this malt, unusual for this distillery in bottled form, is stuff of dreams. Highly unusual Glenfarclas in bottled form and, nose apart, quite outstanding. **46%. ncf.** *Denmark*

**The Lord Balliol Single Cask Aged 20 Years** cask no. 1 **(89) n**23 soft grape but with a feisty malt kick; **t**22 chewy, big, well-matured fruitcake character; **f**22 molassed sweetness topped with singed raisins; **b**22 big, knife and fork malt. There is no way of telling which of the two bottlings they have had so far is cask one or two. Hopefully these not [these notes?] will help. **46%. sc.** *282 bottles.*

**The Lord Balliol Single Cask Aged 20 Years** cask no. 2 **(87) n**21 crushed sultana but a little unsettled; **t**22 immensely sweet barley outperforms the chewy grape; **f**22 light, golden syrup on fruit chocolate; **b**22 not the best of starts on the nose, but the sweet character complements the drier, more roasty elements. There is no way of telling which of the two bottlings they have had so far is cask one or two. Hopefully these not will help. **46%. sc.** *Balliol.*

**MacLeod's Speyside Aged 8 Years (86) n**21 **t**22 **f**21 **b**22. A real delight of a dram: busy and fresh on the tastebuds. Just love the soft coffee tones as the first oak notes kick in. **40%.** *Ian MacLeod (Glenfarclas malt used, though not stated).*

**The MacTarnahan Pure Highland Single Malt 1994 Distillation Season Aged Nine Years (87) n**21 some attractive, lively young sherry; **t**22 first-class malt freshness, mouthwatering and and juicy thoroughout; **f**22 a return to spicier, citrussy, fruitier notes; **b**22 wonderful to see a Speysider this fresh and confident. High quality distilling evident. **46%.** *MacTarnahan's Brewing, Portland, Oregon.*

**The MacTarnahan Pure Highland Single Malt Aged 15 Years (78) n**17 **t**21 **f**19 **b**20. Big, sherried bruiser with enormous burnt raisin and spice but a sulphury shadow spoils the party. **46%.** *MacTarnahan's Brewing, Portland, Oregon.*

**The Whisky Exchange Glenfarclas 1974 Aged 30 Years** cask no. 6041, dist 11 Jul 74, bott 16 Nov 04 **(93) n**24 this sherry cask must have lived in a Spanish orange grove at some stage. Fruitier than a randy Spaniard; **t**23 just so deep ... layer upon layer alternating fruit and oak with some rich malt tossed in now and then for good measure; **f**23 long, spicy and showing excellent mocha; **b**23 a masterpiece from the Old School of Sherry Butts. Flawless. And floorless.... **50.5%.** *246 bottles.*

# GLENFIDDICH
### Speyside, 1887. William Grant & Sons. Working.

**Glenfiddich Special Reserve** (no age statement) db **(88) n**21 **t**23 **f**22 **b**22 no longer produced and now a malt for collectors: one that brings a tear to the eye of us 40-somethings. This is malt that kept us going when none others were obtainable. Never has the term "familiarity breeds contempt" ever been more apposite to any whisky as this. It's become de rigueur in recent years for connoisseurs to rubbish this whisky (though, it has to be said, never by me) as a poor man's malt. A brilliant, effervescent whisky missed more sorely than words can describe. I never thought I would find myself writing those words, but there you have it. I believe in honesty: I have built my reputation on it. And in all honesty, the whisky world is poorer without this unpretentious, landmark malt. The official "Bring Back The No-Age Statement Glenfiddich Special Reserve" campaign starts here. **40%**

**Glenfiddich Aged 12 Years Caoran Reserve** db **(81) n**20 **t**22 **f**19 **b**20. Pleasant enough, but duller and sweeter than before with complexity at a premium. **40%** ☉☉

**Glenfiddich Aged 12 Years Special Reserve** db **(80) n**20 **t**22 **f**19 **b**19. Delicious malt but perhaps a touch too much caramel subtracts from the otherwise juicy maltfest. Just not the same as the old (younger) version. Much flatter and less fun than its predecessor. **40%**

⌐ **Glenfiddich 15 Years Old** db **(95) n**23 beautifully sculpted nose: barley is firm, the oak bourbony, the sweetness controlled; **t**23 as intense as the nose suggests, again with compartmentalization. Early spices flit about while the malt is in concentrate form. Again the sweetness is allowed to progress only so far; **f**25 as deft as it's long, some lovely dark fudge and soft liquorice brushed with high roast Java guarantees the weight; **b**24 one of those stunning expressions this distillery is apt to come up with from time to time to underline the pedigree of its malt. Probably the best and most complete finish of the year: an essay in pure magnificence. **56.8%**

**Glenfiddich Aged 15 Years Cask Strength** db **(80)** n21 t21 f19 b19. Very toffeed: is it the oak or possibly caramel? Big dram, all the same. **51%**

**Glenfiddich Aged 15 Years Solera Reserve** db **(93)** n24 a marriage of citrus notes (especially oranges) subtle spices and oak; t23 honey leads the way with balancing spices and oak. The malt remains fresh and refreshing; f23 medium to long with soft sherry and gently building cocoa; **b**23 this is one of my regular drams, and the one I immediately display to people who rubbish Glenfiddich. Over the years I have noticed a shift in quality in both directions, the best being two marks higher, the worst cropping six points, mainly due to traces of sulphur on the sherry. However, this sample is pretty representative of a quite brilliant Speyside malt of awesome complexity. Just wish they'd up the strength and make it nonchillfiltered and noncoloured. **40%**

**Glenfiddich Aged 18 Years Ancient Reserve** db **(92)** n24 blood oranges, apples, the most gentle of smoke and oaky saltiness: delicate, complex and enormously sexy; t23 those oranges are there again as the malt melts in the mouth. Quite salty still but sherry and sultanas to fatten things up, brown sugar sweetens things a little; f22 a dry finale of medium length with unsweetened mocha: clean, chewy and well-defined; **b**23 another nail in the coffin of those who sniffily insist that Glenfiddich can't make good whisky. Taste this – and Solera Reserve – then find me two distillery-bottled malts of this age anywhere on Speyside that offers this enormity of complexity and sheer élan. ☉

**Glenfiddich Aged 21 Years Havana Reserve** db **(76)** n20 t20 f18 b18. I know a lot of people are jumping up and down about this one in excitement. But, sorry, I just don't get the picture. Cuban rums tend to be light in character, so in theory it should marry with the distillery's elegant character. However, we seem to have everything cancelling each other out leaving a pleasant experience with a decent cream coffee-toffee middle/finish, but little else besides to really get the pulses racing. **40%** ☉☉

**Glenfiddich 1974 Aged 29 Years** cask 2336 db **(88)** n23 softly, softly sherry punctuated by delicate and complex bourbon notes and the most distant hint of peat: sophisticated t23 bourbon theme arrives immediately, with fabulous "small grain" depth; a heavier fruit layer holds the roof of the mouth f19 thins out with grapey vanilla holding court **b**23 not all old Glenfiddich casks show such class: this is a minor gem of almost hypnotic complexity **48.9%** *The Whisky Exchange*

**Glenfiddich 30 Years Old** db **(89)** n22 exotic fruit in custard; t23 a sprightly fruity sweetness gives way to powering waves of barley and chalky vanilla; f21 soft and the most distant echo of smoke; **b**23 a much happier bottling than previously with barley still rampant and some charming complexity. **40%** ☉☉

**Glenfiddich Rare Collection 40 Years Old** db **(92)** n23 curiously and attractively smoked, lots of sweet vanilla and stunning spices: remarkable and beautiful; t24 brimming with oaky, toasty vanilla, malt punching through for silky, rich and mildly honied middle. Signs of oaky wear and tear, but do not detract from the overall beauty; f22 remains silky with a return of peat, mixed with cocoa; **b**23 quite brilliant for a Glenfiddich of this antiquity: rarely does it survive to this age. In fact, brilliant for any distillery. **43.6%.** *600 bottles.*

**Glenfiddich 1937** db **(94)** n24 smoky, almost agricultural farmyardy, with kippers spitting on the range, salted butter melting into them. Quite beautiful, the peat almost hitting perfection. Truly unique; t23 sweet malt that just dissolves around the mouth but leaving traces of the most elegant oak, almost too soft to be true. Again the smoke is just stunning in its elegance; f23 long, silky, soft oak and – amazingly – clean barley; **b**24 when this was distilled my football team,

Millwall, reached the FA Cup semi final. My late dad went to the game in my old mate Michael Jackson's country, 'uddersfield. We lost 2–1. They haven't reached the FA Cup semi finals since. I'll taste this again the next time we do ... it could be a long wait. From a sheer whisky perspective, proof – alongside some older Macallans – that Speyside once made a much peatier dram, one which perhaps only Ardmore can today match. How this whisky has remained this truly fabulous for so long has been entirely in the lap of the Gods. To whoever, whatever, is responsible: thank you!! NOTE TO 2005 EDITION: On April 4th, 2004, Millwall did, miraculously, reach another FA Cup semi-final. And beat the team they lost to in 1937. So my wait to taste it was shorter than I could even dream ... **40%**. *61 bottles only (going for in the region of £10,000 each).*

**Glenfiddich 1961 Vintage Reserve** db **(75)** n20 t19 f18 b18. Hasn't withstood the test of time quite as well as might be hoped. **43.2%. sc**.

**Glenfiddich 1967 Vintage Reserve** db **(87)** n23 t22 f21 b21. An unusually refreshing dram for such age. **43.6%. sc**.

**Glenfiddich Vintage Cask 1972** db **(82)** n20 t19 f22 b21. On the sappy side throughout but good honey depth. **48.9%**

**Glenfiddich 1972 Vintage Cask** cask no. 16031 db **(84)** n19 t22 f22 b21. Quite outstanding spices take weight off the oak and even allow the malt to show. Fights valiantly for its delightful identity with continuous arrivals of increasingly sweet malt. **47.3%**

**Glenfiddich 1972 Vintage Cask** cask no. 16032 db **(78)** n19 t21 f19 b19. Further evidence that this great distillery often struggles at these advanced ages. Apart from a wonderful delivery of exotic fruit and lush malt, this rapidly disappears in a forest of oak. **47.3%**

**Glenfiddich 1973 Vintage Reserve** db **(88)** n23 t23 f21 b21. Intense, crisp and spicy. **49.8%. sc**

⁘ **Glenfiddich 1973 Vintage** cask no. 9874 db **(94)** n23 citrus - made from concentrate: hard as nails nose really pumps out the barley-fruit marriage; t23 mouth-filling, luxuriously mouthwatering and barley, fruit and spice all at full throttle; f24 the oak is driven like a stake through the barley, but there is a fabulous molassed edge to it. The late viscosity carries a delightful hint of liquorice. Wow!; b24 I've been tasting these special casks from this distillery since before my hair went grey. I've sampled some good 'uns. This is possibly the best of the lot. **48.1%**

**Glenfiddich Private Vintage 1976 Exclusively for Queen Mary 2**, cask 21229, bott 04, db **(79)** n18 t22 f19 b20. For all the lovely honey touches, there is so much oak it would have been better designated for the Mary Rose.... **50.3%**

**Glenfiddich Reserve 1984** db **(90)** n21 t24 f22 b23. Glenfiddich at its most exuberant defying its age with a nonchalant charisma. **40%**

**Glenfiddich 1982 Private Collection for The Craigellachie Hotel** cask 3672, bott 03 db **(93)** n23 t24 f22 b24. The kind of star-studded bottling that makes you wonder why Glenfiddich don't do this kind of thing at this kind of age – or younger – more often. *288 bottles available at The Craigellachie Hotel, Speyside.*

**Glenfiddich Vintage Reserve 1991** db **(88)** n22 the first signs of a bourbony edge to the malt; some distinctive citrussy notes lighten it considerably; t22 delicate and malty, again the fruitiness is easily accessed; f22 soft spices and hints of tannins; b22 exceptionally even and elegant, this is from 200-odd bourbon casks...and it shows. Could have done with being bottled at 43 or 46% to take it up an extra notch. **40%**

**Cadenhead's Bond Reserve Glenfiddich-Glenlivet Distillery Aged 32 Years (83)** n19 t21 f22 b21. The nose and early arrival are oaksoaked, but the malty richness on the finish, plus the gathering spice, makes for a decent, if wrinkled, old 'un. **46.9%**

# GLENFLAGLER
## Lowland, 1965–1982. Demolished.

**Glenflagler 29 Years Old** db **(88)** n22 pretty ripe tangerines on vanilla ice cream. The oak makes for just about perfect bitter-sweet balance; t23 massive fresh fruity to start – citrus again – then an astounding intense and clean malty follow-through; f21 a quiet finale with the malt remaining confident, the oak adding a slight bitterness, but all under control; **b22** I've tasted some Glenflagler over the years, but nothing quite as accomplished as this. Lowlander it might be, but this has seen off the years with the grace and élan of the noblest Highlander. Forget about collector's item: eminently drinkable in its own right. **46%.** *A unique malt, as it was run through a Kentucky-type beer still before entering a pot still: a Lowlander made the American way.*

**Killyloch 35 Years Old** db **(80)** n20 thin, malty nose, but strong enough to see off the oak; t20 again a thin, wispy start wth the malt offering sweetness but always in the shadow of something oaky; f20 holds together reasonably well: the oak does play the major role but behaves itself while again the malt makes a valiant stand.; **b20** only the fourth Killyloch I have ever tasted – even including lab sample form – and, I admit, a lot better than I thought it might be. It doesn't have either the muscle or complexity to guarantee a great malt, but very few faults, either. Rather, it hangs on in there proudly – like a frail old lady successfully crossing a busy road – so you can relax and enjoy it for the pretty decent dram it is. **40%**

# GLEN GARIOCH
## Highland (Eastern), 1798. Suntory. Working.

**Glen Garioch 10 Years Old** db **(80)** n19 t22 f19 b20. Chunky and charming, this is a malt that once would have ripped your tonsils out. Much more sedate and even a touch of honey to the rich body. Toffeed at the finish. **40%**

**Glen Garioch 12 Years Old** db **(86)** n21 t22 f22 b21. Little complexity, but just sits very comfortably on the palate. **43%** ⊙

**Glen Garioch 15 Years Old** db **(91)** n22 the most gentle sweet peat dovetailing with sour apple and malt; t23 voluptuous and curvy malt tries to lord it over the gentle sweet peat – and fails; f23 oak is injected in almost perfect proportions; **b23** an enormous improvement on previous bottlings, sticking to a peculiarly Glengarioch character that offers immense chewability. Satisfying dramming, showing the distillery at its most refined and complex. **55.4%**

**Glen Garioch 16 Years Old** db **(88)** n20 fruity and spiced: a real heavyweight with a hint of peat thrown in; t23 clean, fresh oloroso character massively chewy with a fine malt thread; f22 lengthy, sweetening malt, a hint of peat and spice returns; **b23** lovely whisky, setting off a bit like a Dufftown but heading into a galaxy that poor old Speysider can only dream of. Really high grade malt with bags of character and attitude. **55.4%**

⬩⬩⬩ **Glen Garioch 16 Years Old Wine Finish** SL06.002, bott 13 Feb 06 db **(87)** n20 sweetish, wine-dulled and not entirely unlike a Portuguese rose; t23 an "after you, Claude" gentility to the melt-in-the mouth malt, though an on-rush of spice livens things up in towards the middle; f22 very long and works well considering the bitter almond note to the oak. The very faintest of smoke signals gives extra value; **b22** you have to check the label to confirm this is a 'Garioch! **53.8%**

**Glen Garioch 21 Years Old** db **(81)** n20 t21 f19 b20. For the last few years this has been one weird whisky: "cuckooland nuts" was how I think I described it last time. And so it remains. Its one that still has you scrambling through your memory to try and find a comparable malt. You can't. From the smoky-piny nose to the smoky-piny finish it is a dram that never quite feels at home with itself. That said, there is no shortage of entertainment value along the way; one that really has to be tried just for the (weird) experience. **43%**

**Glen Garioch 1958** db **(90) n**24 what a brilliant, heady, almost eccentric mix of once chunky peat, once vivid malt and now beautifully varnished oak; **t**21 loses its early balance but settles on a waxy honey thread to complement the slowly reasserting peat; **f**23 elegance in abundance as the oak plays lip-service to the sweet, chewy malt. Just so charming! **b**22 the distillery in its old clothes: and quite splendid it looks! **43%**. *328 bottles.*

**Glen Garioch Highland Tradition** db **(74) n**17 **t**20 **f**18 **b**19. The soapiness on the nose is a bit of a giveaway. **40%**

**Glen Garioch 12 Years The National Trust for Scotland** db **(77) n**18 **t**21 **d**19 **b**19. Mouthwatering, and would be even more so but for a toffeed intrusion. **43%**

⊰⊱ **Cadenhead's Authentic Collection Glengarioch Aged 13 Years** Bourbon Hogshead, dist 93, bott Sept 06 **(82) n**20 **t**22 **f**21 **b**19. Big barley at times yet just a shade on the thin side. And hot. **57.6%**. *264 bottles.*

⊰⊱ **Duncan Taylor Collection Glen Garioch 1988** cask no. 1554, dist Apr 88, bott May 06 **(80) n**19 **t**21 **f**20 **b**20. Sweet with banana and lime. But a bit leaden-footed and plateaus out. **55.8%**. *283 bottles.*

**Murray McDavid Maverick Glen Garioch 1993 Aged 10 Years** Bourbon cask W0407 finished in Leroy Grand Cru Romanée St Vincent Pinot Noir, bott 04 **(74) n**17 **t**21 **f**18 **b**18. Poor nose, as so often with wine cask interference, though the middle displays a mild, welcome touch of smoke. But for Californian Glen Garioch and Pinot fans it could have been much worse: it could have been finished in Merlot.... **46%**

⊰⊱ **Old Malt Cask Glen Garioch 14 Years Old** dist Nov 91, bott May 06 **(91) n**23 just like the old days: soft peats trundle about the nose though now with a salty, citrussy edge; **t**22 lovely weight with some smoky depth to the sweet, gristy barley. Some spices on this chewathon; **f**23 long with ultra-clean barley and soft cocoa notes to the smoke; **b**23 curiously oily, but so satisfying and sweet. Geary as God intended!! **50%**. *Douglas Laing. 326 bottles.*

**Old Malt Cask Glen Garioch Aged 15 Years** dist Sep 88, bott Oct 03 **(82) n**18 **t**22 **f**21 **b**21. A bourbony edge to the lively malt-rich middle. Good spice, cocoa and overall body feel. **50%. nc ncf sc.** *Douglas Laing. 336 bottles.*

⊰⊱ **Old Masters Glen Garioch 1988 Aged 18 Years** cask no. 1535, dist 88, bott 06 **(90) n**22 an intriguing Bowmore-type peat edge to this: curious as that is its sister distillery...; **t**23 the Bowmore-esque theme continues as the malt generates a freshness not normally associated with such relative old age; **f**22 excellent smoked vanilla and wonderful bitter-sweet balance; **b**23 handsome, weighty yet fresh. A real meal of a malt. **53.9%**. *James MacArthur.*

**Park Avenue Liquor Store Glen Garioch 24 Year Old** db **(90) n**23 lavender and moist ginger cake; **t**23 an eruption of warming spices and calming sweet malt; some herbal notes pitch in for the fun and even the strangest delivery of rye on a malt I've ever seen; **f**21 peat trickles from the base of toasted rye bread and vanilla; **b**23 another Glen Garioch that just heads off on a tangent and that you never quite get to the centre of. Weirdly fascinating, typically unique and genius in a bottle. **52.1%**. *New York.*

**Platinum Old and Rare Cask Glen Garioch Aged 35 Years** dist 68 **(75) n**18 **t**20 **f**18 **b**19. Like watching an ancient rock band having one come back too many. **56%**

**Platinum Old and Rare Cask Glen Garioch Aged 36 Years** dist Mar 67 **(82) n**19 **t**22 **f**21 **b**20. I was expecting something a lot peatier than this; no more than a hint of smoke: not enough to paper over the cracks though the torrid battle between oak and malt is entertaining. **55.5%**. *Douglas Laing.*

⊰⊱ **Provenance Glen Garioch Aged 11 Years** Refill Hogshead 1880, dist Autumn 94, bott Winter 06 **(85) n**20 **t**22 **f**21 **b**22. The refreshing fruits of a Garioch matured in a clapped-out third-fill cask, I assume. Not instantly recognizable as malt from this distillery, a burst of smoke gives some clue. Deliciously light...in every sense. **46%. nc ncf.** *McGibbon's.*

**Signatory Glen Garioch 1988 Aged 16 Years** cask 4107 dist 28 Oct 88, bott 27

May 05 **(90) n**23 at once weighty, yet incredibly delicate. There is the most subtle smoke mixing with barley sugar and varying levels of light oak; **t**22 the barley sugar rises first followed by bite and spice that bare the distillery's teeth; **f**22 soft smoke again, hint of Fishermen's Friend cough sweet, with some barley sugar for good measure; **b**23 only a touch of smoke, but as much barley sugar as you'll ever need. That said, the complexity is stunning. **55.3%.** *272 bottles.*

⦂⦂⦂ **The Spirit Safe & Cask Glen Garioch 1988 Aged 18 Years** Hogshead, dist Apr 88, bott May 06 **(94) n**23 a breakfast of chocolate spread on slightly burnt toast with kippers on a side-dish; **t**24 one of the best deliveries of a 'Garioch I've encountered for year or three: mouthwatering with a fabulous degree of barley-sodden demerara and manuka honey mixing with the smoky grist; rounded body holds exceptionally wonderful weight; **f**23 pulsing spices that begin halfway through the cycle continue towards the death; more vanilla and singed butterscotch generate a fabulous sweet balance to the drying oak; **b**24 almost the complete whisky experience. Wonderful! **56.1%. nc ncf.** *Celtic Whisky Compagnie, France.*

**Usquebaugh Society Glen Garioch Aged 16 Years** cask 1550, dist 18 Apr 88, bott 22 Apr 04 **(93) n**23 bliss ... so rare these days to come across a Glen Garioch still offering peat: the smoke here is delicate amid the sharper barley and citrus; just so much fruit lurking about here and astonishing honey drifts in if the glass is left for a while; **t**23 old fashioned "Geary" with a stupendous buzz of alcohol and malt combined tightly and a few layers of smoky bacon; **f**23 the sweet malt holds ground while cocoa gathers, lashings of chocolate raisins also aids the intensity; **b**24 when this was distilled it would have been a fireball of a spirit. Sixteen years on it has been tamed slightly by the oak but there is still no shortage of attitude. A throwback and one of the most entertaining bottlings from this distillery in quite a while. If you are looking for a reason to join a Dutch Whisky Society, this is it... **54.4% sc ucf.** *Holland 280 bottles.*

**Whisky Galore Glen Garioch 1988 Aged 15 Years (75) n**17 **t**20 **f**19 **b**19. Poor nose; to taste – sweetness on full throttle. **46%**

# GLENGLASSAUGH
**Speyside, 1875. Edrington. Silent since 1986.**

**Glenglassaugh 1973 Family Silver** db **(95) n**23 fruity and exceptionally complex: quite coastal with something vaguely citrussy, orange in particular; **t**24 melt-in-the-mouth malt that intensifies by the second. Never becomes either too sweet or vaguely woody. There is a soft hint of peat around the spices; **f**24 virtually without a blemish as the malt continues on its rich and merry way. Some sublime marmalade follows through on the spice; **b**24 from first to last this whisky caresses and teases. It is old but shows no over-ageing. It offers what appears a malt veneer but is complexity itself. Brilliant. And now, sadly, almost impossible to find. Except, possibly, at the Mansefield Hotel, Elgin. **40%**

⦂⦂⦂ **The MacPhail's Glenglassaugh Selected Single Distilleries Collection Aged 18 Years** dist 86, bott 04 **(85) n**23 **t**21 **f**21 **b**20 the nose may be like walking past a Surrey garden in August after a downpour but a meandering malt that struggles to focus. **40%**

⦂⦂⦂ **Murray McDavid Mission Glenglassaugh 1978 Aged 28 Years** Fresh Sherry/Syrah, bott 06 **(86) n**24 **t**20 **f**23 **b**19. What balance? One of the challenges of cask finishing is that you never know when it will get better or worse: the nature of the beast there is nothing with which you can compare the whisky. This works and fails on two massive levels, but it is worth experiencing for the astonishing nose and charming finale alone. **46.6%. nc ncf.** *500 bottles.*

⦂⦂⦂ **Old Malt Cask Glenglassaugh Aged 27 Years** dist Jan 78, bott Nov 05 **(85) n**22 **t**20 **f**22 **b**21. Straight up and down stuff for something of this antiquity. Plenty of class, though, and the bourbon dimension is appealing. **50%.** *Douglas Laing. 213 btls.*

## GLENGOYNE
**Highlands (Southwest), 1833. Peter Russell. Working.**

**Glengoyne 10 Years Old** db **(88) n**21 beautifully clean despite coal-gas bite. The barley is almost in concentrate form with a marmalade sweetness adding richness; **t**22 crisp, firm arrival with massive barley surge, seriously chewy and textbook bitter-sweet balance; **f**22 incredibly long and refined for such a light malt. The oak, which made soft noises in the middle now intensifies, but harmonises with the intense barley; **b**23 proof that to create balance you do not have to have peat at work. The secret is the intensity of barley intermingling with oak. Not a single negative note from first to last. A little beauty. **43%**

**Glengoyne 12 Year Old Cask Strength** db **(89) n**22 dusty coal scuttles and Dundee fruitcake: busy, earthy and inviting; **t**23 intensity of the malt takes you aback a little; takes time before the grape filters through; **f**22 much quieter as the sweetness makes a late entry; **b**22 the sulphur mentioned previously has gone. Instead we have a genuinely robust, confident yet graceful malt. **57.2%. nc ncf.**

**Glengoyne Limited Edition 15 Years Old Scottish Oak** db **(86) n**22 **t**21 **f**21 **b**22 perhaps not quite as complex as you might expect, but there is good balance and impressive clarity to the simplicity. **43%. nc.**

**Glengoyne 16 Years old** db bott Oct 03 **(85) n**24 **t**23 **f**18 **b**20. One of those real monsters that crop up from time to time: the Chrtstmas cake nose and immediate impact is nothing short of astonishing. But for every action, there's an equal and opposite reaction. **55.5%.** *For Clan Des Grands Malts, Paris*

**Glengoyne 17 Years Old** db **(76) n**19 **t**22 **f**17 **d**18. Elegant and charming at first, but the malt is too light to hold the oak. **43%**

⠴ **Glengoyne Single Cask LE Aged 19 Years** Sherry cask no.1227 db **(93) n**24 sherry as it should be: clean, fully of grapey weight yet light enough for the barley to sing a tune or two; **t**23 brilliant barley on the charm offensive then some real chewy grape kicks in; **f**23 plenty of liquorice seasoned with Demerara sugar: the way old oak should behave; **b**23 absolute bliss. **55.8%. sc.**

**Glengoyne 21 Years Old** db **(79) n**17 **t**22 **f**20 **b**20. The middle is honied, waxy and fabulous, but caramel flattens the fun. **43%**

**The Old 'Glen Guin' Glengoyne 21 Year Old** db **(85) n**21 **t**22 **f**20 **b**22. Another summer would have been one too many for this old chap. A fascinating, juicy improvement on the old 21-y-o version, though. **43%. nc.**

**Glengoyne 22 Years old** db bott 8 Apr 04 **(88) n**23 celery and bread with a jar of honey open somewhere; **t**22 the malt is embracing and stands up manfully against the oak; best though is the background sweetness offering malt at a second level; **f**21 surprisingly quick despite the hint of tannin; **b**22 excellent whisky showing little age damage. **43%.** *For Whisky Festival, Limburg.*

⠴ **Glengoyne Single Cask LE Aged 32 Years** White Rioja cask no.985 db **(92) n**25 unique. In 30-odd years of nosing this stuff, no other whisky has offered such a style which moves across so many oak types. Despite the obvious grape, it is the bourbony theme which underpins the style; next, light and heavy spices buzz the nose.....and then there is the dryness to the grape offset by the naturally sweet barley and bourbon. Fabulous; **t**23 bumbling and somewhat brusque, there is a discreet harshness which is softened by bourbon and barley; **f**23 still quite juicy yet hot and uncompromising; a little milky Java softens the finale; **b**21 Wow! What was all that about? Either there was no balance at all, or it was perfection... **48.7%. sc.**

⠴ **Glengoyne Single Cask LE Aged 37 Years** Sherry butt cask no.975 db **(91) n**24 no ifs to this butt: absolutely as clean and beautifully structured as they come, though oak and barley is at a premium; **t**23 mouthwatering and majestic, the wine digs deep; **f**22 simplistic, though a little barely does peak through; **b**22 in some ways the sherry works too well: so rich and soft is the wine, you cannot help think that some of the complexity has been washed away. **47.6%. sc.**

∵ **Old Malt Cask Glengoyne Aged 16 Years** dist Nov 88, bott Aug 05 **(89)** **n**23 barley and coal fires. Beautifully balanced; **t**22 salivating delivery; slightly uneven towards the middle and a little bitter, but it is the barley that continues to star; **f**22 bitter-burnt raisin and vanilla; **b**22 hints of sophistication, but just a slightly bitter edge. **50%.** *Douglas Laing. 331 bottles.*

∵ **Provenance Glengoyne 10 Years Old** dist Jun 96, bott Aug 06 **(80) n**19 **t**21 **f**20 **b**20. Young, clean, malty: pure blending fodder. **46%.** *McGibbon's.*

∵ **Provenance Glengoyne Aged 11 Years** Refill Hogshead DMG 2403, dist Winter 95, bott Winter 06 **(88) n**22 daises and dank grass; **t**23 charmingly refreshing with simple barley tones; **f**22 soft vanillas over barley; **b**21 clean and simple. **46%. nc ncf.** *McGibbon's.*

# GLEN GRANT
**Speyside, 1840. Campari. Working.**

**Glen Grant** db **(89) n**22 young, clean malt doesn't come much cleaner, maltier – or even younger than this: drooling stuff; **t**23 crisp, brittle grain nibbling at the tastebuds, lovely and mouthwatering; **f**22 more of the same: the intensity of the malt is stunning, yet it remains delicate throughout; **b**22 little oak, so not much complexity, but the balance and quality is nothing short of superb. **40%. nc.** *Italy.*

**Glen Grant 5 Years Old** db **(84) n**21 **t**21 **f**21 **b**21. Enormous malt, much more oily than the non-age-statement version with an unusual lack of crispness for a Glen Grant. Still mouthwateringly delicious, though! **40%. nc.** *Italy.*

**Glen Grant 10 Years Old** db **(87) n**21 fine, flinty grain, quite hard and with limited oak interference; **t**23 really mouthwatering, clean and fresh: not an offnote in sight; **f**21 gentle, almost half sleeping, just malt and a faint buzz of oak; **b**22 a relaxed, confident malt from a distillery that makes great whisky with effortless charm and each mouthful seems to show that it knows it. **43%. nc.**

**Glen Grant 14 Years Old Distillery Edition** db **(89) n**22 Scandinavian cracker bread; a touch salty and big oak; **t**23 you could cut diamonds with the barley: flinty hard with a distant golden sugary glow; **f**21 back to the salt and oak; **b**23 those of you expecting a soft, dreamy, Speyside ride will be in for a shock. Ride the punches and enjoy. **59.5%**

**Berrys' Own Selection Glen Grant 1969 34 Year Old**, Sherry cask, bott 03 **(76) n**18 **t**21 **f**18 **b**19. Sulphured and flawed: a rare dud from Doug. **46%.**

**Berrys' Own Selection Glen Grant 1972 31 Years Old**, Sherry cask, bott 04 **(94) n**24 curious hints of aguave amid the flawless oloroso; **t**24 dry oak at first then blossoms within seconds into a spicy number with the most sensational honeycomb and stewed plum giant; **f**23 long, lengthy, wave upon wave of oak and sherry; **b**23 just one of those spellbinding whiskies which must live in your cabinet. **51%.** *Berry Bros & Rudd.*

**Berrys' Own Selection Glen Grant 30 Year Old Sherry Cask**, bott 04 **(85) n**21 **t**21 **f**22 **b**21. Sweet, delicate: it is the piney and bourbony oak which stars. **46%.**

**Cadenhead's Authentic Collection Glen eGrant-Glenlivet Aged 16 Years** Bourbon Barrel, dist 89, bott May 05 **(94) n**23 granite-like, rock solid malt; just so clean and crisp; **t**24 like geological layers on a cliff face, one flinty note peels aways before another. Mouthwatering barley concentrate. Tastebud invigorating. And entirely mind-blowing; **f**24 successive strata of green-malty, mouthwatering, lip-puckering delight; **b**23 have you any idea how long I have been waiting for Chivas to unleash on us a malt of this stature? Almost a lifetime, it seems. Those of us in the know are aware that fabulous, unsherried casks like this exist from Glen Grant: why must we wait for an independent to show the world just how magnificent this distillery really is?? **61.6%.** *216 bottles.*

∵ **Cask Strength Glen Grant 1990** bott 01.02.06 **(85) n**21 **t**22 **f**21 **b**21. Ultra-intense barley sugar, but the oak keeps tabs on the sweetness. Good spice and body. **59.3%.** *Gordon & MacPhail, US Market.*

**Coopers Choice Glen Grant 1988 Port Wood Finish 15 Years Old** bott 03 **(79)** n22 t20 f18 b19. A natural caramel effect blasts the fruit out of the glass. **46%.**

⟐ **Dewar Rattray Individual Cask Bottling Glen Grant 1985 Aged 19 Years** cask no. 16914, dist Nov 85, bott Sept 05 **(95)** n24 if it wasn't for the firmness of the barley, this could have been raised in Kentucky: just stick your nose in this to discover the meaning of complexity; t24 shimmering barley forces the pace but is soon surrounded by those expected bourbony notes, complete with a rye spiciness – weird!! And beautiful; f23 strands of liquorice dipped in muscovado sugar. So elegant; b24 the new owners of Glen Grant better take a pretty close look at this. This will be hard pressed to produce anything finer. **58.4%.** 240 btls.

**Distillery No. 4 Glen Grant 1989** cask 23057 **(83)** n20 t21 f22 b20. A faultlessly simplistic expression: what it loses in complexity it makes up for with uncomplicated, deliciously honest malt. **46%**

⟐ **Duncan Taylor Collection Glen Grant 1969** cask no. 6232, dist Oct 69, bott Mar 06 **(88)** n23 butterscotch tart – I have just been transported back over 40 years to my primary school in Surrey ...; t23 masterful delivery of gently honeyed barley complete with body you that you so want to explore; dries a tad too quickly; f20 over oaked; b22 delicious at times but bottled about five or six years too late for greatness. **52.3%.** 143 bottles.

⟐ **Duncan Taylor Collection Glen Grant 1970** cask no. 827, dist Feb 70, bott Apr 06 **(92)** n23 lashings of natural toffee lightened by a bourbon-style small grain buzz. Highly complex and rich; t24 big, mouth-filling and immensely chewy early on. Fabulous structure to the barley which is firm enough to hold the oak and spice with comfort; a some lightly roasted Cuban also makes an entry; f22 the cracks that began to appear in the late middle begin to widen; still a lovely bourbon sheen to this; b23 a fascinating bourbony element has appeared. **53%**

**Duncan Taylor Glen Grant 1970 Aged 24 Years** cask 831 **(85)** n22 t22 f20 b21. Very drinkable, very big and very over-aged. **54.2%**

⟐ **Duncan Taylor Collection Glen Grant 1970 Aged 36 Years** cask no. 830, dist Feb 70, bott 17 May 06 **(89)** n23 one assumes sherry, but the enormity of this almost suggests a pre-carameled Demerara rum; t23 seriously big: requires a second mouthful to get a bearing on this: the intensity of the oak with all its burnt fudge tries to confuse, but there is something else in this swamp. Kind of fruity. Miraculously, some barley actually punctures through and salivates the tastebuds; f21 do you know those brown and black liquorice allsorts? Imagine that in concentrate with some extra oak for good measure; b22 good God! What the hell was that? If it was a sherry butt, then that was pretty strange fruit coming from it. A must for whisky clubs all over the globe to muse over. **54.1%.** 140 btls.

⟐ **Duncan Taylor Special Selection No 2 Glen Grant 1970** cask no. 122, dist 1970, bott Nov 05 **(95)** n24 more along the same lines of the 54.1% above, except the oak is less aggressive and the fruit is softer and slightly more raisiny; t24 if I was in my lab blending a rum, I wouldn't bat an eyelid at this: I have seen several species of these from Guyana. Thrillingly intense, with a stunning sweetness, the oak plays a wonderful spicy part. The usual coffee and cocoa notes are there, plus a mild bourbony overture. It is hard to find a glass big enough for this one ...; f23 enormous yet relaxed, sumptuous waves of varying intensity and sweetness wash over the tastebuds for ages; b24 just one of those great old whiskies that pops up from time to time. In exchange for eternal life, it has sold its soul for a rummy depth. But when the result is this astonishing, who the hell cares??? **57.1%.** 548 bottles

**Gordon & MacPhail Glen Grant 1948 (90)** n23 big oranges, oak and smoke; t24 massive malt intensity, with the oak being nothing like as threatening as the nose suggests. Some peat drifts around, filling in some age-cracks, but the malt is quite overwhelming; f21 lots of toffee-vanilla; b22 a real cracker of a malt displaying controlled power and aggression. Stunning. **40%**

**Gordon & MacPhail Glen Grant 1950 (90)** n23 remarkable: oak, presumably, takes the form of newly opened horsechestnuts while soft grapey notes waft around: highly unusual and very enticing; **t**23 massively sweet: both malt and sultana concentrate congregate for a whisky version of the noble rot; **f**22 some smoke and cocoa take a bow; **b**22 no spitting out on this one: has to be one of the world's most extraordinary bottlings. Not only of enormous age, but remains entirely intact and revelling in its sweet glory. Defiant and utterly delightful. **40%**

**Gordon & MacPhail Glen Grant 1952 (85)** n24 Arbroath smokies, sweet and malty: stunning; **t**21 some early oak creates a chalky field in which the fruit and grassy malt works; **f**19 tiring rapidly, the oak is really giving the malt a hard time. Some very late smoke helps cushion the attack; **b**21 in 1992 I bought a bottle of this to mark my wife's 40th birthday. Seven months later we were no longer an item: obviously she didn't like the whisky, so I kept it … **40%**

**James MacArthur Glen Grant 1993 11 Year Old**, bott Apr 05 **(84)** n21 t22 f20 **b**21. Beautiful malt crescendo. **43%. ncf.**

⮞ **James MacArthur Glen Grant 1993 Aged 11 Years** bott 05 **(88)** n22 intense, brittle barley overwhelms the slightest oak overture; **t**22 mouthwatering; limited sweet development; **f**22 more relaxed with subtle oil just softening the barley and traces of golden syrup towards the finale; **b**22 precise, clipped malt. Would you expect anything else? **43%**

⮞ **Lonach Glen Grant 31 Years Old (84)** n21 t22 f21 **b**20. Exceptionally firm barley for its age; enjoys a sugar-coated lustre and good depth. **42.3%.**

⮞ **Lonach Glen Grant 35 Years Old (83)** n20 t21 f21 **b**21. Creaks a bit, but some lovely barley sugar and liquorice. **41.8%.** *Duncan Taylor.*

⮞ **Lonach Glen Grant 1970** cask no. 3487, dist May 70, bott Apr 06 **(78)** n22 **t**19 f19 **b**18. Exotic fruit early on, but age catches up with it. **41.5%.** *168 btls.*

**MacLeod's Extremely Rare Glen Grant 1949** cask no. 3447 **(83)** n24 sweet barley sugar, with a touch of mint and some delicate smoke. The oak offers a dry edge and combines with the smoke to deliver a touch of spice. Beautifully refined but unmistakably ancient; **t**21 almost a sugary arrival and then a big unleashing of controlled oak: a polarised delivery with the move from sweet to dry with extraordinary swiftness; **f**19 dries with some late echoes of soft peat; **b**19 a lost cask found a few summers too late for true greatness, although the nose is fabulously complex. For those born in 1949 a fascinating annual dip into the past. **46%.** *80 bottles: one can be found at TasTToe, Kampenhout, Belgium.*

**Murray McDavid Mission Glen Grant 1969 (80)** n20 t19 f20 **b**21. Tangy, sharp orange coated in chocolate. **46%. nc ncf.**

⮞ **Norse Cask Selection Glen Grant 1967 Aged 38 Years (86)** n21 t23 f21 **b**21. One of those ancient malts hanging on by the slenderest thread to attractiveness and elegance. Another month or two in the cask and this would have gone. **44.2%.** *QualityWorld, Denmark.*

⮞ **Old Malt Cask Glen Grant** Wine finish, dist Nov 92, bott Oct 05 **(92)** n23 crushed green and white peppers give an unexpected twist to the fruity barley; **t**23 beautifully clean delivery and sweet. The crispness of the barley ensures that shape and direction is maintained; **f**23 this has to be one of the cleanest finishes to any wine cask I've ever come across: the barley is pristine and the soft fruits juicy; **b**23 easily one of the better wine finishes around: a malt that is in the pink in every sense… **50%.** *Douglas Laing. 272 bottles.*

**Old Malt Cask Glen Grant Aged 12 Years** dist Apr 91, bott Jan 04 **(84)** n19 t23 f21 **b**21. A bitty, busy malt full of enjoyably stereotypical Speyside characteristics. The malt is well defined and very clean, the oak well behaved and adding a salty twist. Only the surprisingly tired nose loses points. **50%. nc ncf sc.** *324 btls.*

**Platinum Old and Rare Cask Glen Grant 1967** bott 04 **(92)** n22 freshly roasted coffee offers a more Demerara rum characteristic than Speyside. Hints of tired oak but the rich intensity just about conquers all; **t**23 only a lifetime in a fresh oloroso butt can offer this type of bitter-sweet, softly spiced gentle giant; f24 continues on its brilliantly chewy way; liquorice adding to the coffee and sherry. Elephantine stuff; b23 half whisky half Demerara rum: entirely astonishing. The enormity of the dram never quit subtracts from the underlying delicacy of this beast. From the Golden Age of sherry butts, this is now a dying breed. **49.6%**.

**Private Collection Glen Grant 1953 (95)** n24 mountainous oloroso. Pretty crisp and shapely for the great age, though some salt has crept in; t24 salty and spicy, the oloroso develops a life of its own. Loads of coffee notes and excellent bitter-sweet ratio; f23 a silky coating of salty sherry encrusts the tastebuds guaranteeing an amazingly long and deep finale; b24 What can be said? Except that this malt has no right whatsoever to be anything close to this good. G&M have their detractors, and sometimes they do make life hard for themselves. But when it comes to delivering golden treasures from the past they are the Lord Caernarvon of the whisky world. A dry masterpiece. **45%**. *Gordon & MacPhail.*

**Private Cellars Selection Glen Grant 1977** bott 03 **(79)** n20 t21 f18 b20. Firm with an honest, honied edge but the finish is dull. **43%**. *Speyside Distillers.*

**Scott's Selection Glen Grant 1977** bott Jun 03 **(89)** n21 t23 f22 b23. The honey-spice holds off the oak brilliantly. **55.4%**. *Robert Scott & Co.*

# GLEN KEITH
**Speyside, 1957. Chivas. Silent.**

**Glen Keith 10 Years Old** db **(80)** n22 t21 f18 b19. A malty if thin dram that finishes with a whimper after an impressively refreshing, grassy start. **43%**

**Glen Keith Distilled Before 1983** db **(79)** n21 t21 f18 b20. Lemon-drop nose of concentrated malt on palate; fades just too much towards oaky bitterness. **43%**

⫶⫶⫶ **Connoisseurs Choice Glen Keith Aged 36 Years** Refill Sherry Hogshead, dist 67, bott 03 **(85)** n22 t22 f21 b20. A clean dram brimming with cream toffee and attractive spices. Attractive and very drinkable but a bit too closed on the finale and lacking development. **46%**.

⫶⫶⫶ **Connoisseurs Choice Glen Keith 1993 (91)** n22 freshly cut rhubarb, barely ripened apple and crisp barley; t24 a real malt storm, with a blizzard of barley melting 'gainst the tastebuds – a real and rare hard-soft complexity; f22 an almost Glen Grantish follow through of rock hard grain: clean and revitalizing; b23 I had to look twice to check the distillery!! You don't see Glen Keiths like this every day – alas! **46%**. *Gordon & MacPhail.*

**Coopers Choice Glen Keith 1969 36 Years Old** Single Cask Range, bott 05 **(89)** n22 pure bourbon; t23 leathery-liquorice with enormous sweet grains; f22 wave upon wave of sweet malt and spiced oak, almost with rye-style mouthwatering fruitiness and hardness; b22 well, yawl, I plumb had no idea that this here critter distillery was found smack in middle of Blue Grass country. I'll be a son of a gun.... **49.8%**. *Vintage Malt Whisky Co.*

**Duncan Taylor Collection Glen Keith 1971 Aged 33 Years (78)** n21 t20 f18 b19. One of those malts that sherry lovers will shoot me down in flames about. Massive sherry, but for me that's exactly the problem: the distillery character has been obliterated and it's all too one-dimensional. **50.8%**

**Old Malt Cask Glen Keith Aged 14 Years** dist Mar 89, bott Sep 03 **(80)** n19 t21 f20 b20. Thin nose but compensated by sweet and spicy barley attack on the palate; bitter almond finish. 50%. nc ncf sc. Douglas Laing. 378 bottles. Old Master's Glen Keith 1974 (78) n21 t20 f19 b18. Attractive, rich bourbon notes, but never quite gets into gear. **52.7%**. *James MacArthur.*

# GLENKINCHIE
**Lowland, 1837. Diageo. Working.**

**Glenkinchie 10 Years Old** db **(79)** n20 t20 f19 b20. No great shakes on the nose; one-dimensional sweetness on the palate. What the hell was all that about? **43%**

∴ **Cadenhead's Authentic Collection Glenkinchie Aged 18 Years** Bourbon Hogshead dist 87, bott February 06 **(88) n**21 lazy butterscotch; **t**23 juicy, sharp, tangy barley; **f**22 spiced vanilla with a late barley sheen; **b**22 good to see a Lowlander offering so much life at this age – lovely! **56.5%.** *246 btls.*

# THE GLENLIVET
## Speyside 1824. Chivas. Working.

**The Glenlivet Aged 12 Years** db **(83) n**20 **t**22 **f**20 **b**21. A surfeit of apples on both nose and body. The malt is quite rich at first but thins out for the vanilla and thick toffee at the death. **40%**

**The Glenlivet Aged 12 Years American Oak Finish** db **(86) n**21 **t**22 **f**22 **b**21. Stylish and under-stated in every department. **40%**

**The Glenlivet Aged 12 Years French Oak Finished** db **(83) n**21 **t**22 **f**20 **b**20. The oak is extraordinary and offers an unusual style of spiciness, though the finish is flatter than might be expected. Good bitter-sweet sync. **40%.**

**The Glenlivet 12 Years Old First Fill Matured** db **(86) n**23 **t**21 **f**21 **b**21. Delightful, playful malt that is slightly underpowered. **40%**

**The Glenlivet Aged 15 Years** db **(84) n**22 **t**21 **f**20 **b**21. Good spice and complexity. Very well-weighted throughout. **43%**

∴ **The Glenlivet 15 Years of Age** db **(80) n**19 **t**21 **f**20 **b**20. There is an undeniable charm to the countless waves of malt and oak. But don't expect much in the way of complexity or charisma. **40%**

**The Glenlivet Aged 15 Years French Oak** bott 04 db **(86) n**21 **t**22 **f**21 **b**22. A by no means straightforward Glenlivet with an accentuated bitter-sweet theme. **43%**

**The Glenlivet French Oak Reserve 15 Years Old** db **(77) n**20 **t**20 **f**18 **b**19. Half-decent honey, but for me this style is a definite "non". **40%**

**The Glenlivet Distillery Edition 16 Years Old** db **(84) n**19 **t**23 **f**21 **b**21. Very mildly flawed nose translates elsewhere, but the oily, mildly estery kick is really excellent. **58.1%**

**The Glenlivet 18 Years Old** db **(87) n**22 fresh for its age, though the old smoke has gone; **t**22 attractive fruity complexity and quite a decent spice presence; **f**21 quietens and dries rapidly, lots of vanilla; **b**22 another Glenlivet that starts beautifully but lacks stamina. **43%**

**The Glenlivet Archive Aged 21 Years** db **(77) n**21 **t**20 **f**18 **b**18. The more I have got to know this whisky, the more I despair of it. After a lovely fruity start, way too much toffee-caramel, I'm afraid. **43%**

**The Glenlivet Cellar Collection 1959** bott 02 db **(90) n**22 **t**23 **f**22 **b**23. No malt has any right to be this good at this kind of age. Oak has done very little damage, apart from giving a mildly bourbony feel amid some indulgent liquorice, and that can hardly be construed as damage at all. It is the élan of the fruitiness jousting with the rich malt that impresses most. If anyone was born in 1959, this is the bottle you must buy: a 2cl nip every birthday should be enough to see you through to the end in style. **42.28%**

**The Glenlivet Cellar Collection 1964** bott 04 db **(82) n**23 **t**20 **f**19 **b**20. Curious, delightful nose with memories of school at that time: polished floors and plasticine with oranges at break. Too oaky on the palate, though. **45.05% ncf**

∴ **The Glenlivet Cellar Collection 1964** Bottle code 2LBF901, bott 04 db **(93) n**24 unequivocal excellence. The sherry is entirely sulphur free and pulses with grape and sultana richness. This is old-time sherry influence but the barley and oak play their part in maximizing complexity. A treat; **t**23 lush, soft and melts into the tastebuds to offer a chalky, peppered fruitiness. Mouthwatering and mesmerizing, even after 40 years; **f**23 tannins and leather abound, but there is enough muscovado sweetness to edge out the growing oaky-vanilla; **b**23 former distillery manager Jim Cryle selected the casks for this one: he knew exactly what he was doing. **45.1%.** *1824 bottles.*

⁘ **The Glenlivet Cellar Collection 1972** bott Aug 05 db **(93)** n22 pleasing honeycombed fusion of oak and barley also encompasses spice; just a hint of oak tiredness detracts; t24 monumental arrival with searing spices pressing home a slightly bourbony theme. Languid liquorice and honeycomb delight; f23 dries towards cocoa and vanilla; **b**24 there is a brilliance to this which will delight bourbon lovers every bit as much as Scotch drinkers. **52.3%**

**The Glenlivet Cellar Collection 1983** Finished in French Oak, bott 03 db **(88)** n22 t23 f21 **b**22. Sophistication and attitude rolled into one. **46%**

**The Glenlivet Nadurra 16 Years old** db **(94)** n22 caramelised ginger wrapped in bitter chocolate; t24 enveloping, spellbinding, shocking...an immediate outbreak of Deremara sugar before the tastebuds are crept up on by stealthy malt and coshed by a voluptuous outbreak of Fox's ginger chocolate biscuits; the middle arrival of faintly chilli-ish spice combines beautifully with the warming ginger; f24 lengthier and with more ginger than a very lengthy, gingery thing; **b**24 in some respects one of the sweetest single malts of all time. It would be too sweet altogether except for a balancing ginger-led spice attack that drags the oak into action. The closest thing to a liqueur whisky you will ever find: pure entertainment, sheer class and immeasurable fun. **48%**

**The Glenlivet Vintage 1967** db **(85)** n21 t22 f21 **b**21 excellent cocoa-sherry complexity and no over-ageing.

**The Glenlivet Vintage 1968** db **(82)** n20 t22 f20 **b**20. Firm oak, interesting bite.

**The Glenlivet Vintage 1969** db **(89)** n22 t24 f21 ; **b**22. Fruitcake whisky with great but controlled age.

**The Glenlivet Vintage 1970** db **(93)** n24 t23 f22 **b**24. One of the most delicate distillery-bottled Glenlivets I have tasted.

**The Glenlivet Vintage 1972** db **(84)** n21 t22 f20 **b**21. Very dry sherry ensures complexity and maximum spice.

⁘ **Adelphi Glenlivet 1991 Aged 15 Years** Bourbon Hogshead cask 55486, dist 91, bott Jun 06 **(90)** n21 intense, as if there is a high degree of first-fill bourbon influence; t23 stunning! The weight and intensity of the barley works perfectly with the richness offered by the oak. Busy and biting the chewy harmonisation is engrossing; f23 chocolate fudge and walnuts; **b**23 what a glorious bottling this is. Compare this to the lacklustre 15-year-old distillery bottling: you could weep! **59.7%**. *258 bottles.*

**Adelphi Glenlivet 26 Years Old** cask 13120, dist 77, bott 03 **(84)** n21 t22 f21 **b**20. Firm to the point of brittle; the rich malt dominates especially early on. **57%**

**Adelphi Glenlivet 23 Years Old** cask 13743, dist 80 bott 03 **(86)** n21 t21 f22 **b**22. The intensity of the vanilla in conjunction with the barley goes into overdrive **50.6%**

⁘ **Berry's' Own Selection Glenlivet 1972 Aged 32 Years** **(86)** n19 t23 f22 **b**22. A fascinating cask which cherishes its vitality. **46%**. *Berry Bros & Rudd.*

⁘ **Berry's' Own Selection Glenlivet 1974 Aged 32 Years** **(84)** n19 t22 f21 **b**22. A well-mannered dram offering barley-sugar in all the right places. But has a few bags under the eyes. **46%**. *Berry Bros & Rudd.*

**Berrys' Own Selection Glenlivet 1975 Aged 28 Years** bott 04 **(87)** n18 painfully OTT oak; t23 marauding, red-hot spices fizz against the ultra-sweet malt concentrate; f23 exceptional balance towards the death as bourbony-leathery oak makes for a deliciously chewy finale; **b**23 the nose and early arrival points towards one shagged-out dram, but it recovers supremely. **56.8%**.

⁘ **Berry's' Own Selection Glenlivet 1975 Aged 31 Years** **(77)** n19 t21 f18 **b**19. A fraction bland on the nose, shapeless and, early mouthwatering spiced-delivery apart, all background noise and too little structure. **54%**. *Berry Bros.*

⁘ **Cadenhead's Chairman's Stock Glenlivet (Minmore) Aged 30 Years** Sherry butt, dist 76, bott Sept 06 **(95)** n24 sumptuous, seasoned grape; moist fruitcake with the odd burnt raisin. Like sticking your head in a fabulous sherry cask; t24 a delivery to die for: pure grapey silk. The accompanying spices also inject an oaky dryness, but the balance is sublime; **f**23 much drier now with the oak having the major say through a cocoa-dusted finale. Thins out, too; **b**24 I have nosed so many dud sherry casks today this almost brings a tear to the eye when the real thing comes along. Hunt a bottle of this unspoiled nectar down at all costs! Nigh faultless malt. **57.1%**. *432 bottles.*

❧ **Cadenhead's Glenlivet (Minmore) Chairman's Stock Aged 35 Years** Sherry butt dist 70, bott Sep 05 **(63) n**15 **t**18 **f**14 **b**16. Iffy and a not very good butt. **58.2%.** *275 bottles.*

❧ **Cask Strength Glenlivet 1990** American Hogshead casks 26928/9, dist 21 Nov 90, bott 21 Apr 05 **(84) n**19 **t**22 **f**22 **b**21. Only toward the finish does this ultimately satisfying dram begin to talk complexity: the arrival is all about uncomplicated and delicious juicy barley. Quite lovely. **59.4%. ncf.** *G&M*

**Celtic Heartlands Glenlivet 1968 (90) n**22 rickety, creaking oak but bound together by a honey core; **t**23 again it is the honey that binds this malt together, with burnt toast bitterness offering a strangely attractive counterbalance; **f**22 a more civilised landing of doughy grain and custardy oak; **b**23 this is one hell of a journey...hang on to your hats and take a deep breath before setting out on this one. **41.2%.** *Jim McEwan/Bruichladdich. American Oak Hogshead.*

**Coopers Choice Glenlivet 1971 Single Cask 32 Years Old** bott 04 **(93) n**23 clean, spicy sherry; dusty cupboards old leather; **t**23 classy, bitter-sweet arrival with early sherry-malt battles; the middle is slightly flawed as the oak takes too aggressive control but this lasts a few moments only; **f**24 returns to form with the sweet malt battling it out with the burnt raisins; **b**23 just one of those exceptional old casks one is lucky enough to stumble across now and again. **46%. nc ncf.**

**Coopers Choice Glenlivet 1972 Sherry Cask Aged 30 Years** bott 03 **(88) n**22 **t**21 **f**23 **b**22. An oddly behaved sherry butt, but after 30 years strange things do sometimes happen. **46%.** *Vintage Malt Whisky Company.*

**Coopers Choice Glenlivet 1991 13 Years Old Single Cask Range,** bott 04 **(83) n**21 **t**22 **f**20 **b**20. Light and simplistic blend of butterscotch and malt. **43%.**

❧ **D&M Aficionados' Club Bottling Glenlivet Aged 27 Years** cask 6097, dist Mar 79 **(91) n**21 a touch lazy, but sandpaper and barley make an interesting mix; **t**24 absolutely top-of-the-range arrival with an intensity to the sweet malt that has to be tasted to be believed; hints of Demerara and leather sit comfortably within the natural fudge. The spongy mouth-feel orbits perfection; **f**23 a really classy fade-out with hints of honey balancing out the gathering oak; **b**23 a corker of a dram whose arrival on the palate is as profound as it is beguiling. **43%. nc ncf.** *US*

**Duncan Taylor Glenlivet 1968 Aged 35 Years** cask 2840 **(86) n**21 **t**22 **f**21 **b**22. Salty, delicate for age: like Springbank but with only two thirds complexity. **43.6%**

❧ **Duncan Taylor Collection Glenlivet 1968** cask 5240, dist Sept 68, bott Mar 06 **(84) n**19 **t**23 **f**21 **b**21. Put your nose too close to this and you'll get splinters. Creaky, but lip-smacking sophistication on the arrival. **53.4%.** *113 btls.*

❧ **Duncan Taylor Collection Glenlivet 1970** cask 1999, dist Feb 70, bott Apr 06 **(81) n**20 **t**22 **f**19 **b**20. A bit furry around the finish but the arrival radiates spiced barley. **54.8%.** *112 bottles.*

❧ **Duncan Taylor Collection Glenlivet 1988** dist Sept 88, bott Oct 05 **(85) n**20 **t**22 **f**21 **b**22. Enjoyable to the extent of almost being a cliché for the distillery. **46.1%.** *1806 bottles.*

**George & J.G Smith's Glenlivet 1974 (78) n**19 **t**20 **f**20 **b**19. Friendly, docile, liquorice-oak controlled. **40%.** *Gordon & MacPhail.*

**Glenscoma Glenlivet 1986 17 Years Old (88) n**21 nutty, a hint of smoke and a nip of warming sherry; **t**22 mouthwatering, lush malt and then a wall of bristling spice; **f**23 a few estery hints of rye-fruited bourbon; **b**22 quite a dashing fellow with a petulant streak. **57.8%.** *Scoma, Germany.*

❧ **Lonach Glenlivet 37 Years Old (86) n**21 **t**21 **f**22 **b**22 chic and fruity. **43.1%**

⁕ **Old Malt Cask Glenlivet 20 Years Old** dist Dec 85, bott Oct 05 **(86) n**20 **t**22 **f**22 **b**22. Enjoyable, but further proof that this distillery stubbornly refuses to surprise. **50%.** *Douglas Laing. 331 bottles.*

⁕ **Old Malt Cask Glenlivet Aged 25 Years** dist Apr 80, bott Oct 05 **(92) n**23 a flamboyant aroma (for a Glenlivet) with the vaguest nod towards passion fruit and lime; **t**23 silky-textured, the barley coats the mouth before a teasing fanfare of exotic fruit, which never quite arrives; **f**23 lovely balance to this with a wisp of smoke, the oak never offering dryness and the barley and semi-fruit sailing off into the sunset; **b**23 often you can tell a malt that is OTT: all kinds of exotic fruit abound. Here it has been nipped in the bud and the result borders true excellence. **50%.** *Douglas Laing. 260 bottles.*

⁕ **Old Masters Glenlivet 1996 Aged 9 Years** cask 906678, dist 96, bott 06 **(88) n**21 soft banana amid intense barley; **t**22 gushing, mouthwatering barley-sugar jazzed up with spice; **f**23 lovely delivery of passing honey preludes the light oak as the complexity intensifies; **b**22 refreshing to see an honest dram like this at such a sprightly age. A little dazzler. **58.5%.** *James MacArthur.*

⁕ **Old Masters Glenlivet 28 Years Old** cask 19753, dist 77, bott 06 **(89) n**22 crunchy, sprightly barley; **t**23 just so juicy with a soft honey hint adding to the zesty barley; **f**22 soft oils, lingering malt; **b**22 hardly the most complex of malts, but the refreshing youthfulness is a real turn up for the books. **53.6%.** *150 btls.*

**The Peated Malt Old Ballantruan Speyside Glenlivet** (see Tomintoul )

**Private Collection Smith's Glenlivet 1943 (87) n**21 an astonishing mixture of understated oaky notes intertwined with clean, distinctive malt and the most distant aroma of peat: a gentleman of an aroma; **t**20 maintains a malty integrity despite the accompaniment of oak; **f**23 for its age, quite astounding: no over-the-top oak or dryness, just soothing waves of malty-oak which are neither bitter nor sweet; **b**23 remarkable. How a whisky remains this enjoyable after so many years is what makes spending a lifetime investigating the world's greatest drink such a great profession! No off-notes and, whilst it is not the greatest dram you will ever find, it is certainly the finest wartime relic you can find to keep you company whilst watching Whisky Galore. **40%.** *Gordon & MacPhail.*

⁕ **The Queen of the Moorlands Rare Cask Glenlivet 30 Years Old "The Chairman's Bottling" Edition XVI (94) n**24 from the toffee-apple school of sherry butt brilliance: fresh, clean and ripe and just the right degree of herbs and spices for balance. A stunner; **t**24 mouth-watering, melt-in-the mouth delivery which starts sweetness and kind but peppers up spectacularly; **f**23 back to toffee apples and burst of lush barley to boot; **b**23 one of those wonderful sherry casks that leaves most of today's in the shade. An absolute must – even for non-sherry lovers! **54%.** *The Wine Shop Leek and Congleton, UK.*

**Scott's Selection Glenlivet 1977** bott 05 **(88) n**21 peppery, buttery; **t**23 lashings of mildly honied malt against bitter oak: astonishingly rich for its age; **f**22 good late balance with the oak making itself heard but failing to entirely penetrate the malt and marmalade; **b**22 shows signs of tiredness but there are some marvellous moments to this. **47.1%.** *Speyside Distillers.*

⁕ **Scott's Selection Glenlivet 1977** bott 05 **(93) n**23 a soft, citric accent to the refreshing barley; **t**24 just unbelievable! Twenty-eight years old and all the freshness of a malt less than half that age. The barley really is about as mouthwatering as it comes at that age and the malty waves bounce against the tastebuds seemingly for ever. Gentle spices add complexity; **f**23 just a soft vanilla feel to this, but it's the rich malt that remains on show; **b**23 now this is how I dream of old Glenlivets: unmolested by fancy casks and shouting its ultra-intense, mouthwatering barley from the highest, time- and weather-beaten peaks of Speyside. **49%.** *Speyside Distillers.*

**Smith's Glenlivet 1948 (85) n**21 **t**22 **f**21 **b**21. Good whisky which is impressive on its own merits, let alone the great age. *Gordon & MacPhail.*

**Smith's Glenlivet 1951 (82) n**19 **t**21 **f**21 **b**21 silky and sweet with delicious milky, malty depth. Not half as oaky as the nose threatens. **40%**.

**Smith's Glenlivet 1955 (87) n**23 big ripe fruit, sensuously clean within a frame of oak and malt; **t**20 oak immediately asserts itself, then a follow-through of fruit and soft peat, fruitcake rich; **f**22 much more sensible and structured with some mouthwatering malt adding complexity; **b**22 absolutely hypnotic whisky. **40%**.

**The Un-chillfiltered Collection Glenrothes Vintage 1990** cask 10985, dist 11 May 90, bott 23 Jan 04 **(69) n**18 **t**18 **f**16 **b**17. Sulphur spoiled. **46%**. *Signatory*

**Wilson & Morgan Barrel Selection 28 Years Old** hogshead N.5727 dist 75, bott 03 **(87) n**23 **t**22 **f**20 **b**22. No little sophistication. **46%**

**Wilson & Morgan Barrel Selection Glenlivet 28 Years Old** dist 75, bott 03 Hogshead No 5727 **(92) n**22 **t**23 **f**24 **b**23. This whisky has spent 28 years in the kind of characterful cask that us long-in-the-tooth whisky specialists shed a tear or two over. Masterful for its antiquity. **46%**

## GLENLOCHY
### Highland (Western), 1898–1983. Closed.

**Platinum Old and Rare Glenlochy 38 Years Old** dist May 65 **(78) n**21 **t**19 **f**19 **b**19. Fruity and juicy but you are still left picking out the splinters. **42.5%**.

**Platinum Old and Rare Glenlochy 38 Years Old** dist 65 bott 03 **(84) n**22 **t**21 **f**20 **b**21. Softly smoked and sweet. Big oak but remains in bounds. **42.3%**. *Douglas Laing. 171 bottles.*

## GLENLOSSIE
### Speyside, 1876. Diageo. Working.

**Blackadder Raw Cask Glenlossie 29 Year Old** cask 5949, dist 8 Aug 75, bott Apr 05 **(89) n**20 tired and a touch soapy but with compensating honey; **t**23 bourbon and hives-full of honey arrive in a big rush; **f**23 layers of wonderfully rich barley coated in a honied sugar and spice; **b**23 honey is the trademark of this wonderful Speysider, and there is enough here to feed the world's bear population. Remarkable for its age. **52.2%**

**Connoisseurs Choice Glenlossie 1978 (91) n**22 Turkish delight; **t**23 fabulously intense malt with barley sugar leading into some boiled fruit sweets; **f**23 wonderful honey refrain and links beautifully with the late chocolate; **b**23 it's like delving into a candy store! 'Lossie flying at full golden colours. **43%**. *G&M.*

**Duncan Taylor Glenlossie 1978 Aged 25 Years** cask 4802 **(88) n**20 sappy, bacon fat; **t**22 mouthwatering, rich malt; the oak has a mildly bourbony resonance; **f**23 takes off into honey heaven as the oak and barley embrace with passion: more liquorice-honey bourbon notes towards the end; **b**23 enough malts survives to take on the bourbon. A genuinely beautiful whisky. **54%**

**Murray McDavid Mission 2 Glenlossie 1975 (77) n**19 **t**21 **f**18 **b**19. Good, sturdy, mouthwatering arrival on the palate, but runs out of puff. **46% nc ncf**

**Murray McDavid Glenlossie 1993 (86) n**22 **t**22 **f**21 **b**21. Absolutely prime example of Glenlossie at its most malt intense: great example as to why it's such a great blender. This is the Speyside Way. **46%**

**Peerless Glenlossie 1978** ( see Duncan Taylor Glenlossie 1978)

**Provenance Glenlossie 12 Years Old** dist 18 Nov 92, bott, 17 Feb 05 **(84) n**21 **t**22 **f**21 **b**20. Malty, sharp, simplistic: pure undemanding Speyside. **46%**.

·:·· **Provenance Glenlossie 12 Years Old (90) n**22 intriguing waft of distant smoke on the fine barley; **t**23 a stunning malt explosion with crystal clarity to the grassy barley and then a seismic wave of cocoa-spicy oak. The oil is on a slow burner; **f**22 long with those soft, sweet oils; **b**23 say what you like: a well-used cask and would make brilliant blending whisky. All true. But the ebullience of the malt is something to cherish. **46%**. *McGibbon's.*

Provenance Glenlossie Over 14 Years dist Autumn 89, bott Autumn 03 **(85)** n21 t22 f21 b21. Much younger and fresher than its 14 years suggests: delicious stuff, about as good as you will get from a cask this well used. **46%.**

## GLEN MHOR
**Highland (Northern), 1892–1983. Demolished.**

⁙ **Glen Mhor 1976 Rare Malt** db **(93)** n23 pure barley sugar but any excess sweetness is trimmed by a luxuriant oaky-vanilla thread that is dipped in honeydew melon; t24 the delivery on palate edges close to perfection as the natural barley lushness is pricked by oak-induced spice. Oak is very often a detracting factor in an old malt: here it adds depth to the effortless elegance and adds sophistication to the sweetness; f22 long, lithe and lengthened by a surprising puff of peat popping up from nowhere; b24 you just dream of truly great whisky sitting in your glass from time to time. But you don't expect it, especially from such an old cask. This was the best example from this distillery I've tasted in 30 years....until the Glenkeir version was unleashed! If you ever want to see a scotch that has stretched the use of oak as far it will go without detriment, here it is. What a pity the distillery has gone because the Mhor the merrier... **52.2%.**

⁙ **Glenkeir Treasures Glen Mhor 30 Years Old** dist Apr 75, bott Nov 05 **(94)** n24 curiously and attractively rummy: a touch of 13/14 year old Jamaican Long Pond about this. Those esters also help to accentuate the residue barley against the oak. There is a freshness that belies the age; t24 lush with stunning esters coating the palate with coffee-crème brulee. The balance between the sugar-coated, ultra-juicy barley and the deepening oak takes some believing, as does the melt-in-the-mouth quality; f23 long and perhaps slightly over- dependent on a thick chocolate ice cream theme; b23 you just can't fault sensational whisky like this. This distillery is hitting super stardom very late in the day. **51.2%.** *The Whisky Shop. 270 bottles.*

Gordon & MacPhail Glen Mhor 1965 **(74)** n19 t20 f18 b17. Somewhat bitty and unbalanced. **40%**

## GLENMORANGIE
**Highland (Northern), 1843. Glenmorangie plc. Working.**

Glenmorangie 10 Years Old db **(94)** n24 perhaps the most enigmatic aroma of them all: delicate yet assertive, sweet yet dry, young yet oaky: a malty tone poem; t22 flaky oakiness throughout but there is an impossibly complex toastiness to the barley which seems to suggest the lightest hint of smoke; f24 amazingly long for such a light dram, drying from the initial sweetness but with flaked almonds amid the oakier, rich cocoa notes; b24 remains one of the great single malts: a whisky of uncompromising aesthetic beauty from the first enigmatic whiff to the last teasing and tantalising gulp. Complexity at its most complex. **40%**

Glenmorangie 15 Years Old db **(89)** n23 t23 f21 b22. Rich by Glenmorangie standards and very warming. **43%**

Glenmorangie 15 Years Old Sauternes Wood Finish db **(68)** n14 t17 f19 b18. Only the intense fruit and finish saves this sulphury one ... to a degree. Not a patch on the standard Sauternes. **46%.** *Duty Free.*

Glenmorangie 18 Years Old **(87)** n23 big citrus presence: fresh and sparkling; t22 big, yet somehow subdued, as though on best behaviour. The sweet fruit dominates through a silky sheen, though the malt recovers; f21 the oak battles grimly for control, but the malt holds fast, supported by the fruit. The finale is pure custard tart. Lovely! b21 a real sweet, smoothie. **43%**

Glenmorangie 25 Years Old db **(84)** n21 t22 f20 b21. Soft as a baby's bum, but for all its clean tones needs an injection of complexity. **43%**

**Glenmorangie 30 Years Old** db **(72)** n17 t18 f19 b18. From the evidence in the glass the jury is out on whether it has been spruced up a little in a poor sherry cask – and spruce is the operative word: lots of pine on this wrinkly. **44.1%**

✣ **Glenmorangie 30 Years Old Malaga Finish** db **(92)** n23 astonishing: a very similar type of nose to the 25-y-o version, though there is some chalkier oak; t23 ditto; f23 a slight change here, with the smoke vanishing and light liquorice talking its place; b23 a very strange experience: it is so similar to the 25-y-o to be almost untrue, yet that little extra age has upped the quality a notch or two as the components seem to fit that little bit better. **43%**

**Glenmorangie Artisan Cask** db **(93)** n24 playful, teasing malt, very distant carrot juice and evening primroses among other fruity/floral notes. "En perfum de jardinair" my former French girlfriend may have called it, and quite rightly, too (seeing as this most Scottish of malts wants to use French-derivated appendages to its brand names); t23 the arrival doesn't disappoint, with the malt expectedly leading the way with aplomb; in its wake soft spices stir and also an earthy oakiness; f22 relatively simple oak _n' malt with a dash of liquorice; b24 seriously disarming. **46%**

**Glenmorangie Burgundy Wood Finish** db **(76)** n19 t20 f18 b19. Such an improvement on the first, disastrous, bottling (keep a wary eye out for that one by the way – was lucky to get 69 in the last Bible), yet still I can't see the point of this expression. By Glenmorangie's great standards it is (save for an all too brief, mouthwatering purple patch) dull, listless, unimaginative and takes the malt and imbiber absolutely nowhere. **46%**

**Glenmorangie Burr Oak Reserve** db **(92)** n24 burr by name and nature: prickly, nipping, biting but enormous and not without a passing resemblance to a very high quality bourbon; t24 capow!! The enormity of the oak-thrusted malt leaves little to the imagination: the mouth is coated in its radiance and the bitter-sweet richness positively glows; could easily mistake this for a bourbon; f22 relatively bitter and twisted, but a bourbony liquorice-cocoa character; b22 fades on the finish as a slightly spent force, but nose and arrival are simply breathtaking. Wouldn't be out of place in Kentucky. **56.3%**

**Glenmorangie Cellar 13 Ten Years Old** db **(90)** n22 the very first threads of bourbon notes are filtering through; the butterscotch and honey notes mentioned on the label are spot on; t22 more glorious honey makes for an unusually intense maltiness; f23 that wonderful honey swarms all over the finale. The vanilla picks up in weight, as do some spices; b23 oddly enough, as much as this is the most honey-rich Glenmorangie of them all and a tastebud pleaser from first to last, the use of 100% first-fill bourbon has slightly detracted from the all round brilliance and complexity of the standard 10-y-o. **43%**

**Glenmorangie Cote de Beaune** db **(63)** n10 t18 f19 b16. Hard to get past the disastrous nose. Improves towards the end, but too little, too late. **46%**

**Glenmorangie Elegance** db **(92)** n22 quite herbal and soothing; t24 the thinnest layer of icing sugar coats the silk-soft malt; every bit as gentle as the nose suggests; f22 medium to short with some attractive rolling vanilla; b24 a surprise package that is not entirely dissimilar to the Golden Rum, only a tad sweeter. **43%**

**Glenmorangie Golden Rum Cask Finish** db **(94)** n23 much of the usual 'Morangie complexity except there is also a syrupy sweetness to this one; t23 after a hesitant first second or two, the flavours sing in diverse harmonisation like a morning chorus: any more delicate it would snap; f24 some honeyed strands are coated in soft rum notes while the vanilla purrs along contently; b24 as limited a fan of finishes as I may be, a standing ovation here is richly deserved. The complexity fair boggles the mind. **40%.** *Glenmorangie for Sainsbury's.*

**Glenmorangie Madeira Matured** db **(93)** n21 big, wilful, spiced fruit and, despite carrying a slight blemish, big, bruising and belligerent; t24 the enormity of the flavour takes some serious map-making. A moderately-spiced grape leads the way, but beneath this the pulse of the barley beats strongly; sweetens fabulously and unexpectedly around the middle. The most mouthwatering 'Morangie of all time? **f**24 long, with less flaws now but the marrying and then slow fade of the fruit, barley and oak is a treat; **b**24 this is like a scarred, bareknuckled, fist-fighter knocking 50 types of crap out of a classically trained world champion boxer: not one for the purists, but you cannot but admire and gasp in awe ... **56%**

**Glenmorangie Madeira Wood Finish** db **(82) n**17 **t**22 **f**22 **b**21. Like all the Glenmorangie wood finishes the quality can vary dramatically. It's all part of the fun. Here a poor nose is rescued by a wonderful fruit-pastel, candy, mouthwatering arrival. Succulent and sweet. **43%**

**Genmorangie Millennium Malt Aged 12 Years** db **(83) n**21 **t**22 **f**20 **b**20. This is from entirely 100% first fill bourbon barrels and because of this – and the extra two years – the enchanting spell that makes Glenmorangie the most complex malt on mainland Scotland has been broken. Delicious, make no mistake, but simply too much of a good thing. **40%**

**Glenmorangie Port Wood Finish** db **(87) n**22 a lively, peppery attack to the softer, juicier fruit; **t**21 succulent fruit perhaps overshadows the malt; **f**22 quite a bitter finale as the oak really fights its corner: very busy, warming and intricate; **b**22 a big improvement but still not in the league of its first expressions a decade ago. **43%** ☉

**Glenmorangie Sherry Wood Finish** db **(80) n**21 **t**23 **f**17 **b**19. The finish here is more cream toffee than sherry: somewhat disappointing, knowing how good it can be. The initial mouth arrival is superb, though. **43%**

**Glenmorangie Speakeasy** db **(89) n**22 enormous vanilla, dense malt and sawdust; **t**23 bitter-sweet with sharp, acidic fruit hand in hand with even sharper barley; **f**22 some wonderful zesty orange; **b**22 just creaking a little under the oak, but the chewability of the malt is amazing. **63.3%**

**Glenmorangie Speakeasy 1990** db **(83) n**20 **t**22 **f**20 **b**21. Fine malt, as usual, but curiously dry with natural caramel not helping either. **60.2%**

**Glenmorangie Speakeasy 1990** db **(91) n**22 dusty blackboards and floral; even a hint of bourbon here; **t**23 crystal-clean malt launches with a strangely raisiny payload; **f**23 wonderful balance of softly spiced oak and confident malt – again hints of young bourbon towards the finale; **b**23 more oak than normal for a Morangie. But a real delight. **59.7%**

**Glenmorangie Tain L'Hermitage** db **(88) n**22 a busy aroma, full of darting coal gas (at times an improbable hint of very weak peat reek), wild berries crushed in the hand and vanilla-tangerine; **t**21 flat at first, then a rush of ultraripe fruity notes: the middle merges effortlessly into the finish; **f**23 much more together here, with pleasing, mouthwatering fruit outlines against a deepening chocolate kick and those bizarre peat tones again; **b**22 a see-saw of a dram full of rich, mouth-bulging entertainment. **46%.**

**Glenmorangie Traditional** db **(87) n**21 solid, unblemished malt with just a touch of saltiness; **t**23 charming and really outstanding chewability to the rich, biscuity malt; a little raw but great entertainment; **f**22 a return of the drier salty notes; **b**21 young, faultless and probably from second-fill bourbon, it reveals how the extra oak turns this from first-rate blending material into a masterpiece. **57%**

⬩⬩⬩ **Glenmorangie Truffle Oak** db **(96) n**24 a significant aroma: big, powering oak yet controlled with no sign of bitterness or tiredness. Some golden syrup on the barley is toned down by age. If you can find a flaw or off-note, e-mail me; **t**24 bloody hell!!! Now the golden syrup comes out to play, but the intensity of that plus the barley fair takes the breath away. Something very breakfast- cerealy about this experience. But for grown ups...; **f**25 burning embers of honey-nut cereal last forever. Keeping them company are varying shades of golden to molassed sugar. One of the longest un-peated finishes you'll ever find; **b**23 the Glenmorangie of all Glenmorangies. I really have to work hard and deep into the night to find fault with it. If I am going to be hyper-critical, I'll dock it a mark for being so constantly sweet, though in its defence I have to say that the degree of sweetness alters with astonishing dexterity. Go on, it's Truffle oak: make a pig of yourself...!! **60.5%**

⁖ **Glenmorangie Vintage 1975** db **(89) n**23 clementines! It must be Christmas...; **t**23 improbably clean malt for something so aged, then a layer or three of fruit and spiced vanilla; **f**21 bitters out as an oaky trench is found; **b**22 a charming, fruity and beautifully spiced oldie. **43%**

**Glenmorangie Warehouse Three Reserve** db **(92) n**22 dry, yet effervescent malt offers a fruity barley thrust; **t**23 slightly oily perhaps, it's all about thrusting barley and a mouth-puckering sharpness; **f**23 excellent arrival of light oak adding a touch of extra class and charisma to the finale. Lovely cocoa notes radiate warmly; **b**24 another genuinely outstanding expression, a cathartic catalogue of complexity, from a distillery that shows its greatness when allowed. **40%**. *Glenmorangie for Asda.*

# GLEN MORAY
**Speyside, 1897. Glenmorangie plc. Working.**

**Glen Moray** (no age statement) db **(82) n**19 **t**22 **f**21 **b**20. Young, vibrant, fresh malt, beautifully made. Has the feeling of a young blend – without the grain! **40%**

**Glen Moray Classic 8 Years Old** db **(86) n**20 **t**22 **f**21 **b**23. A vast improvement on previous bottlings with the sluggish fatness replaced by a thinner, barley-rich, slightly sweeter and more precise mouthfeel. **40%** ☉ ☉

**Glen Moray 12 Years Old** db **(91) n**23 a comfortable straddle between very light, teasing malt and soft vanilla; **t**23 lazy flavour entry: the malt saunters round the palate as if it owns the place, perfect harmony between sweet malt and drier oak; **f**23 here's where we get to business with the delicate complexity between malt and oak which is simply sublime. Some minor bourbony notes make a subdued approach; **b**23 one of my favourite Speyside malts for the last 17 years simply because it is so unfailingly consistent and the delicate nature of the whisky has to be experienced to be believed. **40%** ☉

**Glen Moray 16 Years Old** db **(88) n**23 pears and passion fruit amid the pounding malt; **t**21 a very soft and even mouth arrival with a barley-sugar middle; **f**22 more complexity here as lazy oak arrives to add a drying depth; **b**22 seriously easy drinking with not a single note out of tune. **40%** ☉

**Glen Moray 16 Years Old Chenin Blanc Mellowed in Wine Barrels** db **(85) n**20 **t**22 **f**22 **b**21. A fruity, oak-shaded dram just brimming with complexity. **40%**

**Glen Moray 20 Years Old** db **(80) n**22 **t**22 **f**18 **b**18. With so much natural cream toffee, it is hard to believe that this has so many years on it. After a quick, refreshing start it pans out, if anything, a little dull. **40%**

**Glen Moray 30 Years Old** db **(87) n**22 a soft touch of smoke mingles well with the citrus and light sap; **t**21 a lovely fruit tart character dominates; **f**22 the smoke returns as some honeycomb liquorice weight brings the curtain down slowly; **b**22 a malt that seems conscious of its old age and delivers carefully and within itself. **43%**

**Glen Moray 1959 Rare Vintage** db **(91) n**25 **t**23 **f**21 **b**22. They must have been keeping their eyes on this one for a long time: a stunning malt that just about defies nature. The nose reaches absolute perfection. **50.9%**

**Glen Moray 1962 Very Rare Vintage Aged 42 Years** db **(94) n**23 the thick oak offers something of the farmyard, but there is a hint of apple, rhubarb and citrus to thin it out a little; **t**24 the orangey/citrussy notes defy the years as the malt delivers some early and surprising blows for youth; by the time the middle arrives the oak has caught up and we have a mishmash of liquorice, bitter chocolate and beautifully controlled spices; **f**23 some banana milkshake and a very late surge of a vague orangey fruitiness as well; **b**24 the first temptation is to think that this has succumbed to age, but a second and a third tasting reveal that there is much more complexity, integrity and balance to this than first meets the tastebuds. The last cask chosen by the legendary Ed Dodson before his retirement from the distillery: a pretty perceptive choice. A corker! **50.9%. sc.**

**Glen Moray 1984** db **(83) n**20 **t**22 **f**20 **b**21. Mouthwatering and incredibly refreshing malt for its age. **40%**

**Glen Moray 1986 Commemorative Bottling** cask 4698 db **(96) n**25 take your time over this: like a week or so! The bourbon notes are unmistakable (nosing blind I might have plumped for Kentucky!) with a series of rich and sharp blood orange/kumquat notes interlaced with dark chocolate. A peculiarly coastal saltiness has also crept in. Amid all this can be found a sharp maltiness. Just one of the great noses of this and many other years; **t**24 spectacular bitter-sweet arrival on the palate shows a glorious harmony between the malt and bourbony oak. Beyond this gentle spices about, as do mouthwatering, candy-fruit riches; **f**23 one of the longest non-peaty fade-outs since "Hotel California"...the ripeness of the malt, enriched by the most fabulous of bitter-sweet molasses lasts until finally replaced by a toasty vanilla; **b**24 Ed Dodson hand-picked this cask from the warehouse to mark the opening of the distillery's visitor centre in late 2004. Ed has now retired but – and this bottling proves the point entirely – he should be brought back to the distillery, as Elmer T. Lee has at Buffalo Trace, and be given his own named brand. You simply cannot buy the experience and natural feel Ed has for Glen Moray. This astonishing single cask proves the point with a delicious and unforgettable eloquence. **64.4%. ncf.**

⟨≈⟩ **Glen Moray 1989** db **(86) n**23 **t**22 **f**20 **b**21. Doesn't quite live up to the fruit smoothie nose but I'm being a little picky here. **40%**

⟨≈⟩ **Glen Moray 1992 Single Cask No 1441** Sherry butt db **(74) n**17 **t**21 **f**18 **b**18. Oops! Didn't anyone spot the sulphur ...? **59.6%**

**Glen Moray Classic** db **(79) n**22 **t**20 **f**18 **b**19. Sweet, malty, amiable, but a bitter finish and short of ideas. **40%**

⟨≈⟩ **Glen Moray The Fifth Chapter Distillery Manager's Choice** cask filled 25 Mar 92, bott 12 Sept 05 db **(87) n**18 bugger! Sulphur alert...; **t**23 an early lick of sulphur is overwhelmed by, at first, salivating barley, and then marauding spices. Enormous and prisoner-free; **f**23 now drops into cocoa overdrive as the fruit at last finds a voice amid the barley sugar and soft molasses. The elegance is breathtaking; **b**23 this bottling was to mark the event of Graham Coull becoming only the fifth (and prettiest) man to put his legs under the Glen Moray Distillery Manager's desk. I'd love to have given him a top-notch welcome, but bloody sulphur has struck again. Still, the recovery on the palate is already the stuff of distillery legend! **59.6%. ncf sc.** *430 bottles.*

**Glen Moray Mellowed in Chardonnay Barrels** db **(84) n**20 **t**22 **f**21 **b**21. Cramped on the nose, it is much more expansive on the palate with juicy grape detectable amid the refreshing, busy malt. **40%**

**Glen Moray Mountain Oak** db **(94) n**24 it must be the Appalachians, because there is a distinct bourbony aroma here; **t**22 a mixture of fresh, lip-smacking barley crashes head-first into something brimming with liquid spice and a smoky, biscuity depth; **f**24 astonishing length and weight; cut-glass barley sparkles to the very end; **b**24 Unquestionably the best Glen Moray I have ever tasted: a masterpiece Speysider that, if this quality can be maintained, is set to become a legend through its sheer complexity and depth. **60.5%**

⟨≈⟩ **Dewar Rattray Individual Cask Bottling Glen Moray 1990 Aged 16 Years** cask no. 4556, dist May 90, bott May 06 **(88) n**22 reminiscent of toasted oak at a Kentucky cooperage; you can almost taste the charred tannins and caramel; **t**23 soft liquorice and hickory feed into the barley, tries to be salivating but the warming oak won't let it; **f**21 buckles slightly under the tannin; **b**22 a classy, individualistic bottling which for the most part holds the oak well. **55.8%**. *64 bottles.*

**MacLeod's Highland Aged 8 Years (89)** n22 t21 f23 **b**23. Wow! This may be a Highlander by name on the label, though the source of the whisky is Speyside. But it is Highland by nature with some enormous earthy, resonance. Absolutely top-class stuff that bites and teases deliciously. Love to have seen this at 46% nonchillfiltered: might have had a minor classic on our hands. Glen Moray, though not stated on label. **40%**

⁙ **Norse Cask Selection Glen Moray 1990 Aged 13 Years (78)** n19 t20 f19 **b**20. A little feinty, which is unusual for this distillery but it is missing its normal charm and is even a tad oily. Still plenty of barley to grip on to, though. **62.1%**. *QualityWorld, Denmark.*

# GLEN ORD
### Highland (Northern) 1838. Diageo. Working.

**Glen Ord Aged 12 Years** db **(81)** n20 t23 f18 **b**20. Just when you thought it safe to go back....for a while Diageo ditched the sherry-style Ord. It has returned. Better than some years ago, when it was an unhappy shadow of its once-great self, but without the sparkle of the vaguely-smoked bottling of a year or two back. Nothing wrong with the rich arrival, but the finish is a mess. I'll open the next bottling with trepidation... **43%** ⊙ ⊙

**Glen Ord 25 Years Old** dist 78 db **(95)** n24 the most narrow seams of peat offer backbone to deeply impressive arrays of fruits, including kumquats, unripe figs and greengages. The oak is firm, as is the malt; **t**24 nectar-plus!! The astonishing mouthfeel is matched only by the perfectly presented fruit, mainly a citrussy affair, that battles for supremacy against grassy malt and spiced oak. Waiting in the wings is wonderfully gentle smoke. A faultlessly choreographed production; **f**23 slightly more simplistic here thanks to some caramel being sucked from the oak, but the spices continue as does a fruity tang; **b**24 some stupendous vatting here: cask selection at its very highest to display Ord in all its far too rarely seen magnificence. **58.3%**

**Glen Ord 28 Years Old** db **(90)** n22 malt and mint bound together by soft liquorice and dark fudge; **t**23 delightful barley-sugar theme that forms a stupendously rigid middle with the most delicate hints of smoke and coffee. The body weight is perfect; **f**22 amazingly long finale with lashings of cocoa to go with the mollassed sugar and powering barley; **b**23 this is mega whisky showing slight traces of sap, especially on the nose, but otherwise a concentrate of many of the qualities I remember from this distillery before it was bottled in a much ruined form. Blisteringly beautiful. **58.3%**.

⁙ **Glen Ord 30 Years Old** db **(87)** n22 shaped by oak, there is a peppery element to the floral thrust; **t**21 molten barley spearheads the arrival before a cumbersome oakiness interferes. Plenty of spice and underpinning sweetness; **f**23 settles down for a really long and delightful finish with a glorious interaction between delicate, velvety barley and vanilla. Charming; **b**21 creaking with oak, but such is the polish to the barley some serious class is on show. **58.8%**

⁙ **Cadenhead's Authentic Collection Ord Aged 22 Years** Bourbon Hogshead, dist 83, bott Feb 06 **(88)** n21 healthy oak entanglement; **t**23 quite lovely barley richness, with beautifully disguised biscuity sweetness; **f**21 estery and a tad salty but otherwise thin; **b**23 a clever and attractive malt that carries its advancing years with aplomb. **55%**. *210 bottles.*

⁙ **Old Malt Cask Glen Ord Aged 15 Years** cask 1335, dist Jan 89, bott Sept 04 **(83)** n21 t22 f20 **b**20. A well-used bourbon cask allows this one to pass off as a juicy and clean 10-year-old. **50%. nc ncf**. *Douglas Laing. 604 bottles.*

**Old Malt Cask Glen Ord 33 Years Old** dist Aug 70, bott Jun 04 **(84)** n22 t21 f20 **b**21. Attractive chocolate orange seeps through the oaky depths. **50%**.

## GLENROTHES

**Speyside, 1878. Edrington. Working.**

**Glenrothes 1972** db **(88) n**23 plump sultanas and suet pudding; **t**23 spectacular marriage between yielding malt and vine fruit; **f**20 dries and dies rather too quickly, with oak having all the say; **b**22 a shy malt for its age, releasing all its complexity on the intrinsic, suety/fruity nose and mouth arrival that is simply to die for. Old age catches up on the flat finish, though. **43%.**

**The Glenrothes 1974** bott 03 db **(94) n**24 **t**24 **f**23 **b**23. I know people who are Glenrothes aficionados: their lives revolve around this distillery. Without this truly classic dram, those lives will be incomplete. **43%**

**Glenrothes 1979 Single Cask** cask 13466 db **(94) n**23 leather armchairs, gentlemen's clubs, dusty libraries, polished oak, oloroso evaporating from a sleeping octogenerian's chair; traces of a burnt match; **t**24 dry oloroso crashing head-first into rich, honied malt; a welter of spicy punches are jabbed around the tastebuds; **f**23 burnt fudge, strings of dark liquorice and hints of coffee-infused Demerara pot still rum; **b**24 creaks around the palate with effortless class. **57%.**

⁘ **The Glenrothes 1979** cask 13470 db **(95) n**24 a basket of toffee apples sitting under a spice rack. Awesome; **t**24 massive spice and hickory start, sweetened with mollased sugar and honeycomb; **f**23 long, with the spices remaining playful and the vanilla intervention soft and empathic; **b**24 that's what you call a sherry cask: big, yet everything just-so. Classic. **57.5%. sc.**

**Glenrothes 1979** bott 05 db **(91) n**22 succulent over-ripe grape, distant white pepper, gentle oak; **t**23 the intensity of the sweet malt belies the nose; a silk body that purrs towards the big, plum-fruitcakey middle; **f**23 fabulous, controlled outpouring of warm spices harmonising perfectly with solid malt and burnt fudge; **b**23 an understated gem, simply because the complexity unfolds almost imperceptibly. **43%.**

**Glenrothes 1984** bott 05 db **(87) n**22 wood shavings and diced greengages; **t**22 tangy, orangey, spicy, busy; **f**21 drying oak arrival complements the fruitier thrust; **b**22 well weighted malt with confident, spicy character. **43%.**

⁘ **The Glenrothes 1985 Vintage** dist 21 July 85, bott 31 May 05 db **(88) n**23 great complexity, offering salty, buttered crumpets and toasted hot cross buns; **t**23 silky sultanas; the spices begin to bombard as the barley and oak jostle for supremacy; **f**20 toasty and ever-drying; **b**22 a lovely old whisky which fades fast. **43%**

**Glenrothes 1987** bott 05 db **(83) n**20 **t**21 **f**21 **b**21. Enticing marmalade on toast, but never quite hits the heights expected. **43%.**

⁘ **The Glenrothes 1991** dist 7.9.91, bott 24.5.05 db **(85) n**20 **t**22 **f**21 **b**22. It is as if this distillery wants to challenge your tolerance levels: a malt that should ebb in the healthy 90s has been pegged back by guess what. **43%**

**The Glenrothes 1992** bott 04 db **(76) n**17 **t**20 **f**19 **b**20. Just a hint of red liquorice on the finale heads it away from the malt. The nose is poor, though. **43%**

⁘ **The Glenrothes Select Reserve (87) n**20 just when you wonder if a touch of sulphur has crept in, all is lost under an avalanche of over-ripe oranges. Jury's out ...; **t**24 one of the softest deliveries in Speyside, the silky barley and citrus caress the tastebuds with rare tenderness; a drop of honey assists; **f**21 again, there is a strange note to the coffee and cocoa finale; **b**22 definitely flawed greatness. **43%**

**Adelphi Glenrothes 13 Years Old** cask 15355 dist 90 bott 03 **(79) n**19 **t**19 **f**21 **b**20. Despite that impressive toffee-apple sherry effect on the middle and finish just the odd flaw marks this one down slightly. **59.6%**

**Blackadder Raw Cask Glenrothes 15 Years Old** cask 18832, dist 19 Oct 89, bott Jul 04 **(87) n**19 niggardly, tight and grouchy; **t**23 much happier now with an immediate impact of malt concentrate and barley sugar: huge delivery and lip-smacking all the way; **f**22 long, less than complex but lovely cocoa on the finale; **b**23 ignore the sulking nose. On the palate it comes alive beautifully. **56.6%**

**Cadenhead's Authentic Collection Glenrothes-Glenlivet Aged 14 Years**

Sherry Butt, dist 90, bott May 05 **(80)** n20 t19 f22 b19. One of those big, spicy butts which completely consume the whisky. Some people like this style. I must admit I don't. No off notes but, excellent finish apart, just nothing interesting going on. **58.8%.** *636 bottles.*

⋅⋅⋅ **Cadenhead's Authentic Collection Glenrothes Aged 15 Years** Sherry butt, dist 90, bott May 06 **(71)** n18 t18 f17 b18. Sulphur tinged. **59.5%.** *582 bottles.*

**Chieftain's Glenrothes 1992 Aged 10 Years Port Finish** bott 27 Mar 04 **(90)** n21 the malt hasn't quite merged with the port; t23 no such problems here: the arrival on the palate is one of harmony with the softness of the wine laying a fruity foundation for the increasingly intense barley; f23 some oak arrives to add a touch of welcome bitterness to the gathering sweet barley; b23 from such an unpromising nose has sprung a port finish that keeps the tastebuds guessing until the last. Brilliant!! **43%.** *Ian Macleod.*

**Chieftain's Glenrothes 1993 Aged 10 Years Rum Finish** bott 25 Mar 04 **(93)** n22 as rum-soaked as a sea wind; t24 from the very start the mouth goes into overtime to come to terms with the sheer enormity of the flavour profile: the sweetness is intense but the barley richness matches the rum richness. Just so wonderfully complex; f23 some extra oak for its age which really does work well with the natural caramel notes which linger with the peppery spices and barley; b24 one that you can chew until your jaw drops off. **43%.** *Ian Macleod.*

⋅⋅⋅ **Dun Bheagan Glenrothes 12 Years Old** Sherry finish **(79)** n20 t21 f19 b19. A cleanish, sound sherry cask but short changes in the complexity department. **43%.** *Ian Macleod.*

⋅⋅⋅ **Duncan Taylor Collection Glenrothes 1970** cask 10574, dist July 70, bott Apr 06 **(79)** n20 t19 f20 b20. Pleasant, but a touch jaded and enormous natural toffee. **43.5%.** *162 bottles.*

**Gordon & MacPhail Glenrothes 1961 (82)** n20 t21 f21 b20. Gooseberries on the nose and malty-silk on the palate. No off-notes or oak deterioration whatsoever. **40%**

**Hart Brothers Glenrothes Aged 10 Years** dist Nov 92, bott Sep 03 **(86)** n18 t22 f23 b22. Nose a horror show; sweetening finish is fabulously memorable. **46%**

⋅⋅⋅ **Lonach Glenrothes 35 Years Old (93)** n23 heading into exotic fruit territory; t24 about as soft a delivery as you'll ever get. Not sure which direction to take at first, though it has to be said the bitter-sweet balance during contemplation and dissolving just couldn't be finer. Decides to pan out, as you might expect, towards drier oak; f22 a vague hint of something smoky and mocha and cream brings the curtain down on this most elegant of old gentlemen; b24 Takes time to really get to understand and appreciate this whisky: once you pick up what it's all about you will be charmed, I'm sure. **40.2%.** *Duncan Taylor.*

**MacPhail's Collection Glenrothes 1965 (87)** n22 the unlikely and delicious combination of carrot juice and young bourbon: fresh, sweet, yet earthy; t23 relaxed, wonderfully rich-textured malt; all delightfully coated with Demerara; f21 drying oak, burnt toast; b21 loses it on the finish somewhat, but the early complexity is a treat. **43%**

**MacPhail's Collection Glenrothes 30 Years Old (82)** n20 t21 f21 b20. Good honey spice, enthusiastic oak. **43%.** *Gordon & MacPhail.*

⋅⋅⋅ **Murray McDavid Mission Glenrothes 1968** Bourbon/Mourvedra/Syrah **(84)** n23 t21 f20 b20. The vivid nose of barely ripened blood oranges is not quite matched by the confused delivery which follows. Still clean and tasty, though. **45.5%.** *300 bottles.*

⋅⋅⋅ **Norse Cask Selection Glenrothes 1988 Aged 15 Years (84)** n21 t22 f20 b21. Rich and pleasantly honeyed. **55.4%.** *QualityWorld, Denmark.*

**Old Malt Cask Glenrothes Aged 17 Years** dist Dec 85, bott Sep 03 **(72)** n17 t19 f18 b18. Sultanas, raisins and high roast Java coffee offer riches, but the lurking sulphur from the sherry has the most telling say. **50%. nc ncf sc.** *Douglas Laing.* *581 bottles.*

⋯ **Old Malt Cask Glenrothes 27 Years Old** Wine finish, dist Apr 79, bott July 06 **(66)** n17 t18 f15 b16. Suicide or murder? Was the sulphur there with an early sherry butt or was it the wine cask that did it? **50%.** *Douglas Laing. 363 bottles.*

**Old Master's Glenrothes 1988 16 Year Old**, cask no. 7022, bott Sep 04 **(82)** n21 t21 f20 b20. The big malt middle thins at the sweet finish. **53.5%**

⋯ **Old Masters Glenrothes 1988 Aged 17 Years** cask no. 6995, bott 06 **(94)** n24 beautiful strata of acacia honey, maple syrup and Lubeck's finest, with just enough chalky oak to balance; t24 the sweetness generated is enormous yet somehow controlled with vivid barley sugar in concentrated form. Remarkable freshness remains; f23 a gentle reduction of all the starring qualities as the oak adds a quality riposte; b23 for that extraordinary number of Glenrothes fans out there, here is a must have...! **54.1%.** *James MacArthur.*

⋯ **Platinum Glenrothes 25 Years Old** dist 21 Apr 79, bott May 05 **(87)** n23 the hint of sulphur is outweighed by the intensity of the toffee apple from what must, originally, have been one helluva butt; t23 more chewy toffee and dried dates: this is sherry influence at its most enormous. A slight flaw detectable, but you cannot be butt amazed; f19 a trace of sulphur tang, butt what toffee-treacle influence we have, right to the bitter end! b22 no ifs or butts here: genuine flawed genius. **51.9%.** *Douglas Laing. 325 bottles.*

**Private Cellars Selection Glenrothes 1974** bott 03 **(89)** n22 t23 f22 b22. Fights every inch against the odds to produce something morishly sweet. **43%.**

⋯ **Provenance Glenrothes Aged 10 Years (86)** n22 t21 f22 b21. Clean, revitalising malt. But the grappa nose is a real surprise! **46%.** *Douglas Laing.*

**Provenance Glenrothes Over 13 Years** dist 1 Nov 90, bott 5 July 04 **(72)** n18 t17 f19 b18. Spoiled by disappointing cask. **46%.** *Douglas Laing*

**Provenance Glenrothes 14 Years Old** dist 20 Nov 90, bott 5 Apr 05 **(83)** n22 t21 f20 b20. Busy, chewy, with mouthfilling fruit. **46%.** *Douglas Laing*

**Scott's Selection Glenrothes 1986** bott 04 **(83)** n20 t22 f21 b20. Typically clean, lightweight, first-class blending fodder. 52.7%. *Speyside Distillers.*

**Scott's Selection Glenrothes 1980** bott 05 **(84)** n20 t22 f21 b21. Such a light malt, the character is changing distinctly in the direction of spicy bourbon. **53.1%.** *Speyside Distillers.*

**The Un-chillfiltered Collection Glen Rothes Aged 14 Years** dist 11 May 90, bott 8 Dec 04 Sherry Butt 11003 **(76)** n18 t20 f19 b19. Dragged down by a sulphur blip. **46%. nc ncf.** *Signatory. 847 bottles.*

**Wilson & Morgan Barrel Selection Glenrothes 1989 Rum Finish** bott 03 **(75)** n20 t19 f18 b18. Mildly cloying and off the pace. **46%.**

## GLEN SCOTIA
### Campbeltown, 1832. Glen Catrine. Working.

⋯ **Glen Scotia Heavily Peated**, cask 518, dist 23 July 99 db **(92)** n22 moist marzipan adds a sweet, nutty element to the pre-pubescent, vaguely Bowmore-style peat. Deliciously young; t23 fresh, enormously sweet and surprisingly oily for this distillery: but, for all this, it is stunningly balanced and charismatic; f23 dries very impressively; there is an imperious flourish to the peaty signature; b24 this is pretty big and quite beautifully made malt. Forget the age. Enjoy a touch of class. **45%**

⋯ **Glen Scotia Heavily Peated**, cask 525, dist 23 July 99 db **(85)** n21 t22 f22 b20. Tasty, but relatively blunt, nothing like so together or complex as cask 518. **45%**

⋯ **Glen Scotia Aged 12 Years** db **(81)** n23 t21 f18 b19. What a whisky: you could write a book about it, a thriller. It'd be called "Murder by Caramel." The early signs on the nose and palate arrival are genuinely awesome. But then...then.....!!! I can't say for sure if it's natural from the oak, or has been added. Unmolested, this malt would be in the very high 80s, possibly low 90s: there is something wondrous in there, not least the richness of the diced apple and honey on the nose: you don't have to hunt too hard to see what I mean. Let's hope I'll be able to give it that score next year. **40%**

**Glen Scotia 14 Years Old** db **(90) n**23 complex, with darting malty notes nipping around, almost like the small grains in a bourbon: really top-quality stuff; **t**22 busy, light maltiness with flickering intensity. The malty sweetness is never more than a passing illumination amid the gathering cocoa oakiness; **f**23 gristy malt and soft oak intertwine; **b**23 if Glen Scotia had been this good in the past it wouldn't have suffered such a chequered career. Absolutely engrossing malt with fabulous complexity. **40%**

⸬ **Cadenhead's Authentic Collection Glen Scotia Aged 14 Years** Sherry Hogshead, dist 91, bott Feb 06 **(84) n**21 **t**19 **f**23 **b**21. A bear-hug of a whisky at times threatening to crush the tastebuds; just enough honey to ease the sherry-oak grip. Fine spice and the odd second or two here is simply sublime. **57.7%.** *198 btls.*

**Cask Glen Scotia 1992 (81) n**18 **t**22 **f**21 **b**20. Not exactly text-book whisky (troubled times at t'distillery) but the excellence of the unexpected peat makes for a delicious dram. **62.1%.** *Gordon & MacPhail.*

**Chieftain's Glen Scotia Aged 30 Years Rum Barrel** bott 31 Mar 04 **(83) n**22 **t**21 **f**19 **b**21. Enormously sweet, salty, oaky with a toffee creaminess. **41.2%.**

**Chieftain's Glen Scotia Aged 30 Years Rum Barrel** cask 991, distMar 74, bott Dec 04 **(82) n**19 **t**22 **f**21 **b**20 . Some highly attractive, beefed-uphoney-spicy moments, but the oak has gone through the top **42.2%. nc ncf.** *204 bottles.*

**Murray McDavid Mission III Glen Scotia 1975 (73) n**18 **t**19 **f**18 **b**18. There are those who will lie down and die for this; however, to me this is more like an OTT flavoured aquavit. **46%**

⸬ **The Whisky Fair Glen Scotia Aged 30 Years** Rum barrel, dist July 75, bott June 06 **(74) n**19 **t**19 **f**18 **b**18. The bubble gum nose gives due warning to the rather messy ride that is to come. **47.5%. nc ncf.** *Germany. 96 bottles.*

⸬ **The Whisky Fair Glen Scotia (Heavily Peated) 1999** casks 541/542, dist Jul 99, bott June 06 **(89) n**22 firm peat gathering depths it warms in the glass; drier than many Islays of its age and a flash of hickory for extra weight. But lovely and young, nonetheless; **t**23 every bit as big as the nose suggests and again the sweetness, though momentarily intense, is kept under leash; more oak depth than might be expected for a 6-y-o; **f**22 chewy peat allows through some firm barley. A touch of coffee simmers, but youth has its way; **b**22 always a treat to come across a dram so brimming with the vitality of youth. **52.7%.** *Germany. 464 bottles.*

# GLEN SPEY
## Speyside, 1885. Diageo. Working.

**Glen Spey Aged 12 Years** db **(90) n**23 the kind of firm, busy malt you expect from this distillery plus some lovely spice; **t**22 mouthwatering and fresh, a layer of honey makes for an easy three or four minutes; **f**22 drier vanilla, but the pulsing oak is controlled and stylish; **b**23 very similar to the first Glen Spey I can remember in this range, the one before the over-toffeed effort of two years ago. Great to see it back to its more natural, stunningly beautiful self. **43%.** *Flora and Fauna range.*

**Adelphi Glen Spey 1977 Aged 28 Years** cask 3655, bott 05 **(93) n**23 light malt and a plate of crushed Alpine flowers; **t**24 poised, classy interaction between absolutely pristine malt and a variety of spices. And even the shyest hints of smoke. Brilliant; **f**23 long, soft development of citrus, orangey fruit and grassy malt: Speyside at its most playfully sublime; **b**23 I have long adored this underrated and little-known distillery, and when a bottling arrives so true to its character I can only sit here and applaud! **51.2%.** *154 bottles.*

⸬ **Connoisseurs Choice Glen Spey 1995 (76) n**19 **t**19 **f**19 **b**19. Vapid blending fodder. **43%.** *Gordon & MacPhail.*

··:·· **James MacArthur Glen Spey 1992 Aged 12 Years** bott 05 **(85) n**22 **t**22 **f**20 **b**21. In so many ways this is the distillery crystallised: one of the cleanest of all Scotland's malts and with an exceptionally sweet barley-sugar kick. But steadfastly refuses to kick on and develop. **43%**

··:·· **Murray McDavid Glen Spey Aged 9 Years** Bourbon/Madeira, dist 96, bott 05 **(87) n**21 robustly meaty; **t**22 lethargic start then, from out of the blue (or pink in this case), a whoosh of oily malt and fruit; **f**22 moist fruitcake and still oily; **b**22 absolutely no other whisky to compare this to: a unique fingerprint to this one. **46%. nc ncf.** *2400 bottles.*

**Murray McDavid Mission Selection Number 4 Glen Spey 1974 Aged 30 Years (84) n**21 **t**20 **f**22 **b**21 . Some fresh mango developes with the white-hot peppers to make for a fascinating and entertaining dram. **46%.**

**Old Malt Cask Glen Spey 12 Year Old** dist Sep 91, bott Aug 04 **(83) n**19 **t**22 **f**21 **b**21. Deliciously clean, malty-sweet and ethereally light. **50%. nc ncf.** *304 btls.*

··:·· **Old Malt Cask Glen Spey 28 Years Old** dist Dec 77, bott Oct 05 **(91) n**23 there must be a shortage of bananas somewhere. And oak... and smoke... ???; **t**22 tied down with some early oak but slowly blossoms, helped along the way by some surprising – but welcome – gentle peat notes that build in intensity; **f**23 with the smoke giving weight and length, everything else falls into place; exotic, silky fruit links beautifully with the juicy barley; **b**23 a surprise package. I have nosed and tasted peated Glen Spey before, and it was usually from this period, but it is a long time since I have seen it take a leading role. Quite beautiful. **50%.** *Douglas Laing. 233 bottles.*

## GLENTAUCHERS
**Speyside, 1898. Chivas. Working.**

··:·· **Gordon & MacPhail Distillery Label Glentauchers 14 Years Old** bott 15.02.05 **(87) n**22 the barley bristles about the nose; vanilla and coal dust interject; **t**22 simmering, mouthwatering barley of stunning freshness; **f**21 cream toffee; **b**22 not the most complex expression but the early delivery has so much energy. **43%.** *US Market.*

**Old Malt Cask Glentauchers 12 Years Old**, dist Mar 93, bott Aug 04 **(80) n**20 **t**20 **f**20 **b**20. Pleasant, sweet, naturally caramelised blending fodder. **50%.**

··:·· **Old Malt Cask Glentauchers Aged 12 Years** dist Mar 93, bott Aug 05 **(89) n**22 don't often get hints of carrot on the nose: you do here; **t**22 bristling malt and a subtle layer of maple syrup; **f**22 a lovely touch of hickory and vanilla rounds off a busy encounter; **b**23 a delightful, ever-shifting malt that plays teasing games with the tastebuds. **50%.** *Douglas Laing. 266 bottles.*

··:·· **Old Malt Cask Glentauchers Aged 15 Years** dist Aug 90, bott Nov 05 **(86) n**22 **t**22 **f**21 **b**21 'Tauchers in its most simplistic mood. **50%.** *Douglas Laing. 270 bottles.*

**Old Master's Glentauchers 1990** cask 14422, bott 04 **(91) n**22 firm, clean, rye-hard nose offering perfect poise; **t**23 brittle, mouthwatering barley explodes on impact. The fallout includes gentle vanilla; **f**22 a sophisticated sweetness lingers with ginger and coffee as the barley-oak balance stays in sync; **b**24 stylish and subtle, this is textbook Glentauchers. **59.2%.** *James MacArthur.*

**Old Master's Glentauchers 1990 14 Year Old**, cask 14426, bott Feb 05 **(92) n**22 oak tries to make headway but barely pierces the oak: very firm and sound; **t**23 malt is lavished on the tastebuds despite a wonderful counterattack of spice and white chocolate; **f**24 back to standard cocoa, and the wonderful texture guarantees a thousand malty send-offs, with drying oak and a puff of distant smoke adding further depth; **b**23 absolutely tip-top stuff, full of fizz and vitality. One of the longest Speyside finishes of the year. I have long adored this distillery and it's great to see it back up its sister bottling with such blistering panache. **58.5%.** *James MacArthur.*

⠵ **The Queen of the Moorlands Rare Cask Glentauchers 1990 Edition No. 10** Hogshead 14431, dist 21 Nov 90, bott 21 Nov 05 **(92) n**23 the clarity here is invigorating: no off notes, no fussiness from the oak. Just Speyside-style malt at its finest; **t**24 cut-glass barley cleanses the palate; the bitter-sweet elements are sublime, the drizzle of oak, just so; **f**22 maintains shape, poise and bristling barley to the last embers; **b**23 if you ever wanted to know exactly what a very good cask from this great distillery tastes like, look no further. **58.6%. sc.** *Available at The Wine Shop, Leek, UK. 195 bottles.*

⠵ **Whisky Galore Glentauchers 1990** cask no. 14430, dist 27 Nov 90, bott 27 May 05 **(89) n**22 a touch of coal dust on the grist; **t**23 the tastebuds go into salivatory overdrive as the barley lets rip; **f**22 oak interjects as a chalky dryness develops; **b**22 firm and steady as a rock. **46.1%.** *Duncan Taylor.*

**Whisky Galore Glentauchers 1990 Aged 12 Years (88) n**21 textbook 'Tauchers with flint-hard malt you could fire bullets with; **t**23 absolutely no give on the palate: the barley thuds meteorite-like into the tastebuds; **f**22 some mouthwatering malt falls out from the blast and some vanilla, too; **b**22 I love this distillery. Clean, delicious and entirely uncompromising. **46%**

**Wilson & Morgan Barrel Selection Glentauchers 1990 Rum Finish** bott 04 **(75) n**20 **t**19 **f**18 **b**18. Rarely has the old adage of "if it ain't broke, don't fix it" been more apposite. The rum character is discernible, but only at the cost of the more complex, delicate malt trying to be heard. **46%**

# GLENTURRET
## Highlands (Perthshire), 1775. Edrington. Working.

**The Glenturret Aged 10 Years** db **(87) n**20 barley sugar and mild feints. Weighty with an attractive oiliness; **t**23 mouth-clinging malt with a honey-vanilla sub-plot; **f**22 more soft honey and gradual delivery of black pepper and caramel; **b**22 really does appear to have something about the "sma' still" about it, which is hardly surprising. A slightly wider cut than normal has has upped the weight all round. And even emphasises a wonderful honey depth. **40%**

⠵ **Glenturret 10 Years Old** db **(75) n**18 **t**21 **f**18 **b**18. Disappointingly feinty. **40%**

**The Glenturret Aged 15 Years** db **(87) n**21 **t**22 **f**22 **b**22 a beautifully clean, small-still style dram that would have benefitted from being bottled at a fuller strength. A discontinued bottling now: if you see it, it is worth the small investment. **40%**

⠵ **Cadenhead's Authentic Collection Glenturret Aged 18 Years** Bourbon Hogshead, dist 87, bott February 06 **(77) n**21 **t**19 **f**18 **b**19. Pretty tight and hot, bouncing between OTT sugar and bitterness. **52.1%.** *234 bottles.*

⠵ **Chieftain's Glenturret Aged 11 Years Port Finish (87) n**22 if all noses were like this, I'd never get this book finished: where does the fruit start and end, how much is the spice due to oak or Port; where the heck is the barley? So many questions...; **t**22 palate entirely cleansed by a thin layer of wine which slowly fills in body as the malt catches up. Half-hearted spices begin to assemble; **f**21 remains light and wine gummy; **b**22 something this outrageous could come from only one company these days...and you can't help loving it. **43%.** *Ian Macleod.*

**Chieftain's Glenturret Aged 13 Years Port Finish** bott 25 Mar 04 **(86) n**23 **t**21 **f**21 **b**21. Never quite lives up to the nose ... but what a nose!! **43%.** *Ian Macleod.*

⠵ **Kingsbury's Single Cask Glenturret 11 Years Old** cask no. 819, dist 92 **(88) n**21 big, bludgeoning body; not always in tune but worth listening to; **t**23 massively chewy malt that begins with a peck of sugar which blossoms into very mild acacia honey; **f**22 vanilla and custard; **b**22 very attractive sma' still malt, revealing the copper-rich intensity to body and finish usually found on stills below a certain size. Delightfully rich. **46%.** *Japan Import System.*

⠵ **Murray McDavid Mission Glenturret 1980 Aged 26 Years** Bourbon/Rioja **(83) n**23 **t**22 **f**19 **b**19. I thought, at first, that this was the best Rioja I had come across since I was in the boardroom at Coventry last season: the clarity of nose and early delivery are scintillating. But, just like my beloved Millwall that afternoon, it promised much then fired blanks. **47.3%. nc ncf.** *680 bottles.*

꧇ **Old Malt Cask Glenturret Aged 15 Years** Hogshead cask 1744, dist Sept 90, bott Nov 05 **(86)** n23 t22 f20 b21. Forget the disappointing finish: concentrate on the big barley nose and arrival. **50%.** *Douglas Laing. 302 bottles.*

**Old Malt Cask Glenturret Aged 17 Years** dist Dec 85, bott Sep 03 **(72)** n17 t19 f18 b18. Oh dear. **50%. nc ncf sc.** *Douglas Laing.*

## GLENUGIE
### Highland (Eastern). 1834–1983. Closed.

**Connoisseurs Choice Glenugie 1967 (89)** n23 tangerines, grist and vanilla: a wonderful combination; t23 softly oiled and massive, sweet malt. The barley just revels. A touch of peat, too; f21 soft vanilla and lingering malt; b22 the first Glenugie I ever tasted: has never been bettered in bottle. **40%** *G&M*

**Old Malt Cask Glenugie 20 Year Old** dist Mar 84, bott Aug 04 **(93)** n23 mango and pawpaw salad; t24 I'd be tempted to refer you to fruit candy, but I can't think of one that is quite fruity enough to fit the bill; f23 just wave upon wave of mildly toasty malt, but the sweetness is deft and refreshing; b23 fruity and fine, the emphasis is very much on the exotic: an expression of one of the rarest malts – one that can never be forgotten. **50%.** *Douglas Laing & Co.*

**Old Malt Cask Glenugie 25 Years Old**, dist 18 Oct 79, bott 14 Mar 05 **(87)** n22 touches of lavender on plasticine; t22 sweet malt firstly, then that strange plasticine quality again. Wonderful greengage follow-through; f21 waxy and warming; b22 highly individualistic, truly unique malt that no other distillery can begin to imitate – or now ever will. **50%.** *Douglas Laing & Co.*

꧇ **Rare Old Glenugie 1968** dist 68, bott 04 **(94)** n23 absolutely clapped out oak. But it somehow happens it has reconstituted itself as a very passable imitation of a Pacific island fruit salad; t24 stunningly soft and melt-in-the-mouth with hints of mangos and pawpaws, but enlivened, somehow, by untainted barley; f23 light and uncomplicated. That is if you can't be bothered to unravel the late fruits and coffee; b24 one of those displays of exotic fruit that works almost too beautifully to be true. By rights should be oak-infested and in its grave. Yet we have here a genuine classic whisky – Peterhead's finest! **43%.** *Gordon & MacPhail.*

## GLENURY ROYAL
### Highland (Eastern), 1868–1985. Demolished.

꧇ **Glenury Royal 36 Years Old** db **(89)** n21 oak interference damages the fruit balance; t23 starts worryingly dull then takes off to fabulous heights on fresh, beautifully textured barley; f22 begins to fall out of sync as some heavyweight hickory is driven home, but lightens with a succession of gentle waves of cocoa; b23 an undulating dram, hitting highs and lows. The finish, in particular, is impressive: just when it looks on its last legs, it revives delightfully. The whole package, though far from perfect, is pretty astounding. **50.2%**

**Glenury Royal 50 Years Old** dist 53 db **(91)** n23 marvellous freshness to the sherry butt; this had obviously been a high quality cask in its day and the intensity of the fruit sweetened slightly by the most delicate marzipan and old leather oozes class; a little mint reveals some worry lines; t24 the early arrival is sweet and nimble with the barley, against the odds, still having the major say after all these years. The oak is waiting in the wings and with a burst of soft liquorice and velvety, understated spice beginning to make an impression; the sweetness is very similar to a traditional British child's candy of "tobacco" made from strands of coconut and sugar; f22 masses of oak yet, somehow, refuses to go over the top and that slightly molassed sweetness sits very comfortably with the mildly oily body; b22 I am always touched when sampling a whisky like this from a now departed distillery. **42.8%**

# HIGHLAND PARK
**Highland (Island–Orkney), 1795. Edrington. Working.**

**Highland Park 8 Years Old** db **(87) n**22 firm young, honied malt with food coke/peat smoke; **t**22 silky honey and excellent complexity for a malt so young; **f**22 complex layers of vanilla and soft peat at first then caramel grabs hold: shame; **b**21 a journey back in time for some of us: this is the orginal distillery bottling of the 70s and 80s, bottles of which are still doing the rounds in obscure Japanese bars and specialist outlets such as the Whisky Exchange. **40%**

**Highland Park Aged 12 Years** db **(92) n**24 sublime: the peat is almost hand-sprinkled in exact measures; honey and vague molasses guaranteeing contolled sweetness, salt, old leather and apples in there, too; **t**22 moderately weighty mouth arrival, sweet yet enough oak to offer some bitter complexity. This fabulour bitter-sweet balance pans out in favour of the honey though there is enough peat around to add extra weight; **f**22 long, spicy, some earthy heather and more oak than usual. Excellent cocoa hangs about with the peat; **b**24 it defies belief that an international brand can maintain this quality, more or less, year in year out. Few drams are as silkily enveloped as this gem. **40%**

**Highland Park Aged 15 Years** db **(80) n**20 **t**22 **f**19 **b**19. The new kid on the block has yet to show the voluptuous expansiveness of its brothers. The nose is surprisingly closed and the flavours never fully open on the palate, either. Even the spice and smoke have deserted it. Indubitably pleasant, but you are left wanting so much more. **40%** ⊙ ⊙

⫶ **Highland Park 16 Years Old** db **(88) n**23 softly softly strains of oranges, honey and vanilla; **t**23 mouthwatering and delightfully weighted barley with soft nuances of liquorice and smoke; **f**20 toffee-vanilla: just a little too quiet; **b**22 I tasted this the day it first came out at one of the Heathrow whisky shops. I thought it a bit flat and uninspiring. This sample, maybe from another bottling, is more impressive and showing true Highland Park colours, the finish apart. **40%** *Exclusively available in Duty Free/Travel Retail.*

**Highland Park Aged 18 Years** db **(95) n**24 an empty honey jar which once held peaty embers. An enormous nose of excellent consistency, with salty butter and burnt honeycomb is always present; **t**23 beautifully sweet, in some ways sweeter than even the 12-y-o thanks to some manuka honey, which is accentuated against the drier oaky tones and rumbling peat towards the back of the palate: beautifully chewy, a touch oily and wholly substantial; **f**24 some citrus, heathery notes, controlled oak and outstanding cocoa and peat: long and rewarding; **b**24 a consistent dram of enormous weight and complexity, bottle after bottle, and never short of breathtakingly brilliant: the ace in the Highland Park pack. **43%**

**Highland Park Aged 25 Years** db **(89) n**23 emphasis on the heatherhoney though significant fruit – apple especially – abounds. Some pulsating oak, but the theme is sweetish and gently spiced. No more than a hint of smoke; **t**23 firm bodied with soft, smoky spices forming a guard around the burnt honey and barley; much more rigid and crisp than normal HP but this doesn't detract from the radiating complexity; **f**21 layers of vanilla and rich honey. Pretty short, though; **b**22 a very different animal to the 50.7% version with less expansion, depth and expression. Not a bad dram, though... **51.5%**

**Highland Park 25 Years Old** db **(96) n**24 nectar. Hang on? Is nectar this good? Honeycomb and toffee-apple combined and lightened slightly with a squeeze of tangerine and a near perfect stratum of delicate smoke. As I once, apparently famously, described a younger HP: not a jagged edge to be found...; **t**24 sits on the palate as if owning the place and sings: the weight is perfect so both the big barley notes are at full throttle, yet remain on the lightish side and heavier oaky-nutty-marzipan offers the weight. Meeting in the middle are warming spices and a swirl of smoke; **f**24 the age shows, but as if botoxed. There are no cracks to the sheened honeycomb and in the balance, as any great HP should be, the bitter-sweet battle is won hands down by the sweetness; **b**24 HP Ambassador Gerry Tosh's hit man has got me and I've gone to heaven....this is the best bottling of HP25 I've ever come across, in this form eclipsing the astonishing 18. You have to work overtime to find fault with this. I suggest you grab a bottle and try... **50.7%** ☺ ☉

**Highland Park 30 Years Old** db **(89)** **n**22 honey and marzipan help keep the oak at bay; **t**23 surprisingly fay with such wondrous softness to the waxy honey; a mild nutty character to the gathering oak; **f**22 remains soft and coy with the vanilla thickening; honey returns as the finish develops a life of its own; **b**22 this has genuinely surprised me. I expected this to be a tired oldie, but though it shows understandable signs of wear and tear, the general effect is quite outstanding. **48.1%**

**Highland Park 1967** cask 10252, db **(87)** **n**22 **t**22 **f**21 **b**22 the sum is better than the parts but this is massive whisky caught at the moment it falls over the oaky edge. **49.7%**. *Exclusive to the Whisky Exchange.*

⚜ **Highland Park Ambassador's Cask 2** cask 1071, dist 96, bott 06 db **(79)** **n**19 **t**20 **f**20 **b**20. There are some lovely coastal qualities to this and the rich honey touches are a delight. But not, I'm afraid, from the best cask ever to hold whisky, this displaying the surprising characteristics of a mild sulphur taint and on the nose in particular a peculiar $CO_2$ tun room kick. If dear Jerry Tosh is still speaking to me I'll try and get a sample of Cask 1 from him. **58.8%**. *594 bottles.*

**Highland Park Bicentenary Vintage 1977 Reserve** db **(93)** **n**24 herbal and salty. The heather is in full bloom; **t**25 the early peat dissolves in the mouth allowing the honey and vanilla the stage. Lovely greengages and salt add to the complexity: truly fantastic, to the point of faultless; **f**21 cocoa and Jamaican coffee compensate for an otherwise lazy though lightly spiced finale; **b**23 should have been bottled at 46–50% for full effect: they were making great whisky at this time at HP and this is a pretty peaty version. **40%**

**Highland Park Capella Special Edition** db **(87)** **n**23 that unique buzz of smoke that so comfortably sits with distinctive heather/gorse and honey. Genuinely awesome how this distillery does it; **t**23 smoke and some grapey, fruity notes, then thick fudge; **f**20 spice but dampened and embittered by toffee; **b**21 the caramel (natural or otherwise) that has arrived towards the middle and end flattens an until then intensely glorious bottling. **40%**

⚜ **Alchemist Highland Park Aged 15 Years** dist May 90, bott Jul 05 **(90)** **n**22 heathery sophistication with soft fruit as it oxidizes; **t**23 mouthwatering and zingy, there is a distinct citrus kick to the malt and late-developing honey; **f**23 some soft smoke swirls around barley and delicate oak; **b**22 this is just how I like to see H: lots of sheen to the barley, plus some tantalizing smoke. **46%. nc ncf.**

⚜ **Battlehill Highland Park 1997** cask no. 5306, dist Sept 97, bott Apr 06 **(76)** **n**20 **t**20 **f**18 **b**18. Highly usual: slightly feinty, massive esters and a metallic finish. Some lovely rich honey, but never quite finds its feet. **43.1%**. *Duncan Taylor. 447 bottles.*

⚜ **Berry's' Best Orkney Highland Park Aged 14 Years (87)** **n**23 buttery, but soft honey and smoke; **t**23 the delivery is as clear as church bell in midwinter: crisp, precise barley with just the right amount of acacia honey; **f**20 some bitter elements to the oak hit hard, but softened by natural caramel; **b**21 one of the few under 15 HPs bottled this year that is entirely unambiguous regarding its style and origin...though the finish is a bit rough. **43%**. *Berry Bros & Rudd.*

**Blackadder Highland Park 10 Years Old** refill sherry cask 20569, dist 11 Nov 92, bott Mar 03 **(80)** **n**19 **t**22 **f**20 **b**19. Very sweet and refreshing. **45%**

**Blackadder Raw Cask Highland Park 12 Years Old**, cask no. 20388, dist 29 Jun 92, bott Nov 04 **(90)** **n**21 almost something Canadian to the oaky interference to the firm grain; **t**23 multi-layered malt with a dollop of honey at the peak; **f**23 wonderful deep coffee and hickory notes pulse against the intense, rampant malt. The length of the sweet finale is almost incalculable; **b**23 monster whisky, not just because of the strength but more for its uncompromising make-up. **62.3%**

**Blackadder Raw Cask Highland Park 14 Years Old** cask 10039 dist Mar 89, bott Nov 03 **(91)** **n**22 bales of straw; a little sappy but some impressive covering peat-reek and honey; **t**23 heads directly into the heather-honey zone without passing go; **f**23 soft peat returns and battles it out with rich, oily spices; **b**24 massive amounts of complexity, and all in the fingerprints of HP despite above average peat: most excellent. **57.1%**

**Blackadder Raw Cask Highland Park 15 Years Old**, Sherry Butt cask no. 11931, 05 Dec 88, bott Nov 04 **(68)** **n**17 **t**18 **f**16 **b**17. The soft sulphur taint on the nose is magnified on the palate. **56.1%**

⟐ **Cadenhead's Authentic Collection Highland Park Aged 16 Years** Bourbon Hogshead, dist 89, bott Feb 06 **(92)** **n**22 coal dust and custard; **t**24 bracing barley fans out into various honey variants, from early acacia to manuka as the oak involves itself; **f**23 playful peats and natural toffee vie for dominance over the spicy barley; **b**23 could be the house dram at a honey conference. Wonderful! **51.6%**. *210 bottles.*

**Cadenhead's Authentic Collection Highland Park Aged 17 Years** Bourbon Hogshead, dist 88, bott May 05 **(81)** **n**21 **t**20 **f**21 **b**19. From a tired cask which dulls the honey somewhat. **56.8%**. *288 bottles.*

⟐ **Cadenhead's Authentic Collection Highland Park Aged 18 Years** Sherry butt, dist 88, bott Sept 06 **(76)** **n**19 **t**20 **f**18 **b**19. There are worse sulphur taints around but pity it's a HP. **58.2%**. *678 bottles.*

⟐ **Cask Strength Highland Park 1994** bott 14 Jun 06 **(94)** **n**23 a confident amalgam of citrus and honey; quite tart but the peat reek is discreet though telling; **t**23 no less lucidity on the palate where rich honey replaces the early barley bite; just a flash of smoke; **f**24 long, toffee-honeycomb and finally a peat flourish to the signature; **b**24 take your time with this cask: astonishingly subtle and complex – at full strength. One of G&M Casks of the Year! **57.8%**. *G&M, US Market.*

**Coopers Choice Highland Park 27 Years Old** Single Cask Range, bott 05 **(91)** **n**24 burning oak, bonfires, a spat-upon hearth; **t**22 ferociously busy, untidy start with little structure and then bountiful waxy-heathery honey points you towards a single distillery; **f**23 relaxes at last to spin a lengthy tale of fruit and soft oak and honeycomb; **b**22 extraordinary and quite memorable for its ordered confusion. **52.1%**. *Vintage Malt Whisky Co.*

⟐ **Dewar Rattray Individual Cask Bottling Highland Park 1981 Aged 24 Years** cask 6061, dist Sept 81, bott Sept 05 **(95)** **n**23 lemon tart, banana milkshake and peat trace; **t**25 sumptuous, about as curvaceous as HP gets; the mouth filling with lightly salted and cured barley that moulds itself to the tastebuds. The bitter-sweet ratio ponders perfection; **f**23 sweet vanilla and smoke begin to gain an oily weight. Long, pulsing and nothing lost to age; **b**24 an attractive if slightly unprepossessing nose offers no warning of the unforgettable beauty that is about to unfold on your palate. For seven or eight mercurial seconds you are entirely enveloped in faultless malt, with no beginning or end to it – in other words, orgasmic... An absolute must have for HP devotees. And not a bad choice for those who aren't. And, perhaps even more germane, it is interesting to note that the best HP of the year does not come from any kind of cask finish or wine involvement... **52.3%**. *263 bottles.*

**Duncan Taylor Highland Park 1966 Aged 36 Years** cask 6410 **(79)** **n**19 **t**20 **f**20 **b**20. A malt straffed by rampaging oak but there is enough honey in there for running repairs. **40.1%**

**Duncan Taylor Highland Park 1966 Aged 37 Years** cask 4637 **(85)** **n**19 **t**21 **f**23 **b**22. Sees off the worst of the oak with waxy honey to spare. **40.9%**

⟐ **Duncan Taylor Collection Highland Park 1966** cask no. 4630, dist May 66, bott May 06 **(82)** **n**19 **t**20 **f**22 **b**21. Recovers wonderfully from a shaky start. The nose, for its hints of smoky exotic fruit, does the malt no favours but such is the deftness of the barley after the first biting oak that you cannot help but close your eyes and enjoy, especially when the spices arrive. **41%**. *156 bottles.*

**Duncan Taylor Collection Highland Park 1980 Aged 24 Years** cask no. 9266, dist Nov 80, bott Feb 05 **(87) n**21 steamy suet pudding; dense malt and white chocolate...but the oak is tired; **t**23 estery with intense rich malt and strands of honey – an absolutely outstanding delivery for something so old; **f**22 remains lush and with an almost copper-rich sheen to the honey-oaty finale; **b**22 the nose suggests that time may have defeated this one. But it comes back to life on the plate with aplomb, though a drier HP. **55.1%**

⊰⊱ **Duncan Taylor Collection Highland Park 1992** dist Mar 92, bott Mar 06 **(88) n**21 sluggish if unusually firm; **t**23 outstanding explosion of intense malt and peat; **f**22 gentle whispers of spiced-up smoke on the toffee; **b**22 allows the peat an open road. **46%**. *471 bottles.*

⊰⊱ **Glenkeir Treasures Highland Park 21 Years Old Refill** sherry butt, dist May 84, bott Nov 05 **(91) n**21 toffee and raisins; **t**23 the oily creaminess is a lovely backdrop to the spotted dog pudding lead and delightful light smoke; soft honey waves in and out; **f**23 lots more cream toffee and a fabulous crescendo of mouth-watering malt and warming spice; **b**24 a genuinely pulsing HP choc-a-bloc with intense barley and the late spices are a joy. **54.1%**. *The Whisky Shop. 450 bottles.*

**Gordon & MacPhail Cask Strength Highland Park 1991 (94) n**22 linseed and hickory with perhaps the slightest touch of smoke; **t**24 close your eyes and lie back for the most wonderful delivery of classic heather-honeysmoke. HP not so much in essence as in pure form; **f**24 now goes into orbit as the complexity confounds. All those well-known HP points, but flighting around the palate with bitter marmalade for company; **b**24 slow coming out of the blocks so far as the nose is concerned, but what happens next is pure joy! **59%**

**Hart Brothers Highland Park Aged 10 Years** dist July 93 bott Sep 03 **(82) n**21 **t**22 **f**19 **b**20. One of the most intense citrus noses I've come across with slight pine and peat giving it a character the like of which I guarantee you've never seen before from this or probably any other distillery! **46%**

**Jack Wiebers Whisky World Old Train Line Highland Park 30 Years** cask 8396 dist Jun 73, bott Aug 03 **(91) n**22 **t**24 **f**22 **b**23. Rarely does one cask nutshell Highland Park so comprehensively as this. A must have. **58.7%**. *Germany. 168 bottles.*

**Jim McEwan's Celtic Heartlands Highland Park 1967 (87) n**22 **t**22 **f**21 **b**22 I have drunk some '67 HP over the years, but nothing quite as oily, as this curious – and delicious – chap. **40.1%**. *Bruichladdich.com.*

**The MacPhail's Collection Highland Park 30 Years Old (89) n**22 quite some honeyfest; **t**21 decidedly off-balance at first, but regains its poise towards the middle as some smoke arrives; **f**24 now goes into overdrive as all the old suspects, honey, heather and smoke combine like old pros to steer the dram home to a near perfect conclusion; **b**22 starts unpromisingly but finishes a thoroughbred. **43%**. *Gordon & MacPhail.*

⊰⊱ **Murray McDavid Mission Highland Park 1967 (93) n**22 creaking under the oak but holds out enough for a gently-smoked barley twinkle; **t**24 stupendous! The entire Highland Park works: it is all here, acacia honey in hotel-sized pots with a distinctly heathery drizzle and just the right depth of smoke. This, ladies and gentleman is Orkney at its most auspicious: HP dressed up to the nines; **f**23 the oak which threatens on the nose has now gone home. Instead we have honeycomb ice-cream, with the sweetness beautifully controlled by the vanilla; **b**24 it's drams like these that makes falling in love with whisky such an easy affair. A celebration of a great distillery. **40.1%**. *500 bottles.*

**Murray McDavid Mission IV Highland Park 1979 Aged 25 Years (91) n**23 crushed primroses suggest good age, the delicate malt suggests good breeding; **t**23 beautifully aligned malt that offers a stream of controlled sweetness and tart green apple; **f**22 some strands of honey and liquorice, but it's all very underplayed; **b**23 so delicate, a malt that could snap in half on your tastebuds. **46%**

⸬ **Murray McDavid Mission Highland Park 1979 Aged 27 Years** Bourbon/Syrah, bott 06 **(78) n**22 **t**19 **f**18 **b**19. Decent nose and the first few nano-seconds of the delivery. But, frankly, I don't get the point of this. HP luxuriates in a unique style of honey and peat and the odd brush with heather. This, though, after such a promising nose, leaves you with a pleasantish but disjointed malt that could be from any inferior distillery and, by HP standards, is pretty one dimensional. One of the leading lights of Murray McDavid comes from an exceptional wine background. I have known him years and have much time and respect for him. But, as a friend, I say to him this: how would you feel if I was tipping a splash of Highland Park into a '82 Margaux? **46.2%. nc ncf.** *500 bottles.*

⸬ **Murray McDavid Highland Park 1989 Aged 16 Years** Bourbon/Grenache Blanc, bott 06 **(86) n**23 **t**22 **f**20 **b**21 the voluptuous body of HP perhaps takes to Grenache better than other malts; the curious bonfire/coal/peat smokiness guarantees a complex nose. **46%. nc ncf.** *2500 bottles.*

⸬ **Old Malt Cask Highland Park Aged 10 Years** Refill Hogshead 2168, dist June 95, bott Oct 05 **(79) n**20 **t**22 **f**18 **b**19. Bright barley start but a dull follow-through. **50%. nc ncf.** *Douglas Laing.*

⸬ **Old Malt Cask Highland Park 12 Years Old** dist 30 Nov 92, bott Jul 05 **(85) n**21 **t**22 **f**21 **b**21. Rich, estery and mildly metallic; very little smoke to this one. **50%.** *Douglas Laing. 370 bottles.*

**Old Malt Cask Highland Park 13 Years Old** dist Mar 91, bott Aug 04 **(89) n**21 malty but surprisingly neutral; **t**22 the honey doesn't take long to kick into action, though some vanilla seems to hold it back a little; **f**24 absolutely comes into its own as some smoke drifts in to add depth and balance; a touch of sweet liquorice also adds weight to the gathering malt; **b**22 takes a little time to get going, but once it does, it's a real corker. **50%.** *Douglas Laing & Co.*

**Old Malt Cask Highland Park Aged 16 Years** cask 984 dist Apr 87, bott Sep 03 **(82) n**20 **t**22 **f**20 **b**20. A delicious honeyball at times, but the oak has fraction too loud a shout. **50%, nc ncf sc.** *Douglas Laing. 306 bottles.*

**Old Malt Cask Highland Park Aged 16 Years** dist Dec 87, bott Mar 04 **(91) n**21 warming and honeyed if a little thin; **t**23 brilliant combination of spicy punches softens you up for the gushing honey; **f**24 just a hint of vanilla is all that shows of the oak; the honey and very soft smoke have the field to themselves: maximum effect with minimum effort – outstanding! **b**23 HP at its most abstract and alluring: the secret is the minimum oak interference. **50%. nc ncf sc.**

**Old Malt Cask Highland Park Aged 19 Years** dist May 84, bott Jun 03 **(78) n**19 **t**21 **f**19 **b**19. Attractively sweet at times, but otherwise fuzzy and illdefined. **50%. nc ncf sc.** *Douglas Laing. 636 bottles.*

⸬ **Old Malt Cask Highland Park Aged 21 Years** Sherry **(92) n**22 caramel wafers and dank sultana; **t**23 lively delivery but is becalmed by waves of softening honey; **f**23 the spice picks up beautifully and goes hand-in-hand with the juicy malt and wispy smoke; **b**24 a not dissimilar bottling to the Glenkeir expression. A really big HP to take as much time as you like over. **54.1%.** *Exclusively for Vintage House.*

**Old Master's Highland Park 1989** bott 04 cask 10535 **(83) n**21 **t**21 **f**20 **b**21. Blood orange vies with the pounding oak for the honeyed hand. **53.5%.**

⸬ **Old Masters Highland Park 1992 Aged 13 Years** cask no. 20359, bott 05 **(88) n**21 bananas and barley; **t**23 refreshing, ultra-intense barley; the most delicate waves of golden syrup; **f**22 a tad bitter but some late smoke sooths; **b**22 mouthwatering clarity. **50%.** *James MacArthur.*

**Park Avenue Liquor Store Highland Park 24 Years Old (75) n**17 **t**20 **f**19 **b**19. The intense sherry fights valiantly against the annoying (and, in whisky terms, tragic) suphur. Oh, for what might have been.... **59%.** *Old Malt Cask.*

**Private Cellars Selection Highland Park 1985** bott 04 **(74)** n18 t20 f18 b18. Furry and unattractive. Not from the greatest cask in the world. **43%.**

**Provenance Highland Park 10 Years Old** dist 13 Jun 94, bott 23 Mar 05 **(85)** n22 t22 f20 b21. Enjoyable, but virtually nil oak input is compensated for by peat: a must for HP collectors. **46%.** *Douglas Laing & Co.*

⋅⋅⋅ **Provenance Highland Park 10 Years Old** dist Jun 95, bott Oct 05 **(79)** n21 t20 f19 b19. The nose is pure grist; nascent peat adds weight but otherwise thin. **46%.** *McGibbon's.*

⋅⋅⋅ **Provenance Highland Park 10 Years Old** dist 29 Mar 95, bott 21 Jun 05 **(84)** n22 t21 f20 b21. An almost identical story to the June bottling, except this has just a little extra bounce and balance. **46%.** *McGibbon's.*

⋅⋅⋅ **Provenance Highland Park 12 Years Old** dist Jun 94, bott Autumn 06 **(86)** n22 more from the HP gristmill; t22 excellent controlled sweetness to the barley; f20 disappointingly dull and fragmented; b22 this would have been so good at a fuller strength. **46%.** *McGibbon's.*

**Scott's Selection Highland Park 1986** bott 05 **(79)** n19 t21 f19 b20. Mildly hot and lacking the distillery's usual grace and charisma: at times rather rum-like. **55.7%.**

**The Un-chillfiltered Collection Highland Park Vintage 1990** cask 3925, dist 23 Apr 90, bott 23 Jan 04 **(87)** n22 t22 f21 b22. Sweet and spicy throughout. **46%.**

**The Un-Chillfiltered Collection Highland Park Aged 14 Years** Hogsheads 3942 and 3943, dist 23 Apr 90, bott 9 Dec 04 **(88)** n21 bonfires and barley; t23 the most delicate build-up of soft honey imaginable, an essay in subtlety; f22 returns to some spice and smoke; b22 entirely underplayed, understated HP that only whispers its charm and beauty. Listen hard.... **46%. nc ncf.** *Signatory.*

⋅⋅⋅ **Vintage House Highland Park Aged 16 Years** Natural Cask Strength **(87)** n22 esters that wouldn't be out of place at Jamaica's Hampden Distillery...!!; t23 a real mouthful of toffeed barley and lemon cake; f21 burnt fudge and a vague marzipan depth; the smoke appears as an almost apologetic afterthought; b21 charming, but almost too well behaved for its own good. **50.1%.** *from Douglas Laing for Vintage House. 159 bottles*

**Whisky Galore Highland Park 1987 Aged 17 Years** cask 1527, dist Jan 87, bott 04 **(81)** n21 t21 f20 b19. Sweetly malted; missing its usual special charisma. **46%.**

**Whisky Galore Highland Park 1989 Aged 15 Years** cask 6 **(58)** n18 t15 f12 b13. If the whisky was attached to a cardiograph, there would be a straight line. **40%.** *Duncan Taylor.*

**Whisky Galore Highland Park 1990 Aged 13 Years (87)** n21 t23 f22 b21. With this pale, second (or even third) fill bourbon expression, proof were it ever needed that the heather-honey effect does not come from maturation. **46%.** *Duncan Taylor.*

**Whisky Galore Highland Park 1991 Aged 14 Years** cask 8, dist Feb 91, bott Mar 04 **(90)** n23 the smoke signals are clear and stark against the malty sweetness. Excepionally refined; t23 wonderful smoke gently holds together firm malt and shards of honey; f22 lightly roasted Santos and Blue Mountain (believe me!) blend perfectly with the lingering smoke; b23 now this is how you want HP to be: gently smoked and running soft, honied fingers over your tastebuds. Not easy to spit this one out. **46.1%.** *Duncan Taylor & Co Ltd.*

**Whisky Galore Highland Park 1994 Aged 11 Years** cask 1, dist Feb 94, bott Mar 05 **(87)** n22 teasing honey; t23 sweet, simple malt. Lethargic and lush, just so gently honied; f21 butterscotch and vanilla; b21 a honey barrel in every sense but pretty simplistic. **46.1%.** *Duncan Taylor & Co Ltd.*

## HILLSIDE ( see Glenesk)

## IMPERIAL
### Speyside, 1897. Chivas. Silent.

⋅⋅⋅ **Berry's' Own Selection Imperial 1976 Aged 29 Years (91)** n23 tight little nose, excellent firm honey edge. Shows virtually no sign of wear and tear; t23 again there is a clipped and polished element to the barley, steadfastly refusing to allow the oak to get too dominant; lovely hints of melon on the soft manuka honey; **f22** some toasty notes show that this whisky does doff its cap, if only briefly, to advancing years; **b23** unbelievably comfortable in old age; in human terms you'd have expected this to have had the full nip and tuck treatment. A wonderful cask. **46%.** *Berry Bros & Rudd.*

⋙ **D&M Connoisseurs' Club Bottling Imperial Aged 15 Years** cask no. 11968, dist Dec 90 **(93) n25** one of the noses of the year: just stick your beak in a glass of this for about half an hour and discover just how astonishing Speyside can be. The balance between barley and oak is textbook, the levels of sweetness offered by the barley defies belief; **t23** envelops the tastebuds in enormous waves of barley which span between marmalade and under-ripe apple. All brushed with honey; **f22** some bitterness to the fade, but a buttery oil; **b23** what a fabulous advertisement for this unjustly silent distillery. **60.4%. nc ncf.** *US by Angus Dundee Distillers plc.*

⋙ **Duncan Taylor Collection Imperial 1994** cask no. 2111, dist Mar 94, bott Mar 06 **(74) n19 t20 f17 b18.** An entirely unsympathetic cask which does the distillery few favours. **46%.** *286 bottles.*

⋙ **Gordon & MacPhail Imperial 1991 (77) n21 t20 f18 b18.** Hmmmm. After the initial sweet burst, curiously flat or out of tune. The citric-laced nose needs some time to settle. **43%.** *Gordon & MacPhail.*

**Gordon & MacPhail Imperial 1993** bott 04 **(91) n22** hints of bourbon and honeycomb edged by the faintest smoke; **t23** beautifully crafted, crisp malt continues with the delicate honey theme; **f23** a surprising degree of oak for one so young adds a dry vanilla and delicate spice to the runaway malt; **b23** a sensuous, honey-crested dram with more weight than normally associated with this tragically silent distillery. A collector's must-have. **45%**

⋙ **Old Masters Imperial 1976 Aged 27 Years** cask 10171, bott 04 **(90) n22** curious, peaty edge takes a little time to unravel. Also some odd fruit on there. Highly unusual combination and needs oxidization to work; **t23** a sweeter more intense barley than you might expect for a whisky of this vintage; the smoke arrives in mid stream and the mouthwatering properties are close behind; **f22** some of the coffee notes are rather spellbinding; **b23** to be honest, I didn't much care for this when I first tasted it. However, I was drawn back, for I realized there was something very different about it and it needed longer investigation. A wise choice. A particularly idiosyncratic cask. **57.2%.** *James MacArthur.*

⋙ **Private Collection Imperial Calvados 1990** bott 28.06.05 **(83) n22 t21 f20 b20.** The punchy aroma has no little bourbon but after a big malty chewfest the finish is lacking. **46%.** *Gordon & MacPhail, US Market.*

**Private Collection Imperial Calvados Finish 1990 (56) n14 t15 f14 b13.** Just doesn't work. A disaster that should have been tipped (with care) into a blend. **40%.**

⋙ **The Single Malt of Scotland Imperial Aged 11 Years Vintage 1994** Sherry butt cask no. 1537 **(83) n20 t22 f21 b20.** Imperial in sherry is as rare as hen's teeth. And appears to have more bite as this is a full-on no holds barred, old-fashioned duff up of the tastebuds. And, for its rock hardness and imbalance...it's wonderful...!! **59.2%.** *The Whisky Exchange.* 165 bottles.

⋙ **Whisky Galore Imperial 1994 Aged 12 Years** cask nos. Part 2112, 2113, dist Mar 94, bott 28 Jun 06 **(85) n22 t21 f21 b21.** Big barley theme that remains clean and chewy throughout. **45.98%.** *Duncan Taylor.* 480 bottles.

# INCHGOWER
### Speyside, 1872. Diageo. Working.

**Inchgower Aged 14 Years** db **(77) n19 t20 f19 b19.** A vague hint of peat and a sprinkling of spice lifts the dram above something treacly and over-sweet. **43%.** *Flora and Fauna.*

**Inchgower 27 Years Old Rare Malts 2004** db **(84)** n21 t22 f20 b21. Oily, decently spiced, but at times heavy going. Some charming, sharp barley, though. **55.6%**

⸬ **Adelphi Inchgower 1980 Aged 24 Years** Sherry butt cask no. 14152, dist 80, bott Jun 06 **(86)** n22 t21 f22 b21. Usually my memo to independent bottlers – and drinkers – is: stay away from this distillery for anything casked in the late 70s and early to mid 80s. The wood policy was, at best, horrific. But there are always exceptions, and here we have a chunky expression with just enough Demerara on the nose and early bite to make for an unusually enjoyable experience from this distillery. **60.4%**. *576 bottles.*

⸬ **The Coopers Choice Inchgower 1980 Sherry Wood 24 Years Old** bott 06 **(75)** n18 t21 f18 b18. A shuddering nose is offset by the silky mouth arrival. But the finish is pure Inchgower from this period. Or perhaps I should say impure... **46%**. *The Vintage Malt Whisky Co.*

⸬ **Dewar Rattray Individual Cask Bottling Inchgower 1980 Aged 25 Years** Sherry cask no. 14161, dist Dec 80, bott May 06 **(65)** n15 t18 f15 b17. I originally gave this 69. What was I thinking? That might have suggested that something went down here as even vaguely enjoyably... **53.2%**. *486 bottles.*

Duncan Taylor Collection Inchgower 1968 Aged 36 Years cask no. 5575, dist Oct 68, bott Feb 05 **(88)** n21 dragging the first strands of sap, but some wonderful marmalade citrus compensates; t23 silky malt woven on avelvety grassiness; a wonderfully understated sweetness throughout; f22 remains improbably mouthwatering for its enormous age to the very last; b22 that rarest of beasts: an Inchgower made in the days before it had been run into the ground and the warehouses had been swamped with sub-standard wood. Charming and delicious. **46.3%**. *142 bottles.*

⸬ **Usquebaugh Society Inchgower Aged 20 Years** cask no. 5633, dist Jun 85, bott 16 Aug 05 **(80)** n22 t20 f18 b20. Technically not great. Raw and "dirty" in that old-fashioned Bells style, there is still a wonderful resonance – some of it distinctly bourbony – that bites and nips and swamps; a whisky where the sum is infinitely better than the parts. **60.8%. ncf sc.** *250 bottles.*

## INCHMOAN ( see Loch Lomond)

## INCHMURRIN ( see Loch Lomond)

## INVERLEVEN
### Lowland, 1938–1991. Demolished.
⸬ **Cadenhead's Dumbarton (Inverleven Stills) 18 Years Old (94)** n22 old parchment and barley water; t25 beautiful, intact malt that starts confidently but with a dozen graceful, mouthwatering sweeps of the palate becomes something intense and glorious. With a charming citric and barley fruitiness, too, this is sheer perfection as far as an 18-year-old Lowlander goes; f23 the vanilla never overdoes it, though the barley backs off with the same grace with which it initially sweeps the palate; unsalted butter coats toasted fresh bread; b24 while the label might be somewhat confusing, what isn't is the élan of this glorious bottling. Often the malt from this distillery was too light to withstand too long an inquisition from the oak; here it has not only survived but thrived. Not just stunning. But also outranked only by an exceptional Rosebank as Scottish Lowlander of the year. **57.9%**

Duncan Taylor Inverleven 1977 Aged 26 Years **(78)** n20 t18 f20 b20. They rarely come much more warming than this, though when the flames are doused the sweet malt is attractive. **57%**

⸬ **Duncan Taylor Collection Inverleven 1977** cask 3099, dist Sept 77, bott Mar 06 **(85)** n20 t23 f21 b21. Some lovely lemon-zesty life still in this one. A bit battered, but in much better shape than the distillery. **56.5%**. *175 bottles.*

**Gordon and MacPhail Inverleven 1989 (79)** n19 t20 f20 **b**20. Though thin and shy, it is also clean, barley-rich and refreshing. **40%**

**Gordon and MacPhail Inverleven 1990 (84)** n21 t22 f21 **b**20. Delicate, malty, playfully sweet and grassy. Such a soft, courteous, unassuming yet charming memory of this recently demolished distillery. **40%**

**Old Malt Cask Inverleven 16 Years Old** dist 17 Jan 89, bott 24 Feb 05 **(84)** n19 t23 f21 **b**21. Attractive, if simplistic, fare where the oak has gone through the nose slightly but is compensated for by the wonderful mouthwatering quality of the concentrated malt arrival: a delicious requiem for a recently lost distillery. **50%.**

**Peerless Inverleven 1977** (see Duncan Taylor Inverleven 1977)

## ISLE OF ARRAN
**Highland (Island–Arran), 1995. Isle of Arran Distillers. Working.**

**Arran First** db dist 95, bott Apr 04 **(87)** n21 melt-in-the-nose gently sweetened malt; t22 a double layer of malt – one hard, juicy and purposeful, the other soft, sweet and undisciplined; f22 some almost chalky vanilla puts the brake on the malty celebrations; **b**22 quite beautifully made malt. **46%.** *2,784 bottles.*

⊰⊱ **The Arran Malt Aged 10 Years** L140206 db **(93)** n23 charming, delicate; varying citrus notes hand-in-hand with rich, butterscotch-barley; the odd youthful note things out; t24 the palate coated in caressing oils, to which stick the cleanest and most profound barley. You can chew your jaw off here; f23 developing vanillas dovetail with some of those younger new-makish notes but still cannot escape the clutches of the fat barley. Some fizzing spice decides to make an appearance; **b**23 at last! The distillery feels confident enough to put an age statement to their malt, although it's been good enough to do that for the last four or five years. This bottling of some of Arran's first casks entertains and delight. It won't be long before the world's malt connoisseurs add Arran to their list of must haves. Because if it's character and quality you want, it's here by the malt shiel load. **46%. ncf.**

⊰⊱ **The Arran Malt 100° Proof** L210806 db **(91)** n23 complex not just in aroma but weight: both firm yet soft; the barley offers varying degrees of intensity. Youthful and deeply desirable; t23 just so barley rich! That lovely hint of youth embracing something older and more oakily complex as it develops; the early barley offers a fruit edge, some natural toffees and then cocoas develop; f22 much drier, though with enough moistening barley, and waves of mocha; **b**23 different, intriguing, style of Arran; some excellent use of bourbon cask allows a relaxed meeting of barley and oak. Sheer class. **57%. ncf.**

**The Arran Malt Bordeaux Finish** db **(90)** n22 awkward and cumbersome, though the salty element appeals; t23 wonderful delivery on gently fruited malt, but then it unravels clumsily and falls apart to reveal its intricate workings; f22 the eclectic style here continues with a burnt raisin and chocolate finale; **b**23 bloody hell! I'm exhausted after that lot. Whatever balance it has is by fluke rather than design. Never settles down and the palate can't quite get a grip. Yet we have a slapdash masterpiece. Arran has gone all French with its Calvados, Bordeaux and Cognac finishes. This is probably the most intriguing of the lot. And the unconventional colour should appeal in San Francisco, Soho and Sydney.... **59.6%.**

⊰⊱ **The Arran Malt Brandy Finish** Lepanto Px Brandy cask from Gonzalez Byass, bott 17.1.06 db **(74)** n18 t19 f19 **b**18. Intense but irritatingly off-key. **59.4%.** *705 bottles.*

⊰⊱ **The Arran Malt Cream Sherry Cask** from Gonzalez Byass, bott 01.2.06 db **(90)** n22 chunky malt with spicy apple and sour under-ripe cherry; t24 a delivery from heaven with perfect weight to the barley; a bitter-sweet delivery to die for. The natural oiliness of the barley sits comfortably with the "cream" grape, the most enormous spice explosion blasting apart any chance of a cloying nature; f21 surprisingly lightweight grape; **b**23 make sure your chair has arm-rests... **57.5%.** *812 bottles.*

⋄ **The Arran Malt Finished in Port Cask** bott 28.6.05 db **(90)** n23 the port shines from the very first; perhaps the most distant waft of sulphur but fails to significantly detract; **t**23 well structured and calm – behaved fruit suddenly gives way to a rip-tide of pulsating pepper; some malt-fruit notes intertwine towards the late middle. Fabulously mouthwatering throughout; **f**22 firm traces of oak dry this one out, but it's a long journey; **b**22 at a tasting in Canada, where both this and the 4th July bottling can be found, I at first favoured the lighter-coloured bottling of just 218. However, on reflection, this one may just edge it – if you find them side-by-side, it's a close call!! **58.4%.** *770 bottles.*

⋄ **The Arran Malt Finished in Port Cask** db **(89)** n22 mildly peppered fruit; delicate and with youthful, malty resonance; **t**23 simple, brilliant, very young arrival: suppressed fruit on the nose arrives in concentrated form before backing off to allow those peppers full play; **f**22 lightens out dramatically with cocoa and vanilla leaning towards dryness; **b**22 genuinely lovely whisky showing both youth and maturity in its broad-sweeping mouthfeel. **58.5%.** *218 bottles.*

**The Arran Malt Non-Chill Filtered** db **(89)** n22 quite feisty barley kicking up a rumpus; good age now and some real character to the mildly gristy freshness; **t**23 massive barley delivery, a few half-hearted spices and then a lovely oiliness creeps in to intensify the malt; **f**22 gentle vanilla, greengages and dry but big barley; **b**22 a vastly improved dram with some apparent extra age and body, though less spice. A real meal from the real deal. **46%** ⊙ ⊙

⋄ **The Arran Malt Premier Cru Bourgogne Cask Finish** db **(86)** n21 t22  f21 **b**22. An entertaining dram which some would do somersaults for, but marks docked because we have lost the unique Arran character. **56.4%**

**The Arran Malt Single Cask (92)** n22 very thinly spread marmalade, vanilla and fresh malt; this freshness even hints slightly at sliced cucumber; **t**23 a breathtaking assortment of malty notes of varying sweetness and intensity; oak also pounds through and a gentle, citric fruitiness is woven into the rich tapestry; **f**24 a gentle wave of salt to go with the gentle oak and vanilla; late hints of cocoa on the death; **b**23 the bottle doesn't give the vintage or cask number (something to be addressed?) but this malt is only about eight and shows maturity way beyond those years. The depth of intensity is outstanding and from first to last not even the whimper of an off note: a glorious advert for a distillery just coming of age. For the record, it was a 1998 vintage and cask no. 640. **58.9%.** *Drawn from cask at the Isle of Arran Distillery and available only in visitor centre.*

**The Arran Malt Single Bourbon Cask Strength** db **(88)** n23 highly unusual mixture of Irn Bru and stewed ginger on a bed of young bourbon: surprisingly delicate and complex; **t**22 the enormity and intensity of the malt take some believing; **f**21 dries considerably with a comparatively bitter edge to the oak; the lingering spices are attractive; **b**22 on this evidence Arran is confidently formulating its own style. **56.6%**

**Arran Single Malt Calvados Finish**, bott 03 Feb 05 db **(86)** n19 t22 f23 b22. The unerring sharpness of this may make it the apple of some Arran fans' eyes, but not mine. **60.1%.** *620 bottles.*

**Arran Single Malt Cognac Finish** bott 08 Apr 05 db **(87)** n22 looking for Frenchified stuff? Forget it; the sallow peat offers enough to charm; **t**22 one of the bigger Arrans doing the rounds, with the malt packed with smoke and honey; enormously oily: perhaps too much so; **f**21 vanilla and natural caramel; **b**22 the Cognac plays no role whatsoever here (unless it once boasted a phenol level): the star – and real shock – is the gentle peat. **59.4%.** *506 bottles.*

**The Arran Malt Single Cask Strength Marsala Finish** db **(82)** n21 t20 f21 **b**20. Pleasant, gentle spiced fruit but otherwise flat and charisma-free by Arran standards. **56.9%**

**The Arran Malt Single Cask Strength Rum Finish** db **(87)** n20 clean, dull and non-committal; **t**22 leaps into life with the most glorious volleys of bitter-sweet barley; at once mouthwatering and spicy; **f**23 the bitter-sweet spiciness lasts the course; **b**22 a tastebud-provoking extrovert – but only on the palate. **58.5%**

**The Arran Malt Single Sherry Cask Strength** db **(91) n**23 tangy orange and crushed grape; has come from top-draw cask because there is still enough clarity to see the usual Arran trademark intense malt; **t**23 weighty and takes time to really find its bearings: when it does, the tastebuds are crushed under an avalanche of enormous malt and fruit in equal measures; **f**22 lightens to allow vanilla and spice to flourish; **b**23 heartening to see a latter-day sherry butt come through so brilliantly; the complexity and bitter-sweet balance is fabulous. **57.3%**

⚜ **The Arran Malt Single Sherry Cask** cask 98/44, dist 19 Jan 98, bott 7 Nov 05 db **(94) n**24 freshly opened conkers; nutty with a jaffa/marzipan/cocoa complexity. Wonderful; **t**25 the best Arran delivery yet. Tastebuds blitzed by a relentless barrage of high propane barley notes; mouthwatering and beguiling as the grape finds a various fissures to gain a toe-hold. Almost, but not quite overwhelmed: total brinkmanship and brilliance; **f**22 surprisingly hard and metallic; **b**23 there is not a whisky even close to this in character. A stunning one-off. **58.3%**

**The Arran Malt Limited Edition 1996** dist 12 Aug 96, bott 14 Apr 03 db **(88) n**22 **t**23 **f**21 **b**22. When Arran whisky was little more than an embryo, I predicted rapid maturation. Even I didn't expect something quite like this from a six-year-old. Astonishing and massively drinkable. **57%**. *175 bottles.*

**The Arran Malt Single Cask Finished in Calvados** db **(83) n**19 **t**22 **f**21 **b**21. A strange, indecisive whisky that never quite settles on the character it wishes to be. Undermined by a slight soapiness on the nose it still has one or two astonishing moments of wanton wild, fruity passion, especially on the early mouth arrival. One that may terrify you at first but will grow on you. **62.1%**

⚜ **The Arran Malt Single Montepulciano D'Abruzzo Sherry Cask** bott 06 db **(76) n**19 **t**20 **f**18 **b**19. The odd butyric note reveals a cask not entirely in sympathy with the distillery. **56.9%.** *315 bottles.*

⚜ **The Arran Malt Trebbiano D'Abruzzo Cask Finish** db **(93) n**22 a jazzed-up, fruity, spicy number, but astonishingly clean; **t**24 thundering, spiced malt but entirely in sync with the massive, chewy body; **f**23 long with subtle re-emergence of fruit and a hint of honeycomb; **b**24 a cask finish that works uncommonly well with the malt and fruit being very much on the same wavelength. If enormous complexity doesn't come naturally to this distillery, then it certainly has the weight and charisma to absorb agents that will help. **56%**

**The Arran Malt Vintage Collection 1996** db **(88) n**22 charming and elegant with just-so measures of marmalade, malt and oak and even the most deft touch of smoke; **t**22 softest of mouth arrivals with the emphasis on sweet malt. Gentle vanilla and spice towards middle; **f**21 dry digestive biscuit and ginger nuts; **b**23 all the early promise from this distillery is coming to fruition. **46%.** *6,000 bottles.*

**Arran Port Finish** bott 14 Jun 04 db **(87) n**19 raw, fruity yet imbalanced; **t**22 an astonishing transformation on the palate, the malt is still amazingly young but the port effect is like boiled candy, especially as the intense, sweet malt congregates; **f**23 very long, immensely fruity and then a delicious chocolate-cherry finale; **b**23 a highly unusual Scotch that is like weak cranberry juice on the eye and a malty fruitfest on the palate thanks most to most probably a first-fill port pipe. Just ignore the nose. **57.5%**

**Robert Burns World Federation Arran Single Island Malt** db **(84) n**19 **t**22 **f**22 **b**21. Fat, creamy, full-bodied. The malt sweetens by the second to become something like a good old-fashioned American malt milkshake: amazing but there is enough oak for a drying balance. One of the most intense young malts on the market, only the naivety of the nose preventing it from hitting the heights. A delightful, tastebud-massaging malt experience. **40%.** *Isle of Arran.* ⊙

**Blackadder Raw Cask Arran-Lochranza 8 Years Old** cask no. 43 dist 24 Jan 96, bott Jun 04 **(90) n**22 very tight malt, the barley locked solid with only a hint of honey and oak to offer balm; **t**23 rock-hard arrival and then, after missing a few beats, opens up spectacularly with several layers of gristy sweetness offset against sharp grassy notes; **f**22 big bitter-sweet finale; **b**23 weird: I have just tasted a whole array of Arran finishes, and all but one of them have impressed me more than this standard bourbon cask bottling which is so full of pent-up, malty aggression. Tells a tale, that.... **55.2%**

⋅⋅⋅ **Cadenhead's Authentic Collection Arran Aged 10 Years** Bourbon Hogshead, dist 95, bott Feb 06 **(93)** **n**23 a flawless aroma of the most intense barley imaginable, yet friendly and lightly oiled; **t**24 the palate is swamped with barley at its most concentrated, charismatic yet clean; the degree of sweetness hits perfection; **f**23 soft spices appear as does vanilla and natural cream toffee; **b**23 this distillery has so come of age. Spectacular! And a more intense, if less complex, version of the distillery's own 10-year-old. **53.6%.** *348 bottles*

⋅⋅⋅ **Mac Y 10th Anniversary Isle of Arran Aged 10 Years** cask no. 718, dist 96, bott 06 **(95)** **n**23 firm barley and sultana softened by a sprinkling of grist and most distant rumblings of peat. Proud, high quality stuff; **t**24 immediately crisp and salivating with a glorious crescendo of intense barley; the layering is cleverly structured with the malt offering varying intensity of sweetness. Just so subtle and perfectly weighted...; **f**24 long with a late grapey reprise; fades as the spices and cocoa arrive. Again, supreme structuring and complexity; **b**24 this is the kind of malt, when writing a book like this, you have to wait a long time to find. In this case, it's among the very last whiskies tasted and is on new ground as Arran is still finding its feet. And was it worth the wait! Arran in one of its most compelling guises yet; a stunning way for Danish whisky importers Mac Y to mark their first ten years. And further, indisputable, evidence of Arran taking on the status of one the Great Distilleries. **48%. nc ncf.** *Denmark. 450 bottles.*

⋅⋅⋅ **Old Malt Cask Isle of Arran Aged 9 Years** Sherry butt 2309, dist July 96, bott Jan 06 **(87)** **n**19 intense barley despite the butt, but also a tad feinty; **t**23 one of the richest most intense barley deliveries in the business with echoes of marmalade and butterscotch; **f**23 long, oily and just the faintest speck of peat to add body. Lovely whisky; **b**22 don't be put off by the very slight feintiness on the nose as, is so often the case, it is followed by untold riches on the body. **50%. nc ncf.** *Douglas Laing.*

**Provenance Arran 7 Years Old** dist Spring 97, bott Autumn 04 **(90)** **n**24 honey, lemon and honeydew melon; **t**22 beautifully weighted malt with a riveting, understated butterscotch sweetness that works perfectly with a gentle sherry dryness; **f**21 relatively short with the emphasis on developing oak; **b**23 stunning whisky which entirely mocks its youthfulness. **46%.** *Douglas Laing & Co.*

**Vom Fass Isle of Arran 6 Years Old** **(87)** **n**22 butterscotch and honey; **t**22 excellent malt arrival with soft vanilla drifting through the muscovado sugar; **f**22 neat, tidy and with many layers of gentle sweetness; **b**21 a bit of wimp whisky-wise, with no spice or telling oak. But if your tastebuds want a sweet, barley-laden massage, this is your boy. Or girl. **40%.** *Austria.*

## ISLE OF JURA
### Highland (Island–Jura), 1810. Whyte and Mackay. Working.

**Isle of Jura 5 Years Old** 1999 db **(83)** **n**19 **t**23 **f**21 **b**20. Absolutely enormously peated, but has reached that awkward time in its life when it is massively sweet and as well balanced as a two-hour-old foal. **46%** *The Whisky Exchange*

**Isle of Jura 10 Years Old** db **(77)** **n**18 **t**19 **f**21 **b**19. A tangy malt that seems younger than its 10 years. The finish is long and offers the faintest hint of smoke on the rich malt. **40%**

**Isle of Jura 16 Years Old** db **(80)** **n**18 **t**22 **f**20 **b**20. Some lovely, mildly salty honey thorough the middle. But an indefinable something is missing. A variable dram at the best of times, this expression is pleasant but ... variable. **40%**

**Isle of Jura Aged 21 Years** db **(78) n**20 **t**21 **f**19 **b**18. Pleasant enough, but surprisingly short of charisma. **40%**

**Isle of Jura 21 Years Old Cask Strength** db **(92) n**22 something hard and grainy against the ultra-clean fruit; **t**24 fabulous mouth arrival, just such a brilliant fruit-spice combo held together in a malty soup; **f**23 long and intensely malty; **b**23 every mouthful exudes class and quality. A must-have for Scottish Island collector ... or those who know how to appreciate a damn fine malt **58.1%**

**Isle of Jura Aged 36 Years** (dist 1965) db **(96) n**25 **t**25 **f**23 **b**23 I remember 20-odd years ago being taken into a corner of Jura's warehouse and tasting a cask of something big and smoky. It was different to all the other Juras around, but had none of this honey. Is this the same cask, a generation on? Most probably. I then returned to the hotel opposite for a dram (and a bottle) of their own Jura and wondered what would become of that peaty one-off. Now I know. **44%**

**Isle of Jura 1984** db **(69) n**15 **t**18 **f**18 **b**18. Big brother ... with sulphur. All whiskies are equal, but some are more equal than others. Oops, wrong book. **42%**. Bottled to commemorate George Orwell who wrote the book 1984 while on the island.

**Jura Festival of Malt and Music Distilled 1989** dist Mar 89, bott 04 db **(87) n**19 the two year influence of the young "Anada" sherry butt has left a slight blemish though an agave pepperiness is interesting; **t**23 very unusual delivery of barley, almost glass textured at first and mildly cooling before those massive peppers return to torch the outside of the tongue; **f**23 opens up later on to reveal a saltier tang to the storming spice and a distant waft of smoke; **b**22 not entirely flawless but one of the most unusual, fascinating and, it must be said, at times delicious drams of the year. **57.9%**. 850 bottles.

**Isle of Jura 1989** bott 23/2/03 db **(66) n**16 **t**17 **f**17 **b**16. Wrong kind of sherry influence: off-key. Not my cup of tea at all. **57.2%**

**Isle of Jura Legacy** db **(82) n**19 **t**22 **f**20 **b**21. Some very chewy honeycomb on the middle. Pretty big stuff. **40%**

**Isle of Jura Stillman's Dram Limited Edition Aged 27 Years** db **(90) n**24 **t**23 **f**21 **b**22. One of the most complex Juras yet bottled. **45%**

**Isle of Jura Superstition** db **(86) n**21 **t**22 **f**20 **b**23. A rare case of where the whole is better than the parts. Wins through with superb balance between peat and sweeter barley. Distinctive to the point of being almost unique. **45%**

**Cadenhead's Authentic Collection Isle of Jura Aged 13 Years** Bourbon Hogshead, dist 92, bott May 05 **(87) n**21 sea-salty malt; **t**22 refreshing, mildly salty malt and good oily structure; **f**22 excellent juicy depth with late cocoa oils to complement the vanilla; **b**22 Jura at its most islandy. **54.8%**. 270 btls.

⋰ **Cadenhead's Authentic Collection Jura Aged 14 Years** Bourbon Hogshead, dist 92, bott May 06 **(78) n**20 **t**21 **f**18 **b**19. A bitter, metallic experience, though not too unusual for this distillery. **56.3%**. 276 bottles.

**Connoisseurs Choice Jura 1991 (74) n**18 **t**21 **f**17 **b**18. Pleasing barley kick, but otherwise not happy with itself. **43%**. Gordon & MacPhail.

**Coopers Choice Single Cask Bottling 1993 10 Years Old** bott 04 **(73) n**18 **t**19 **f**18 **b**18. Flat and inert although in a natural state. **46%. nc ncf.**

⋰ **Dun Bheagan Isle of Jura Aged 17 Years (76) n**19 **t**20 **f**18 **b**19. Another off-key offering: by and large, not a classic period for Jura. **43%**. Ian Macleod.

⋰ **Dun Bheagan Isle of Jura 18 Years Old (92) n**24 gorgeous citrus and marzipan; **t**23 melt-in-the-mouth malt offering perfect, understated sweetness; **f**22 decent vanilla offers a sexy, soft landing; **b**23 hurrah! A delightful, delicate Jura absolutely worth investing in...!!! **43%**. Ian Macleod.

**Murray McDavid Isle of Jura 1989 13 Years Old** Bourbon cask **(77) n**18 **t**20 **f**19 **b**20. Decidedly unscintillating fare. **46%**

⋰ **Old Malt Cask Jura 15 Years Old** dist 4 May 90, bott Jul 05 **(69) n**17 **t**18 **f**17 **b**17. Sulphur... so bad... **50%**. Douglas Laing. 718 bottles.

**Old Malt Cask Jura 16 Years Old** dist 16 Nov 88, bott 23 Mar 05 **(87) n**21 like sticking your head in the barrel, complete with bung and gause; **t**23 brilliant, really wonderful richness and sheen to the malt that sees off that usual, lurking Jura tangy note; **f**21 a touch of fruit to the vanilla; **b**22 an above average Jura with loads of intense malt character. **50%**. *Douglas Laing & Co.*

**Old Master's Isle of Jura 1991 Aged 13 Years** cask 681, bott May 04 **(84) n**20 **t**22 **f**21 **b**21. Sheer Jura: undulating between moments of prime, ultra-tender, juicy malt and strange, tangy, off-citrussy tones that really shouldn't be there. This really is the most frustrating distillery. **55.1%**

**Royal Mile Whiskies Isle of Jura 5 Year Old** cask 19 dist 18 Jan 99 **(78) n**20 **t**19 **f**20 **b**19. Hints of coriander and juniper in this peaty free-for-all which is evident on both nose and taste: odd. Not in the same league as either Whisky Exchange or Whisky Fair bottlings, especially with the dull, oily finish.

**Signatory Isle of Jura 1988** cask 2679, dist 21 Dec 88, bott 23 Jan 04 **(82) n**19 **t**22 **f**21 **b**20. Unexciting. **46%**. *Signatory 268 bottles.*

**Spirit of the Isles Isle of Jura 1988 Rum Cask Finish** bott 03 **(75) n**18 **t**20 **f**18 **b**19. Teasingly smoked, oily malted but ultimately lazy dram. **40%**.

**The Whisky Fair Isle of Jura 5 Year Old** cask 144, dist 27 Jan 99 **(88) n**22 imagine raw peat reak, barley rubbed with lashings of salt, armpit sweat and wild young oak being tossed mindlessly together: that gives you some idea of the chaos involved here; **t**23 enormous launch of myriad young notes with praline binding together the sweetness and the drier tones; **f**22 long and lush with the peat continuing its fiery dance. Wonderful fun; **b**21 young, robust, raw and eclectic, it holds together very well. **61.3%**

# KNOCKANDO
**Speyside, 1898. Diageo. Working.**

❁ **Knockando Aged 18 Years** Sherry casks, dist 87 db **(77) n**19 **t**21 **f**18 **b**19. Bland and docile. Someone wake me up. **43%**

**Knockando 1990** db **(83) n**21 **t**22 **f**20 **b**20. The most fruity Knockando I've come across with some attractive salty notes. Dry, but a little extra malty sweetness these days. **40%**

# KNOCKDHU
**Speyside, 1894. Inver House. Working.**

**AnCnoc 12 Year Old** db **(90) n**22 an aggressive pepperiness bites deep into the usual grassy maltiness and coal smoke. Excellent depth and complexity, though slightly more aggressive, if younger, in style than of old; **t**23 absolutely fabulous, near-perfect, malt arrival, perhaps the most clean, yet intense of any in Scotland. The complexity is staggering with not only multi-layers of malt but a distant peat and oak infusion; **f**22 deliciously spicy; **b**23 if there is a more complete 12-year-old Speyside malt on the market, I have yet to find it. A malt that should adorn a shelf in every whisky-drinking home. ☺☺

**AnCnoc 13 Year Old Highland Selection** db **(85) n**21 **t**23 **f**20 **b**21. A big Knockdhu, but something is dulling the complexity. **46%**

**AnCnoc 1990** bott Mar 04 db **(90) n**21 dry-ish and sawdusty; the barley puts up firmer than usual resistance; **t**23 pure Knockdhu with its sturdy barley lines offering a mouthwatering embrace; **f**23 a faint hint of bourbon as the oak adds a cocoa-tinged edge to the oily and enormously long finish; **b**23 strikingly attractive and textbook clean; the extra oak has detracted slightly from the usual honeyed complexity but has provided instead an interesting weight. Speyside at its most alluring. **46%. ncf.**

❁ **AnCnoc 1991** bott Aug 05 db **(76) n**18 **t**22 **f**17 **b**19. Some eloquent and delightful moments early on but for a true World Great distillery, there is something very wrong here with the odd sub-standard cask having somehow made its way to the bottling hall and spoilt the party. As disappointing, flawed and under par as an England World Cup performance. **46%. ncf.**

**AnCnoc 26 Years Old Highland Selection** db **(89)** n23 profound. Everything is big, but perfectly proportioned: massive grapey fruit and malt concentrate; t22 pure Knockdhu: intense malt carrying some beautiful spices and an obscure but refreshing fruit; f23 the lull after a minor storm: rich vanilla and echoes of malt; **b**21 there is a little flat moment between the middle and finish for which I have chipped off a point or two. That apart, superb. **48.2%**

**AnCnoc 30 Years Old** db **(85)** n21 pipe smoke, old leather armchairs and a sprig of mint: this seems older than its years; t23 wonderfully thick malt, beefed up in intensity by drawing in as much oak as it comfortably can; the honeycomb and molassed sweetness adds a lovely touch; f19 big natural caramel and some pretty rough-stuff oak; **b**22 seat-of-the-pants whisky that is just on the turn. Still has a twinkle in the eye, though. **49%**

**Knockdhu 23 Years Old** db **(94)** n23 t24 f23 **b**2. Pass the smelling salts. This is whisky to knock you out. A malt that confirms Knockdhu as simply one of the great Speysiders, but unquestionably among the world's elite. **57.4%.**

**Cadenhead Authentic Collection Knockdhu 16 Years Old** dist 89, bott May 05 **(88)** n22 mint on malt; t23 immediate spices and then, of course, the honey thread and fresh plucked grass; f21 lush, vanilla laden and oiled; **b**22 independent versions from this distillery are rarer than hens' teeth, but I can't remember, even in the lab, the last time I came across a Knockdhu with such an oily grip. **50.1%.** *282 bottles.*

⠿ **Harrods Knockdhu Aged 12 Years (84)** n19 t23 f21 **b**21. One can assume only that caramel (or an exceptional dull sherry cask) has been added here because it is otherwise impossible to find such a flat nose from a Knockdhu. However, the arrival on the palate is bliss, with dates combining with glossy honey and marzipan, but again the finish is only a dull echo of what it should be. Shackled greatness. **40%.**

**Provenance Knockdhu 10 Years Old** dist 12 Dec 94, bott 21 Feb 05 **(88)** n23 heathery, wet tweed jackets, celery, salady; t22 usual honey arrival followed by a spreading of spicy malt; loses a little balance as the malt kicks in; f21 big oak implosion for one so young-ish; **b**22 nose is nothing short of amazing. **46%.**

**Provenance Knockdhu Aged Over 10 Years**, dist Spring 94, bott Winter 05 **(91)** n23 the cleanest malt imaginable, kissed by strands of honey and the most distant rumble of smoke; t23 malt makes the softest imprint at first and then a wonderful explosion of spices follows; remains clean and blessed with effortless complexity; f22 layers of oak and barley take turns to wash against the tastebuds; **b**23 the subtlety and complexity of this show exactly why it is so outstanding, both as a blending and a single malt. **46%. nc ncf.** *Douglas Laing.*

## LADYBURN
### Lowland, 1966–1974. Closed.

**Ladyburn 1973** db **(60)** n15 varying shades of light oak have not entirely dimmed the malt, just a tad spirity but pleasant with minimum complexity; t15 oak, oak and more (spicy) oak; f17 oak; **b**13 this has lost all trace of shape and form. Pretty one-dimensional yet easily drinkable thanks to a singular malty sweetness, especially towards the very end. Don't bother opening.

**Old Rare Malt Ayrshire Distillery 1970 (71)** n16 t17 f21 **b**17. A mildly soapy nose, uncomfortably hot on the palate but redeemed by a superb, clean malt surge at the end that is deliciously out of character. **40%.** *Gordon & MacPhail.*

## LAGAVULIN
### Islay, 1816. Diageo. Working.

**Lagavulin 12 Years Old** db **(93)** n24 disarmingly gentle peat, much of its younger oils have miraculously vanished, lots of fresh fruit – including mandarin – available and mildly nutty, too. Pretty faultless material; t23 the smokescreen of the nose is laid bare on the palate: oil enough for heart attacks, peat laid on thickly and the oak offering an extra surge of spice that is man-marked by gristy, sweet barley; f23 long and at times almost too soft to be heard. Impressive vanilla to thin out the smoke, but the peat with the cocoa still lingers for a good five or ten minutes; b23 really, all you can ask from a Lagavulin at this age: weighty yet delicate enough for impressive complexity. Just try not having a second of this ... **57.8%**

**Lagavulin 12 Years Old** db **(92) n**24 clean sea-brine and peat: first class; t23 explosive peat and soft barley make delicious bedfellows; f22 cocoa and smoke. The barley hangs sweetly around; b23 really charming Islay with a frisky peatiness that is sweet and lingering. One to savour and reminisce for those of us who were hooked on the Lagavulin in pre-Classic Malt era. **58%**

**Lagavulin 12 Years Old** db **(91) n**22 marauding peat on a very greasy base – compelling but lacking complexity; t23 sweet malt arriving in droves and sliding around the palate on a pan of oil; some wonderful liquorice and toasty notes add depth; f23 sweetens out with a nutty dimension to the coastal feel; b23 some extra oil makes this a slightly less complex beast than its predecessor. And the last one was oily enough! **58.2%**

**Lagavulin Aged 16 Years** db **(95)** n24 wave upon surging wave of giant peat; delicate spices interject with hints of malt and liquorice. Heavy roast Jamaican Blue Mountain coffee and medium roast Java blend (35/65) help spin out the smoke; t24 the chewiest of sweet peats, a touch of burnt grist and sugared smoke, with maximum chewing required; f23 bitter chocolate on the death, almost a touch of chocolate cup cake, but with layers of sweet peat reek to add extra sturdy depth; b24 much more like the Lagavulin of old with unfettered development and delivery. Befitting the great distillery this unquestionably is. Forget some recent disappointing bottlings: this is the real thing! **43%**

**MacLeod's Islay 8 Years Old (90)** n24 an astonishing array of citrus (lime and orange) battles with some success against the crashing waves of clean peat that is iodine-rich and enticingly green. Something that no true whisky lover should fail to experience; t22 fresh-faced and tender, there is an enveloping sweetness that is like liquid grist. The peat almost pings around the mouth, so crisp is it. Only on the middle does the lack of age seem to offer an unfilled hole; f21 lengthy and lusciously, it is still spritely and fun and boasts massive liquoricey chewability, but so very green and immature – fabulous all the same! b23 the nose is Islay, pure Islay. At half the age of what you would normally taste Lagavulin this effervescent malt helps you learn so much more about this great distillery. No Islay malt on the market comes cleaner than this: only the old Bowmore 5-y-o used to show such childish abandon. This dram should be in every serious collector's or Islay-phile's home. I'm 100% certain this is Lagavulin. **40%**

꽃 **The Whisky Fair "Vanilla Sky" Aged 13 Years** (Lagavulin) Hogshead no. 5341, dist Nov 92, bott Mar 06 **(95)** n23 get a chisel to cut through the dense peat, though a touch of citrus helps. Islay in a sniff...; t24 enormous delivery, yet clean, mouthwatering and barley rich over and beyond the obvious smoke; f24 just stays on course with countless waves of iodine sweetened with a small dab of maple syrup and barley sugar; wonderful vanillas arrive late on and see it through – with the smoke – to the glorious end; b24 Lagavulin on cruise control: definitely no ice with this one... **53.6%**. *Germany. 138 bottles.*

# LAPHROAIG
## Islay, 1820. Fortune Brands. Working.

**Laphroaig 10 Years Old** db **(92) n**24 impossible not to nose this and think of Islay: no other aroma so perfectly encapsulates the island – clean despite the rampaging peat-reek and soft oak, raggy coast-scapes and screeching gulls – all in a glass; **t**23 one of the crispiest, peaty malts of them all, the barley standing out alone, brittle and unbowed, before the peat comes rushing in like the tide: iodine and soft salty tones; **f**22 the peat now takes control for a sweet, distinguished finish; **b**23 has reverted back slightly towards a heavier style in more recent bottlings, though I would still like to see that old oomph at the very death. Even so, this is, indisputably, a classic whisky. The favourite of Prince Charles, apparently: he will make a wise king ... **40%** ⊙

**Laphroaig 10 Years Old Original Cask Strength** db **(80)** n20 t20 f21 b19. Would never have marked this down as a Laphroaig. For all the oil, thin and disappointing. **57.3%**

**Laphroaig 10 Years Old Original Cask Strength** db **(90)** n22 an alluringly precise, almost dense smokiness with lovely strands of chocolate marzipan oak; **t**23 overtly sweet as the malt really goes to town, but the peat digs deep, chewy trenches; **f**23 more semi-bourbony oak, then slow delivery of a late wave of peat; **b**22 it is amazing when compared with different expressions of the same whisky (see below). Where the 57.3% version fires blanks, this presses just the right buttons in the right order to ensure this one is a treat of a dram and so worthy of the great Laphroaig name: just so sophisticated. **55.7%**

⠿ **Laphroaig 10 Years Old Original Cask Strength** (with UK Government's Sensible Drinking Limits boxed on back label) db **(92)** n22 a duller nose than usual: caramel reducing the normal iodine kick; **t**24 recovers supremely for the early delivery with some stunning black peppers exploding all over the palate leaving behind a trail of peat smoke; the controlled sweetness to the barley is sublime; **f**23 again there is a caramel edge to the finish, but this does not entirely prevent a fizzing finale; **b**23 caramel apart, this is much truer to form than one or two more recent bottlings, aided by the fresh, gristy sweetness and explosive spices. Wonderful! **55.7%**

**Laphroaig Aged 15 Years** db **(79)** n20 t20 f19 b20. A hugely disappointing, lacklustre dram that is oily and woefully short on complexity. Not what one comes to expect from either this distillery or age. **43%** ⊙

**Laphroaig 17 Years Old Islay Festival of Malt and Music 2004** db **(93)** n23 just a whimper of smoke by Laphroaig standards – and smoked cod at that – but the malt itself if thick and gristy, the soft intensity of the oak offers a bitter-sweet narrative, **t**24 lush and loaded with malt, there is almost a sugarcane element to this one with the smoke gathering in intensity as the mouth is coated; **f**22 the demerara sugar-peat combination lingers with some soft vanilla acting as the perfect foil; **b**24 reminds me very much of the original Ardbeg 17- year-old I created with the peat hiding at first and then slowly trying to take command ... but failing. Most probably will be panned by those looking for in your face peat, but this is a sophisticated and highly unusual single cask Laphraoig that needs time to get to know. Congratulations to blender Robert Hick on spotting a real one off. **55.2%**. *250 bottles.*

**Laphroaig Aged 30 Years** db **(94)** n24 t23 f23 b24. The best Laphroaig of all time? Nope, because the 40-y-o is perhaps better still... just. However, Laphroaig of this subtlety and charm gives even the very finest Ardbeg a run for its money. A sheer treat that should be bottled at greater strength. **43%**

**Laphroaig Aged 40 Years** db **(94)** n23 t24 f23 b24. Mind-blowing. This is a malt that defies all logic and theory to be in this kind of shape at such enormous age. The Jane Fonda of Islay whisky. **43%**

⠿ **Laphroaig 1994 Islay Festival of Malt and Music 2006** db **(90)** n22 no shortage of salt and a twist of lemon to the sturdy smoke; **t**23 a beautifully refreshing citrus edge accentuates the clarity of the barley; the peat hovers but refuses to attack; **f**22 delicate and remains mouthwatering; soft spices compensate for the lazy peat; **b**23 a beautifully complex malt and one not depending on peat alone for charm and charisma. A pleasant touch, this coming from casks filled (as an apprentice) and emptied by new distillery manager John Campbell. **56%. 600 bottles.**

**Laphroaig 1/4 Cask** db **(95) n**22 burning embers of peat in a crofter's fireplace; sweet intense malt and lovely, refreshing citrus as well; **t**24 mouthwatering, mouth-filling and mouth-astounding: the perfect weight of the smoke has no problems filling every crevice of the palate; builds towards a sensationally sweet maltiness at the middle; **f**24 really long, and dries appropriately with smoke and spice. Classic Laphroaig; **b**25 a great distillery back to its awesome, if a little sweet, self. Layer upon layer of sexed-up peatiness, this is the closest to how I remember it some 30 years ago! **48%**

**Cadenhead's Authentic Collection Laphroaig Aged 13 Years** dist 91, bott Feb 05 **(95) n**24 if you want to know how this distillery should nose at this age, have a sniff of this. It's embers and gentle smoking peat at its most complexly pungent. The malt offers nothing but ballast. Near perfection; **t**24 so delicate it defies belief; the peat is there by the bucket load, but presents itself with a series of gentle, bitter-sweet, cocoa-crusted layers; **f**23 more gentle mauling from the malt. The smoke now gets into the late mouthwatering quality that defies such age; **b**24 miss out on this bottling and you'll regret it for the remainder of your days: an absolute 24 carat gem. **55%. 228 bottles.**

**Cadenhead's Authentic Collection Laphroaig Aged 13 Years** dist 91, bott Feb 05 **(82) n**22 **t**21 **f**19 **b**20. A half-decent cask, but one I would have earmarked for blending. **55.4%. 234 bottles.**

**Cadenhead's Authentic Collection Laphroaig Aged 14 Years** dist 91, bott May 06 **(93) n**23 pure Laphroaig!; **t**24 the gristy sweetness is the perfect balance to the rumbling oak and smoke; mildly molassed but the coastal tang to the barley is sublime; **f**23 long, clean, layered with vanilla and the smoke just keeps on rolling; **b**23 Authentic...??? And some!!! **56.1%. 234 bottles.**

**Cadenhead's Authentic Collection Laphroaig Aged 16 Years** Bourbon Hogshead, dist 90, bott Sept 06 **(87) n**20 pretty closed and hard to recognize at a typical Laphroaig; **t**23 sweetish delivery with some pounding barley and a lucid, light oiliness to the smoke; **f**23 long, a touch of the Bowmores with hickory and smoke; **b**21 without seeing the cask numbers (we'll get them later) this appears to be a sibling of the 53% version: very much as usual but this one has an extra degree of attitude and complexity. **58.4%. 246 bottles.**

**Cadenhead's Authentic Collection Laphroaig Aged 16 Years** Sherry Hogshead, dist 90, bott Sept 06 **(86) n**21 **t**22 **f**22 **b**21. Very different from the norm with almost a Bowmore-ish style peat to it. Restricted in development but always drinkable. **53%. 156 bottles.**

**Distillery No 1 Laphroaig 1988** cask 3881 **(89) n**22 clean, uncluttered Laphroaig that's a little young for its age but enjoys excellent depth; **t**23 again, brilliant distillate with no off notes and after the initial peaty exclamation, some sweeter barley-liquorice notes arrive; **f**22 shows its age now with plenty of oak to soften the peaty, seaweedy blows; **b**22 a touch of natural (?) caramel at the death but until then a warts-and-all, macho bottling. **62.9%**

**Murray McDavid Laphroaig Aged 17 Years** dist 88, bott 05 **(69) n**19 **t**17 **f**16 **b**17. Noses wrong and tastes....well, that's me done for an hour or three. **46%**

**Old Malt Cask Laphroaig 10 Years Old** dist 28 Sep 94, bott 22 Jun 05 **(85) n**22 **t**21 **f**21 **b**21. Gentle, clean and gristy. **50%.** Douglas Laing. 632 bottles.

**Old Malt Cask Laphroaig Aged 11 Years** dist Apr 92, bott Nov 03 **(89) n**23 **t**23 **f**21 **b**22. A near faultless template for all Laphroaigs of this age with a gristy, mealy edge to the smoke. **50%. nc ncf sc.** Douglas Laing. 540 bottles.

**Old Malt Cask Laphroaig Aged 12 Years (89) n**23 two-toned peat both light and ashy and with deep base; **t**23 very young style with mouthwatering fruitiness to the barley and a spice bite to the peat; **f**21 thins out fast; **b**22 probably a third-fill blending cask showing Laphroaig in un-oaked beauty. Light, but early on fantastic. **50%.** *Douglas Laing.*

**Old Malt Cask Laphroaig Aged 14 Years** dist Mar 89, bott Sep 03 **(79) n**19 **t**21 **f**19 **b**20. Astonishing, delicate Laphroaig with about the lowest phenol level I have seen in a bottle. Sugary in part with the smoke drifting around the palate. The bitter finale doesn't help. **50%. nc ncf sc.** *Douglas Laing. 300 bottles.*

**Old Malt Cask Laphroaig Aged 15 Years** dist Apr 88, bott Jan 04 **(93) n**23 liniment; a leaking bottle of bromine; a hint of salt; **t**23 the peat dissolves on the palate with ripples of clean malt carrying with it a spicy flotsam; **f**23 the sweetness continues for a minute or two more before some drier wafer-notes start dissolving again; the spices are persistent but harmonious; **b**24 a memorable Laphroaig in top form. **50%. nc ncf sc.** *Douglas Laing. 162 bottles.*

**Old Malt Cask Laphroaig Aged 15 Years** dist Apr 88, bott Mar 04 **(83) n**22 **t**21 **f**20 **b**20. An oily, machine-room nose but the palate, though sweet, never quite gets out of third gear. **50%. nc ncf sc.** *Douglas Laing. 112 bottles.*

**Old Malt Cask Laphroaig Aged 15 Years** dist Mar 89, bott Apr 04 **(90) n**23 farmyards and haystacks plus plenty of cottage peat-reek **t**22 sweet oils even catch a honeyed strand amid the ultra-clean peat; **f**23 one of the softest finishes to a Laphroaig for quite a few years: the malt and peat are inextricably intertwined, it is all very soft yet the oak advances no more than a distant hint of vanilla while the peat becomes supremely assertive; **b**22 Laphroaig at its cleanest and best behaved while still displaying its unique charms. **50%. nc ncf sc.** *Douglas Laing. 289 bottles.*

**Old Malt Cask Laphroaig Aged 15 Years** dist Feb 87, bott Jan 04 **(90) n**18 tainted and sweet, not exactly the perfect nose; **t**24 time to sit down: the intensity of the sweet sherry backed to the hilt by writhing peat makes this one hell of an experience; **f**24 big sprinkling of spices still cannot dampen the enormous, mind-blowing sherry-peat theme; **b**24 if you went by the nose alone, you'd probably not go any further. But do. Your reward will be a one-off, an oral orgy, for all bottlings in the last year. Brilliant ... very few whiskies have been awarded a 90 after such a poor start on the nose. Hey, but that's whisky ...! **50% nc ncf sc.** *Douglas Laing. 309 bottles.*

**Old Malt Cask Laphroaig Aged 16 Years** dist Feb 87, bott Sep 03 **(83) n**22 **t**20 **f**20 **b**21. A strangely synthetic nose while the malt is dazzlingly sweet. **50%. nc ncf sc.** *Douglas Laing. 270 bottles.*

**Old Malt Cask Laphroaig 16 Years Old** dist 24 Nov 87 bott 18 Mar 04 **(91) n**21 diesel oil and coal sheds; not as indulgently peaty as some but intriguingly attractive; **t**23 thumping peat-barley mix; gristy for its age but the spice follow-through is a delight; the oak makes an early entry and stays the course; **f**23 this telling oak adds subtle extra spice; excellent mocha adds sweetness to the building dry notes; **b**24 a charming Islay, which starts off breezy and then kicks up a peaty storm. First-class complexity and balance throughout. **50%** *158 btls*

**Old Malt Cask Laphroaig 17 Years Old** dist 16 Mar 88, bott 27 Apr 05 **(91) n**23 lightly seasoned with the peat showing a salty edge. Big, yet seriously delicate; **t**23 the malt has already melted by the time some spicy, smoky depth appears; **f**23 the clarity on the palate continues despite some hints of cocoa to go with the peat; **b**22 a fascinating Laphroaig and as delicate as they come: rarely do you find one of this age with so little oak attached. Here we get a great view of the workings of the malt – and it is something beautiful to behold. **50%.** *141 btls*

☼ **Old Malt Cask Laphroaig Aged 18 Years** dist Nov 87, bott Oct 05 **(89) n**21 undemonstrative, relaxed; **t**22 crisp barley; a touch of coffee to the smoke; **f**23 restrained but drying oak tinged with excellent citrus; **b**23 one of those drams that gets better as it goes along. **50%.** *Douglas Laing.*

☼ **Old Malt Cask Laphroaig 18 Years Old** dist Apr 88, bott Sept 06 **(83) n**20 **t**21 **f**22 **b**20. Laphroaig coming in any kind of finish is rarer than nominations for

George W Bush to receive the Nobel Peace Prize. But to turn up in rum...!!! It is both rock-hard and at times syrupy sweet. Some very drinkable moments, but a real collector's item to Laphroaig lovers. **50%.** *Douglas Laing. 327 bottles.*

⋄ **Premier Barrel Laphroaig 7 Years Old** dist Oct 98, bott Nov 05 **(87) n**21 kiddies' plasticine; **t**22 gentle oils intensify the grist; **f**22 citrus lightens the gentle smoke further; **b**22 compare a bottle of this with the March 06 bottling and discover first hand how peating intensity and effect can vary at an Islay distillery. **46%.** *Douglas Laing. 406 bottles.*

⋄ **Premier Barrel Laphroaig 7 Years Old** dist May 98, bott Mar 06 **(94) n**23 gristy, cold malt kilns; **t**24 mouthwatering, fresh barley seems to be kept apart from the cindery peat which fills the palate. The controlled sweetness is excellent; **f**23 medium length and cotton soft; **b**24 just so wonderful to see this distillery bottled at an age it should have been available at for the last 20 years and showing so much zest. **46%.** *Douglas Laing. 385 bottles.*

⋄ **The Queen of the Moorlands Rare Cask Laphroaig 12 Years Old** dist 25 Mar 93, bott 10 Jun 05 **(81) n**21 **t**20 **f**20 **b**20. Too subtle for its own good: remains closed where it should be open and developing; most telling contribution is from a fruit-jam attack, rather than the uninspiring peat. Drinkable and enjoyable. But Laphroaig should offer more. **54.7%. sc.** *The Wine Shop, Leek, UK.*

**The Un-chillfiltered Collection Laphroaig Vintage 1992** cask 3613, dist 16 Mar 88, bott 23 Jan 04 **(91) n**22 young in character but the peat really is of the most well-proportion type imaginable, lovely; **t**23 text-book mouth arrival with the peat at first arriving in a dense cloud, vanishing momentarily to allow in the barley and then returning slowly again; **f**23 long, delicate, late sawdusty, flasky smoke; **b**23 the epitome of a gentle giant. **46%.** *Signatory. 819 bottles.*

⋄ **The Whisky Fair Artist Edition Laphroaig Aged 8 Years** Bourbon Hogshead, dist Apr 98, bott June 06 **(88) n**21 a strange mixture of the $CO_2$ from the tun room and dying peaty embers in the furnace; **t**23 brilliant distribution of softly oiled, sweet peats, all enriched by golden-syrup sweetened barley; **f**22 drier and a tad oakier than one might expect – or hope – for; **b**22 lovely malt that lacks a little in balance but makes up for with an enchanting peatiness. **48.5%.** *Germany. 420 bottles.*

**The Whisky Fair Laphroaig Aged 16 Years** dist 88, bott Feb 05 **(69) n**16 **t**18 **f**17 **b**17. A feinty disaster. **50.1%. nc ncf.** *150 bottles.*

**The Whisky Shop Laphroaig 1988 Vintage 16 Years Old** dist Apr 88, bott Nov 04 **(90) n**22 something to stand your spoon in: mega-intense and chunky; **t**23 sweet peat that's thick and true to the distillery; almost a Demerara sweetness develops; **f**23 layers of oily smoke with tangy, salty, seaweedy riches and very late caramel; **b**22 big and uncompromising, this has the stamp of just one distillery running through it. Lacking in subtlety...but so what!! Who the hell looks for subtlety with Laphroaig?? **52.5%. sc.** *614 bottles.*

## LEDAIG (see Tobermory)

## LINKWOOD
**Speyside, 1820. Diageo. Working.**

**Linkwood 12 Years Old** db **(79) n**21 **t**22 **f**17 **b**19. Not a patch on previous bottlings, with the usual clarity lost to a very confused fruit-caramel theme. Especially on the finish. **43%**

**Adelphi Linkwood 13 Years Old** dist 90, bott 03 **(76) n**18 **t**20 **f**19 **b**19. Aggressive, hot and off-key but not entirely without merit. **56%**

⋄ **Linkwood 1974 Rare Malt** db **(79) n**20 **t**21 **f**19 **b**19. Wobbles about the palate in search of a story and balance. Finds neither but some of the early moments, though warming, offer very decent malt. The best bit follows a couple of seconds after – and lasts as long. **55%**

**Blackadder Raw Cask Linkwood 15 Years Old** Sherry butt cask 5625, dist 30 Oct 89, bott Nov 04 **(74)** n19 t21 f16 b18. Sorry. You will rarely find me championing Linkwood in sherry. And there is no chance here. **59.3%**

⊹ **The Bottlers Linkwood 31 Years Old** Refill sherry cask 12228, dist Aug 74, bott Dec 05 **(87)** n22 sultanas, vanilla and barley refreshed by freshly sliced cucumber; t22 big barley and muscovado delivery with spices fizzing in all directions; the sweetness intensifies for a while then some grape lightens the load; f21 soft vanilla and hickory; b22 these guys don't bottle much. But what they do has a tendency to be way above the norm. So I was intrigued to see how they would tackle one of the trickiest distilleries of them all. And I have to say: the Bottlers did good... **54.3%**

**Cadenhead's Authentic Collection Linkwood-Glenlivet Aged 15 Years** dist 89, bott 05 **(80)** n20 t20 f21 b19. Lots of natural caramel. **53.5%.** *246 bottles.*

⊹ **Cadenhead's Authentic Collection Linkwood Aged 16 Years** Bourbon Hogshead, dist 89, bott May 06 **(79)** n20 t19 f20 b20. Hot stuff: the stills must have been screaming when they made this. Decent balance, though, and even an enjoyable touch of marmalade. **55.8%.** *264 bottles.*

⊹ **Chieftain's Linkwood Aged 13 Years** French oak **(72)** n19 t18 f17 b18. Overly sweet and latterly furry. **43%.** *Ian Macleod.*

**Coopers Choice Linkwood 1990** bott 03 (12 Years Old) **(79)** n18 t21 f20 b20. Slightly syrupy, but decent spices. **43%.** *The Vintage Malt Whisky Co.*

⊹ **Dewar Rattray Individual Cask Bottling Linkwood 1985 Aged 20 Years** cask no. 4544, dist Nov 85, bott Jan 06 **(85)** n21 t22 f21 b21. A biting, sugary maltfest. Eye-wateringly intense but for its ability to stay fresh at this age, complexity, as ever, remains at a premium. **60.2%.** *231 bottles.*

⊹ **Dun Bheagan Linkwood 10 Years Old American Oak (85)** n21 t22 f21 b21. An attractive, light cask but the real star quality is found on the arrival and soft cereal-cocoa fade. **43%.** *Ian Macleod.*

⊹ **Dun Bheagan Linkwood 11 Years Old Port Finish (91)** n22 some peppery prickle to the fruit; t23 spectacular arrival on the palate, about all you could ask from a Port finish: enormous complexity and variance in weight, flipping between light and heavy in a nanosecond; f23 mocha and raisin – which make themselves heard earlier – really now play out a slow finish; b23 a complex, seductive dram played out at first in double quick time and then slows for the finish. Wonderful. And it ain't often I can say that about Linkwood... **46%** *Ian Macleod.*

**Dun Bheagan Linkwood 1991 Aged 12 Years Port Finish** bott 15 Mar 04 **(79)** n21 t20 f19 b19. Many years back I discovered the now famous "green" whisky, the port-cask Springbanks. Now, ladies and gentlemen, I unveil the first-ever truly pink whisky, followed by the later bottled Glendronach – also from port. Here the listless Linkwood is outgunned by the mildly unbalanced wine. **43%.** *Ian Macleod.*

⊹ **Gordon & MacPhail Linkwood Aged 15 Years** First fill and refill sherry **(76)** n18 t19 f20 b19. Some decent gristy maltiness links with the toffee. **40%.**

⊹ **Gordon & MacPhail Linkwood 15 Years Old (82)** n21 t21 f20 b20. By far one of the better Linkwoods around. A bit aggressive and hot in places, but some lovely natural caramel and, dare I say it, a touch of elegance to the barley sugar. **43%.**

**Gordon & MacPhail Linkwood 1954 (69)** n18 t16 f17 b18. One for birthdays and anniversaries only. **40%**

**Gordon & MacPhail Linkwood 1969 (69)** n17 t18 f16 b18. Old, tired and awaiting the grim reaper. **40%.** *Gordon & MacPhail.*

⊹ **Gordon & MacPhail Linkwood 1972 (87)** n22 burnt raisin, crisped barley; t22 juicy fruit and barley mix: salivating but remains rock-hard; f21 sharp, flinty, metallic at death; b22 no yield to this hard-as-nails but fun bottling. **43%.** *Rare Vintage range.*

**Gordon & MacPhail Linkwood 1972 (72)** n20 t18 f17 b17. Decent vanilla, but just a shade too heavily oaked. **40%.** *Gordon & MacPhail.*

⟐ **Kingsbury's Single Cask Linkwood 13 Years Old** cask 10432, dist 91 **(76)** n20 t19 f18 b19. A bit more complexity than the average Linkwood, but... **46%.** *Japan Import System.*

⟐ **Kingsbury's Valdespino Linkwood 16 Years Old (84)** n23 t21 f20 b20. Clean, well structured; caramelized biscuit. The nose, though, stars by displaying sufficient raw oak to get into the sharp barley. **46%.** *Japan Import System.*

**Murray McDavid Linkwood 1990 (69)** n17 t18 f17 b17. Screwed by mild sulphur. **46%.**

**Murray McDavid Mission 2 Linkwood 1973 (84)** n21 t20 f22 b21. Hints of citrus and honey plus background smoke amid the pounding vanilla. **46%. nc ncf.**

⟐ **Murray McDavid Mission Linkwood 1983 Aged 23 Years** Bourbon/Madeira, bott 06 **(94)** n23 forget the Madeira; the age really comes through with traces of exotic fruit amid the grape and malt; t23 a concoction of golden sugar, sultanas, ultra-intense barley sugar and even a touch of coconut milk makes for controlled sweetness; f24 levels out with the fruity touch of a truffle bar and searing white pepper; b24 leave in the glass for a full five minutes to allow the complexity to settle. On of the best cask finishes of the year. **52.1%. nc ncf.** *700 bottles.*

⟐ **NMWL Single Cask Malt Whisky Linkwood** Hogshead cask 1835, dist 4 Apr 89, bott 6 Apr 05 **(84)** n21 t22 f20 b21. Pssst! Looking for some decent Linkwood? Try Norway. Revels in the usual weird combination of big barley sweetness and hot distillate. But this one appears to have been nurtured in a way above average cask, allowing the malt to blossom. Still don't expect too much, though... **58%.** *Norsk MaltWhisky Lag, Oslo. 388 bottles.*

⟐ **Old Malt Cask Linkwood 16 Years Old** dist Dec 89, bott June 06 **(82)** n21 t20 f21 b20. Some wonderful lavender spruces this one up. **50%.** *Douglas Laing. 302 bottles.*

**Old Malt Cask Linkwood 21 Years Old** dist Apr 83, bott Jul 04 **(84)** n21 t22 f21 b20. Sweet, malt, fresh and clean, one of the better Linkwoods of late. **50%.** *Douglas Laing.*

⟐ **Old Malt Cask Linkwood 22 Years Old** dist 24 Apr 83, bott Jul 05 **(78)** n21 t19 f18 b20. A remarkably soft Linkwood which battles hard to find a rhythm and depth and not entirely with success. **50%.** *Douglas Laing. 213 bottles.*

**Old Master's Linkwood 1989 15 Year Old** cask 2010, bott Sep 04 **(88)** n21 touches of fruit; t24 stupendous mouth arrival: clean malt unmolested by any other outside interference; f22 oak arrives, offering a toasty edge; b24 few whiskies offer such intense malt as this. Forget about complexity here. **54%**

**Provenance Linkwood Over 11 Years** dist Winter 93, bott Winter 04 **(82)** n20 t22 f20 b20. Youthful, fresh, mouthwatering barley and zesty. **46%.** *Douglas McGibbon.*

⟐ **The Single Malt of Scotland Linkwood Aged 12 Years Vintage 1993** Sherry butt cask 3517 **(76)** n20 t19 f18 b19. Intense, syrupy and a little hot. Pretty normal early 90s Linkwood, then. **59.1%.** *The Whisky Exchange. 180 bottles.*

**Vom Fass Linkwood 10 Years Old (78)** n20 t19 f20 b19. Good natural weight and malty chewability. But pretty underdeveloped for its age. **40%**

**The Wee Dram Linkwood Aged 12 Years (85)** n21 t22 f21 b21. Twelve years ago I was discussing with United Distillers the strange effect their rather unnatural sherry wood policy will have further down the road. They said no-one would spot the difference; I said they would. The result has been a clutch of Sellafield-style sulphured monsters (especially from Mortlach), and a few disarmingly eccentric chaps like this. One for every collector. **43%.** *The Wee Dram, Bakewell, UK.*

⟐ **Wilson & Morgan Barrel Selection Linkwood 1991 Sherry Wood** dist 91, bott 05 **(70)** n18 t18 f17 b17. It's sherry, Jim. But not as we know it... **46%**

## LINLITHGOW (see St. Magdalene)

## LITTLEMILL
**Lowland, 1772. Demolished.**

**Littlemill Aged 8 Years** db **(84) n**20 **t**22 **f**21 **b**21. Aged 8 Years, claims the neck of the dumpy bottle, which shows a drawing of a distillery that no longer exists, as it has done for the last quarter of a century. Well, double that and you'll be a lot closer to the real age of this deliciously sweet, chewy and increasingly spicy chap. And it is about as far removed from the original 8-y-o fire-water it once was as is imaginable. **40%.** *Loch Lomond Distillers.*

**Littlemill 1964** db **(82) n**21 **t**20 **f**21 **b**20. A soft-natured, bourbony chap that shows little of the manic tendencies that made this one of Scotland's most-feared malts. Talk about mellowing with age ... **40%**

⊰⊹⊱ **Berry's' Best Lowland Littlemill 12 Years Old (71) n**17 **t**19 **f**17 **b**18. Astonishingly tame by Littlemill standards. But, though bad form to speak ill of the dead, pretty naff. **43%.** *Berry Bros & Rudd.*

⊰⊹⊱ **Cadenhead's Authentic Collection Littlemill Aged 16 Years** Bourbon Hogshead, dist 89, bott Feb 06 **(82) n**19 **t**23 **f**19 **b**21. Classically fiery as the delivery is, it has to be said, a fabulous ultra intense malt delivery of near perfect sweetness. Then tapers away towards something more off-key. **59.7%.** *294 bottles.*

**Coopers Choice Littlemill 1984 20 Years Old** Single Cask Range, bott 05 **(81) n**21 **t**22 **f**19 **b**19. Some early, graceful malt, then it becomes a roughhouse. **56.7%**

**Dun Bheagan Littlemill 1984 Aged 19 Years** bott 14 Jul 03 **(81) n**20 **t**19 **f**21 **b**21. The years have been kind to this dram: a stylish fresh-barley intensity that was never evident in its youth, despite recognisable early blemish. **43%.**

⊰⊹⊱ **Dun Bheagan Littlemill Aged 21 Years Sherry Finish (74) n**20 **t**19 **f**17 **b**18. Mutton dressed as lamb. **46%.** *Ian Macleod.*

**Dunglas (17) n**6 classic butyric (baby sick) qualities and something else besides: soapy beyond belief; **t**7 malty, but the off-key oils suggest a still out of control **f**0 oak fails to save an impossible situation: it might even be adding to it. The soapiness will be with you for days. I had to stop tasting for the day after this one; **b**4 the stills at Littlemill often caused problems at the best of times. When they experimented with the rectifier to produce Dunglas it was as if they were trying to perfect the art of making bad whisky. This is one of the rarest whisky bottlings in the world and worth being in any collection. Buy it for the experience and to learn. But don't expect to enjoy that experience. Interestingly, and in fairness to Littlemill, I have discovered these same faults with some casks in Scotland and beyond. An educated guess is that the stillman had major problems keeping the still under control and used large chunks of soap to calm down the frothing wash. There was probably a soap shortage in the area for some months after. **46%.** *Bravely bottled by The Whisky Exchange, London. www.thewhiskyexchange.com. 102 bottles. For serious whisky devotees or people with a serious grudge against their tastebuds.*

⊰⊹⊱ **Old Malt Cask Littlemill Aged 16 Years (89) n**22 a rum, surely? **t**23 no, the fist-fighting barley confirms the distillery, though the juiciness of the barley is a shock; **f**21 thins down in house style but none of the usual rough edges; **b**23 Littlemill as never seen before. It is passed the hell-fire days of its youth that brought its demise. But there is enough attitude to jab through the barley-rum theme to land some delicious punches. A little cracker. Had only the distillery bottled such malt when still standing. **50%.** *Douglas Laing.*

**Private Cellars Selection Littlemill 1984** bott 04 **(83) n**22 **t**21 **f**20 **b**20. Fruity and lively but a little rough around the edges. **43%.** *Speyside Distillers.*

**Scott's Selection Littlemill 1984** bott 05 **(86) n**22 **t**21 **f**22 **b**21. Just great, lip-smacking fun. **61.1%.** *Speyside Distillers.*

Whisky Galore Littlemill 1992 Aged 10 Years **(77)** n18 t21 f19 **b**19. An attractive malty early mouth arrival outshines the indifferent nose and finish. **46%.** *Duncan Taylor.*

## LOCH LOMOND
### Highland (Southwestern), 1966. Glen Catrine. Working.
꞉꞉꞉ **Craiglodge** American oak barrel 223, dist 26 Feb 01, bott 8 Sept 05 db **(84)** n19 t22 f21 **b**22. Big, intense malt coats the palate entirely for a seriously delicious chew. The nose isn't great, though. **45%.** *442 bottles.*

꞉꞉꞉ **Craiglodge** American oak barrel 329, dist 13 Sept 92, bott 15 Sept 05 db **(80)** n19 t21 f20 **b**20. A vaguely Fettercairnish rubbery nose picks up with the sweet smoke on the palate. Craiglodge should be – and usually is – a whole lot better than this. **45%.** *191 bottles.*

꞉꞉꞉ **Craiglodge** Sherry wood cask 139, dist 26 Mar 98 db **(72)** n17 t19 f18 **b**18. Cloying, off-key, rough...and they're the good points. The nose of sherry and smoke don't gel and it never recovers. **45%**

**Craiglodge Distillery Select Peated Malt** cask 061, dist 19 Feb01, bott 14 Apr 05 db **(91)** n22 young, frisky, earthy peat; t23 big, wonderfully bodied peated grist, where the sweetness looks set to run but then dries [?] with some unexpected oak; f23 wonderful shock waves lasting several minutes of smoke and spice; **b**23 a little-known style of whisky from Loch Lomond that is likely to become world-famous in future years. Astonishingly compact and stable for its age. **45%. nc ncf.** *Loch Lomond Distillers. 400 bottles.*

꞉꞉꞉ **Croftengea** cask no. 18, dist 22 Jan 97, bott 09 Sept 05 db **(76)** n19 t19 f20 **b**18. Hot, less than happy with itself...or the cask it has lived in. **45%**

꞉꞉꞉ **Croftengea** cask no. 24, dist 22 Jan 97 db **(87)** n22 pungent young peat, bracing, clean and even mildly salty; t22 refreshing barley with coffee/smoke double act; f21 vanilla and dry toast; **b**22 what a difference a cask makes: entirely together and charming. **45%**

꞉꞉꞉ **Croftengea Aged Over 9 Years** Sherry finish, cask 283, dist Jan 96, bott 6 Sept 05 db **(79)** n20 t21 f19 **b**19. The sherry flattens out the contours. **45%. nc ncf.** *380 bottles.*

꞉꞉꞉ **Glen Douglas** American oak barrel no. 337, dist 27 June 01, bott 12 Sept 05 db **(89)** n22 mildly gluey, but also a staggeringly complex maltiness intrigues; t23 beautiful delivery with a delightful intermingling of pillow-soft esters and spice; f22 the precocious complexity continues with a touch of honeyed vanilla and marmalade; **b**22 not only do I love blending with this stuff, but it makes a pretty tasty single malt, even at this age! **45%.** *315 bottles.*

꞉꞉꞉ **Inchfad 2001 Heavily Peated** cask 665 dist 14 Feb 01 db **(80)** n20 t21 f19 **b**20. Pretty atypical of this particular malt. Missing the fruity ester kick that comes with the big peat. In fact, what big peat? An underwhelming example. **45%**

꞉꞉꞉ **Inchfad 2001 Heavily Peated** cask 666, dist 14 Feb 01 db **(87)** n22 a real youngster, but with all the charm a child can bring. Smokey, though to call it heavily peated stretches the imagination somewhat; t23 sweet, gristy, soft esters and a wonderful barley rounding. High quality distillate; f21 the oak grabs far too large a hold and the balance is compromised; **b**21 one cask on and so much more in tune. From the same distillate, but an excellent example of how a better quality cask can allow the malt to thrive. Perhaps the cask numbers are the wrong way round...!! **45%**

꞉꞉꞉ **Inchmoan 2001 American Oak Barrel no. 53** dist 5 Mar 01, bott 7 Sept 05 db **(88)** n21 a toddler of a nose with alternating wispy and punchy smoke; t23 the most mouthwatering malt imaginable... with glorious smoke at fore and aft; f22 citrussy and refreshing; **b**22 the fact this is probably a second-fill cask ensures a wonderful rawness to this. A refreshing change – in every sense. And there is probably only a handful of us in the world who can vouchsafe this: but the closest thing to peated new make Lammerlaw, from New Zealand, on the planet. **45%**. *397 bottles*.

❖ **Inchmoan 1992 American Oak Barrel no. 151** dist 4 Sept 92, bott 14 Sept 05 db **(90) n**23 excellent smoky balance, but a lot younger than its years; **t**23 beautifully oiled and delicate, gristy sweetness to the smoked barley; **f**22 a drier send-off as oak bites; **b**22 another lovely malt from this little-known distillery. **45%**. *269 bottles*.

**Inchmoan Distillery Select** cask 48, dist 15 Mar 01, bott 14 Apr 05 db **(88) n**21 a touch feinty but the sweet peat offers attractive compensation; **t**23 like most mildly feinty drams, the enormity of the arrival is magnificent, with the gristy young malt clinging smokily to the roof of the mouth; **f**22 much cleaner and refreshing with little oak interference and the dying embers of peat glowing deliciously; **b**22 not quite in the league of Craiglodge, but worth a place in any collection. **45%. nc ncf.** *Loch Lomond Distillers. 400 bottles*.

❖ **Inchmurrin** Spanish oak butt cask 1-708, dist 20 July 01, bott 12 Sept 05 db **(76) n**18 **t**20 **f**19 **b**19. A malt equivalent of Les Dawson playing the piano. **45%**. *963 bottles*.

❖ **Inchmurrin** American oak butt cask 1-173, dist 20 June 01, bott 13 Sept 05 db **(80) n**20 **t**21 **f**19 **b**20. A typically nutty affair. **45%**

**Inchmurrin 10 Years Old** db **(81) n**21 **t**21 **f**19 **b**20. A sturdy, sweet and indulgently complex malt that struggles very slightly on the mildly bitter finale. **40%**.

❖ **Inchmurrin Aged 12 Years** db **(80) n**19 **t**21 **f**20 **b**20. Peas from the same pod as the 10-year-old. A tad more citrus, though. **40%**

**Loch Lomond** db **(74) n**18 **t**19 **f**18 **b**18. Oops! Not quite what was intended here, especially on the peaty but farmyardy nose. I have a distinct feeling that future bottlings will come together with less awkwardness. **40%**.

**Loch Lomond 21 Years Old** db **(89) n**22 attractive, confident grape intermingling with a spiced bourbony oak and malt; **t**23 real Dundee cake properties: full of fruit and nuts, only with some extra molassed sugar stirred in; **f**22 soft liquorice and delicious cocoa; **b**22 a quality, big-hearted malt from an unfashionable distillery. To be taken by big mouthfuls only and chewed until your jaw aches! **43%**

**Old Rhosdhu 5 Years Old** db **(77) n**18 **t**21 **f**19 **b**19. Big, ungainly, molassed, caramelised chewing whisky. **40%**. *Loch Lomond Distillers*.

**Murray McDavid Mission III Old Rhosdhu 1979** (81) **n**20 **t**21 **f**20 **f**20. Typically well built and chewy; a handsome milk-toffee richness to the barley. **46%**

❖ **Murray McDavid Mission Old Rhosdhu 1984 Aged 21 Years** Bourbon/Viognier, bott 06 **(82) n**21 **t**21 **f**20 **b**20. A bit fierce – especially on the nose - when first poured but calms down a treat. **49.3%. nc ncf.** *400 bottles*.

**The Whisky Fair Croftengea 1993** dist 23 Aug 93, bott 15 Jan 04 **(86) n**18 **t**22 **f**23 **b**23 this is the first time I have tasted Croftengea in bottled form, though it has changed little since I first tasted it at the distillery about eight years ago. All the main peaty components are still there – as are the feinty flaws. An enormous, curious dram that challenges and entertains and hangs around the palate for hours on end... **54.8%**. *Germany. 208 bottles The Limburg Whisky Fair*.

❖ **The Whisky Fair Inchmoan 1994** cask no. 646, dist 25.11.94, bott 26.01.05 **(82) n**21 **t**20 **f**21 **b**20. A bit dirty and out of tune, but enough coffee and smoke for some fun. **54.8%**. *Germany. 210 bottles*.

## LOCHSIDE
### Highland (Eastern), 1957–1992. Closed.

**Berrys' Own Selection Lochside 1981 22 Year Old**, bott 04 **(87) n**21 a bag of boiled sweets; **t**23 lovely lychee sweetness mingles well with the malt and banana-oak; **f**21 thins out but the malt remains constant; **b**22 a fruity, stylish dram that captures the true Lochside style better than most. **46%**.

Blackadder Raw Cask Lochside 23 Years Old cask 616, dist 23 Feb 81, bott Nov 04 **(78)** n20 t19 f20 b19. Some pleasant vanilla and typical Lochside fruit. **55.4%**

Cadenhead's Authentic Collection Lochside Aged 23 Years dist 81, bott Feb 05 **(95)** n25 fabulously scented: apple strudel with nutmeg, pine nuts and uncooked Christmas pudding for good measure. One of the great noses on the whisky market today and entirely unique; **t23** forget the port: this has the delivery of a pretty old bourbon, complete with red liquorice, red currant jam and then an astonishing build-up of very warming spices; **f23** happy to allow soothing vanilla-oak to dampen down the fire; returns to a sweeter, maltier tempo; **b24** the influence of the port pipe delivers extra spice but, really, single malt whisky doesn't come any more complex than this. Take all the time in the world over this one: just don't rush it. There are only 246 bottles of this stuff – make sure one has your name on it. **56.7%**. *246 bottles.*

·:· Cadenhead's Authentic Collection Lochside Aged 24 Years dist 81, bott Sep 05 **(75)** n17 t21 f18 b19. There is something not quite 100% clean on nose or palate with this one, as if from poor sherry rather than a bourbon cask. But there is just enough versatility and fruit on the barley to make for an interesting dram. **59.1%**. *276 bottles.*

Connoisseurs Choice Lochside 1991 **(85)** n20 t22 f21 b22. Fruity, spicey, deceptively complex and rewarding. **43%**. *Gordon & MacPhail.*

Jack Wiebers The Lochside 37 Years cask 7543 dist Dec 66, bott Mar 04 **(87)** n21 t22 f22 b22. A cask picked just in the nick of time shows delicious insight into this lost distillery. **58.7%. nc ncf sc.** *Germany. 168 bottles.*

Old Malt Cask Lochside 14 Years Old dist Jul 89, bott Mar 04 **(78)** n19 t21 f19 b19. Just too intensely sweet ever to be a great whisky, but a jolly exhibitionist all the same. **50%. nc ncf sc.** *Douglas Laing.*

·:· Old Malt Cask Lochside Aged 14 Years dist Oct 90, bott Sept 05 **(94)** n24 bedazzling with a rare firmness to the barley and lucid grassy presence which suggests a whisky considerably younger; **t23** every bit as mouthwatering and charming as the nose suggests with a delicate digression from the barley towards a neat cocoa influx; **f23** really beautifully balanced with a light infusion of vanilla and toast – and a dash of marmalade? – to make for a serene finale; **b24** when a distillery capable of making whisky this good is lost to us for ever, I could almost weep. **50%.** *Douglas Laing. 275 bottles.*

# LONGMORN
### Speyside, 1895. Chivas. Working.

Longmorn 15 Years Old db **(93)** n23 curiously salty and coastal for a Speysider, really beautifully structured oak but the malt offers both African violets and barley sugar; **t24** your mouth aches from the enormity of the complexity, while your tongue wipes grooves into the roof of your mouth. Just about flawless bitter-sweet balance, the intensity of the malt is enormous, yet – even after 15 years – it maintains a cut-grass Speyside character; **f22** long, acceptably sappy and salty with chewy malt and oak. Just refuses to end; **b24** these latest bottlings are the best yet: previous ones had shown just a little too much oak but this has hit a perfect compromise. An all-time Speyside great. **45%**

Longmorn 17 years old Distillery Edition db **(92)** n23 exceptionally salty with big oak presence. The malt, though, remains firm and almost serene; **t22** really good fruit, mainly orangey-citrus before the middle begins leaking big oak; **f24** the tongue aches as the complexity not only nudges up a gear but seemingly goes on for ever; loads of cocoa and toast; **b23** one of those drams which really knows how to milk the audience. **58.3%**

·:· Berry Brothers & Rudd Longmorn Aged 15 Years Bourbon casks no. 30111 & 30112, dist 90, bott 05 **(87)** n20 bizarre...!!! Corn oil...; **t22** lots of early oak kicks in with the oily barley; **f22** excellent sweetness to the finale with oak now taking a back seat; **b**23 a very curious expression: lots of bourbony-oak influence yet it's almost like a corn whisky on the nose. And the oiliness on the palate is also exaggerated by this distillery's standards. That said, still quite excellent stuff!! **46%. nc ncf.**

**Blackadder Raw Cask Longmorn 14 Years Old** cask no. 30050, dist 26 Feb 90, bott Dec 04 (86) **n**22 **t**21 **f**22 **b**21. Clean and simple. **54.3%**

**Cadenhead's Longmorn-Glenlivet 18 Years Old** (86) **n**20 **t**22 **f**22 **b**22. The oak fails to overcome the more mouthwatering properties. **54%.** *234 bottles.*

❖ **Chieftain's Longmorn Aged 11 Years Manzanilla Finish** (83) **n**19 **t**21 **f**22 **b**21. Clunks and thuds around the palate as about as an unwieldy a malt as you are likely to find from this distillery. But for all its flaws - and there a few – you cannot but help enjoy its rugged nature and bold, sweeping maltiness. A very enjoyable bit of rough and tumble. **43%.** *Ian Macleod.*

**The Coopers Choice Longmorn 1988 Aged 14 Years** bott 03 (86) **n**22 **t**21 **f**22 **b**21. Bedazzling array of muted dark sugars amid the rich malt;. a more than passable example of Longmorn at this age. **43%.** *Vintage Malt Whisky Co.*

❖ **The Coopers Choice Longmorn 1996 Matured for 9 Years** bott 06 (91) **n**21 a surprising dose of bourbon is injected into the prime barley; **t**23 Enormous! The intensity of the barley is sublime while again the oak dives in much more quickly than you might expect at this age; **f**23 calms down to allow the malt to arrive in waves while the sluggish spices develop into something more profound; **b**24 fabulous whisky and make no mistake. What a breath of fresh air to see this distillery at such an excellent age. Faultless and fantastic. **46%.**

❖ **D&M Aficionados' Club Longmorn Aged 31 Years** cask 3965, dist Mar 75 (88) **n**22 maybe a bit oak-tired but enough caramelized ginger, honey and even salted celery to make for an interesting sniff; **t**23 early confirmation of big oak but quickly gets into a honeyed stride with sweet spice and rich, telling and endearing oils; **f**22 long, still an extra dollop of oak but some coffee kicks in late; **b**21 from a purist and technical point of view, a cask several years beyond greatness. But here's the rub: warm the whisky well up to body temperature – and even beyond - and a quite beautiful thing emerges in the glass. The score above is a midway score between traditional tasting – and the way the whisky needs to be. **46%. nc ncf.** *US by Angus Dundee Distillers plc.*

❖ **Dun Bheagan Longmorn Aged 11 Years Madeira Finish** (82) **n**21 **t**22 **f**19 **b**20. A pretty whisky but, for all its mildly fruity make-up, lacks personality. **43%.**

**Duncan Taylor Collection Longmorn 1973 Aged 31 Years** cask 8912, dist Oct 73, bott Mar 05 (86) **n**21 **t**22 **f**22 **b**21 hangs on for grim death as age has really caught up, but holds out for a graceful finish. **51.3%**

**Duncan Taylor Longmorn 1978 Aged 25 Years** cask 5556 (96) **n**23 dream-like complexity with near perfect salt seasoning the vanilla-dried, barley sweetened theme **t**24 wow...!!! No easy task to get to grips with what is happening here: that saltiness peppers the mouth but the honey edge to the barley quietens the liquorice/coffee oak **f**24 some fruit edges into the equation but still we have a briny quarter to the barley; the oak is dry and has weight and purpose and some late honeycomb arrives to even it up a little **b**25 ladies and gentleman, I introduce to you complexity... **58.1%**

**Gordon & MacPhail Longmorn-Glenlivet 1963** bott 03 (87) **n**23 **t**22 **f**20 **b**22. Just one of those little beauts that pop up now and again: not a stone's throw in style from those wonderful 1967 Caperdonichs – not least because they come from the same cask base and home. Mildly over-oaked, but still a nugget. **40%**

**Gordon & MacPhail Longmorn 1971** (91) **n**22 whistle-clean sherry has soaked up rich oak comforatably; **t**23 again the grape is towering but such is the clarity the malt makes delicious inroads; **f**23 laced with cocoa and prunes, the bitter-sweet finish is a joy; **b**23 one of those exceptional Seagram sherry butts of the early '70s. Unmistakable and unmissable. **40%.** *Gordon & MacPhail*

**James MacArthur Longmorn 1990 14 Year Old**, cask 30110, bott Sep 04 **(94)** n24 The balance of the sweetness is beyond man's creativity: Longmorn at its most beautifully natural; t24 the weight of the malt almost grinds the tastebuds to a halt: refreshing grassy notes enrich some growing sawdusty oak and mocha – all you can expect from what must have been a near perfect cask; f22 a gentle finish that has lost the early viscosity; b24 a lush and vibrant example of why this is one of Speyside's great distilleries: if you want a template for great Longmorn at its most relaxed, this is it. **59.7%.**

⸭ **Murray McDavid Longmorn 1990 Aged 15 Years** Bourbon/Rioja, bott 05 **(76)** n19 t20 f18 b19. Full-on, fat but somewhat flat. **46%. nc ncf.** *1200 bottles.*

⸭ **Norse Cask Selection Longmorn 1990 Aged 15 Years** Cognac finish, bott Aug 05 **(94)** n22 vivid barley with a light brush of fruit; t25 concentrated liquidised essence of barley-sugar. This is almost too beautiful for word paintings because it is so rare to find a malt in this near perfect, unruined form. It may have been in a Cognac cask, but that has not had the slightest jot of influence on the barley, except, maybe, for keeping off the oak, as many Cognac casks are, frankly, way over the hill; f23 just the lightest sprinkling of cocoa powder adds an aging depth to the waves of faultless malt; b24 only a slight tiredness to the nose and some missing complexity detracts from a glorious whisky experience. Obviously I am being picky. With that, or a touch of smoke, we would be looking at probably one of the top five whiskies of the last couple of years. **54.9%.** *QualityWorld, Denmark.*

**Old Malt Cask Longmorn Aged 15 Years** dist Nov 88, bott Feb 04 **(91)** n23 first-class interplay between busy coal-gas/peaty smoky notes, soft honey, unripened oranges and unmalted barley flour; t22 really delicate malt with waferthin strands of oak underpinning it at first and then attempting to take control; bitter oranges and honey form a complex diversion. Mouthwatering throughout; f22 the odd waft of peat reek sweetens the lightly charred toast; b24 this is something to spend time over: a bitter-sweet tale if ever there was one. **50%. nc. ncf sc.** *Douglas Laing.*

⸭ **Old Malt Cask Longmorn 18 Years Old** dist Oct 87, bott Sept 06 **(89)** n22 rock solid barley; a vague Irish potstill firmness; t23 crackling barley with a wonderful diffusion of gristy sweetness; wonderfully salivating; f22 hard-as-nails barley offers late oils and oak; b22 lip-smacking despite the obvious rigidity. Unusual for Longmorn and an excellent early-evening dram. **50%.** *314 btls.*

**Private Cellar Longmorn-Glenlivet 1970** bott 03 **(93)** n23 t24 f22 b24. Some say there is no such thing as vintages: let's just say that in the late 60s and early 70s the whisky gods smiled benevolently on Longmorn. **43%.** *Forbes Ross Co.*

**Private Cellars Selection Longmorn Glenlivet 1983** bott 03 **(80)** n19 t21 f20 b20. Some high quality malt punches through the oak and caramel. **43%.**

⸭ **The Queen of the Moorlands Rare Cask Longmorn 12 Years Old (95)** n24 toffee apples dipped in very high quality sherry; a fabulous buzz of spice and dank, north-facing gardens. Exquisite; t24 sweet sherry bombarded by ground white peppers; the middle thrust comprises intense barley and deft oak; the bitter-sweet ratio offers pure textbook harmony. To term it sensational hardly does all this justice; f23 long, excellent cocoa development and lashings of natural, sweet caramel; b24 I thought truly great sherry butts like this were history, but Longmorn has come up trumps again. The most startling aspect is that it has taken an excellent though barely-known little whisky outlet off the beaten track in rural England to show the world something that Chivas, with all its might, should have made available the world over. **55.4%. sc.** *The Wine Shop, Leek, UK*

**Royal Mile Whiskies Longmorn 1995 Aged 9 Years** bott 05 **(92)** n21 t20 f21 b20. This is one of Speyside's weightier, slower-maturing malts. Here we have a rare glimpse in bottled form of a giant just waking up and getting some curiously toffeed sleep out of its eyes. **58.4%. nc ncf.**

**Scott's Selection Longmorn-Glenlivet 1983** Sherry Wood bott 03 **(89)** n23 t22 f22 b22. No prisoners taken here in this unusual chewathon. **54.5%**

⋙ **The Single Malt of Scotland Longmorn Aged 15 Years Vintage 1990** Bourbon cask 30091 **(92)** n23 the wood influence is striking as there is a distinct bourbon edge to this. The malt, meanwhile, shimmers; t22 stunning mouth arrival, firstly radiating rich barley and then, close behind, comes that Kentucky-style thrust. A liberal dose of spices help the two meld; f23 tingling with oak-induced mini-explosions, the barley still has intensity enough to regroup and blow you away; b24 left to its own devices, this distillery will come up trumps 99 times out of 100. Here's a fine example of very good whisky matured in a very good cask. But the results are way beyond very good... **60.4%**. *The Whisky Exchange. 129 bottles.*

⋙ **The Single Malt of Scotland Longmorn Aged 36 Years Vintage 1970** Sherry cask no. 28 **(78)** n19 t21 f19 b19. A borderline malt. This has any number of good things to be found but countless weeknesses. **56.1%**

⋙ **The Whisky Fair Longmorn Aged 31 Years** Bourbon Hogshead no. 3494, dist Apr 74, bott Mar 06 **(74)** n19 t18 f19 b18. Lots of exotic fruit. And we know what that means. But so thin is the line between success and failure: and this isn't exactly a success... **49.8%. nc ncf.** *Germany. 135 bottles.*

## LONGROW (see Springbank)

## MACALLAN
**Speyside, 1824. Edrington. Working.**

**The Macallan 7 Years Old** db **(89)** n23 beautifully clean sherry, lively, salty, gentle peppers; t23 mouth-filling and slightly oily. Some coffee tones intertwine with deep barley and fruit; f21 unravels to reveal very soft oak and lingering fruity spice; b22 an outstanding dram that underlines just how good young malts can be. Fun, fabulous and in recent bottlings has upped the clarity of the sherry intensity to profound new heights. **40%** ⊙⊙

**Macallan 10 Years Old** db **(86)** n20 t21 f23 b22 improved by slightly thinning out and accentuating the spice. **40%** ⊙

**Macallan 10 Years Old Cask Strength** db **(94)** n24 a fleck of smoke harmonises with the bitter blood orange, marzipan and ripe fig: sublime; t23 big, yet always keeping perfect shape on the palate with alternating waves of malt and fruit; f24 long, hints of spiced cocoa and Seville oranges; b23 brings tears to the eyes – and it isn't just the strength. A sherried Macallan draw from the cask coopered in heaven. Find, buy and be consumed.... **58.4%**

⋙ **The Macallan 10 Years Old Cask Strength** db **(85)** n20 t22 f22 b21. Enjoyable and a would give chewing gum a run for its money. But over-egged the sherry here and not a patch on the previous bottling. **58.8%.** *Duty Free.*

⋙ **The Macallan 12 Years Old Sherry Oak Elegancia** db **(86)** n23 t22 f20 b21. Promises, but delivers only to an extent. **40%**

**Macallan 18 Years Old** db **(95)** n24 compelling, crystal clear sherry notes with not a single blemish; massive fruitcake character fortified by a dry oloroso theme; t24 there are several layers working in tandem here: there is the dry oloroso forming the backbone, there is sweeter malt flitting butterfly-like around the palate; and lighter, fresher, grapey notes lighten the entire load. The whole almost overloads the tastebuds and senses; f23 just so deft and subtle: the enormity of the mouth arrival settles down now for a series of cross skirmishes between sweetened cocoa, ripe plum and even the softest wave of apologetic peat. Glorious; b24 it's been at least ten years since I've come across a Macallan 18 with such flawless depth. Beyond brilliant: a must for the Macallan purist who will be relieved by this expression following last year's unveiling of the Fine Oak range.... **43%**

⋄ **The Macallan 18 Years Old** dist 87, bott 06 db **(89)** n22 marmalade and freshly trimmed rhubarb. A dab of grape, too. Not entirely without blemish, though; t22 caressing and teasing in texture, the grape, vanilla, natural caramel and barley have melted into one indistinguishable lump; f23 long and languid, the tastebuds are sent to sleep by the sheer comfortableness of it all; **b**22 another essay in silk. **43%**

**Macallan 25 Years Old** db **(78)** n20 t20 f19 b19. After some early orangey pleasantries, goes strangely off-key and bitter. Having tasted so many classics over the years, an extremely disappointing expression. **43%**

**The Macallan 30 Years Old** db **(92)** n24 orange pith and oak, really charming and incredibly sexy and complex; t23 mouth-filling with a mixture of full fruits and beguiling spices, brilliant layer of honied barley; f22 slightly medium to short after the brilliance of the palate, but lovely vanilla and lingering, silky sweet malt; **b**23 a greatly improved dram than a few years back. An astounding mixture of age and quality. **43%**

⋄ **The Macallan 40 Years Old** dist 10 May 61, bott 9 Sep 05 db **(90)** n23 no shortage of oak, as you might expect. But nutty, too (chestnut pure, to be precise). The scope is broadened with a distracted smokiness while oak maximizes the longer it stays in the glass; t23 soft and yielding, with a lovely dovetailing of vanillins and delicate sherry. The grape appears to gain control with a sweet barley sidekick before the oak recovers; f22 soft oils formulate with some laite and slightly salted, Digestive-style biscuit. Gentle spices delight; **b**22 very well-rounded dram that sees off advancing years with a touch of grace and humour. So often you think the oak will take control, but each time an element intervenes to win back the balance. It is as if the dram is teasing you. Wonderful entertainment. **43%**

⋄ **The Macallan 50 Years Old** dist 29 Mar 52, bott 21 Sep 05 db **(90)** n25 we all have pictures in our minds of the perfect grandmother: perhaps grey-haired and knitting in her rocking-chair. Or grandfather: kindly, gentle, quietly wise, pottering about in the shed with some gadget he has just made for you. This, then, is the cliched nose of the perfect 50-year-old malt: time-defying intensity and clarity; attractive demerara (rum and sugar!) sweetened coffee, a tantalizing glimpse at something smoky and sensationally rich grape and old fruit cake. So that the sweetness and dryness don't cancel each other out, but complement each other and between them tell a thousand tales. Basically, there's not much missing here... and absolutely all you could wish to find in such an ancient Speysider...; t23 dry delivery with the oak making the early running. But slowly the grape and grain fights back to gain more than just a foot-hold; again telling wisps of smoke appear to lay down a sound base and some oily barley; f19 now the oak has taken over. There is a burnt-toast and burnt raisin bitterness, lessened in effect marginally by a sweeter vanilla add-on; **b**23 loses it at the end, which is entirely excusable. But until then it has been one fabulous experience full of passion and complexity. I nosed and tasted this for over an hour. It was one very rewarding, almost touching, experience. **46%**

**The Macallan 1851 Inspiration** db **(74)** n19 t19 f17 b19. Uninspirational in 2007.

**The Macallan 1876 Replica** db **(83)** n21 t21 f21 **b**20. Lovely oak-malt nose while the palate is silky and relaxed. **40.6%**

**The Macallan 1937** bott 69 db **(92)** n23 an outline of barley can eventually be made in the oaky mist; becomes better defined as a honeyed sweetness cuts in. Fingers of smoke tease. When nosing in the glass hours later the fresh, smoky gristiness is to die for ... and takes you back to the mill room 67 years ago; t22 pleasantly sweet start as the barley piles in − even a touch of melon in there; this time the oak takes second place and acts as a perfect counter; f24 excellent weight with soft peat softening the oak; **b**23 a subtle if not overly complex whisky where there are few characters but each play its part exceptionally well.

One to get out with a DVD of Will Hay's sublime Oh Mr Porter which was being made in Britain at the same time as this whisky and as Laurel and Hardy were singing about a Lonesome Pine on the other side of the pond; or any Pathe film of Millwall's FA Cup semi-final with Sunderland. **43%**

**The Macallan 1937** bott 74 db **(83)** t19 t24 f20 b20. It's all about the superb, silky initial mouth impact. **43%.**

**The Macallan 1938** bott 73 db **(90) n**21 hint of apple blossoms on oak; **t**23 stupendous balance and poise as the barley rolls, wave after wave over the palate bringing with it a sweet sugar-almond biscuity quality; **f**23 fabulous finish of great length. Spices dovetail with an almost perfect barley-oak charm; **b**23 no hint of tiredness here at all: a malt that has all the freshness and charisma yet old-world charm and mystery of Hitchcock's The Lady Vanishes, which was made at the same time as this whisky. **43%**

**The Macallan 1938 (31 Years Old)** dist 38, first bott 69, re-bottled 02 db **(83) n**20 t22 f20 b21. Some wonderful trills of barley early on but the oak dominates. **43%.**

**The Macallan 1939** bott 79 db **(90) n**23 pleasing peaty edges to the thick malt; a touch of hickory for extra weight and Highland Park-esque heather-honey; **t**22 spot on barley gives an unmolested mouthwatering performance; the oak tags on reluctantly drying towards cocoa at the middle; **f**22 the integrity is kept as the oak backs off and little wisps of smoke re-surface; some brown sugar keeps the bitter-sweet pot boiling; **b**23 enormous complexity confidence to a whisky distilled at a time of uncertainty; one to accompany the original Goodbye Mr Chips, though the whisky seems nothing like so faded. **43%**

**The Macallan 1940** bott 75 db **(83) n**20 t22 f21 b20. Easily the most modern style discernible from this distillery; a Macallan recogisable as an ancestor of today's famous dram, even with one or two warts apparent. **43%**

**The Macallan 1940 (37 Years Old)** dist 40, first bott 77, re-bottled 02 db **(91) n**22 not dissimilar to an old sherried Irish of this era with the barley having a firm, crisp, almost abrasive quality. Rather lovely especially with the most subtle wisps of peat imaginable; **t**23 bracing, full-on barley where the flintiness from the nose is transferred perfectly to the palate; a touch of spice and hint of smoke towards the middle; **f**23 clean, long finale where the barley pulsates its rock hard message; **b**23 blind-tasting I would have declared this Irish, though slightly mystified by the distant hints of peat. Hard to believe that something so sublime could have been made by a nation under siege. Obviously nothing can distract a Scotsman from making great whisky ... **43%**

**The Macallan 1945 (56 Years Old)** cask 262, bott 02 db **(89) n**22 extraordinary to the point of improbability: the sherry is fresh and keeping at bay logjams of chunky oak, though the fruitiness burns off the longer it remains in the glass; the smoke hovers and soars like pin-prick eagles on the wing; **t**23 battling oak fizzes against the sweeter, mouthwatering barley; the fruit is subtle though there is a pineapple sharpness amid the still lush grape; **f**22 really impressive, slow development of peat that offers no spice but a smoky overlay to the oak; **b**22 how can a whisky retain so much freshness and character after so long in the cask? This game never ceases to amaze me. **51.5%**

**The Macallan 1946 Select Reserve** db **(93) n**25 does peat arrive any more delicately than this? The sherry, barley and oak offer perfect harmony: perfect and faultless; **t**23 teasingly mouthwatering and fruity. Crushed sultanas cruise with the peat; **f**22 the oak makes inroads at the expense of the barley. Remains chewy and tantalisingly smoky, though; **b**23 I have never found a finer nose to any whisky. Once-in-a-lifetime whisky. **40%**

**The Macallan 1946 (56 Years Old)** cask 46/3M, bott 02 db **(84) n**21 t21 f20 b22. The most peat-free '46 I've come across yet **44.3%**

**The Macallan 1948 (53 Years Old)** cask 609, bott 02 db **(77) n**18 t21 f19 b19. Drinkable, but showing some major oaky cracks. **45.3%**

**The Macallan 1948 Select Reserve** db **(75)** n22 t19 f17 **b17**. What a fabulous nose! Sadly the package trails behind the '46. **40%**

**The Macallan 1949 (53 Years Old)** cask 136 bott 02 db **(95)** n23 wonderfully lively fruit interwoven with waxy, polished wooden floors and acacia honey; a touch of salt sharpens it further; t24 nothing extinct about this old Scottish volcano as oak-led spices assert their grip on the tastebuds while soft, sultry sherry tries to act as placator; f24 oaky-cocoa/liquorice and intense barley; remains mouthwatering yet spicy for seemingly hours; b24 hold on to your trilbies: this punchy malt knows exactly where it is going. What a year: Carol Reed makes the incomparable The Third Man and Macallan can come up with something like this. Oh, to swap Orson Welles for H. G. Wells and his time machine. Sheer, unrepeatable class. **49.8%**

**The Macallan 1949 (52 Years Old)** cask 935 bott 02 db **(82)** n23 t21 f19 **b19**. Faded and slightly tired, it has problems living up to the heaven-made nose. **41.1%**

**The Macallan 1950 (52 Years Old)** cask 598 bott 02 db **(83)** n22 t22 f18 **b21**. Charmingly delicate peat but probably about two or three summers past being a truly excellent whisky. **46.7%**

**The Macallan 1950 (52 Years Old)** cask no.600 bott 02 db **(91)** n20 the early fruit quickly evaporates to leave a clear path for the oak; t24 stunning sherry: the grape absolutely sparkles yet is soft enough to allow through a tidal wave of malt, on which peat is sensuously surfing; f23 spices from the middle carry through as does the chewy peat. Some fabulous undercurrents of burnt raisin and healthy malt continue; b24 only two casks apart, but this is almost a mirror image of the first, in the sense that everything is the other way round... **51.7%**

**The Macallan 1951 (51 Years Old)** cask 644 bott 02 db **(93)** n23 a minor fruitfest with withering grapes and raisins the main attraction but over-ripe greengages and raspberries bulk up the sub-plot: needs this to see off the firm oak. A gentle, barely discernible peatiness drifts over it all with absolutely no signs of over-aging; t24 fascinating detail to the barley: it is fresh and still mildly gristy at first but the sherry builds a dark path towards it. All the time the sherry remains clean and in harmony; some confident peat weaves a delicious path through the complexity; f23 unrefined brown sugar digs in with the barley to see off the encroaching oak; the most delicate wafts of peat imaginable caress the senses; b23 a malt instantly recognisable to Macallan lovers of the last two decades. Simply outstanding. **52.3%**

**The Macallan 1952 (50 Years Old)** cask no.627 bott 02 db **(80)** n20 t20 f21 **b19**. Good, clean sherry but it all seems a little detached **50.8%**

**The Macallan 1952 (49 Years Old)** cask 1250, bott 02 db **(74)** n19 t19 f18 **b18**. Ye olde weirde Macallane. **48%**

**The Macallan 1953 (49 Years Old)** cask no. 516, bott 02 db **(92)** n22 a shade meaty with the oak offering a big counter to the thumping sherry and delicate smoke; t24 full sherry alert as the fruitcake richness goes into overdrive, as do the spices; f23 some medium roast Santos lightens the oak while enrichening the barley; b23 deliciously big and unflinching in its Christmas pudding intensity. **51%**

**The Macallan 1954 (47 Years Old)** cask 1902, bott 02 db **(77)** n19 t18 f21 **b19**. The line between success and failure is thin: outwardly the '53 and 54 are similar but the 53 controls the oak much tighter. I love the coffee finale on this, though. **50.2%**

**The Macallan 1955 (46 Years Old)** cask 1851 49, bott 02 db **(88)** n21 more burnt raisins and apples; t22 the tastebuds get a good spicy peppering as the barley rootles about the palate; the sherry is clear and intact; f23 amazingly long with the oak falling short of its desired palate domination; b22 close call: one more Speyside August and this dram would have been matchwood. **45.9%**

**The Macallan 1958 (43 Years Old)** cask 2682, bott 02 db **(86)** n17 t22 f24 **b23**. One fears the worst from the sappy nose but the taste is sheer Highland Park in its honey depth. **52.9%**

**The Macallan 1959 (43 Years Old)** cask 360, bott 02 db **(79)** n19 t21 f19 **b**20. The oak is giving the malt a good hiding but it just hangs on to a delicious sub-plot. **46.7%**

**The Macallan 1964 (37 Years Old)** cask 3312 bott 02 db **(86)** n24 t22 f20 **b**20 butterscotch and honey: a real chewing whisky if ever there was one. **58.2%**

**The Macallan 1965 (36 Years Old)** cask 4402 bott 02 db **(91)** n22 pretty well oaked but wonderful balance from blood oranges; t23 again lovely mouthfeel as the fabulously balanced and lush barley hits the palate; fruit and oak are dished out in even measures with the spice: this is top notch whisky; f22 after the big bust comes the ample arse: heaps of chewy barley fortified by sultanas and raisins; **b**24 if this was a woman it would be Marilyn Monroe. **56.3%**

**The Macallan 1966 (35 Years Old)** cask 7878 bott 02 db **(83)** n21 t22 f20 **b**20 a malt which never quite works out where it is going but gives a comfortable ride all the same. **55.5%**

**The Macallan 1967 (35 Years Old)** cask 1195 bott 02 db **(93)** n23 top notch uncompromised sherry with some lovely nutty touches; t24 the sherry deftly flicks each individual tastebud while the burnt fudge offers a bitter-sweet distraction; f23 coffee ice cream but a whole lot warmer as the spices pop about the mouth. Vanilla and raisins gather around the spicy centrepiece; some lovely salt towards the finale; **b**23 this is what happens when you get a great sherry cask free of sulphur and marauding oak: whisky the way God intended. Unquestionably classic Macallan. **55.9%**

**The Macallan 1968 (34 Years Old)** cask 2875 bott 02 db **(92)** n23 lemon curd tart and barley; t23 full frontal barley with a grape chaperone; f22 continues to mouthwater now with late cocoa adding depth and finesse; **b**24 possibly the most sophisticated and delicate malt in the pack despite the strength. **51%**

**The Macallan 1968 (33 Years Old)** cask 5913 bott 02 db **(84)** n17 t23 f22 **b**22. Flawed genius: how can a whisky with such a poor nose produce the goods like this? **46.6%**

**The Macallan 1969** cask 9369 db **(75)** n19 t18 f20 b18. One of those ungainly sherry butts that swamps everything in sight. **52.7%**

**The Macallan 1969 (32 Years Old)** cask no. 10412 bott 02 db **(76)** n18 t20 f18 **b**20. One small sip for man, one ordinary vintage for Macallan. Splinters. anybody? **59%**

**The Macallan 1970 (32 Years Old)** cask no. 241 bott 02 db **(95)** n23 another heavyweight but this time with some honey and ripe fig to offer complexity; passable impersonation of ancient bourbon blended with old Demerara rum; t24 quite massive with strands of brown sugar bringing out the best of the grape; f23 very long and so subtle: the barley and vanilla stretch a long distance with some natural toffee rounding things off; **b**25 Brazil win the World Cup with the finest team and performance of all time, my girlfriend born there soon after and Macallan receive a butt from Heaven via Jerez. 1970 was some year ... **54.9%**

**The Macallan 1970 (31 Years Old)** cask no. 9033 bott 02 db **(81)** n20 t20 f22 **b**19. A butt bottled on its way down. **52.4%**

**The Macallan 1971 (30 Years Old)** cask no. 4280 bott 02 db **(86)** n21 t22 f22 **b**21. Imagine the trusty 10 years old from about 1980 with a grey beard ... **56.4%**

**The Macallan 1971 (30 Years Old)** cask 7556 bott 02 db **(91)** n22 delicate salt helps develop the barley; t22 vivid barley with rather soft sherry and then spice; f24 lengthy, subtle end with waves of rich sherry carrying a Demerara sweetness and coffee; **b**23 a complex dram that is comfortable with its age. **55.9%**

**The Macallan 1972 (29 Years Old)** cask no. 4041 bott 02 db **(92)** n23 hell's teeth!!! This is probably what an explosion in a bodega would smell like. The most awesomely powerful sherry I can probably ever remember on a whisky, much more one dimensional than cask 4043, though; t24 that trademark coffee-ness is there (in this case something of a heavy roast Costa Rican) then some tomato and burnt raisin; **f**22 bitter and slightly nutty as the oak begins to gain some control; **b**23 once, I would have hated this type of malt. But I have come across so many sulphur-tainted casks over recent years that I have learned to have fun with monsters like this. Snatched from an awesome clutch of butts. **49.2%**

**The Macallan 1972 29 Years Old** cask 4043, bott 02 db **(93) n**25 well, it has to be said: a quite faultless nose. The spices are entirely in true with the perfect sherry-oak balance. This is big stuff, but perfectly proportioned: seems almost a shame to drink it ...; **t**24 stupendous spice-plum-giant-boiled-Italian-tomato: enormous with a waft of smoke through the middle; **f**21 slightly bitter as the oak nibbles but still lots of complexity; **b**23 the sherry butt used for this was a classic: the intensity of the whisky memorable. If, as Macallan claim, the sherry accounts for only 5% of the flavour, I'd like to know what happened to the other 95.... **58.4%**

**The Macallan 1973 (30 Years Old)** cask no.6098 bott 03 db **(93) n**23 the grape is brittle and nestles behind barley and honey; some ripe pears add to the freshness; **t**24 the honey is at the vanguard of a brilliant display of intense, sugarcoated barley; **f**23 the sweetness vanishes to leave the more mouthwatering, grassy malt elements; **b**23 a superbly chosen cask for those with a sweet tooth in particular. If you know any women who claim not to like whisky, seduce them with this. **60.9%**

**The Macallan 1989** cask no 552 db **(94) n**23 stunningly clean sherry with wonderful nuttiness amid spice and oak; moist Melton Hunt cake at its most subtle; **t**23 explosive entrance with spices and a superbly full-on oakiness that bathes in the luxuriant, simply flawless, leathery sherry; the sweetness is not entirely unlike Demerara rum; **f**24 calms down for wave upon wave of chocolate fruit and nut ... only without the excessive sweetness; **b**24 there are countless people out there who cut their whisky teeth 20 years ago on Macallan. Battle to get a bottle of this and the grey hairs will return to black, the eyesight will improve and your clothes will fit more easily. This is timewarp Macallan it its most dangerously seductive. **59.2%**

**The Macallan Cask Strength** db **(94) n**22 cranked-up, sweet, clean sherry; **t**24 absolutely spot-on delivery with grape concentrate, thickened further by intense barley. Wonderful spices arrive on cue; **f**24 long with the taste buds storm-lashed by juicy sherry for some time. And still those spices rock ...; **b**24 one of those big sherry babies: it's like surfing a massive wave of barley-sweetened sherry. Go for the ride. **58.6%**. *USA.* ☉☉

⠿ **Macallan Cask Strength** db **(82) n**20 **t**20 **f**22 **b**20. I could weep. What could have been an absolute classic is just one less-than-perfect cask away from greatness. Even so, an enjoyable and memorable ride for the most part. **57.8%**. *Canada.*

**The Macallan Distillers Choice** db **(80) n**21 **t**20 **f**19 **b**20. Sweeter, less sherried and more bashful than previous bottlings. **40%** ☉☉

⠿ **The Macallan Easter Elchies Seasonal Cask Selection Winter Choice 14 Years Old** db **(94) n**24 you can almost picture the butt before it was filled: large, dripping with dampness inside and smelling as sweet as a nut. Nothing has changed in 14 years, except some exquisite marmalade and honeycomb has been added; **t**24 sizzling spices cut rapier-like through the intense grape; juicy barley seeps through the wounds; **f**23 lilting, rich-textured natural caramel and vanilla; **b**23 from a faultless cask and one big enough to have its own Postcode... **54%**. *Exclusive to visitor centre.*

**The Macallan Gran Reserva 1981** db **(90) n**23 **t**22 **f**22 **b**23. Macallan in a nutshell. Brilliant. But could do with being at 46% for full effect. **40%**

**The Macallan Gran Reserva 1982** db **(82) n**21 **t**22 **f**20 **b**19. Big, clean, sweet sherry influence from first to last but doesn't open up and sing like the '81 vintage. **40%**

**The Macallan Elegancia 1991** db **(79) n**19 **t**21 **f**19 **b**20. Distinctly citrusy with fresh-squeezed blood orange intermingling with vanilla and fresh malt; sadly, a distant murmer of sulphur on both nose and finish docks a point or three. **40%**

**The Macallan Elegancia 1992** db **(85)** n19 t21 f23 **b**22. A marvellous improvement on the '90 edition **43%**

**The Macallan Fine Oak 8 Years Old** db **(89)** n21 entirely different to any other Macallan around: the brash freshness of the sherry appears to be magnified by the young barley, playful, kindergarten stuff; t23 the youthful exuberance on the nose is matched by the live-wire arrival on the palate. The shape it takes in the mouth is fascinating with the initially mouthwatering grape effect at first breathlessly rushing in and then calming to dissolve in every corner of the palate, gentle spices trickle down as does the very faintest of honey notes; f22 a lot of cocoa butter as the oak shows a surprising depth, burnt raisins also guarantee a bitter edge to the sweet malt; **b**23 a distinctly different, young and proud Macallan that settles into a satisfying middle and finish where the soft grapey tones break through for a mottled effect with the intense malt. Seriously tasty stuff and great fun. **43%**

**The Macallan Fine Oak 10 Years Old** db **(83)** n20 t21 f21 **b**21. The faintest blemish on the grass and citrus nose disappears after the bottle's been open a day or two; elsewhere soft malt dissolves leaving a more bitter biscuity oatiness in its wake. The malt-fruit combination is mouth-cleansing as it gathers in intensity. A pleasingly delicate Macallan. **40%**

**The Macallan Fine Oak 12 Years Old** db **(89)** n22 clean, dry sherry is bolstered by competent fresh barley and even a hint of ginger when warmed; t23 seriously mouthwatering with the barley coating the palate with its ultra-clean bitter-sweet charms; vanilla arrives earlier than usual – especially for a Macallan; f21 quite a dry, chalky finish but only after the barley is given an almost free run. If you have chewed malt, then you will recognise this beautiful character; late natural toffee muscles in on the vanilla fade; **b**23 a dram to be taken at body temp for best results: when sampled cold the balance edges towards subtle fruit and crispness; when warmed the barley makes the most stunning impact. A suave dram of near flawless character. **40%**

**The Macallan Fine Oak 15 Years Old** db **(95)** n24 over-ripe bananas on toast with freshly-picked spring grass as a side dish and plenty of floral notes to round it off: a sublime and probably unique official Macallan aroma! t23 the malt, complete with distant peat, simply dissolves in the mouth; beautifully weighted with the distinctive Macallan brown-sugar sweetness hitting the red zone for a while before it is pulled back by drier vanilla; f24 just so, so long!! Excellent playful peaty spice development late on helps punctuate the continuation of the rich barley theme that expands out into low key butterscotch/toffee; dovetailing is a distant grapey sub-plot; **b**24 true story: I have for years played about in my lab with bourbon and sherry cask Macallan and come to the conclusion that a truly great whisky was waiting to happen. This could be it. You have to travel a long way to find a whisky with quite the same refreshing all round harmony as this. The balance is the stuff of legend ... and genius. **43%**

⠶ **The Macallan Fine Oak 17 Years Old** db **(84)** n21 t21 f21 **b**21. A curious, pleasant but not entirely convincing addition to the Fine Oak family, having neither the 15-year-old's outrageous complexity or the deftness of the 18. An expression too far? **43%**

**The Macallan Fine Oak 18 Years Old** db **(91)** n23 inside the dry sherried shell is sweeter malt and vanilla; a touch of salt gives a slightly coastal air, even with some far-off peat-reek on the breeze; t22 myriad malt characteristics on varying levels of sweetness; there is mesmerising spice and grape varying between pungent and juicy; f23 remains young at heart with the barley dominating; mouthwatering to the end, distant smoke returns flanked by spineless grape juice and toffee plus oak that lays bitterness on sweet; even a touch of bourbon-style ageing at the death; **b**23 a dram much truer to the old Macallan style but with enough overt barley to make a difference. **43%**

**The Macallan Fine Oak 21 Years Old** db **(89) n**22 an attractive honeyed thread weaves through the oak and grape; some beautiful marmalade off-cuts toys with a ghostly peatiness; **t**22 oily and sultry with some stiff oak softened by the barley which is yielding and mouthwatering; **f**23 remains butter-creamy, that vague, ethereal peatiness plays peak-a-boo but the vanilla continues as does the marmalade on toast; **b**22 by far the richest textured Macallan of all time with a fascinating distant peatiness. **43%**

**The Macallan Fine Oak 25 Years Old** db **(94) n**24 probably the first Macallan since '46 to show such little shyness with peat, though here it is more fleeting; the second wave is proud, clean sherry. The third is vanilla ice-cream with pears and peaches; the fourth is pure bourbon. Speyside bliss; **t**23 the oak offers a framework in which the sherry thrives while the barley punches its weight; an assortment of fruit also make an entrance as does an almost underground spiciness; **f**23 back to vanilla for the undetectable touchdown; I can think of no whisky this age which has such a velvety feel right to the very end. Guys, if it were a woman you wouldn't know whether to make love or snuggle up in a silky embrace and go to sleep: I suggest both; **b**24 the blenders have obviously worked overtime on this: what a star! **43%**

**The Macallan Fine Oak 30 Years Old** db **(90) n**23 lots of nose-nipping oaky weight softened by crushed gooseberries and grape; a mild and deeply attractive bourbony character develops **t**23 delicate spices arrives from nowhere, there is a quick flash of half-hearted peat and then we are left in a custard-sweet and enormous world of malty-oaky-grapiness; a certain fatness to the whisky develops **f**22 where's the oak? An improbable finale that is all about barley arm-inarm with sherry and nut oil. At last the oakiness appears but immediately tapers out **b**22 the oak threatened on the nose never quite materialises. Few whiskies of this maturity are quite so polite regarding the age **43%**

◦➣ **The Macallan Fine Oak Whisky Maker's Selection** db **(92) n**22 good age with the oak determining a dry course; the barley carries delicate grape; **t**23 distinctively Speyside-style with an early avalanche of spice; there is a barley-juiced fruitiness and perhaps a fino touch, too; **f**23 long, with all the vanilla you'd expect from such a well oaked dram; the clean-ness of the barley and grape is stunning, as is the light oily sheen that carries the dim sweetness; **b**24 those who cannot see Macallan in anything other than chestnut oloroso will be having sleepless nights: this is a dram of exquisite sophistication. The ultimate pre-prandial dram with it's coy, mildly cocoaed dryness, set against just enough barley and fruit sweetness here and there to see off any hints of austerity. Some great work has gone on in the lab to make this happen: fabulous stuff, chaps! **42.8%.** *Duty Free.*

**The Macallan Millennium 50 Years Old** (1949) decanter db **(90) n**23 **t**22 **f**22 **b**23. Magnificent finesse and charm despite some big oak makes this another Macallan to die for. **40%**

**The Macallan Travel 1920s** db **(67) n**17 **t**18 **f**15 **b**17. Does absolutely nothing for me at all. Totally off-key, no finish. Nothing roaring about this one. **40%**

**The Macallan Travel 1930s** db **(91) n**22 beautiful peat and sherry combo; **t**23 the cleanest, most mouthwatering sherry you could pray for; **f**23 soft vanilla and lingering, lazy smoke; **b**23 an essay in complexity and balance. Clean sherry at its finest. You little darling! **40%**

**The Macallan Travel 1940s** db **(81) n**21 **t**22 **f**17 **b**21. Lovely smoke and complexity, but let down by the sherry and a faltering finish. **40%**

**The Macallan Travel 1950s** db **(92) n**24 intense, immaculate sherry and blood orange with playful spices adding nose prickle; **t**22 massive but voluptuous sherry, then a wave of malt concentrate; **f**23 more barley, a touch of smoke and then juicy sultanas and lingering spice; **b**23 sit back, take a deep, mouth-filling draught, close your eyes and listen to Hogie Carmichael's "Stardust", for this is just what this whisky is. **40%**

·:· **Alchemist Macallan Aged 14 Years** dist Apr 91, bott Jul 05 **(91) n**22 floral and grassy; **t**23 marauding, mouth-watering barley; **f**23 classy, cocoa and barley-laced vanilla; **b**23 Macallan at it's unsherried best: the richness is sublime. **46%. nc ncf.**

**Cadenhead's Macallan-Glenlivet Authentic Collection Aged 14 Years** Butt, dist 90, bott May 05 **(75) n**19 **t**19 **f**18 **b**19. Some decent fruit and chewability despite the flaw. **57.6%.** *654 bottles.*

·:· **Cadenhead's Authentic Collection Macallan-Glenlivet Aged 16 Years** Bourbon Hogshead, dist 89, bott Sept 06 **(95) n**24 glorious interlinking between golden-syrup and honey on one hand and crisp barley on the other. All this is on a bed of distant smoke and ice cream cones; **t**24 sweetness on nose translates automatically to palate where a mouthwatering barley middle is deeply embedded; **f**23 a gathering of spices which add to the honeyed gloss of barley; **b**24 showing some of the extraordinary DNA which makes Macallan Fine Oak 17 such a world-beater. Stunning. And for the thousands of Macallanophiles out there – you'd better get the next plane to Campbeltown!! **53.3%.** *282 bottles.*

**Cadenhead's Authentic Collection Macallan-Glenlivet Aged 17 Years** dist 87, bott Feb 05 **(94) n**24 bitter orange and wild strawberries crushed in the hand; some cocoa-oak perfectly sprinkled; **t**24 a bourbony oak kick, then it's back to the multi-layered fruit followed by thick malt; **f**23 much drier but never too dry, returning to bitter chocolate and bitter orange; a hint of spice; **b**23 very unprofessional, I know, but I just couldn't spit this one out – just too damn good! **56.1%.** *630 bottles.*

**Celtic Heartlands Macallan 1969 (92) n**23 Macallans rarely get more exotic than this: passion fruit and gala melon. The perfect breakfast malt...; **t**24 fantastic interplay between malt brushed with peat and sympathetic oak: wave upon wave of beautifully weighted malt; **f**22 cocoa and smoke; **b**23 proof that a Macallan from a great bourbon cask is as good as one from sherry. **40.3%.** *Jim McEwan/Bruichladdich.*

·:· **Dewar Rattray Individual Cask Bottling Macallan 1989 Aged 17 Years** cask no. 2819, dist Feb 90, bott May 06 **(89) n**23 textbook sherried Macallan; **t**21 dry toffee-nut; **f**23 sweetness as barley gets a juicy grip; dries and bitters out after some while; **b**22 rich and full-bodied. **58.4%.** *256 bottles.*

**Distillery No 7 Macallan 1990 (81) n**19 **t**20 **f**21 **b**21. Attractively malty and mouthwatering with some chewey cocoa notes **46%**

**Duncan Taylor Macallan 1968 Aged 35 Years** cask 5593 **(90) n**20 a hint of citrus **t**24 massive injection of barley leaves the tastebuds gasping **f**23 amazingly long with an irresistable combination of cocoa and very late smoke **b**23 all understated and gentle, this oozes class **53.1%**

·:· **Duncan Taylor Collection Macallan 1968 Aged 38 Years** cask no. 5586, dist Jun 68, bott 4 July 06 **(79) n**23 **t**20 **f**18 **b**18. The debonair marzipan and cocoa nose raises the profile of an otherwise over-aged malt. **50.94%.** *103 bottles.*

·:· **Duncan Taylor Collection Macallan 1968** cask 5589, dist Jun 68, bott Mar 05 **(83) n**21 **t**23 **f**19 **b**20. Beautifully sensual malty start, but tires out. **54%.** *151 bottles.*

·:· **Duncan Taylor Collection Macallan 1969** cask no 7191, dist Jun 69, bott Dec 05 **(94) n**24 toffee-vanilla massages the nose; some coffee, too; **t**23 lush and luscious with rich barley-toffee lead; massive spices jolt the tastebuds back to life; **f**23 lightly roasted Java brushed with demerara; **b**24 great age, but alive and kicking to fabulous effect. **55.8%.** *116 bottles.*

·:· **Duncan Taylor Collection Macallan 1969** cask no 8377, dist Sept 69, bott Dec 05 **(88) n**23 fruity and beautifully aged; **t**22 silky barley then some devilish spices: a mouthful and a half; **f**21 burnt toast; **b**22 a lovely malt that was just beginning its descent in the barrel. **49.3%.** *203 bottles.*

**Duncan Taylor Collection Macallan 1986 Aged 18 Years**, cask 10195, dist Nov 86, bott Feb 05 **(94) n**23 the oak tries to go a little soapy but fails; instead we are seduced by a bouquet of wild early Spring flowers with just enough earthiness to complete the effect; **t**24 oh yes! a seductive outpouring of intense malt that is sweetened to just the right degree: barley sugar but going easy on the sugar; **f**23 now a drier side to the dram with the oak integrating beautifully; **b**24 quite masterful whisky which gives your tastebuds one damned good seeing to.... **56.7%**

⟴ **Duncan Taylor Collection Macallan 1989-91** cask vx3 **(89) n**24 classy and complex with soothing butterscotch and barley sugar; **t**21 light, varying shades of malt but big oak surge; **f**22 the oak calms down and behaves itself enough for the malt to return for a long, ultra-delicate finish; **b**22 surprising degree of oak in the middle but, over-all, sheer quality. **46.1%**

⟴ **Gordon & MacPhail Speymalt Macallan 1938 (94) n**25 can this really be over 65-years of age? How, after all these years, does the dynamic of the millroom fit so comfortably with pulped citrus and lavender? And, lurking at the very back, almost wishing not to be noticed, a waft of the softest peat imaginable. I have spent over half an hour nosing this. I cannot fault it. True legend...; **t**22 an oaky barrage doesn't auger well, but soon it runs out of ammunition. It doesn't take long for accompanying spices and following barley-sugar and burnt honeycomb to unite and link with the pithy orange which has kept the oak in check from the off; **f**23 amazingly, the oak remains on the retreat and now we get to the real serious bit. Soft peats return to offer little more than a smoky echo but the sweetness continues for dozens more waves. There is a lingering dryness, totally in sympathy with the leading malt but, most of all, the tangy orange remains sharp and delicious; **b**24 when a malt is bottled at this near unbelievable age you expect the worst. And, even if it doesn't come, you have to be hyper-critical because such whisky doesn't come cheap and tasting notes written in awe of age rather than giving a true, honest assessment of its quality is not worth the ink used to print it. So, I have taken a long time to study this. And to find fault. Naturally, there are faults: every whisky has them, and at this age is expected to have more than most. But was it the quality of the wood they used in those days, or the peat involvement? Somehow, this malt has come through the best part of seven decades without any fatal flaws. The nose, in fact, is perfect. And although it wobbles on the palate on the start of its journey, by the end you cannot but be astounded. This is nature-defying whisky, very much like the 62-year-old Dalmore. Few people will be lucky enough ever to taste this. But those that do will be one of the truly privileged. And that includes me. **41.4%**

⟴ **Gordon & MacPhail Speymalt Macallan 1950 (91) n**24 a swirl of peat beds down into the firm barley; the fruit is masterful with blood orange lightened by plums and juicy sultana. Oak is present but refuses to unbalance the delightful tranquillity and weight; **t**22 wonderfully fruity pulse but there is still a gristy youth hanging on in there, allowing a subtle touch of peat to weave into the fabric. Again the oak holds back from doing any damage and the off wave of tangy kumquat is there to be found; **f**22 does it's best to take an oaky route, but hasn't the heart to do it. Instead, light barley recovers to mingle playfully with the vanilla. Dry and sawdusty, but always in tune and balanced; **b**23 I always taste these ultra-ancient whiskies with trepidation. Nature suggests that they should not be that good as barley – even with the aid of sherry – can see off only so much oak. But fortified with a delightful touch of peat, this holds itself together like an old Shakespeare first in original buckskin. It creaks. It's delicate. But take the time and handled carefully, this will amaze you. **43%**

⟴ **Gordon & MacPhail Speymalt Macallan 1967 (93) n**23 fruitcake fortified, curiously, with a dash of rum; **t**24 stunningly soft delivery of mixed fruits – especially sultana – and almost gristy barley; **f**22 just the right sprinkling of chalky oak to counter the rising spice and suet; **b**24 a mighty classy malt which has withstood the years with aplomb. **40%**

⚜ **Harris Whisky Co. "No Ordinary" Aged 16 Years** cask 5436, dist 89, bott Jan 06 **(90)** n22 medium malt; t23 big malt; f22 little malt; b23 malty. And magnificent. **53.1%. nc ncf.** *The Harris Whisky Co. Doesn't say on label, but this is Macallan.*

**Hart Brothers Macallan Aged 15 Years** dist Oct 88, bott Nov 03 **(92)** n21 t23 f24 b24. For a Macallanophiles out there: this is bourbon-Macallan at its finest for its vintage. **46%**

**Jim McEwan's Celtic Heartlands Macallan 1968 (84)** n19 t23 f21 b21. Although from bourbon cask, this is a very curious re-run of Macallan '54, only without quite so much honey; the early freshness of the barley is excellent. **40.2%**

⚜ **Murray McDavid Macallan Aged 8 Years** Bourboun/Syrah cask enhanced in Guigal Hermitage Rouge, dist 96, bott 05 **(73)** n18 t20 f17 b18. Guigal...but no Brueghel. Way too much polarised bitterness and sweetness. **46%. nc ncf.** *1200 bottles.*

**Murray McDavid Macallan 1990 Aged 13 Years (70)** n18 t18 f17 b17. Sulphur blighted and off-key. **46%**

⚜ **Murray McDavid Macallan 1990 Aged 15 Years** Bourbon/Grenache, bott 06 **(74)** n17 t20 f19 b18. A softie, but never gets out of the starting blocks. **46%. nc ncf.**

⚜ **Murray McDavid Mission Macallan 1969** Bourbon/Marsanne/ Roussanne **(84)** n24 t21 f19 b20. Fabulous, busy and entirely unique nose. To taste, though, the malt never quite finds its compass and spends much of its time fending off the oak. Never less than juicy and enjoyable, though. **41%.** *900 bottles.*

⚜ **Murray McDavid Mission Macallan 1985 Aged 21 Years** Bourbon /Sauternes (Chateau d'Yquem), bott 06 **(96)** n25 sweet, cleverly spiced (cinnamon mainly), grape underpinned by firm, rich barley. The best Macallan nose this year – by the distance from Speyside to Sauternes; t24 entirely sure-footed grape and grain in complete harmony; the tastebuds are swamped at first by the élan of this juicy, tongue-tying combination, then deft spice arrives to attack in waves and with panache; f23 long, continuing along the mouth-watering path with the oak finally getting a word in, a slightly bitter one but softened by natural caramel and tannins; b24 when I tasted this, my researcher had written only "bourbon/sauternes" after the name of the whisky (she had correctly copied directly from the label). When I had nosed, tasted, spat and found a safe route down from the ceiling, I inspected the sample bottle a little more carefully and spotted "Chateau dYquem." If all wine-finished whiskies were of this calibre you'd never hear a dissenting voice from me. Sadly, they aren't. But this one is and all I can do is savour every last drop of a truly great malt. Oh, and put the spittoon into temporary retirement... **52.4%. nc ncf.** *600 bottles.*

**Old Malt Cask Macallan Aged 13 Years** dist Jun 90, bott Feb 04 **(88)** n22 flakes of honey enrich the lazy barley and soft oak: relaxed and enticing; t23 sumptuous mouthfeel with that honey really making its mark from early on; soft additions of vanilla and peach work well with the faintest of smoke tones; f21 not quite so complex as the early arrival and dries as the oak broadens, but a lingering sweetness does the trick; b22 really lovely Macallan shorn of sherry and bringing about the exhibitionist in its nudity. **50%. nc ncf sc.** *307 bottles.*

⚜ **Old Malt Cask Macallan 15 Years Old** dist 23 Jan 90, bott 15 Jun 05 **(86)** n21 t22 f21 b22. About as gentle and clean as they come. **50%.** *Douglas Laing.*

**Old Malt Cask Macallan 15 Years Old** dist 23 Jan 90, bott 6 May 06 **(87)** n21 coal smoke and thick malt; t22 deeply intense malt; f22 harmonious vanilla to the malt contentrate; b22 good quality without ever testing the tastebuds. **50%**

⚜ **Old Malt Cask Macallan 21 Years Old** dist Apr 85, bott May 06 **(92)** n24 soft citrus further sweetens a gentle stem ginger-based spice buzz; t23 wonderfully layered, fruity barley refuses to bow to its age; the spices are busy and intriguing; f22 outstanding esters guarantee length and depth; b23 the freshness and complexity to this bottling is astounding. A real treat. But don't expect a sherry onslaught. **50%.** *Douglas Laing. 302 bottles.*

**Old Malt Cask Macallan Aged 25 Years** dist Oct 78, bott Dec 03 **(89) n**21 **t**23 **f**22 **b**23. Macallan unplugged: confirmation that it has weight enough to hold its own in a non-sherried environment. **50%. nc ncf sc.** *138 bottles.*

**Old Malt Cask Macallan 25 Years Old** dist Nov 79, bott Oct 04 **(79) n**19 **t**21 **f**20 **b**19. Pleasant but rather thin and hot for a Macallan. **50%.**

**Old Malt Cask Macallan 25 Years Old** dist 1 Jun 79, bott 16 May 05 **(89) n**23 faint peat reek clinging to ripe pears and malt; **t**23 incredibly powerful malt enriched by a teasing fruitiness; **f**22 tingling spices, echoes of peat and drier toasty notes; **b**22 a thoughtful Macallan that requires and repays solitude and time. **50%.**

⋅❖⋅ **Old Malt Cask Macallan 25 Years Old** dist Oct 80, bott Dec 05 **(89) n**23 rice pudding with honey stirred in; **t**23 early, crisp, lightly sugared sweetness ; big barley surge; **f**21 lazy spices and vanilla; **b**22 a laid-back joy. **50%.** *296 bottles.*

**Old Malt Cask Macallan Aged 26 Years** cask no DL988 dist May 77, bott Oct 03 **(76) n**18 **t**20 **f**19 **b**19. Overly honey sweet, off-balance, ordinary fare with a bit of a kick. **50%. nc ncf sc.** *Douglas Laing. 240 bottles.*

**Old Malt Cask Macallan Aged 26 Years** dist Jun 90, bott Feb 04 **(85) n**19 **t**23 **f**22 **b**21 Creaking and patched up, there is just enough class and lingering sweetness to make this a very decent dram. **50%. nc ncf sc.** *Douglas Laing. 240 bottles.*

**Old Masters Macallan 1989 15 Year Old** cask no. 1249, bott Sep 04 **(91) n**22 great evidence of that "sma' still" aroma: intense with a coppery edge to the sweetness; a curious carroty freshness adds to the intrigue; **t**24 big, decent esters then a wave of onrushing malt: absolutely tip-top bitter-sweet shape; **f**22 complex, rich and at last allowing soft oak to arrive, bringing with it some natural caramel; **b**23 Arthur Winning must have danced a small jig when he found this cask. **62.2%.** *James MacArthur.*

**Platinum Macallan 27 Year Old** dist May 77, bott Jul 04 **(84) n**21 **t**20 **f**22 **b**21. Caught in no man's land: no longer fresh and sexy, yet with not quite enough enriching oak (or sherry) to make it extra distinguished and alluring. **51%.**

⋅❖⋅ **Platinum Selection Macallan 26 Years Old Rum Finish** dist 20 Oct 78, bott May 05 **(94) n**23 sherry, it ain't!! A heavy-duty bitter-sweet delight; **t**24 really lovely light sugary sheen to the barley; the deep, clean punchiness of the malt is matched by the perfectly matched oak weight; **f**23 lashings more of rich malt of near-perfect sweetness. A rare treat; **b**24 explosive and brimming with character. A bottle that has to be found and experienced. **55.4%.** *Douglas Laing. 262 bottles.*

⋅❖⋅ **Platinum Selection Macallan 27 Years Old** dist 30 May 77, bott May 05 **(88) n**23 an intriguingly rummy aroma; **t**23 exceptionally firm malt with a delicious sugary sheen; **f**20 bitters up as oak arrives; **b**22 a much flintier Macallan than most. **53.9%.** *Douglas Laing. 298 bottles.*

⋅❖⋅ **Platinum Selection Macallan Aged 27 Years** dist May 77, bott Nov 04 **(85) n**22 **t**22 **f**20 **b**21. Attractively citrussed and malty. **49.6%.** *Douglas Laing. 211 bottles.*

⋅❖⋅ **Platinum Macallan 29 Years Old** dist May 77, bott Sept 06 **(90) n**22 a tad tired in the oak department but some lovely floral notes (including Bluebells, the poseur in me regrets to note); **t**23 some exotic, tangy fruit darts in and then crumbles under a welter of barley-rich blows; **f**22 lovely depth to the barley-oak marriage with a vague coffee depth and warming spice. Wonderful structure and poise; **b**23 the oak is absorbed with something approaching reverence: a magnificent Macallan for its antiquity. **50.3%.** *Douglas Laing. 185 bottles.*

⋅❖⋅ **Platinum Selection Macallan 1977 Sherry Finish** dist May 77, bott Mar 06 **(78) n**20 **t**19 **f**20 **b**19. The nose is a curious mixture of blood orange and spinster aunts' water closets. Old fashioned and scented. But cumbersome on the palate. **48.4%.** *Douglas Laing. 249 bottles.*

**Private Cellars Selection Macallan 1985** bott 04 **(77) n**19 **t**20 **f**19 **b**19. A bit furry and unimpressive. **43%**

**Provenance Macallan Over 10 Years** dist Autumn 93, bott Spring 04 **(88) n**21 fresh, grassy, new make-ish; **t**22 despite the overall lightness, there is a weightiness to the malt; f23 stupendous clarity and goes into mouthwatering overdrive; **b**22 an outstanding example of Macallan without make up: no sherry, little oak to speak of due to old bourbon cask. Top notch distillate and so delicious! **46%**. *Douglas McGibbon*.

**Provenance Macallan Aged 10 Years** dist 13 Dec 94, bott 12 Apr 05 **(86)** n21 t22 f21 **b**22. Naked Macallan, as you may never have seen it before: 10-y-o, not a trace of sherry, a second or even third-fill sherry cask and its maltiness exposed entirely. Fascinatingly delicious. **46%**. *Douglas Laing & Co*.

**Provenance Macallan Over 12 Years** dist Summer 92, bott Winter 04 **(77)** n18 t21 f20 **b**18. A distant hint of sulphur, sadly. Sweet, robust arival on the palate works well with peppery finish, though. **46%**. *Douglas McGibbon*.

❖ **Provenance Macallan 12 Years Old** dist Nov 93, bott Feb 06 **(86)** n20 t22 f22 **b**22. Forget the neutral nose. Just dive into to the malt!! **46%**. *McGibbon's*.

**Provenance Macallan 13 Years Old**, dist Summer 91, bott Summer 04 **(87)** n22 a gentle waft of peat on the rigid malt; t21 lazy malt, soft and yielding, revealing a mouthwatering, grassy underbelly; f22 even more interesting as the oak arrives and with that distant smoke offers wave upon wave of bittersweet malt; **b**22 great to see Macallan unplugged and revelling in its relatively weighty self. **46%**. *Douglas Laing & Co*.

**Provenance Macallan Over 14 Years** two cask bottling dist Summer 90, bott Summer 04 **(77)** n17 t21 f19 **b**20. Sulphur-spoiled, but recovers some ground thanks probably to the malt-honey richness of a top quality cask included. **46%**. *Douglas McGibbon*.

**Royal Mile Whiskies Macallan 25 Years Old (88)** n22 gristy and clean and very lightly peated, no sign of a quarter of century's work in barrel; t23 slight oily texture to the massive, gristy maltiness; f21 some citrus amid the barley and then the; **b**22 Macallan in aspic: this must have come from a second fill bourbon. **40%**

**Scott's Selection Macallan 1985** bott 03 **(94)** n23 t23 f24 **b**24. Macallan at its cleanest, most bullish and recognisable. A rare bottling that takes me back 30 years to its finest days. Brilliant. **51.2%**

**Scott's Selection Macallan 1986** bott 04 **(82)** n21 t20 f21 **b**20. An attractive degree of smoke, but perhaps too sweet on delivery. **53.7%**. *Speyside Distillers*.

**Scott's Selection Macallan 1987** bott 05 **(91)** n23 freshly diced Coxes, crushed grass and grist; t23 absolutely stunning gristy freshness to the malt, complete with a distant rumble of smoke. As the malt melts in the mouth, soft vanilla and butterscotch come on board; f22 custard and vanilla top the lingering fresh barley; **b**23 a real youngster for its age, with the freshness of the malt never failing to dazzle. **58.8%**. *Speyside Distillers*.

**Speymalt from Macallan 1973 (88)** n21 a must for those into toffee apples; t22 sound, rich sherry with the most gentle sub-stratum of toasty malt; f23 attractively complex, and the sherry-malt theme now hits just the right balance, with the drying oak coming quite late on; **b**22 a very well-behaved and flawlessly spoken malt that refuses to wallow too self-indulgently in the sherry. **40%**. *Gordon & MacPhail*.

**Speymalt from Macallan 1996 (79)** n21 t20 f19 **b**19. The nose is a curious embrace between green grape and green malt; the body is pretty uninspiring. **40%**. *Gordon & MacPhail*.

❖ **Speymalt from Macallan Distillery 1997** bott 15.06.06 **(85)** n22 t22 f20 **b**21. Juicy and no shortage of early barley. **40%**. *Gordon & MacPhail, US Market*.

**The Vintage House Macallan (93)** n22 the input of European oak is more telling than the wine; the grapiness is gentle and in tandem with intense barley guarantees a delicate bitter-sweet thrust. Intriguingly, there is even more than a hint of barley wine about this; t23 at first intense malt, then a shock wave of dry, fruity oak. Distinctive and beautifully weighted; f24 almost immeasurably long, with a fabulous silkiness kissing the roof of the mouth. Very dry and demanding in attention and detail; **b**24 an almost freakish one-off, the style of which I have never encountered before. The quality of the oak is beyond question; the shape and personality of the ensuing confusion will be a good reason for much study. **56.9%**

**Wilson & Morgan Barrel Selection Macallan 12 Years Old** dist 90 **(87)** n22 t23 f20 b22. A thoughtful, busy dram that demands time for exploration. **57.7%**

**Wilson & Morgan Barrel Selection Macallan 1990 Rum Finish** bott 04 **(84)** n20 t21 f22 b21. A diamond of a Macallan: not that it particularly dazzles, just that it is the hardest on the palate I've ever come across. Has its attractively fruity, mouthwatering moments, though: even with a hint of peat thrown in. **46%**

⋙ **Wilson & Morgan Barrel Selection Macallan 1991** Refill Sherry dist 91, bott 05 **(86)** n20 t22 f22 b22. Exceptionally easy going. **46%.**

## MACDUFF
### Speyside, 1963. Dewar's. Working

⋙ **Glen Deveron Aged 10 Years** dist 95 db **(83)** n19 t23 f20 b21. The enormity of the third and fourth waves on delivery give some idea of the greatness this distillery could achieve perhaps with a little more care with cask selection, upping the strength to 46% and banning caramel. We'd have a malt scoring in the low to mid 90s every time. At the moment we must remain frustrated. **40%**

**Cadenhead's Authentic Collection MacDuff Aged 16 Years** dist 89, bott May 05 **(78)** n19 t21 f19 b19. Sherried, sweet, oily, mildly phenolic: just doesn't quite work. **59.8%.** *678 bottles.*

**D&M Connoisseurs' Club Bottling Macduff Aged 15 Years** cask no. 7118, dist Dec 90 **(87)** n21 signs of a tired cask but the fizzing malt perseveres; t22 the dullness of the cask fails to extinguish the rich-textured, softly spiced honey theme; f22 lively towards the end and that honey continues, heading towards a raspberry-jam sweetness; b22 only less than perfect oak manages to lessen the impact of the honey. **59.2%. nc ncf.** *US by Angus Dundee Distillers plc.* ⊙ ⊙

**Duncan Taylor Collection Macduff 1969 Aged 35 Years** cask 3686, dist Apr 69, bott Jan 05 **(89)** n22 a nose I have come across only once before in a very old cask in Japan: the oak is profound and leathery, with a responding, gently sweetened maltiness on a bed over soft and very distant scents. Pure bathroom; t22 again the oak is up for it and again the malt responds, this time with a huge Demerara kick; f23 liquorice and sweetened Columbian medium roast; b22 the sort of beautiful old dram you need many hours to fathom. Another year in the cask might have wrecked this one. Excellent plucking! **61.1%**

⋙ **Duncan Taylor Collection Macduff 1969** cask 3684, dist Apr 69, bott Feb 06 **(78)** n20 t20 f19 b19. No shortage of orange...or oak. For those who prefer their scotch bourbony. **59.4%.** *135 bottles.*

⋙ **Duncan Taylor Collection Macduff 1969** cask no 3680, dist Apr 69, bott Apr 06 **(79)** n19 t21 f19 b20. Has some pleasant, sweet malty and spicy moments. Silky and attractive but just off the pace. **54.9%.** *197 bottles.*

⋙ **Harris Whisky Co. Macduff Aged 14 Years** cask no.1382, dist Mar 91, bott Jan 06 **(94)** n23 clean, green and keen; t24 stunning: mouth-watering barley begins crisp and juicy then adopts the distillery's honeyed style; f23 remains beautifully intense and salivating; vanilla almost apologetically enters the fray. Just so refined and fragile; b24 a stunning opening from a new whisky company which, at first attempt has succeeded in showing this under-rated distillery in all its glory and magnificence. As fresh and thirst-quenching as any malt whisky gets. One can only hope the distillery owners take a lead from this. **46%. nc ncf.**

⋙ **Harris Whisky Co. Macduff Aged 14 Years** cask 1383, dist 91, bott Jan 06 **(88)** n21 a dense, busy nose is somewhat claustrophobic but a gooseberry tart fruitiness does emerge; t22 that intenseness is magnified as the barley clusters around the tastebuds leading to something of an oaky cul-de-sac; f23 waves of vanilla and barley sugar; b22 this is the sister cask of the above. An although the oak is fractionally less impressive, this remains high quality malt. **58.7%. nc ncf.**

**Vom Fass MacDuff 23 Years Old (91)** n23 mildly smoked gingerbread; t23 silky and honied in that inimitable MacDuff way, showing not a single malevolent sign of old age: fresh and chewy from first to last; f22 back to ginger again for the most soporific yet delightful of finishes; b23 if you ever wondered why William Lawson blends are so damn good, grab hold of this...!! **40%.**

## MANNOCHMORE
**Speyside, 1971. Diageo. Working.**

**Mannochmore Aged 12 Years** db **(84)** n22 t21 f20 b21. As usual the mouth arrival fails to live up to the great nose. Quite a greasy dram with sweet malt and bitter oak. **43%.** *Flora and Fauna.*

⋰ **Cadenhead's Authentic Collection Mannochmore Aged 14 Years** Sherry butt, dist 92, bott Sept 06 **(95)** n24 top-notch sherry; no off-notes, just sublimely confident and so sexily spiced. Breathtaking...; t24 big, butch and beautiful. The grape is exploding from the glass but this is controlled quality with the barley and liquorice also having a full say; f23 barley-sugar and molasses with strands of grape. Late vanilla and dates; b24 highly unusual rendition of this little-known and criminally under-rated malt and the best I've ever found bottled. **54.6%.** *486 bottles.*

⋰ **Connoisseurs Choice Mannochmore 1990 (85)** n20 t22 f21 b22. Perhaps overly sweet and slightly featureless. **46%.** *Gordon & MacPhail.*

**Old Malt Cask Mannochmore Aged 14 Years** Sherry Finish dist Feb 90, bott Oct 03 **(88)** n19 t22 f24 b23. A less demanding person than I would be slightly more forgiving with the nose. **50%. nc ncf sc.** *Douglas Laing. 354 bottles.*

⋰ **Old Malt Cask Mannochmore 15 Years Old** dist 5 Feb 90, bott Jul 05 **(92)** n23 guava and pears; the fruity opening gives way to improbably soft barley; t24 little more could be asked of a malt this age; the oak remains at bay whilst the barley offers simpering waves of varying sweetness and refinement. Just so damned beautiful!; f22 lazy spice and hints of tangy oak that points to something older than its age; b23 such a gentle, refined dram, you can scarcely believe the strength. **50%.** *Douglas Laing. 339 bottles.*

**Private Cellars Selection Mannochmore 1978** bott 03 **(88)** n22 t23 f21 b22. The most gentle of rides imaginable. **43%.** *Speyside Distillers.*

⋰ **Provenance Mannochmore 11 Years Old** dist Jan 95, bott July 06 **(92)** n23 unique and unmistakable Mannoch. Flinty in the style of Glen Grant, but with a trademark weightiness that no more than hints at smoke; t23 textbook barley brittleness and then an outpouring of salivating juiciness; f23 wonderful interplay between barley and vanilla; b23 one of the few botlings I have seen that reflects the quality I find in the blending lab. **46%.** *McGibbon's.*

**Provenance Mannochmore Over 12 Years** dist Spring 91, bott Winter 04 **(87)** n23 fluting barley notes that never hit a bum note; textbook clarity and bitter-sweet charm; t22 green and young in part, the mouthwatering elements contrast sharply with the abrupt arrival of chunky oak; f21 more bitter than sweet, the barley-sheen remains profound although the oak has a surprisingly big say; b21 most probably a first-fill bourbon cask to the fore here: it's older than its age should suggest but the all-round complexity is quite wonderful. **46%.**

**Scott's Selection Mannochmore 1978** bott 04 **(89)** n23 clean malt with an attractive, unusual and entirely spotless green vegetable sub-plot; t22 pretty hot, but the depth of the sugared malt impresses; f22 malt and vanilla combine for a sweet finale; b22 fabulous blending whisky that has enough guts and attitude to make for a challenging dram. **55.3%.** *Speyside Distillers.*

## MILLBURN
**Highland (Northern), 1807–1985. Closed.**

⋰ **Millburn 1969 Rare Malt** db **(77)** n19 t21 f18 b19. Some lovely bourbon-honey touches but sadly over the hill and declining fast. Nothing like as interesting or entertaining as the massage parlour that was firebombed a few yards from my office twenty minutes ago. Or as smoky... **51.3%**

**Blackadder Raw Cask Millburn 1974** cask 4615, dist Nov 74, bott Nov 03 **(90)** n24 t23 f21 b23. A top-notch dram that has experienced a summer or two: in Nov 74 I was a £5-a-week cub reporter still working on the Lord Lucan case and took my first driving lesson; in Nov 03 I celebrated my 46th birthday with my 32-year-old Brazilian girlfriend and launched the 2004 Whisky Bible: tough call on whether the Millburn or I had aged the better in the passing 28 years ... **56.8%**

**The Bottlers Millburn 1982 Aged 20 Years** cask 1971 **(78)** n20 t21 f18 b19. The nose reminds me of freshly sharpened school pencils, and although the fruity malt shines for a short while it does, overall, succumb to age. **63%**. *Reaborn Fine Wine.*

-:::- **Cadenhead's Millburn 31 Years Old (88)** n22 an attractive sprinkling of fresh sawdust over the very softest of peats and custard tart; t23 lush malt coats the mouth before a bombardment of spicy oak keeps the barley at bay; f21 an oaky echo; b22 a rumbustuous, red-hot affair which is ensuring the distillery is not disappearing with a whimper. Now a must have cask: decent bottlings of any of the old Inverness distilleries are few and far between. **52.3%**

**Mackillop's Choice Millburn 1981** cask no. 353, dist Feb 81 **(76)** n18 t18 f21 b19. I know some people like this type of sherry style, but I'm afraid to me it strikes a sharp, rancid tone I have major problems with, even if the malt does fight back impressively and stylishly at the very finish. Sorry. If you want to put me up against a wall, I understand. **61.5%**. *Angus Dundee.*

-:::- **Platinum Selection Millburn Aged 34 Years** dist Nov 70, bott 04 **(81)** n22 t19 f20 b20. Some pleasantly rich moments, but not faring quite as well as its sister Inverness distillery, Glen Albyn, also lost to us. **50.9%**. *Douglas Laing. 171 bottles.*

**Private Cellars Selection Millburn 1983** bott 03 **(79)** n19 t21 f20 b19. A forgotten Christmas stocking: rotting oranges and old nuts. Decent in parts, though. **43%**. *Speyside Distillers.*

**Scott's Selection Millburn 1983** bott 03 **(77)** n19 t21 f19 b18. The watercress spice is fine, but thin overall and just not enough complexity to see it through. **58%**

# MILTONDUFF
**Speyside, 1824. Chivas. Working.**

-:::- **Miltonduff Aged 15 Years** Bott code L00/123 db **(86)** n23 t22 f20 b21. Some casks beyond their years have crept in and unsettled this one. But some real big salty moments to savour, too. **46%**

-:::- **Cask Strength Miltonduff 1993** Sherry butt no. 9400, dist 17/6/93, bott 21/4/05 **(91)** n21 moist Melton hunt cake; a very distant hint of something sulphurous; t24 the intense, sticky sherry is driven home into the tastebuds partly thanks to the strength. And the experience is stunning!!; f23 more of the same, except now the intensity has gone and the structure of the fruity layers become easier to detect; b23 not the easiest distillery to find these day. And G&M have done us proud with a very decent sherry butt (though one or two might detect the most minor flaw). **61.8%**. *Gordon & MacPhail.*

**James MacArthur Miltonduff 1994 10 Year Old**, bott Apr 05 **(84)** n20 t21 f22 b21. Deliciously clean malt with a big sweetness to the fade. **43%**

**Old Malt Cask Miltonduff 20 Years Old** dist 13 Jun 84, bott 24 Feb 05 **(89)** n23 brilliant, sharp, zesty, thick-cut marmalade igniting the complex and sweeter malt; t23 the mouthfeel is stunning: near perfect delivery of tangy malt followed by a quick injection of oak and the most delicate whiff of smoke; f21 a little tired, as a Speysider of this age has every right to be. But the bitter-sweet essence remains; b22 another unsubtle reminder of how Allied have shot themselves in the foot over the years by failing to market this, like Ardmore, the way it deserves. **50%**. *Douglas Laing*

**Private Cellars Selecton Miltonduff 1987** bott 03 **(85)** n23 t22 f19 b21. Shame about the finish: this had the hallmarks of something quite lovely. **43%**. *Speyside Distillers.*

⊰⊱ **Scott's Selection Miltonduff 1987** bott 2005 **(87)** **n**20 caramel cake; **t**23 sweet barley strata but a voluminous increase in intensity: a real chewy number; **f**22 back to caramel notes alongside the powering malt; **b**22 rather a delicious, intense bottling that gets over its inclination towards toffee rather impressively. **58.6%**. *Speyside Distillers.*

## MORTLACH
**Speyside, 1824. Diageo. Working.**

**Mortlach Aged 16 Years** db **(87)** **n**20 big, big sherry, but not exactly without a blemish or two; **t**23 sumptuous fruit and then a really outstanding malt and melon mouthwatering rush; **f**22 returns to heavier duty with a touch of spice, too; **b**22 once it gets past the bold if very mildly sulphured nose, the rest of the journey is superb. Earlier Mortlachs in this range had a slightly unclean feel to them and the nose here doesn't inspire confidence. But from arrival on the palate onwards, it's sure-footed, fruity and even refreshing ... and always delicious. **43%**. *Flora and Fauna range.*

**Mortlach 32 Years Old** dist 71 db **(88)** **n**22 burnt fudge and cola; **t**22 full-bodied, molassed malt with enormous spice and sweetening early vanilla; **f**22 the spice continues...for a long time. A touch of liquorice arrives, too; **b**22 big and with attitude.... **50.1%**

⊰⊱ **Cadenhead's Authentic Collection Mortlach Aged 14 Years 1992** Sherry butt, dist 92, bott Nov 06 **(82)** **n**22 **t**21 **f**19 **b**20. Adore the fruitcake dough nose and a rich sherry purple patch but the rest is typically roughhouse and hot. **58.3%**. *600 bottles.*

**Cadenhead's Authentic Collection Mortlach Aged 16 Years** dist 88, bott May 05 **(66)** **n**16 **t**18 **f**16 **b**16. Guess what! Spooky! Having just given it 66, I've just spotted there are 666 bottles...well, there had to be when the devil's been so busy with his matches. **58.1%**. *666 bottles.*

⊰⊱ **Cask Strength Mortlach 1993** bott 07 July 05 **(79)** **n**19 **t**21 **f**20 **b**19. An act of bravery by G&M to offer an untreated Mortlach to the world... and they get away with it. The flaws are for all to see, but the intensity of the barley, especially in the eye-watering middle, wins the day. **60.7%**. *G&M, US Market.*

⊰⊱ **Chieftain's Mortlach Aged 15 Years** Sherry wood **(69)** **n**17 **t**18 **f**17 **b**17. This sweet and sulphurous effort is one 69 I don't like... **46%**. *Ian Macleod.*

⊰⊱ **Craigellachie Hotel Quaich Bar Range Mortlach 12 Years Old** 1st release **(79)** **n**21 **t**20 **f**19 **b**19. A few moments of barley-rich lucidity, otherwise slightly over-sweet. **46%**. *Craigellachie Hotel.*

**Dun Bheagan Vintage Bottling Mortlach Aged 10 Years** Refill sherry cask no. 9679, dist 93 bott 04 **(65)** **n**15 **t**18 **f**16 **b**16. Ooops!! Like a match, the dreaded S-word has struck. The exact reason I avoid this once great distillery like the plague these days. **43%**. **nc ncf.** *Ian Macleod. 936 bottles.*

⊰⊱ **Dun Bheagan Mortlach Aged 11 Years** Port finish **(91)** **n**23 peaty and porty; **t**22 soft, barley-led delivery with a thickish amalgam of smoke and wine; **f**23 complex finale with the smoke drifting into delicious shapes and variants of intensity; **b**23 unusually smoky with big fruit and sugar. Excellent for a latter-day Mortlach. **43%**. *Ian Macleod.*

⊰⊱ **Duncan Taylor Collection Mortlach 1988** cask no 4743, dist Nov 88, bott Nov 05 **(74)** **n**18 **t**19 **f**18 **b**19. Dirty nose, vicious arrival on palate...but it does have some character. But then so did Billy the Kid... **57.9%**. *632 bottles.*

**Fortnum & Mason Old Malt Cask Mortlach Aged 13 Years** dist Jun 90 bott Nov 03 **(71)** **n**17 **t**20 **f**16 **b**18. Not a great vintage at Mortlach for sherry butts. **50%**

**Gordon & MacPhail Mortlach 1954 (78)** **n**20 **t**20 **f**18 **b**20. Survived the oak attack well — enough character to enjoy on a cold night.

**Gordon & MacPhail Mortlach 1959 (82)** **n**22 **t**20 **f**21 **b**19. What it lacks in complexity it makes up for in effortless charm. **40%**

⟨∴⟩ **Gordon & MacPhail Mortlach 1970 (83) n**23 **t**21 **f**19 **b**20. The nose takes me back to Niger and sumptuous dates; the confused palate and bitter finish returns me to Dufftown....with a bump. **43%**. *Rare Vintage range.*

⟨∴⟩ **Gordon & MacPhail Reserve Mortlach 1991** cask no. 7880, bott 04 **(75) n**18 **t**20 **f**18 **b**19. Generally cloying and dysfunctional. **46%**. *For Juuls Vinhandel, Denmark. 334 bottles.*

**Hart Brothers Mortlach Aged 12 Years** dist May 90, bott Jan 03 **(69) n**15 **t**18 **f**18 **b**18. United Distiller's sherry wood policy of the early 90s leaves a little to be desired. Well, a lot, actually. **46%**

**Murray McDavid Mortlach 1990 (70) n**17 **t**18 **f**17 **b**18. Whatever passed for sherry butts in those days at UDG should be taken out and unceremoniously torched. Give me the match. **46%**

⟨∴⟩ **Murray McDavid Mortlach 1993 Aged 11 Years** Bourbon/Port, bott 05 **(86) n**21 **t**22 **f**22 **b**21. A way-above-average Mortlach, still mildly flawed from the original cask, I guess. Some of the characteristics I could recreate using a Trinidadian rum as base – and it's those impurities that help make it interesting. **46%. nc ncf.** *1800 bottles.*

⟨∴⟩ **Norse Cask Selection Mortlach 1994 Aged 10 Years (73) n**19 **t**18 **f**18 **b**18. Not even the citrus can save it. **58.7%.** *QualityWorld, Denmark.*

⟨∴⟩ **Old Malt Cask Mortlach Aged 12 Years** dist Sep 92, bott Dec 04 **(72) n**19 **t**18 **f**17 **b**18. A seriously cloying dullard. **50%.** *Douglas Laing.*

**Old Malt Cask Mortlach Aged 13 Years Sherry Cask** dist Jun 90, bott Jan 04 **(78) n**17 **t**23 **f**19 **b**19. A brilliantly bullish mouth arrival offers all kinds of natural dark sugars and rich barley. But the bitter, off-key fade is in tune with the poor nose. **50%. nc ncf sc.** *Douglas Laing. 384 bottles.*

**Old Malt Cask Fortnum and Mason Mortlach Aged 13 Years** (*see* Fortnum & Mason OMC Mortlach)

⟨∴⟩ **Old Masters Mortlach 1989 Aged 16 Years** cask no. 969 **(77) n**19 **t**20 **f**19 **b**19. Furry, bitter, harsh and hot: one of the better Mortlachs from this period... **56.5%.** *James MacArthur.*

**Old Malt Cask Mortlach Aged 20 Years** dist May 83, bott Aug 03 **(90) n**23 **t**23 **f**22 **b**22. This is big stuff, a type of Mortlach I have not found in the best part of a decade and I was wondering if lost to us. One to take your time over. **50%. nc ncf sc.** *Douglas Laing. 384 bottles.*

**Old Malt Cask Mortlach Aged 30 Years** dist Dec 73, bott Oct 04 **(79) n**20 **t**21 **f**18 **b**20. A touch sappy and over age. But at least it's a sulphur-free zone. **50%.** *Douglas Laing & Co.*

**The Peebles Malt Mortlach 12 Years Old (75) n**18 **t**20 **f**18 **b**19. A pleasant honeyed thread does its best to mend the sulphured tear. **43%.** *Villeneuve Wines.* ⊙

⟨∴⟩ **Private Collection Mortlach 1968** Sherry hogshead cask no. 4836, dist 25.07.68, bott Mar 06 **(85) n**22 **t**22 **f**20 **b**21. Nose within first seconds of pouring – it oxidizes fast!! Fabulous sherry delivery for the first few seconds, then loses control to spicy oak; the late middle and finish is like chewing coffee liquorice allsort and Fisherman's Friend simultaneously. Some beast! **45%.** *Gordon & MacPhail. 148 bottles.*

**Provenance Mortlach Aged 11 Years** dist 1 Oct 92, bott 8 Jun 04 **(87) n**22 stunningly clean, quite complex malt firmed up with unripened banana and carrot juice! **t**22 mouthwatering malty Mortlach completely un-fucked with sulphur. A miracle!! **f**22 simplistic, but rather delicious waves of barley on rye bread and vanilla; **b**21 thank God! Mortlach in a bourbon cask. A pretty tired one, but my word it's good!! **46%.** *Douglas Laing & Co.*

**Provenance Mortlach Over 12 Years** dist Spring 92, bott Winter 04 **(85) n**22 **t**22 **f**20 **b**21. One of the better Mortlach expressions of recent years. **46%.**

**Provenance Mortlach Over 13 Years** dist Summer 90, bott Autumn 03 **(61) n**12 **t**17 **f**16 **b**16. Never survives the sulphurous wounds. **46%.** *Douglas McGibbon.*

**Raeborn Fine Wines Mortlach 1983 18 Years Old** cask 2378 **(87)** n22 blood oranges, caramelised biscuit and very thick barley; t21 a slightly hot but heart-warming delivery of firm oak and firmer barley; f22 lovely distant smoke to the layers of high roast coffee and toast; b22 uncompromising and almost too big for the glass. **51%**

⸰⸰⸰ **Un-Chill Filtered Collection Mortlach Aged 13 Years** Sherry butt 4776, dist 31 May 91, bott 8 Dec 04 **(74)** n19 t20 f17 b18. Some honey, but here is a serious case for filtration!! **46%. nc ncf.** *Signatory. 831 bottles.*

⸰⸰⸰ **Whisky Galore Mortlach Aged 12 Years** dist 93, bott 06 **(84)** n21 t22 f21 b20. Even those with a sticky tooth might struggle with this one. Ultra sweet and intense barley that is always attractive and drinkable though complexity suffers. Even so, there are signs that one or two half-drinkable Mortlachs are beginning to surface. Still a long way to go, though. **46%. nc ncf.** *Duncan Taylor.*

**Whisky Galore Mortlach 1993 Aged 10 Years (87)** n22 the second fill bourbon cask has left a clear path for the sparkling, apple-juicy, grassy barley; t23 mouthwatering and refreshing barley-sugar; f21 a touch of spice to the barley; b21 at last! For almost the first time in a decade a Mortlach not screwed by being filled into a cask of the very crappiest order. Wonderful to show what this distillery can really do without someone doing their best to ruin it. Look forward to a few more. **46%.** *Duncan Taylor.*

**Wilson & Morgan Barrel Selection Mortlach 10 Years Old** dist 89 **(73)** n18 t19 f18 b18. Spot the difference between this and a typically inept Dufftown: blowed if I can. **57.2%**

## MOSSTOWIE
**Speyside, 1964–1981. Two Lomond stills located within Miltonduff Distillery. Now dismantled.**

**Connoisseurs Choice Mosstowie 1975 (85)** n22 t21 f20 b22. A busy dram with massive malt influence. **40%.** *Gordon & MacPhail.*

**Connoisseurs Choice Mosstowie 1979 (86)** n20 t23 f22 b21. Not the most complex of drams, but the weight of the malt is amazing: not entirely unlike an old-fashioned Scottish heavy ale but in sweeter form. **40%.** *Gordon & MacPhail.*

⸰⸰⸰ **Rarest of the Rare Mosstowie 1975** cask no. 5814, dist May 75, bott Apr 06 **(88)** n22 takes time to open out; perfumed braised apples eventually arrive; t22 soft barley delivery with lovely tags of honey; f22 delicate vanillas sit comfortably with the laid-back barley and soft oils; b22 a wonderful surprise: the nose at first indicated that it might be beyond greatness. Not a bit of it – a rare treat, indeed! **48.1%.** *Duncan Taylor. 191 bottles.*

## NORTH PORT
**Highland (Eastern), 1820–1983. Demolished.**

⸰⸰⸰ **Brechin 1977** db **(78)** n19 t21 f18 b20. Fire and brimstone was never an unknown quantity with the whisky from this doomed distillery. Some soothing oils are poured on this troubled – and sometimes attractively honeyed – water of life. **54.2%**

⸰⸰⸰ **Cadenhead's Chairman's Stock North Port (Brechin) Aged 29 Years** Bourbon Hogshead, dist 77, bott Sept 06 **(83)** n21 t21 f20 b21. Fishermen's Friend cough sweets by the bag-load. Hints of hotness but pretty good for this usually harsh and unforgiving malt. **51.4%.** *174 bottles.*

**Connoisseurs Choice North Port-Brechin 1981 (89)** n22 clean with refreshing malt and lychees; t23 mouthwatering and delicate in the most traditional of Speyside styles (even though it's not a Speysider). Even with a puff of smoke to complete the experience; f21 thins out with waves of vanilla; b23 is this really North Port? My mouth isn't on fire and I'm still alive. What's going on? Easily the best bottled NP I've come across in over 20 years. **43%.** *Gordon & MacPhail.*

**Private Cellars Selection North Port 1982** bott 03 **(83) n**19 **t**21 **f**22 **b**21. Gets off to a wobbly start but settles down impressively. Wonderfully silky, malt-intense yet fruity delivery. **43%.** *Speyside Distillers.*

**Scott's Selection North Port 1980** bott 04 **(86) n**20 **t**22 **f**22 **b**22. Stings like clawmarks on your back. And just as pleasurable. **58%.** *Speyside Distillers.*

**Scott's Selection North Port 1982** bott 03 **(86) n**21 **t**22 **f**22 **b**21. Hot as Hades. But, d'ya know, for all the fire this is serious fun and worth enduring the tastebud blitz. A rare North Port worth finding. **52.5%**

··∵· **The Whisky Fair North Port Aged 25 Years** Sherry wood, dist Apr 81, bott Apr 06 **(85) n**22 **t**21 **f**21 **b**21. A brave malt for any small outfit to bottle. Rips out only about half the tastebuds – great going by Brechin standards – but those left functioning will detect a genuine honey deliciousness. **56.1%. nc ncf.** *Germany. 120 bottles.*

## OBAN
### Highland (Western), 1794. Diageo. Working.

**Oban 14** db **(84) n**20 **t**22 **f**21 **b**21. Slick and fruity, you can close your eyes and think of Jerez. Oban seems a long way away. A very decent dram. But I want my old, bracing, mildly smoky, fruitless Oban back!! Those who prefer malts with a sheen, sweet and with enormous fruit depth won't be disappointed. **43%**

**Oban 20 Years Old** dist 84 db **(89) n**21 large oak but kept in check by salt, pepper and malt; **t**23 buttery on arrival, and then an explosion of massive and pretty sharp malt. Sweet mallows balance out the oak; **f**23 French toast and hints of light roast coffee; **b**22 wonderfully complex and challenging. A west coast treat. **57.9%**

## OLD RHOSDHU ( see Loch Lomond)

## PITTYVAICH
### Speyside 1975–1993. Closed.

**Pittyvaich Aged 12 Years** db **(64) n**16 **t**18 **f**15 **b**15. It was hard to imagine this whisky getting worse. But somehow it has achieved it. From fire-water to cloying undrinkability. What amazes me is not that this is such bad whisky: we have long known that Pittyvaich can be as grim as it gets. It's the fact they bother bottling it and inflicting it on the public. Vat this with malt from Fettercairn and neighbouring Dufftown and you'll have the perfect dram for masochists. Or those who have entirely lost the will to live. Jesus.... **43%.** *Flora and Fauna.*

**Pittyvaich Aged 12 Years** (new stock circa 03 – bottling number L19R01941144, dark brown print) db **(84) n**22 **t**21 **f**20 **b**21. For a dram that will tear your throat out as soon as look at you, this has been tempered dramatically by the use of some exceptionally clean sherry casks which show to their best on the nose. Pittyvaich in a form I thought I'd never see it in my lifetime ... drinkable! And deliciously so. **43%.** *Flora and Fauna range.*

··∵· **Connoisseurs Choice Pittyvaich 1993 (79) n**21 **t**20 **f**19 **b**19. Decent, simple barley... though subdued: it is if the malt knows that it from the last year it was ever made. **43%.** *Gordon & MacPhail.*

··∵· **Duncan Taylor Collection Pittyvaich 1979** cask no. 5631, dist Apr 79, bott Feb 06 **(79) n**19 **t**20 **f**20 **b**20. Like an old old lag who's done his time: obviously a bit rough around the edges, from the lower classes, and has relished a few scraps in his time but now, in old age, has a certain defiant dignity. **52.3%.** *189 bottles.*

## PORT ELLEN
### Islay, 1825–1983. Closed.

··∵· **Port Ellen 1979** db **(93) n**22 mousy and retiring; a degree of oak fade and fruit on the delicate smoke **t**23 non-committal delivery but bursts into stride with a series of sublime, peat-liquorice waves and a few rounds of spices; **f**24 a surprising gathering of oils rounds up the last traces of sweet barley and ensures an improbably long – and refined – finish; **b**24 takes so long to get out of the traps, you wonder if anything is going to happen. But when it does, my word...it's glorious! **57.5%**

**Port Ellen 24 Years Old** dist 79, bott 03 db **(90) n**23 **t**24 **f**21 **b**22. Pow!! Port Ellen at something over its usual 35ppm phenols here, acting like a 50ppm monster. On a blind tasting I'd swear it was Lagavulin! **57.3%.** *9000 bottles.*

**Port Ellen 4th Release Aged 25 Years** dist 78, bott 04 **(95) n**22 much less smoky than previous release, with greater emphasis on fruit, especially cinnamon-sprinkled apple. The oak offers perhaps the firmest thread, marginally threatening to dominate; **t**25 just so, so stunning! The immaculate balance between the peat-malt and oak hits home from the very first second. Somehow, after 25 years, it has retained the trademark gristiness with the peat being released in controlled waves. Hints of honey help fend off any advancement of oak, and the threat from the nose never materialises. Instead there is a steady throbbing of perfect spices; **f**24 honey-vanilla and more lapping waves of peat and spice bring a gentle end to proceedings...eventually; **b**24 for those of us who can remember it in its original younger form, this is almost something to give you a lump in the throat and a watery eye: it remains just so true to character and form, cocking the most elegant and contemptuous snook at those who decided to kill the distillery off. When they closed the distillery I remember being told by the decision-makers there was no difference in quality between PE and Caol Ila. I disagreed then, strongly. Today, my argument is mute: the eloquence belongs to the contents of this bottle. **56.2%.** *5100 bottles.*

**Blackadder Raw Cask Port Ellen 21 Years Old**, Sherry butt cask 2734, dist 3 Nov 82, bott Jun 04 **(89) n**22 a busy, bready, hot-cross bun, confused nose with the peat dabbing on a hint of pepper and bonfires. Intriguing; **t**24 an eruption of spice which has heavily impacted on a thick fruit shield. Massive, though slightly softened by puny waves of liberated smoke. The oak arrives early and threatens but remains controlled; **f**21 still the spice has a say, but it's a pretty lengthy delivery of a flat-fruit-fudge. No shortage of oak – but all within acceptable bounds; **b**22 an old distillery going down with a fight. **62.7%**

⚬ **Dun Bheagan Port Ellen 23 Years Old (94) n**23 soft grist and vanilla; a touch of lime and the gentlest of smoke; **t**23 salivating, fresh barley; minimal oak interference allowing a slow crescendo of peat; **f**24 it appears relatively short, but if you listen, the gentle smoke rumbles on almost relentlessly; **b**24 Port Ellen in aspic. One of the most delicate Islays of this age to hit the market in years. **45.9%.** *Ian Macleod.*

**Old Malt Cask Port Ellen Aged 20 Years** dist Feb 83, bott Dec 03 **(87) n**23 **t**20 **f**23 **b**21. Limps about in old age a bit but still has style. **50%. nc ncf sc.**

⚬ **Old Malt Cask Port Ellen 22 Years Old** dist Mar 83, bott Sept 05 **(87) n**22 **t**22 **f**21 **b**22. An almost identical pea from an identical pod as the Provenance 22-y-o below. Spooky!! This one is perhaps a shade smokier and juicier. **50%.** *Douglas Laing. 659 bottles.*

**Old Malt Cask Port Ellen Aged 25 Years** dist Sept 78, bott Feb 04 **(95) n**24 this is prime Port Ellen: absolutely perfectly balanced peat, offering a mild sweetness that just sings with the oak-induced vanilla and sprig of lavender; **t**23 very few 25-years-olds can be so delicate on the palate; the peat, like the underlying barley is fragile yet the building medium roast Java coffee cannot dislodge it; **f**23 lengthy, with a delicate sprinkling of Muscovado sugar helping to counter the formulating liquorice and strengthening coffee; **b**25 one of those great whiskies you search for and rarely find. It has captured the gentle magnificence of Port Ellen that very few bottlings, not least because of a later downgrade in cask quality, are ever ever likely to again. **50%. nc ncf sc.**

**Old Malt Cask Port Ellen Aged 25 Years** dist 8 Sep 78, bott 6 Apr 05 **(84)** n20 t21 f22 b20. A curious bipolar attack of bourbon and peat on both nose and palate never quite harmonises, but the intensity of the smoked mocha is some treat. Very oily for a Port Ellen. **50%.** *Douglas Laing.*

⚬ **Old Malt Cask Port Ellen 25 Years Old** dist Nov 80, bott Apr 06 **(95)** n24 on the brink of perfection, there is a complexity to the peat that almost defies description. Those who know Fishermen's Friends cough sweets will recognise one direction it takes; there is a heathery angle to this equally. Beautiful weight and poise, this is ancient elegance; t24 melt-in-the-mouth peats with the trademark gristy barley even after all these years. Soft oils develop and expand slowly; f23 long, showing a degree of age, but the lines show maturity and grace rather than evidence of seismic turbulence. Helped along the way by some sweetened cocoa and soft vanilla; b24 Quite stunning; a malt to stir the emotions. How wonderful to find this truly great old distillery's whisky in a cask which allows all its natural character to sparkle. A treasure. And from this distillery, there can't be too many left... **50%.** *Douglas Laing. 201 bottles.*

⚬ **Old Malt Cask Port Ellen 26 Years Old** dist 15 May 79, bott Jul 05 **(89)** n24 light and exceptionally gristy: it is like sticking your head in a Porteus; t23 melt-in-the-mouth, delicate and again the grist is simply filling every last crevice with smoke and sweet barley. A joy; f20 rather tired as the oak bites slowly and bitterly; b22 a docile but proud old malt that has had a great innings, has some splendid stories to tell on the palate and is awaiting the great Spirit Receiver in the sky. A dram to salute. **50%.** *Douglas Laing. 332 bottles.*

⚬ **Old Malt Cask Port Ellen 26 Years Old** dist Nov 79, bott July 06 **(83)** n22 t21 f19 b21. An odd bird, this. Chopped tobacco on nose and (I guess) delivery. There are some real mouth-watering moments, but the malt never seems to relax or find a rhythm, especially at the finish. **50%.** *Douglas Laing. 602 bottles.*

⚬ **Old Malt Cask Port Ellen 26 Years Old** **(92)** n24 fantastic mix of coal-peat ashes and malt kiln. Amazing...; t24 lively, fresh barley hits the salivation butter first time; the peat is firm but keeps to the background; spices ping around happily; f21 oak rubs out some of the barley's finer points, though soft peat continues; b23 even after 26 years, this Port Ellen is still doing all it can to keep its unique, gristy style. There is such grace and near defiance in each mouthful I could almost weep! **50%.** *Douglas Laing.*

**Provenance Port Ellen 21 Years Old** dist Winter 82, bott Summer 04 **(78)** n20 t21 f19 b18. Attractive and chewy in part but has obviously lost its way regarding balance and direction. **46%.** *Douglas Laing & Co.*

**Provenance Port Ellen 21 Years Old** dist 3 Nov 82, bott 30 Jun 04 **(94)** n25 a miraculous nose entirely intact after all these years and for all the peat: apples and pears thin out the smoke, but it's all in perfect proportions and as enticing and delicate as a sexy 21-year-old can be; t22 soft layers of peat, but some oak has been given a slight head start; soft fruits sweeten things; f24 the tastebuds are caressed by the softest march-past of saluting peat you'll ever see; b23 distilled from smoked feathers.... **46%.** *Douglas Laing & Co.*

**Provenance Port Ellen Over 21 Years** dist Winter 82, bott Autumn 03 **(76)** n19 t19 f19 b19. As spicy as a Cumberland sausage but a bit murky and lacks guile. **46%.** *Douglas McGibbon.*

⚬ **Provenance Port Ellen 22 Years Old** dist Mar 83, bott Aug 05 **(87)** n22 unusual oils for a PE; cold kilns; t22 delicate lime and honey and lazy smoke; f21 bitter cocoa; b22 understated, lightly smoked, though much to chew on. **46%.**

⚬ **The Whisky Fair Port Ellen 27 Years Old** dist May 78 **(89)** n22 mildly over-oaked, soft peats and butterscotch tart...with lots of crust; t23 delightful interplay between a valiantly gisty peatiness and encroaching vanilla; f22 sweetens and oils out surprisingly well though some burnt toast creeps in; b22 just starting to creak with age. But still fabulous malt. **52.3%.** *Germany. 198 bottles.*

## PULTENEY
### Highland (Northern), 1826. Inver House. Working.

**Old Pulteney Aged 12 Years** db **(82) n**20 **t**22 **f**20 **b**20. Much changed from the old bottlings, with greater emphasis on early brown sugar sweetness. Sadly, the finish has dulled further in the last year. **40%** ⊙⊙

**Old Pulteney Aged 12 Years** db **(88) n**22 incisive malt and wonderfully tangy; **t**23 yesss!! Spot-on Pulteney character with the malt bristling the tastebuds, and then a fruitier, gently sweeter layer, sharpened by a touch of citrus; **f**21 dries off as chalky oak grows; **b**22 now this is much, much closer to what I expect from this outstanding distillery! **43%**

**Old Pulteney 15 Years Old** cask 2341 db **(91) n**22 toasty, almost like old parchment. The balancing sweetness is like French toast (on brown bread); **t**24 mesmerising mouth arrival: subtle citrus ranging from kumquats to lime and then wave upon wave of pounding oak, softened by something very slightly peated; **f**22 hints of vanilla and lime; **b**23 this distillery is genuinely one of the little-known, undiscovered gems of Scotland. Your reward for finding it is this: from the second cask ever sold in bottle form to visitors to the distillery. It is a better dram all round than the first! **62.8%**

**Old Pulteney Aged 15 Years Old Single Cask Selection** cask 2340, dist 23 Jun 89, bott 23 Jun 04 db **(88) n**22 sharp, clean and lively; citrus abounds, with salty, bourbony notes adding further riches; **t**23 every bit as busy and biting as the nose suggests, only with more oil and much earlier oak than you might expect, even a hint of smoke seems to be in there, a little hot, maybe, but forgivably so; **f**21 long, with lashings of dark chocolate; **b**22 a mouthful of a dram that is delightful reward for making the long trip north. **63.2%**. *Available exclusively from distillery where drawn directly from cask.*

**Old Pulteney 17 Years Old** db **(91) n**22 distant hints of cut grass and citrus, but all under a soft oaky shadow; **t**24 absolutely flies! Just such an invigorating delivery of citrussy malt, with the barley showing extraordinary intensity and clarity for its age; **f**22 remains mouthwatering and now some spices, inevitably, arrive with hints of toffee and chocolate; **b**23 dangerous whisky: one glass is never enough as the combination of aged complexity and youthful freshness forms a heady cocktail. **46%.** ⊙

**Old Pulteney Cask Strength Sherry Wood 18 Years Old** cask 1500 db **(91) n**22 sharp sherry; spiced fruitcake; **t**22 early fresh sherry, ultra-clean green grape and lumps of brown sugar; **f**24 mildly bitter at first and then a clarion call of spices reverberating around the palate; **b**23 a malt that cleverly builds up into something a little special. **58.8%**

**Old Pulteney 21 Year Old** db **(85) n**20 **t**22 **f**21 **b**21. Always spicy and enjoyable but always the feeling that it's nearing the end of its life. **46%**

**Old Pulteney Cask Strength Sherry Wood 1983** cask 929 db **(85) n**23 **t**21 **f**20 **b**21. After the pungent sherry nose a touch too predictable on the palate. **58.4%**

**Adelphi Pulteney 19 Years Old** cask 2610, dist 84, bott 03 **(84) n**23 **t**22 **f**19 **b**20. Nose to die for and taste absolutely mercurial, but let down by the short, thin finish. **51.9%**

‐∷‑ **Cadenhead's Authentic Collection Pulteney Aged 15 Years** dist 90, bott May 06 **(87) n**21 malty, but bourbon in there, too, as oak takes a firm grip; **t**22 seriously concentrated malt with lashing of oaky spice; **f**22 a defter, more subtle finale with a touch of custard to soften the spice; **b**22 in your face oak but such is the enormity of the barley it works well. Big stuff though not exactly what you expect from this distillery. **59.5%**. *228 bottles.*

‐∷‑ **Duncan Taylor Pulteney 1977** cask no. 1377, dist July 77, bott Nov 05 **(78) n**19 **t**20 **f**19 **b**20. Does its best not to be too oaky, but fails gallantly. **58.6%**.

**Duncan Taylor Pulteney 1977 Aged 26 Years** cask 3078 **(86) n**20 **t**22 **f**22 **b**22. Slick, bready and sweet. **58.3%**

⠿ **Gordon & MacPhail Old Pulteney 1969 (92)** n24 an aroma freshly prepared in the kitchen: slivers of cucumber, an orange and passion fruit puree, all topped with vanilla. Mmmm!!; t23 the mouthfeel is simply glorious, as is the slowly building intensity of the barley; toasty oaky notes offer an early vanilla and mocha counter; f22 medium length with more of the same; b23 one of those casks that threatens to go over the oaky edge, but keeps stepping back from the precipice at the very last moment. Sheer class from good ole G&M! **43%.** *Gordon & MacPhail.*

**Private Collection Old Pulteney 1973 (72)** n19 t19 f16 b18. An entirely odd fish, this, with some attractive sweet coffee notes at times but a mysterious, bitter off-note that gives it an irony, Fisherman's Friend character. **45%** *G&M.*

**Scott's Selection Pulteney 1977** bott 04 **(90)** n20 dry marzipan; t23 dazzling, textbook malt-oak arrival for this age with just so much fudgy sweetness: a touch of salt brings out the sharper semi-fruit tones vividly; f24 fabulous finish: peppery-toasty-salty notes continue to thrive with some beautiful cocoa towards the end. Rarely does oak play such an outstanding role. There's some magic in this bottle; b23 from the north it may be, but few signs of it heading south.... **53.2%**

**Scott's Selection Pultney 1977** bott 05 **(88)** n22 rich bourbon notes and almonds; t23 a hot dram for all its age, and still the bourbon shape continues. But some lovely salty-malt notes abound; f21 dries too effectively with the big oak; b22 some wonderful depth, but a cask dumped just in the nick of time. **55.9%.** *Speyside Distillers.*

⠿ **Whisky Galore Pulteney 1989** cask no. 10254, dist Jan 89, bott Jun 05 **(89)** n22 a touch of apple to the barley; t23 mouth-watering and intense malt with some early spices; f22 remains tingling and a drop of oil adds length; b22 not too dissimilar to cask 10256, except this shows a touch more oil and less complexity. Still a beauty, though. **46.1%.** *Duncan Taylor. 161 bottles.*

⠿ **Whisky Galore Pulteney 1989** cask no. 10256 **(91)** n22 a touch of oak and sea air amid the vivid barley; t23 excellent clarity and deftness of touch to the barley; mouth-watering and massively fresh and lip-smacking; f23 some lovely salt is detectable amid the golden syrup; a touch of spice with the developing cocoa; b23 what a wonderfully bright portrait of this great distillery. **46%.** *Duncan Taylor.*

# ROSEBANK
### Lowland 1840–1993. Closed. (But if there is a God will surely one day re-open.)

**Rosebank Aged 12 Years** db **(95)** n24 strands of honey and honeycomb entwine around a softly herbal, but enormously weighted maltiness: the type of nose you can stick your head in and wallow about for a few minutes; t24 this has to be near perfection in regard to texture and not far off with the way the honeypolished malt trips around the palate with an almost apologetic spiciness for accompaniment. Just so accomplished and breathtaking; f23 long, more honeycomb, with hints of liquorice and soft herbs; b24 infinately better than the last F&F bottling, this is quite legendary stuff, even better then the old 8-y-o version, though probably a point or two down regarding complexity. The kind of whisky that brings a tear to the eye...for many a reason.... **43%.** *Flora and Fauna.*

**Rosebank 22 Years Old Rare Malts 2004** db **(85)** n22 t23 f19 b21. One or two Rosebank moments of joyous complexity but, hand on heart, this is simply too old. **61.1%**

**The Wee Dram Rosebank 15 Years Old** db **(81)** n20 t20 f21 b20. Probably from a third-fill bourbon cask, showing early vitality and then rich cocoa-oak influence. A wafer-light dram, so reminiscent of a Scapa half its age. **40%.** *The Wee Dram, Bakewell, Derbyshire.*

**Aberdeen Distillers Rosebank 12 Years Old** cask no. 236, dist Feb 91, bott Oct 03 **(96)** n25 t24 f23 b24. Last year I tasted this from a leaking sample bottle of which barely 2cl remained. So I have reevaluated it – and thank God I did! As far as Lowland malt whisky is concerned, I will be surprised if it ever gets better than this. If Rosebank really is to be left to rot, I hope whoever decided that should be the case gets a bottle of this at Christmas, along with the latest Flora and Fauna expression for good measure. And no, not choke on them, but wonder if their wisdom was so great after all. And if, in the grand scheme of things, there is something even more important than the bottom line of a pretty bottomless company accounts sheet. **43%**

⌐☞ **Berry's Own Selection Rosebank 1990 Aged 15 Years (93) n**23 elegant, wispy barley; playful, perfectly weighted oak; barely ripened greengages and the most distant echo of coriander and....juniper?; **t**24 oh yeah, baby! Just honey me...!!!; **f**23 those beautiful waves of honey which saturate the tastebuds from the very first moment carry on, only allowing through unsweetened custard and a dash of rhubarb juice (honestly – see for yourself!); **b**23 if there is a woman in your life who says she doesn't like whisky, give her a shot of this: she'll be addicted for life. **46%**. *Berry Bros & Rudd.*

**Cadenhead's Authentic Collection Rosebank Aged 15 Years** dist 89, bott Feb 05 **(88) n**21 polished floors, dank sawdust and a trace of smoke; **t**24 soft smoke permeates the glorious mixture of barley sugar and fruit candy; **f**21 rapid oak explosion; **b**22 shows signs of exhaustion towards the end, but the early complexity is awesome. **56.1%**. *318 bottles.*

⌐☞ **Cadenhead's Authentic Collection Rosebank Aged 16 Years** dist 89, bott Sep 05 **(87) n**22 fresh barley, fresh grass, freshly sawn tree; **t**23 voluptuous malt offering the normal honey sweetness and depth; the middle is a bit fuzzy due to some unexpected oils; **f**21 the oil hangs around to blur the oak/barley interplay; **b**21 the oiliest Rosebank I've seen for a long time. The result is a slight dip in complexity. **55.3%**. *294 bottles.*

⌐☞ **Cadenhead's Rosebank 17 years Old (90) n**22 a teasing spice buzz to this; **t**23 the hallmark honey takes little time to say hullo; **f**22 lovely fade, which is slow and befitting the gentle, yet quietly intense nature, of this lovely malt; a delicious touch of liquorice and prunes at the death; **b**23 well mannered, gentle and classy. **54.2%**

⌐☞ **Cask Strength Rosebank 1990** Sherry butt nos. 1605/1606, dist 27.6.90, bott 30.3.06 **(95) n**24 confident, structured and beautifully balanced: nothing too sweet or dry despite the powering barley; **t**24 like the nose, perfect structure: controlled acacia honey, barley that is far more mouth-watering than can be possible for its age and a softening marriage of natural toffee and spices which add further solidity; **f**23 layers of vanilla of varying intensity; a late gristy maltiness and a deft sprinkling of muscovado sugar; **b**24 another cask which reinforces the fact that Rosebank has to be one of the top ten distilleries in the world. So why is it silent? **61.1%**. *Gordon & MacPhail.*

⌐☞ **The Coopers Choice Rosebank 1992 Sherry Wood 14 Years Old (72) n**17 **t**19 **f**18 **b**18. Gooseberries, barley and sulphur. This is spooky: it could almost be the Chieftain's 14...!!! Except this has slightly more sulphur. Otherwise, peas in a pod! **46%**. *The Vintage Malt Whisky Co.*

⌐☞ **Chieftain's Rosebank Aged 14 Years Hogshead (75) n**18 **t**20 **f**18 **b**19. A fascinating unification of barley and gooseberries try to fight through the a sulphur-type off-note. Such is the brilliance of this spirit, it nearly wins... **46%**.

**Connoisseurs Choice Rosebank 1990 (86) n**23 **t**23 **f**20 **b**21. A delicious but frustrating Rosebank that for a brief moment threatens greatness but never achieves it. **40%**. *Gordon & MacPhail.*

**The Coopers Choice Rosebank Single Cask 1992 Aged 12 Years** bott 04 **(83) n**20 **t**22 **f**21 **b**20. Drawn from one of those lazy, second or third-fill ex-bourbon casks used latterly at Rosebank, which adds little colour or oak weight. Despite this, the mouth arrival is a marmalade and lime fruitfest of the top order. **46%**. **nc ncf.** *The Vintage Malt Whisky Co Ltd.*

**Dun Bheagan Rosebank Aged 13 Years Bourbon Barrel** dist 91, bott 05 **(82)** n20 t22 f20 b21. A whiff of smoke helps iron out some of the oaky creases. **46%. nc ncf.** Ian Macleod. 600 bottles.

⋯ **Dun Bheagan Rosebank 14 Years Old (91)** n23 it is as you are standing in between the doors of two shops – one a florist , the other a confectioner; t24 the most ingratiating arrival imaginable: the barley is about as intense as it gets, yet a perfect harmonization between oak and honey adds an extra weight and ferocity you wouldn't believe; toffee and Demerara-sweetened coffee towards the late middle; f21 lots of natural caramels dampens the fun; b23 a bold Rosebank this is slightly off the wall. But superb! **46%.** Ian Macleod.

**Hart Brothers Rosebank Aged 13 Years Cask Strength** dist Nov 90, bott Nov 03 **(89)** n21 t23 f22 b23. At once energetic yet delicate whisky of very high quality. **58.3%**

⋯ **Murray McDavid Mission Rosebank 1989** Bourbon/Guigal **(91)** n22 moist earth; spiced, tangy lime peel; t22 the enormity of the barley-fruit takes time to sink in – and unravel on the palate. A real mess at first but sanity arrives with some structured barley-vanilla waves thinning out the thudding fruit; f24 now a gentlemanly and refined procession of complex oak-dusted and gently spiced and alternating waves of barley and apricot; b23 Rosebank as you have never before seen it... **55.3%**

**Old Malt Cask Rosebank 11 Years Old** dist Mar 93, bott Oct 04 **(91)** n22 citrus and weak pipe smoke; t24 holy Lowlanders! This just so reminds me of the old Rosebank 8-y-o of 20 years ago: the oak acts as the perfect catalyst for the malt to display its entire gamut from honey-rich to much drier cereal tones; f22 perhaps a shade too dry as the vanilla kicks in; still the citric elements about, though; b23 vivid confirmation of Rosebank as a true great. **50%.** Douglas Laing.

**Old Malt Cask Rosebank Aged 12 Years** dist Jan 91, bott Nov 03 **(71)** n15 t20 f18 b18. Unusually robust for Rosebank but off notes have crept in from somewhere. **50% nc ncf sc.** Douglas Laing. 354 bottles.

⋯ **Old Malt Cask Rosebank 12 Years Old** dist 26 Mar 93, bott 15 Jun 05 **(79)** n21 t21 f18 b19. Attractively gristy but a touch bitter and fragile. **50%.** Douglas Laing.

⋯ **Old Malt Cask Rosebank Aged 15 Years** dist July 90, bott Sept 05 **(90)** n21 gooseberry perhaps, but a little closed – clean malt apart; t23 that's more like it: a silky delivery followed by a continual upping of barley intensity, topped with the softest hint of honey; f23 long and luxurious with that intense barley continuing to pulse with wonderful Java/Indian low roast blend seeing you through to the finish; b23 yet another glorious example of a great distillery. **50%.** Douglas Laing. 242 bottles.

⋯ **Old Malt Cask Rosebank 16 Years Old Rum Finish** dist July 90, bott Sept 06 **(85)** n22 t21 f21 b21. Unrecognisable as Rosebank with the usual complexity reduced significantly and bogged down in a most un-Rosebank-ish sugary squabble. Still a pretty cultured dram. **50%.** Douglas Laing. 358 bottles.

**Old Malt Cask Rosebank 23 Years Old** dist 26 Feb 81, bott 17 Jan 05 **(94)** n24 primroses, bluebells, the uplifting if slightly earthy aroma of a northfacing summer garden; t24 the only Lowlander that offers such glorious weight, the pristine malt seducing the tastebuds with its faultless estery riches; f23 enormous depth with a wonderful crescendo of spice; b23 sublime Rosebank: quite extraordinary for its age. **50%.** Douglas Laing & Co.

⋯ **Old Malt Cask Rosebank 28 Years Old (91)** n24 big oak, but the fabulous Kentucky/Canadian charge is met by stout marzipan-topped fruitcake resistance; t23 beautifully sweet with molten Demerara and boiled plums; f22 a darker, drier, oakier experience all round; b22 good grief! I forgot anyone ever kept Rosebank this long! Usually a malt is at its best when young though the odd old 'un does surface, and usually with excellent results. This is no exception. **50%. nc ncf sc.** Douglas Laing.

**Provenance Rosebank 11 Years Old (79)** n19 t22 f19 b19. Slightly soapy on the nose: the old cask refuses to further the malt's complexity. **46%.**

✦ **Provenance Rosebank 12 Years Old** dist Mar 93, bott July 05 **(87)** n24 if all whiskies had a nose like this, this Bible would never get finished! A bowl of fruits arranged by angels. One of the most delicate noses of the year; t22 doesn't quite translate as well onto the palate as the lack of oak fails to reinforce the brittle barley; f21 a sprinkling of vanilla and spice; b20 the nose is a legend: what follows is perhaps just a little too delicate. **46%.** *McGibbon's.*

**Provenance Rosebank Over 12 Years** dist Summer 91, bott Summer 03 **(93)** n22 t24 f23 b24. I was tut-tutted by some a decade ago when I wrote that Rosebank at its best can match anything most other Scotch distilleries can offer. Well, try this. The early bourbon theme is rendered a side-show: the balance between honey and spice is equal to Highland Park at its most sophisticated and eloquent. Absolutely tastebudsmackingly brilliant. **46%.** *Douglas McGibbon.*

✦ **Provenance Rosebank Aged Over 12 Years** Refill Hogshead DMG 1907, dist Spring 93, bott Summer 05 **(91)** n22 fresh grist enlivened by diced apple and pear t23 wonderful weight and lift to this send the barley soaring; toasty vanilla and then a fresh wave of mouth-watering malt; f23 lovely layers of cocoa sweetened slightly by a sprinkling of brown sugar; b23 another reminder of what we will shortly never see again... **46%. nc ncf.** *McGibbon's.*

**Provenance Rosebank Over 13 Years** dist Winter 91, bott Spring 04 **(83)** n20 t21 f22 b20. The coal dust nose is followed by prisoner-shooting barley: a hard and bitter little cuss **46%** *Douglas McGibbon*

✦ **The Single Malt of Scotland Rosebank Aged 14 Years Vintage 1991** cask no 2024, dist 01 July 91, bott 05 Apr 06 **(93)** n24 another tapestry of faint apple and cinnamon amid the near perfect fresh barley; t24 acacia honey is interwoven through the rich barley juice; spices batter at the roof of the mouth; f22 thins out and dries as the oak interjects; b23 another stunning cask from this stunning distillery. **46%.** *The Whisky Exchange. 305 bottles.*

**Whisky Fair Rosebank 1974 30 Years Old Sherry Cask (92)** n23 big sherry, clean, old, nutty and faultless; t22 just slightly off-key at first, but then an explosion of honey and oloroso comes to the rescue; f24 a brilliant balance of major fruit and glossy, coppery malt; a perfection of sweetness helps to dazzle; b23 probably Rosebank as you've never seen it before: I can count on the fingers of one hand the times I've seen something quite like this. One of the biggest Lowlanders in recent times. **55.8%.** *The Whisky Fair, Limburg.*

✦ **Whisky Galore Rosebank 1990** cask no. 3413, dist Nov 90, bott Apr 06 **(85)** n21 t22 f21 b21. As Rosebanks go, this one is pretty introverted. **55.4%.** *Duncan Taylor. 253 bottles.*

**Whisky Galore Rosebank 1990 Aged 13 Years (83)** n19 t23 f20 b21. Weighted beyond a Lowlander with thick, mildly honeyed, malt, but just a fraction too much age for a Rosebank to fully blossom. **46%.** *Duncan Taylor.*

# ROYAL BRACKLA
**Speyside, 1812. Dewar's. Working.**

**Royal Brackla Aged 10 Years** db **(73)** n18 t20 f17 b18. A distinct lowering of the colours since I last tasted this. What on earth is going on? **40%** ☹ ☉

**Royal Brackla Aged 25 Years** dist 78, bott Mar 03 db **(88)** n23 t22 f21 b22. A very complex malt that for a light Speysider has survived the passing summers much better than can be expected and is bold enough to display its own richness of style. Some excellent cask selection has gone into this one. **43%**

**Cadenhead's Authentic Collection Royal Brackla Aged 12 Years** dist 92, bott Feb 05 **(92)** n24 outstanding bourbon-style sweetness with malt and tart stewed apple: nosing blind you would mistake it for a high quality, middle-aged Kentuckian; t23 faultless mouth arrival for a Brackla with wave upon wave of clipped malt that allows the vanilla-oak dryness to act as a perfect counterweight; **f**22 threatens to become a shade too dry, but a soft estery sheen helps see off any excess; **b**23 sophisticated and demanding on the palate, a connoisseur's dram if ever there was one. **59%**. *234 bottles.*

Cadenhead's Chairman's Stock Royal Brackla Aged 30 Years 1976 Sherry hogshead, dist 76, bott Nov 06 **(93) n**24 pithy, exceptional dryness counters the juicier barley: top dollar sophistication; **t**23 maybe the dryness is a tad too profound on delivery but a vivid bourbon/sherry hybrid develops and compensates fabulously; **f**22 returns to dry sherry and papery oak; **b**24 who needs Martinis? Sheer class. **53.6%**. *126 bottles.*

**Connoisseurs Choice Royal Brackla 1976 (84) n**19 **t**21 **f**22 **b**22. Bit thick on the oak early and very late on but all in between is a riot of weighty barley sugar ripping off in a warming, bourbony direction. **46%**

**Connoisseurs Choice Royal Brackla 1991 (84) n**22 **t**21 **f**20 **b**21. Wonderful honey thread on the nose, but the oak jumps in a little early. **46%**. *G&M.*

**Coopers Choice Single Cask Range Royal Brackla 1979 25 Years Old** bott 04 **(88) n**23 surprisingly fresh and gristy for its age, the oak evident but outflanked by honey; **t**22 deft sweet malt with some sharp citrus; **f**21 layers of vanilla that begin to head into a forest of oak; **b**22 big oak at the finish suggesting that it was bottled just in time. **63%**. *Vintage Malt Whisky Co.*

**Mackillop's Choice Royal Brackla 1976** cask no 6924, dist Oct 76 **(84) n**21 **t**19 **f**23 **b**21. Massive malt, big bold and brassy with excellent honey to soften the oaky blows; an intriguing latent smokiness adds extra depth. **59.6%**.

**Murray McDavid Royal Brackla 1975** cask ref MM0421, bott 2004 **(86) n**22 **t**21 **f**22 **b**21. This is one very unusual Brackla. Had I tasted this blind and not known from the label, I would have put this down as second-fill sherry. Some rough edges, but you can't but rather like its cheeky character. **46%**. *Bottled exclusively for Willow Park Wine and Spirits, Alberta. 240 bottles.*

## ROYAL LOCHNAGAR
**Highland (Eastern), 1826. Diageo. Working.**

**Royal Lochnagar Aged 12 Years** bott lott 4330 db **(83) n**21 **t**22 **f**19 **b**21. More care has been taken with this than some other bottlings from this wonderful distillery. But I still can't understand why it never quite manages to get out of third gear...or is the caramel on the finish the giveaway...? **40%**

**Royal Lochnagar Rare Malts 30 Years** Old bott 04 db **(83) n**21 **t**22 **f**20 **b**20. A wonderful thread of honey battles heroically against the invading oak. **56.2%**

**Royal Lochnagar Selected Reserve** db **(89) n**23 superb oloroso, clean and spicy with apples and pears; **t**23 stupendous spice lift-off which really starts showing the malts to great effect; **f**21 the malts fade as the toffee progresses; **b**22 quite brilliant sherry influence. The spices are a treat. **43%**

**Old Malt Cask Lochnagar 14 Years Old** dist Feb 90, bott Dec 04 **(82) n**22 **t**21 **f**19 **b**20. Begins with an attractive honey sheen and then fades fast. **50%**. *Douglas Laing & Co.*

Old Malt Cask Royal Lochnagar Aged 14 Years Single Cask Bottling for a Fine Cigar's Pleasure **(84) n**19 **t**21 **f**22 **b**22. Curiously, before I even saw what this whisky was, I thought I was getting tobacco smoke off the nose. Strange... but a sprightly, zesty dram if ever there was one. **50%. nc ncf sc.** *Douglas Laing.*

Platinum Selection Lochnagar 30 Years Old dist 10 Dec 74, bott May 05 **(83) n**22 **t**20 **f**21 **b**20. One of those suet pudding and custard jobbies; a touch of the fruitcakes, too. But it lucks out on the oak, which is altogether too forceful on landing. **60.2%**. *Douglas Laing. 224 bottles.*

**Platinum Old and Rare Lochnagar 32 Years Old** dist 72, bott 04 **(85) n**23 **t**19 **f**22 **b**21. A malt that hangs in there by the skin of its teeth but most extraordinary is the strength for the age. **60.5%**. *Douglas Laing.*

**Platinum Lochnagar 32 Years Old** dist May 72, bott Jul 04 **(93) n**23 moist Jamaica cake with a layer of Danish marzipan; a fabulous cocoa-laced thread of smoke weaves through it; **t**24 busy spice throughout as the malt settles towards a Jaffa-cake fruit, honied theme; gorgeous copper and gentle peat involvement; **f**23 honeycomb, cocoa and a touch of smoke; **b**23 as lush and rich as you could pray a whisky this age to be: really seems to have that "sma' still" body. **60.5%.** *Douglas Laing & Co.*

⋙ **Provenance Lochnagar Aged 11 Years** Sherry butt DMG 2675, dist Winter (Nov) 94, bott Summer 06 **(79) n**19 **t**19 **f**21 **b**20. A temperamental malt at the best of times, this one's a bit sulky by refusing to really get going. **46%. nc ncf.** *McGibbon's.*

**Provenance Lochnagar 12 Years Old** dist 28 Apr 93, bott 23 May 05 **(94) n**23 fresh, breezy, mildly salty: marvellous balance between clear barley and soft oak; **t**25 the wonderful Lochnagar honey I have sampled in so many casks is caught perfectly here, but the mildly oily lushness of the malt, the charm of the spiced, exotic fruit, the development of the spices, the waft of gentle smoke make for a classic; **f**23 the late-developing peat continues and blossoms well against the malt and vanilla; **b**23 this is the independent Lochnagar I've been waiting years to find. Absolutely spot-on, capturing the curiously delicate yet heavy style in one glass. Majestic: Queen Victoria would be very amused.... **46%.** *Douglas Laing & Co.*

⋙ **Provenance Lochnagar 12 Years Old** Sherry matured, dist Mar 93, bott Nov 05 **(84) n**20 **t**22 **f**21 **b**21. A thoroughbred of a cask showing the cleanest, most excellent sherry. But to nitpick, perhaps it could do more on the complexity side. **46%.** *McGibbon's.*

⋙ **Provenance Lochnagar Aged Over 12 Years** Sherry butt no. 1790, dist Winter 93 (Spring distillation label), bott Spring 05 **(74) n**18 **t**19 **f**18 **b**19. Sweet barley fights to overcome a sulphured edge. **46%. nc ncf.** *McGibbon's.*

⋙ **Provenance Lochnagar 12 Years Old Sherry Finish** dist Jun 94, bott Autumn 06 **(86) n**21 **t**22 **f**22 **b**21. Decent, sharp barley but slightly awkward and tight at times in delivery **46%.** *McGibbon's.*

# ST MAGDALENE
**Lowland, 1798–1983. Closed.**

**Linlithgow 30 Years Old** dist 73 db **(70) n**18 **t**18 **f**16 **b**18. A brave but ultimately futile effort from a malt that is way past its sell-by date. **59.6%**

**Duncan Taylor Linlithgow 1982 Aged 21 Years** cask 2211 **(80) n**19 **t**20 **f**21 **b**20. Thin and hot, but the clarity of the malt is without question. **63%**

⋙ **Gordon & MacPhail Reserve St Magdalena 1975** bott 01.11.05 **(82) n**22 **t**19 **f**21 **b**20. Slightly overcooked on the oaky front, as one might expect, but not enough to ruin those sparkling barley notes that gather attractively on the finish. **46%.** *US Market.*

**Hart Brothers St. Magdalene Aged 21 Years Cask Strength** dist Sep 82, bott Nov 03 **(86) n**20 **t**22 **f**22 **b**22. There are two types of St Magdalene. Vicious or serene. Here you taste with angels. **56.6%**

**Murray McDavid Mission IV Linlithgow 1975 Aged 29 Years (81) n**20 **t**21 **f**20 **b**20. Gone fractionally through the top with oak, but recovers thanks to a relaxed malty and slightly citrussy theme. **46%.** *Bourbon Cask.*

⋙ **Old Malt Cask St Magdalene 23 Years Old** dist Dec 82, bott June 06 **(84) n**22 **t**21 **f**20 **b**21. Well preserved and really belts out the malty notes. **50%.** *Douglas Laing. 329 bottles.*

# SCAPA
**Highland (Island–Orkney), 1885. Chivas. Working.**

**Scapa 12 Years Old** db **(88) n**23 honeydew melon, soft salt and myriad styles of barley: really complex with a sprinkling of coal dust on the fruit; **t**22 truly brilliant mouth arrival: the most complex display of malt and cocoa, the fruit is ripe figs with a thread of honey; **f**21 a slight bitterness with some developing toffee, but the malt stays the distance; **b**22 always a joy. **40%**

**Scapa 14 Years Old** db **(89) n**22 hints of honey and kumquats; the sappiness from last year has gone; **t**22 relays of mouthwatering barley sprinting between the shards of honey; **f**22 toasty, a subtle bitterness blends well with the lingering barley-honey; some caramel flies in from somewhere to beat down an important degree of complexity. Otherwise the entire scoring would be two or three points higher; **b**23 the tongue works overtime trying to work out the multi-layered structure of a superb malt from a distillery at last being recognised for its excellence. **40%** ⊙ ⊙

∷ **Chieftain's Scapa Aged 22 Years** Sherry **(90) n**23 one of those noses which is a bit awkward and top heavy when poured but after 5-10 mins of airing reveals a wonderful honey side to the fruit; **t**22 ditto the palate: a bit closed at first but opens up gloriously for a light fruitcake effect; **f**22 elegant, with a touch of brown sugar; **b**23 fabulous whisky deserving as much time as you can afford. **46%**. *Ian Macleod.*

∷ **Duncan Taylor Collection Scapa 1977** cask no. 2831, dist Oct 77, bott Apr 06 **(83) n**20 **t**21 **f**22 **b**20. Sharp, tangy, lively. Has fended off obvious old age with a touch of fruity panache. **57.9%**. *164 bottles.*

**Duncan Taylor Collection Scapa 1977 Aged 27 Years** cask no. 2828, dist Oct 77, bott Mar 05 **(94) n**24 a mesmerising amalgam of ordinary and manuka honey salted down and then given a gristy, malty blast. Astonishing, and something you can keep your nose stuck in for an age; **t**24 the very arrival spells brilliance with the most extraordinary complexity sitting on the tongue as the saline notes are swamped by the sharp, bitter-sweet battles between oak, curvaceous malt and citrus. Spice has to arrive and it does! **f**22 long, but a degree of oiliness mildly dampening down the early mayhem, and some late, mildly bitter oak sees off the last of the honey; **b**24 I have long felt that Scapa has been poorly served by the independents. However, most of the older bottlings have been classic and this just about tops the bill. Pure drama on the tastebuds. Fabulous!!! **61.1%**

**Gordon & MacPhail Scapa 1993 (85) n**20 **t**21 **f**22 **b**22. If people still insist that G&M colour their standard malts, have a look at this! **40%**

**Old Malt Cask Scapa 13 Years Old** dist Feb 91, bott Aug 04 **(79) n**19 **t**21 **f**20 **b**19. A touch of paraffin and ungainly oak. **50%**. *Douglas Laing & Co.*

**Old Malt Cask Scapa Aged 14 Years** dist Oct 89, bott Mar 04 **(83) n**20 **t**21 **f**21 **b**21. A neat and tidy dram with a rich cocoa finale but perhaps just a shade too fierce in places. **50%. nc ncf sc.** *Douglas Laing. 269 bottles.*

**Old Malt Cask Scapa 14 Years Old** dist 29 Apr 91, bott 9 May 05 **(88) n**22 fruity barley woven around vanilla; **t**23 mouthwateringly delicate: Speyside in form, but a touch of salt and earth suggest maybe not; **f**21 layers of vanilla and playful spice; **b**21 a very light Scapa that at times tries to shout but raises only a loud whisper. **50%**. *Douglas Laing & Co.*

**Provenance Scapa 11 Year Old** dist 4 Nov 93, bott 21 Apr 05 **(85) n**21 **t**22 **f**21 **b**21. Hints of papaya but very similar, if memory serves me correctly, to a Douglas Laing Macallan from a long-in-the-tooth cask which reveals a warts an' all whisky. **46%**. *Douglas Laing and Co.*

∷ **Provenance Scapa 12 Years Old** dist Nov 93, bott Summer 06 **(87) n**21 lazy: the oak is offering little sympathy to the salted barley; **t**22 better as the lush body generates a barley sweetness; **f**22 indifferent oak cramps the finer, classier notes. But there is a lovely coppery gloss that impresses; **b**22 attractive, as usual, for this wonderful little distillery. But the oak input could be better. **46%**.

**Provenance Scapa Over 14 Years** dist Autumn 88, bott Winter 04 **(86) n**19 **t**22 **f**23 **b**22. Devilishly complex with some fruit and honey mixing well with the oaky cocoa. **46%. nc ncf.** *Douglas McGibbon.*

## SPEYBURN
### Speyside, 1897. Inver House. Working.

**Speyburn 10 Year Old** db **(81)** n21 t22 f18 **b**20. Soft, slightly smoked, sweet, syrupy, simple: Speyburn so stylish. **40%**. *Inver House Distillers.* ☉

⋅⋅⋅ **Speyburn 25 Years Old** db **(81)** n19 t23 f20 **b**19. A Hyde and Jekyll malt: starts and ends ugly, but some deliciously honeyed normality on the early arrival. **46%**

**Connoisseurs Choice Speyburn 1974 (77)** n18 t22 f19 **b**20. Pity that an off note from the cask has got in to spoil what would have been an exceptionally honied party. **43%**. *Gordon & MacPhail.*

## SPEYSIDE
### Speyside, 1990. Speyside Distillers. Working.

**Drumguish** db **(64)** n15 t17 f16 **b**16. Feinty, cloyingly sweet and poorly made. Rubbish, frankly. **40%**

**Speyside 10 Years Old** db **(81)** n19 t21 f20 **b**21. Plenty of sharp oranges around; the malt is towering and the bite is deep. A weighty Speysider with no shortage of mouth prickle. **40%**

**The Speyside Aged 12 Years** db **(90)** n23 wonderful apple brandy fruitiness combined with cinnamon and malt; t23 velvety malt casting an apple and peach spell on the tastebuds. Waves of wonderful malt arrive latterly; f21 vanilla with developing spice cut short by caramel; **b**23 confirmation, as I suspected, that they really did make some top quality malt in those early days. **40%**

**Scott's Selection The Speyside 1991** bott 04 db **(89)** n22 apple turnover; t23 sweet, sticky malt with magnificent spice infusion and the vaguest hint of smoke and feints; f22 heads off in a soft oaky, burnt toasty, bitter chocolate direction; **b**22 a lovely cask full of fat, malty riches. **61.1%**. *Speyside Distillers.*

**Hart Brothers Speyside Aged 10 Years Sherry Cask** dist Oct 93, bott Nov 03 **(73)** n17 t18 f20 **b**18. A slight feintiness to the nose and early mouth arrival but the grapiness magnifies and prospers the longer it remains on the palate. **46%**

**Cu Dhub (73)** n18 t19 f18 **b**18. This is one of the few whiskies I had been trying to avoid in recent years as previous encounters had not been particularly enjoyable. Some in the past have been a touch feinty, a fault too many with so much caramel. But this is much cleaner and therefore makes for a tolerable experience. So much caramel, though, could easily be mistaken for a Scottish West Coast rum! **40%**. *Mac Y, Denmark.* ☉☉

⋅⋅⋅ **Cu Dhub 10 Years Old (82)** n19 t22 f20 **b**21. Not too sure how they have achieved this. Threateningly dark and hardly shy of caramel but there is real juice abounding. A lot more engaging than it looks. **46%**. *Mac Y, Denmark. 100 bottles.*

## SPRINGBANK
### Campbeltown, 1828. J&A Mitchell & Co. Working.

⋅⋅⋅ **Hazelburn Aged 8 Years** 2nd Edition, release 2006 db **(90)** n22 big, concentrated barley. Much more complex than first sniff suggests and there is enough oak layering to really impress; t23 kabooom!! The barley absolutely explodes around the palate; just a touch of salt brings out the full intensity; f22 soft oils help project the advancing oak. Simple, but good balance; **b**23 I adore this ultra-intense barley style: something you can devour for an age. Wonderful stuff!! **46%**. *6000 bottles.*

**Longrow 10 Years Old 1994** db **(95)** n25 never in all the years of nosing whisky have I come across one that is a complete replica of sitting on a Scottish shore by a rock pool surrounded by seaweed and evaporating salty seawater. The pungency of the peat is deft and astonishing; t24 velvetcushioned malt gracefully coats the mouth while sweet peat offers waves of gentle intensity; f22 laid-back, with banana and caressing layers of smoky grist; **b**24 it is incredible how the present Springbank 10-y-o have problems finding their feet, yet add some peat to the mix and you have on your hands a malt of such subtlety and complexity that you need simply hours to try and fathom it out. Whisky for the gods. **46%**. *Limited availability.*

⋙ **Longrow Tokaji Wood Aged 10 Years** 8 yrs refill, 2 yrs fresh Tokaji, dist Feb 95, bott Aug 05 db **(69) n**17 **t**18 **f**17 **b**17. Why..? **55.6%**

⋙ **Longrow Aged 14 Years** db **(89) n**25 a strap-on-to-the-head aroma with so many barley-peat nuances at so many levels it almost defies comprehension; and it wouldn't be a Longrow if there wasn't some salty goings on, too; **t**21 mildly tart delivery with the smoke and oak refusing to gel; **f**21 where the hell is the peat on the nose? No shortage of natural toffee, though; **b**22 hard to get a bearing on this one. The nose, though... **46%. nc ncf.**

⋙ **Longrow 1995 Aged 10 Years** db **(91) n**24 distant peat reek of a coastal village carried on the wind; salty smoked bacon. Just so delicate and delicious...; **t**23 sweet grist and bursting spices; **f**22 hollows out as vanilla chimes in; again the smoke refuses to entirely vanish; **b**22 a graceful malt, almost lethargic by comparison with the legendary '94, but a whisky education in its own right. **46%**

⋙ **Longrow 1996 Aged 10 Years** db **(86) n**23 **t**22 **f**20 **b**21. If I was a gambling man I'd say some very fresh bourbon is involved here, because the balance has been compromised. I think this needed a few more years to find its natural balance. That said, remains very drinkable. **46%**

⋙ **Springbank 9 Years Old Marsala Wood Expression** dist Oct 96, bott Aug 06 db **(88) n**21 pungent, biting spices; a hint of something smoky and piny; **t**23 heavy on the wine at first, but as the barley picks up the pace and the body lightens a fabulous injection of swarming, buzzing, piny spices kick in; **f**22 long with lots of wine sticking to the cocoa-sprinkled finale; **b**22 easily one of the spiciest Springbanks for a long time: the Sicilian influence makes this an offer you can't refuse... **58%**. *7740 bottles.*

**Springbank 10 Years Old** db **(74) n**18 **t**19 **f**18 **b**19. Woahhh...!! Way off key. But, really, that's no criticism: this is a malt on its way to greatness, but like the most glorious butterflies must go through its ugly larva stage. For these casks, this is it... **46%** ☺ ☺

**Springbank Aged 10 Years** db **(84) n**20 **t**22 **f**21 **b**21. A much better fist than the 46% version, though this is dripping in natural caramels which distances it from the complexity of previous bottlings. But it pulses with its trademark malt. **57% (100 proof).** ☺ ☺

**Springbank 10 Years Old 100 Proof Bourbon Matured** db **(85) n**19 **t**23 **f**21 **b**22. Another brain-busting expression. At this tender age, Springbank has no set rules: it can disappear on any tangent it sees fit. Today it has decided to take the big oak route. **57%**. *Not available in USA or Canada.*

**Springbank 12 Years Old Bourbon Wood Expression** dist 91, bott Feb 04 db **(82) n**20 **t**22 **f**21 **b**19. Springbank is one of the most complex and probably the slowest maturing single malt in Scotland. Here is a priceless example of a dram that cannot find its equilibrium yet at the same time generates flashes of pure genius. **58.5%**. *5986 bottles.*

**Springbank 12 Years Old 175th Anniversary** db **(86) n**20 **t**24 **f**21 **b**21. An unusually soft Springbank with less complexity than usual but displaying amazing intensity. **46%**. *12000 bottles worldwide from Apr 03. The age may not be stated.*

**Springbank 1989 14 Years Old Port Wood Expression** bott Sep 04 db **(89) n**22 fruity and salty, there's a bit of a directional crisis here! **t**23 astonishing spice explosion to start, followed by a surprisingly orderly procession of malt, fruit and coffee; **f**21 the malt at last finds a more gristy, sweeter gear, but that salty oak holds it back a little; **b**23 a strange beast that is nothing if not unpredictable and entertaining after an indifferent start on the nose that needs time in the glass to come alive. **52.8%**. *12 years re-fill sherry, 2 years fresh port. 7,200 bottles.*

**Springbank 15 Years Old Sherry Matured** db **(77)** n19 t21 f18 **b**19. Very unusual, in fact almost a first. But I think a dodgy sherry butt has got in here somewhere. **46%**

**Springbank Aged 25 Years (91)** n24 t22 f22 **b**23. I think complex is the word. **46%**

**Springbank FFF 25 Year Old** db **(90)** n23 t22 f22 **b**23. The words Springbank and complexity seem conjoined: they are again here. **46%**

**Springbank 32 Years Old** bott Oct 04 db **(93)** n24 a startling and unusual overture of redcurrant jam and salted porridge; a distant hint of medium roast Java coffee underlines the complexity; **t**24 that unique combination of intense sweet malt and intense salty malt go into overdrive; f22 more oak and some natural crème brûlée douse the intensity somewhat; **b**23 for those Springbank diehards out there, here's a must-have for the collection. **46%**. *2400 bottles.*

**Springbank Private Bottling for Distillery Visitors 2005** db **(79)** n21 t21 f18 **b**19. This is a ten-year-old but very curiously flat, especially towards the finish.

**Adelphi Springbank 1970** cask 1622 **(92)** n23 a warming, peppery nose has a Demerara rum and sugar edge and a touch of sweetened tequila; look carefully and malt seeps out, too; **t**22 a big, threatening oakiness is checked by a sherry-malt resistance and overcome by gentle brown sugar; f24 mouthwatering, chewy with layers of plummy fruit and liquorice; **b**23 brilliant, complex whisky that two years earlier may have been quite exceptional. **54.4%**

⟨⟩ **Accura Engineering Springbank** cask no. 66, dist may 95, bott Sep 05 **(85)** n21 t22 f21 **b**21. A real turn up for the book Down Under, with this massive, fruit-fuelled beaut. Perhaps just a little sharp in places, especially on the finish, for greatness, but this is less a whisky and more an adventure... **57.1%. nc ncf sc.** *Australia. 12 bottles.*

⟨⟩ **Cadenhead's Authentic Collection Longrow Aged 11 Years** dist 93, bott Sep 05 db **(91)** n23 distinct Arbroath Smokie; **t**23 high-class gristy delivery with all the sweetness that brings; a touch of sugared lime, too; f22 loads more fruit with a golden syrup glaze and the faintest smoke; **b**23 another sweetie, literally and figuratively. **54.1%**. *270 bottles.*

⟨⟩ **Cadenhead's Authentic Collection Springbank Aged 14 Years** Sherry butt, dist 91, bott Sept 06 **(84)** n20 t20 f23 **b**21 Only towards the back of the astonishingly elegant and long finish do things fall into place. And how! **53.9%**. *654 btls.*

⟨⟩ **Cadenhead's Bond Reserve Hazelburn Aged 8 Years** Sherry Hogshead, dist 97, bott May 06 db **(84)** n21 t22 f20 **b**21. A sherry hoggy it may be, but this behaves like a dram freshly poured from a pre-carameled PM Demerara cask, complete with give-away coffee notes. Rather lovely, but finesse is at a premium. **58.4%**. *288 bottles.*

⟨⟩ **Cadenhead's Bond Reserve Longrow Aged 10 Years 1996** Cream sherry butt, dist 96, bott Nov 06 db **(75)** n18 t20 f18 **b**19. A real shame: the cream sherry has curdled. Sulphur at work. **59.4%**. *654 bottles.*

⟨⟩ **Chieftain's Springbank Aged 31 Years (94)** n23 salty barley meets sugary barley head on: no shortage of splinters in the explosion; **t**24 cripes! My slumbering tastebuds – barely disturbed by the majority of the "young" Springbanks - get a rude awakening as the most astonishingly clean and intense malt crashes head first into them with myriad glorious waves of lessening intensity; f23 real complexity with the salt catching up with the golden syrup. About 20 different shades of vanilla cannot dampen the developing spices; **b**24 one the sweetest Springbanks I've yet across. Book a dental appointment before buying a bottle. **57.2%**. *Ian Macleod.*

⟨⟩ **Chieftain's Springbank Aged 34 Years (86)** n21 t22 f21 **b**22. Just so light for its age. **43%**. *Ian Macleod.*

**Chieftains Springbank 1969 Aged 34 Years** Rum barrel, bott 27 Nov 03 **(92)** n24 t23 f22 **b**23. A bigger finish would have made this one of the all-time greats. As it is, just enjoy the astonishing early harmony. **43.2%**

⬥ **Chieftain's Springbank Aged 36 Years (82) n**20 **t**20 **f**21 **b**21. Remarkably high strength for age but a bit raw irrespective of this. **57.3%**. *Ian Macleod.*

**Da Mhile Organic Springbank 1992 Aged 7 Years** dist June 92, bott Sept 99 **(74) n**17 **t**20 **f**19 **b**18. Really big, oily and chewy. Also a bit feinty, but a real one-off. **46%**. *Made for organic farmer John Savage-Onstwedder.*

⬥ **Dewar Rattray Individual Cask Bottling Springbank 1993 Aged 12 Years** cask no. 212, dist May 93, bott Jan 06 **(89) n**22 nutty, salted butter and vague smoke; **t**23 stunningly fresh and mouth-watering with a citrus and grist sweetness combining and a swirl of smoke adding depth; **f**22 lightly salted and spicy; **b**22 a really wonderful cask, probably second or even third fill so the caramels have been kept in check. **57.5%**. *282 bottles.*

**Dun Bheagan Springbank 1969 Aged 35 Years** bott 15 Mar 04 **(94) n**24 **t**23 **f**23 **b**24. When a Springbank can stand the test of time, little can live with it for sheer élan and complexity. **50%**

⬥ **Duncan Taylor Collection Springbank 1967** cask no. 1941, dist May 67, bott Dec 05 **(78) n**19 **t**20 **f**20 **b**19. The soft, exotic fruit doesn't quite save it from the ravages of time. **41.3%**. *196 bottles.*

⬥ **Kingsbury's Single Cask Springbank 11 Years Old** cask no. 378, dist 93 **(84) n**21 **t**22 **f**20 **b**21. A short surge of honey and citrus reveals the first tentative step towards greatness. **46%**. *Japan Import System.*

⬥ **Kingsbury's Valdespino Springbank 14 Years Old (87) n**22 spiced grape; **t**21 grassy and grapey but toffees out early on; **f**22 chewy and warming if a little bitter; **b**22 enormously busy; the odd kink but enough plusses to make for an enjoyable and, at times, classy dram. **46%**. *Japan Import System.*

**Duncan Taylor Springbank 1967 Aged 37 Years** cask 1943 **(82) n**21 **t**21 **f**20 **b**20. Some barley-rich moments but just a shade sappy. **41%**

⬥ **Murray McDavid Springbank Aged 9 Years** Bourbon/Marsanne/ Roussane casks enhanced in Guigla Hermitage Blanc, dist 96, bott 05 **(82) n**20 **t**20 **f**21 **b**21. Considering how off the pave young Springbank can be, this thrives with the extra fruity-sweetness. **46%. nc ncf.** *480 bottles.*

⬥ **Murray McDavid Springbank Aged 12 Years** Bourboun/Marsanne Roussanne enhanced in Guigal Hermitage Blanc, dist 92, bott 05 **(84) n**20 **t**22 **f**21 **b**21. Does Springbank come softer than this? The deft fruitiness is quite enchanting. **46%. nc ncf.** *480 bottles.*

**Old Malt Cask Springbank Aged 10 Years** dist Jun 93, bott Jan 04 **(81) n**19 **t**22 **f**20 **b**20. Disappointingly sappy nose translates to the finale. Some bright, typically weighty, salty and complex moments on the early arrival and middle, though. **50%. nc ncf sc.** *Douglas Laing. 628 bottles.*

⬥ **Old Malt Cask The Argyll Malt (Hazelburn) 1997 Aged 8 Years (82) n**20 **t**21 **f**21 **b**20. It's no secret that the malts from this slow-maturing distillery wobble about like Bambi until they get into double figures. This is no exception, though the malt intensity is marked. **58.8%**. *Exclusively for Vintage House. 296 bottles.*

**Peerless Springbank 1967** cask 1940, dist May 67 36-y-o **(86) n**22 **t**19 **f**23 **b**22. Takes time to settle but well worth the wait. **41.1%**. *Duncan Taylor*

⬥ **The Queen of the Moorlands Rare Cask Springbank 1991 Committee Bottling (87) n**23 mildly salty, tangy barley with a squeeze of citrus and fudge; **t**23 jarring, juicy barley; **f**20 lots of natural caramels and tannins flattens it; **b**21 hats off again to this bottler: they very rarely let you down. **46%. sc.** *Available at The Wine Shop, Leek, UK.*

**The Whisky Fair Limburg Springbank 1975 29 Years Old (88)** bott 04 **n**21 a tad soapy, but also salty and honied; **t**23 a sweet, enriching arrival with the big malt lightly sweetened with golden syrup; **f**22 long vanilla and some late salty tannins; **b**22 Springbank rarely comes quite as well-behaved as this. **49.2%**

⬥ **The Whisky Fair Springbank 35 Years Old** Bourbon Hogshead, dist May 70 **(89) n**21 salty and a tad sappy; **t**23 classy entry with intense, salivating malt which is mouth-puckeringly saline; f22 soft spices and yet more waves of ridiculously fresh barley; b23 even taking the less than perfect nose into account, this is truly great stuff. The annual Whisky Fair Springbanks are becoming an important fixture in the whisky world. **59.5%.** *Germany. 120 bottles.*

**The Whisky Fair Springbank Aged 36 Years** Bourbon Hogshead 402, dist Feb 69, bott Feb 05 **(89) n**21 hickory and slightly burnt toast; **t**23 malt brushed with Demerara; thin honey on toast; excellent bitter-sweet charm; **f**22 lots of vanilla and very dry, unbuttered toast; **b**23 typical Springbank, so polarised yet together. **45.6%. nc ncf.** *197 bottles.*

**Whisky Galore Springbank Aged 10 Years (79) n**19 **t**21 **f**20 **b**19. No screaming off-notes except perhaps a strange tobacco character. A brief flash of peaty smoke, but pretty half-baked by Springbank standards. **46%**

# STRATHISLA
**Speyside, 1786. Chivas. Working.**

**Strathisla 12 Years Old** db **(87) n**21 a dab of distant peat adds even more weight to something that is malt-heavy already; **t**22 pleasant, sultana-fruity with a very rich malt follow-through; **f**22 some almost apologetic oak breaks into the rich maltiness. Some hints of cocoa and more smoke elongate the finale; **b**22 an infinitely better dram than a few years back that was a bit oily and shapeless. Today the heavily-weighted, full-bodied malt engages the tastebuds from first to last with a complexity and richness of genuine class. **43%.** *Flora and Fauna.*

**Strathisla Distillery Edition 15 Years Old** db **(94) n**23 flawlessly clean and enriched by that silky intensity of fruity malt unique to this distillery; **t**23 the malt is lush, sweet and every bit as intense as the nose; a touch of toffeespice does it no harm; **f**24 just so long and lingering, again with the malt being of extraordinary enormity: these is simply wave upon wave of pure delight; **b**24 what a belter! The distillery is beautiful enough to visit: to take away a bottle of this as well would just be too good to be true! **53.7%**

**Aberdeen Distillers Strathisla 13 Years Old** dist Nov 89, bott Nov 03 **(87) n**21 **t**22 **f**23 **b**21. Anaemic-looking but unmasked. **43%**

**Blackadder Aberdeen Distillers Strathisla 13 Years Old** cask no. 9412, dist 6 Nov 89, bott Nov 03 **(84) n**20 **t**22 **f**21 **b**21. Attractive, simplistic, topgrade blending fodder. **43%**

**The Bottlers Strathisla 1977 Aged 27 Years** cask 4472 **(90) n**23 refreshing sultanas and apple; **t**23 soft, bitter-sweet sherry influence in conjunction with developing thick malt that is never less than mouthwatering; **f**22 relatively flat thanks to some over-egging of the sherry, but makes an elegant farewell and there is even a fascinating late juniper development as it takes on a curiously ginny quality at the death; **b**22 the more I taste from the independent company, the more impressed I become. **43.9%.** *Raeborn Fine Wines.*

⠿ **Cadenhead's Strathisla Aged 18 Years** Bourbon wood **(93) n**23 lively, with a buttress of oak groaning against the wall of barley; beautifully buttery, too; **t**23 succulent: stunningly juicy with a lovely thumbprint of the delicate oils so typical of Strathisla; **f**23 much more of an oaky theme, as should be the case but still that bitter-sweet barley rumbles; **b**24 if you want to sample exactly how this excellent distillery should be at 18, here's your man....but it takes it perhaps a notch further. The sheer élan of the layers, the intensity to the body; the absolute mmmm-i-ness of this makes it among the best single malts of the year, though not quite the best Strathisla... **58.4%**

**Cadenhead's Authentic Collection Strathisla-Glenlivet Aged 18 Years** Bourbon Hogshead, dist 87, bott May 05 **(94) n**24 an astonishing complexity of bourbon-assisted citrus and barley. Oh, and apple. Both bitter and sweet, this repays a good ten minutes' sniffing; **t**24 dream-like balance between myriad malty tones and vanilla. Mouthwatering and succulent; **f**22 errs on the side of age here, with the soft oak tones having the final, softly spoken say; **b**24 Strathisla at its most tart, busy and mercurial. **58.4%**. *198 bottles.*

· **Cadenhead's Authentic Collection Strathisla-Glenlivet Aged 19 Years** Bourbon Hogshead, dist 87, bott Spet 06 **(89) n**22 stunning esters; not a million miles from a Long Pond rum; **t**23 lush, continuing the rummy theme with a golden sugar edge to both the oak and barley; **f**22 continues its lengthy tale with more of the same and a gradual build up of drier vanilla; **b**22 a strange and delicious beast for rum lovers. **59.5%**. *264 bottles.*

· **Cask Strength Strathisla 1985** bott 4 Jul 05 **(94) n**24 gorgeously floral with a touch of African violet. Honeyed and a tad spicy, too. Shimmering and fabulous; **t**23 wonderfully layered, there is a touch of rich copper adding lustre to the barley and honey. The intensity defies belief, but it is the layering that makes this so special; just so clean, too; **f**23 long, barley-sugar dotted again with acacia honey and that intense copper-effect; **b**24 absolutely everything you can ask for from this great distillery, and a little more besides. **62.8%**. *G&M USA .*

**Coopers Choice Strathisla 1969 Aged 36 Years Single Cask Range**, bott 05 **(95) n**25 a perfection of unblemished sherry, spiced apple tart, scalded raisins, molassed-sweet malt (even slightly Demerara rummy to that effect) and ripe, crushed sultanas. Nose for at least 10-15 minutes before drinking...; **t**23 big, pounding, sweet malt all wrapped in drying hickory and cocoa; **f**23 the enormity of the body continues but in pulsing waves of spice and other nuances of beautiful oak; **b**24 quite awesome: if you want to see what a sherry used to be able to do to whisky, exactly what perfection from Jerez means, then here is a malt that is both a stunning experience and an education to the uninitiated. This is one the likes of which we are unlikely ever to see again. And a primer as to why I often mark modern sherry butts so low. Easily one of the whiskies of the year. **55%**. *Vintage Malt Whisky Co.*

**Coopers Choice Strathisla 1976 Aged 27 Years** bott 03 **(87) n**22 t22 f21 **b**22. What us Surreyites would call a "little darling", were that not now considered sexist. **46%**. *Vintage Malt Whisky Co.*

· **D&M Aficionados' Club Bottling Strathisla Aged 30 Years** cask no. 4215, dist May 76 **(78) n**21 t19 f19 **b**19. Sound nose, but once on the palate starts wheezing a bit and has a furry finish. **43%. nc ncf.** *US by Angus Dundee.*

· **Duncan Taylor Strathisla 1967** cask no.1881, dist Mar 67, bott 15 Mar 06 **(91) n**24 wonderful bourbon depth; leather armchairs, dates and walnuts topped by honeycomb: the way an old malt should be; **t**22 oak shapes the attack, first gently and then permitting toasty barley; drier towards the middle with roast malt. The secret, though, is the gentle honey background; **f**22 maintains its class despite the big oak thanks to a drizzle of maple syrup; **b**23 a glorious old 'un that has gone as far as it can and kept its charisma. A serious must have for bourbon lovers, too! **48.8%**

· **Gordon & MacPhail Distillery Label Strathisla 1960** bott 12.08.05 **(83) n**19 t23 f20 **b**21. The nose suggests a procession of splinters should follow but the grand old distillery retains a surprise smoke package which for about 45 glorious seconds lifts the malt into a glorious wrinkly world. The finish is dry and oak infested, but just hang on to those few glorious moments when you are transported back nearly 40 years and softly peated Speyside barley reigns supreme. **46%**. *US Market.*

· **Kingsbury's New Celtic Strathisla 15 Years Old** dist 89 **(77) n**20 t19 f19 **b**19. Although sulphur has, sadly, got in among the grape, it must originally have been a supreme sherry butt *Japan Import System*

· **Murray McDavid Mission Strathisla 1967** Bourbon/Grenache Banyuls **(85) n**22 t21 f21 **b**21. From the school of exotic fruit via bourbon college. Has just about controlled on the oak, but needed a few fruit salad/black Jack nails to help keep the lid on. **43.6%**. *300 bottles.*

**Murray McDavid Mission Strathisla 1976 (83) n**20 **t**23 **f**20 **b**20. The barley-rich fullness of the body has helped overcome some upfront oak: a genuine tastebud pleaser. **46%**

⁖ **Old Malt Cask Strathisla Aged 10 Years** Refill hogshead no.1497, dist Nov 93, bott Oct 04 **(86) n**22 **t**22 **f**21 **b**21. No complications here: just decent malt with a lovely barley richness. **50%. nc ncf.** *Douglas Laing.*

**Old Malt Cask Strathisla Aged 28 Years** dist Nov 75, bott Dec 03 **(79) n**18 **t**23 **f**19 **b**19. A summer or two too many for this one. Still sparkles with the fabulous mock bourbon on the fruity mouth arrival and offers a glorious mouthful. But the nose and tail show some cracks. **50%. nc ncf sc.** *Douglas Laing.*

**Private Collection Strathisla 1955 (84) n**23 coffee iced biscuit; thick, sweetish sherry and biting spice: classic ye-olde sherry butt and one, in its day, of the very highest order; **t**23 hold on to your seat: the spice latches on to your throat and tastebuds and refuse to let go; the sherry really is heavyweight stuff that is brilliantly balanced between sweet toffee and bitter pear-drops; **f**18 pretty shattered: an oak-exhausted bitterness softened by liquorice; **b**20 full tasting notes because this old timer deserves it. **59.2%.** *Gordon & MacPhail.*

**Provenance Strathisla Over 10 Years** dist Winter 92 bott Autumn 03 **(86) n**21 **t**20 **f**23 **b**22. Brilliant mouthfeel combines well with a delicious finish. **46%. nc**

**Provenance Strathisla 12 Years Old** dist 4 Jun 92, bott 15 Mar 05 **(80) n**19 **t**21 **f**20 **b**20. Malty but disappointingly flat and tired. **46%.** *Douglas Laing & Co.*

# STRATHMILL
## Speyside, 1891. Diageo. Working.

**Strathmill Aged 12 Years** db **(79) n**21 **t**21 **f**18 **b**19. A big malt for a normally light, delicate Speysider. Brilliant spice and rich mouthfeel but fatally let down by caramel-toffee. Strathmill, but not as God intended. **43%.** *Flora and Fauna range.*

**Cadenhead's Authentic Collection Strathmill 12 Years** dist 92, bott Feb 05 **(77) n**19 **t**21 **f**19 **b**18. Off-balance and hot (and that has nothing to do with the strength). There is a wall of early malt, but it's just not up to this distillery's usual excellent standards. **63.9%.** *216 bottles.*

⁖ **Chieftain's Choice Strathmill Aged 11 Years** Refill sherry no. 226, dist Mar 94, bott Apr 05 **(75) n**18 **t**19 **f**19 **b**19. Even this great distillery can't win against a sulphur-nipped cask. **43%.** *Ian Macleod. 702 bottles.*

⁖ **Dewar Rattray Individual Cask Bottling Strathmill 1989 Aged 15 Years** cask no. 10303, dist Oct 89, bott Nov 04 **(94) n**23 wonderful spice buzz tries to disrupt the precision of the barley which in equal measures dishes out cut grass and honey on toast. Fascinating and fun; **t**24 the best body I have seen away from a French beech; the light oils help build the astonishing intensity to the barley. The tastebuds almost swoon under the attack; **f**23 sandalwood and demerara sugar unite for a long and delightful finale; **b**24 how long have I argued that this is an undiscovered jewel? Grab a bottle of this and see what I mean. **63.5%.** *407 bottles.*

**Duncan Taylor Strathmill 1975 Aged 28 Years** cask 1891 **(79) n**18 **t**21 **f**20 **b**20. Some lovely nougat-honey moments, but also hot and ungainly: the make is too delicate to take the weight. **48.7%**

**James MacArthur Strathmill 1992 12 Years Old** cask no. 10908, bott Sep 04 **(84) n**21 **t**22 **f**20 **b**21. Another hot '92 vintage, but this time the sweetness of the malt softens the blow. Overall, chewy, delicious but demanding. **63.4%**

**Old Malt Cask Strathmill Aged 40 Years** dist Apr 63, bott Aug 03 **(89) n**22 **t**23 **f**22 **b**22. On the edge of going over the top, we have almost nerveless brinkmanship here. Quite superb malt and rare to see such a light and delicate dram last the pace. **50%. nc ncf sc.** *Douglas Laing.*

**Old Masters Strathmill 1992** bott 03 **(81) n**19 **t**22 **f**20 **b**20. Real highpropane, heavy-duty Speysider at its very maltiest. **64.2%. nc ncf.** *James MacArthur.*

## TALISKER
### Highland (Island–Skye), 1832. Diageo. Working.

**Talisker Aged 10 Years** db (**93**) n23 Cumberland sausage and kipper side by side; t23 early wisps of smoke that develop into something a little spicier; lively barley that feels a little oak-dried but sweetens out wonderfully; f24 still not at full throttle with the signature ka-boom spice, but never less than enlivening. Some wonderful chocolate adds to the smoke; b23 it is wonderful to report that the deadening caramel that had crept into recent bottlings of the 10-y-o has retreated, and although that extraordinary, that wholly unique finale has still to be re-found in its unblemished, explosive entirety, this is much, much closer to the mark and a quite stupendous malt to be enjoyed at any time. But at night especially. **45.8%**

**Talisker Aged 18 Years** bott 21 Mar 05 db (**94**) n22 a curious delivery of soapy smoke and almost over-ripe nectarines; t23 wonderful, almost unbelievable softness to the arrival: the palate is met by a wall of brown-sugartinged malt and then a gradual build-up of smoke and spice; the middle is infiltrated by just enough oak to confirm its age; f24 a gentle series of muffled explosions as the spice is almost, but thankfully not quite, contained by the richness of the fruit and malt; b25 you can forgive the odd old blemish on the nose: what happens on the palate is a masterful telling of the Talisker tale: all what should be is there and in perfect proportions. Exceptional. **45.8%**

**Talisker Aged 20 Years** db (**95**) n24 t24 f23 b24. I have been tasting Talisker for 28 years. This is the best bottling ever. Miss this and your life will be incomplete. **62%**

**Talisker 20 Years Old** db bott 03 (**93**) n21 t24 f24 b24. This is major whisky for most the demanding of palates. Absolutely no signs of weakness for its age. **58.8%**

**Talisker 25 Years Old** db (**94**) n21 for all its strength, relatively docile and shy with sweet vanilla to the fore and some peek-a-boo smoke and a strand of honey; t24 sweet malt with more than a hint of exotic fruit, and then the most wonderful multiplying of smoke towards the middle, starting off as a suggestion and ending as a statement; oak also arrives in the first nanosecond but is controlled and adds structure; f25 fizzing, buzzing spices on a bed of Old Jamaica fruit chocolate. Soft oils help ensure this is the most faultless of finales...; b24 the nose lulls you into thinking this will be a dull affair. My God! It is anything but! Magical and enchanting. **57.8%**

⠿ **Talisker 175 Anniversary** db (**88**) n23 subtle and restrained by Talisker standards, with plenty of orange peel to complement the unusually even peats. There is a lovely Talisker buzz, though, if not particularly loud; t22 a toffeed, gentle sweetness accompanies the smoke and though some of the trademark peppers and spices escape the creamy clutches, it's all pretty restrained stuff; f21 a return of the marmalade but it's a relatively dull affair; b22 very good whisky? Yes. Great Talisker? No. Someone told me that a prominent website in France gave this 19/20. They could be right: everyone's opinion is valid. (Well, with the exception of one or two self-appointed duds I could name). But I'd happily wager £1,000 to charity that most people taking that lofty score to heart will be greatly disappointed. **45.8%**

**Black Cuillin 8 Years Old** (**78**) n19 t21 f18 b20. Pleasant initial peatless sweet malt but lacking telling depth or cutting edge. **40%.** *The Highlands and Islands Scotch Whisky Co.*

**Old Malt Cask Director's Tactical Selection 1977 Aged 25 Years** bott 03 (**92**) n22 t25 f22 b23. A stunningly structured Talisker showing sweetness in just the right places and a mouth arrival that has to be tasted to be believed. **50%. nc ncf.** *Douglas Laing. 300 bottles.*

**Old Malt Cask Director's Tactical Selection 1982 Aged 23 Years** Sherry dist 21 Jan 82, bott 31 Jan 05 (**79**) n20 t21 f19 b19. The kind of sherry cask which, for me, is just too in your face and over the top. The distillery character has entirely vanished under the grape. **50%.** *Douglas Laing & Co.*

**Old Malt Cask Director's Tactical Selection 1982 Aged 23 Years** dist 1 Apr 82, bott 14 Apr 05 **(84) n**20 **t**21 **f**22 **b**21. Beautifully intense malt, although the oak is a bit too indulgent. **50%.** *Douglas Laing & Co.*

⇌ **The Whisky Fair Artist Edition Talimburg Aged 20 Years** Bourbon Hogshead, dist May 86, bott June 06 **(86) n**24 **t**22 **f**20 **b**20. Breathtaking nose and start, but the cask hadn't read the script. **43.8%.** *Germany. 240 bottles.*

⇌ **The Whisky Fair Talimburg 23 Years Old** Bourbon Hogshead, dist May 82 **(92) n**23 a right old duff up between some vicious peats and bruising oak. Sit back, close the eyes and sense the spectacle...!!; **t**23 some real fire with the peat ripping into the tastebuds with trademark brio; the sweetness feathers perfectly with the developing smoke; **f**23 an oilier than usual finale for this distillery with grist and citrus seeing off the vanilla; **b**23 sheer, undiluted quality ...! **49.5%.** *Germany. 222 bottles.*

# TAMDHU
**Speyside, 1897. Edrington. Working.**

**Tamdhu** db **(87) n**23 grassy, fresh, juicy, youthful, boiled fruit candy, coke smoke: pure Speyside in a sniff; **t**22 very light malt, extremely clean, newly cut grass, deliciously chewy; **f**21 perhaps a hint of toffee but the malty show rumbles on with good weight and late burst of non-peated smoke; **b**21 nothing like as oily as of old; charmingly refreshing, non-threatening and enjoyable. **40%**

⇌ **Tamdhu 25 Years Old** db **(88) n**22 citrus showing now a more orangey based style to the lemon of its youth; **t**22 typically fat and intense; the barley eventually escapes the gravitational pull of the oils to offer a wonderful barley sweetness; **f**21 dried dates vanilla; **b**23 radiates quality. **43%**

**Adelphi Tamdhu 1982 Aged 22 Years** cask no. 2453, dist 82, bott 05 **(88) n**22 something Kentuckian here: the oak takes control and offers liquorice and over-ripe dates; **t**23 young Buffalo Trace? or Heaven Hill? No, Tamdhu at its richest with the controlled sweetness of the oak sitting beautifully with the barley; **f**21 layers of vanilla and cocoa; **b**22 one of those drams that have theoretically gone OTT, but work rather beautifully. **55.2%.** *212 bottles.*

⇌ **Chieftain's Tamdhu 12 Years Old Sherry Finish (80) n**18 **t**22 **f**20 **b**20. The sherry offers a pleasant, fruity weightiness and spice but the natural oiliness of the spirit limits the scope of complexity. **43%.** *Ian Macleod.*

⇌ **Dun Bheagan Tamdhu 12 Years Old Rum Finish (87) n**22 the most distant hint of coal smoke anchors the grist and sprinkled sugar; **t**22 an unusual and level sweetness rounds the barley's natural juiciness; **f**21 soft, slightly sweetened vanilla and barley; **b**22 much crisper than the standard Tamdhu, with a vague, brittle sugariness driving the style: complex and needs some patience. **43%.** *Ian Macleod.*

**Dun Bheagan Tamdhu Aged 14 Years Medoc** dist 90, bott 04 **(80) n**20 **t**21 **f**20 **b**19. Pleasantly spiced and some glowing fruitiness, but never entirely at home with itself. **50%. nc ncf.** *Ian Macleod. 696 bottles.*

⇌ **Dun Bheagan Tamdhu Aged 15 Years Port Finish (84) n**22 **t**20 **f**22 **b**20. Enormously winy and a bit sticky around the gills; the malt has lost the space to breath. Conjures some lovely moments, though. **43%.** *Ian Macleod.*

**Duncan Taylor Tamdhu 1969 Aged 34 Years** cask 7314 **(83) n**21 **t**21 **f**20 **b**21. Oily, malt younger than its years and sweet vanilla; attractive whisky displaying little sign of great age. **42.6%**

⇌ **Harris Whisky Co. Tamdhu Aged 14 Years** cask no. 14085, dist Dec 91, bott Jan 06 **(86) n**23 **t**22 **f**20 **b**21. Another desirable malt from this excellent new company, but would have been at optimum ripeness for picking three or four summers earlier. **58.5%. nc ncf.** *The Harris Whisky Co.*

⇌ **Old Malt Cask Tamdhu Aged 10 Years** Refill Hogshead no. 1925, dist Nov 94, bott Oct 05 **(93) n**23 very delicate peat enhances the clarity of the barley:

genuinely classy; **t**23 the landing would barely cause a ripple on a pond: again the smoke shows early and acts as a buffer for the oily, mouth-watering barley; **f**23 mocha and Demerara offer countless juicy waves in the very long finale; **b**24 this malt in its natural blending colours – and age – knocks the crap out of the majority of fancy finishes. A lesson to be learned? **50%. nc ncf.** *Douglas Laing.*

⋅⋅⋅ **Old Malt Cask Tamdhu 29 Years Old** dist Feb 77, bott Jan 06 **(89) n**21 pretty ripe mango and calvados; **t**23 luxuriant fruit again, especially bitter marmalade, but this time weighed down with a dash of peat and mocha; **f**22 the chocolaty theme continues and even some barley reveals itself for a juicy burst at the death; **b**23 first impression on the nose suggest a spent force; it's performance on the palate is a revelation! **50%.** *Douglas Laing. 211 bottles.*

**Old Master's Tamdhu 1989 15 Year Old** cask no. 8132, bott Sep 04 **(85) n**21 **t**22 **f**21 **b**21. Clean, concentrated malt that is top-grade, slightly simplistic blending fodder. **58.2%.** *James MacArthur.*

⋅⋅⋅ **Provenance Tamdhu Aged 10 Years** dist Nov 94, bott Sept 05 **(77) n**20 **t**19 **f**19 **b**19. Oily and clean. But my God it's dull. **46%.** *McGibbon's.*

## TAMNAVULIN
**Speyside. 1966. Whyte and Mackay.**

**Tamnavulin 12 Years Old** db **(79) n**19 **t**20 **f**21 **b**19. Quite weighty for a Speysider with a deliciously massive malty kick. But missing out on complexity somewhat. **40%**

⋅⋅⋅ **Cadenhead's Authentic Collection Tamnavulin-Glenlivet Aged 14 Years** Bourbon Hogshead, dist 92, bott Sept 06 **(87) n**21 unusual, clipped European style. Hints of tobacco and fruity barley; **t**22 spice kick to the marauding, mouth-watering barley; **f**22 long, leafy and lingering; the freshness of the barley is a constant; **b**22 has the curious tobacco edge found in some mainland European malts. Entertaining. **58.2%.** *258 bottles.*

⋅⋅⋅ **Cadenhead's Authentic Collection Tamdhu-Glenlivet Aged 15 Years** Bourbon Hogshead, dist 91, bott Sept 06 **(79) n**20 **t**21 **f**19 **b**19. Barley emphatic but unusually oil-less and coarse. **58.9%.** *318 bottles.*

**Connoisseurs Choice Tamnavulin 1989 (82) n**20 **t**21 **f**20 **b**21. Delicate and retiring despite the intense malt holding court. For those with a penchant for egg custard. **43%.** *Gordon & MacPhail.*

**Old Malt Cask Tamnavulin Aged 13 Years** dist Nov 90, bott Feb 04 **(88) n**21 some stewed apples go well with the intense barley **t**23 really beautifully weighted malt with just slightly gristy sub-plot allows the barley full play; the oiliness is almost Caol Ila-ish in effect **f**22 slightly fresh bready with gathering vanilla and spice **b**22 thoroughly enjoyable and tastebud provoking. **50% nc ncf sc**

⋅⋅⋅ **Old Malt Cask Tamnavulin 14 Years Old** dist 31 May 91, bott Jul 05 **(91) n**22 Marigolds growing from a bed of grist..??? A mixture of something astonishingly floral and the Porteus; **t**23 a sensational ebullience to the ultra refreshing barley; liquidized grist; **f**23 a tiny speck of smoke and spices make for an amazingly long, chewy finale with not a hint of bitterness or oaky over-excitement. Just lovely...! **b**23 now this is simple and, quite simply, great malt... **50%.** *Douglas Laing. 328 bottles.*

**Provenance Tamnavulin Over 10 Years** dist Autumn 93 bott Winter 04 **(81) n**20 **t**21 **f**20 **b**20. Enjoyable blending fodder. **46%. nc ncf.** *McGibbon's.*

**Provenance Tamnavulin 10 Years Old** dist 9 Dec 94, bott 23 Feb 05 **(88) n**23 coal dust and freshly mown grass; green tomatoes, salt on celery, salady; **t**21 clean, flinty barley; **f**22 sweetens out as the malt really takes a grip; **b**22 clean, hard, yet entertaining and stylish. **46%.** *Douglas Laing & Co.*

**Scott's Selection Tamnavulin 1977** bott 04 **(87) n**22 Seville oranges and hints of bourbon; **t**23 a typical full-frontal Tamna malt orgy; **f**20 tires with some salty oak and spice; **b**22 some decent spices mix up the malt and vanilla fest. **47.6%.**

# TEANINICH
**Highland (Northern), 1817. Diageo. Working.**

**Teaninich Aged 10 Years** bott 18 Feb 05 db **(84)** n21 t21 f21 b21. A very even, ultra-malty, outwardly light dram with some pleasantly lurking spice. **43%.**

**The Bottlers Teaninich 1982 Aged 21 Years** cask 7202 **(96)** n24 t24 f24 b24. Near faultless malt from the type of sherry butt that deserves worshipping. A genuine masterpiece bottled at an age that encompasses the brilliance of both the malt and the cask: one to remember for the rest of your life. **62.3%.** *Raeborn*

⠿ **Cadenhead's Authentic Collection Teaninich Aged 12 Years** Bourbon Hogshead, dist 93, bott Sept 06 **(88)** n21 a curious grape and citrus freshness slightly out of sync; t23 beautiful construction to the intensity of the barley and also those unusual fruit edges; f22 thins out slightly to allow attractive oak dryness; b22 juicy and attractive throughout. **58.3%.** *282 bottles.*

**Cadenhead's Authentic Collection Teninish Aged 22 Years** dist 83, bott May 05 **(71)** n18 t18 f17 b18. Less than perfect sherry influence. **55.3%.** *252 bottles.*

**Connoisseurs Choice Teaninich 1983 (85)** n22 t22 f20 b21. Refreshing and never dull **46%.** *Gordon and MacPhail.*

**Connoisseurs Choice Teaninich 1991 (83)** n21 t21 f21 b20. A basic, pretty simple banana and custard affair. **46%.** *Gordon & MacPhail.*

⠿ **Dewar Rattray Individual Cask Bottling Teaninich 1975 Aged 30 Years** cask no. 9419, dist Aug 75, bott May 06 **(86)** n23 t22 f20 b21. Too old, frankly. But there are some really excellent, highly complex moments to savour. **60.8%.** *486 bottles.*

**Dun Bheagan Teaninich 1984 Aged 18 Years** Sherry wood, bott 11 Sep 03 **(94)** n24 t24 f23 b23. Always had a soft spot for this distillery. But when it appears like this, one can only swoon. Stick your head in a trough of this and you won't re-surface for some weeks. **59%.** *William Maxwell.*

⠿ **Lombard Brands Teaninich 12 Years Old Single Malt (85)** n21 t22 f21 b21. An agreeable, chewy malt with some good barley sugar. But it feels as though someone left the hand brake on... 43%. *Lombards Brands.*

**Part Nan Angelen Teaninich 25 years old (83)** n21 t22 f19 b21. Softly smoked and floral nose, well supported by the early freshness of the banana and malt mouth arrival; very dry, tired finish. **43%**

# TOBERMORY
**Highland (Island–Mull), 1795. Burn Stewart. Working.**

**Ledaig** db **(83)** n18 t22 f22 b21. A tad feinty (especially on the nose), though the extra oils help spread the dense peat. Interesting at this central European strength. **42%**

**Ledaig Aged 7 Years** db **(81)** n19 t21 f21 b20. Young, off balance, off key, though the salty nose might get those more red-blooded bulls among us purring...if you get my drift, lads! Enormously sweet, a hint of feint but quite a lip smacking experience, so to speak. 81/100 for a Ledaig. 181/100 if it's Miltonduff you're after... Meeeoww!! **43%**

**Ledaig Sherry Finish** db **(79)** n19 t22 f19 b19. Sherry fails to master the feints. **42%**

**Ledaig Vintage 1972** Oloroso Sherry Cask Finished, cask filled 21 Dec 72, bott 08 Sep 04 db **(92)** n23 where worlds collide: massive sherry goes head first into solid peat; t24 wonderful: as good an arrival as any sherry cask in the last 12 months, with faultless oloroso caressing the vast expanse of smoky barley; f22 a bit thinner at the death but long and crisp; b23 like a smoky Macallan, but with some extra salt added. **48.5%. ncf.** *1000 bottles.*

**Ledaig 1974 Vintage** db **(77)** n20 t20 f18 b19. Good looking, sweet but overly polite peat and a bit of a stuffed shirt. Bottled some time ago; some bottles still doing the rounds. **43%**

**Tobermory Aged 10 Years** db **(90)** n21 less floral than last year's bottling, a tad more youth but the salt still straps itself to the barley; t22 refreshing malt cleanses the palate; but now much heavier with some substantial oils bubbling up and, again, some youthfulness apparent; f24 the late middle and early finish offers a mind-blowing display of honey, helping cement the lush personality; b23 a slightly different character to previous bottlings with big honey through the middle making up for some under-developed areas. But the whole remains genuinely a great experience. **40%** ⊙ ⊙

⋙ **Berrys' Own Selection Tobermory 1995 Aged 11 Years (89)** n21 ordinary and unassuming; t23 young at first followed by gorgeous honey-salt delivery and then complex waves of bitter-sweet barley; f23 long, with a magnificent saline tail. The vanilla arrives late, but the salt still tenderly dominates; b22 busy, demanding malt full of riches: one that needs three or four mouthfuls before the enormity begins to bite. Seriously scrummy. **46%.**

**Blackadder Raw Cask Ledaig 13 Year Old** cask no. 123, dist 5 May 92, bott May 05 **(94)** n23 but for the soft smoke this would be a bourbon on the nose...; t23 Buffalo Trace with peat: immensely sweet and complex, though the malt unravels more towards the middle; glazed cherries and greengages offer the fruity accompaniment; f24 immeasurable complexity on the finish, with Dundee fruitcake meeting soft peat meeting ancient bourbon; b24 what the hell is this freakish whisky?? Whatever it is, I want a full bottle, not this useless 10cl sample. Magnificent! **46.1%.** *Only 30 bottles.*

⋙ **Cadenhead's Authentic Collection Ledaig Aged 14 Years** Bourbon Hogshead, dist 92, bott May 06 **(91)** n21 crazy, confused nose: a hint of smoke, but it is swamped in an oaky-god-knows-what; t23 a pause on arrival and then a shuddering delivery of sharp intense barley and spice. Again the smoke struggles to find its place; f23 much better once it has calmed and some peat relaxes into the rich vein of barley and then rich, dry cocoa; b24 somewhat anarchic and enormous, this does not follow any pattern. The result, though, is wonderful: it is so diverse, so multi-layered, it is has many of the attributes of a fine blend! **59.6%.** *294 bottles.*

**Chieftain's Ledaig 31 Years Old** sherry hogshead **(94)** n24 strikingly beautiful with a faint smokiness linking arms with the faultless and intense grape t23 like jewels glittering in a golden crown juicy grape fills the mouth as intense, crisp barley and sweeter smoke add wonderfully to the clutter, the start of something spicy; f23 a little toffee intervenes as the grape wins back control for a long, gently peated finale that can be counted over a great many waves; b24 an essay in depth and balance; by far the best Ledaig I've come across since the late 1980s. **54.8%.**

**Dun Bheagan Leidaig Aged 29 Years** dist 74, bott 04 **(94)** n23 cordite, malt and salt: bonfire nights by the sea; t24 just such an extraordinary delivery of peach-infested malt with a slow fuse of peat reek; f23 sweet malt divested of its smoke links with bourbony oak...and a late, inevitable, delivery of peat; b24 the old-styled pre-closure Ledaig to a smoky T.... *Ian Macleod.* **50%. nc ncf.** *396 bottles.*

**Iona Atoll (69)** n16 t18 f18 b17. Young and for all the heavy peating the lack of structure, plus the fact this is not a particularly well-made batch of whisky, cannot be disguised. **40%**

⋙ **Murray McDavid Tobermory Aged 9 Years** cask MM0420, dist 95, bott 04 **(79)** n19 t21 f20 b19. Lacking cohesion, but the marzipan's a treat. **46%. nc ncf.**

⋙ **Old Malt Cask Tobermory 10 Years Old** dist Apr 96 bott Jan 06 **(79)** n18 t21 f20 b20. Fresh and recovers with stimulating barley from a so-so nose. **50%.** *Douglas Laing. 359 bottles.*

**Old Masters Ledaig 10 Years Old (82)** n20 t21 f21 b20. The superbly rich, malty-dark fudge, roasty middle and curtain call makes up for some overly youthful smudges. **56.7%.** *James MacArthur.*

**Old Master's Ledaig 1993 11 Year Old** cask no. 272, bott Sep 04 **(79)** n18 t21 f19 b20. Feinty but with plenty of smoky grist. **56.1%.** *James MacArthur.*

⠐⠂ **Provenance Ledaig Aged 8 Years (86) n**21 **t**23 **f**21 **b**21. Thundering peat but new-makey and a tad feinty. An early juice-fest, though. **46%.**

**Provenance Ledaig 12 Year Old** dist 1 Apr 92, bott 3 Jun 04 **(88) n**20 restrained and shy, the peat fails to find its legs; **t**23 the understated bourbon cask helps amplify the rich texture of the sweet malt and developing smoke; vanilla arrives early towards the middle; **f**22 overlapping of the gentle smoke and drying oak; **b**23 a second-fill bourbon cask, most probably, helps reveal Ledaig in all its glory. **46%.** *Douglas Laing & Co.*

**Signatory Ledaig 1974 Aged 30 Years** cask 3223, dist 25 Jun 74, bott 11 Mar 05 **(83) n**21 **t**22 **f**20 **b**20. Lots of toffee apple and spice ... and oak. **48.7%.**

**The Whisky Shop Ledaig 8 Years Old (88) n**21 burnt toast and smoke; very young gristy malt; **t**22 full-bodied, silky sweet malt dragging with it massive smoky bacon and iodine; **f**23 more balanced and thoughtful, the peat dovetailing with the relaxed vanilla and malt; **b**22 young yet confident, there are no significant feints: the distillery is deliciously back on track! **40%.** *(bottled in store) Scotland.*

⠐⠂ **Wilson & Morgan Barrel Selection Tobermory 1995 Sherry Wood** dist 95, bott 06 **(84) n**20 **t**21 **f**22 **b**21. Some honey on the salty sherry. **46%.**

# TOMATIN
## Speyside, 1897. Working.

**Tomatin 12 Years Old** db **(79) n**21 **t**20 **f**19 **b**19. A much happier and better proportioned dram than of old, having eschewed its sherry weirdness for something a lot more mouthwateringly malty and vibrant. **40%**

**Tomatin 25 Years Old** db **(89) n**22 amazingly green and lively with the vanilla at arm's length; **t**22 mouthwatering, fresh with hints of lychee, syrup of pear and grist; **f**22 astonishingly soft, with a very late, long spice delivery; **b**23 one of those understated, deftly fruited numbers that defy age.

⠐⠂ **Tomatin Malt 25 Years Old** bott 05 db **(88) n**22 pleasant citrus sharpens the straw and sawdust; **t**21 a beautiful, fresh fruit delivery....then goes flat. Revives after a few seconds to sweeten; **f**23 spicy cocoa balances the sweet barley marvellously; **b**22 a worrying fade to this dram and you think it's going to die on you. But fear not: loads of life in this gentle and lucid old timer! **43%**

⠐⠂ **Cadenhead's Authentic Collection Tomatin Aged 17 Years** Bourbon Hogshead, dist 89, bott Sept 06 **(84) n**20 **t**22 **f**20 **b**22. Competent and enjoyable malt though the bitter ill-at-ease finale no way reflects the mouth-watering, tangy barley with a barley sugar theme. **56.4%.** *294 bottles.*

**Connoisseurs Choice Tomatin 1988 (83) n**20 **t**21 **f**22 **b**20. Docile, simplistic malt but with an unusual yeasty nose. **43%.** *Gordon & MacPhail.*

**Duncan Taylor Collection Tomatin 1965 Aged 40 Years** cask no.1903, dist Jan 65, bott Jan 05 **(85) n**22 **t**22 **f**20 **b**21. Either my tastebuds have gone deaf or this is one of the quietest 40-year-olds for a long time. **47.6%**

⠐⠂ **Duncan Taylor Collection Tomatin 1965** cask no. 1904, dist Jan 65, bott Mar 06 **(77) n**18 **t**19 **f**20 **b**20. Hangs on in there thanks to a surprising injection of Demerara and barley sugar. But it's a close call. **45.9%.** *181 bottles.*

⠐⠂ **Norse Cask Selection Tomatin 1989 Aged 15 Years (85) n**21 **t**21 **f**22 **b**21. Exceptionally oily and creamy with massive chewiness to both barley and fruit. Big stuff. **57.7%.** *Quality World, Denmark.*

⠐⠂ **Norse Cask Selection Tomatin 1996 Aged 7 Years (79) n**20 **t**21 **f**19 **b**19. I must be one of the biggest advocates for young malt going. But this narrowly misses the mark, perhaps by being, despite the obvious youth on the nose, a tad too advanced for its years. The big malt thrust on arrival is wonderful, but it is far flatter than one might otherwise expect. Curious. **50%.** *Quality World, Denmark.*

**Part Nan Angelen Tomatin 1962 Vintage** bott 03 **(79) n**20 **t**19 **f**20 **b**20. Though faded and somewhat threadbare in places, there is enough charm left to make this a pleasant enough birthday treat. **42.6%**

Signatory Un-Chillfiltered Collection Tomatin 1989 Aged 14 Years dist 30 Nov 89 bott 18 Aug 04 **(77) n**19 **t**20 **f**19 **b**19. Not from Speyside's greatest-ever cask. **46%**

# TOMINTOUL
**Speyside, 1965. Angus Dundee. Working.**

Tomintoul Aged 10 Years db **(79) n**20 **t**21 **f**19 b19. A fresh, clean, malty dram but leading to toffee fudge simplicity. **40%** ☉

Tomintoul Aged 16 Years db **(88) n**22 a sharper, zestier aroma than before with diced apple where there was once raisins; **t**22 crisp, juicy barley to start and a wonderfully impressive array of sweet notes, becoming heavier and more demerara and toffee in style as it wears on; **f**22 much more bitter yet still within range of those deft sweet notes; some very late, lethargic spice; **b**22 it is always interesting to see a whisky change its shape slightly. No better or worse than before in quality, the emphasis has moved slightly away from the old soothing delivery to something a bit sharper and more pronounced. Yet at times still has all the grace of Peter Osgood in his prime. **40%** ☉ ☉

Tomintoul Aged 27 Years db **(86) n**21 **t**23 **f**20 **b**22. An accomplished malt that shows few cracks despite the obvious great age for a Speysider. **40%** ☉

Adelphi Tomintoul 1967 cask 4479 **(78) n**19 **t**20 **f**19 **b**20. Feels its age. **47%**

Adelphi Tomintoul 1967 cask 4481 **(85) n**22 **t**21 **f**21 **b**21. A malt hanging on for dear life, but succeeds rather attractively where a cask two down the line fails. **47.3%**

🞜 Adelphi Tomintoul 1967 Aged 38 Years Bourbon Hogshead cask no. 4485, dist 67, bott Jun 06 **(79) n**21 **t**19 **f**19 **b**20. A real pity: one of those vaguely exotic fruity whiskies that has gone a couple of summers too long in the cask. Perhaps four or five years ago this would have been a minor classic dripping in honeycomb. Still, here's one for Chelsea supporters: the distillery is owned by a lifelong Chelsea season ticket holder, the Blues between 1924-28 had a full back called Alphonse Adelphi (23 appearances, 0 goals), the club were FA Cup Finalist in '67 under Tommy Docherty (who has been to one of my tastings) and won the Premiership in 2006. When put like that, what's a few splinters...? (Actually, I made one of those facts up. But which one?). **49.2%**. *Adelphi Distillery. 196 bottles.*

Mackillop's Choice Tomintoul 1966 cask no. 5259, dist Sep 66 **(92) n**24 a gentle salt and spice seasoning stirs up the sleepy oak and honey-tinged barley; impressively adroit – in a sluggish kind of way; **t**23 beautiful and dignified mouth arrival with almost malt concentrate heading off the mild hint of fruitcake topped with marzipan: as graceful as you could expect of so ancient a malt; **f**22 a little bit of oak and marmalade bitterness creeps in, but it's all rather oncepaced; **b**23 lethargic, though showing remarkably few wrinkles until the end; leave it in the glass to breathe for half an hour to unleash a lurking degree of sophistication. About as close as you'll ever come to feeling like a tortoise making love.... **43%**. *Angus Dundee.*

Murray McDavid Tomintoul 1973 Mission IV Aged 31 Years **(94) n**23 a fruity scent: melons, passion fruit and papaya, sprinkled with honied malt. Alas, no figs...; **t**24 melts in the mouth, licks around the tastebuds with a demure spice and soft barley sugar; **f**23 gentle spasms of soft oak embedded in a malty frame; **b**24 aaahhhhh...oh,yes! At the end of a long tasting day – week, come to that – this is exactly the kind of dram you need before heading to bed: soothing, gentle, with perfectly understated curves and showing that touch of class, breeding and energy that serves you well under the covers and until the next morning...and just the right age, too.... **46%**

🞜 The Peated Malt Old Ballantruan Speyside Glenlivet **(88) n**21 young, a tad feinty, but with bubbling peat complementing the barley/fruity fudge; **t**22 some serious oils where the cut has been so wide. The peat has little coastal quality but instead imparts a delightful sweetness which clamps itself to every corner of the palate; **f**23 pretty long, skimping slightly on complexity but the developing spices dovetail sexily with the light muscovado-tinted malt; **b**22 I had tasted the new make smoked Tomintoul, but this was my first look at it as the finished article. A Speyside Young Ardbeg, I have heard some day. Hmmm, I think not. The soft feints are still there, as though the stillman has tried to extract every last drop out of the still, but this is malt that ultimately succeeds on its gifts rather than the fortitude of its failings. Worth an investigation. **50%. ncf.**

⁘ **Scott's Selection Tomintoul 1989** bott 05 **(78)** n20 t20 f19 **b**19. Despite the rich malt start, this is otherwise hot and Spartan. Older whisky lovers will remember Glen Scotia being almost identical in taste and style many years ago. **56.9%**

**Vom Fass Tomintoul 8 Years Old (78)** n19 t19 f21 **b**19. Pleasant but frustratingly light and non-committal. **40%.** *Austria.*

**The Whisky Castle Tomintoul 1992** cask 3085, dist 20 May 92 **(87)** n23 brilliantly inventive nose full of marzipan scraped over slightly burnt toast; t22 the early malt explosion heads towards a saltier, more honied middle; f21 a touch of spiced cocoa; **b**21 sound, confident malt. **63.5%.** *The Whisky Castle.*

# TORMORE
**Speyside, 1960. Chivas. Working.**

**Tormore 12 Year Old** db **(79)** n19 t21 f20 **b**19. The influence of then distillery manager John Black is showing: this is now a tolerable malt with a clean, well-defined malty backbone. **40%**

**Blackadder Raw Cask Tormore 14 Years Old**, cask no. 1965, dist 02 Feb 90, bott Nov 04 **(83)** n20 t22 f21 **b**20. Stunningly clean, intense malt that is evenly distributed, but lacks form and complexity. **65.1%**

**Cadenhead's Authentic Collection Tormore Aged 20 Years** dist 84, bott Feb 05 **(76)** n18 t21 f18 **b**19. Harsh, brittle, slightly hot and unforgiving; there is also an attractive sub-stratum of candy and oak which lessens the pain. **60.4%.** *258 bottles.*

**Old Malt Cask Tormore 15 Years Old** dist Feb 89, bott Nov 04 **(81)** n19 t22 f21 **b**20. A real collector's item this: a slightly but unmistakably peaty Tormore that never quite finds its equilibrium, but the attractive smoke helps paper over the cracks. **50%.** *Douglas Laing & Co.*

**Provenance Tormore Aged 10 Years** dist Autumn 93, bott Autumn 04 **(86)** n20 t22 f23 **b**21. A quite excellent Tormore with an appealing natural toffee fade which also emphasises the malt: easily the best expression I have ever seen bottled. **46%.** *Douglas Laing & Co.*

⁘ **Signatory Vintage Single Malt Scotch Whisky Tormore Aged 11 Years** Refill sherry butt no. 920260, dist 11.5.89, bott 20.2.01 **(81)** n19 t21 f20 **b**21. Rich, dense and biscuity by Tormore standards. **43%**

# TULLIBARDINE
**Highland (Perthshire), 1949. Tullibardine Ltd. Working.**

**Tullibardine 1964** dist 64, bott 04 db **(78)** n21 t20 f18 **b**19. Fruity, buttery nose but it's seen a few summers too many: the finish in particular shows its oaky gums. **44.6%**

⁘ **Tullibardine 1964 Best Procurable** Ex sherry Hogshead cask no. 3359, dist 64, bott 04 db **(81)** n22 t20 f19 **b**20. "Best Procurable". Great term – sounds like we are going back to the Glendronach 12...But in truth, this whisky is hanging on by its bleeding finger nails to the very last vestiges of good form. Some exotic fruit – just! – does the trick. Enjoyable and refreshing, all the same and hard work not to enjoy this. **44.6%. nc ncf sc.** *166 bottles.*

⁘ **Tullibardine 1965 Best Procurable** Hogshead cask no. 949, dist 65, bott 05 db **(79)** n21 t20 f18 **b**20. A light and fruity offering for a sherry butt with good countering spice. Rather tired, though. **48.3%. nc ncf sc.** *225 bottles.*

⸭ **Tullibardine 1966** Ex sherry butt cask no. 1112, bott 06 db **(90) n**23 a delightful, mildly rummy, experience; **t**23 beautiful delivery of sherry-soaked barley, then a confused presentation of over-aged oak and dark cherries; **f**21 burnt fudge and cocoa at first, then the toffee really piles in; **b**23 the natural caramels have taken hold and, with the sherry, make for an enjoyable experience but lacking a few features. But if that sounds picky, I have been spoiled by the World Cup edition. In its own right, this is a wonderful stuff. **49.8%**

⸭ **Tullibardine 1966 World Cup Edition** Ex sherry butt cask no. 2132, bott 06 db **(96) n**24 one of those gold nugget, pure magic casks with the marks of Hurst and Moore upon it. Forty years on and the sherry is still lashing it out with rich toffee apple, soft natural caramels and moist fruitcake. Not even the hint of an off note to be had; **t**24 mouth-watering barley...after all this time!! And then layer upon layer of sherry of varying viscosity and intensity. Lush, lithe and latently spicy; the oak is naturally deep but never gets caught out of position and knows exactly when to pass; **f**24 still developing as a touch of Jaffa cake sweetens the vanilla and coating of dark chocolate. After an almost world record number of taste waves for a non-peated cask, very late on even lighter, fresher fruits. There's some peaches running on to the palate. They think it's all over: it is now...; **b**24 this cannot be in any way confused with England's bid to win the 2006 World Cup. Because this has style, charisma, shape, purpose, the ability to attack, plenty in reserve and the unmistakable pedigree and aura of something that can not only match just about anything else in the world, but beat it. Ironically, the label says Butt – which sums up to the English France's World Cup comeuppance. And WC, which nutshells to the French (and everyone else) England's quality of management and play...This is one of the great single cask malts of our lifetime. Sven, being a Caol Ila man, would have no idea how to change tactics to understand this. But the rest of us can see what a World Cup winner this is... **48%**

**Tullibardine 1973** cask no. 2519, bott Sep 04 db **(95) n**24 bizarrely, despite being ex-sherry, the initial outpourings from the nose are those of very old – and extremely good – bourbon! A heady mix of fresh leather, crushed sultana, acacia honey and a distant rumble of ginger. Extraordinary; **t**23 big oak, yet refuses to dominate or spoil and we are back with a curious, and quite beautiful balance between fruitcake richness and a more leathery, profound malt; **f**24 have you ever tasted malt wrapped in such high-class white chocolate? Usually the oiliness can be a downer, but here it works to near perfection, and extends the lingering finale. With layer upon layer of the most sumptuously fruity malt, a kind of high alcohol white chocolate and succulent raisin orgy; **b**24 I slipped this unknown bottling into a few tastings I did around Europe. The result was a succession of spellbound audiences. **47.5%. ncf.** *234 bottles.*

**Tullibardine 1973** db **(91) n**22 no shortage of tangerines, which lifts the groaning oak; **t**23 the fruit influence develops from the first moment with that sublime citrussy freshness forming a wonderful counter-balance to the sawdusty oak; just a hint of spice works well with the dull, dry marzipan sweetness; **f**23 a hint of custard with a sprinkling of cinnamon; **b**23 never quite kicks its shoes off and relaxes like the 47.5% version, but the complexity rises as it works all the harder to hurdle the bigger oak. **49.2%**

⸭ **Tullibardine 1973** Ex sherry butt cask no. 4138, bott 05 db **(77) n**19 **t**21 **f**18 **b**19. Snatched moments of fruit/barley deliciousness, but feeling the oaky strain. **50.2%**

⸭ **Tullibardine 1973** cask no. 2518, bott May 05 db **(91) n**23 a lovely fruitiness: kiwi/passion fruit; **t**23 big barley delivery then quickly into silky fruit; **f**22 playful vanilla; **b**23 big age but very few wrinkles. Quite a treat. **45.7%. ncf.** *239 bottles.*

⸭ **Tullibardine 1986 John Black Selection** Ex sherry Hogshead cask no. 697 db **(95) n**25 blackberries, freshly-made fudge, lichen-covered rocks, fresh grape, mildly burnt raisin. It is all there...and so much more. Some 500 whiskies into the

2007 edition and this is the best nose of the year so far; t24 dark, intense and slightly foreboding on arrival it lightens with a firm injection of toasted toffee and sweetening, intense barley; f22 sherry dulls things down but spices form and crème brulee sees us to the end; b24 there is good reason why John Black has long been one of the most respected distillers in Scotland. Here is liquid, 92 proof why....And though he may not have made it, there's now no doubt he knows what a stunning whisky should nose and taste like. **46%. nc ncf sc.** *255 bottles.*

**Tullibardine 1987** db **(82) n**21 **t**21 **f**20 **b**20. Good, solid, ultra-malty and oily dram that just fails to go up that extra gear. **46%**

**Tullibardine 1988** db **(88) n**20 a touch of honey on the oak-weighted malt; **t**22 good bitter-sweet combination; **f**24 comes into its own as some kumquat and elderberry take on the big malt-oak combo. Very fat and chewy with a fabulous bitter chocolate fudge finale; **b**22 in the great Tulli tradition, the complexity and subtlety demand that you take several good looks before making your mind up about this one. And each re-visit rewards you handsomely. This is big stuff! **46%. ncf.**

**Tullibardine 1991** db **(89) n**22 the seasoning oak does just enough to dry out the vivid malt; **t**20 again the dry oak is very upfront, suppressing the exuberance of malt; **f**24 settles down beautifully at last for a teasing interplay between cocoa and barley with a thin sugar and salt-coated veneer. Silence while you listen to sophisticated manoeuvring of the subtle bitter-sweet balance; **b**23 so delicate, you are frightened it might shatter. **46%**

⠫ **Tullibardine 1992** H/H & ex bourbon barrel vatting, bott 06 db **(89) n**22 young, citrussy and light but with just a glimmer of pre-pubescent bourbon; **t**23 undercooked, but as delicious as a doughy Maryland cookie..and with some of its attributes; **f**22 soft vanilla and crisp barley...for a long time; **b**22 spookily like the original Glenfiddich no age statement bottlings of a decade ago. For those who miss that little gem, this is a must. **46%. ncf.**

⠫ **Tullibardine 1992** cask 1871 (1st fill Bourbon barrel) db **(93) n**24 how do you measure such complexity? Despite the cask type, fruits abound: over-aged apple and simmering citrus plus grassy barley and sultana cake; **t**22 light, dusting the palate with barley and gentle vanilla; **f**24 gets more into its stride with some raspberry jam playing with the late, mouth-watering barley and drier cocoa. Brilliant; **b**23 there are first fill bourbons and first fill bourbons...this one probably came from a cask that held a bourbon for a dozen years or more, so measured is the oaky influence. The nose is whisky heaven. **46%. nc ncf sc.** *270 bottles.*

**Tullibardine 1993 Port Wood Finish** db **(91) n**22 spicy tomato, pork (or should that be port?) scratchings; all very salty and savoury; **t**23 initially dry liftoff, then a warming spread of sweeter malt, followed by a third layer of something fruitier, softer and more estery; **f**22 very long and silky with a late vanilla-malt surge; **b**24 not sure about this one at first, but as your palate acclimatises you realise that the complexity and balance here are of rare depth. **46%**

**Tullibardine Vintage 1993** db bott 03 **(79) n**21 **t**22 **f**18 **b**18. Lots of early spicy fruit and vanilla but, sadly, the caramel dumbs it down and embitters it. **40%**

⠫ **Tullibardine 1993** (H/H & ex bourbon barrel vatting) dist 93, bott 05 db **(85) n**21 **t**22 **f**21 **b**21. Putty-nosed, the delivery is sensuous and gossamer light if a little under-developed. **40%. nc.**

⠫ **Tullibardine 1993 Marsala Wood Finish** H/H cask db **(89) n**22 a sharp fruitiness: sultanas and under-ripe pears; **t**22 a mouthwatering and quite vivid fruit kick adorned with spice; **f**22 lush finale with some extra cocoa to the spice; **b**23 sophisticated, with enough complexity to keep you quiet for quite a few minutes. **46%. nc ncf.**

⠫ **Tullibardine 1993 Muscatel Wood Finish** H/H cask db **(91) n**23 distinctly grapey in that double-edged Muscat style that seems simultaneously both sweet and dry; **t**22 dry and mouth filling with some pounding barley that has somehow had the sweetness removed: strange but very attractive; **f**23 remains bone dry and now some lovely spice begins to tingle the roof of the mouth; **b**23 seriously classy whisky which really does exploit a wine finish to the nth degree. And very different. **46%. nc ncf.**

⠿ **Tullibardine 1993 Port Wood Finish** Portpipe cask no. 15012, bott 06 db **(86) n**20 **t**21 **f**23 **b**22. A bit like a concert orchestra tuning up before four minutes of Beethovian bliss. **46%**

⠿ **Tullibardine 1993 Sherry Wood Finish** Ex oloroso butt cask no. 15004, bott 06 db **(94) n**25 stunning oloroso: one of the best butts I've come across in an age. Resplendent in toffee apple and ripe barley; and if that isn't enough there is also the most sublime bourbon edge. It is hard to ask for or expect more; **t**23 succulent fruit/barley mix, some early vanilla and cream toffee; **f**22 dried dates, busy spices and extra-dry vanilla; **b**24 forget about spitting this one out. A sherry-kissed wet dream. We are getting to the stage where Tullibardine is now becoming one of the true great single malts of Scotland. Even the younger vintages are showing a degree of brilliance some thought impossible. **46%**

⠿ **Tullibardine 1994** H/H cask no. 677, dist 94 db **(88) n**23 relaxed and floral. Citrus undertones cranks up the complexity; **t**22 evenly weighted barley with a delicate flourish; **f**21 thins out slightly complexity-wise, perhaps because of the lethargic sherry; **b**22 such a fragile thing for something that has spent time in a sherry hogshead. **46%. nc ncf sc.** *352 bottles.*

**Connoisseurs Choice Tullibardine 1994 (94) n**24 stupendous aroma of juicy white grape and near-exploding gooseberries, almost too fresh and mouthwatering to be true; **t**24 what a treat! The intensity of the barley mixed with the juicy fruit misses only some soft smoke for harmony ... until it arrives; **f**22 gentle oils roll over the hint of smoke and drying, vanilla-rich oak; **b**24 when they closed this distillery soon after the barrel was filled, I was left scratching my head in perplexity. On this mouthwatering evidence, my belief in this distillery was by no means misplaced...**46%.** *Gordon and MacPhail.*

⠿ **Dewar Rattray Individual Cask Bottling Tullibardine 1972 Aged 33 Years** cask no. 2597, dist Dec 72, bott Jan 06 **(84) n**20 **t**23 **f**21 **b**20. Stylish, especially on the silky fruit/barley delivery, but there is marked fade on nose and balance. Still, an unforgettable dram: a few minutes after tasting this I met for the first time unquestionably the most naturally beautiful English girl I have encountered in over a decade....and also, as fate would dictate, a 1972 vintage. Sadly (for me), Georgia (97) n24 t24 f24 b25 is freshly married to one of the most relentlessly decent guys I've ever known. So I'll have to make do with this. Sigh... **43.1%.** *141 bottles.*

**Old Malt Cask Tullibardine Aged 14 Years** dist Jun 89, bott Jan 04 **(90) n**23 steaming suet pudding with freshly mashed barley malt; clean and sharp; **t**24 astonishingly clean and refined barley of the very top order; the mouth waters as the malt and then sensual spices play havoc with the tastebuds; **f**21 a cross between European bitters and pungent marmalade; **b**22 a refreshing and at times explosive concoction. **50%. nc ncf sc.** *Douglas Laing. 360 bottles.*

⠿ **The Queen of the Moorlands Rare Cask Tullibardine 1994 Edition XV** Hogshead no. 676 **(89) n**23 different from the Tulli of 20 years ago: a heathery job, this, crisper than the norm and excellent oak involvement; **t**21 chaotic barley and oak battle for a foothold; **f**23 beautiful simmering of busy barley and earthy oak. The slow cocoa crescendo is a joy; **b**22 pretty wild, and it has nothing to do with the strength. The delivery is scrambled but finds a rhythm late on and genuinely impresses. **57.7%.** *The Wine Shop Leek and Congleton, UK.*

⠿ **Scott's Selection Tullibardine 1989** bott 05 **(88) n**21 fighting juice, with some real sharp edges to the barley; **t**22 pulsing barley simutaneously heavy and refreshing. Big spice kick towards the middle; **f**23 oils add a lustre to the fizzing malt; the fade is long and classy, offering a delicious dose of Horlicks; **b**22 classically oily Tully: a bit rough and ready, but good slap and tickle. **55.1%.**

## UNSPECIFIED SINGLE MALTS (Campbeltown)

⁖ **Cadenhead's Campbeltown Malt (92) n**22 a touch of cordite to the barley; **t**24 as explosive as the nose suggests as the taste bud-ripping barley produces a pyrotechnic display. Gung-ho spices kick in with the advancing oak; **f**23 long, enormous depth to the spices while eye-watering orange rind completes the complexity; **b**23 on their home turf you'd expect them to get it right...and, my word, so they do!! **59.5%**

⁖ **Cadenhead's Classic Campbeltown (92) n**23 balance at a premium but, my word, the salty liveliness to the malt is worth a few extra minutes to enjoy; **t**24 you can drown in your own saliva, so mouth-watering is the barley; a touch of salt accentuates the enormity; **f**22 pretty mainstream by comparison, with boring ole salty vanilla tucking in; **b**23 what a dram! Must be what they gave Lazarus... **50%**

## UNSPECIFIED SINGLE MALTS (Highland)

⁖ **Adelphi Breath of the Highlands 1985 Aged 20 Years** cask no. 1065, dist 85, bott Jun 06 **(86) n**22 **t**21 **f**22 **b**21. Loses way in middle but sprightly for its age. **54.8%.** *Adelphi Distillery. 176 bottles.*

**"As We Get It" Highland 8 Years Old (92) n**22 way beyond its years with massive oak, but the richness of the malt keeps it young; very bourbony in style except for a clever, latent dryness; **t**24 genuinely astounding in its malt richness, there is a tantalising, mouth-puckering, copper-rich quality; **f**23 long, custard and butterscotch tart sweetness with molten Demerara sugar for topping; **b**23 macho to start, but really one for the ladies. **57.2%. nc ncf.** *Ian Macleod.*

**"As We Get It" Aged 8 Years (85) n**18 **t**23 **f**22 **b**22. Ker-pow, zap, kaboom... Batman stuff for a good punch up on the tastebuds. Despite the distant threat of sulphur, appeals to the Millwall supporter within me ... **58.5%.** *Ian MacLeod.*

**Asda Single Malt** (*see* Douglas MacNiven)

**Auld Edinburgh Highland 10 Years Old** cask AE 003 **(83) n**22 **t**22 **f**19 **b**20. The wonderful marzipan on the nose and enriching malt on arrival is let down slightly by the dull, natural caramel towards the finish. **43%.** *Blackadder.*

⁖ **Cadenhead's Classic Highland (82) n**19 **t**22 **f**21 **b**20. The trace of fusel oil on the nose guarantees a big delivery. Highly malty! **50%**

⁖ **Cadenhead's Highland Malt (90) n**22 malt concentrate; **t**23 ditto for the delivery; soft oaks and apple develop countering complexity; **f**22 hard, fresh barley, vanilla and malt milk-shake all the way; **b**23 does barley come any more pure or intense than this...? **60.2%**

**Celtique Connexion 1993 11 Years Old Highland Monbazillac Finish** dist Mar 93, bott Sept 04 **(79) n**20 **t**19 **f**21 **b**19. An entirely new experience for me, this. Of the thousands of whiskies I've tasted over the years the profile here is unique. Enormously spiced, lots of probing, mouthwatering qualities and yet...and yet.... **43%. nc ncf.** *Distilled and aged in Scotland, and then, maturation being completed in Brittany, sold, as is their right, as "Produit de France".*

⁖ **Celtique Connexion 1993 Coteaux du Layon Finish 13 Years Old** dist Mar 93, bott May 06 **(78) n**18 **t**21 **f**19 **b**20. Highly unusual style: gives the impression of wanting to burst out but seems tied down. The nose is particularly off key. **46%.** *Celtic Whisky Compagnie. Distilled and aged in Scotland, and then, maturation being completed in Brittany, sold, as their right, as "Produit de France".*

⁖ **Celtique Connexion 1994 Quarts de Chaume Finish 11 Years Old** dist Apr 94, bott Mar 06 **(86) n**23 **t**23 **f**19 **b**21. A brilliant whisky at first, frustratingly halted in its tracks by caramel. **46%. nc ncf.** *Celtic Whisky Compagnie. Distilled and aged in Scotland, and then, maturation being completed in Brittany, sold, as their right, as "Produit de France".*

**Douglas MacNiven Highland Highland Single Malt 12 Years Old (84) n**20 **t**22 **f**21 **b**21. Firm and bold throughout with chewy vanilla amid the malt. **40%.** *Asda UK.*

**Dun Bheagan Highland Single Malt 8 Years Old (89) n**22 **t**22 **f**22 **b**23. Further evidence, were it needed, that fabulous, nigh-on faultless single malt whisky doesn't have to come with a two-figure age statement. **43%**

⸭ **Glenalmond Highland Malt** dist 96, bott 06 **(91) n**23 wonderful soft fruit and sugar crystals speckled with grist; **t**23 the sweetness remains, as does the gristy quality; beautifully refreshing and injecting just the right amount of oak when required; **f**22 blood oranges help break up the malt dominances; **b**23 I confess: I have no idea what this is...other than absolutely bloody excellent. **40%**. *The Vintage Malt Whisky Co.*

**Glen Andrew Single Highland Malt 1983** bott 04 **(84) n**20 **t**22 **f**21 **b**21. Just enough body to the sweet malt to see off the encroaching oak. **46%**. *The Highlands & Islands Scotch Whisky Co.*

**Glen Andrew Single Highland Malt 1988** bott 04 **(86) n**19 **t**23 **f**22 **b**22. The rich, honied palate makes a nonsense of the poor nose. **46%**.

**Glen Andrew Single Highland Malt 1991** bott 04 **(83) n**23 **t**20 **f**20 **b**20. Really great nose, this is simple but deliciously refreshing throughout. **43%**.

**Glen Andrew Highland Single Malt 10 Years Old (87) n**22 **t**22 **f**22 **b**21. What a pleasant, fun, unpretentious malt. More, please! **40%**.

**Glenbeg Single Highland Malt (82) n**21 **t**21 **f**20 **b**20. Young, tasty stuff that might be tastier still without the evident toffee. **40%**. *MacDuff International.*

⸭ **Glen Burn Single Highland Malt (81) n**20 **t**20 **f**21 **b**20. Pleasant, gentle if simplistic pub fodder. **40%**. *Glen Burn Distillers*

⸭ **Glenfinnan Highland Scotch Single Malt Over 12 Years Old (84) n**22 **t**23 **f**19 **b**20. Starts beautifully with citrus and rose petals among other delights. But then stops dead just as you pass the middle. Damn!! **40%**. *Celtic Whisky Compagnie, France.*

**Glenfoyle Highland Single Malt Aged 12 Years (82) n**20 **t**22 **f**20 **b**20. Barley sugar on the nose; to taste clean malt, rich in texture and sweetens by the second. The finish is a bit fudgy. **40%**. *Longman Distillers for Tesco UK.*

**Glenfoyle Highland Single Malt Aged 17 Years** dist 85 **(72) n**17 **t**19 **f**18 **b**18. Sweet, ungainly and bitter towards the finish. I know those who love this style of malt – but not my cup of tea, so to speak. **40%**. *Longman Distillers for Tesco.*

**Glen Gordon 1957 Single Highland Malt (88) n**23 beautiful spices dart out from the rich sherry; **t**22 intense from the start, the spice bringing with it dry oak and a hint of liquorice; **f**21 pretty dry and tired around the edges, but still impressive; **b**22 that supreme Glen Grant/Glenfarclas sherry style that displays sheer class despite the age. **40%**. *Gordon & MacPhail.*

⸭ **Glen Torran Highland Single Malt 8 Years Old (75) n**17 **t**21 **f**18 **b**19. Sparkles briefly on arrival, helped along the way by lovely spice. But the caramel on the nose and finish does it in. **40%**. *Roderick & Henderson for London & Scottish International.*

⸭ **Glen Turner Single Highland Malt Aged 12 Years** L616656B **(84) n**22 **t**23 **f**19 **b**20. There's a really lovely malt trying to escape there, but its wings are clipped by some over hefty caramel on the finish. But the nose and delivery sing beautifully and are joyously mouth-watering. I feel a Bible-thumping trip to France coming on....they must realize that because Cognac has spent the last few decades using caramel as a crutch for its own lack-lustre spirit, it doesn't mean to say that Scotch needs it. Absolutely the contrary! Right, down from my soapbox. **40%**. *Glen Turner Distillery for La Martiniquaise, France.*

⸭ **Glen Turner Single Highland Malt Aged 18 Years** L532556A **(87) n**21 **t**23 **f**21 **b**22. A wonderfully clean and characterful malt that lays it on thick with the barley but, again, could do with keeping the caramel at bay. **40%**. *Glen Turner Distillery for La Martiniquaise, France.*

**Ian MacLeod's "As We Get It"** (*see* As We Get It)

⸭ **Inverey Single Highland Malt Aged 12 Years (73) n**17 **t**19 **f**20 **b**17. A complete change in style, and nothing like the "light bodied" whisky described on the label. This is vaguely smoked but is wayward and off-balance, especially on the nose. **40%**. *Burn Stewart for Marks and Spencer, UK.*

**The Lord Balliol Single Aged 20 Years** (*see* Glenfarclas)

**Majestic Wine Warehouse Mature Highland Malt Aged 8 Years (77) n**20 t20 f19 b18. Decent malt struggles to penetrate the caramel. **40%**. *Majestic UK.*

⌐ **McClelland's Highland (82) n**21 t20 f21 b20. Good body and malty sheen. **40%**. *Morrison Bowmore.*

**McClelland's Highland Single Malt Sherry Cask (78) n**19 t21 f19 b19. Silky and succulent but limited complexity. **40%**. *Morrison Bowmore.*

**McClelland's Highland Single Malt Aged 10 Years (76) n**17 t21 f20 b18. A malty, spicy recovery after an indifferent start on the nose. Too sweet in places, though, and the balance suffers. **40%**. *Somerfield Stores UK.*

**McClelland's Highland Single Malt 16 Years Old (79) n**20 t21 f19 b19. A rich dram with lots of chewability. **40%**. *Morrison Bowmore.* ☉

**MacLeod's Highland Aged 8 Years** ( *see* Glen Moray)

**Wm Morrison Highland Single Malt Aged 10 Years (78) n**19 t21 f18 b20. A much duller, less integrated dram from Morrisons than once was. Not worth standing an hour in the queue for this.... **40%** ☉

**Sainsbury's Sherry Cask Malt Whisky 8 Years Old (69) n**16 t18 f17 b18. Why oh why do they do it? Why must they insist on pratting around with sherry butts? Hasn't anyone got the message yet? It's like playing Russian roulette these days. Sulphur-tainted and less than pleasant. What a surprise.... **40%**

**Sainsbury's Single Highland Malt Aged 12 Years (84) n**21 t23 f19 b21. An impressively tempered dram allowing full vent to a complex range of malty-vanilla tones. Cut the finish-deadening caramel and it would be right up there. **40%**. *UK.* ☉

**Stronachie Single Highland Malt Aged 12 Years (82) n**18 t21 f22 b21. An enjoyably busy dram with impressive soft spice follow-through. The nose is so-so, but some decent esters make for a chewy mouthful. Very slightly smoked, but seeing how this is meant to be the spirit of a malt distillery closed in 1928 a little more peat wouldn't go amiss for authenticity's sake. **43%**. *A Dewar Rattray.*

**Tantallan 10 Years Old Highland Single Malt (89) n**22 fresh figs and moist barley, a hint of clove; **t**23 the nose tells you what's coming and there is no disappointment: massive malt surge, mouthwatering and refreshing; **f**21 beautifully textured finish as the barley unites with the light oak; **b**23 the sheer brilliance of this whisky is its simplicity. Limited colouring interference and a severe lack of sherry means that the barley can do as it pleases. And pleases, it does. **40%**. *The Vintage Malt Whisky Co.*

⌐ **Tesco Highland Single Malt 12 Years Old (87) n**22 t22 f21 b22. A quite lovely malt displaying no shortage of character and charm. **40%**. *Tesco, UK.*

**Waitrose Pure Highland Malt (84) n**21 t23 f19 b21. Well weighted with an impressive honey-marmalade thread running through it: wonderful improvement. **40%**. *Waitrose Stores, UK.*

**Waitrose Highland 12 Year Old (80) n**20 t22 f19 b19. Some decent honeycomb and spice poke through the lighter caramel than of yore. **40%**. *Waitrose Stores.*

## UNSPECIFIED SINGLE MALTS (Island)

**Auld Edinburgh Island 10 Years Old** cask AE 005 **(84) n**19 t23 f21 b21. Firm and sturdy, the arrival and deployment of mouthwatering malt on the palate is a joy. **43%**. *Blackadder.*

**Berrys' Own Selection Best Orkney 14 Years Old (89) n**23 complex: a tad smoky but the strands of honey invigorate the malt; **t**23 soft and sensual, there is the most wonderful sharpness to the malt; **f**21 quietens with the spiced oak; **b**22 Orkney honey throughout; seriously high quality. **43%**. *Berry Bros & Rudd..*

**Majestic Wine Warehouses Island Single Malt 8 Years Old (88)** n24 a nigh-faultless, clean, crisp peat aroma dovetails some youngish oaky notes: really fabulous; t22 complex interplay between fresh but mature sweet peat and first-class oak; f20 dies slightly and becomes a little bitter as complexity is lost; b22 although delivered to my tasting lab in May 2003, the bottler's date suggests early November 1999. Surely a malt as deliciously good as this hasn't been hanging around on the shelves that long? **40%.** *Majestic Wine Warehouses UK* ⊙

**Waitrose Island 10 Year Old (92)** n23 ravishing malt wrapped in diaphanous peat; t24 Highland Park, surely, at its most heather-honied. The tastebuds can only purr at the silky caress; f22 flattens slightly but some late citrus tones work well with gathering spice; b23 easily one of the best superstore malts around, and that thanks to a superstar distillery. One very odd thing: the label says, "Allergens: contains maize." How can a single malt whisky contain maize, one wonders? Not changing filters between blends and malts at the bottling hall? Or just legal covering of the backside gone completely "allergens nuts"? **40%.**

## UNSPECIFIED SINGLE MALTS (Islay)

**Ardnave Single Islay Malt Aged 12 Years (88)** n22 t23 f21 b22. If this isn't Bruichladdich, then my name's Ricardo Patermismo. Having gone non-chill filtered, just wish they had the confidence to go non-coloured. **41.2%. ncf.** *Tesco UK.*

**As We Get It 8 Years Old Islay (85)** n22 t21 f21 b21. A teasing malt lacking the peat some might buy it for, but showing fresh, lively barley throughout. **57.9%. nc ncf.** *Ian Macleod.*

**Auld Edinburgh Islay 10 Years Old** cask AE 004 **(88)** n22 as salty and bracing as a fizzog full of fish; t22 really complex malt and barley delivery; f22 long, set in vanilla but with such a wonderful saline depth; b22 not one for the peat-heads. But should you ever get cramp.... **43%.** *Blackadder.*

**Auld Reekie Islay 12 Year Old (82)** n21 t21 f19 b21. For its 12 years remains as raw as the wind that rips down Caol Ila on a January night. Oily and a fraction flat. **46%.** *Duncan Taylor & Co. Ltd.*

⠿ **Auld Reekie Islay Malt (95)** n24 a near-perfect nose with indecipherable complexity, though salt and peat are at the nucleus; t24 breathtakingly scrummy: bitter-sweetness – perfect; peat-levels – perfect; degree of oak weight – perfect; spice injection – perfect. Perhaps could just do with an addition of a surprise element for true perfection; f23 long, chewy; Fisherman's Friends dipped in Camp Coffee and hickory; b24 my last whisky of the day and a dram I shall be tasting all the way to when I clean my teeth. On second thoughts...I'll do them in the morning. Only kidding. But this is a must dram for Islayphiles: true genius. **46%.** *Duncan Taylor.*

**Berrys' Own Selection Best Islay 8 Years Old (82)** n21 t21 f20 b20. Slick and smoky. Look for effect rather than complexity. **43%.** *Berry Bros & Rudd.*

**Blackadder Smoking Islay** cask 2004/2 **(91)** n24 citrus amid the weighty smoke; softly oiled, but not overly so, and still pretty malt; t23 fabulous delivery of fresh malt thumping into the tastebuds with the weight of smoke behind it; f22 vanilla inlaid into persistently mouthwatering barley; b22 a peaty, perky cherub. **55%. nc ncf.**

**Blackadder Smoking Islay** cask 2004/4 **(83)** n21 t22 f20 b20. Entertaining, but the salt and oak can't find the right balance together. **55%. nc ncf.**

**Blackadder Smoking Islay** cask 2004/5 **(80)** n20 t21 f19 b20. Thin, for all the peat, and so sharp and dry your eyes water. **55%. nc ncf.**

⠿ **Cadenhead's Classic Islay (91)** n23 young, light and revealing viperish clarity. The smoky grist is such a delight; t23 gentle oils and lumbering smoke; the sweetness intensifies and displays a liquorice honeycomb quality; f22 soft and delicate with gentle smoky brush-strokes; perhaps a tad too bitter for its own good; b23 I admit: totally baffled by this one. Just can't read the distillery at all: a completely different take on any of them: kind of Ardbegian, but a Lahphraogish blast and a hint of Caol Ila's oils. Yet it is all, yet none of them. Oddly enough, it reminds of Port Ellen when about eight years old. But, obviously, can't be. Classic, indeed! **50%**

⋄ **Cadenhead's Islay Malt (84) n**22 **t**21 **f**20 **b**21. Fat, well enough peated but lacks ambition and complexity. **58%.**

⋄ **Classic of Islay** cask nos. 3910/3911, bott 05 **(93) n**23 brooding peat; dank and salty; **t**24 puckering sharpness to the malt; the dry oakiness meets the lemon-lime citrus with a puffed out chest. The peats play happily meanwhile; **f**23 continues to confuse slightly with the big salty blast and limp sweetness. Soft oils and thick peat abounds; **b**23 there really is only one place on earth this could come from...this is major whisky! **58%.** *The Vintage Malt Whisky Co.*

**Dun Bheagan Islay Single Malt 8 Years Old (91) n**23 **t**23 **f**22 **b**23 when you get faultlessly clean and supremely made distillate, the matter of age seems to matter not. This is outstanding stuff. **43%**

⋄ **Finlaggan Islay Single Malt 10 Years Old (82) n**21 **t**21 **f**20 **b**20. Beautiful citrus notes mildly tempered with smoke: an enormous improvement from the caramel-ruined previous "Lightly Peated" bottlings. **40%.** *The Vintage Malt Whisky Co.*

**Finlaggan Islay Single Malt 17 Years Old (72) n**20 **t**20 **f**15 **b**17. Sweet and chewy, but lots of toffee drowning out the complexity. Can't say I'm that impressed. **46%.** *The Vintage Malt Whisky Co.*

**Finlaggan Islay Single Malt 21 Years Old (75) n**20 **t**19 **f**18 **b**18. Some chewy moments, but overall strangely off-beam. **46%.** *The Vintage Malt Whisky Co.*

**Finlaggan Old Reserve Islay Single Malt (94) n**23 big breakfast fruitiness (Old Preserve, more like), plus nuts and chocolate. What a start! **t**23 fat mouth arrival, more chocolate and ... oh, peat, lashings of it; **t**24 back to fruit again, then a chocolate mousse; all interlocked by peat. Brilliant; **b**24 this is simply awesome. Someone has had access to one or two of the best casks the east coast of Islay has to offer. If you don't get a bottle of this, you'll regret it for the rest of your life. **40%.** *The Vintage Malt whisky Co.*

**Glenscoma Single Cask Single Islay Malt 5 Years Old (85) n**22 **t**22 **f**21 **b**20. One dimensional peat, but great fun. **46%.** *Scoma, Germany.*

**The Ileach Peaty Islay Single Malt (94) n**24 a thick chunk of peat has been dissolved in my glass; **t**24 the oil-peat-barley balance is spot on, as is the bitter-sweet tone: just stunning; **f**23 the peat dissipates slowly to leave a slightly bitterish, oaky influence. But the spices compensate; **b**23 Fabulous stuff, a bottle of which should sit in every household cabinet. A wonder dram. **40%.** *The Highlands & Islands Scotch Whisky Co.*

⋄ **Islay Storm (76) n**19 **t**20 **f**19 **b**18. More of a drizzle. **40%.** *C.S. James & Sons.*

⋄ **Islay Storm 12 Years Old (81) n**20 **t**21 **f**20 **b**20. Some lovely spice emphasis the seaweed kick. Decent oak weight, too. **40%.** *C.S. James & Sons.*

**The Islay Whisky Shop Islay Single Malt Aged 9 Years (85) n**21 **t**22 **f**21 **b**21. Try and convince me this isn't a Bruichladdich.... **43%.** *Islay only.*

**McClelland's Islay Single Malt (87) n**23 **t**21 **f**21 **b**22. What a really elegant and gentle whisky this is, quite unlike what the nose at first suggests. A reflective dram. **40%.** *Morrison Bowmore.*

**MacLeod's Islay 8-y-o** (*see* Lagavulin)

**Majestic Wine Warehouses Islay Malt Whisky 8 Years Old** ("this whisky was aged in oak casks at the distillery") **(85) n**21 **t**22 **f**21 **b**21. This bottling from 2004 and still doing the rounds, apparently, just doesn't have the sheen of the previous one. Quite Bowmore-ish in style. **40%.** ☉ ☉

**Marks and Spencer Islay Single Malt Aged 10 Years (90) n**23 buttered kippers with a side plate of smoked Alpine cheese...all lightly salted; **t**23 just one of those malts which just sings to your tastebuds with a sweet, if smoky, voice; the peat is multilayered and offers many variations of intensity over the course of just a minute or two; f22 dries for the perfect counterpunch with chalky oak; b22 a grand improvement on the old bottling and although this is from Burn Stewart, Bunnahabhain in style this is simply not!! **40%**. *UK.* ☺ ☺

⟨⠿⟩ **Wm Morrison Islay Single Malt Aged 10 Years (84)** n21 t22 f21 b20. A uniform Islay which, though pleasant and initially sweet, fails to trouble the imagination or pulse. **40%**. *Wm Morrison Wines & Spirits Merchant.*

**The Pibroch 12 Years Old Islay Single Malt (87)** n22 t21 f22 b22. This was the name I wanted to launch my own Islay single malt brand with, some 20- odd years ago. But I have been beaten to it: damn! This is classical Caol Ila-style: oily with the peat subdued but still pretty rich. A very evocative dram in many ways. **43%**. *The Highlands & Islands Scotch Whisky Co.*

⟨⠿⟩ **The Queen of the Hebrides Islay Single Malt Whisky (85)** n22 t22 f20 b21. Big, rolling fat peats: any fatter and it'd be declared obese. **40%**. *Available at The Wine Shop, Leek, and The Islay Whisky Shop.*

⟨⠿⟩ **Smokehead Islay** db **(92)** n24 even iodine doesn't come more iodiney than this. Also salty, youngish and bracing; t23 sweet grist at first, moves into sharp citrus and back into malt; f22 the complex peats begin to fade as vanilla and caramel kick on; b23 this company does this kind of whisky so well. A little gem. **43%**. *Ian Macleod.*

⟨⠿⟩ **Tamifroyg Islay Single Malt Scotch Whisky: The Vaccine to Bird Flu (91)** n23 Few Islays so largely depend on dense citrus for the lead role, though the underlying peat possibly stretches back to the ice age. Big, but subtle...sort of; t23 remains fruity, but massive oils dredge up some serious oak and praline; f23 succulent oils sweetened by weakened mollased sugar and decent natural caramels; a slight raspberry jam sharpness titillates the tastebuds in the mid of this profound heaviness; b22 from the guys who brought you the original Papal Ardbeg, another enormous Islay that could – and if not, should - have been named after one of the people most seriously dear to my heart, the Islayphile extraordinaire Tammy Secor (please, darling, say yes to marrying me in my next life). This, very sensibly, has been brought out to ward off bird flu, though several glasses of this would probably mean that you would neither know – or indeed care – if you had it or not. Curiously, after I wrote these notes I was pointed in the direction of the website of the Lindores Whisky Society: a conclave of 12 noble souls in northern Belgium, I think, who have embraced the Jim Murray scoring system with a zeal demanding official blessing. I'm proud to report that they, like me, scored 91, though they have given 23-23-22-23 (as opposed to 23-23-23-22). However, they have spotted on the nose; "sqaushed (sic) strawberries...fine horsemeat..horseleather." Boys, it is nearly 25 years since I lived with a French girl, so I will bow to your Continental in-knowledge. But compared to you, and the amassed genii of Regensburger Whisky Club, I am not worthy... **49%**. *Regensburger Whisky Club. 26 bottles.*

⟨⠿⟩ **Tesco Islay Single Malt 12 Years Old (89)** n23 mottled peat vying with a salty, tangy barley and dryish toffee; t23 sumptuous and mouth coating, the sweetness threatens to overload but holds back. Some toffee notes dig in; f21 varying degrees of smoke, happily embracing the gathering oak; b22 timeless whisky: this is like going back 25 years and onto the island when the peat was thick and caramel was thicker!! Had this been at natural colour, I think we'd have a malt closer to about 92: this has come from some wonderful casks. **40%**. *UK.*

**Waitrose Islay Aged 10 Years (88)** n23 head-thumping, unforgiving peat with a lovely salty depth; t22 sweet, silky and oily; f21 complexity come to a standstill under the massive oil; b22 unquestionably Islay this time **40%**

⟨⠿⟩ **W&M Born on Islay House Malt** casks no. 655-672, dist Jan 95, bott Jan 04 **(71)** n20 t18 f16 b17. Unusually dull and disappointing from what is normally an excellent independent bottler. Rightly or wrongly, one detects the evil, nullifying hand of caramel at work here. **43%**. *Wilson & Morgan Barrel Selection.*

## UNSPECIFIED SINGLE MALTS (Lowland)

**Auld Edinburgh Lowland 10 Years Old** cask AE 001 **(79) n**18 **t**22 **f**19 **b**20. The nose never quite settles but the body is clean, intensely malty and washes over you. **43%**. *Blackadder.*

**Berrys' Own Selection Best Lowland 12 Year Old (85) n**23 **t**22 **f**19 **b**21. Easy drinking stuff. **43%**. *Berry Bros & Rudd.*

⁕ **Cadenhead's Classic Lowland** Bourbon wood **(82) n**19 **t**21 **f**21 **b**21. Much juicier and fortified with rich barley than the nose suggests. **50%**

⁕ **Cadenhead's Lowland Malt (90) n**22 delightful division between bourbon and citrus; **t**23 again the citrus rattles the taste buds with grassy alt not far behind; **f**22 soft waves of tidy vanilla sprinkled with demerara; **b**23 one of the best lowlanders around. Fabulously fresh! **56.4%**

**Dun Bheagan Lowland Single Malt 8 Years Old (87) n**19 **t**23 **f**23 **b**23. Just shows you: don't read a book by its cover ... I think it has to be said that the present Dun Bheagan regional range is about the best I have ever encountered outside Classic Malts. Knocvks you off your seat! **43%**

**McClelland's Lowland Single Malt (85) n**21 **t**22 **f**21 **b**21. Never spectacular, this is always just very good whisky with a steady development of complexity: in others words, a lovely dram. **40%**. *Morrison Bowmore.* ☉

**MacLeod's Lowland Single Malt Aged 8 Years** (*see* Auchentoshan)

## UNSPECIFIED SINGLE MALTS (Speyside)

**Asda Speyside Single Malt 12 Years Old (81) n**19 **t**21 **f**20 **b**21. A vast improvement on previous years though the aroma hints at some casks whose next stop are flower pots; good verve to the beautifully balanced barley, though. **40%**. *Douglas MacNiven for Asda.* ☉☉

**Ben Bracken 12 Years Old (88) n**20 **t**20 **f**19 **b**20. Engagingly light with a real malty fizz. A tobacco hint amid the spice and cocoa. **40%**. *Clydesdale Scotch Whisky Co.* ☉☉

**Celtique Connexion** (*see* Unspecified Single Malts (General))

**Celtique Connexion 14 Years Old 1990 Speyside Cadillac Finish** dist May 90, bott Oct 04 **(76) n**21 **t**19 **f**17 **b**19. A shrug of the shoulders here, guys. Pardon! But for me there is just too much oak dominance. **43%. ncf.** *Distilled and aged in Scotland, and then, maturation being completed in Brittany, sold, as is their right, as "Produit de France".*

⁕ **Celtique Connexion 1990 Armagnac Finish 15 Years Old** dist May 90, bott June 05 **(85) n**20 **t**22 **f**21 **b**22. I don't know for certain if these guys use caramel or not. But three out of three of their malts have witch's tit finales, though this one does retain some late pulse. Frustrating, especially if avoidable. Especially in this case where the mouth-watering delivery and early spices are superb! **54.4%. nc ncf.** *Celtic Whisky Compagnie. Distilled and aged in Scotland, and then, maturation being completed in Brittany, sold, as their right, as "Produit de France".*

**Glen Darbach Single Speyside Malt Aged 12 Years (86) n**21 **t**23 **f**20 **b**22. A much better fist than the boring disaster this brand used to be. Ticks all the expected boxes for a Speysider. **40%**. *Burn Stewart for Marks and Spencer, UK.* ☉☉

**Glen Marnoch Aged 12 Years (77) n**20 **t**20 **f**18 **b**19. Pleasant, but the over indulgence in caramel limits its scope badly. **40%**. *Alistair Graham for Aldi Store, UK.* ☉☉

**Glen Parker** (*see* GlenParker)

**GlenParker Speyside Single Malt (72) n**18 **t**19 **f**17 **b**18. Oh dear. Has lost some of its old charm: this is an adolescent whose voice is breaking – entirely off key and mildly irritating. The liberal dose of caramel exacerbates matters. **40%**. *Angus Dundee Distillers plc.* ☉☉

**Glinne Parras Single Speyside Malt Aged 12 Years (86) n**22 **t**22 **f**21 **b**21. Solid, chewy, well-made whisky. **40%**. *Eaux de Vie.*

**Jenners Speyside Aged 10 Years** bott lott 03/10013 **(92) n**22 big bourbon influence with acacia honey on slightly singed toast; **t**23 sublime mouthfeel to the sweet, confident, blemish-free malt; a touch of muscovado sugar sweetens the early vanilla; **f**23 long, with a touch of friendly spice to balance the continuing gristy sweetness. More toast on the finale and this time with some marmalade; **b**24 an excellent and massively impressive Speysider that keeps its shape and richness throughout. Complex and wonderfully structured. Yet another reason to visit Edinburgh.... **40%.** *Jenners, Edinburgh.*

**Lochruan Speyside Single Malt Scotch Aged 12 Years (86) n**21 **t**22 **f**21 **b**22. A charming malt with good weight despite the citrus sub-stratum. I guess from the finish this has been coloured: would have been a belter in natural form. **40%.** *Leith Distillers for Tesco UK.*

**McClelland's Speyside (76) n**19 **t**19 **f**19 **b**19. A distinct improvement on the last bottling of this I came across. But the charisma bypass was still a complete success. **40%.** *Morrison Bowmore.* ⊙ ⊙

**McClelland's Speyside Single Malt Aged 10 Years (73) n**19 **t**19 **f**17 **b**18. Surprisingly heavy for the region; oily and rumbustious but ultimately lacking the aplomb the region desires. **40%.** *Exclusive to Somerfield Stores UK.*

**MacLeod's Speyside Aged 8 Years** (*see Glenfarclas*)

**The Queen of the Moorlands Aged 12 Years (89) n**23 toffee apple and multiple layers of molassed malt; **t**23 just so big and chewy; again with thin, tasteful layers of brown sugar coating the malt; **f**21 spices and developing oak; **b**22 what a lovely whisky for a small shop to have as their own label. Some serious quality here. **40%.** *The Wine Shop, Leek, UK.*

**Wm Morrison Speyside Single Malt Aged 10 Years (85) n**21 **t**22 **f**21 **b**21. A lighter, more honeyed affair than previous years. **40%.** *Morrison's, UK.* ⊙ ⊙

⋯⋰⋯ **Pebble Beach 12 Years Old (78) n**19 **t**20 **f**20 **b**19. The malt fits with the allusion to something rounded and smooth. But I also presume it's a beach to fall asleep on while sucking a toffee... **43%.** *Lombard Brands.*

**Sainsbury's Single Speyside Malt Aged 12 Years (78) n**18 **t**21 **f**19 **b**20. Above-average fruitiness and sweetness. **40%.** *UK.*

**Sainsbury's Speyside Single Malt Matured for 15 Years Claret Finish (87) n**23 **t**23 **f**20 **b**21. An intriguing and on the whole pretty enjoyable dram. To be churlish and technical, could do with a little tightening up: that said, no way I'd say, "No." if offered a second one. Fun and fruity! **40%.** *UK.*

**Sainsbury's Speyside Single Malt Matured for 15 Years Cognac Finish (88) n**22 complex; light, busy, floral tones with sound vanilla; **t**21 quite a biting, nippy arrival that seems a little ill-at-ease; **f**23 now finds its path with a luxuriant, never-ending bathing of cocoa over myriad fruity-floral notes; **b**22 for a moment it appears the Cognac barrels have thrown this out of sync, but its recovery is stunning. **40%**

⋯⋰⋯ **Tesco Speyside Single Malt 12 Years Old (88) n**21 some stressed oak is becalmed by subtle smoke and firm barley; **t**22 outstanding delivery with a sheen to the barley as it glides over the palate; the spices mass as the oak concentrates; **f**22 a gentle return of smoke sits comfortably with the cocoa and barley; **b**23 no shrinking violet here: a Speysider with a touch of attitude – and class. **40%.** *Tesco, UK.*

**Waitrose Speyside Aged 12 Years (76) n**19 **t**20 **f**18 **b**19. Another Waitrose single malt that, according to the matter-of-fact label, "Contains maize" – rather than the more precautionary "May contain maize". More intriguing than the whisky, frankly. Because despite some pleasant passages this is just not a heart-stopper. Unless you are allergic to maize, of course.... **40%**

## UNSPECIFIED SINGLE MALTS (General)

**Celtic Whisky Malt Scotch 12 Years Old (89) n**21 some quality oak sits comfortably with the rich barley; **t**22 crisp, clean barley which develops in a honied direction; **f**23 more honey and then a gradual increase in spicy oak; **b**23 genuinely first-rate whisky of a Highland-meets-Perthshire style, massive complexity and balance. **40%.** *From the Celtic Spirit Company – that's the Celtic race: not to be confused with football club. Although doesn't say so on the label, I can confirm this is a single malt.*

**Celtique Connexion 1990 Double Maturation Affinage En Fut De Sauternes** bott 03 **(87) n**22 **t**23 **f**21 **b**21. A clean malt with no shortage of charming flavour development. **43%.** *Celtic Whisky Compagnie.*

**Cu Dhu** (*see* Speyside Distillery)

**Fiskavaig 1977 Vintage 27 Year Old (90) n**23 sharp, grassy, and lingering peat; **t**22 smoky, yet with plenty of young malt that defies the age statement completely; **f**22 two left jabs and peaty uppercut leave you floored; **b**23 what the hell is this stuff? From Islay almost certainly. But the intensity of the pure cocoa (75% at least) leaves you gasping. **51.3%.** *The Whisky Shop.*

**Glen Shira** (distillery, age unspecified) **(77) n**19 **t**21 **f**19 **b**18. A young, barely pubescent dram full of refreshing, uncomplicated but mouthwatering malt. Without the caramel, which guarantees a cream-toffee finish, it would have been a stormer. **40%.** *Exclusive to Asda UK.*

**Glentromie 17 Years Old** (distillery unspecified) **(68) n**19 **t**17 **f**16 **b**16. Charisma-free. **40%.** *Speyside Distillers. Not from own distillery.*

**Stonefield Castle Hotel Single Malt Whisky (84) n**21 **t**22 **f**20 **b**21. A very pleasant, undemanding, gently-spoken dram that offers the most surprising prune-stone, fruit-spirit quality. **40%.** *Tarbert, Argyll.*

⠿ **Wilson & Morgan Barrel Selection House Malt** cask nos. 8586-8589 **(92) n**24 beautifully salted and coastal peats with enough youth to remain refreshing and profound; **t**22 lime juice lightens the smoke; **f**23 returns to a more gristy sweetness and depth; **b**23 a high quality (presumably) Islay of distinctive, compelling clarity. **43%**

## Scottish Vatted Malts
## (also Pure Malts/Blended Malt Scotch)

⠿ **100 Pipers Aged 8 Years Blended Malt (73) n**17 **t**19 **f**18 **b**19. All those outstanding Speyside distilleries and we get this...??? **40%.** *Chivas Brothers.*

**Anchor Bay Pure Malt Scotch Whisky (81) n**20 **t**22 **f**19 **b**20. A significantly improved brand with much fresher, more stark barley....though I wish they'd do something about that furry finish. **40%.** *Lombards Brands.* ☉ ☉

**Asda Islay Pure Malt 10 Years Old (82) n**21 **t**22 **f**19 **b**20. Sweet, chewy, excellent mouth arrival and fresh. Can simply do with losing the toffee at the death. **40%.** *Douglas MacNiven for Asda.* ☉

**Ballantine's Pure Malt 12 Year Old (91) n**24 a spicy mixture of honey and light smoke; **t**23 stupendous mouthfeel with a fruity outline unable to quite get the better of varying malt tones, including a gentle peaty one; **f**21 the oak has been compartmentalised to the finish and shows well with a late gristy, peaty surge but dies as some unwelcome toffee arrives; **b**23 a real mixed bag with every conceivable malt type taking the lead role, if only at times momentarily. Docked points for the toffee finish, but whoever put this together knew exactly what they were doing. Excellent blending, guys! **40%.** *Allied.*

**Baxter's Malt (88) n**21 simple, clean, uncluttered fresh malt; **t**22 beautiful mouth arrival, refreshing clean malt; **f**23 outstanding development continuing on the same theme; **b**22 no great age to this but it's all about classic, soft Speyside character. Lovely stuff. **40%.** *Gordon & MacPhail for Baxter's. Found in the famous soup company's shops on Speyside and at Aberdeen Airport.*

**Baxter's 8 Years Old Malt (83) n**20 **t**22 **f**20 **b**21. Good weight and oil with some citrus on the malt. The oak adds a late dash of bitterness. **40%.** *Gordon & MacPhail for Baxter's. Found only in the Baxter's shops at Aberdeen Airport and at Fochabers, Speyside.*

**Bell's Special Reserve Pure Malt (87)** n22 t23 f20 b22. Absolutely excellent vatting, let down only by the pointless caramel denuding the gold leaf from the edges. Another example of this style of whisky coming out of the doldrums with some very careful and skilful mixing. Shame about the caramel, though. **40%**

**Berrys' Best Islay Vatted Malt Aged 8 Years (82)** n20 t21 f20 b21. Smoky, raw, sweet, clean and massive fun! **43%**. *Berry Bros & Rudd.*

**Berrys' Own Selection 25 Year Old Blue Hanger Second Limited Release (90)** n24 gooseberries and apricot on a butterscotch tart; t23 busy, spicy arrival with some chuntering oak trying to outdo the malt. Mildly estery and oily weight with a lighter, playful thread of honey; f21 vanilla and manuca honey; b22 a majestic and seamless transformation from blend to vatted malt. **45.6%. nc ncf.**

**The Big Smoke 40 Islay Malt (83)** n20 t21 f21 b21. Keeps it sweet, simple...and very smoky! **40%**. *Duncan Taylor.*

**The Big Smoke 60 Islay Malt (86)** n20 t23; f22 b21. Big and bolshy, the peats remorselessly thump anything in their path **60%**. *Duncan Taylor.*

**Black Ribbon 10 Years Old Lowland, Highlands and Islay (78)** n20 t21 f18 b19. The promising mouthwatering malt vanishes under a welter of caramel blows. **40%**

**Black Ribbon 21 Years Old Highlands and Islay (83)** n22 t22 f19 b20. Starts with a brilliantly chewy, deliciously spiced sweetness, but fades fast. **43%**

**Blairmhor 8 Years Old (84)** n22 t22 f20 b20. Reconstituted and a wonderful improvement. Some lovely smoke on the nose and excellent weight to mouth arrival, but the caramel flattens it latterly. **40%**. *Inver House.*

**Cardhu Speyside Pure Malt Aged 12 Years (88)** n22 superbly complex: no shortage of citrus and apple and pear notes to complement the deep malt, but there is also significant, almost dry, chalky oak – far more than the original Cardhu single malt – taking it off in a vaguely bourbony direction. Some spice buzz, too; t23 much more punchy and spicy than its single malt predecessor with some weighty cocoa arriving early as the oak bites. The intensity and mouthfeel of the chewy, sweet malt is exceptional, the cleanliness awesome; f21 the cocoa remains constant with a soft drying from the earlier sweet barley; a fraction too much oak at the death; b22 this controversial and discontinued vatted malt, using the established name of a working distillery, caused ructions in the industry and is now collectors' item. **40%**

**Century of Malts (94)** n23 t24 f23 b24. Tragically, a brand now discontinued: certainly the most complete vatted malt I have come across in my lifetime. Having malts from 100 distilleries is one thing, vatting them in harmony for near perfect weight and texture is something else. This was probably Colin Scott and his team's finest moment: an art form and treasure. By the way, the little book that comes with it is a work of genius, too ... **40%**. *Chivas.*

**Clan Campbell 10 Years Old Vatted Malt (83)** n20 t22 f20 b21. Fruitier, less feisty than the blend, as one might expect. But much less fun! Competent as drinking malt all the same. **40%**. *Chivas.*

**Clan Denny (Bowmore, Bunnahabhain, Caol Ila and Laphroaig) (94)** n24 mildly awesome: a mixing of varying grists – peaty, but on so many planes...; t23 still on the grist blitz with a powdery smokiness working well with a veiled honey theme; f23 dries out at first but a smoky butterscotch balances things out; b24 a very different take on Islay with the heavy peats somehow having a floating quality. Unique. **40%**. *Douglas Laing.*

**Compass Box Eleuthera** bottle identification L3350 **(85)** n21 t22 f21 b21. Enjoyable but clumsy by usual Compass Box standards. **46%**

**Compass Box Eleuthera Marriage** Married for nine months in an American oak Hogshead **(86)** n22 t22 f20 b22. I'm not sure if it's the name that gets me on edge here, but as big and robust as it is I still can't help feeling that the oak has bitten too deep. Any chance of a Compass Box Divorce...? **49.2%**. *Compass Box for La Maison du Whisky in commemoration of their 50th Anniversary.*

**Compass Box Eleuthera All Malt** (first bottling with star compass points and orange/brown label, called "All Malt".) **(93)** n23 t24 f22 b24. Quite simply, one of the most complex and truly magnificent vatted malts of all time. A collector's piece. Not least because this was the first bottling to show that Compass Box was a brand and company worth keeping a very close eye on. They have rarely let us down in the intervening years. **46%. ncf nc.**

**Compass Box Eleuthera Vatted Malt** (second bottling (2003) with mauve central illustration, called "Vatted Malt".) **(87)** n22 t21 f22 b22. A slightly smokier, oilier version. Delicious, but lacking that previous touch of genius. **46%. ncf nc.**

**Compass Box Juveniles (95)** n23 t23 f24 b25. They've done it again!!! Almost an essay in delicate, sweet malt at its most complex. This is Scotch at its most erotic; a wand has been waved over these six casks. Simply fabulous. **44%**

**Compass Box Juveniles** Lot Code L5021 **(93)** n23 fresh, grassy and salivating. There is a touch of soap, but in almost attractive proportions, which adds to a subtle, scented fruitiness; t24 just so light – almost flimsy – in body, yet with oily malt sturdy enough to bless it with a sweet charm; a touch of passion-fruit adds lustre; f23 soft, playful spices arrive quite early and intensify, and then layers of rich cocoa; b23 so subtle you won't get the full picture until the fourth of fifth mouthful. Less honied than the last bottling and with more stealthy weight towards the finish. But just fabulous all the same...! **43%. nc ncf.**

⋯ **Compass Box Magic Cask Limited Edition** bott Oct 06 **(89)** n20 confused, jaded and just a bit top-heavy with fruit; t24 almost liqueur-like in body: more silk than a High Court Judge riffling through a Madame's underwear draw; distinctly intense malt but the juicy, grapey fruits are such a treat; f23 magically buzzing spices kick in and add layers to the sultana; b22 disappointing nose, but beyond that you enter a world of unbridled, peatless enormity with a distinct sma' still richness. What a glassful!! **46%.** *480 bottles for the LCBO, Canada.*

**Compass Box Monster (89)** n22 the oily peat thuds unambiguously against the nose; t23 massive. The peat is sweet and oiliness keeps it crushed to the roof of the mouth; f22 drier now as some oak kicks in; b22 there has to be some Caol Ila in there somewhere amid all that oil. And may be Lagavulin for all the depth? Massive ... a monster!! **54.9%.** *Park Avenue, New York.*

⋯ **Compass Box Oak Cross Malt Scotch Whisky** bott 06 **(94)** n23 the spiced French oak has been cleverly tamed thanks to an understated lustre to the barley; t24 such delicate fruit, not entirely unlike Payne's Raisin Poppets, then an oak surge towards the middle; throughout subtle spices pop and tickle around the palate. The oak/spice/barley/fruit ratio is just about perfect; f23 some wonderful semi-dry marzipan at the death is cloaked in cocoa; b24 a vatting of exceptionally high class malts which have embraced the oak without ever yielding to it. Superb! Ignore entirely the instructions on the back to add ice, water or whatever: this is genius whisky that must be drunk exactly as nature intended. **43%. nc ncf.**

**Compass Box The Peat Monster** Lot Code L4337 **(88)** n22 someone's taken the fangs out: a monster breathing relatively little smoke, let alone fire! That said, the delivery of the peat is deft and suggests genuine quality; t22 the oily peat arrives first and is then backed up by a stunning surge of pure barley....barleysugar, even. A mouthwatering monster! f22 the density of the peat thickens, butit's still a very subdued and well-mannered experience; b22 this ain't no monster...it's pure pussy! **46%. nc ncf.** ☺

⋯ **Compass Box The Spice Tree Inaugural Batch (93)** n23 a thick nose, almost offering the botanicals of gin but without the juniper. Oak influence is all-consuming, the barley acting as a thinning agent for the pungent spices and vanilla; t23 immediately warming yet almost syrupy-sweet; the accent is on spiced orange (I think I can see where they are coming from cinnamon-wise, but not cloves); f23 such is the intensity and enormity, it is hard to pick out individual flavour: we have a marriage of styles in which the key is beautiful, bitter-sweet integration; **b**24 the map for flavour distribution had to be drawn for the first time here: an entirely different whisky in shape and flavour emphasis. And it is a map that takes a long time to draw... **46%**. *4150 bottles.*

⋙ **Compass Box The Spice Tree** 2nd release, Apr 06 **(94)** **n**22 lighter, more citrussy gathering of complex aromas; barley is refreshing and grassy; **t**24 astonishing dexterity to the sweetness and though well oiled, not quite as thick in body as the first bottling. But this allows the honeyed elements to flourish. And with aplomb...; **f**24 spicy, but not as fizzing as the inaugural bottling with a roasty honeycomb flourish; **b**24 I think this probably wins it over the first bottling, but only on account of the better finish helped along by slightly more sympathetic oak. Either way, make the most of either or both of them. They have been outlawed as illegal Scotch by the industry's association because of the use of oak staves. How dare you produce whisky like this, Compass Box? You are a disgrace to whisky: what were you thinking of? You should have darkened and flavoured it with caramel, instead. Or even a sherry butt humming with sulphur. **46%**

**Co-operative Group (CWS) Blended Malt Aged 8 Years** **(82)** **n**19 **t**22 **f**21 **b**20. With its intense syrup thrust, one of the sweetest malts on the market: a touch of spice and vanilla add welcome relief. Book your visit to the dentist after this one...! **40%**. *Watson & Middleton for Co-operative Group (CWS).* ⊙ ⊙

**Douglas MacNiven Islay Pure Malt 10 Years Old** **(82)** **n**21 **t**21 **f**20 **b**20. Chunky, raw, green and young for its age but unmistakably from just one particular place in the world. **40%**. *Asda UK.*

**Dram House Age 12 Years** "Vatted from 12 Distilleries" **(86)** **n**20 **t**22 **f**22 **b**22. An almost perfect oiliness and barely perceptable smokiness helps see this big 'un over the big oak: session stuff of frightening moreishness. **46%**. *ncf. John Milroy.*

**Driftwood Highland Pure Malt Scotch Whisky** **(82)** **n**20 **t**22 **f**19 **b**21. Just like driftwood, this is hard to get a fix on. One minute you think you have it, then it disappears for a bit. Certainly a better mixing than two or three years back, with a curiously smoky edge to some shimmering honey. The finish, though, is duller than it should be. That said, it is something to hold on to... **40%**. *Lombard Brands.* ⊙ ⊙

**Dun Bheagan Pure Malt Aged 8 Years** **(81)** **n**19 **t**22 **f**20 **b**20. Big, malty, sweet and very full flavoured. **43%**. *ncf. William Maxwell.*

⋙ **Duncan Taylor Regional Malt Collection Highland 10 Years Old** dist 1995, bott 05 **(78)** **n**20 **t**21 **f**18 **b**19. Must be the region that's in the middle of the road. **40%**. *920 bottles.*

⋙ **Duncan Taylor Regional Malt Collection Islay 10 Years Old** **(81)** **n**21 **t**22 **f**19 **b**19. Soft citrus cleanses the palate, while gentle peats muddies it up again. **40%**. *888 bottles.*

⋙ **Duncan Taylor Regional Malt Collection Speyside 10 Years Old** dist 1995, bott 05 **(79)** **n**19 **t**22 **f**19 **b**19. Decent enough, but irritatingly non-committal and Tandhu-ish oily on the finish. Come on guys: you are in the heart of Speyside – give us something to get our pulses racing!! **40%**. *838 bottles.*

**The Famous Grouse Malt** **(79)** **n**19 **t**21 **f**19 **b**20. Very sweet, intense malt, but a slight but noticeable blemish spoils the party. **40%**. *Taiwan.*

⋙ **The Famous Grouse Malt 10 Years Old** **(86)** **n**22 **t**21 **f**21 **b**22. One of those attractive drams where the sum is better than the parts. **40%**

**The Famous Grouse Malt 12 Years Old** **(90)** **n**23 stunning mixture of kumquat and blood orange diluted on a malty-gristy base: genuinely complex and charming; **t**22 big malt kick-off, and then a development of pastel vanilla notes and some sawdusty oak; **f**22 medium length, light with hints of oats; **b**23 vatted malt at its most delicate and intricate. A wonderful experience. **40%**. *Taiwan.*

⋙ **The Famous Grouse Malt 15 Years Old** **(91)** **n**23 some major sherry, not always spotless, generating a big blood orange kick; **t**23 beautiful – and pretty enormous – malt/fruit overload on delivery; massively fresh and invigorating; **f**22 milky coffee and pulsing spices; **b**23 some seriously clever creativity went into this one. **40%**. *Edrington* .

**The Famous Grouse 18 Years Old Malt (84) n**19 **t**23 **f**21 **b**21. Mildly flawed sherry, but the honied melt-in-the-mouth malt on the palate is such a treat. **43%**. *Taiwan.*

··· **The Famous Grouse Malt 21 Years Old (92) n**24 candy jar spices, green apple and crisp barley. So beautiful!; **t**23 spot on oak offers a platform for the myriad rich malty notes; **f**22 flattens slightly but muscovado sugar keeps it light and sprightly; **b**23 a very dangerous dram: the sort where the third or fourth would slip down without noticing. Wonderful scotch! And an object lesson in how vatted malt whisky should be. **43%**. *Edrington Group.*

**The Famous Grouse 30 Years Old Malt (94) n**25 the level of complexity here rockets off the scales: swirling, distant peat-reek, acacia honey, pipe smoke, French toast...it simply goes on and on – flawless and fabulous; **t**23 lush, honey-enriched barley weighted down with a smokiness almost too delicate to register; **f**23 it's all about the oak, yet again the molten honey sweetens any possible excess; **b**23 I have been trying hard to think of any whisky quite so delicate – and failed. Blending at its most sublime. **43%**. *Taiwan.*

**The Famous Grouse Vintage Malt 1990** bottled 03 **(78) n**17 **t**21 **f**20 **b**20. Pity about the poor sherry nose. The mouth arrival is scrummy. **40%**

**Fortnum & Mason Highland Malt 12 Years Old (74) n**19 **t**20 **f**17 **b**18. A bland dram floored, it seems, by caramel and perhaps (though impossible to tell) sherry in tandem. **40%**. *UK.*

**Glenalmond Highland Malt (83) n**21 **t**21 **f**20 **b**21. At times impressive. **40%**. *Vintage Malt Whisky Co.*

**Glencoe Aged 8 Years** ( *see* MacDonald's Glencoe)

**Glen Drumm (78) n**18 **t**22 **f**19 **b**19. The nose slightly off-key but decent youthful barley freshness; the sweetness on the palate is as surprising as it is even. **43%**. *Langside Distillers.*

**Glen Martin Pure Highland Malt 5 Years Old (76) n**18 **t**20 **f**19 **b**19. A slightly feinty nose underscores the obvious youth here. Not as well balanced as before but the puckering maltiness delights. **40%**. *James Martin for Sainsbury's, UK.* ☉☉

**Glen Nicol (80) n**20 **t**20 **f**20 **b**20. An honest Joe of a malt: lots of lively character and straight as a die. **40%**. *Inver House.*

**Glen Roger's Pure Malt Aged 8 Years Old Reserve (63) n**18 **t**17 **f**13 **b**15. About as dead as a whisky gets. *For French market.*

**Glenstone (71) n**17 **t**19 **f**17 **b**18. Raw and full on. **40%**. *Kyndal.*

··· **Glen Turner Pure Malt Aged 8 Years** L525956A **(84) n**20 **t**22 **f**22 **b**20. A lush and lively vatting annoyingly over dependent on thick toffee but simply brimming with fabulously mouth-watering barley and over-ripe blood oranges. To those who bottle this, I say: let me into your lab. I can help you bring out something sublime!! **40%**. *Glen Turner Distillery for La Martiniquaise, France.*

··· **Grand Macnish Vatted Malt Scotch Whisky (82) n**19 **t**24 **f**19 **b**20. A real shame: a vatting which offered so much has been done to death with caramel. The mouth-watering ultra-intense and beautifully sweet malt which just makes the heart pound on delivery deserves so much more. **40%**. *MacDuff International. Taiwan.*

··· **Grand Macnish 12 Years Old Vatted Malt Scotch Whisky (78) n**18 **t**23 **f**18 **b**19. The oak and caramel carry out a nifty pincer movement on the barley. Dull. **40%**. *MacDuff International. Taiwan.*

··· **Grand Macnish 21 Years Old Vatted Malt Scotch Whisky (86) n**21 **t**23 **f**21 **b**21. After the velvety landing remains firm throughout but a persistent touch of class is there to see. **40%**. *MacDuff International. Taiwan.*

··· **Glen Orrin 6 Years Old Highland Blended Malt (83) n**21 **t**21 **f**20 **b**21. Value-for-money-wise, you can't go wrong. Some sturdy malts in there with sufficient give to allow an attractive biscuity sweetness. **40%**. *Alistair Graham for Aldi, UK.*

**Golden Harvest (75) n**19 **t**20 **f**18 **b**18. The rich early barley-fest apart, still seems a little flat to me. **40%**. *Lombard Brands.* ☉☉

**Hammer Village No.12 Hammerby F.C. (87) n**21 **t**23 **f**22 **b**21. This is a special bottling for the supporters of the Swedish football side Hammerby FC. Made from the turf, on this evidence...!! **43%.** *Blackadder.*

**Hankey Bannister Pure Malt (87) n**23 **t**22 **f**20 **b**22. The mammoth intensity of the malt enjoys a rare balance. **40%.** *Inver House.*

**Highland Fusilier 8 Years Old (78) n**19 **t**20 **f**19 **b**20. Well-balanced and plenty of body. **40%.** *Gordon & MacPhail.*

**Hogshead Pure Malt (73) n**18 **t**19 **f**18 **b**18. Ordinary and toffeed. **43%.** *Inverheath.*

**Inverarity Islay 10 Years Old (85) n**22 **t**21 **f**21 **b**21. A teasing dram, so soft the flavours barely make it round the mouth. Delightfully different. **40%** ⊙

**Islay Connection Scotch Vatted Malt Over 10 Years Old (76) n**21 **t**20 **f**17 **b**18. Enjoyable last time round. Now the big peat has gone, what little complexity it had has vanished with it. Surprisingly dull, especially the toffeed finish. **40%.** *Celtic Whisky Compagnie, France.* ⊙ ⊙

⋙ **Islay Trilogy 1969** (Bruichladdich 1966, Bunnahabhain 1968, Bowmore 1969) Bourbon/Sherry **(91) n**23 sooty embers in a hearth; kiwi fruit and peaches offer sweetness; **t**23 pure silk that melts and moulds into the tastebuds, with the best bit coming about ten seconds in as creamy cocoa tries to usurp the barley-sugar and fruits. And fails...; **f**22 much drier with chalky, salty vanilla and the weakest hint of peat imaginable; **b**23 decided to mark the 700th tasting for the 2007 edition with this highly unusual vatting. And no bad choice. The smoke is as elusive as the Paps of Jura on a dark November morning, but the silky fruits and salty tang tells a story as good as anything you'll hear by a peat fire. Take your time...the whiskies have. **40.3%.** *Murray McDavid. 1200 bottles.*

⋙ **J & B Exception Aged 12 Years (80) n**20 **t**23 **f**18 **b**19. Very pleasant in so many ways. A charming sweetness develops quickly, with excellent soft honeycomb. But the nose and finish are just so...so....dull...!! For the last 30 years J&B has meant, to me, (and probably within that old company) exceptionally clean, fresh Speysiders offering a crisp, mouth-watering treat. I feel this is off target. **40%.** *Diageo/ Justerini & Brooks.*

⋙ **J & B Nox (89) n**23 classy Speyside thrust, youthful and crisp with a wonderful strand of honey. Gentle oak balances pleasingly; **t**23 the nose in liquid form: exactly the same characteristics with some extra, gently peppered toast towards the middle; **f**21 dries just a little too much as the barley tires; **b**22 a teasing, pleasing little number that is unmistakably from the J&B stable. **40%.** *Diageo.*

**The Jacobite Highland Malt (84) n**20 **t**21 **f**22 **b**21. A mouthwatering, fresh, effervescent and complex malt, especially towards the finish. **40%.** *Malt House Vintners.*

**James MacArthur Pure Islay 1991 Aged 12 years (87) n**22 **t**21 **f**22 **b**22. A perfectly smoky little begger for peat freaks. **59.7%**

**James Martin's Vintage 1984 (83) n**21 **t**20 **f**21 **b**21. An orangey number with pleasing toast-barley complexity. **43%.** *Glenmorangie.*

**James Martin 8 Year Old Malt (87) n**21 **t**22 **f**22 **b**22. A discreet, thoughful vatting quite beautifully constructed. **40%.** *Glenmorangie for Oddbins UK.*

**Johnnie Walker Green Label 15 Years Old (92) n**24 this is one of the best vatted noses on the market: superb complexity, relatively peatless but still boasting big weight amid some fresher Speyside notes; **t**23 bingo! Serious flavour explosion which leans towards malty sweetness with a gradual fade-in of drier oak; **f**22 now some oils arrive, plus a little mint suggesting good age; **b**23 this is easily one of the best vatted malts in the market, pretty sweet, too. **43%** ⊙

**Jon, Mark and Robbo's The Rich Spicy One (89) n**22 a real fruitcake nose; clean and complete with spices and cooked, pithy fruits; **t**23 pretty rich, again with a raisiny fruit density and excellent bitter-sweet balance; **f**22 half-hearted spices tag along with the vanilla; **b**22 so much better without the dodgy casks: a real late night dram of distinction though the spice is perhaps a little on the subtle side... **40%.** *Edrington.* ⊙ ⊙

**Jon, Mark and Robbo's The Smoky Peaty One (92)** n23 a faultlessly clean aroma where the reek enjoys a distinctive salty, coastal rock-pool edge; t22 again the peat is delicate yet coastal with a build-up of intense barley; f23 beautiful honey tones accompany the peat like a high phenol Highland Park; b24 genuinely high-class whisky where the peat is full-on yet allows impressive complexity and malt development. A malt for those who appreciate the better, more elegant things in life. **40%.** *Edrington.* ⊙

**Kelt Tour du Mond Very Rare Extra Old Pure Malt** 1995 Shipment **(93)** n24 freshly ground orange peel, covert nutmeg and profound salty-oaky tang; t23 beautifully weighted arrival, a background hint of smoke and spice that offers sweetness to the drier, even deeper, oak softened by vanilla caramel; f22 some sweetening custard on the lengthy deftly oaked finale; b24 the casks to this whisky spent a couple of months crossing the world by ship. And it shows: its sea legs have given it extraordinary balance.

**Label 5 Pure Highland Malt Aged 12 Years** L534956A **(78)** n19 t20 f20 b19. Crushed by caramel, this never quite gets off the ground despite some promising moments. Won a Gold medal at the International Spirit Competition. I am mystified. **40%.** *The First Blending Co for La Martiniquaise, France.* ⊙ ⊙

**The Living Cask Anniversary Offering (79)** n20 t21 f20 b18. Not a happy bunny, this. Intense and chewy but never finds its rhythm or the usual degree of charm. **59%.** *Loch Fyne Whiskies.*

**Loch Dhup (86)** n22 t22 f21 b21. A charming vatting needing some attention on the finale; strength debatable. A special bottling solera vatted on the spot at Royal Mile Whisky in Bloomsbury, London, and blended by Duncan Ross, tasted by the store's more valued customers. You've heard of the Living Cask: this is the living bottle...

⋯∷⋯ **Loch Fyne Whiskies Living Cask Volume XXIV** bott 26 June 06 **(92)** n22 t24 f23 b23. Another snapshot from this wonderful, ever-evolving cask at Loch Fyne. No point doing full notes, as it'll be quite different when you get there. But this one comes alive on the palate with the most wonderful marriage of great age and something young enough to salivate yourself to death with. Always a highlight of the year when I get a sample! **57.5%.** *Loch Fyne Whiskies.*

**Lochinvar Pure Malt (83)** n18 t22 f22 b21. The careless nose is more than made up for by the scrambled delivery on the palate. There is no rhythm to this whisky and absolutely no plot. It feels like a bunch of casks slung together at random...but the result, though confused, has some deliciously spicy and barley-rich moments. A fun dram. **40%.** *Roscow Greig & Co for Somerfield, UK.* ⊙ ⊙

**Lodhian Founders Choice First Edition Aged 10 Years (72)** n18 t19 f17 b18. Malty but bland. **40%.** *For Lodhian Distillery, Sweden.*

**MacDonalds Glencoe Aged 8 Years (81)** n19 t22 f19 b21. Invigorating and enjoyable if slightly out of sync. Much more honeycomb than before and a tad oilier. **58%. nc.** *Ben Nevis Distillery.* ⊙ ⊙

**Matisse Pure Malt Over 12 Years (73)** n16 t21 f18 b18. Explosive on the palate, but too much caramel. **40%**

**Monkey Shoulder (93)** n23 busy, complex and wonderfully weighted: the theme is orangey-citrus softened by vanilla. Excellent malt-oak ratio; t24 soft mouth arrival and then a steady increase in malt intensity; shards of Demerara sweetness help counter the vanilla; some firm grain early on also guarantees a degree of mouthwatering freshness and bite to balance against the creamy softness; f22 enormous length with layer upon layer of gently oiled malt slowly diminishing in sweetness; b24 outstanding vatting here by David Stewart, who clearly has the malts in the palm of his hands. Pity a freak accident in a bottling hall should deprive him of a Bible award! A joy. **40%.** *William Grant & Sons.*

⋯∷⋯ **Norse Cask Selection Vatted Islay 1991 Aged 12 Years (89)** n24 stonking peat. The barley must have been grown on a peat bed and then dried over a peat fire for about three years. Bloody hell's-peaty-bells...; t23 no prizes for guessing what's first to show, but a massive spice kick is not far behind; **f**21 sweetens out towards a toasty-gristiness; **b**21 fabulous, but not much going in the way of complexity. But if you're a peat freak, I don't think you either notice...or much care...!! **59.5%.** *Quality World, Denmark.*

**Old Elgin 8 Years Old (82) n**21 **t**20 **f**21 **b**20. Lush, lengthy, honied and a little spicy. A good anytime, anywhere whisky. **40%.** *Gordon & MacPhail.*

**Old Elgin 15 Years Old (71) n**17 **t**19 **f**17 **b**18. A tad sulphury and off-key. **40%.** *Gordon & MacPhail.*

⠿ **Old Master's Islay Pure Malt 1991 12 Year Old** bott May 04 **(93) n**22 **f**24 **t**23 **b**24. Some very clever vatting makes for a diamond of a bottling. **59.3%**

⠿ **Old Masters Islay Pure Malt Aged 14 Years** dist 91, bott 05 **(86) n**22 **t**22 **f**20 **b**22. I'd hazard that there's a cask of Caol Ila in there somewhere, and it's a bit too much for the better Islays in this bipolar mix. **58.3%.** *James MacArthur.*

**Poit Dhubh 8 Bliadhna (83) n**22 **t**22 **f**19 **b**20. Generously peated and rich in the middle but foiled by very un-Gaelic toffee. **43%.** *Praban Na Linne. Conduct their business, whenever possible, in Gaelic: bliadhna means "years old".* ☺☺

**Poit Dhubh 12 Bliadhna (82) n**20 **t**22 **f**20 **b**20. The bitterness of old has been eradicated, though the deliciously mouth-watering start comes to grief on caramel. **43%. ncf.** *Praban na Linne.* ☺☺

**Poit Dhubh 12 Bliadhna Unchillfiltered (88) n**23 oranges and juicy pears combine spectacularly wth a peat sub-stratum; **t**21 a mildly flat, toffeed arrival but then an eruption of smoky spices; **f**22 more spice, sweetening malt and then vanilla; **b**22 an exceptionally fine vatted malt with considerable attitude, complexity and personality to get over the low-key mouth arrival. Great stuff. **46%. ncf.**

**Poit Dhubh 21 Bliadhna (84) n**21 **t**21 **f**21 **b**21. A couple of years back you might have spotted me enjoying this once seriously complex dram in a Scottish bar. Now it has lost a degree of its buzz and heart with the removal of all the old peat; the attractively fruity remains are still enjoyable, though toffeed. **43%. ncf.** ☺☺

**The Pot Still 8 Years Old Pure Malt (88) n**22 clean, mildly honeyed and fresh; **t**23 a seriously beautiful palate arrival, silk-textured malt that builds into a fabulously spiced honey middle; **f**21 lengthy with just enough sweetness; **b**22 an enormously charming malt: the way vatted drams should be. **43.5%. ncf.** *Celtic Whisky Compagnie.*

⠿ **The Pot Still Scotch Vatted Malt Over 8 Years Old (90) n**22 excellent oak sub plot to the ballsy barley; **t**24 goes down with all the seductive powers of long fingernails down a chest: the wonderful honey and barley richness is stunning and so beautifully weighted; **f**22 a lazier finale, allowing the chalky oaky notes to make folly of those tender years; **b**22 such sophistication: the Charlotte Rampling of Scotch. **43.5%. ncf.** *Celtic Whisky Compagnie, France.*

**Pride of Islay 12 Years Old (88) n**22 real hospital antiseptic stuff here, oily, too; **t**22 comes to life with a soft upping of peaty intensity after some original fruity notes wear thin; **f**23 quite long and enjoys fine integration between peat and oak; **b**21 I love the gentle but firm nature of the peat with this one. Unusual as an Islay but then, as a vatted version, so it should be. **40%.** *G&M.*

**Pride of the Lowlands 12 Years Old (77) n**20 **t**18 **f**20 **b**19. Lively and the character of a certain distillery shines clearly through. **40%.** *Gordon & MacPhail.*

**Pride of Orkney 12 Years Old (72) n**18 **t**19 **f**18 **b**17. A vatting from Orkney ... now I wonder which distilleries they used? As it happens, there is a very slight soapiness to this one. **40%.** *Gordon & MacPhail.*

**Pride of Speyside (91) n**22 **t**23 **f**23 **b**23. This is a one-off whisky vatted by David Urquhart in aid of charity. As part of his recuperation after undergoing emergency major heart surgery he, quite amazingly, cycled some 150 miles to all 44 working distilleries in his beloved Speyside, collecting samples of their malt from each of them. He then vatted the whiskies together to produce a very limited number of bottles which will eventually be auctioned off for worthy causes including the Moray Cardiac Project. This really is a nuggety little fighter brimming with character and style – and the same can be said about the whisky.... **57.6%.** *Gordon & MacPhail.*

**Pride of Speyside 12 Years Old (87)** n21 t22 f22 b22. Well if good ol' G&M can't get it right with a vatted Speysider, no-one can. A lovely dram. **40%**.

**Prince Lordon Old Malt (79)** n21 t20 f19 b19. Clean, lively energetic malt, sharp grassy notes, refreshing on the nose, with enormous cream-toffee body and finish. **40%**. *VDB Spirit. A specially prepared kosher whisky, in which no sherry is used barrels are cleaned and so on. For US market.*

**Royal Swan 10 Years Old Pure Malt (70)** n18 t19 f16 b17. Fun at first, let down by dodgy finish. **40%**. *Quality Spirits International.*

**Sainsbury's Malt Whisky Finished in Sherry Casks (72)** n19 t19 f17 b17. Never the best, this still remains somewhat cloying with over-indulgent sweetness and an aggressive bitterness. The finish remains a mess. **40%**. *Sainsbury's, UK.* ⊙ ⊙

**Sainsbury's Pure Islay Malt Aged for 10 Years (92)** n24 the iodine reeks from the glass: there is a wonderful balance between oily, soft smoke and something altogether more punchy and complex; t22 still mouth-watering – early on. Then the smoke grabs hold and offers an oily cloak; f23 cocoa and hickory adds to the chewy iodine. Wonderful; b23 I wonder if they took note of my bitching about this brand in a previous Bible. Easily one of the most improved UK supermarket brands of the year, for now there is no doubts about where this whisky hails from: the peat oozes from the glass with class. **40%**. *Sainsbury's, UK.* ⊙ ⊙

⊹⊱ **Scottish Leader Imperial Blended Malt (77)** n20 t20 f18 b19. Now don't be confused here: this isn't Imperial malt from Speyside. And although it says Blended, it is 100% malt. What is clear, though, is that this is pretty average stuff. **40%**. *Burn Stewart.*

⊹⊱ **Scottish Leader Aged 14 Years (80)** n21 t21 f19 b19. A cleaner, less peaty version than the no-age statement vatting, but still fails to entirely ignite the tastebuds **40%**. *Burn Stewart.*

**Scottish Pride 12 Years Old Pure Malt (80)** n20 t21 f19 b20. A lively, lovely and busy vatted malt of some character. **40%**

**Serendipity (96)** n23 do giant noses come any more gentle than this? The peat is thumping, wide-ranging and of the style unique to when Ardbeg was cut from its own peat bogs; but this peat is harnessed by layers of sweet, soothing malt; t25 I have tried. Believe me, I have tried, but I cannot find a single fault, a single crack on the palate. It is perfect: just like the nose, the peat arrives with a fanfare, it caresses with great might, but never leaves a mark. The intensity of the maltiness and the opaqueness of the peat are the only things that can control the enormity of the oak. Yet control it they do. And with something to spare; f23 much drier, the oak begins to get away slightly from the malt, but it remains in check and delivers the most exquisitely complex sensations imaginable; b25 the story behind this whisky beggars belief. If you made it up no-one would believe you. But it was an accident – a major one in whisky terms. Standard common or garden Glen Moray 12 years old is mixed by accident in the bottling hall with genuinely antique Ardbeg: yes, we are talking some of the rarest, most priceless whisky in the world. It works out at just 20% Glen Moray, but it is still vatted whisky and Ardbeg lovers are deprived of casks of the most sought-after malt this universe has ever seen. The result is this. Something, by sheer chance, that borders perfection. The blender in me wants to weep. Whatever you have to do, do it. Just get a bottle. **40%**. *Glenmorangie Co.*

**Sheep Dip (84)** n19 t22 f22 b21. Young and sprightly like a new-born lamb, this enjoys a fresh, mouthwatering grassy style wth a touch of spice. Maligned by some, but to me a clever, accomplished vatting of alluring complexity. **40%**

**The Six Isles Pure Island Malt Uisge Beatha (94)** n24 fresh, alluring, sensuously smoked with an underlying intense barley charisma; t23 a gentle massaging of young peat malt never becomes overly sweet, beautifully oily and lush; f23 long, increasingly spicy: a glorious array of vanilla and barley; b24 Wow! For all the peat, the strength of the whisky is its masterful balance: never sweet, never dry. About as charming and charismatic a vatted malt as you are likely to find. Contains malt from Islay, Jura, Skye, Mull, Orkney and Arran. Together they make unquestionably the best standard, non-deluxe vatted malt I have found in my lifetime. **43%.** *William Maxwell.* ⊙

**Smoking Ember (81) n**22 **t**20 **f**20 **b**19. The nose is glorious, fresh, straight from the malt kiln. But the full follow-through fails to materialise. **40%.** *Lombard Brands.* ⊙

**Stewarts Pure Malt (68) n**16 **t**18 **f**17 **b**17. Loads of flavour but, for me, just doesn't gel **40%.** *Kyndal.*

**Tambowie Highland Pure Malt (75) n**18 **t**20 **f**19 **b**18. Don't think that this is the old Tambowie distillery come back to life. Just a vatted malt put together to bring the old name back to life? It's claimed that this is what they think the old distillery (built in 1885 – great year: that's when Millwall FC were founded) would have produced. My own feeling is that this is a degree too light in character. **40%.** *The Vintage Malt Whisky Co.*

**Tambowie Highland Pure Malt 12 Years Old (73) n**18 **t**18 **f**19 **b**18. Slightly fusty; has some bright fruity moments but fades too quickly. **40%.**

**Tidal Ebb Islay Distillation Area (83) n**21 **t**22 **f**20 **b**20. Some lovely peaty tones softened by light muscovado sugar. **40%.** *Lombard Brands.* ⊙

**Tulchan Lodge 12 Year Old Speyside Malt (80) n**19 **t**20 **f**21 **b**20. Pretty rich and builds up well; the toffee dictates at the last. **40%.** *Tulchan Estate.*

**Vintner's Choice Highland Aged 10 Years (60) n**18 **t**15 **f**13 **b**14. Staggeringly flat and unimpressive. **40%**

**Vintner's Choice Speyside Aged 10 Years (73) n**16 **t**19 **f**19 **b**19. Malty; some fruit. **40%**

**Waitrose Pure Highland Malt (78) n**20 **t**21 **f**18 **b**19. Highly intense, delicious malt with some spice. *Waitrose Stores UK.*

⋙ **Wemyss Vintage Malt The Peat Chimney Hand Crafted Blended Malt Whisky (80) n**19 **t**22 **f**20 **b**19. The balance is askew here, especially on the bone-dry wallpapery finish. Does have some excellent spicy/coffee moments, though. **43%.** *Wemyss Vintage Malts Ltd.*

⋙ **Wemyss Vintage Malt The Smooth Gentleman Hand Crafted Blended Malt Whisky (83) n**19 **t**22 **f**21 **b**21. Not sure about the nose: curiously fishy (very gently smoked). But the malts tuck into the tastebuds with aplomb showing some sticky barley sugar along the way. **43%.** *Wemyss Vintage Malts.*

⋙ **Wemyss Vintage Malt The Spice King Hand Crafted Blended Malt Whisky (84) n**22 **t**22 **f**20 **b**20. Funnily enough, I've not a great fan of the word "smooth" when it comes to whisky. But the introduction of oily Caol Ila-style peat here makes it a more of a smooth gentleman than the "Smooth Gentleman." Excellent spices very late on. **43%.** *Wemyss Vintage Malts.*

**Whisky Galore Pure Malt Aged 10 Years (60) n**16 **t**16 **f**13 **b**15. Featureless. One to forget … had there been anything to remember in the first place. **40%.** *Duncan Taylor.*

⋙ **Whisky Galore Pure Malt Aged 10 Years** dist 95, bott 05 **(89) n**22 gristy, grassy and classy; **t**22 mouth-watering but there is weight to the mildly honeyed barley; **f**23 real complexity as soft citrus and vanilla rye with the malt. A superb mid-day dram; **b**22 talk about the Power of the Whisky Bible. When I first reviewed this brand, it marked up a staggering 60 points....and was lucky to get that. It was a dram scuppered by the OTT use of caramel which left it flatter than an East Anglian pancake. My comments brought shockwaves to Huntley, and the town's drains filled with discarded pots of caramel. (Not really, but you get the drift...) Here is a direct result. Not a whisky that you would jump off a rushing train to retrieve (mind you, thinking about it, the company's owner is about as Scottish as you can get) but one unspoiled that you can genuinely enjoy. **40%.** *Duncan Taylor. 120 bottles.*

⋙ **Wild Scotsman Aged 15 Years Vatted Malt (95) n**23 a seriously attractive marriage between gentle oaky vanilla and preening barley; diluted honey and spiced apple abound; **t**24 you really can't ask for more from a malt delivery than this.

Soft and vaguely lush, the taste buds are overrun by an enchanting Danish-style moist marzipan in dark chocolate. It is impossible to fault the intensity and beauty of the early barley charge; **f**24 settles down to drier marzipan and pistachio oil. The interplay between barley and oak is exceptional and even proffers some very late and welcome spices. One of the longest finishes in the business; **b**24 if anyone wants an object lesson as to why you don't screw your whisky with caramel, here it is. Jeff Topping can feel a justifiable sense of pride in his new whisky: for its age, it is an unreconstituted masterpiece... **46% (92 proof)**. **nc ncf**. *USA*.

**Wm Morrison Islay Pure Malt Aged 10 Years (84) n**20 **t**22 **f**21 **b**21. A very delicate and well-structured Islay for reflective moments. Doesn't paint the peat with a tar brush.; maybe an extra layer than previous years. **40%**

**Wm Morrisons Pure Malt Aged 8 Years (77) n**20 **t**22 **f**17 **b**18. Starts with a shock wave of stunning young grassy malt, but then a curtain of caramel descends and life in the glass is extinguished. What a shame. What a waste. **40%**

## MYSTERY MALTS

**Blackadder Raw Cask Blairfindy** (*see* Glenfarclas)

⠿ **Chieftain's Limited Edition Aged 40 Years** Hogshead **(78) n**22 **t**22 **f**16 **b**18. Oak-ravaged and predictably bitter on the death (those of you who enjoy Continental bitters might go for this..!). But the lead up does offer a short, though sublime and intense honey kick. The finish, though... **48.5%**. *Ian Macleod.*

**Gordon & MacPhail Christmas Malt 10 Years** bott 02 **(85) n**20 **t**22 **f**21 **b**22. Quality malt, worth drinking more than once a year. **40%**

**Inverarity 10 Years Old** (*see* Aultmore)

**Inverarity Ancestral 14 Years Old** (*see* Balmenach)

**Old St Andrews 5 Years Old Malt** (in miniature bottle encased in plastic barrel) **(83) n**19 **t**22 **f**21 **b**21. A refreshing, mouthwatering dignified young dram of good stock. **40%.**

**Old St Andrews 15 Years Old Malt** (in miniature bottle encased in plastic barrel) **(81) n**20 **t**22 **f**19 **b**20. Malty and chewy with lots of vanilla and toffee. **40%.**

# Scottish Grain

It's a bit weird, really. Many whisky lovers stay clear of blended Scotch, preferring instead single malts. The reason, I am often told, is that the grain included in a blend makes it rough and ready.

Yet I wish I had a ten pound note for each time I have been told in the last year how much someone enjoys a single grain.

The ones that the connoisseurs die for are the older versions, special independent bottlings displaying great age and often a Canadian or bourbon style.

Like single malts, grain distilleries produce whisky bearing their own style and signature. And, also, some display characteristics and a richness that can surprise and delight. Most of the grains available in (usually specialist) whisky outlets are pretty elderly. Being made from maize and wheat helps give them either that Canadian or, depending on the freshness of the cask, an unmistakable bourbony style. So older grains display far greater body than is commonly anticipated.

Light whiskies, including some Speysiders, tend to adopt this north American stance when the spirit has absorbed so much oak that the balance has been tipped. So overtly Kentuckian can they be, I once playfully introduced an old single grain Scotch whisky into a bourbon tasting I was conducting and nobody spotted that it was the cuckoo in the nest ... until I revealed all at the end of the evening. And even had to display the bottle to satisfy the disbelievers.

Younger grains may give a hint of oncoming bourbon-ness. But, rather, they tend to celebrate either a softness in taste or, in the case of North British, a certain rigidity. Where many malts have a tendency to pulverise the taste-buds and announce their intent and character at the top of their voice, younger grains are content to stroke and whisper.

Scotch whisky companies have so far had a relaxed attitude to marketing their grains. William Grant has made some inroads with Black Barrel, though with nothing like the enthusiasm they unleash upon us their blends and malts. And Diageo are apparently content to see their Cameron Brig sell no further than its traditional hunting grounds, just north of Edinburgh, where the locals tend to prefer single grain to any other whisky. Hats off to Kyndal, though, for actually bringing out an impressive vintage version of their Invergordon.

The news for grain lovers has not been good lately with the demolition of Dumbarton. I hope Chivas, as a mark of respect for the lost and, for my money, best grain distiller to operate out of Scotland following the closure of Cambus, each year launch a special vintage of this crisp grain. As a distillery that distilled from both wheat and corn, it would make a fascinating addition for whisky lovers to be able to try and spot the difference in style from the same age.

The tastings notes here for grains – both single and vatted – cover only a few pages, due to their scarcity. However, it is a whisky style growing in stature, helped along the way by Compass Box's recent launching of a vatted grain. And we can even see an organic grain on the market, distilled at the unfashionable Loch Lomond Distillery.

At last the message is getting through that the reaction of this relatively lightweight spirit - and please don't for one moment regard it as neutral, for it is most certainly anything but - to oak can throw up some fascinating and sometimes delicious possibilities. Blenders have known that for a long time. Now public interest is growing. And people are willing to admit that they can enjoy an ancient Cambus, Caledonian or Dumbarton in very much the way they might celebrate a single malt. Even if it does go against the grain...

# Single Grain Scotch
## ALLOA (see North of Scotland)

### CALEDONIAN

Cadenhead's Caledonian Aged 31 Years dist Jan 63, bott Feb 94 **(88)** n22 t23 f21 b22. The last hurrah of a grain that obviously put a metal backbone into many a blend. **48.7%**

⁙ **Clan Denny Grain Caledonian 40 Years Old** dist Aug 75, bott Aug 05 **(94)** n25 does the aroma of grain get better than this? No, I don't think it does. What we have here is bourbon at its most honeycombed, leather armchaired and toffee-appled. But the oak hasn't even remotely gone OTT. It was for this that nature gave us a nose...It even makes you forget about drinking the stuff...; t23 soft and lush, the corn gives up a wonderful Demerara sheen to the oak-controlled sweetness; again soft honey flitters about. Not a jagged edge, the tastebuds have rarely been so tenderly caressed; f22 fades more quickly than one might expect from a 40-year-old, but that is because the oak is controlled and doesn't offer a shred of bitterness; instead, delicate vanillins abound as do the well manicured sugars; b24 Grain is an inferior type of whisky...? Yeah, right...!! **47.4%**. *Douglas Laing.*

### CAMBUS

Cadenhead's Cambus Aged 31 Years dist 63, bott 94 **(87)** n21 t23 f21 b22. An impressive grain that has taken the years in its stride and remained upbeat and full of character. **53.2%**

### CAMERONBRIDGE

Cameron Brig db **(79)** n19 t21 f19 b20. Toffee on the light, sweet finish. **40%**. *Diageo.*

Duncan Taylor Cameronbridge 1979 cask 3523, dist Feb 79, bott Jan 05 **(83)** n21 t22 f19 b21. Few whiskies in the world can boast quite so much natural caramel. **59.9%**

⁙ **Duncan Taylor Cameronbridge 1979** dist 79, bott 3 Mar 06 **(94)** n23 wonderfully firm nose with soft muscovado sugar and playful oak spices; t24 blind-tasted, this could be exceptionally fine Canadian with the oaky-grain inter-play being a picture of harmony. The soft-firm delivery is also exceptional; f23 long, with soft oils fanning out the coffee and corn; b24 a wonderful, stylized grain of the highest quality. This bottling is unmistakably from this distillery, so true to type is it. Sensational. **59.5%**

### CARSEBRIDGE

Duncan Taylor Collection Carsebridge 1979 Aged 25 Years cask no. 32901, dist Mar 79, bott Jan 05 **(90)** n22 subtle spices and crushed pine nuts; t24 exceptional arrival with wonderfully weighted corn enriched in its own sweet oil; f22 soft vanilla and corn; b22 never understood why this was not bottled more often. Well done to Duncan Taylor for helping to show what we have been missing... and shall continue to miss. **56.4%**

### DUMBARTON

Cadenhead's Dumbarton Aged 32 Years dist Feb 62, bott Feb 94 **(85)** n21 t22 f21 b21. Amazingly firm grain with a lovely fruity edge. **49.9%**

⁙ **Clan Denny Grain Dumbarton 40 Years Old** dist Dec 64, bott Nov 05 **(90)** n22 if you adore sticking your nose in an over-ripe mango, then this is the one for you...some orangey-bourboney notes also bubble up as it oxidizes; t23 mouth-watering and fresh to start, the soft delivery is fruit accented and a near perfect sweetness; f22 the corn offers enough oil to accept the growing, drier oak; b23 a proud grain with no buckling at the knees to oak and a luxurious lift off. **44.1%**. *Douglas Laing.*

# GIRVAN

⋆ **Berrys' Own Selection Girvan 1989 Aged 17 Years (87)** n21 creamy vanilla; t23 skydivers landing in a lake of blancmange wouldn't get a softer touchdown than this; the oak-grain interplay is impressive; f22 lashings of vanilla and a touch of spice; b21 pure silk: beautifully soft and a must for Canadian whisky lovers. **46%.** *Berry Bros & Rudd.*

**Black Barrel** db **(82)** n20 t20 f22 b20. Dangerously drinkable, moreish grain oasting a soft, Canadian-style oakiness. Light, spicy fizz on the long finish. **40%**

**Girvan 1964** casks filled 30/4/64, bott 10/10/01 db **(88)** n22 beautiful, rich corn notes: sweet, deep, yet clean and crystal clear despite age; t23 sweet, oily, bourbony, sensual. Brilliant mouthfeel; f21 lots of liquorice, oak and subtle vanilla; b22 a luscious, classical well-aged grain straight from the top drawer. **48%.** *1200 bottles.*

**Old Master's Girvan (87)** n21 flaky oak and vanilla; t23 sweet, soft arrival that just sticks to the roof of the mouth; f22 long, clean and fabulously yielding with just a touch of late sugar to see off the oaky arrival; b22 standard, high quality Girvan at its sexiest. **60.4%.** *James MacArthur*

⋆ **Old Masters Girvan Aged 16 Years** cask no. 110632, dist 89, bott 06 **(89)** n22 untypically Girvan-esque tough cop-soft cop approach. But, overall, fresh and seriously tender; t23 beautifully, intense, sweet grains softly oiled and alluring; f22 bitters down as the oak takes hold. Good length and poise; b22 Quality whisky: Girvan at its most forthright. **58%.** *James MacArthur.*

# INVERGORDON

**Invergordon Single Grain** db **(84)** n20 t21 f22 b21. High-quality, sweet, velvety grain: a fine representative of medium-aged stock from this distillery. **40%**

⋆ **Dewar Rattray Individual Cask Bottling Invergordon Aged 40 Years** cask no. 57633, dist 14.8.64, bott 29.6.05 **(91)** n23 you can almost hear the pack ice cracking on Lake Winnipeg. Nosed blind, it's pure Canadian; t23 startling, lush and mouth-watering corn laced with maple syrup; perfect vanilla undercurrent; f22 relatively short and docile but the honey remains intact; b23 more Canadian in style than a Film Board. **48.1%.** *270 bottles.*

**Duncan Taylor Collection Invergordon 1965 Aged 39 Years** cask no. 15504, dist Dec 65, bott Dec 04 **(87)** n21 massively intense corn while the oak is vanilla incarnate; t22 err...corn; f23 corn, but this time beautifully sweetened: sweet corn, perhaps; b21 it's as though the corn and oak have cancelled each other out to give a highly enjoyable but relatively featureless experience. **49.6%**

⋆ **Duncan Taylor Collection Invergordon 1965** cask no. 15508, dist Dec 65, bott Feb 06 **(86)** n21 t22 f22 b21. Needs a good prod to show it's still alive but when it does wake up the spices excel. **50.3%.** *243 bottles.*

**The Whisky Fair Invergordon Aged 39 Years** dist Dec 65, bott Feb 05 **(89)** n22 floral, even a touch herbal; t24 massive and complex arrival of firm oak and even firmer corn with the bitter-sweet complexity of epic proportions; weirdly estery for a grain – almost like a rum; f21 slightly tired and vanilla-rich; b22 a bit of a spent force by the finish, but the early delivery is stupendous. **49.8%. nc ncf.** *90 bottles.*

# LOCH LOMOND

**Da Mhile Organic (88)** n21 soft, lush and sweet with distant echoes of bubblegum; clean, rich and honest; t23 fat in the mouth with the most beautiful coating of silky grain; uncomplex, but the oak delivers a vanilla sheen to the middle; f22 remains velvety-textured despite gentle waves of spice and late, oaky bitterness to balance out the simple, underlying sweetness; b22 a calm, genteel grain up to the usual very high Loch Lomond standards and always exuding a certain, effortless touch of class. **46%.** *Da Mhile. 1000 bottles.*

⋆ **Dà Mhìle Loch Lomond Organic** dist July 00, bott Mar 06 **(90)** n23 gentle sweetness that sits well with vanilla; curiously firm yet soft at same time; **t23** beautifully chewy with teasing, subtle vanilla and butter tones; **f21** pretty short but refuses to lose balance; **b23** great to get a chance to see Loch Lomond's high class and complexly bodied grain – organic or not. **46%. nc ncf.** *6500 miniatures bottles.*

⁙ **Loch Lomond Organic Single Grain in Organic wine Hogshead** cask no. 37700, dist 24 July 00, bott 27 July 05 db **(86) n21 t22 f21 b22.** Astonishing for a 5-year-old whisky. Amazing for a grain. And is one of the "must experience" whiskies of the year. But it can be even better when not rounded off...believe me! **45%.** *402 bottles.*

## LOCHSIDE

⁙ **Clan Denny Grain Lochside Aged 42 Years** dist Nov 63, bott Nov 05 **(89) n23** I'm in deepest Kentucky and just opened up a 17-year-old barrel: it's tired and groaning but the hickory and muscovado sugar are such a treat; nice chestnuts, too; **t23** silky, mesmerising oak with splinters in every direction; lovely heavy roast Java coffee at the very centre; **f21** fades and becomes mildly bitter and tired with the coffee-bourbon theme continuing; **b22** a bit like clapped out bourbon on the nose and even more clapped out bourbon on the finish. My researcher put this under single malts, but as soon as I tasted it, I smelt (and tasted!) a rat. Proof positive that old grain Scotch can produce vintage bourbon!! **44.1%.** *Douglas Laing.*

## NORTH BRITISH

**Adelphi North British 13 Years Old** cask 52640, dist 90, bott 03 **(87) n22 t22 f21 b22.** Faultlessly rich and chewy grain: fascinating that when compared with previous bottlings the scores are almost identical – 100/100 for consistency!! **63.5%**

**Adelphi North British 13 Years Old** cask 52640 **(87) n21** soft, Canadian style corn and oak: enticing; **t21** delicious fat toffee with growing oak offering soft spice. Some fruit hangs around, too; **f23** long, chewy with a hint of cocoa and increasing sweetness: stunning; **b22** exemplary. **63.5%**

⁙ **Clan Denny Grain North of Scotland 39 Years Old** dist Jun 66, bott Nov 05 **(76) n21 t20 f17 b18.** Curious, farm-yardy nose and early grain arrival, but then the off-key development is startling; almost like some experimental rye whiskies I have seen in Europe go slightly wrong. Odd. **44.4%.** *Douglas Laing.*

**Scott's Selection North British 1974** bott 05 **(86) n22 t23 f20 b21.** Attractive, but lacking in complexity towards the end. **43.6%.** *Speyside Distillers.*

## NORTH OF SCOTLAND

**Hart Brothers Alloa 1964** cask 30296, dist Jul 64, bott Feb 05 **(89) n24** toasted marshmallows, natural vanilla and sweet Muscovado sugar all in a Canadian coating; **t23** silky; begins in a bourbon sweetness, then dries more towards very old Canadian: the mildly spicy corn is paramount and rich; **f20** although feeling a bit tired there is enough custardy vanilla to see it through; **b22** better in bottled form than the sampler I received last year, it's like being transported to the lakes of Winnipeg or Manitoba: outstanding quality and very Canadian in style. An absolute quality straight grain of the highest magnitude. Alloa grain was made at the North of Scotland distillery but tankered and filled into cask at their Dillichip Bond. Very rare stuff. **44.1%.** *Hart Brothers Ltd.*

**Private Cellars Selecton North of Scotland 1970** bott 03 **(91) n23 t23 f22 b23.** One of those great old grains that are a class apart. **43%.** *Speyside Distillers.*

**Scott's Selection North of Scotland 1964** bott 03 **(90) n22** buttery, sweet corn: slightly bourbony with a dash of Canadian; **t23** extraordinary early sweetness that maintains balance and corn richness: the oak is a distant rumble; **f22** Demerara sugar abounds, a touch of liquorice but the corn still blossoms even at the death; **b23** is this really almost 40 years old? One hell of a cask for one hell of a whisky ... **43.6%**

Scott's Selection North of Scotland 1971 bott 02 **(81) n**21 **t**21 **f**19 **b**20. Soft, sweet Canadian/bourbony notes are overpowered on the finale by an offkey bitterness. **49.9%**

Scott's Selection North of Scotland 1973 bott 05 **(90) n**22 firm grain and soft vanilla; **t**22 mouthwatering with a real juicy edge; **f**23 long, cornlaced and sweetening; **b**23 mouthwatering, fresh and relaxed. About as entertaining as they come: yet another classic from this lost distillery. **45%**. *Speyside Distillers.*

## PORT DUNDAS

Duncan Taylor Collection Port Dundas 1973 Aged 32 Years cask no. 128316, dist Jan 73, bott Feb 05 **(87) n**23 am I going insane, or is this grain whisky in a thundering sherry butt? **t**19 the sherry dominates and the lightness of the spirit provides for a warts-and-all experience; **f**23 much better now with some sticky raisin and developing sweetness; **b**22 I've experienced some strange whiskies in my time, but this almost takes the fruity biscuit. Pass me a straightjacket.... **59.3%**

## STRATHCLYDE

Duncan Taylor Strathclyde 1973 Aged 31 Years cask no. 74061, dist Nov 73, bott Jan 05 **(80) n**20 **t**21 **f**19 **b**20. Lots of peaches and tropical fruit, but the shape and balance are all over the shop. **62.8%**

Duncan Taylor Strathclyde 1980 Aged 24 Years cask no. 1462, dist Aug 80 , bott Jan 05 **(75) n**18 **t**19 **f**19 **b**19. Harsh and puckering. **62.6%**

# Vatted Grain

⁃⁙⁃ Clan Denny Speyside (Mortlach; Glendullan; Linkwood and Dufftown) **(84) n**22 **t**21 **f**20 **b**21. When I saw Mortlach and Dufftown in there I feared the worst. But a genuine Speyside grassy nose is backed up with a malty charge on the palate. **40%**. *Douglas Laing.*

Compass Box Hedonism bott 04 (bottle identification L4097) **(89) n**22 soft, circular vanilla with a spec of honey; **t**22 soft landing but enough chew in there to make it entertaining; **f**23 good length and spice; **b**22 grain again shown to its advantage. **43%**

Compass Box Hedonism Vatted Grain (second bottling, small central illustration, described as "Vatted Grain") **(87) n**21 **t**22 **f**22 **b**22. Really mouthfilling and intense. Canadian style. **43%. nc ncf.**

Compass Box Hedonism Vatted Grain (third bottling, same label as second bottling, but laser jet bottling code number L3 136) **(89) n**22 **t**22 **f**22 **b**23. This is the other side of the same Hedonism coin: really classy, but in this case light and spicy rather than the overtly sweeter, oilier, more velvety texture of the previous bottling. This one, though, wins hands down for eye-closing, contemplative complexity. **40%**

Compass Box Hedonism bott lot no L5035 **(88) n**22 sticky toffee pudding and distinct layers of bourbon; **t**22 incredibly sweet, oily grain (seems like corn), then a deployment of soft spices and drying oak; **f**21 lazy oils and a continuation of vanilla; **b**23 a drier version of Hedonism, but the gentle complexity is a treat. **43%**

⁃⁙⁃ Jon, Mark and Robbo's The Fresh Fruity One **(84) n**21 **t**22 **f**20 **b**21. Lovely to see vatted grains coming into vogue after years of campaigning for distillers to take such a course. Enjoyable drinking. But Fresh and Fruity? Well, a touch too much oak for this ever to be fresh and not estery enough to be fruity. Doesn't do what it says on the tin. **40%**. *The Easy Drinking Whisky Company.*

# Scottish Blends

**W**ith a Scottish blend for the first time being named the Bible's Whisky of the Year the time surely has come for re-evaluating this most misunderstood and undervalued of whiskies. For it really is quite extraordinary how people the world over, with refined palates and a good knowledge of single malts, are so willing to dismiss blends out of hand.

Perhaps it is a form of malt snobbery: if you don't drink malts, then you are not a serious Scotch whisky connoisseur ... or so some people think. Perhaps it is the fact that something like 94 out of every 100 bottles of Scotch consumed is a blend that has brought about this rather too common cold-shouldering. Well, not in my books. In fact, perhaps the opposite is true. Until you get to grips with blends you may well be entitled to regard yourself knowledgeable in single malts, but not in Scotch as a whole. Blends should be the best that Scotland can offer, because with a blend you have the ability to create any degree of complexity. And surely balance and complexity are the cornerstones of any great whisky, irrespective of type.

Of course there are some pretty awful blends created simply as a commodity with little thought going into their structure – just young whiskies, sometimes consisting of stock that is of dubious quality and then coloured up to give some impression of age. Yes, you are more likely to find that among blends than malts and for this reason the poorest blends can be pretty nasty. And, yes, they contain grain. Too often, though, grain is regarded as a kind of whisky leper – not to be touched under any circumstances. Some writers dismiss grain as "neutral" and "cheap", thus putting into the minds of the uninitiated the perception of inferiority.

But there really is nothing inferior about blends. In fact, whilst researching The Bible, I have to say that my heart missed more than one beat usually when I received a sample of a blend I had never found before. Why? Well, with single malts each distillery produces a style that can be found within known parameters. With a blend, anything is possible. There are many dozens of styles of malts to choose from and they will react slightly differently with certain grains.

For that reason, perhaps, I have marked blends a little more strictly and tighter than I have single malts. Because blends, by definition, should offer more.

And they do not have to be of any great age to achieve greatness. Look at the brilliance of the likes of Johnnie Walker Gold, Royal Silk, Black Bottle, Bailie Nicol Jarvie, Grant's and, of course, the all-conquering Old Parr Superior. Look, also, at the diversity of style from crisp and light to peat dominant and myriad styles between. Then you get others where age has also played an astonishing role, not least a 50-years-old, such as Royal Salute.

Just like malts, blends change in character from time to time. In the case of blends it often has much to do with the running availability of certain malts and grains. The most unforgivable reason is because the marketing guys reckon it needs a bit of extra colour and precious high notes are lost to caramel or sherry. Subtlety and character are the keys for any great blend without fail.

The most exciting blends, like White Horse 12 (why, oh, why is that restricted mainly to Japan?) and Grant's show bite, character and attitude. Silk and charm are to be appreciated. But after a long, hard day is there anything better than a blend that is young and confident enough to nip and nibble at your throat on its way down and then throw up an array of flavours and aromas to get your taste-buds round? Certainly, I have always found blends ultimately more satisfying than malts. Especially when the balance simply caresses your soul.

With Blended Scotch the range and possibilities are limitless. All it takes is for the drinker not just to use his or her nose and taste-buds. But also an open mind.

# Scottish Blends

**100 Pipers (67)** n17 t17 f16 b17. 100 Pipers: zero harmony. Young, less than pleasant grain and now lashings of caramel on top. Was called 100 Pipers, then re-named Black Watch – now appears to be 100 Pipers again, though there is still a Black Watch. They keep changing the name but the same bloody awful whisky keeps appearing. **40%.** *Chivas.*

⟨ **100 Pipers** Batch no. 391, bott Dec 05 **(81)** n20 t21 f20 b20. Now this is pretty good: excellent citrussy grain and the odd wave of Speysidey freshness. Now I know where to get some decent 100 Pipers... **42.8%.** *Chivas Bros./Seagram Distilleries India.*

**Aberdour Piper (83)** n21 t21 f20 b21. For an economy bar whisky, this offers unusual depth with satisfyingly lucid crunchy grain, excellent bite and just the right addition of smoke. A real clean mouthful and an attractive and cleverly blended one at that. **40%.** *Haymon Distillers.*

**Acing Superior (76)** n18 t22 f18 b18. A really enjoyable and impressive 5-y-o-style blend with decent malt and sparkling grain, but let down for the purists by the colouring. **40%**

**Adelphi Ben Nevis Blend 1970 Aged 24 Years** cask no. 4640, dist 70, bott 05 **(92)** n24 hypnotic malt and oak intensity: wonderful age and harmonisation here, together with stunning (kiwi?) fruit lightness; t23 lush body again, with the barley and oak absolutely as one; some strands of fruit here but entirely [OK?] non-specific; f22 much drier with the malt offering required sweetness; b23 what the hell is this stuff? I'd better consult The Bible...oh, hang on...this is The Bible! It turned up after I had been away for a month – haven't had the official word. But it feels like something that has been married in oak for a long, long time. Can't spot any discernible grain here at all. **50.3%.** *186 bottles.*

**Aged Blend** (*see* Duncan Taylor Aged Blend)

**Ailsa Craig (77)** n18 t22 f19 b18. The strangely anarchic, smoky yet mildly off-key nose for a blend is compensated by an extraordinary and quite delicious mouth arrival that heads in two distinctly different directions. The grain is hard and unyielding while the malt is oily and aided by sharp and intense barley and no little smoke. Hardly a blend: more of a delicious-tasting accident. Weird and, in part, wonderful. **40%.** *A Dewar Rattray.*

**Alistair Graham Scotch Whisky (71)** n17 t19 f18 b17. Spot the malt contest. Decent enough grain, though. **40%.** *For Sainsbury's, UK.*

**Ancient Clan (75)** n17 t20 f19 b19. Furry on the plate and, despite a lovely clean-malt purple patch in the middle, suffers from a rough periphery. **40%.** *Tomatin Distillery Co.*

**The Andrew Usher Memorial Blend (92)** n23 beautifully firm grain which seems attached to succulent fruit. The malts are busy and spicy: a real blender's blend; t24 explosive, mouth-enveloping stuff. The malts go hand-inhand with the grain to create complex patterns all around the palate while the fruit ensures softness reigns; f22 much lighter with toffee-vanilla gentleness against the foraging spice; b23 one for the Andrew Usher hall of fame. The old man would have been proud of a blend that has it all. **49%.** *Kyndal.*

**The Antiquary 12 Years Old (92)** n23 a stunning Speyside top note reflects perfectly off the crisp, clean grain; t24 mouthwatering, sweet grain refreshes and re-ignites the tastebuds. Just so salivating and delightful with the grain crackling around the palate; f22 long, with the malt-grain interplay sending continuous shock waves; b23 enormously improved in recent years with a growling, purring interplay between grain and quite stunning malt. The caramel has been ditched and it's a delight! This is just how I see many blends before they are ruined in the bottling hall when colour is added. **40%.** *J & W Hardie Ltd.*

**Antiquary 21 Years Old** bott 05 **(95)** n25 some lovely honey interlaced with pure barley and crisp grain; and where before there was an off-key note, now we have something almost too harmonious for words. A wonderful injection of bourbon-laden grain offers supreme depth to counter the light fruitiness; **t**23 big, booming malt with honey at its centrefold and succulent white grape juice in the wings; **f**23 just layers of interwoven acacia honey and grape with barley hunkering down with the vanilla; the grain offers a firm background for the malts to rebound from with interest; **b**24 probably the most improved blend of the year: nigh on faultless. This is erotic whisky: dab it behind the ears of the one you love. Viagra has a rival. **43%.** *The Tomatin Distillery.* ☺ ☺

**Asda Blended Scotch (83) n**21 **t**21 **f**20 **b**21. Sound, honest, whisky with excellent grain bite adding steel to the softer Speyside malt: all you could ask and more from a standard own label. **40%**. *Glenmorangie for Asda.*

**Asda Finest Old Scotch Aged 8 Years (79) n**19 **t**22 **f**19 **b**19. A more than competent supermarket blend that positively shimmers on the tastebuds with a wondrous delivery of fresh, mouthwatering malt aided and abetted by crisp yet well aged grain. A sightly bitter finish, though. **40%**

**Asyla** (*see* Compass Box)

**Avonside (74) n**17 **t**20 **f**19 **b**18. Pleasant, but a little flat. **40%**. *Gordon & MacPhail.*

**Avonside 8-years-old (81) n**18 **t**21 **f**22 **b**20. Beautifully honeyed: much more evidence of oak and age than on standard 8-y-o version. **57%**. *Gordon & MacPhail.*

**The Bailie Nicol Jarvie (B.N.J.). (89) n**22 decidedly Speysidey with caressing grain; **t**23 where the malt and grain rebounded and sparred off each other, we now have two distinct cultures trying to harmonise and bringing in the faintest smoke to help. Delicious, but...; **f**22 the extra oak flattens out the blend further and adds a degree of bitterness; **b**22 lovely blending still but the crisp, shrapnel-sharp edge to the grain and malt has blurred to become something softer and less heart-pounding. Just too damned civilised! All armchairs slippers and pipes hen you are looking for juicy action. **40%**. *Glenmorangie.*

**Ballantine's Aged 12 Years (87) n**21 distinctly grapey and sweet, with kumquats and buttered toast; **t**22 lashings of cream-toffee punctuated by the occasionally exposed strata of Speyside-clean barley; **f**21 beautifully layered at first, with even the odd hint of something vaguely smoky. The toffee has too great a say, though; **b**23 the kind of old-fashioned, mildly moody blend Colonel Farquharson-Smythe (retired) might have recognised when relaxing at the 19th hole back in the early 50s. Too good for a squirt of Soda, mind. **40%** *Allied.*

**Ballantine's Gold Seal 12 Years Old (88) n**23 gently smoked with the most distant hints of very clean sherry: just beautiful; **t**21 the fruit ensures a rather too gentle entry onto the tastebuds, but excellent grain does some catching up to land a vanilla punch. The malt is lazy and relaxed; **f**22 some cocoa and rousing complex malty-oaky-smoky tones ensure a bitter-sweet ending; **b**22 very complex and alluring. **40%**. *Allied.*

**Ballantine's Royal Blue 12 Years Old (90) n**23 fabulous chalky-oak and big malt presence; **t**22 mouthwatering, fat, some dazzling citrus notes and then cocoa/coffee towards the spiced, complex middle; **f**22 sweetens with both malt and soft brown sugar The texture remains lush without ever being oily; **b**23 this blend has improved beyond recognition since I last tasted it: my hats off to the blender. This is for the Japanese market and, had I tasted this blind, I would have marked it down as a Japanese blend of the top order... which is some compliment. **43%**. *Allied.*

**Ballantine's 17 Years Old (96) n**24 a floral lavender-mint combination balance with aplomb with the most intrinsic peat and grain: beguiling and wonderfully sexy. Only a coating of ultra-clean sherry deviates from earlier bottlings; **t**25 this is it: balance, charm, guile, charisma ... the entire works in one voluptuous mouthful. First a sweet sheen coats the mouth then some grassy notes get you salivating before soft smoke provides the weight. Enormous with wave upon wave of intense barley sugar and peat but never heavy enough to snap a twig. This is masterful blending; **f**23 some oaks finally settle like sediment. Raisins and walnut complete the rich picture and spices add that extra dimension ... as if it was needed; **b**24 it's amazing that out of one lab comes two blends that give masterclass performances: Ballantine's 17 and Teachers. Both are outwardly weighty but reveal so much more that is gentle and complex. The point about this whisky is that you feel you never quite get to the bottom layer: labyrinthine liquid genius. **43%.** *Allied.*

**Ballantine's 21 Year Old (93) n**22 suet pudding laced with gentle oloroso and molasses, with a few fresh figs to freshen things up a little; **t**24 silky arrival on palate as the charming grain magnifies the rich barley presence; the bittersweet theme is glorious; **f**23 pulsating oaky vanilla soothed by the firming cocoalaced grain and developing spices; **b**24 an entirely different animal to before, sensual and supremely balanced: top draw blending. **43%.** *Allied.*

**Ballantine's 30 Year Old (84) n**21 **t**21 **f**22 **b**20. Changed dramatically from of old, with sterner, more dominating, drier oak and an overall much crisper, less embracing character. Lovely malty, Horlicky finish, though. **43%.** *Allied.*

**Ballantine's Black (85) n**22 **t**23 **f**20 **b**20. Could be so much more elegant and complete if that early smoke-wafting malt stretched a bit further. **40%.** *Allied.*

**Ballantine's Finest (87) n**22 sweet, subtle smoke softening the firm grain; **t**22 immediate peat impact, then a delicious delivery of biting grain and lilting malt; **f**20 the grain softens with developing oak; **b**23 always a classy, classic act, this has softened and become a little smokier, fuller bodied and significantly more complex in recent times. **40%.** *Allied.*

**Ballantine's Limited (89) n**22 excellent clarity of fruit and barley; **t**24 early grain and then a slow, complex delivery of malt surrounded by soft grape and the lightest coating of muscovado sugar; **f**21 dryer with some bitter-almond and cocoa on the oak; **b**22 a quality newcomer that is beautifully textured, fabulously constructed and an almost teasing rum-like quality. **43%.** *Allied.*

**Ballantine's Master's (82) n**21 **t**22 **f**19 **b**20. Excellent lively grain and chewy malt, but the always suspect, grain-drizzled finish has become even more nondescript in recent bottlings. **40%.** *Allied.*

**Ballantine's Original Character (94) n**22 chunky, almost thick in its heady malt richness; the grain chips in with deft oak; **t**24 near perfect mouth arrival with an explosion of spices that sends sweet malt to all parts of the palate. The grain comfortably criss-crosses the malt to lighten the load on the tastebuds; **f**24 more grain involvement now, but the burnt caramel/mild roast Java coffee effect adds another degree of glorious complexity. The finale is near endless with some Demerara digging of further depth; **b**24 this is big, bold blending from the old school that really rattles the tastebuds.A stunner. **47%.** *Allied.*

**Bell's Aged 8 Years (83) n**19 **t**22 **f**21 **b**21. The soapiness on the nose and late finish are compensated for by a surprisingly rich malt, biscuity backbone. **40%.** *Diageo/Arthur Bell & Sons.*

**Bell's Extra Special (75) n**19 **t**19 **f**18 **b**19. A faded dram that shows overdependence on a nondescript fruitiness. **40%.** *Diageo/Arthur Bell & Sons.*

**Bell's 12 Years Old (90) n**22 new leather and a hint of honey; **t**23 both grains and malts arrive in just about equal measures for very busy, complex start. Silky mouthfeel and some wonderful gently smoked spices; **f**22 long and clean with vanilla dominating; **b**23 absolutely quality blending, and pretty remarkable considering the mass scale on which it is achieved. No one style dominates, though it would be fair to say this is on the light side of medium in weight. **40%.** *Diageo/Arthur Bell & Sons.*

**Bell's Islander (82) n**21 **t**21 **f**20 **b**20. A blend that has been discontinued a little while, though in 2003 I have spotted it in bars as far apart as Copenhagen and Oxfordshire. These later bottlings were softer than the first run with the added Talisker not showing to great effect. Chewy, but a little toffeed. **40%**

**Ben Aigen (68) n**17 **t**18 **f**16 **b**17. Sweet caramel; bland and dusty. **40%**. *G&M*.

**Ben Alder (85) n**20 yielding and sweet; **t**23 an absolute avalanche of complex fruit and barley flavours, stretched out by silky grain; **f**21 sweet and rich with much toffee and spice; **b**21 a delicious dram, especially with the massive mouth arrival. But not quite what it was at the moment. **40%**. *Gordon & MacPhail*.

**Beneagles (67) n**17 **t**18 **f**16 **b**16. Flat and lifeless. **40%**

- **Benmore (74) n**19 **t**19 **f**18 **b**18. Underwhelming to the point of being nondescript. **40%**. *Diageo*.

- **Ben Nevis "Blended at Birth" 40 Years Old** Matured in sherry cask, dist 1962, bott 2002 **(91) n**22 what an intriguing overture: coal smoke and apricots add weight and softness to the ultra-firm grain. A very soft waft of bourbon adds to the mix; **t**24 this is where it hits top gear: the stunning arrival on palate and immediate impact. The gristy malt sweetness radiates in all directions taking with it a gooseberry-like fruitiness. The grain, though cumbersome, then strikes home bringing with it oak and spice; **f**22 delicate cocoa at first, then bitters; **b**23 the Ben Nevis distillery manager sent me another bottle of this, as he was a bit miffed I wasn't too impressed by this blend when I first tasted it in 2002. Oddly, I can't find any previous reference in the Bible, so gave it another shot. And am I glad I did. This would have been better called "Married at Birth" because the Ben Nevis grain and Ben Nevis malt were blended as new make and then allowed to mature for 40 years in sherry butts. There is nothing else like it on the market, and there are still some of these to be had at the distillery. **40%**. *Ben Nevis Distillery*.

**Ben Roland Five Years Old (81) n**19 **t**21 **f**20 **b**21. Caramel led, sweet, spicy and quietly complex. **40%**. *For Unwins, UK*.

- **Berrys' Blue Hanger 30 Years Old (88) n**22 curiously, a touch of the Blue Mouse distillery in Germany about this one, such is the way the bitter-ish oak is grabbed in. Attractive with a tantalizing degree of exotic fruit, but distinctly curious for a blended Scotch; **t**22 an unusual, bitter start, despite the near perfect body; then a starburst of malt and kiwi fruit and then back to some oily oak; hard to spot the grain: it must be here somewhere; **f**22 an attractive fall out of vanilla and dusty barley; **b**22 just a shade too oily for it to blossom to its full potential, perhaps. Stunningly beautiful in part but is it good enough to bear the Blue Hanger badge of brilliance? You decide. **45.6%**. *Berry Bros & Rudd*.

- **The Best 8 Years Old Scotch Whisky** (*see* Morrison's The Best)

**The Big Ben Special Reserve (83) n**20 **t**22 **f**20 **b**21. Bong: big caramel. Bong: rock hard and irresistible grain fortified by Speysidey malts. Bong: fabulous bite. Bong: the most outrageous bottle on the market moulded as the famous London landmark. Bong: if you've seen an old black and white film of the place, this is just the kind of whisky they would have been drinking – as this is a style recognizable 50 or 60 years ago. Bong: who needs a clock? This should live on the mantelpiece and every home should have one. **40%**. *Angus Dundee*. ⊙ ⊙

**Big "T" (77) n**19 **t**20 **f**19 **b**19. Not long ago I would drink this with anyone, anywhere. Something drastic has happened and some pretty poor standard whisky has crept into this to disrupt the pristine elements that can still be spotted. Still has its moments, but would the real Big T please come forward.... **40%**. *Tomatin Distillery*.

**Black & White (88) n**24 sublime aroma of pears and oak couched in gentle but significant peat; **t**22 decent malt thrust early on ensures a chewy haughtiness. The grains filter through slowly to lighten the experience, though a soft waft of smoke generates further complexity; **f**20 vanilla and caramel; **b**22 such is the enormous jump in quality from a couple of years back, I had to taste this one three times. Just wonderful blended whisky, not only of the old school but of a style I remember from this brand 20 years ago and I feared lost for ever. The return of a minor classic. **40%**. *Diageo/James Buchanan & Co*.

**Black Bottle (91)** n22 some gnawing grains make the teasingly smoked malt work hard for its money; t23 a battling fizz reveals some youngsters having fun in there. Like the nose, the grain really does fight its corner and the fault line where it meets the malt is marked by a spicy, smoky sweetness; f23 the buzz continues and there is a touch of demerara sweetness and coffee to the chewy smokiness; b23 it has taken me a bit of time to get used to this slight change in style for this persistently brilliant blend. This one's been reduced in smoke and roughed up a little: the intervening grain which restrained the battling malts has now become a bit of a bruiser in its own right. Ignore the nonsensical claim of "Original Blend" on the label: this is a very old brand that has gone through many changes in its lifetime and will be unrecognizable from the modest whisky concocted over a century ago in an Aberdeen shop. And there are any number of us who are so glad it is nothing like the seething firewater it was 20-30 years ago. But it has kept true-ish to its re-birth under Allied when they turned it into a peaty beast and is probably closer to that in style that Highland's subsequent, lush re-working of it. **40%.** *Burn Stewart/Gordon Graham & Co.* ☉ ☉

**Black Bottle 10 Years Old (89)** n22 so age-weightedly peaty it could be almost a single malt: the grains make little discernible impact; t23 soft, deft malt and firmer grain. The peat arrives after a short interval; f22 more vanilla and other oaky tones; b22 a stupendous malt of weight and poise, but possessing little of the all-round steaming, rampaging sexuality of the younger version ... and like the younger version showing a degree less peat: here perhaps even two. Not, I hope, the start of a new trend under the new owners. **40%.** *Burn Stewart/Gordon Graham's.*

**Black Cock (78)** n19 t20 f19 b20. Overtly grainy but a surprisingly malty mouthwatering quality makes for a half-decent blend. **40%**

⋙ **Black Dog 12 Years Old** Batch no. 015, bott Nov 05 **(92)** n21 distinctly nutty – especially walnuts – with no more than a hint of citrus lightening the deep vanilla and toffee. Gentle and attractively layered; t23 soft grains delve gently into the tastebuds offering light oak and a distinct toastiness. The barley sweetness is relaxed and clean; f24 traces of soft honey and a strand of marmalade welcome the visiting spices which cling to the subtle oils clamped to the roof of the mouth. Almost a near perfect finish for a blend this age. Stunning!; b24 an altogether thinner style than Century but offering genuine sophistication and élan. This minor classic will probably require two or three glass-fulls before you take the bait... **42.8%.** *United Distillers India Ltd.*

⋙ **Black Dog Century (89)** n21 a big nose displaying grainy teeth at first but chunky fudge and dried dates weigh in impressively; t23 mouth-filling and distinctly viscous, chocolate fudge clamps itself to the roof of the mouth allowing a lighter, teasingly spicy pulse to do its work around the back of the tongue. Meanwhile, a well-mannered sweetness lurks around every corner ensuring the oak is on its best behaviour. Big and no shortage of complexity; f23 brilliantly long and chewy with the chocolate fudge b22 I adore this style of no-nonsense, full bodied bruising blend which amid the muscle offers exemplary dexterity and finesse. What entertainment in every glass!! **42.8%.** *McDowell & Co Ltd, India. Blended in Scotland/ Bottled in India.*

**Black Douglas (83)** n20 t20 f22 b21. Big, chewy, well weighted and fat. Pretty long, decently smoked nose and finale. **40%.** *Australia.*

**Blackpool (73)** n18 t19 f18 b18. Grain and sweet toffee. Easy going but never hits the bright lights. **40%.** *Invergordon.*

**Black Prince (68)** n16 t19 f17 b16. One rich flourish apart, way off target. **40%.** *Burn Stewart.*

**Black Prince 12 Years Old (80)** n19 t22 f19 b20. Soft and silky, there is good fruit and crisp grain. A spicy but toffeed finish. **43%** *Burn Stewart. A discontinued blend now: a collector's item if you see it.*

**Black Top Finest De Luxe (77)** n19 t21 f18 b19. Silky, sweet and rich, but a touch too much caramel dulls the complexity. **40%**. *Aberfoyle & Knight.*

**Black Watch** (*for tasting notes see* 100 Pipers)

**Blue Hanger 25 Years Old** bott 03 **(93)** n23 a silky sheen makes for the softest of nasal impacts; ripe grape and mango to the fore with a barley-sugar sub plot. Real fruit cake fodder; t24 lush arrival and then a slow unravelling of subtle spices; the fruitiness clings to the roof of the mouth as an obviously high malt percentage makes its mark; f22 some grain and oak are visible at last as a gradual thinning out of flavours begins; b24 an exceptional blend that offers a subtle bite to balance perfectly the lush intensity. The biter-sweet balance is exemplary. Brilliant. **45.6%. nc ncf.** *Berry Bros & Rudd.*

⋅⋅⋅ **Blue Hanger 30 Years Old** (*see* Berry's Blue Hanger)

**Bruce and Company Scotch Whisky (79)** n19 t21 f20 b19. The minimalist label – "Scotch Whisky" in black on white – somehow perfectly summarises a minimalist dram. This, for all intents and purposes, is young grain whisky with a dash of malt – and I do mean a dash. And topped up with some colouring. Yet, it's sweet, has a rich mouthfeel, there are no off-notes and perfectly enjoyable – providing you are not on the hunt for complexity. **40%**. *Exclusive to Tesco UK.*

**Buchanan's De Luxe Aged 12 Years (91)** n23 freshly-squeezed grape and profound clean barley. Excellent; t23 luxurious and lucid with a wonderful development of classy Speysidey-malt weighed down by a burst of peat and cocoa; f22 the grains move in offering vanilla and a drying shelter from the mouth-watering malts; b23 a significantly improved blend over recent years and some time since I've come across the duff sherry that used to mar it. Genuine elegance and now back up there with the world's classier blends. **40%**. *Diageo Venezuela/James Buchanan & Co.* ☺ ☺

⋅⋅⋅ **Buchanan's Red Seal (90)** n22 clean with almost equal portions of grain, malt and oak; t23 wonderful malt clarity guarantees a rare charm; the grains are crisp and amplify the barley sweetness; f22 lovely sweet vanilla complements the persistent barley; b23 exceptionally good, no-frills blend whose apparent simplicity paradoxically celebrates its complexity. **40%**. *Diageo.*

**Buchanan's Special Reserve Aged 18 Years (86)** n22 t22 f21 b21. Has flattened out slightly in recent years and become somewhat dull. **40%**. *Diageo* ☺ ☺

**Budgens Scotch Whisky Finely Blended (84)** n20 t21 f22 b21. A quite dramatically improved blend from the old grain and caramel fest it once was. Stirring a decent amount of peat into the mix has helped the cause no end. **40%**. *Budgens, UK.* ☺ ☺

**C & J Fine Old (89)** n22 the soft grains help further the marmalade and malt; t23 absolutely spot-on malt integration: sparkling and fresh on the palate with delicate oak notes popping in; f22 vanilla and more citrus; b22 I didn't get where I am today without spotting a surprisingly spacious, excellently blended, high quality dram when I see one. Super. Great. And I raise my sample glass to toast: Happy 70th Birthday, David Nobbs! And, also, Henry Pratt! **43%**. *Diageo.*

**Campbeltown Loch (90)** n22 sparkling barley; t23 clean, crisp grain helps accentuate the mouthwatering malt; f22 lightens with vanilla; b23 restored to its former classical grace and beauty. A blend-lover's blend. **40%**. *Springbank.* ☺ ☺

**Campbeltown Loch 21 Years Old (91)** n24 stunning depth here: the oak seems to be part of the barley, which in turn folds neatly into the silky grain. A gentleman; t22 the light grains show first, and then the malt arrives to offer soft waves of more complex but restrained substance; f23 fabulous fade: long with a development of fruit and very mild smoke; b22 there's 60% malt in this one. And, my word, it shows...!! **40%**

**Catto's Deluxe 12 Years Old (81)** n19 t22 f20 b20. Appears to have changed shape considerably: the nose has a sulphury catch and after a delicious sparkle to the palate settles down slightly **40%**. *Inver House.*

**Catto's Rare Old Scottish Highland (89) n**22 fresh, sensual. The grains are brilliantly chosen to allow full malt impact; **t**22 adorable formation of sweet Speysidey malts just melt in with the lush grain; **f**23 long and spicy and a touch of chalky oak adds to the balance; **b**22 silky and rich, this is delicious everyday fare of considerable charm. A truly classic, crisp young malt that is way above its station. For confirmation, smell the honey on the empty glass. **43%.** *Inver House.*

**The Charles House (73) n**18 **t**19 **f**18 **b**18. Sweet and sticky. **40%**

**Chequers De Luxe** bott lott L5108 **(76) n**19 **t**20 **f**18 **b**19. Standard, uncomplicated fare for Venezuelans with big grain lead and toffee finish. **40%**. *Diageo/John McEwan & Co.*

**Chivas Brothers 1801 (92) n**23 **t**24 **f**22 **b**23. The kind of dram you just can't say no to. Quality. **50%.** *This, tragically, has now been lost to us and has evolved into Chivas "Revolve".*

**Chivas Brothers Oldest and Finest (94) n**24 beguiling stuff of most untypical Chivas style: smoke and peat blending in with the fruit, nutmeg and allspice. The sherry influence is sublime; **t**24 just flows on from where the nose left off. The sherry is clean and weighty and beautiful spices arrive to flit around the palate. The malt is big with a degree of smoke and the grains do what grains should do best: polish the malts and marry the styles. Absolutely breathtaking; **f**22 long with smoke and a sound structure. The spices continue to sparkle and the fruit also gathers intensity; **b**24 it breaks my heart to announce that the blend has been discontinued, though a search through specialist outlets should reveal the odd bottle or two lurking about. Make no mistake: this is testimony to the art of brilliant, sympathetic and intuitive blending. What we have here is a masterpiece. **43%**

**Chivas Regal 12 Year Old (82) n**19 **t**20 **f**23 **b**20. A great improvement on recent years. But 30 years ago this used to be my house whisky and I still expect a lot more from it than this. The nose is much repaired, with a distinct Speyside thread now visible through the grain, but after a muddled, slightly dull arrival on the palate it is the finish that stars, and that owing mainly to some decent oak (offering stunning mocha and praline) and malt. The grain remains a headache and the whisky staggers around unbalanced for the most part. Still, at least it is heading in the right direction, though a bottle I tasted earlier this year, a few months before this sample, was a bit of a horror show. Let's pray it is heading in the right direction because this does have one or two truly classy moments. **40%.** *Chivas.*

**Chivas Regal 18 Year Old (77) n**20 **t**20 **f**18 **b**19. The 12 may have picked up, but this has regressed badly. Good fruit on the nose, but it is hard to escape from the bitter grain and caramel. A massive disappointment. **40%.** *Chivas.*

**Chivas Revolve (79) n**18 **t**22 **f**19 **b**20. Although tasting significantly better than it noses (some pretty tired casks have made it into this one), this brand is going backwards. **40%.** *Chivas Brothers.* ☉ ☉

**Clan Campbell (84) n**20 **t**22 **f**21 **b**21. Genuinely enjoyable whisky, but much too dependent on the caramel. The puckering, mouthwatering Speyside and spice of yore have been seen off by an altogether silkier dram. **40%.** *Chivas.*

**Clan Campbell Legendary Aged 18 Years (89) n**22 accomplished oloroso notes are thinned by attractive grain-led vanilla: stylish stuff; **t**23 superb: a real outbreak of all things complex with soft grain at the centre but fruit heading from one malt to another and a very subtle smokiness from elsewhere; **f**22 more simple but the gentle vanilla and distant echo of spice is a tease; **b**22 greatly improved on recent years and now a dram of unquestionable distinction. **40%**

**Clan MacGregor (92) n**22 superb grains allow the lemon-fruity malt to ping around: clean, crisp and refreshing; **t**24 as mouthwatering as the nose suggests with first clean grain than a succession of fruity and increasingly sweet malty notes. A brilliant mouthful a tad oilier and spicier than of old; **f**23 yielding grain;

and now, joy of joys, an extra dollop of spice to jolly it along; **b**23 just gets better and better. Now a true classic and getting up there with Grants. **43%**. *William Grant & Sons.* ⊙ ⊙

**Clan MacGregor 12 Years Old (84) n**21 **t**20 **f**22 **b**21. The suspicion is that the grains are a lot older than 12: there is a lot of bourbon-oaky character on the nose and on the mouth arrival. Great finish, but lacking the all-round fresh-faced charisma of the young MacGregor. *Wm Grant's US.*

⸬ **Clan Murray Rare Old (84) n**18 **t**23 **f**21 **b**22. The wonderful malt delivery on the palate is totally incongruous with the weak, nondescript nose. Glorious, mouth-watering complexity on the arrival, though. Maybe it needs a Murray to bring to perfection... **40%**. *Benriach Distillery.*

**Clan Roy (87) n**20 gritty and grainy, still too much caramel here; **t**22 the peaty influence of Bowmore takes a little time to arrive and takes second place to some pretty attractive grassy malt and firm grain; **f**23 wonderfully long and perfectly spiced. A lingering sweetness allows the finish to continue in its soft and silky vain; **b**22 a vastly improved, chunky and now hugely enjoyable blend showing big malt on the palate despite the grainy nose. Terrific session whisky. **40%**. *Morrison Bowmore.* ⊙ ⊙

**The Claymore (76) n**17 **t**20 **f**19 **b**20. A much more tastebud-friendly blend than the old cut-and-thrust number of yore. Still can't say the nose does much for me but the developing fruitiness on the middle and finish is silky and complex. **40%**.

**Cluny (85) n**20 **t**21 **f**22 **b**22. I adore this kind of slightly rough-edged blend: every time you take a mouthful something slightly different happens. If I were to find fault, a touch too much caramel is evident at the very death. **40%**. .

**Compass Box Asyla** (second bottling (2003) – small picture, fluted bottle 40% abv) **(93) n**23 **t**23 **f**23 **b**24. So sexy, you could almost make love to it. Unquestionably one of the best light blends on the market. **nc ncf**.

**Compass Box Asyla** bottle identification L4097 **(92) n**22 like a trifle ... but without the sherry; **t**23 very clever strands of sugar-honey intertwine with both grassy malt and clean grain; **f**23 long and laid-back with no weight whatsoever but an erogenous caressing of the tastebuds with an almost covert flavour attack; **b**24 subliminal whisky that may wash over you unnoticed for the first two or three mouthfuls but then you wake up to what is happening to you: and that is pretty sexy stuff, believe me ... **40%**

⸬ **Compass Box Asyla Marriage** Married for nine months in an American oak barrel **(88) n**22 a soup of a nose, though slightly over oaked for perfect harmony; **t**23 a big, sweet cherry tart kick off with custard and spices galooped on top; **f**21 warming, spiced vanilla; **b**22 a lovely blend, but can't help feeling that this was one marriage that lasted too long. **43.6%**. *Compass Box Whisky for La Maison du Whisky in commemoration of their 50th Anniversary.*

**Compass Box The Double Single (83) n**21 **t**22 **f**20 **b**20. This is a lively blend consisting of a single cask of malt and a single cask of grain. For all the brightness, doesn't entirely work because of the nose prickle, early hotness and slightly ungainly finish. But refreshing and chewy all the same. **46%**. *Compass Box for The Craigellachie Hotel, Speyside.*

**Co-operative Group (CWS) Scotch Whisky (86) n**20 **t**23 **f**21 **b**22. Always great to see a standard blend going up in quality – in this case rising dramatically. A beautifully clean Scotch (and would be a real pale stunner if they ditched the caramel), refreshing, salivating and bursting with excellent grain and Speyside-style malt. Has every right to stand by the big boys in the family cupboard. **40%**. ⊙ ⊙

**Co-operative Group (CWS) Premium Scotch Whisky Five Years Old (73) n**17 **t**21 **f**17 **b**18. Complex middle, but let down by poor cask selection. **40%**. *Co-op UK.*

⸬ **Corney & Barrow No. 1 Scotch Whisky 12 Years Old (85) n**20 **t**23 **f**20 **b**22. Attractive and beautifully structured, this would be a real classy stunner but for the overuse of caramel. **40%**.

⟐ **Corney & Barrow No. 6 Scotch Whisky (76)** n18 t20 f19 b19. A raw, viperish blend that strikes immediately but sooths with an overly sweet, oily fade. **40%**

**Covent Garden 10 Years Old (88)** n22 the style is classical and one of crystal clarity; t23 the marriage between those crisp, clean Speyside malts and refreshing grain is one of harmony and bliss: seems younger than its 10 years thanks to minimal oak interference; f21 which arrives towards the finish and dumbs down the rampaging complexity; b22 what an outstanding blend this is: pity – though no surprise – that the Cadenhead's shop in Covent Garden that sells it runs out so quickly. **40%** *Cadenhead's.UK.*

⟐ **Craigellachie Hotel Quaich Bar Range (81)** n20 t21 f20 b20. A delightful malt delivery early on, but doesn't push on with complexity as perhaps it might. **40%**

**Crawford's (79)** n19 t21 f19 b20. An attractive, delicate little creature until the caramel takes hold. **40%.** *Whyte and Mackay Ltd.*

**Crawford's 3 Star (87)** n22 punchy grain with malty depth not far behind; some smoke adds weight; t21 big body and pleasant oils; f22 wonderfully long, with rich dark chocolate for afters; b22 an honest, complex and characterful dram that's worth a shout. **40%.** *Diageo.*

**Crown Whisky Co. Very Rare Highland Special Reserve (74)** n18 t19 f18 b19. A competent grainy blend with a hint of oak. **40%.** *Denmark only.*

**Custer's Imported Scotch Whisky (81)** n19 t21 f20 b21. For an ultra cheapy there is surprising dexterity to this caramel-rich but otherwise clean and attractive dram. **40%.** *Pierre Charles, Europe.*

**Cutty Sark (88)** n23 light and floral with firm grain accentuating the malt; t22 big grain surge then a slow build-up of Speyside maltiness. Grassy and sharp throughout with a lovely Tamdhu-esque oiliness; f21 lots of vanilla and a thread of cocoa on the finale; b22 always been light, but virtually all peatiness has vanished of late. Even so, a real cracker of crispy grain. **40%**

**Cutty Sark Aged 12 Years (82)** n18 t22 f21 b21. A blemish on the nose, but an otherwise lovely, fresh blend showing more sherry than of old and excellent spices throughout. **40%**

⟐ **Cutty Sark Aged 15 Years (78)** n19 t20 f19 b20. Drinkable and at times charming, but an off sherry butt has upset the delicacy and rhythm somewhat. **40%.**

**Cutty Sark Aged 18 Years (93)** n24 outstanding clean sherry influence, softly smoked and good oak, almost bourbony, input. Beautiful; t23 big, spicy and immensely chewy; f22 lots of cream toffee, and a hint of tiring oak, but the grain is really high quality and delicious; b24 absolutely stunning. The clever use of the grain is simply breathtaking. **43%**

**Cutty Sark Aged 25 Years (90)** n23 massive acacia honey and vanilla sing sweetly; t23 as intense as an old pot-still demerara with absolutely stunning mouthfeel and fruity richness; f22 long, with gathering spices and a hint of smoke. The grains are minute but exemplary and chocolate-coated; b22 heavy and honeyed, chewy and charming, the oak has a fraction too big a say but still quite delicious! **45.7%**

**Cutty Sark Discovery** (*see* Cutty Sark Aged 18 Years)

**Cutty Sark Emerald** (*see* Cutty Sark Aged 12 Years)

**D Steven & Son (Wick) Ltd Finest 8 Years Old (80)** n20 t21 f19 b20. A solid, firm blend with satisfying smoke, bite and spice. Big grain finish. **40%**

**Da Mhile Organic Blended Scotch (89)** n21 the grain is typically Loch Lomond-ish in its embracing style, wrapping soft arms around the flintier, more energetic malt; not exactly perfect harmony but an endearing overture nonetheless; t23 now the blend comes together with the malt – sharp, mouthwatering, grassy and fresh – battling for independence from the enveloping grain but failing. Lots of complexity and character; f22 waves of soft vanilla and spice sit comfortably with the enduring malt; b23 a delicious blend against the odds: the grain and malts were mixed together from what was available from an organic point of view and make for a light, singular but highly attractive style. By no means perfect but it has worked, perhaps helped by liberal use of Springbank, making this probably the only blend made from organic Springbank malt you are ever likely to come across! **46%.** *Da Mhile. 1000 bottles.*

**Dewar's White Label (83) n**21 **t**22 **f**19 **b**21. A decent, punchy, mildly biting blend where the grains are proud to show themselves and the malt makes enjoyable, soothing and sweetening noises. The toffee dims the sparkle somewhat, though. **40%.** *Curiously, White Label is now the possessor of a pale yellow one...*

**Dewar's Ancestor Aged 12 Years** db **(77) n**18 **t**20 **f**19 **b**20. Usually this was, as old man Dewar might have said, a Ramble Round the Gob. This strange animal, though, a weird mix of enchanting complexity and several freshly struck sulphur matches, graphically underlines that nowadays using sherry butts can be tantamount to playing cricket with hand-grenades. **43.5%**

**Dewar's Special Reserve Aged 12 Years** batch 0403 db **(91) n**23 exceptionally well designed with the heavier smoke and fruit notes adding only a background noise to the slightly more three-dimensional grain and soft honey-malt; **t**23 big and mouthwatering with spices developing fast. Beautiful integration of the harder grains and a developing oakiness; **f**21 way too much toffee undoes some of the intricate complexity. The spices carry on unabated, though; **b**24 an unashamedly old-fashioned type of blended Scotch and closest to the traditional Dewar's style of pre-Second World War days. A seriously delicious transportation back in time to the days when blends were cherished. **43%**

**Dewar's 18 Years Old** db **(93) n**22 the oak from the grain leads the way on this with some soft malt and citrus fruit playing catch-up; surprisingly light and elegant for the colour; **t**24 the Dewar's signature of rigid complexity strikes from the off; a rock-hard wall of grain at first seems impenetrable then a fizzing, breathtaking and quite glittering array of malty-oaky tones of varying degrees of sweetness batter the grain into submission. Again some citrus bares its teeth in the middle; **f**23 there is a delicate cocoa dustiness to the malt that at last has broken free of the grain and fruit; **b**24 like all better blends, this is a whisky that needs re-visiting and listening to to get the best results. Handsome, distinguished and displaying almost immeasurable complexity. **43%**

**Dewar's Signature** bott code A 13122 **(95) n**23 distinctive and lucid despite some obvious age around. Very firm, almost crisp apples with sweeter malt softening the sharpness. The most subtle hint of something smoky ensures weight to the elegant, flighty complexity. One to take your time over and get to know; **t**24 an adorable attitude and edge to this one: the tastebuds are immediately pounded by jagged, busy spices; the grain is hard as nails with fabulous nip and bite and allows the truly mouthwatering malts to ricochet around the palate. Lusty and luscious, this is great stuff which gets even better as the cocoa-smoky middle emerges; **f**24 again the grains are confident enough to have their say, offering, amid clarity, a firm, cocoa-dusted hand that points to some serious age; the finale is at first slightly estery but at last unusually clean and clear; **b**24 a blend-drinker's blend that is uncompromising and not stinting on old-fashioned sophistication. Just love that spice kick and the biting boldness of the grains that hold their own amid some mouthwatering malt. This is serious whisky, of a style easily identified in the East by connoisseurs of Suntory's freshest and finest. An outstanding addition to the highest echelons of the blended Scotch and in recent bottlings has remained true to type but added an extra dimension of juicy exotic fruit which reveals itself randomly, as though there are now older whiskies being used. The result is a greatly improved and much longer finale that even shows some delicate peat. To keep its mind-boggling complexity and integrity, the age profile should go no higher. And to drink, there is now only one way: do not sip, take a large mouthful and keep it on the palate for about 12-15 seconds and then swallow whole. Welcome to the world of superblends!! **43%**. *John Dewar & Sons.* ⊙ ⊙

**Dewar's Signature** Batch 0403 db **(93)** n23 t24 f22 b24. As above, except for the most subtle, barely perceptible replacement of some smoke with top-notch, clean-as-a-whistle sherry. **40%**

**Dew of Ben Nevis (76)** n18 t19 f20 b19. Heavy duty stuff with a sweet finish. **40%**. *Ben Nevis Distillery.*

**Dew of Ben Nevis Hector's Nectar** (*see* Hector's Nectar)

**Dew of Ben Nevis Special Reserve (81)** n19 t20 f22 b20. Very firm malt, sweet, full-bodied and punchy grain – even a hint of honey on the spicy finale. **40%**. *Ben Nevis Distillery.* ⊙

**Dew of Ben Nevis Aged 12 Years (86)** n21 t22 f22 b21. An enormous improvement: a richer, roastier, all-round more delicious blend. **40%**. Ben Nevis Distillery. ⊙ ⊙

**Dew of Ben Nevis Aged 21 Years (90)** n23 citrus 'n' salt; t23 fabulous complexity wth illuminating malt showing sweetness to a salty depth and toasty oak; f21 thins out towards vanilla and milky coffee, but with a little orange to lighten the load; b23 a really lovely aged blend where the complexity is mindblowing. Go get...!! **43%**. *Ben Nevis Distillery.*

⋯ **Dew of Ben Nevis Blue Label (82)** n19 t22 f20 b21. A busier, lighter blend than the old Millennium one it replaced. The odd off-key note is handsomely outnumbered by deliciously complex, mocha tones with a touch of demerara. Ditch the caramel and you'd have a sizzler! **40%**. *Ben Nevis Distillery.* *Replacement for Dew of Ben Nevis Millennium Blend.*

⋯ **Dew of Ben Nevis Supreme Selection (77)** n18 t20 f20 b19. Some lovely raspberry jam swiss roll moments here. But the grain could be friendlier, especially on the nose. **40%**. *Ben Nevis Distillery.*

**Dimple 12 Years Old (83)** n21 t20 f21 b21. A puff of smoke adds a touch of clout to an otherwise light yet gently spiced and deliciously grained blend. **43%**

**Dimple Years 15 Old (79)** n18 t20 f21 b20. A sturdier dram than before, but over-sweet and still fails to get my pulse racing. **40%**. *Diageo.*

**Diners Deluxe Old Scotch 12 Years Old (85)** n21 t22 f21 b21. Genuinely classy stuff with attitude. **43%**. *Douglas Denham for Diners Club.*

**Diners Supreme Old Scotch 21 Years Old (82)** n20 t21 f21 b20. A massive blend with no little bourbony-oaky style. **43%**. *Douglas Denham for Diners Club.*

**The Dowans Hotel (88)** n22 t22 f22 b22. A marginally lighter (in character), fruitier version of The Inverarity (see below). Not quite so smoky as previous bottlings but remains a stylish treat. **40%**. *Inverarity Vaults for The Dowans Hotel, Aberlour.* ⊙ ⊙

**Duggans (76)** n17 t20 f19 b20. A young, high-grained blend which enjoys a short malty, spicy blast early on before settling for grainier, safer ground. **40%**. *Morrison Bowmore.* ⊙

**Duncan Taylor Aged Blend 35 Years Old** (Bourbon) **(81)** n18 t22 f20 b21. Worn and weary but just enough honeyed touches to keep it impressive. **46%**.

**Duncan Taylor Aged Blend 35 Years Old** (Sherry) **(83)** n20 t19 f23 b21. Exceptional chocolate honeycomb on the fruity finish. **43%**.

⋯ **Duncan Taylor Auld Blended Aged 35 Years** dist Pre 1970 **(93)** n23 a knife and fork nose appears too oaked but time in the glass allows some excellent marmalade and marzipan to appear; t24 glorious delivery: amazing silk, lots of gentle, natural caramel but topped with honeycomb; f22 chocolate malt and burnt toast; b24 only a handful of companies could come up with something like this. An infinitely better dram than previous bottlings, due mainly to the fact that the dangers of old oak appear to have been compensated for. **46%**. *131 bottles.*

⋯ **Duncan Taylor Auld Aged Blend 38 Years Old** dist 68, bott Mar 06 **(86)** n22 t22 f21 b21. Incredibly soft for all those years, but not a patch of the 35-y-o. **40%**. *623 bottles.*

**The Dundee (78) n**19 **t**21 **f**19 **b**19. A slight improvement on previous years but the caramel still undoes slightly the deliciousness of the bright, grainy arrival. Not a bad dram, though, with the excellent spice and bite doing a grand job. **40%.** *Angus Dundee.* ☉ ☉

**Dunfife (75) n**18 **t**20 **f**19 **b**18. Refreshing and chewy. **40%.** *William Maxwell.*

**EH10 (86) n**22 **t**23 **f**20 **b**21. From the same charm school as Bailie Nicol Jarvie, but lacks finish. Otherwise delicious. **40%.** *Sainsbury UK (from Glenmorangie).*

**The Famous Grouse (87) n**21 brusque, flinty grain which anchors the flighty malt; **t**23 comes into its own here with a fabulous heather-honey malt arrival which is at once soft but with a rod of steel through its spice with Speysiders bouncing off the grain. A flutter of busy spices help see off any early caramel involvement; **f**21 a touch sweeter and maltier than of late; at the death back to being much drier and Spartan; **b**22 remains sexy, elegant and refined with a stunning opening on the palate. The balance has improved of late with some extra, subtle spices, punching through the threatening caramel making for an altogether busier blend. **40%** ☉ ☉

**The Famous Grouse Cask Strength (87) n**22 amazingly big, fresh clean sherry for a light blend: the grains cut into the fruit with precision and no little grace; **t**22 seriously fruity at first then a wave of malt and toffee. The grain reforms towards the middle; **f**21 quite soft with lots of toffee and vanilla; **b**22 a chewy, stylish dram that absorbs the strength easily. Again the toffee is a bit on the heavy side but the overall grain-malt balance is deft and delicious. **59.4%**

**The Famous Grouse Gold Reserve Aged 12 Years (85) n**19 **t**23 **f**21 **b**22. A much more honeyed, richer and improved dram than of old. But the caramel could be cut considerably. **43%** ☉

**The Famous Grouse Islay Cask Finish (88) n**21 beautifully weighted with kippery tones amid nipping grains; **t**22 a real chewy mouthful: sweet with lots of obvious malt; **f**23 more grain presence with vanilla drying out the sweeter barley. Remains smoky and very long; **b**22 if ever you wondered what a peaty Grouse would be like, here you go. What makes it work is the alluring softness of the smoke. Genuinely graceful for all its weight. **40%**

**The Famous Grouse Port Wood Finish (75) n**20 **t**20 **f**17 **b**18. A surprising hint of smoke, but otherwise fruity and flat. **40%**

⋯∵⋯ **The Famous Grouse Scottish Oak Finish** bott Nov 05 **(95) n**23 not dissimilar to the European oak of Czech whiskies, but better control. This seems to accentuate the smoke slightly and the grain is lost in a fusion of malt and butter. Really lovely – and very different: in fact unique to any blend I've come across; **t**24 wow, wow, wow, wow, wow, wow...!!! The mouth arrival is memorable and truly orgasmic: just wave upon wave of something beautiful, seamless and spicy. A kind of half-sweet honeycomb – all roast and chewiness – stars with the grains at last making themselves heard with a string of vanilla thrusts. Those spices pound the sides of the tongue and the roof of the mouth and the bitter-sweet balance is sensational. Just to make things better still, there is just the right degree of bite one desires in a blend; **f**23 long, with mounting signs of oak dominance, but those glorious toasted-barley waves, now topped with muscovado sugar keep the blend honest. The final embers offer a surprising hint of juniper. Is that the oak...or the bottling hall?; **b**25 what a stunner! What a one off...!!! Sadly, this is a limited edition blend...and once those 7,092 bottles have been drunk, that's it! I sincerely hope they are already planting new Caledonian oak to make this a fixture on the whisky shelves for future generations! **44.5%.**

**Findlater's Finest (69) n**17 **t**18 **f**17 **b**17. A furry, sticky palate; mildly rubbery. **40%.**

**Findlater's Deluxe 15 Years Old (81) n**21 **t**20 **f**20 **b**20. The fruity nose is followed by a chunky arrival on the palate where the malt is thick and chewy. Some coffee on the finale. Takes time to acclimatise to this style of blend, but worth every second. **40%.** *Whyte and Mackay.*

**Findlater's Deluxe 18 Years Old (91)** n22 a hint of dry Lübeck chocolate marzipan; t23 decent soft malt sprinkled with light muscovado sugar; f22 back to bitter almonds and bourbon amid the lush grain; b24 the cleanest, lightest yet most comfortably weighted of the Findlater clan by some margin; supremely balanced with a lush texture and lilting complexity. Some serious blending went into this one. **40%.** *Kyndal.*

**Findlater's Deluxe 21 Years Old (89)** n22 subtle sherry, clean with simmering spice just below the surface; t23 lazy and demure for a blend of such age: the malt does possess a certain countering brittleness to the softer grain; f21 vanilla and a hint of sultana and toffee fudge; b23 dreamy, end-of-day blend when you want your tastebuds featherdusted before retiring. **40%.**

⋄ **The Formidable Jock of Bennachie (82)** n19 t22 f21 b20. "Scotland's best kept secret" claims the label. Hardly. But the silky delivery on the palate is worth investigating. Impressive roastiness to the malt and oak, but the caramel needs thinning. **40%.** *Bennachie Scotch Whisky.*

**Fortnum & Mason Choice 5 Year Old (83)** n20 t21 f22 b20. Good, solid grain helps propel a decent percentage of malt to rich, gently spicy deeds. An impressive 5-y-o by any standards. **40%.** *UK.*

**Frasers Supreme (77)** n19 t19 f20 b19. A dash of smoke helps add weight. **40%.**

**"Frisky Whisky" Macho 60% (81)** n19 t20 f21 b21. Big, grainy caramel: a standard, mildly smoky blend apart from the warehouse strength delivery and excellent finish. Possibly the best label on the market, though. **60%.** *John Milroy.*

**Gibson Glengarry (68)** n16 t18 f17 b17. Tough going. **40%**

**Glen Alba (76)** n20 t18 f20 b18. Changed shape slightly of late, with heaps of toffee. **40%.** *Duncan Taylor.* ☺ ☺

**Glen Calder (71)** n18 t19 f17 b17. Sweet; middle of the road. **40%.** *Gordon & MacPhail.*

**Glen Catrine De Luxe (77)** n17 t22 f19 b19. A dusty nose, but recovers for a rich, softly honeyed middle before caramel intervenes on the finish. **40%.** *Glen Catrine.*

**Glen Crinan (72)** n17 t19 f18 b18. Oily; full in places. **40%.** *Edrington France.* ☺

**Glen Crinan 12 Years Old (75)** n17 t20 f19 b19. Maybe I'm being fanciful, but I'm sure I'm detecting Glenturret's hand in there somewhere. A little soapy at first, honey and spice later. **40%.** *Edrington..*

**Glen Clova (70)** n18 t18 f17 b17. Grain and caramel all the way. I'm sure there must be some malt in there somewhere, but the grain is clean and decent quality, at least. *Ewen & Co for Oddbins UK.*

**Glendarroch Finest 15 Years Old (91)** n21 very firm grain surrounded on all sides by peaty ancient malt and bourbon oak; t24 impressive mouthfeel and early spice arrival, then a glorious expansion of quite stunning malt of a richness that needs tasting for comprehension. You can lose yourself in this one for some time; f23 the grains bite back and are quite welcome to rescue you from a malty trance: you will appreciate it more if you wallow in the bourbony afterglow; b23 this is exceptionally high-quality blending and a marriage of malts and grains that were meant for each other. **43%.** *William Gillies & Co.*

**Glen Dowan (79)** n18 t21 f21 b19. Does Scotch whisky come any sweeter than this? **40%** ☺

**Glen Dowan 21 Years Old (89)** n21 fresh, coastal and lively; t22 a real live wire around the palate with big malt presence; f23 lovely spices and exceptional oak control: truly brilliant; b23 big, bold and a little salty. Delicious, especially the finale. Out of this world bitter-sweet balance. **43%.** *J&G Grant Taiwan/Jap/Asia.*

**Glengarry** (*see* Gibson Glengarry)

**Glen Grigg (71)** n16 t19 f18 b18. Heavy; subtlety at a premium. **40%.** *Spar UK.*

**Glen Heather (90)** n22 hard, unyielding and grain-heavy it may be but the ginger nut bite is engaging. Enticing, confident stuff with the faintest touch of peat; t23 fresh, young and mouthfilling. The grains remain brittle and reflect perfectly the Speysidey malts which ensure maximum salivation. Some really excellent spice. Exceptionally clean and crisply defined; **f**22 pretty long with a slight sweetening and softening towards the finale. Some late evidence of age; **b**23 a quite lovely and lively blend from the old school. Clean and distinctive with a marauding spiciness, this is a blend that takes me back 25 years in style. The colour suggests caramel should be lurking somewhere and it does show very briefly and causing virtually no damage at the death. But as a whole this is a throwback, a minor classic blend worthy of discovery. **40%.** *SH Jones at their shops in Banbury and elsewhere in the heart of England.*

**Glen Lyon (78) n**20 **t**19 **f**20 **b**19. Light, clean and non-committal except, perhaps, for the hint of juniper on the nose. **43%.** *Diageo.*

**Glenmonarch (63) n**16 **t**17 **f**15 **b**15. Grim nose despite a inconclusive hint of peat; untidy mouth arrival while grain sweetens and then embitters for an awful finish. If there is malt in there I can't spot it other than possibly on the nose. And is it Scotch for sure? Doesn't say so on the label and although it is heavily implied, I'd be surprised if it is. All horribly synthetic. **40%.** *Belarus Bottling Co.*

**Glen Niven (79) n**20 **t**19 **f**20 **b**20. Way above average supermarket stuff: the nose shows superb grain qualities while the decent malt reveals itself in the finish. Overall, silky and complex. Rip out the OTT caramel and you would have a quality blend here. *Douglas MacNiven (Asda) UK.*

**Glen Osprey (71) n**17 **t**18 **f**18 **b**18. A pageant of young grain that is generally pleasant enough, especially towards the finish. Beware, though. Another I tasted earlier in the year was off-key and seriously awful. **40%.** *Duncan MacBeth & Co.*

**Glen Rosa (74) n**19 **t**18 **f**19 **b**18. Disappointing, oversweet and banal. Still room for improvement. **40%.** *Isle of Arran Distillers.* ☉ ☉

**Glen Rossie (68) n**18 **t**18 **f**15 **b**17. A marked deterioration with lower-grade grain and heightened superficiality. Massively disappointing: the significantly increased caramel cannot make up for the dramatic extraction of character while the finish is abysmal. I mourn the passing of a once good whisky. **40%.** *Quality Spirits International for Thresher Group, UK.* ☉ ☉

**Glen Shira (79) n**20 **t**21 **f**19 **b**19. A young blend that shows delicious citrusfruit qualities. **40%.** *Burn Stewart.*

**Glenshire (69) n**17 **t**18 **f**17 **b**17. Clean, young and caramelised. **40%.**

**Glen Stuart (79) n**18 **t**20 **f**21 **b**20. Honest whisky despite the caramel with an excellent grain lead: good session stuff. **40%.** *For Unwins, UK.*

**Glen Urquhart (82) n**20 **t**21 **f**20 **b**21. Gentle and mouthwatering with a touch of spice. **40%.** *Gordon & MacPhail.*

**Glinne Parras (85) n**23 **t**23 **f**19 **b**20. Brilliant nose and oily-coated malt mouth-start: the real enjoyment is all upfront. The finish could do with some attention. *Eaux de Vie.*

**Glob Kitty (77) n**17 **t**20 **f**19 **b**21. Clean, firm-grained, light and biting. Good standard whisky. **40%.** *Lehar Aus.*

**Golden Blend (88) n**21 a teasing aroma, one minute heavy the next of a fleeting grainy lightness: intriguing and attractive; **t**22 honeyed and complex, major chewy sweet malt against melting grain; **f**22 enters overdrive here, as the softness of the grain is stupendous. The malt has every chance to form a complex liaison with the gentle oak; **b**23 a sound, sophisticated blend of excellent weight and evenness. At no time either bitter or sweet. **40%.** *Kyndal.*

**Golden Dew (78) n**20 **t**20 **f**19 **b**19. High apparent grain and caramel. But pretty decent grain, it must be said. **40%.** *Burn Stewart.*

**Gordon Graham's Black Bottle** (*see* Black Bottle)

**The Gordon Highlanders (85) n**21 **t**22 **f**21 **b**21. A seemingly light whisky but with a weighty middle of some aplomb. The arrival on the palate is almost brain-exploding: in many ways one of the most complex drams on the market. But I suspect a big caramel presence prevents this from being a genuine classic. Glorious, creamy, sweet and lip-smacking stuff. **40%.** *Wm Grant.* ☉

**The Grand Bark (84)** n22 t22 f20 b20. The nose and malty-spicy arrival on the palate are to die for. *Symposium International.*

**The Grand Bark 21 Year Old (74)** n18 t20 f18 b18. The malt and grain just don't get on. **40%.** *Symposium International.*

**Grand Old Parr Aged 12 Years** batch no. L33P00063748 **(90)** n21 the sherry notes help cover a slight soapiness. The addition of the black pepper, though, is a masterstroke; t23 succulent mouth arrival: almost an Oregonian Pinot Noir in its burst of mouthwatering fresh fruit that is tempered by firm grain and gently spiced malt; f23 the spices continue as the vanilla arrives with a wonderful sunset of cocoa-imbued grain; b23 just such a massive improvement on the unwieldy mess that was Old Parr a couple of years back. Much more refined and dignified. **43%.** *Diageo.*

**Grant's** (*see* William Grant)

**Green Plaid (90)** n22 soft strains of Bowmore-style young peat; t23 remains youthful, and the smoke is still there, but the overall complexity as the crisp grains enter is worth a fanfare; f22 more kindergarten smoke while the barley remains fresh and mouthwatering; b23 has kept true to style but is now one of the best young blends around; very old-fashioned and a real cracker. **40%.** *Inver House.*

**Green Plaid 12 Year Old (87)** n22 peated but darkly so, with really impressive grain softness; t21 early vanilla and toffee with a malty thrust towards the end; f22 a shade of extra peat has lengthened the finale and improved the overall balance; b22 a very subtle, almost whispering whisky. **40%.** *Inver House.*

**Haig Gold Label (86)** n21 t22 f21 b22. A much lusher blend than of old, with nothing vague regarding its quality. **40%.** *Diageo/John Haig & Co.*

**Hamashkeh (79)** n21 t21 f18 b19. A good old-fashioned blend with a delightful grain bite. Love it, but could do with dropping the caramel slightly for a crisper flavour. The only blended Scotch kosher whisky on the market. **40%.** *The Hamashkeh Co. (VDB Spirits Ltd). Specially prepared whisky, ensuring that the entire system is sherry-free, with barrels and even the bungs being thoroughly cleaned for use.*

**Hankey Bannister (87)** n21 stoic grain reflecting a soft malty glow; t23 fantastic mouth arrival displaying a subtlety that would astound malt lovers: the even-handedness between the massaging grain and the more biting malt makes for a real lip-smacker; f21 the finish is slightly undone by caramel; b22 from an ordinary Joe to damned fine blend in the space of two years. You get the feeling that Inver House are reaping the rewards of some inspired distillery buying. **40%.** *Inver House.*

**Hankey Bannister Aged 12 Years (82)** n20 t22 f19 b21. The best bottling of this for a while: much cleaner and slightly cavalier on the palate with Speyside-style malts given much better support by the grain. Still needs to get the finish sorted, but a decent mouthful. **40%.** *Inver House Distillers.* ⊙ ⊙

**Hankey Bannister 21 Year Old (91)** n21 fruity, clean and lush but a hint of sap; t24 mouthwatering and improbably soft for its age, with the grain showing no claws whatsoever: you get the feeling this has been married for some time; f23 minimum oak fuss as the fruit continues for a very long finish; b23 for those who prefer their blends to purr rather than hiss and scratch. Quite magnificent. **43%.**

**Harrods Finest Blended Aged 5 Years (83)** n21 t21 f21 b20. Gives an impression of something older and wiser than five years in this one. Silky and old-fashioned in style, the grains have the leading edge and jag around the palate impressively. Too much toffee for this age, though: cut the caramel and you'd have something better still. Love it. **40%**

**Hector's Nectar (84)** n19 t22 f22 b21. A giant of a blend that takes no prisoners: young and pretty generous with the malt thrust, leaving complex grains for the biting finish. A good, rich, sweet session dram to be chewed and then the empty glass thrown in the fire!. **40%.** *Ben Nevis Distillery.* ⊙

**Hedges & Butler Royal (75)** n18 t20 f18 b19. Mouthwatering and crisp. **40%**

**Hedges & Butler Royal 15 Years Old (87)** n21 heavy and fruity with real grainy bite; t22 no less weight: again the grain bites deep but there is a lot of viscous fruit to soften the impact; f22 long and chewy, delicious bitter-sweet finish; b22 bit of a throwback: not an uncommon style of blend before the Second World War. **43%**

**Hedges & Butler 21 Years Old (91)** n24 gently smoked and generously honeyed, this is an essay in subtlety and complexity; t23 mouth-filling, rich and lush, the grains then begin biting and nipping; f22 shows some silky ageing, offering a hint of top-order bourbon with lots of butter-toffee but also some caramel; b22 As a taster, just about impossible to spit out! Absolutely classic stuff. You cannot ask for more from an aged blend. Except the strength to be at 46% and to be non-filtered or coloured. **40%**. *Ian MacLeod.*

**Henry Mason Scotch Whisky (72)** n17 t19 f18 b18. Dusty; overly sweet. **40%**

**High Commissioner (74)** n17 t21 f18 b18. A ubiquitous blend of spectacularly variable quality. This latest sample is mid-range with the usual rubbery nose, but the sweetness of the grain is a joy. Big stuff. **40%**. *A Bulloch.*

⊹ **Highland Bird (79)** n19 t20 f21 b19. An entirely competent whisky with a soft, malty strand amid the clean grains. Enjoyable. **40%**. *Robert McKie Neil Co.*

**Highland Black 8 Years Old Special Reserve (81)** n18 t22 f20 b21. Dramatically changed direction in the last year or two, offering increased spice to cut through the caramel and far better balance and chewability. Clean the nose, cut the caramel and you would have a blend up in the healthy 80s. **40%**. *Alistair Graham for Aldi.* ☉ ☉

**Highland Choice (74)** n17 t19 f20 b18. Soft, silky grain, sweet and attractive. **40%**. *Alistair Graham Ltd (Aldi Stores).*

**Highland Cross (89)** n21 a very comfortable grain firmness; t22 mouthwatering malts arrive early and make a soft landing for the gathering grain; f22 there is a rich Speyside thread amid the oily grain; b24 This is a wonderful blend: deceptively complex and always refreshing. Love it! **40%**. *Edrington Group.* ☉

**Highland Dream 18 Years Old (87)** n21 busy with the grain lively and enlivening; t23 brawny at first then a wonderful pell-mell of malty tones of varying intensity. Soft spice add further illustration; f21 a little toffee on the big grain-vanilla finale; b22 a handsome blend of the old school: my kind of relaxed session stuff. **43%**. *J & G Grant.*

**Highland Earl (82)** n20 t21 f21 b20. Rock-hard grain softened by caramel; the malt is pure Speyside. A little gem. **40%**. *Alistair Graham Ltd (Aldi Stores).* ☉

⊹ **Highland Gathering Blended Scotch Whisky (78)** n19 t20 f19 b20. Attractive, juicy stuff, though caramel wins in the end. **40%**. *Lombards Brands.*

**Highland Gold (80)** n20 t19 f21 b20. A very clean if slightly oversweet blend boasting soft, yielding grain and even a hint of peat and age. Not at all bad. **40%**. *Australia.*

⊹ **Highland Harvest Organic Scotch Whisky (76)** n18 t21 f19 b18. A very interesting blend. Great try, but a little bit of a lost opportunity here as I don't think the balance is quite right. But at least I now know what organic caramel tastes like... **40%**. *London & Scottish International.*

**Highland Poacher (81)** n18 t20 f22 b21. Young, grainy, mouthwatering. The nose and early arrival are odd, the development, though, is excellent and displaying early hints of smoke and delicious cocoa on finale. **40%**.

**Highland Queen (82)** n20 t22 f20 b20. A clean, grassy, Speyside-led young blend, the crispness clipped by caramel. **43%**. *MacDonald & Muir.*

⊹ **Highland Reserve (78)** n20 t21 f18 b19. Simplistic, untaxing, clean, sweet, over- dependent on caramel at the death....and thoroughly enjoyable! **40%**. *Quality Spirits International.*

**Highland Rose (83) n**20 **t**22 **f**21 **b**20. Firm, high-quality blend with superb grains. Nothing withered about this one. I adore this style of whisky for everyday dramming. **40%**

**Highland Stag (74) n**17 **t**19 **f**20 **b**18. Grainy, biting, raw... but fun. **40%**. *R.N MacDonald. US.*

**Highland Way (83) n**20 **t**21 **f**22 **b**20. A lush, clean dram with a rich middle and brilliantly spiced finish. For a duty free blend, you can't go wrong. **40%**. *Highland Way Whisky Co.*

**Highland Wolf (83) n**19 **t**21 **f**22 **b**21. Firm to crisp grain with impressive bite and spice. Good weight and late arrival of malt on finale. Well blended but let down a little by caramel. **40%** *Longman Distillers*

**House of Campbell Finest (73) n**18 **t**18 **f**19 **b**18. Very grainy and hard. **40%**. *Campbell Distillers.*

**House of MacDuff Gold Rush Scotch Whisky (81) n**20 **t**20 **f**21 **b**20. Clean, grain-laden and slight caramel. An acceptable and enjoyable blend, but is it whisky? This blend actually has tiny slivers of gold added and, strictly speaking, to be called whisky nothing outside caramel can be added ... time to pour yourself a glass and have a 24 carat debate. **40%**

**House of Peers (88) n**21 a soft wave of peat is the perfect go-between as grain and malt collide; **t**21 the marriage between delicious, biting grain and sweet malt is harmonious; **f**23 really goes into overdrive as that gentle smoke returns. Additional tingling grain helps make this a long, classical finish; **b**23 delicate smoke gives this attractive dram something extra to chew on. A really excellent example of how to make an outwardly light blend go a long way. **43%**. *Douglas Laing.*

**Ian MacLeod's Isle of Skye** (*see* Isle of Skye)

**Immortal Memory (69) n**17 **t**18 **f**17 **b**17. Easily forgotten. **40%**. *G&M.*

**Imperial Classic 12 Years Old (83) n**20 **t**22 **f**21 **b**20. A two-toned dram that is hard as nails on one hand and yielding and succulent on another. Tasty stuff on both levels. **40%**. *Chivas.* ⊙

**Imperial 17 Years Old** db **(82) n**19 **t**21 **f**21 **b**21. Seems lethargic at first, but it's so complex in the middle it's difficult to say where the middle ends and the end starts ... a real mouth-pleaser. **40%**. *Chivas. Korea only.* ⊙

**The Inverarity (90) n**22 pungent and waspish, there is a welcome degree of peat to overcome the grains; **t**22 mouth filling and chewy, the malt has much to say and dominates the weight and shape. Thrilling throughout; **f**23 the grains return but no balance is lost as the tangy barley and subtle smoke fight to the last; **b**23 truly wonderful complexity swamps the palate offering a vaguely orange-citrus theme to be replaced by something smokier: what a true classic this could be without the caramel dumbing things down slightly just as it promises so much. A real old-fashioned blend and a vast improvement on the last bottling I encountered. **40%**. *Inverarity Vaults.* ⊙⊙

⁘ **Iona Royale 25 Years Old (89) n**22 the rigid grain nails the malt to the glass. Yet there is something attractively of the dank forest about this; **t**23 hold on to something tight: several tidal waves of oak-spattered malt crash about the palate; a second wave of barley remains fresh and salivating before drying with the warming grain; **f**21 lots of burnt fudge and vanilla softened by an evasive sweetness; **b**23 a massively malt-rich blend that piles on the complexity early on. **43%**. *J&G Grant.*

**Islay Hallmark 8 Years Old (76) n**19 **t**20 **f**19 **b**18. Pleasant whisky that's just a bit too subtle with the Islay for it's own good. **40%**. *Morrison Bowmore.* ⊙⊙

**Islay Legend (86) n**22 **t**22 **f**21 **b**21. Threatens to go on the rampage, but behaves itself perfectly thanks to the most velvety grain imaginable. **40%**.

**Islay Mist Aged 8 Years (85) n**19 **t**22 **f**22 **b**22. Excellent weight and peaty freshness. Despite the youth, there is big character. **40%**. *MacDuff International.*

**Islay Mist Premium Aged 17 Years (93) n**23 one gets the feeling something very much older is lurking around: the gingery oakiness is big but kept in shape by the vastness of the peat. This is a balls-gripping blend you don't mess about with; **t**23 arms-behind-the-head, lean-back-and-close-the-eyes stuff. Meticulous citrus notes are bang in tune with the depth of rich, iodine-y peat. The grain is in evidence just lightening the load and offering vanilla oak; **f**23 the beautiful, lush, mildly oily texture continues. More citrus, especially lime, to combat the peat; **b**24 this is great, brave blending. I have compared it to one or two older samples of 17-y-o Islay Mist and this wins by several lengths. Brilliant. **43%**

**Islay Mist Deluxe (82) n**19 **t**22 **f**21 **b**20. For a blend, the grain is barely in evidence – texture apart – massacred under the weight of the fresh, young-ish peaty malt. Sweet, mildly citrussy chewy and lush. Great fun. **40%**. *MacDuff International.*

**Isle of Skye 8 Years Old (93) n**22 layers of peat dovetail with barley and solid grain while a wisp of honey sweetens things; **t**23 stunning. Magnificent fresh, oily peat pings round the palate, but leaves a smoky, toasty, oaky trail with a hint of marmalade fruitiness; **f**24 ridiculously long, remaining sweet and viscous with no shortage of oak and malt to bring the curtain down – eventually; **b**24 A textbook blend and an absolute must for any Islay-philes out there – in fact, a must for everybody! Your tastebuds are beaten up and caressed simultaneously. One of the most enormous yet brilliantly balanced whiskies in the world. **40%**. *Ian Macleod & Co.*

**Isle of Skye 12 Years Old (91) n**23 buttered kippers, big malt presence – even a hint of bourbon; **t**22 firm grain holds together the deft peat and intense vanilla; **f**23 one of the great blend finishes: smoky but allowing both oak and grain to shine for a sweetening finale; **b**23 This is a simmering blend of the very highest order: there is so much more beyond the peat. A real classic. **40%**. *Ian Macleod .*

**The Jacobite (76) n**19 **t**20 **f**19 **b**18. A young, clean, no-nonsense, enjoyable blend with a big grain presence that puts the "bite" in Jacobite. **40%**. *Malt House Vintners.* ☉

⫶ **James King 12 Years Old (81) n**19 **t**23 **f**19 **b**20. Caramel dulls the nose and finish. But for some time a quite beautiful blend soars about the taste buds offering exemplary complexity and weight. **40%**. *Quality Spirits International.*

⫶ **James King 15 Years Old (87) n**21 attractive amalgam of sawdust, crisp grain, grassy malts and a vague smoky toffee; **t**23 stunningly lush with fabulous weight attached to the malt, which just pings of the firm grains; **f**21 vanilla and toffee; **b**22 an impressive blend. **40%**. *Quality Spirits International.*

⫶ **James Martin's 20 Years Old (76) n**20 **t**19 **f**18 **b**19. A bucking bronco of a blend: wild, feisty and never properly tamed. **43%**. *Glenmorangie Co.*

**Jas Gordon Choice Highland Blend (77) n**19 **t**20 **f**19 **b**19. Beautiful grains from an eight-year-old. **40%**. *Gordon & MacPhail.*

**J&B –6C (87) n**23 proudly young in style and lively with green shoots of Speyside scampering all over the fresh grain. About as clean as it gets; **t**23 every bit as mouthwatering as the nose suggests with a crisp delivery of firm grain and even firmer barley. Not a matter of complexity, more one of effect, though there is a welcome buzz of spice; **f**19 thin to almost non-existent. Clean, still some naked, Speysidey barley doing the roads. But where's the oak? In fact, where is anything? **b**22 Quite a bizarre whisky because even youngsters often show more oak than this: it has been entirely deforested. A whisky that has been cleaned maniacally, yet there is still enough beautiful freshness within the barley to make this delightfully mouthwatering. I have to say this, though: give me this little belter any day over a blend lost in caramel. A dram I have become fond of (and would be fonder if they could sort the finish out) – even slightly chilled! **40%**.

**J&B Jet (88) n**21 good, firm grain with a light Speyside shadow; **t**23 sublime mouth arrival with mouthwatering Speyside-esque malt leaping around the palate with enormous freshness, youth and energy; **f**21 mildly disappointing as some vague toffee notes dull the complexity, though gentle grainy-spice brightens the finale; **b**23 very much in the traditional J&B mould with some livewire malt and grain keeping the tastebuds on their toes. **40%**. *Diageo*.

**J&B Rare (90) n**21 firm grain with a gentle Speyside edge; **t**22 mouthwatering and brittle, light yet stupendously rich as the malts fan out in all directions – other than a peaty one; **f**24 this is getting serious: the vanilla is spot on while shards of sharp malt and flinty grain rattle around the tastebuds; **b**23 for a while directly after the merger/takeover this blend went flat on us and I thought one of the great blends had been lost for good. Good news, folks, it's back! That wonderfully crisp Speyside freshness has been re-established and the blend is just like the old days. This is precious stuff: a bit of whisky heritage. Don't lose it again!!! **43%**. *Diageo/Justerini & Brooks*.

⠿ **J & B Reserve Aged 15 Years (78) n**23 **t**19 **f**18 **b**18. What a crying shame. The sophisticated and demure nose is just so wonderfully seductive but what follows is an open-eyed, passionless embrace. Coarsely grain-dominant and unbalanced, this is frustrating beyond words and not worthy to be mentioned in the same breath as the old, original J&B 15 which, by vivid contrast, was a malty, salivating fruit-fest and minor classic. **40%**. *Diageo/Justerini & Brooks*.

**John Barr (74) n**18 **t**20 **f**17 **b**19. Attractive, mouthfilling start, but marred by a bitter finale. **40%**. *Whyte and Mackay*.

**Johnnie Walker Black Label 12 Years (89) n**23 the fingerprint smoke has returned, yet the grains are making a bigger impression than of old; still the fruit offers further body, with citrus and apple to the fore; **t**23 mouthfilling and chewy, deftly peated and boasting more lush grain; **f**21 more than normal fruit around, a bit on the sherry-ish side; **b**22 a hugely complex blend that has struggled to find its old cocksure form in recent years but is beginning to show signs of its former, stunning self. The peat is better dispersed, but still some fruity flatter notes refuse to allow it to quite reach its once classic status. Tastebud seducing stuff all the same. **40%**

**Johnnie Walker Blue Label (88) n**21 the old, cleverly peated nose has been lost to us and now the accent falls on fruit though this is hardly as cleanly endearing as it might be; **t**24 but the magnificence of the mouth arrival is back with a bang with the most sumptuous marriage of over-ripe figs, voluminous malt and lightly sprinkled peat all bound together and then expanded by a brilliant use of firm and soft old grain. Spices also sparkle tease. Magnificent...; **f**21 oh, so disappointing again, with the plot played out on the arrival and there being insufficient reserve to see off the broodier elements of the slightly bitter oak; **b**22 what a frustrating blend. Just so close to brilliance but the nose and finish just being slightly out of kilter. Worth the experience of the mouth arrival alone. **43%**. *Diageo/John Walker & Sons*. ☺ ☺

**Johnnie Walker Gold Label (90) n**23 strands of honey hold together some clean, firm grain and Speyside grassiness and the most distant toll of peat: meticulous and refined; **t**23 spicy and sweet malt arrival on the palate with some much harder grains following up close behind; **f**21 relatively thin and bitter with the grains dominating to an unfair degree, though some peat smoke rumbles on to ensure weight and balance; **b**23 I have tasted any number of these since the very first bottling, and this is the first time it has out-scored Black Label – not least because it is so crisp, clean and beautifully defined. Also just slightly more peaty than most expressions which has guaranteed a superb balance. A blendconnoisseur's blend. **40%**

⠿ **Johnnie Walker Gold Label The Centenary Blend 18 Years Old (96) n**24 at first it seems a level nose with little happening. But look again...deeper. Stirring in the glass are diced apples and moist raisins, a squirt of something peaty, and a honey and golden syrup mix. Sweet yet weighty with just enough smoke and oak to anchor; **t**24 the silky arrival magnifies the smoky edge to this: some Caol Ila here, I guess, doing what Caol Ila does best – buck up blends. But also that hallmark honey thread is there to savour, linking beautifully with soft grains carrying vanilla and fudge; meanwhile playful spices...play!; **f**23 a beautiful denouement in which the vanilla-edged oak refuses to hide, but smoke and barley dovetail in wonderful counterbalance; **b**25 at the moment I would say that the blending lab at Diageo is going through a kind of legendary period. In years to come people will look back at it fondly and with a healthy degree of awe and ask: "do you remember when?"; or they will point to this era and say: "that's when it all started." White Horse 12, Old Parr and Johnnie Walker Gold: three blends where the gauntlet has been laid down to all: blenders and drinkers alike. And also where I say to Scotch lovers: well, you might love malts, but just how many can match these for brain-exploding complexity? This is another astonishing whisky which just has to be included in people's must have lists. Some of you I was talking to at a tasting in San Francisco, I think, will remember when I answered a question about age and blends: how I said that Walker's Gold appears to have older whiskies than when it was launched. Well this is because it slipped my radar that it was now a 18-year-old, rather than the original 15. Sorry about that. Age, as I have often argued, is as likely to do a whisky down as improve it. Certainly, though, not in this case... **40%.** *Diageo/John Walker & Sons.*

**Johnnie Walker Premier (89) n**22 leathery and waxy with distant hints of honey and peat; **t**23 big age on the malt, chewy nutty-toffee and quiet spices; **f**22 more peppery now with excellent oak amid the grain with toffee returning with some sweet coffee; **b**22 a luxurious blend with firm grain and big weight. A dram to take your time over. **43%**

**Johnnie Walker Red Label (84) n**20 **t**21 **f**22 **b**21. The Striding Man has taken enormous steps in the last year or so to compensate for the caramel with some voluptuous fruity notes and more comfortable smoke. The clarity of the grain on the finish is excellent. **43%.** *Diageo/Johnnie Walker.*

**Johnnie Walker Swing (79) n**19 **t**22 **f**18 **b**20. Grainy, biting and explosive, this blend sets itself apart from the other JW brands but is ultimately too well toffeed for its own good. **43%** ☉

**John Player Special (89) n**23 plenty of grassy fresh malt softens the grain. Genuinely wonderful and unfettered; **t**22 beautiful thirst-quenching fresh malt is lightened by good quality, clean grain; **f**22 clean, long, very soft vanilla but impressive malt; **b**22 Why can't more young blends be like this? Refreshing and mouthwatering, it positively basks in its youth. Of its type, utterly superb. **40%.** *Douglas Laing.*

**John Player Special 12 Years Old (81) n**20 **t**21 **f**20 **b**20. Solid and quite weighty, there are some teasing spices to go with the chewy malt. **43%**.

**John Scott's Superior Blended Aged 35 Years** bott 03 **(87) n**22 **t**22 **f**20 **b**23. Works incredibly well considering the big oak presence. Just enough smoke and honey to make this one to find and savour. **43%.** *675 bottles (two Highland Park quarter casks from 1965 and three more from '68, with a cask of 37-y-o Invergordon thrown in).*

**Kenmore Special Reserve (77) n**19 **t**20 **f**19 **b**19. Pleasant, but a thinner, sweeter, less demanding dram than of old. **40%.** *Marks and Spencer, UK.* ☉ ☉

**Kenmore Gold Special Reserve Deluxe Aged 10 Years (79) n**18 **t**21 **f**20 **b**20. Rich, well malted with a little spice and grain-cocoa on the finish. Done down by too much caramel, though. **40%.** *Marks & Spencer UK.*

**King George IV (70) n**18 **t**18 **f**17 **b**17. Sweet but caramel dominated. **40%.** *Diageo/John McEwan & Co.*

**King of Scots (84) n**20 **t**21 **f**21 **b**22. This is pretty raw whisky in places but what makes it a top-notch youngster is the superb balance. The grains dominate, but the malts really do make their weighty mark. Some good oiliness acts as a rich and tasty buffer. Great fun. **43%**. *Douglas Laing.*

**King of Scots 12 Years Old (80) n**19 t22 f19 b20. Some lovely oak involvement as well as rich malt and spice. But some toffee in there flattens the party somewhat. **43%**. *Douglas Laing.*

**King of Scots 25 Years Old (90) n**22 bourbon territory – age has given the nose a rare sheen: fruity and malty, too; t23 really excellent use of oak: acts as a counter to the sweet, silky grain enveloping the grapey malt; f23 long and richly textured with some bitter oaky tones but again the grain is absolutely outstanding; **b**22 supremely structured whisky with a most judicious and enterprising use of grain. The malts are clean and mouthwatering. A stunner. **40%**. *Douglas Laing.*

**King Robert II (71) n**17 t20 f17 b17. An otherwise honest, decent and mouthwatering blend spoiled somewhat by caramel. **40%**. *Ian MacLeod & Co.*

⁑ **King's Crest Scotch Whisky 25 Years Old (83) n**22 t22 f19 b20. A silky middle weight. The toffee-flat finish needs some attention because the softly estered nose and delivery is a honey-rich treat and deserves better. **40%**. *Speyside Distillers.*

**King's Pride (85) n**20 t23 f20 b22. Take away some of the toffee effect and you have a chewy, old-fashioned complex blend. **43%**. *Morrison Bowmore.* ⊙

**Kings Scotch (71) n**18 t19 f17 b17. Thin, with few surprises. **40%**. *The High Spirits Co.*

**Kuchh Nai (81) n**19 t22 f20 b20. Big, bold, spicy and immensely enjoyable. **40%**. *Kuchh Nai Marketing.*

⁑ **Label 5 Classic Black** L617456A **(75) n**18 t20 f18 b19. The off-key nose needs some serious re-working. Drop the caramel, though, and you would have a lot more character. Needs some buffing. **40%**. *The First Blending for La Martiniquaise, France.*

⁑ **Label Five Aged 18 Years** L606133A **(87) n**22 compare the nose with a fruit smoothie and try and spot the difference....! Some wonderful bourbony notes accentuate the age; t22 the oils could not have been better placed and the integration of the soft grain and the slowly pulsing malt is a joy: simple but sumptuous; f21 just loses its sure footedness with an overdose of flattening caramel; **b**22 a lovely little blend with a genuinely first-rate mouthfeel. **43%**. *The First Blending for La Martiniquaise, France.*

**Lancelot 12 Years Old (81) n**19 t22 f20 b20. A more succulent blend than of old. **40%**. *Edrington Group.* ⊙ ⊙

**Lancelot 17 Years Old (77) n**19 t21 f18 b19. The old honey has been lost, but better grain balance. A slight fruity bitterness (perhaps from a sulphured cask) warps the finish. **40%**. *Edrington Group.* ⊙ ⊙

**Langs Supreme Aged 5 Years (89) n**23 diced apples and sultanas, some uglifruit in there, too. Hint of something spicy and the grain is soft and crisp in equal proportion. Supreme, indeed; t23 soft, yielding and mouthwatering young malts are reined in by hardening grains: a bloodless coup; f21 some spice and vanilla but a tad too much caramel; **b**22 this is perhaps an object lesson in how to balance malts and grains. Hopefully the new owners, Ian Macleod's, will cut the caramel and raise my markings even higher next year. **40%**. *Lang Bros.*

**Langs Select Aged 12 Years (77) n**21 t21 f17 b18. Frumpy and, for all the building spice, ultimately a little passionless. **40%**. *Lang Bros.*

**Lauder's Blended Scotch Whisky (74) n**18 t21 f17 b18. Standard, caramel-rich fare. Delicious if shortlived mouth arrival, though. **40%**. *Macduff International.* ⊙ ⊙

**Lauder's 12 Year Old (85) n**21 t21 f22 b21. A really beautifully constructed blend offering finesse. **40%**. *MacDuff International.*

**Lauder's 15 Year Old (86) n**21 t23 f21 b21. Oddly enough it needs the grain to inject complexity into a blend that is otherwise seamless. **43%**.

**Little Frog (84)** n21 t22 f20 b21. A big, succulent Speysidey number with considerable charm. France only. **43%**. *William Maxwell for Société Dugas France*.

**The Loch Fyne (85)** n21 t22 f21 b21. Any peat about is now covertly operating within the spice. A good session dram, a little lighter than it once was. **40%**. *Loch Fyne Whiskies, Inveraray, UK*.

**Loch Lomond Single Blend (85)** n21 t22 f21 b21. A real heavyweight with a massive punch. A blend of malts and grains from the Loch Lomond distillery, including some crisp peaty stuff. Not exactly an exhibition of finesse, but real fun all the way. **40%**

**Loch Ranza (two words, old all blue label) (83)** n19 t22 f21 b21. A good, solid chewy blend of some panache. But a tad more bitter and toffeed than the present new bottling. **40%**. *Isle of Arran Distillers. Still found in miniatures*.

**Lochranza (all one word, cream and blue label) (78)** n20 t19 f20 b19. Has dived a bit over the last year or two, with the malt far harder to fathom. **40%**. *Isle of Arran*.

**Logan (83)** n22 t22 f20 b19. Great nose and mouth arrival but vanishes towards the end, though it is not without a certain complexity. It seems like it's the end of Logan's run. It's been discontinued, I understand. Worth adding to a collection, though. **40%**

⬙ **Lombard's Gold Label (88)** n22 chunky with a good malt depth; t22 silky and mouth-filling with the malts weaving beautifully into the grains; honeycomb towards the middle; f22 delicate spice and toffee-nut; b22 excellently weighted with some wonderful honeycomb and spice making their mark. **40%**. *Lombards Brands*.

**Long John (72)** n17 t20 f18 b17. Grainy, fruity, lush but throat-gripping. **40%**. *Allied*.

**McAndrews (66)** n17 t18 f15 b16. The old rum effect has gone on this. Now it's just a rum whisky. Dirty and cluttered around the palate. Seriously grim. **40%**. *Malt House Vintners*. ☉☉

**McArthurs (77)** n18 t21 f19 b19. A decent touch or two, but basic. **40%**. *Inver House*.

**McArthurs 12 Year Old (79)** n19 t21 f19 b20. A decent touch or two, but dull. **40%**. *Inver House*.

**McCallum's Perfection (80)** n20 t21 f18 b21. Pretty competent and clean of no great age. Lovely malty sweetness combining with soft smoke for a fullbodied start and then finishing with firm grain. **40%**. *D & J Wallum, Australia*.

**McDonalds (74)** n18 t19 f18 b19. Any thinner and it would be on a drip. **43%**. *Diageo*.

**McGibbons (79)** n19 t19 f21 b20. A pretty fat yet medium weighted blend that gathers momentum as the complexity builds. Good spicy finale. **43%**. *McGibbons*.

**Mackinlay's** (*see* Original Mackinlay)

**MacLeod's Isle Of Skye** (*see* Isle of Skye)

**Mac Na Mara (88)** n21 salt and soft fruits; t22 changed shape with softer, more yielding grains and malts now but still attractively assembled; f22 remains malty and complex; b23 a very impressive blend which I adore for its mildly rugged, macho character and superb complexity. **40%**. *Praban na Linne*. ☉☉

⬙ **Mac Na Mara Rum Finish (93)** n22 as is often the case, the rum has hardened the aroma; t24 beautifully crisp with fragile malts clashing with equally crisp barley; the touch of golden syrup works wonders; f23 serious depth to the malt; the grains soften out with vanilla; b24 this is high quality blending, and the usage of the rum appears to have retained the old Mac Na Mara style. Sublime. **40%**. *Praban na Linne*.

**Majestic Wine Fine Oak Cask Matured Scotch (78)** n20 t20 f19 b19. Youthful, biting grain forms the backbone and much of the meat of this pretty tasty and easily drinkable dram. **40%**. *Majestic Wine UK*.

**Major Parka (76)** n16 t20 f21 b19. Poor nose, but refreshing grain on the palate. A light but solid and enjoyable blend. **40%**. *Lehar Austria*.

**Marshal (72) n**17 **t**19 **f**18 **b**18. Very decently spiced. The nose has enough caramel to be a rum. **40%**. *Wm Maxwell Ltd.*

**Martins VVO (76) n**19 **t**20 **f**18 **b**19. Pleasant, sweet, non-committal. **40%**.

**Martins 20 Years Old (87) n**22 clean, intricate and lightly spiced; **t**23 massive malt presence for a blend; the grain offers a brick wall hardness from which some Speyside reflects beautifully; some superb slap and prickle; **f**20 short and quite dull; **b**22 such an improvement on the sherry-ruined previous bottling, this has great charm but the finish needs attention. **43%**. *Glenmorangie.*

**Martins 30 Years Old (87) n**22 clean, ripe sherry, grains very soft, mildly spiced; **t**22 silky, melt-in-the-mouth grain gives way to some sherry and sweet ginger; **f**22 soft vanilla and spices; **b**21 it's unlikely many drams are quite as laidback as this. What it misses in complexity (where the 20-y-o wins hands down) it makes up for in succulent, sherried sloth. **43%** *MacDonald & Muir.* ☉

**Matisse 12 Years Old (89) n**22 distinctly fruity with diced orange peel and hints of Lubec's finest marzipan. Subtle and increased complexity with clean and both soft and firm grains: very clever; **t**22 big grain statement from earliest mouth arrival; good age and intensity of chewy malt towards middle; **f**23 stunning array of beautifully composed grain guarantees the most vivid bitter-sweet cocoa finale. Excellent length with very slow and equal fade; **b**22 distinct improvement on the old-style, lumbering, heavyweight Matisse, with a wonderfully oldfashioned, ultra-traditional grain bite that accentuates the crispy-malt middle. A quietly classy dram. **40%**. *Glenmorangie for UIES, Taiwan.*

**Matisse 21 Year Old (92) n**24 stunningly complex citrus notes link wonderfully with the gentle oak and grains. Sheer seduction...; **t**23 the oak arrives first but lays a sawdusty platform for trilling malt and more lethargic grain. Again, this just works the palate so beautifully; **f**22 some coffee notes and spice offer a deft finale; **b**23 wonderful blending: quality here is never an issue. Worth a trip to Taiwan just to find! **40%**. *Angus Dundee for UIES, Taiwan.*

**Matisse "Old" (84) n**21 **t**20 **f**22 **b**21. Grain-led and lithe, the malts blossom towards the middle and finish with a wave of beautifully textured sweet grassiness. Crisp and enjoyably chewy. **40%**. *Inver House for UIES, Taiwan.* ☉

**Matisse Royal (86) n**20 **t**22 **f**22 **b**22. A haughty but interesting and entertaining blend where the oak has been taken to its limits. **40%**. *Angus Dundee for UIES, Taiwan.*

**Mitchell's 12 Years Old (93) n**23 pounding sea-spray of Springbank offset by hard grain: oaky, clean yet brilliantly complex; **t**23 vigorous, juicy malt and quite stunning bitter-sweet banter; **f**23 too long to be true. Some oak drifts in but can't dislodge the salty grain. Softer yet older than before: stunning! **b**24 almost too complex and beautiful to be true. Magnificent. An already great malt has got even better. **43%**. *Springbank.* ☉ ☉

**Monster's Choice (69) n**18 **t**19 **f**16 **b**16. Lots of liquorice and grain. **40%**. *G&M.*

⁙ **Morrison's The Best 8 Years Old (93) n**23 dry toast, grain and caramel to start but as it warms honey and a vague smokiness begin to take shape; **t**24 chewy and sweet, grain takes first hold though this is fleeting as the integration, and then build up, of malt is gradual but profound: as arrivals go this is superstar stuff! The texture is truly exemplary as it the weight and bitter-sweet balance: stunning!; **f**23 remains outstanding as the honey and smoke linger and then give way slightly to the vanilla. It's like a blended Highland Park but the caramel does come into play, as dies the grain; **b**23 a seriously excellent blend which shines on the palate as some refreshing Speysiders let rip before that stunning wave of honey takes hold. Some roasty notes impress and as economy supermarket blends go there is enough honey and complexity to make this a legend of a whisky. A truly great whisky fit for a world audience: easily one of the best supermarkets blends of all time. **40%**. *Wm Morrison Supermarkets, UK.*

**Muirheads (83) n**19 **t**22 **f**21 **b**21 A beautifully compartmentalised dram that integrates superbly, if that makes sense. In other words, the nose is crisp grain but the flavours display big Speyside malt – mouthwatering and lush. With the aid of a fatty mouthfeel, the two meet on the finish: quality blending. Old fashioned and delicious. **40%**. *MacDonald & Muir.*

**Northern Scot (68)** n16 t18 f17 b17. Heading South bigtime. **40%**. *Bruce and Co. for Tesco UK.* ☉ ☉

⋰ **Old Crofter Special Old Scotch Whisky (83)** n18 t22 f21 b22. A very decent blend, much better than the nose suggests thanks to some outstanding, velvety grain and wonderfully controlled sweetness. **40%**. *Smith & Henderson for London & Scottish International.*

**Old Glen (81)** n20 t21 f20 b20. The grain stars despite the 60% malt content. *V&S Sweden.*

**Old Glenn (78)** n20 t20 f19 b19. Young, clean, refreshing house whisky. **40%**

**Old Inverness (71)** n17 t18 f19 b17. Annoyingly cloying and heavy-handed in parts, but the spice on the finish does offer relief. **40%**. *J G Thompson & Co.*

**Old Masters Deluxe (78)** n17 t22 f19 b20. The odd blemish here and there doesn't detract from the rich-textured malt-rich sweetness that charms. **40%**. *James MacArthur.*

**Old Mull (83)** n22 t21 f20 b20. The nose offers fight and bite, but the body is lush and yielding. A real contradictory dram. **40%**. *Kyndal.*

**Old Orkney "OO" 8 Years Old (79)** n19 t21 f19 b20. A great improvemnet on the old "OO", with intense, delicious malt bouncing off the grain. Too much caramel, though. **40%**. *Gordon & MacPhail.*

**Old Parr Aged 15 Years (84)** n19 t22 f21 b22. Absolutely massive sherry input here. Some of it is of the highest order. The nose, reveals, however, that some isn't... **43%**. *Diageo/MacDonald Greenlees.* ☉ ☉

**Old Parr Superior 18 Years Old** Batch no. L5171 **(97)** n25 here's a nose with just about a touch of everything: especially clever smoke which gives weight but allows apples and bourbon to filter through at will. Perfect weight and harmony while the complexity goes off the scales; t25 voluptuous body, at times silky but the grains offer enough jagged edges for a degree of bite and bourbon; mouthwatering and spicey with the peats remaining on a slow burner. Toasty and so, so chewey; f23 the vanilla is gentle and a counter to the firmness of the combined oak and grain. A flinty, almost reedy finish with spices and cocoa very much in evidence; b24 year in, year out, this blend just gets better and better. This bottling struck me as a possible Whisky of the Year, but perhaps only an outsider. Familiarity, though, bred anything but contempt and over the passing months I have tried to get to the bottom of this truly great whisky. Blended whisky has long needed a champion. This grand old man looks just the chap. This is a worthy, if unexpected (even to me), Jim Murray' Whisky Bible 2007 World Whisky of the Year. **43%**. *Diageo/MacDonald Greenlees.* ☉ ☉

**Old Parr Classic 18 Year Old** bott 11 Apr 05 **(86)** n22 t23 f20 b21. A strange whisky that promises so much but while always interesting fails to live up to its early glory. **46%**. *Diageo.*

**Old St Andrews 5 Years Old (77)** n19 t21 f19 b18. Very soft, sweet, safe and friendly. Good middle with expansive texture. Caramel bowed. **40%**

**Old St Andrews 8 Years Old (69)** n16 t19 f17 b17. A flat, lifeless blend being phased out of existence. **40%**

**Old St Andrews 12 Years Old (88)** n21 fresh for age, clean, big malt and fine, clipped grain, distant hint of smoke; t23 outstanding Speyside-style clarity of malt, rich but never too sweet; f22 tapering finale with excellent vanilla; b22 an impressive newcomer for 2003. Loads of malt character, ironically, to some excellent grain selection. Superb. **40%**. *Old St Andrews Japan.*

**Old St Andrews Clubhouse (90)** n22 clean as a whistle: both malts and grains are young but proudly so. A Speyside influence comes through loud and clear: mouthwatering; t23 the early arrival is identical to the nose: clear as the morning dew on the first green and no less grassy; **f**22 long with some grain gaining hold but bringing with it some soft vanillas; **b**23 a fair way to start any day. How I love young blends: fresh and lacking any sort of pretensions. It has quality enough. **40%**

**Old St Andrews Golf Ball Miniatures** (see Old St Andrews Clubhouse)

**Old Smuggler (79) n**18 **t**21 **f**20 **b**20. Remains enjoyable fare, but much more emphasis now on the caramel softness than the old cutlass hardness and sharpness that I once so loved. **40%**. *Allied*.

**Old Spencer (73) n**18 **t**19 **f**18 **b**18. Attractive and clean but ultimately rather too sweet for its own good. **40%**. *Australia*.

**The Original Mackinlay (76) n**19 **t**20 **f**18 **b**19. Toffee, anyone? Some thought Fettercairn was in this. The talentless know-nothings... **40%**. *Whyte and Mackay*.

**The Original Mackinlay 12 Years Old (80) n**19 **t**21 **f**20 **b**20. Quite hefty with a spicy buzz and lingering complexity. **40%**. *Kyndal*.

**Parkers (78) n**17 **t**22 **f**20 **b**19. The nose has regressed, disappearing into ever more caramel, yet the mouth-watering lushness on the palate remains and the finish now holds greater complexity and interest. **40%**. *Angus Dundee*. ☉☉

**Parkers 12 Years Old (81) n**18 **t**19 **f**24 **b**20. Don't expect a mass market sop. Real bite to this, and for what it lacks in grace it makes up for with a finish of pure roast Brazilian coffee. Some real demerara rum style in there. **40%**. *Angus Dundee*. ☉

**Passport (82) n**21 **t**21 **f**20 **b**20. Much tidied up since I last tasted it. But when will it ever return to the virtually non-coloured Speyside-sharp work of art that I used to worship as a regular dram all those years back? **40%**. *Chivas*.

**Peaty Craig** (see Tanner's Peaty Craig.)

**Peter Dawson (74) n**18 **t**19 **f**19 **b**18. Toffee, anyone? **43%**. *Diageo*.

**Pig's Nose Aged 5 Years (79) n**20 **t**22 **f**18 **b**19. A big, sweet, chunky, gawky, grain-lashed but hugely enjoyable blend which needs a little tweaking at the finish. Lots of caramel gives this little piggy a strange, overly dark complexion for its age. Hopefully the new owners will tidy this up. **40%**. *Spencerfield Spirit Co*.

**Pinwinnie Royale (83) n**19 **t**23 **f**20 **b**21. An absolutely classic, fresh young blend with crisp, rock-hard grain forming the frame on which the clean, mouthwatering malt hangs. Then a slow gathering of complex spices for good measure. Only a tad of caramel on the finish can be detected that lessens the allround complexity and charm. **40%**. *Inver House*.

**Pinwinnie Royale 12 Years Old (85) n**20 **t**22 **f**21 **b**22. Finely-textured and attractive throughout with greatr spice finale. **40%**. *Inver House*.

**Potters (aged 36 months) (64) n**15 **t**17 **f**16 **b**16. Awful. **40%**

**Prince Charlie Special Reserve (73) n**17 **t**20 **f**18 **b**18. Thankfully not as cloyingly sweet as of old, but remains pretty basic. **40%**. *Somerfield, UK*. ☉☉

**Prince Charlie Special Reserve 8 Years Old (81) n**18 **t**20 **f**22 **b**21. A lumbering bruiser of a dram; keeps its trademark shapelessness but the spices and lush malt ensure an enjoyable experience. **40%**. *Somerfield, UK*. ☉☉

**Prince Consort (78) n**19 **t**20 **f**20 **b**19. Enjoyably honest, clean and pleasant if a little conservative. **40%**

**Queen Elizabeth (78) n**20 **t**20 **f**18 **b**20. Pleasant, grainy, toffeed and easy-going. **43%**. *Diageo/Burn Brae*.

**The Queen's Seal (73) n**18 **t**19 **f**18 **b**18. Mildly dusty but decent Speyside input. **40%**. *Wm Maxwell Ltd*.

**Real Mackenzie Extra Smooth (81) n**18 dull; **t**22 a silk landing with crystal clear grains for a second or two, then the honied malt really takes off, and with it some peppers. A wonderful battle ensues; **f**20. Where the battle once played out, the malt and grain become friends and smooch under a toffee umbrella; **b**21 once, the only time the terms "Real Mackenzie" and "Extra Smooth" were ever uttered in the same sentence was if someone was talking about the barman. Now it is a genuine descriptor. Which is odd, because when Diageo sent me a sample of their blend last year it was a snarling beast ripping at the leash. This, by contrast, is a whimpering sop. "Killer? Where are you...???" **40%.** *Diageo.* ☺ ☺

**Real Mackenzie (80) n**17 **t**21 **f**20 **b**22. Gets off to a flyer on the palate with fabulous grain helping the young malts to go for it. Never the gentlest of drams; great to see it maintaining its raucous spirit. **40%.** *Whyte and Mackay.*

**Red Seal 12 Years Old (82) n**19 **t**22 **f**20 **b**21. A mouthwatering blend that starts with a lovely grain kick. Overall balance is charming, but toffee numbs it down towards the finish. Still, a pretty good pub blend. **40%.** *Charles Wells UK.* ☺ ☺

**Reliance PL (83) n**20 **t**20 **f**22 **b**21. Some really lovely spices complement the green apple fruitiness. Juicy and never less than charming. **43%.** *Diageo.*

**Rob Roy (88) n**21 lots of malt activity but the grain is firm and biting; **t**23 the tastebuds are given a good going over with a really delightful array of malty tones ranging from fresh and grassy to subtly peated; **f**22 tends towards dry with vanilla, cocoa, some rising peat and toffee; **b**22 a profound whisky with big malt character and impressive complexity. A real no-nonsense, blend-drinker's dram. **40%.** *Morrison Bowmore.*

**Robbie Dhu 12 Years Old (83) n**21 **t**21 **f**20 **b**21. Maintains its hallmark fruitiness but the usual soft peat is much reduced and silkiness has replaced complexity. This brand some years ago replaced the old Grant's 12-y-o. **40%.** *Wm Grant's.*

**Robert Burns (78) n**19 **t**20 **f**19 **b**20. If Burns were alive today perhaps his tasting notes might be something like this. Ode to a blend: Och, wee shimmering noblest blen', tha most braken heart ye men', and this'n sets oot with grain so soft, til malt an' spice are heild aloft. **40%.** *Isle of Arran.* ☺

**Robert Burns Superior 12 Years Old (88) n**21 excellent, refreshing, tingling, early clarity to both grain and malt; **t**23 mouth-tingling complexity is well weighted behind some very decent malts; no little fruit either; **f**22 the oak on the grain wrestles with the malt but never gains the upper hand; **b**22 a teasing blend that needs a second glass before it comes alive. **43%.** *Isle of Arran.*

**Robert Burns Superior 17 Years Old (73) n**18 **t**19 **f**18 **b**18. An awkward, lumbering dram that lost its compass. **43%.** *Isle of Arran.*

**Robert Burns Superior 21 Years Old (87) n**23 thick cut marmalade on salt-buttered, slightly singed toast; distant peat smoke binds in almost imperceptibly; **t**22 excellent richness and little stinting on the honey; a lovely buzz; **f**21 high coppery-malt presence; a delicious sheen rounds off the charm and some late grain bites wonderfully; **b**21 out of a very similar, impressive, pod to the 12-y-o. **43%.**

**Robertson's of Pitlochry Rare Old Blended (82) n**19 **t**21 **f**21 **b**21. Handsome grain bite with a late malty flourish. Classic light blend available only from Pitlochry's landmark whisky shop. **40%**

**The Royal & Ancient (91) n**21 grainy, clean, firm and traditional; **t**24 oh yea!!! Absolutely mind-blowing complexity from about the third wave on the palate in. The grains arrive first – but of ultra-high quality – then a procession of subtle, gently-spiced malt, tailing off with wonderful honeycomb; **f**23 luscious cocoa digs into the Demerara sweetness and vanilla; **b**23 what an improvement! Far less caramel than of old (thank you!!) but it could still be toned down slightly more. My kind of old-fashioned, honest, top-quality blend! **40%.** *Cockburn & Campbell.* ☺ ☺

**The Royal & Ancient 28 Years** malt content 50% **(95) n**24 enormously rich, floral, softly peated with stunning oak: a few molecules from perfection; **t**24 big malt arrival that just swamps the mouth with the enormity of its richness. Intense bitter-sweet barley along with something smoky, but honeyed enough to keep fabulous harmony; **f**23 signs of tiring oak, but forgivable. The malt is toasty, roasty, lightly peated and chewy. The grains, firm yet light, begin to glow as all else fades; **b**24 an incredible blend. The mouthfeel is spot on: the whole is a sheer masterpiece! **40%.** *Cockburn & Campbell.* ☺

**Royal Castle (51) n**15 **t**14 **f**10 **b**12. Mustiness and caramel: genuinely unappealing. **40%.** *Arcus Norway.*

**Royal Household (88)** n22 a natural harmony between crisp grain and crisper malt, wonderfully refreshing and refined; **t23** the translation onto the palate is spot on with a Speyside-style maltiness clipping alongside the rock-hard grain and a swirl of peat just about noticeable in the far distance; **f21** taken down a peg by the late caramel; **b22** this is a wonderfully sophisticated blend, far too delicate and high class to be able to support something as trade door as caramel. **43%.** *Diageo.*

**Royal Salute 21 Years Old (91)** n23 where there was once smoke there is now extra fruit, but this remains sensual and glorious; **t24** your tastebuds are caressed by grains that give themselves entirely to your desires, the malts provide the background music while vanilla-rich oak expresses maturity; **f22** a simplistic, light landing, with a rich vanilla balancing well against the malt and lightening grains; **b22** not as smoky or full-bodied as it once was, but kind of reminds me of a Canadian whisky from the same stable, Seagram's Crown Royal, of about 20- 25 years ago, in the way that a soft caramel touch is imbued in the rich complexity of the grains. Just a tiny shift in caramel (either natural or added) could ruin this balance, but just now it works wonderfully. **40%.** *Chivas.*

**Royal Salute Destiny 38 Years Old (92)** n22 some sappy, soapy, oaky grumbling, but this is overwhelmed eventually by the playful barley; **t24** fabulous delivery of ripe dates and thick maltshake. Chew this for hours! **f23** the oak returns here but actually slightly lightens the loads with some gentle vanilla; **b23** an enormous blend that is half drink, half meal.... **40%.** *Chivas.*

**Royal Salute 50 Years Old** distilled before 1953 **(95)** n24 t24 f22 b25. A decade ago I tasted the Royal Salute 40 Years Old. It was probably the finest blend I had ever tasted. Now they have the 50-year-old. And it has ripped up and laughed at every rule in the book: finish apart, it has just got better and better. The most extraordinary thing here is the oak involvement. At 50 years you should be picking it out of your teeth. Not here. Instead, after its appearance on the wonderful nose, it all but vanished. Instead we are left to deal with an essay in balance. This is going for £6,000 a bottle. In reality a blended whisky showing this degree of balance and élan is truly priceless. **40%** *Chivas. 255 bottles.*

**Royal Salute The Hundred Cask Selection (92)** n23 some serious age here but attractively tempered by sober herbal-floral tones. Busy, complex and lightly spiced with just a dash of something tart and vaguely marmalady to add extra life; **t23** fabulous weight as the malt-grain combination arrives hand-in-hand. The sweetness is initially propelled by very precise, clean malt and counters effortlessly the early oak. Some white chocolate heralds the spicier bourbon cask influence while the late middle enjoys a degree of fruitiness; **f22** long, velvety textures with gentle hints of some bourbon-oaky tones from the grain and lingering more mouthwatering freshness from the malt. Some oaky-cocoa bitterness at the tapering finish; **b24** knife-edge whisky: serious brinkmanship. The oak so often threatens to dominate, but the diffusion of Speysidey clean malt and sharper fruitiness guarantees a stunning experience. Almost a novel of a blend, with you rapidly turning the pages trying to unravel the mystery of what's going on and what's going to happen next: the way blended whisky should be. And because this is an addition to the lofty Royal Salute stable, I've tried to be hypercritical. But this is worthy of the great name. **40%.** *Chivas.*

**Royal Silk Reserve (93)** n22 classically light yet richly bodied under the clear, crisp ethereal grains. The freshly-cut-grass maltiness balances perfectly; **t24** crystal clear grains dovetail with intense, mouthwatering and refreshingly sweet malt to create a perfect pitch while the middle is heavier and livelier than you might expect with the very faintest echo of peat; **f24** delicate oils and wonderful grainy-vanilla ensures improbable length for something so light. Beautiful spices and traces of cocoa offer the last hurrah. Sheer bliss; **b23** I named this the best newcomer of 2001 and it hasn't let me down. A session blend for any time of the day, this just proves that you don't need piles of peat to create a blend of genuine stature. A must have. **40%**. *International Whisky Company.* ⊙

**Sainsbury's Scotch Whisky (82)** n19 t21 f20 b22. Thinned out significantly over the last year allowing a pleasing degree of complexity amid the agreeable chewability. A great improvement: pretty good, indeed! **40%**. *Sainsbury's, UK.* ⊙ ⊙

**Sainsbury's Finest Old Matured Aged 5 Years (72)** n19 t19 f17 b17. A comfortable dram until the caramel kicks in. **40%**

**Sainsbury's Finest Old Matured Aged 12 Years (84)** n20 t22 f21 b21. Great stuff: once past the caramel the honey blossoms in all directions. A hint of smoke does no harm, either. No shame in having this around the house. **40%**. *UK.*

⠿ **Sandy Mac (76)** n18 t20 f19 b19. Basic, decent blend that's chunky and raw. **40%**. *Diageo.*

**Savoy Blended Scotch (75)** n18 t20 f18 b19. A pleasant young malt lift in the early middle palate. **40%**. *Savoy Hotel UK.*

**Scoresby Very Rare** (aged 36 months) **(69)** n17 t19 f16 b17. Furs the teeth. **40%**

**Scotch Brothers (70)** n17 t19 f17 b17. Grainy, hard, biting and young. **40%**. *Russia.*

**Scotch Blue 17 Years Old (78)** n21 t20 f18 b19. Salty and biting complexity makes for impressive blend, but a little too sappy and caramelised. **40%**. *Korea.*

**Scotch Blue Aged 21 Years (80)** n21 t20 f19 b20. A pleasingly spiced, rich blend with agreeable chewability. **40%**. *Korea.*

**Scots Club (72)** n17 t19 f18 b18. Young, pleasant, basic fare. **40%**. *Kyndal.*

**Scots Earl (83)** n19 t22 f21 b21. A characterful, mildly disharmonised blend that is so full of mouth-bulging character that you cannot fail to be entertained. Love it! **40%**. *Loch Lomond Distillers.*

**Scots Grey De Luxe (83)** n19 t22 f21 b21 The toffeed nose is less than promising but the quality of their grain is outstanding with very impressive malt infusion. Chewy and desirable, despite the so-so aroma. **40%**

**Scottish Collie (73)** n18 t20 f17 b18. Starts promisingly, even showing an improved degree of sparkle, but splutters at the caramel-laden finish. **40%**. *Quality Spirits International.* ⊙ ⊙

**Scottish Collie 12 Years Old (82)** n19 t22 f21 b20. A big change over the last few years. Clumsier now but some lovely spice to the attractive, intense, toasty grain. **40%**. *Quality Spirits International.* ⊙ ⊙

**Scottish Glory** dist 02, bott 05 **(85)** n21 t21 f22 b21. An improved blend now bursting with vitality. The ability of the grain to lift the barley is very pleasing. **40%**. *Duncan Taylor. 960 bottles.* ⊙ ⊙

**Scottish Leader (77)** n19 t21 f18 b19. Formerly the "Supreme". Revamped both inside and out, this has much more vitality than recent bottlings but is brought down by too heavy-handed use of caramel for a dull finish. The new label with its "Deanston Estd 1785" is somewhat misleading: the buildings may date from then but it became a distillery only in 1966. **40%**. *Burn Stewart.*

**Scottish Leader 12 Year Old (77)** n19 t22 f18 b18. Fruity nose and lovely, complex mouth arrival but falters latterly. **40%**. *Burn Stewart.*

**Scottish Leader 15 Year Old (87)** n22 fabulous, supreme mixture of deep fruity tones, soft oak, rich barley and a wisp of smoke; t22 brilliant texture: sweet with malt and plummy fruit and natural oak-caramel; f21 long, oily, chewy with lots of vanilla; b22 this is big stuff, sweet and yet gentle with it. **40%**. *Burn Stewart.*

**Scottish Leader 22 Years Old (86)** n23 t22 f21 b20. This is a lovely dram, but would be better if it wasn't quite so sweet. Much of its complexity is hidden. **40%**. *Burn Stewart.*

**Scottish Leader Aged Over 25 Years (91)** n24 charismatic peat offers the most sublime aroma you could imagine for a blend of this age. No off-notes whatsoever: what little grain can be detected stands firm and clean; t22 chewy, massively intense malt framed by succulent grain; f23 the peat returns, dovetailing with vanilla and lingering sweet barley; b22 a changed character from a few years back: heavier and fuller yet refusing to let age dim its innumerable qualities. A real belter of a blend. **40%.** *Burn Stewart.*

**Scottish Leader Blue Seal (82) n**21 **t**22 **f**19 **b**20. Impressive grain bite on the nose softened by rich malt. A fine dram by any standards. **40%.** *Burn Stewart.*

**Scottish Leader Platinum (73) n**19 **t**19 **f**18 **b**17. Rather bland. **40%.**

**Scottish Leader Supreme (80) n**21 **t**21 **f**18 **b**20. Lush and delicious on the nose and mouth arrival, but the hoped-for big finale is flattened by some outrageous use of caramel. Pity, as there is so much to get your teeth into early on. Enjoyable when all's said and done. **40%.** *Burn Stewart. Gold label for export, especially Japan.*

**Scottish Prince Aged 19 Years (86) n**22 **t**22 **f**21 **b**21. Not a single off-note: nothing like as foppish as the Prince on the label. **40%.** *Forbes Ross & Co Ltd.*

**Scottish Prince Aged 21 Years (86) n**20 **t**22 **f**23 **b**21. If I was a gambling man, I'd say there was a decent amount of ancient grain. No matter: this is stunning entertainment for the tastebuds. **43%.** *Forbes Ross and Co Ltd.*

**Shieldaig The Classic Uisge Beatha (66) n**15 **t**19 **f**16 **b**16. Thin and grainy. **40%.** *William Maxwell and Son (Ian Macleod).*

**Shieldaig Collection Finest Old Uisge Beatha** (*see* Shieldaig The Classic). *William Maxwell and Son France.*

**Silver Barley (84) n**20 **t**22 **f**21 **b**21. Pre-pubescent even to the point of a slight new-makish quality. A blend, but no sign of the grain: just lots of invigorating, mouthwatering barley. Forget about mixers, one to start the day with. **40%.** *John Milroy.*

**Something Special (84) n**21 **t**22 **f**20 **b**21. Changed shape, yet still about the same quality as before. Much lighter, friendlier nose now and the grains are real fun. But lacks that degree of extra complexity. Enjoyable and worth drinking for all that. **40%.** *Chivas.*

⋅∷⋅ **Something Special Premium Aged 15 Years (89) n**22 a vague, distant smokiness sits prettily with some fruity caramel; **t**23 boisterous delivery with unshackled malt adding a wonderful, zesty spiciness amid much more mouth-watering Speyside-style fresh grass; the grain offers the desired cut-glass firmness; **f**21 lots of vanilla and too much caramel, but remains busy and entertaining; **b**23 a hugely enjoyable, fun whisky which pops around the palate like a crackerjack. Fabulous malt thread and some curious raisiny/sultana fruitiness, too. A blend-lover's blend. **40%.** *Chivas/ Hill Thompson, Venezuela.*

**Spar Finest (80) t**20 **t**21 **f**19 **b**20. A standard blend, but of a superblybalanced style I adore. The exquisite clean grains show nip and attitude – as they should – but there is sufficient malt for depth. Love to see the toffee effect go, though, and have it raw and refreshing. **40%.** *UK.*

**The Spey Cast 12 Years Old (81) n**18 **t**22 **f**21 **b**20. Lovely, complex, fruity dram. **40%.** *Gordon & MacPhail.*

**Spey Royal (76) n**18 **t**20 **f**19 **b**19. Quite a young blend with a big toffee effect but not without a delicious and lush early malt-grain explosion. **40%.** Diageo *Thailand.*

**SS Politician Finest (89) n**21 pretty sharp grains softened by first-class crisp malt: light and flighty; **t**22 really excellent used of clean young malt – probably the most of it Speyside - to refresh the tastebuds and make for a lip-smacking middle; **f**23 excellent complexity here as the malt and grain battle it out. It's, literally, clean fun all the way; **b**23 this is a terrific young blend. With its obvious reference to my favourite film of all time, Whisky Galore, it needed to be good – even go down well, if you pardon the pun – and hasn't disappointed in the slightest way. Stand up that blender and take a bow! **40%.** *Duncan Taylor.* ☉

**Standard Selection Aged 5 Years (92) n**22 the rock-hard grain deflects the delicate smoke: uncompromising and enticing; **t**23 fabulous collection of fruity tones, balanced by an ever-increasing peat presence, brilliantly subtle with honey-barley; **f**23 the oak seems more than five years and softens the smoke;

**b**24 a brilliant blend that appears a lot older than its five years: a stupendously stylish interpretation of peat with sweet barley. **40%**. *V&S Stockholm*.

**Stewarts Cream Of The Barley (74) n**19 **t**20 **f**17 **b**18. A dram that's improved a lot since its grimmer days, with passable early malt delivery. But the grain remains unwieldy and stand-offish. **40%**. *Allied*.

**Stewart's Finest (75) n**17 **t**20 **f**19 **b**19. Raw nose; body sweet, curvaceous, toffeed and chewy. Annoyingly and dangerously drinkable. **40%**. *Kyndal*.

**Sullivan's Cove Premium Blend Scotch Whisky (69) n**16 **t**18 **f**17 **b**18. Sweet and fat on the palate with caramel and late grain bite. Shame about the nose. **40%**. *Tasmania Distillery Pty. Australia only*.

**Swords (78) n**20 **t**21 **f**18 **b**19. Beefed up somewhat with some early smoke thrusting through and rapier grains to follow. **40%**. *Morrison Bowmore*. ☺☺

**The Talisman (81) n**20 **t**22 **f**19 **b**20. Good grain and Speyside early delivery, but a lot of the sparkle has vanished from this, and the caramel, once a bit-part player, now dominates. **40%**. *J & W Hardie Ltd*.

**Tam Touler's Dram (79) n**19 **t**21 **f**19 **b**20. A shade too much caramel and grain, but the immediate, malty arrival on the palate does sing. **40%**. *The Whisky Castle, Tomintoul*.

**Tanner's Peaty Creag Aged 8 Years (94) n**23 Lordy me! Just such an astonishing delivery of heavyweight aromas from molten liquorice to top-rate peat; **t**24 sensational arrival of intense, thick malt with both the gristy barley and peat on full display; the grain offers a welcoming thinning but it's all amazingly integrated; **f**23 one of the few blends that has enough smoky, malty clout to carry the caramel with it and land wave after wave of peaty punches. Superb! **b**24 if I lived in the Shrewsbury/Hereford area of the UK this would be a daily tipple for me. Instead I'll have to make do with the closely related Isle of Skye. **40%**. *Tanners Wine Merchants, Shrewsbury & Hereford*

**Teacher's Highland Cream (90) n**23 firm, flinty grain; a tad fruity with gently smoked malt-ensuring weight; **t**23 mouth-filling with a tender sweetness; the grains seem softer than the nose suggests; **f**22 toffee and lazy smoke; **b**22 not yet back to its best but a massive improvement on the 2005 bottlings. So harder grains to accentuate the malt will bring it closer to the classic of old. **40%**. *Fortune Brands*. ☺☺

···⊱ **Teacher's Highland Cream** Batch no. T073, bott Nov 05 **(88) n**22 busy with limited harmonization but attractive weight; **t**21 excellent delivery but the sweetness and grains run amok; **f**23 finally finds its range and now we have super-charged complexity: wonderful spice buzz as the peats begin to kick on; **b**22 the finish entirely outclasses the British version. If they could get a marriage of the two styles: what a blend...!! **42.8%**. *Allied Domecq Spirits, India*.

**Te Bheag (84) n**19 **t**22 **f**21 **b**22. Well balanced with good spice bite. **40%**. ☺

**Te Bheag Connoisseurs' Blend (87) n**21 coastal and salty; **t**22 more oily textured than of late with the accent on the malt and toffee; **f**22 beautifully coastal finally, but fat and sweet; **b**22 an attractive, relaxing dram, but not a patch on what it was. It as if the peat has been surgically removed. **40%**. *Praban na Linne*. ☺☺

**Tesco Special Reserve (80) n**16 **t**22 **f**21 **b**21. The sweaty armpit nose is relieved by the massively improved, rich, chewey and silky body. **40%**. *Tesco UK*. ☺☺

···⊱ **Tesco Scotch Whisky Finest Reserve Aged 12 Years (80) n**19 **t**21 **f**20 **b**20. A thumping, thudding blend as hard as the granite rocks over which the waters ran to the Speyside distilleries used in the recipe. Value-for-money-wise, not a bad blend at all but for all the charm and mouth-watering properties of the malt, the grains are seismic. **40%**.

**Ubique (82) n**20 **t**22 **f**21 **b**19. Fresh, juicy, Speysidey, classy. **40%**

**Upper Ten (68) n**17 **t**18 **f**17 **b**16. Makes a point of peat on the label, but fails to deliver balance. **40%**. *Arcus Norway*.

**Ushers Green Stripe (83) n**20 **t**21 **f**21 **b**21. Light, mouthwatering and with more than a hint of Speyside controlling its style. **43%**. *Diageo*.

**VAT 69 (86)** n20 t22 f21 b23. Exemplary young blend: fresh, clean and mouthwatering. This, to me, offers the kind of balance and style that encapsulates a light blend. No problems with water and even ice on the hottest days. **43%**. *Wm Sanderson/Diageo.*

**Waiting Thirty Three Years** (*see* The Whisky House)

**Waitrose Scotch Three Years Old (76)** n17 t21 f19 b19. A dirty nose, which makes the clarity on the palate all the more remarkable. **40%**

**Walker and Scott Finest (82)** n20 t21 f20 b21. Rock-hard and brittle grain gives a clean shape for the malts to develop around. High grain content, but a Speysidey grassiness is quite delicious as is the mildly citrussy nose; marks docked only for late toffee. Impressive and old-fashioned. **40%**. *Sam Smith's UK.*

**The Watsonian Club Whisky (77)** n19 t20 f19 b19. A soft, sweet, clean blend with a dry finish. **40%**

**The Whisky House 33 Years Old 1969 (92)** n23 some serious age here, but the integrity of the malt never wavers. The grain is barely discernible except maybe that bourbony background; t24 a series of explosions, controlled and uncontrolled, offer pace and thrust to the mouth arrival: the delivery and diversity of flavours is fast and complex. Again there is a slick bourbony edge, not to mention some very distant smoke amid the Demerera sweetness; f22 more spices as the vanilla bites deep; b23 a very unusual blend of no little antiquity. Perfect for bourbon-loving Scotch drinkers. Its overall finesse, however, is unambiguous. **50.5%**. *The Whisky House, Belgium.*

**White Horse (92)** n23 beautifully smoky: big weight with the grains shrinking by comparison; t24 magnificently rounded at first then wave upon wave of varying characteristics ranging from clean, fresh malt to heavier, smoky notes with even room for a little vanilla and sultana; f22 long, vanilla-rich with some light peat still drifting around; b23 this is one of the greatest young blends on the market: only the oiliness presented by, probably, Caol Ila, takes it out of a mark in the mid-90s. When Lagavulin was used there was a cleaner, crisper feel. But I am nit-picking: it is not entirely unknown for me to have a less than harmonious reltionship with some of the world's bigger distillers. But if I were Holmes, I would doff my deerstalker to this masterpiece of a blend, as it is one even he would fail to fathom and one that proves that greatness is not achieved by the age of the whisky but the understanding and feel for how the elements combine and interact. Proof, were it needed, that even among the big boys there are still quality blenders around who know how to make a pulse race. **43%**. *Diageo.*

**White Horse Aged 12 Years (94)** n23 chunky, heather-honied and smoky. A few staves of oak visible, too; t23 big malt content apparent here and the liquorice-led honey show an age greater than the stated 12. Multi-layered, with the firm grain making a belated and complex introduction; f24 incredibly long, with the smoke re-establishing itself, though very subtly. The vanilla has a wonderfully gentle honey glow to it; b24 brilliant blending from the highest echelons. A masterful balance of great age and something a little younger, and one of the most deft uses of peat in the business. A real thoroughbred. **40%**. *Diageo.*

**Whyte and Mackay (86)** n21 t23 f20 b21 while the odd bottling can be pretty bland fare, overall this is a very subtly changed and much improved blend. This last bottling, though, was distinctly on the dull side. **40%** ☉

**Whyte and MacKay 12 Years Old (84)** n21 t21 f20 b22. Beautifully wallowing grain offers little shelter to some rollicking malty notes: curiously light yet weighty – totally intriguing. **40%**. *Kyndal.*

**Whyte & Mackay 15 Years Old Select Reserve (86)** n21 t23 f21 b21. A really neat blend with slightly more toffee effect than the old version. **40%**

**Whyte & MacKay 18 Years Old (89)** n22 dried dates moistened by sultanas: the malt hangs firm; t23 voluptuous and silky, sweet grain and malt marriage made in heaven; f22 simplifies and reverts back to the dates again; b22 a stylish, tamed brute of a blend. A whisky as expansive as its creator. But a whole lot sexier. **40%.** *Kyndal.*

**Whyte & Mackay 21 Years Old (85)** n20 t22 f21 b22. A blend so well married it wears slippers and smokes a pipe. **43%.** *Kyndal.*

**Whyte & MacKay 30 Years Old (93)** n24 flawless fruit, amazingly intense clean malt and the softest of vanilla-laden grain, all entwined with a waft of light smoke; t22 a very fresh sherry feel dominates at first, then behind that arrives a procession of muted malty notes; f23 so soft and gentle you could wash a baby in it. Probably the result of W&M's marrying process, the subtlety is quite astonishing. Some treacle toffee on the very finish is still outflanked by some gathering spice; b24 there is no evidence of a tired cask here at all: the tastebuds are entirely engulfed by something enormous and deeply satisfying. **40%.** *Kyndal.*

**Whyte & Mackay High Strength (87)** n18 rubbery, the weak link; t22 beautifully sweet with lashings of lightly molassed sugar forming the bridge between the soft grain and harder, more rigid malts; f24 long and caressing, massively intense with hints of liquorice and malt concentrate. One of the best finishes of any blend on the market: positively sensual; b23 only the poor nose prevents this from being one of the greatest blends of them all. It has enormous character and confidence and flavours attack the tastebuds from all angles. Damn it: forget the nose, just go for it and enjoy something a little special. **52.5%.** *Kyndal.*

**William Grant's 100 US Proof Superior Strength (92)** n23 sublime chocolate lime nose, decent oak; t24 big mouth arrival, lush and fruity with the excellent extra grain bite you might expect at this strength, just an extra degree of spice takes it into even higher orbit than before; f22 back to chocolate again with a soft fruit fade; b23 a fruitier drop now than it was in previous years but no less supremely constructed. **50% (100 US proof).** ☺ ☺

**William Grant's Ale Cask Reserve (89)** n21 old, peculiar aroma of spilt beer: pretty malty to say the least at this strength; but now with some vivid grain poking through; t23 enormous complexity with myriad malt notes varying from sweet and chewy to bitter and biting; f22 quite long with some toffee and hops(??) Yes, I really think so; b23 a real fun blend that is just jam-packed with jagged malty notes. The hops were around more on earlier bottlings, but watch out for them. Nothing pint-sized about this: this is a big blend and very true in flavour/shape to the original with just a delicious shading of grain to really up the complexity. **40%.** *William Grant & Sons.* ☺ ☺

**William Grant's 12 Years Old Bourbon Cask Reserve (89)** n22 a hard nose until warmed, then the malts blossom with sweeter balance; t23 delicate wafer dissolving in the mouth; the oak arrives quite early but behaves impeccably; padded out further by teasing smoke; f22 only towards the finish can the grain really be picked out, being one of a number of chewy layers; lovely cup cake death; b22 clever weight, but not one for the crash, bang, wallop merchants. **40%**

**Grant's Cask Selection Over 15 Years Old (90)** n23 firm, dry oak balances well against the fresher, fruity elements; delicate and distinguished; t23 very good grain on the arrival and middle with a distinct evenness throughout; f22 lots of chocolate character as the oak and grain gang together; b22 wonderful blending, as one might expect from this stable, but perhaps the finishing in sherry has just flattened slightly any pulse-quickening peaks that that may have been there. Even so, sheer quality. **40%.** *William Grant & Sons.*

⋯❖⋯ **William Grant's 15 Years Old (85)** n21 t23 f20 b21. The grain and, later, caramel dominates but the initial delivery reveals the odd moment of sheer genius and complexity on max revs. **43%.** *William Grant & Sons.*

**William Grant's 18 Years Old Port Cask Reserve (86)** n22 (apologies in advance, but ...) bluebells in a dank, earthy, north-facing garden enlivened by beautifully fresh fruit; t23 it would probably not be possible to make the landing on the palate any softer: a mixture of firm and soft grain play their part in keeping the complexity going; **f**20 lengthy, but flattened rather by a prolonged toffee effect; **b**21 doesn't quite unravel the way you might wish or expect. **40%**

**William Grant's Classic Reserve 18 Years Old (93) n**24 salty, aroma of crashing waves on a beach, seaweed, yet no more than a hint of peat. Grains are crisp and biting but the malt blunts them: sensational; **t**23 big fruit kick-off followed by wave upon wave of breaking malt. The grain bites now and again. The complexity, especially with the arrival of the peat, is nothing short of mindboggling; **f**23 long, fruity and still softly peated. The grains offer gentle oak and a drifting sweetness; **b**23 few whiskies maintain such high levels of complexity from nose to finish. A true classic. **40%**

⬡ **William Grant's 25 Years Old (95) n**23 some serious oak, but chaperoned by top quality oloroso, itself thinned by firm and graceful grain; **t**24 sheer quality: complexity by the shovel-load as juicy fruits interact with darting, crisp barley; again the grain shows elegance both sharpening increasingly mouth-watering malt and softening the oak; **f**24 medium length, but not a single sign of fatigue: the sweet barley runs and runs and some jammy fruits charm. Just to cap it all, some wonderful spices dazzle and a touch of low roast Java enriches; **b**24 absolutely top-rank blending that appears to maximize every last degree of complexity. Most astonishing, though, is its sprightly countenance: even Scottish footballing genius Ally MacLeod struggled to send out Ayr Utd. sides with this kind of brio. And that's saying something! A gem. **43%**. *William Grant & Sons.*

**William Grant's Family Reserve (94) n**25 this, to me, is the perfect nose to any blend: harmonious and faultless. There is absolutely everything here in just-so proportions: a bit of snap and bite from the grain, teasing sweet malts, the faintest hint of peat for medium weight, strands of oak for dryness, fruit for lustre. Even Ardbeg doesn't pluck my strings like this glass of genius can; **t**23 exceptionally firm grain helps balance the rich, multi-layered malty tones. The sub-plot of burnt raisins and peek-a-boo peat adds further to the intrigue and complexity (if it doesn't bubble and nip around the mouth you have a rare sub-standard bottling); **f**22 a hint of caramel can be detected amid returning grains and soft cocoa tones: just so clean and complex; **b**24 there are those puzzled by my obvious love affair with blended whisky – both Scotch and Japanese – at a time when malts are all the rage. But take a glass of this and carefully nurture and savour it for the best part of half an hour and you may begin to see why I believe this to be the finest art form of whisky. For my money, this brand – brilliantly kept in tip-top shape by probably the world's most naturally gifted blender – is the closest thing to the blends of old and, considering it is pretty ubiquitous, it defies the odds for quality. It is a dram with which you can start the day and end it: one to keep you going at low points in between, or to celebrate the victories. It is the daily dram that has everything. **40%** ☉

**William Grant's Sherry Cask Reserve (82) n**20 **t**22 **f**20 **b**20. Raspberry jam and cream from time to time. Very attractive, but a somewhat plodding dram that's content in second gear. **40%**. *William Grant & Sons.* ☉ ☉

**William Lawson's Finest (83) n**19 **t**21 **f**21 **b**22. Not only has the label become more colourful, but so, too, has the whisky. However that has not interfered with the joyous old-fashioned grainy bite. A complex and busy blend from the old charm school. **40%**

**William Lawson's Scottish Gold Aged 12 Years (88) n**22 soft yet weighty with dulcet citrus, fruity notes; **t**23 crisp grains interlink superbly with very clean grape and some sweet malt; **f**22 a smattering of cocoa aids the spices towards a drying finish after the sweetish build-up; **b**21 for years Lawson's 12 was the best example of the combined wizardry of clean grain, unpeated barley and good bourbon cask that you could find anywhere in the world: a last-request dram before the firing squad. Today it is still excellent, but just another sherried blend. What's that saying about if it's not being broke...? **40%**

**William Lawson's 21 Years Old (90) n**23 soft apple-cinnamon overture with deft malt; **t**24 the grain arrives early and is clean and precise; the malt forms an alliance with softer grains while the crisper ones cuts like a knife through the palate; **f**21 the malt falls away quickly leaving clean grain; **b**22 the stunningly complex nose and first minute on the palate is a hard act to follow – too hard for the finale. Only a small tinker away from being an absolute must-have-at-allcosts classic. **40%**

**William Lawson's Founder's Reserve Aged 18 Years (96) n**24 just so gloriously intricate and with teasing aromas; never less than spellbinding....etc etc; **t**25 {remove "yes, its Lawson's....am stunned} {after "caressed with honeytoasted malt" add} The subtlety has been cranked up beyond belief, almost beyond scale, by the most enormously skilful use of dissolving peat. Best taken as a pretty decent mouthful and open the mouth to let in the air; **f**23 long vanilla notes with soft, smoky spice: the finish is short-ish ... probably all the excitement; **b**24 sensual and seductive, this quite extraordinary dram was just what I needed after the relative disappointment of Lawson's 12. Such is the sheer élan, the brilliance of the whisky and the blending behind it, a bottle of this sits in my living-room as an everyday, tangible, drinkable reminder that in a world that can often be so crushingly average and crass, we are still capable at times of genius and the creation of beauty. And hopefully the ability to appreciate it. **40%**

**William Peel Founder's Premium Aged 7 Years (77) n**18 **t**20 **f**20 **b**19. A decent, solid blend. **40%**. *France.*

**Windsor Aged 12 Years Premier (84) n**20 **t**22 **f**21 **b**21. A sweet, jam-tart of a blend that offers silk and grace but also a tad too much blandness. **40%**. *Diageo.* ☉☉

**Windsor Aged 17 Years Super Premium (89) n**23 a fabulous aroma which bombards the nose with both luxurious grain and a hint of something smoky above the butter-honey theme; **t**22 sweet, as is the house style, with a Demerara coating to the crisp malt and gathering vanilla; silky and voluptuous throughout; **f**22 a gentle, soft-textured landing with an echo of spice; **b**22 still a little on the safe side for all its charm and quality. An extra dose of complexity would lift this onto another level altogether. **40%**. *Diageo.* ☉☉

⋰⋰ **Windsor 21 Years Old (90) n**20 fruity and weighty but something a bit lactic and lethargic from some old bourbon casks has crept in; **t**23 excellent oils surround the silk to help amplify the intensity of the fruit and drifting smoke; **f**24 some spiciness that shows towards the middle really takes off now as drying vanilla counters the sweet grains; **b**23 recovers fabulously from the broken nose and envelopes the palate with a silky-sweet style unique to the Windsor scotch brand. Excellent. **40%**. *Diageo.*

**Wm Morrisons Finest Scotch (71) n**18 **t**18 **f**17 **b**18. A lot of the old caramel this was caked in has been stripped away. What it reveals, though, isn't too pretty!! Supermarket fodder. **40%**

**Ye Monks** bot lot L5110 **(83) n**21 **t**20 **f**21 **b**21. "A Curious Old Whisky," claims the front label. Not really, unless you regard finding such a decently complex yet light blend in Venezuela a curiosity. Just enough fruit and malt plus cocoa on the finale to demand a refill at the bar. **40%**. *Diageo/Donald Fisher.*

# Irish Whiskey

**A**s is the way with Empires, they grow then blossom and, finally, fall. And so it is now in Ireland.

Until the advent of the Cooley distillery in the late '80s, all Ireland's whiskey was made under the umbrella of Irish Distillers. And for a short period in the '90s it looked like it would be so again when ID tried to consume Cooley whole. But they choked on it and had to spit out when the Irish Government ruled against the move in the interests of competition. Cooley continues to this day as a maverick distiller helping forge new interest and markets in Irish whiskey.

That left Irish Distillers' owners, Pernod Ricard, with Ireland's two other distilleries. In the south they held Midleton, near Cork, where their stupendous pot still whiskey is made. And in the north, just two miles from the cliffs of Antrim, the malt distillery of Old Bushmills dating all the way back to 1784. That was until last year. Then, as part of Great Whisky Merry-Go-Round following Pernod's acquisition of Allied and all the resultant sell-ons, Diageo parted with the stunning sum of £200 million and in return got The Old Bushmills Distillery (Established 1874) and all its satelite blends and brands.

For a year or so Irish Distillers' blender Billy Leighton has been travelling to Midleton and back to Bushmills in a dual role as blender for both companies, though of course being an Irish Distillers man through and through but helping Diageo create their own blending team. His work is just about complete and soon he will be letting go of the ties that have held him to Bushmills most of his professional life. Though his imput at Midleton has already seen some interesting developments, with an apparent improvement in Midleton Very Rare and his putting together of the stunning Redbreast 15, I cannot believe that there will not be a major tweak in Billy's big heart when he says goodbye at Bushmills for the last time.

Without doubt Redbreast 15 is the most significant development in Irish whiskey for the last few years. Long have I wailed and gnashed my teeth that more was not done with their pot still stocks, as relatively low as I know they are. For 15 years I have been pearching myself on the shoulder of every Irish Distillers executive I can find asking them to bring out pot still (that type of whiskey made from a mixture of malted and unmalted barley unique to Ireland - and now Midleton distillery in particular) as something above the usual Irish Distillers norm of 40abv and at a variation of ages. Yes, I was told. Great idea. It would happen one day, I was reassured. Just needed the stock. And the market.

They have at last responded, I am told, to a request from by Le Maison du Whisky in Paris who required something similar to sell. The result is Jim Murray's Whisky Bible 2007 Irish Whiskey of the Year. And a lot of interest from drinkers who before rarely gave Irish a second glance. Or chance. Now, if I can get a result for my constant beseeching them to tone down - and one day remove - colouring from Midleton Very Rare and Powers in particular....

Finally, a change not for the better. One of Dublin's greatest landmarks, the wondrous Georgian wine shop in Kildare Street, home to the excellent Mitchell and Sons is about to be no more. The 200-year-old company which brings us that other great Irish pot still whiskey, Green Spot, are at last moving out of their quaint headquarters. I for one will feel that Dublin won't quite be the same place again. Disappearing into ithe shop's deepest recesses was like going back in time. To a day when Irish was sold from the cask and 2 Kildare Street shared with Jameson's Bow Street distillery and the Powers' plant in John's Lane a place in Irish whiskey present not its past. Another pricelessly rare link has been broken....

## Pure Pot Still
### MIDLETON (old distillery)

**Midleton 25-y-o Pot Still** db **(92) n**24 **t**24 **f**21 **b**23. A really enormous whiskey that is in the truest classic Irish style. The un-malted barley really does make the tastebuds hum and the oak has added fabulous depth. Interesting when tasted against an American rye – the closeness of the character is there to be experienced, but also the differences. A subtle mature whiskey of unquestionable quality. Superb. **43%**

**Midleton 30-y-o Pot Still** db **(85) n**19 **t**22 **f**22 **b**22 a typically brittle, crunchy Irish pot still where the un-malted grains have a telling say. The oak has travelled as far as it can without having an adverse effect. A chewy whiskey which revels in its bitter-sweet balance. An impressively tasty and fascinating insight into yesteryear. **45%**

**Midleton 1973 Pure Pot Still** db **(95) n**24 **t**24 **f**23 **b**24 the enormous character of true Irish pot still whiskey (a mixture of malted and unmalted barley) appears to absorb age better than most other grain spirits. This one is in its element. But drink at full strength and at body temp (it is pretty closed when cool) for the most startling – and memorable effects. I have no idea how much this costs. But if you can find one and afford it ... then buy it!!

### MIDLETON (new distillery)

**Green Spot (93) t**23 mouthwatering and fresh on one level, honey and menthol on another; **t**24 crisp, mouthwatering with a fabulous honey burst, alarmingly sensuous; **f**23 faint coffee intertwines with the pot still. The thumbprint thread of honey remains but a touch more caramel than yore; **b**23 this honeyed state has remained a few years, and its sharpness has now been regained. Complex throughout. Unquestionably one of the world's greatest branded whiskies. **40%**. *Irish Distillers for Mitchell & Son, Dublin.* ⊙ ⊙

**Green Spot 10 Year Old Single Pot Still** dist 93 **(92) n**23 firm barley and orangey fruit with gentle hints of early bourbon: some serious ageing effect on this; **t**22 mouthwatering and firm, then a gradual increase in the barley input and spices; **f**24 shafts of honey throws a sweetening light on the bitter marmalade; **b**23 launched to celebrate the 200th anniversary of this wonderful Dublin landmark, this is bottled from three mixed bourbon casks of Irish Pot Still. The extra age has detracted slightly from the usual vitality of the standard Green Spot (an 8-y-o) but its quality still must be experienced. **40%.** *Mitchell & Son. 1000 bottles.*

**Green Spot 12 Year Old Single Pot Still** dist 91 **(93) n**24 spices and zesty oranges abound, even a distant trace of coriander; uncompromising barley sugar and heather; **t**24 a stunningly wonderful arrival: layers of sweet malt at first, but that takes a battering from much sharper, more prickly grains and spices. An enormous, vigorous mouthful; **f**22 a degree of bourbon-style liquorice, vanilla and caramel; **b**23 a single cask restricted to exactly 200 bottles to mark the 200th anniversary of the grand old man of Kildare Street, this is the first Middleton pot still I have seen at this strength outside of a lab. A one-off in every sense. **58%.**

**Redbreast 12 Years Old (90) n**23 unhurried display of ripe fruits which, together with the sharpness of the pot still, reminds me of a firm, pure rye, only this is a tad spicier; **t**23 more lazy spice, though not before the shock waves of complex, juicy barley notes on a field of clean sherry; **f**22 lingering fruity toffee-sherry; **b**22 remains an all-Ireland institution: one of the few pure pot-still whiskeys still around. Amazing to think this was a dead duck until my book Jim Murray's Irish Whiskey Almanac was released in 1994 when the brand was due to be withdrawn. The only change over those passing dozen years is that the sherry now is a tad lighter, the heavy effect once being similar to that found in the equally glorious Jameson 1780. Not to be confused with the rare blend Redbreast Blend (see Irish Blends) **40%.** *Irish Distillers.*

☆☆ **Redbreast 15 Years Old** db **(94) n**23 seductive soft fruit wrapped in a hard barley shell. A slight soapy blemish, but minor; **t**24 such enormity and depth fair takes the breath away; soft hints of citrus amid the pulsing grain. Stunning clarity and delicate spice. Extraordinary; **f**23 multi-layered, panning out with barley-edged cocoa; **b**24 for years I have been pleading for Irish Distillers to launch a pot still at 46%, natural colour and unchillfiltered. Well, I've got two out of three wishes. And what we have here is a truly great Irish whiskey and my pulse races in the certain knowledge it can get better still... **46%. ncf.** *France.*

## OLD COMBER

**Old Comber 30 Years Old Pure Pot Still (88) n**23 **t**24 **f**20 **b**21. A classic example of a whiskey spending a few summers too many in wood: increasing age doesn't equal excellence. That said, always very drinkable and early on positively sparkles with a stunning mouthfeel. Out of respect for the old I have made the markings for taste cover the first seven or eight seconds ... **40%**

## TULLAMORE

**Knappogue Castle 1951** bott 87 **(93) n**23 heady mix of over-ripe – almost black – banana and big oak. Molasses and demerara sugar mixed with honey, ripe greengages and pepper ... almost rum-like; **t**24 big, booming. Rich start, attractively oily and juicy. The unmalted barley and even oats show well while the middle provides plenty of estery Jamaican pot-still rum; **f**22 long, hard and brittle – as to be expected from an Irish of this genre. Bourbon-style vanilla with chewy liquorice. An estery, vaguely honeyed finale; **b**24 highly individualistic. Another year in cask might have tipped this over the edge. We are talking brinkmanship here with a truly awesome display of flavour profile here ranging from traditional Irish pot to bourbon via Jamaican pot-still rum. A whiskey of mind-boggling duplicity, tricking the tastebuds into one sensation and then meandering off on a different tangent altogether. About as complex and beguiling as a straight Irish whiskey ever gets. **40%.** *Great Spirits.*

# Single Malt
## COOLEY

**Connemara** bott code L5045 db **(85) n**22 **t**20 **f**22 **b**21 better, but still not quite at its best as its finds balance hard to come by. **40%.** *Cooley.*

**Connemara Cask Strength** db **(94) n**23 a mixture of turf smoke and bonfires; **t**23 unbelievably sweet at first despite the close attention of drying oak, but the smoke chimes in with an outrageously spicy attack; **f**24 burnt toast and liquorice; a mixture of medium and heavy Java coffee, lightly sweetened with Demerara sugar, makes for one giant finale; **b**24 at first it is hard to see the direction this malt is taking. Give it a while, and on about the third tasting you realise there is more to the madness than meets the eye. Superb, so it is!! **58.9%**

**Connemara Aged Twelve Years** bott code L5044 db **(91) n**23 youthful, with myriad citrus notes trying to outdazzle the gathering peat; shows great subtlety and fun; **t**22 refreshing, with the barley insisting on behaving half the age it actually is. The smoke appears lethargic but grows into a spicy crescendo; **f**22 lots of vanilla amid the dusty malt; lots of coffee fudge to balance the smoke; **b**24 the best bottling yet with complexity a byword here. **40%.** *Cooley.*

⁛ **Cadenhead's Cooley Aged 13 Years** bott 05 **(93) n**24 attractively smoked: orange and mango juice with the kippers; **t**23 multi-shaded smoke fighting on varying levels with an influx of natural oaky-caramel and unusual oils; **f**23 prickly spices and then a rerun to a semi-gristy sweetness; **b**23 absolutely top-rate peaty Irish. **60.6%.** *228 bottles.*

⁛ **Cadenhead's Cooley Aged 13 Years** bott 05 **(93) n**24 attractively smoked: orange and mango juice with the kippers; **t**23 multi-shaded smoke fighting on varying levels with an influx of natural oaky-caramel and unusual oils; **f**23 prickly spices and then a rerun to a semi-gristy sweetness; **b**23 absolutely top-rate peaty Irish. **60.6%.** *228 bottles.*

⁛ **Cadenhead's Cooley Aged 14 Years** bott May 06 **(80) n**20 **t**21 **f**19 **b**20. Slightly hot and perhaps not from the best bourbon barrel to visit Ireland. **58.7%.** *222 btls.*

**Locke's Aged 8 Years Crock (92) n**23 pounding, intense, grassy-sweet barley; **t**24 excellent mouth arrival and almost immediately a honey-rich delivery of lush, slightly oily malt: wonderful, wonderful stuff! **f**22 soft oak tempers the barley and a degree of toffee digs in and flattens the .....; **b**23 much, much better cask selection than of old: some real honey casks here. A crock of gold...! **40%.**

**The Tyrconnell** db **(89) n**22 oranges and cedar, clean malt and courteous oak; **t**23 blemish free, so clean and mouthwatering but with a hint of something almost salty; **f**21 pretty long with the malt continuing to buzz around the palate. The vanilla also begins to show well; **b**23 this is easily the best Tyrconnell yet. The quality of The Tyrconnell has been maintained impressively over the last couple of years and the score might rise higher should they manage to lose that caramel flatness towards the middle and finish. **40%**

**The Tyrconnell (Limited Edition)** db **(84) n**19 **t**21 **f**22 **b**22. Lovely citrus on nose and palate, but goes curiously flat at point of entry. Even so, lots of charm and sophistication, especially on the finish. **40%.** *Cooley. 5000 bottles. Confusingly, the label says "Single Malt" and "Pure Pot Still".*

**Avoca (76) n**19 **t**20 **f**18 **b**19. Chewy and sweet at first but turns bitter as the grain and oak bite. **40%.** *Cooley for Aldi.*

**Cadenhead's World Whiskies Cooley Peated Single Malt Individual Cask Aged 12 Years** bott Feb 05 **(93) n**23 bonfires and grist. Just so attractive! **t**24 the sweet smoke laps around the tastebuds with some wonderful fresh barley and oranges lightening things up; **f**23 long, spicy waves of oak and barley. Relaxed and completely in tune with itself; **b**23 an exceptionally fine cask of very well made whiskey. **59.7%.** *216 bottles.*

**Clonmel (78) n**19 **t**22 **f**18 **b**19. Starts beautifully, brightly but dies under a welter of toffee blows. Won a Gold Medal in Brussels, apparently ... amazing:

shows you what a lifetime of drinking Cognac does to some people ... Claims to be "Pure Pot Still". It isn't (in Irish terms): it's malt. **40%**. *Celtic Whisky Co.*

**Clonmel Peated Aged 8 Years (86) n**22 **t**23 **f**20 **b**21. Take the toffee away and you would have one hell of an Irish. Claims to be "Pure Pot Still". It isn't (in Irish terms): it's malt. **40%**. *Celtic Whisky Compagnie.*

**Glen Dimplex (88) n**23 solid malt with a hint of honey; charming, blemish-free; **t**22 gentle development of the malts over simple dusty vanilla; **f**21 quite dry, spiced and a little toffeed; **b**22 overall, clean and classically Cooley. **40%**.

**Jon, Mark and Robbo's The Smooth Sweeter One Irish Malt (89) n**22 a dry, oak-rich vanilla aroma with barley, dried pine nuts and distant honeybourbon to balance; **t**23 much more fresh and mouthwatering than the nose suggests with a thick dollop of honey for the main theme: pretty young, almost embryonic, whiskey; **f**22 decent spice, nut oils and then more vanilla and late cocoa-caramel; **b**22 seriously enjoyable whiskey for all its youth, especially for those with a sweet tooth. **40%**. *Easy Drinking Whisky Co.*

**Knappogue Castle 1990 (91) n**22 **t**23 **f**22 **b**24. For a light whiskey this shows enormous complexity and depth. Genuine balance from nose to finish; refreshing and dangerously more-ish. Entirely from bourbon cask and personally selected and vatted by a certain Jim Murray. **40%. nc.** *Great Spirits.*

**Knappogue Castle 1991 (90) n**22 **t**23 **f**22 **b**23. Offers rare complexity for such a youthful malt especially in the subtle battles that rage on the palate between sweet and dry, malt and oak and so on. The spiciness is a great foil for the malt. Each cask picked and vatted by the author. **40%. nc.** *Great Spirits.*

**Knappogue Castle 1992 (94) n**23 **t**23 **f**24 **b**24 a different Knappogue altogether from the delicate, ultra-refined type. This expression positively revels in its handsome ruggedness and muscular body: a surprisingly bruising yet complex malt that always remains balanced and fresh – the alter-ego of the '90 and '91 vintages. I mean, as the guy who put this whiskey together, what do you expect? But it's not bad if I say so myself and was voted the USA's No. 1 Spirit. Virtually all vanished, but worth getting a bottle if you can find it (I don't receive a penny – I was paid as a consultant!). **40%. nc.** *Great Spirits.*

**Knappogue Castle 1993** (*see* under Bushmills)

**Knappogue Castle 1994** (*see* under Bushmills)

**Magilligan Cooley Pure Pot Still Single Malt (88) n**22 slightly waxy and honeyed: Cooley at its softest; **t**23 beautiful arrival of highly intense, spotlessly clean malt. The sweetness level is near perfect; **f**21 some spices develop but fade quickly; **b**22 "Pure Pot Still," shouts the label. Well, no it isn't in Irish terms. Pure Pot Still Irish is a mixture of malted and unmalted barley. This is 100% malted barley, therefore a single malt. I know there has been much confusion over this, if my e-mail bag is anything to go by. I am sure the nice people at Macleod's will sort this out very soon...! **43%**. *Ian MacLeod.*

**Magilligan 8 Years Old Peated (82) n**21 **t**22 **f**19 **b**20. Lightly peated by Cooley standards; sweet throughout; finish is disappointingly dim. **43%**. *Ian MacLeod.*

**Magilligan Vintage 1991 Sherry Finish (79) n**22 **t**19 **f**19 **b**19. The rare experience of a Cooley in sherry butt. But one doesn't quite hang together. **46%**

**Merry's Single Malt (83) n**20 **t**22 **f**20 **b**21. Ultra-clean barley rich nose is found on the early palate. The finish is flat, though. **40%**

**Sainsbury's Single Malt Irish Whiskey (84) n**21 **t**22 **f**20 **b**21. A decent spice buzz to the lively malt and coal smoke. **40%**

**Shanagarry (76) n**19 **t**20 **f**18 **b**19. Pleasant, but lacks depth. **40%**. *For Intermarche France. Note: Label says "Pure Pot Still". But it is single malt.*

**Shannahan's (92) n**23 beautifully young, fresh and zesty: this distillery's best style; **t**22 refreshing, clean barley that tries to be little else; **f**24 excellent late complexity as some first-class soft vanilla appears; more citrus cleans the palate; **b**23 Cooley natural and unplugged: quite adorable. **40%**

**Slieve na gcloc Single Peated Malt (84)** n21 t20 f22 b21. No, I wasn't drunk when I typed the name. And I was sober enough to detect a slight feinty note that reappears towards the death. Until then, curiously thin. A pleasant cocoa and peat malt, but one not quite gelling as it perhaps might. **40%. For Oddbins.**

**The Spirit Safe & Cask Selection Cooley 1991 12 Years Old** dist Sept 91, bott Oct 03 **(89)** n22 t23 f22 b22 struggles to find a rhythm but the acacia honey holds it together. **43%. nc ncf. Celtique Connexion.**

**Vom Fass Cooley 4 Years Old (82)** n22 t21 f19 b20. Wonderfully clean; for a Cooley, actually has extra sheen and copper richness. Just fades towards the finish and lacks depth. **40%. Austria.**

**Vom Fass Cooley Peated 8 Years Old (89)** n22 gently smoked; lightly cured bacon; t23 sweet delivery with a wonderful honey shadow to the smoke; f22 oily liquorice and vanilla; b22 much more recognisable. This is a treat from an above average cask, though the peating is subtle and subdued. **40%. Austria.**

**Waitrose Irish Single Malt (83)** n20 t22 f20 b21. Pulsating sweet malt: clean as an Irish whistle and beautifully mouthwatering. Really impressive. With the slightly flat finale I suspect it has caramel: without it, it would be better still. **40%. UK.**

## OLD BUSHMILLS

**Bushmills 10 Years Old** Matured in Two Woods db **(82)** n22 t21 f19 b20. A beefed-up, sherried number compared to a few years back; attractive but in need of finding some complexity from somewhere. **40%. Irish Distillers**

**Bushmills 12 Years Old Distillery Reserve** db **(87)** n22 a near sneezeinducing black pepper bite to the rolling citrus and malt; t23 intense, marmaladesharp malt and big spice; f21 vanilla and caramel; b21 improved in recent years with a distinct fruitiness now to the middle. **40%**

**Bushmills Select Casks Aged 12 Years** Married with Caribbean Rum cask db **(95)** n23 unusual moist rum and raisin cake effect: effective and just enough spice to deliver extra complexity. Just the very slightest hint of bourbon, too; t24 adorable malt richness; biscuity and stupendously seasoned yet always remains fresh and mouthwatering. The sweetness is very cleverly controlled; f24 there are just so many layers to this: the oak is a growing force, but restricts itself to a vanilla topping; b24 one of the most complex Bushmills in living memory, and probably since it was established in 1784. **40%**

**Bushmills Aged 16 Years** Matured in Three Woods db **(88)** n20 a touch of sulphur detracts somewhat from the fresh fruit delivery. Still get pomegranates, though! t24 seismic waves of spicy fruit, juicy and salivating in effect; f21 that haunting of poor sherry just takes the edge off the fun; b23 until the advent of the wonderful Bushmills Select Casks 12 and the extraordinary improvement in the awesome Bushmills 21 this was leader of the distillery tribe. Would have been overthrown irrespective of the sulphur, which is hardly the norm for this distillery whose sherry casks are usually the finest in the world's whisky businesss. **40%**

**Bushmills Rare Aged 21** Years Matured in Three Woods Madeira Finish, bott 04 db **(96)** n25 it doesn't come much better than this as a variable but unbelievably clean grape intensity flickers like twinkling lights. Yet for all this the malt still has much to say and the oak butts in with some teasing mocha and spice; t24 amazing! After three mouthfuls or so, it's still impossible to pinpoint what is happening exactly. What I do get is a chocolate effect, like the chocolate the ice-cream man pours on your whipped ice-cream. There are also sultanas in there and walnuts and drier Madeira-induced coffee notes, which then sweeten to give the effect of iced coffee-flavoured biscuits. To complete the harmony youwould need spice...and it turns up on cue; f23 after further layers of grape and spice, becomes much more serene with oakiness taking a slight chalky effect; b24 it looks as though the early gremlins that got into the first bottlings of this expression have been overcome. The harmony here defies description, let alone belief, especially in a golden period about ten seconds after it hits the mouth through to the early part of the finish. Is this a one-off vatting that has hit heights hitherto thought impossible: a one-off freak? Or will the 2005 bottling somehow capture this improbable brilliance? I wouldn't take the chance: if you can find this bottling now, get a case!! **40%**

The **Old Bushmills Single Cask 1989 Bourbon Barrel** cask 7986 **(88) n**22 big vanilla thrust; **t**23 quite an outstanding intensity to the buttery malt with the sweetness almost on a precise curve upwards; some oak offers countering dryness; **f**21 surprising toffee late on; **b**22 perhaps a better malt than the early nose suggests, but very unusual in style for this distillery and would mark higher but for the debilitating toffee. **56.5%. ncf.** *Specially selected for Canada.*

The **Old Bushmills Distillery Single Cask Bourbon Barrel 1989** db cask 8139 **(88) n**21 fruity, but otherwise languid, with some dry, solid age apparent; **t**23 juicy malt that really allows the barley to shine; **f**22 long and revelling in its fresh barley richness; some very late, papery and dry oak at the death; **b**21 Old Bushmills really springing a surprise with its depth for the age. **56.5%.** *USA.*

The **Old Bushmills Distillery Single Cask Bourbon Barrel 1989** db cask no 8140 **(84) n**20 **t**22 **f**21 **b**21. Quite a fiery number, closed early on but with excellent cocoa finale. **56.5%.** *USA.*

The **Old Bushmills Distillery Single Cask Bourbon Barrel 1989** db cask no 8141 **(88) n**20 dry; soft barley; **t**23 pure Bushmills in all its chalky yet oaky barley richness: distinctive and delightful with a bit of a nip; **f**23 seriously impressive on the barley front with better balanced cocoa; **b**22 the only one of the three bourbon casks to scream "Old Bushmills" at you for its unique style. **56.5%.** *USA.*

The **Old Bushmills Distillery Single Cask Rum Barrel 1989** cask no 7110 db **(81) n**21 **t**20 **f**20 **b**20. Big, biting and hot but some serious malt. **53.7%.** *USA.*

The **Old Bushmills Distillery Single Cask Rum Barrel 1989** cask no 7112 db **(84) n**20 **t**21 **f**22 **b**21. Sweet and attractively simple with excellent late malt. **53.7%.** *USA.*

The **Old Bushmills Single Cask 1989 Rum Barrel** cask no. 7115 **(93) n**22 delicate coating of sugar over malt; **t**24 a uniquely complex series of wonderful, prickly, banana-essence, liquorice-hinting waves of malt and spice: labyrinthine hardly does it justice; **f**23 the honied, mildly toffeed richness of the malt seems to multiply in intensity, as does the gentle hint of bourbon: a finish from near the top echelon; **b**24 some in Canada may have seen me taste this for the first time with the country's most effortlessly beautiful and charming tv presenter Nancy Sinclair. I said then I thought we had a great malt on our hands, and a later tasting of it under more controlled – and private – conditions confirmed those initial suspicions. A real honey: elegant, deeply desirable, lip-smacking, memorable and something to get your tongue round and experience slowly at least once in your lifetime. And the whiskey's not bad, either.... **53.7%. ncf.** *Canada.*

The **Old Bushmills Distillery Single Cask Rum Barrel 1989** db cask no 7122 **(77) n**18 **t**19 **f**21 **b**19. Hot and refuses to hang together although the finale is a late delight. **53.7%.** *USA.*

The **Old Bushmills Distillery Single Cask Sherry Butt 1989** db cask no 7428 **(79) n**19 **t**20 **f**20 **b**20. Rich and malty in parts but hot and just not quite gelling. **53.7%**

The **Old Bushmills Distillery Single Cask Sherry Butt 1989** db cask no 7429 **(90) n**22 passion fruit among the citrus. Sensual and gentle; **t**22 gets into a malty stride from go then a slow burning sherry fuse; **f**23 delightful finish that is long, vanilla-rich but with the most subtle interwoven fruit and barley and natural caramel; **b**23 charismatic, charming, self-confident and supremely elegant. **53.7%.** *USA.*

The **Old Bushmills Distillery Single Cask Sherry Butt 1989** db cask no 7430 **(91) n**21 slightly sweaty armpit but a good malt recovery **t**23 sweet, enormously malty for a sherry-influenced dram **f**24 mildly salty, with many layers of sweet malt and spice that go on almost endlessly **b**23 this is a massively complex and striking Bushmills well worth finding: casks 7429 and 7430 could be almost twins...!! **53.7%.** *USA*.

**The Old Bushmills Single Cask 1989 Sherry Hogshead** cask no. 7431 **(78)** **n**20 **t**20 **f**19 **b**19. Wake me up when something happens: a real dullard. **53.7%. ncf.** *Specially selected for Canada.*

**Clontarf Single Malt (94) n**22 intense barley but clipped slightly; **t**24 mouth-watering, young, fresh and wonderfully busy. Outstanding blood orange clinging to the sharp barley edges; soft spices buzz and the juiciness intensifies; **f**24 long with myriad waves of fruity barley of varying intensity, sometimes bringing with them cocoa and mocha; **b**24 young, steady as a rock yet wonderfully perky: just so great to taste Bushmills at this sexily tender yet ripe age. Irish most excellent! **40%** ☉ ☉

**Knappogue Castle 1990** (*see* Cooley)

**Knappogue Castle 1991** (*see* Cooley)

**Knappogue Castle 1992** (*see* Cooley)

**Knappogue Castle 1993 (91) n**22 b22 f23 b24. A malt of exceptional character and charisma. Almost squeaky clean but proudly contains enormous depth and intensity. The chocolate finish is an absolute delight. Quite different and darker than any previous Knappogue but not dwarfed in stature to any of the previous three vintages. Created by yours truly. **40%. nc.** *Great Spirits.*

**Knappogue Castle 1994 (95) n**24 teasingly delicate and complex: first with a mouthwatering intertwining of fresh cut grass enlivened by hints of zesty lemon, then a mild floral tone. The sharpness is not blunted even by soft oaky vanilla. The whole is crisp, clean and vivid: a Bushmills nose that will leave you gasping; **t**24 soft, malty arrival at first which is delicately sweet, then an on-rush of lively barley notes flood around the tastebuds. The oak ties in with the natural zestiness to help form a wonderful bitter-sweet feel to the proceedings; **f**23 barley and oak remain in harmony as soft spices add extra warmth; unbelievably clean despite the subtle cocoa notes indicating advancing years. A shy oiliness keeps the sweeter notes locked to the roof of the mouth. Some late natural toffee/butterscotch dulls the brittleness of the barley; **b**24 the blender, I can tell you with uncanny insight, aimed at re-creating the delicate, complex feel of the K92 and this has been achieved with something to spare. Now the big question for him is: how the bloody hell does he improve on this? Perhaps by plugging the small gap between vatting and bottling where the extra time in the cask saw a minor degree of toffee develop, docking the brand by a point. But this remains the most sophisticated Knappogue of them all not least because of the extra depth. And the one of which I am most proud as there are 150 ex-bourbon casks here and not a single peep of an off-note. **40%.** *Castle Brands.*

⋅⋅⋅ **Knappogue Castle 1994** Lot no. L6 **(89) n**23 clean, pleasantly crisp barley; soft vanillas dance with the fresh grass; **t**24 beautifully weighted, multi-layered delivery where the clarity of barley is almost eye watering. Stunning...; **f**20 remains salivating at first, then goes slightly wrong as an annoyed oakiness dries things too fast and injects an off-key bitterness; **b**22 a wonderful whiskey in the Knappogue tradition, although this one was not done by its creator. That said, it does have an Achilles heel: the finish. This is the most important bit to get right, especially as this is the oldest Knappogue yet. But not enough attention has been paid to getting rid of the oak-induced bitterness. **40%.** *Castle Brands.*

# Single Grain
## COOLEY

**Greenore 8 Years Old** db **(89) n**23 soft, sweet corn, delicious hints of bourbon; **t**22 rich, soft oils, melt-in-the-mouth grain and just a hint of barley for good measure; **f**22 crisps up as the oak returns; **b**22 just a lovely grain whiskey from one of the world's finest grain distilleries. **40%.**

# Blends

**Asda Finest Irish Whiskey (79)** n21 t20 f19 b19. Sweet, chunky, chewy: not unlike a chocolate toffee. Minimal complexity except for some lovely citrus on the nose. **40%.** *Cooley for Asda.*

**Ballygeary (80)** n20 t21 f20 b19. Fresh and mouthwatering with an impressive malty thrust. Decent oak, too. **40%.** *Cooley for Malt House Vintners.*

**Black Bush** (*see* Bushmills Black Bush)

**Brennan's** bott code L5033 **(86)** n21 t22 f21 b22. A very well put together blend with impressive malt magnitude. **40%.** *Cooley for Shaw Ross USA.*

**The Buena Vista** bott code L5051 **(84)** n20 t21 f22 b21. A much lighter, brighter, more integrated whiskey with attractive malt bite linking to the softer grain. Very decent blending for San Franciscans. Mr Delapre would have been proud. **40%.** *USA.*

**Bushmills Black Bush (91)** n24 amazingly spicy – a bit like the old 1608! – with clean but lively sherry and freshish malt. This is one crackerjack nose; t23 stunning: the sweetness is exemplary as it sits snugly between the enormity of the fruit and the clarity of the malt. Somewhere in there is a raisiny sheen; f21 dropped points for a toffee-caramel finale, which undermines some of the complexity. Even so, the sherry remains lip-smacking and the spices behave themselves; b23 the quality of the sherry used boggles the mind. Remains a true classic. My word, though, what I would do to see a 46% non-coloured, non-chill filtered version. **40%.** *Diageo.*

**Bushmills** (formerly Original) **(79)** n19 t20 f19 b21. A light blend that has improved dramatically in recent years. The aroma is of Fox's Biscuits Party Rings, as is the finish topped with some toffee and chocolate. **40%.** *Diageo.*

**Bushmills 1608 (88)** n22 massive surge of fruit and malt, intermingling with light spices with hardly any grain evidence; t23 pure silk: sherry holds the foreground allowing spices to build up from the rear; f22 at last a little grain appears, accentuating the sherry; b21 beautiful Irish that on the evidence of this bottling has turned away from big'n'spicy to a more velvety sherry number. **40%**

**Cassidy's Distillers Reserve (89)** n23 genuine balance and harmony between soft grain and even softer, fresher barley; caramel weighs it down: without that it would be a rare treat; t22 brilliant interaction between stunning grain and top quality malt is evident early on; f22 lush and waxy, still the malt flourishes as the oak provides spice and vanilla; b22 some lilting, fresh complexity on nose and mouth arrival and even the toffee on the finish can't tellingly detract from a very high grade Cooley blend. **40%.** *Marks & Spencer, UK.*

**Castelgy Gold Shield (81)** n20 t20 f20 b21. Strange name, familiar blend style from Cooley. This one does have a little extra fruit from somewhere on the nose and excellent young malt grip on the finish. **40%.** *Cooley for Lidl.*

**Clancey's** bott code L5037 **(87)** n22 really lovely grain firmness with soft oaky, floral interjection; t22 deft and as soft as the nose; f21 just an extra shade of oaky bitterness at the death; b22 the excellent grain nose sets it up well and the rest is honest and very enjoyable. **40%.** *Cooley for Wm Morrison UK.*

**Clontarf Classic Blend (86)** n18 t23 f23 b22. This has to be treated as a new whiskey. Many moons back I created this as a 100% grain from Cooley, a velvet-soft job of real subtlety. These days, with me having no involvement, the whiskies are from Irish Distillers. This is no longer all grain, though the malt content is no more than fractional. And it really underscores the difference in style between Midleton and Cooley grain. For every degree Colley is soft and yielding, Midleton is unremittingly rigid. The nose (though not the taste) is recognizable to devotees of White Bush and Paddy. Which means aroma-wise, with the caramel, it's pretty austere stuff. But you cannot fault the delivery which is crisp, salivating and offering surprising sweetness and big citrus. Not bad once you adapt: in fact, seriously entertaining. **40%.** *Clontarf Irish Whiskey Co.*

**Clontarf Reserve (84)** n19 t22 f21 b22. Frighteningly similar to the Classic

Blend with the rock-solid grain gouging into the tastebuds. Some extra, softening oil helps soften the blows. In fact, the palate doesn't have quite the same all-round charisma and snarling attitude. **40%.** *Clontarf Irish Whiskey Co.* ⊙ ⊙

**Coleraine (74) n**18 **t**21 **f**18 **b**17. Another improved offering than compared to recent years: less firebrand and more sweet and sultry. Still lacks any real complexity although the mouth arrival is much, much more fulfilling than it once was. **40%.** *Irish Distillers.*

**Crested Ten** (*see* Jameson Crested Ten)

**Dunphys (68) n**16 **t**18 **f**17 **b**17. Hard-as-nails blend: rigid grain allows little other development. At least what appears a little pot still does give an Irish feel to it. **40%.** *Irish Distillers IR.*

**Delaney's Special** Reserve bott code L5036 **(89) n**23 the oak offers a surprising degree of floral subtlety, with pansies slightly outweighing the distant citrus: genuinely sophisticated; **t**22 silky early malt arrival but the malt gathers fast: quite sweet and lush; **f**22 subtlety the name of the game here, with the gentle oak adding a dusty finale; **b**22 vast, almost immeasurable improvement in this blend, with the grain showing beautifully and the malt really sharp and precise. In fact, this is really charming and a little classy. **40%.**

**Dundalgan Irish Gold Shield (80) n**20 **t**20 **f**19 **b**21. Light and refreshing. **40%.**

⁘ **Feckin Irish Whiskey (81) n**20 **t**21 **f**20 **b**20. Tastes just about exactly the feckin same as the Feckin Strangford Gold... **40%.** *The Feckin Drinks Co.*

**Finnegan (75) n**19 **t**19 **f**18 **b**19. A simple blend with good malt showing. **40%**

**Golden Irish (93) n**24 firm yet deeply complex with fabulous malt/grain texture. Text-book stuff; **t**22 voluptuous, silky, ultra malty and fresh; **f**23 long, with gathering grains and sublime vanilla; **b**24 a stunning, brilliantly balanced blend that groans with mouthwatering complexity. **40%.** *Cooley Distillers for Dunne's Stores IR.*

**Hewitts (87) n**22 big, intense, heavy malt-rich with some clean fruity-grapey notes in the background. Dark cherries and chocolate complete the mix; **t**22 intriguingly deep, packed with even more grapey fruitiness. The malt clings to the mouth in tandem with crisp grain, though the body is curiously oily and full; **f**20 custard creams and dry, thinner grain with just a late hint of malt; **b**23 a lovely blend that somehow manages to be light, medium and heavy at various stages. **40%** *Irish Distillers. The only blend from Midleton using exclusively malt and grain and no pot still (mixture of malted and unmalted barley).*

**Inishowen (86) n**21 **t**22 **f**22 **b**21. The peat has returned, but still not quite like the old, smoky days. **40%.** *Cooley.*

**Jameson (95) n**23 crisp pot still bounces off some firm and clean grain. Fresh sherry offers a softer dimension; **t**24 melt-in-the-mouth sherry is the prelude to brilliant pot-still sharpness. A real mouthful that you can suck and chew at the same time with some real bite in there; **f**24 vanilla, fruit and some prickly spice; **b**24 from a pretty boring bit-of-a-nothing whiskey to a sheer classic in the space of a decade: not bad going. The inclusion of extra pot still is one thing; getting the balance as fine as this is something else. Truly magnificent: this is the current Irish masterpiece. As classically Irish as someone called Seamus O'Crimmins. **40%.**

**Jameson 12 Years Old (94) n**24 much greater emphasis on the pot still which launches earlier before the second stage of sherry fires. The grains are extremely firm and marshal the constituent parts superbly; **t**24 a quite wonderful marriage between the cleanest sherry and the most rigid pot still imaginable. The result is plate-cleansing stuff, with the bitter-sweet fruit making you salivate; **f**22 slightly bitter as cocoa kicks in, but still the pot still rumbles on; **b**24 this has taken on a slightly new shape, but the quality of both the sherry butt and pot still begs credibility. Outstanding, to be sure!! **40%.** *Irish Distillers.*

**Jameson 15** (*see* under Pot Still section)

**Jameson 18 Years Old** third batch JJ18-3 db **(89) n**21 **t**23 **f**22 **b**23. This is big Irish with attitude. Much closer to the first bottling, it cuts down on the honey slightly and offers a more bourbony character. That said, the pot still guarantees this as uniquely Irish. The spices amaze. Beautiful stuff. **40%**

**Jameson 18 Years Old Fourth Batch (83) n**21 t21 f20 b21. Very pleasant but limited degree of sparkle: the age is evident, as is the toffee. **40%.** *Irish Distillers.*

**Jameson 18 Years Old Fifth Batch (89) n**22 some enlivening pot still moments; very deep and fruity; **t**23 really delightful meeting between friendly pot still, oaky spice and fruit; **f**22 some toffee seeps in but the slight liquorice depth compensates slightly as the age really begins to sing ballads of yesteryear; **b**22 great to see this charming blend back on track; understated to the point of shyness. **40%.** *Irish Distillers.*

**Jameson 1780 Matured 12 Years (94) n**23 lush and confident, spicy and warming: there is a prevailing oloroso undercurrent head on against some sharp pot still; **t**24 a whiskey that fills the mouth with thick, bitter-sweet sherry, then the unmistakable delights of old pot still coupled with a short but effective flypast of spice. The pot still dominates – towards the middle after the early sherry lead; **f**23 pretty long with neither pot still nor sherry showing any signs of wanting to leave; **b**24 now discontinued and if you should see one hanging around an old off licence grab it with both hands. The 12-y-o that has taken its place appears to be using as much sherry, but it appears to be a lighter style, as is the pot still. The 1780 was the last commercial link with the old Irish whiskies I fell in love with in the early 70s. A colossus of an Irish, of a sherry type now entirely lost which couldn't come from any other country in the world. **40%**

**Jameson Crested Ten (88) n**23 the enormity of the pot still is awesome: lovely sherry-ginger balance; **t**23 amazingly clean sherry then traces of malt and vanilla; **f**19 too much toffee but some decent spice helps compensate; **b**23 a beautifully balanced whiskey let down only by the weak finish. **40%.** *Irish Distillers.*

**Jameson Distillery Reserve** (available at Jameson, Dublin) **(74) n**20 t20 f17 b17. Starts well but becomes flatter than the Irish Midlands. Nothing like as good as previous bottlings I have tasted. Just a one-off, I am sure. **40%.** *Irish Distillers.*

**Jameson Distillery Reserve** (*available at Midleton. See* Midleton Distillery Reserve)

**Jameson Gold (94) n**24 layered elements of soft honey and subtle, mildly bourbony oak criss-crossing the crisp pot still; **t**24 honey and barley all the way, wonderfully rich and silky, cocoa shows early too with a fruit chocolate character; **f**22 some age apparent towards the bitter-sweet finale, as is butterscotch; **b**24 if you don't enjoy this, then you just don't get what Irish whiskey is all about. Vattings vary from bottling to bottling, but this is quite representative and falls comfortably within its colourful spectrum. **40%.** *Irish Distillers.*

**Kilbeggan** bott code L5054 **(80) n**19 t20 f21 b20. An improvement on recent years, though the nose is a bit dodgy. Just love the malt thrust half-way through the proceedings. **40%.** *Cooley, John Locke & Co. Ltd.*

**Kilgeary** bott code L4168 **(78) n**20 t21 f18 b19. Pleasant, especially the fleeting delicate grain on arrival, but this is way too feeble-bodied a blend to withstand the caramel onslaught. **40%.** *Cooley.*

**Locke's** bott code L5039 **(72) n**18 t19 f17 b18. Does a job of sorts, but never quite finds its character and finishes poorly. **40%.** *Cooley, John Locke & Co.*

**Merry's Special Reserve (75) n**20 t19 f18 b18. Dull. **40%**

⋄ **Michael Collins A Blend (79) n**21 t20 f19 b19. Michael Collins was known as the "big fellow". This pleasant, impressively spiced dram, might have enjoyed the same epithet had it not surrendered to and then been strangled by caramel on the finish. **40% (80 proof.** *Cooley Distillery.*

**Midleton Distillery Reserve (85) n**22 t22 f20 b21. A whiskey which, for all its muscovado sweetness offers some memorable barley moments. **40%.** *Irish Distillers Midleton Distillery only. Was once bottled as Jameson Distillery Reserve exclusive to Midleton. Changes character slightly with each new vatting. This one is some departure.*

**Midleton Very Rare 1984 (70)** n19 t18 f17 b16. Disappointing with little backbone or balance. **40%.** *Irish Distillers.*

**Midleton Very Rare 1985 (77)** n20 t20 f18 b19. Medium-bodied and oily, this is a big improvement on the initial vintage. **40%.** *Irish Distillers.*

**Midleton Very Rare 1986 (79)** n21 t20 f18 b20. A very malty Midleton richer in character than previous vintages. **40%.** *Irish Distillers.*

**Midleton Very Rare 1987 (77)** n20 t19 f19 b19. Quite oaky at first until a late surge of excellent pot still. **40%.** *Irish Distillers.*

**Midleton Very Rare 1988 (86)** n23 t21 f21 b21. A landmark MVR as it is the first vintage to celebrate the Irish pot-still style. **40%**

**Midleton Very Rare 1989 (87)** n22 citrussy and spicy, the malt is hardchiselled into the overall chararacter: some formidable pot still, too; t22 very vivid pot still which follows the firm grain; f22 the hard, brittle unmalted barley makes itself heard: you could break your teeth on it; b21 a real mouthful but has lost balance to achieve the effect. **40%.** *Irish Distillers.*

**Midleton Very Rare 1990 (93)** n23 carrying on from where the '89 left off. The pot still doesn't drill itself so far into your sinuses, perhaps: more of a firm massage: t23 solid pot still again. There is a pattern here: pot still first, sweeter, maltier notes second, pleasant grains third and somewhere, imperceptibly, warming spices fill in the gaps; f24 long and Redbreast-like in character. Spices seep from the bourbon casks; b23 astounding whiskey: one of the vintages every true Irish whiskey lover should hunt for. **40%.** *Irish Distillers.*

**Midleton Very Rare 1991 (76)** n19 t20 f19 b18. After the Lord Mayor's Show, relatively dull and uninspiring. **40%.** *Irish Distillers.*

**Midleton Very Rare 1992 (84)** n20 t20 f23 b21. Superb finish with outstanding use of feisty grain. **40%.** *Irish Distillers.*

**Midleton Very Rare 1993 (88)** n21 pot still with sub plots of honey and pepper; t22 the pot still makes use of the dry hardness of the grain; t23 beautiful elevation of the pot still towards something more complex and sharp balancing superbly with malt and bourbony-oak texture; b22 big, brash and beautiful – the perfect way to celebrate the 10th-ever bottling of MVR. **40%.** *Irish Distillers.*

**Midleton Very Rare 1994 (87)** n22 pot-still characteristics not unlike the '93 but with extra honey and ginger; t22 the honeyed theme continues with malt arriving in a lush sweetness; f21 oily and a spurt of sharper, harder pot still; b22 another different style of MVR, one of amazing lushness. **40%.** *Irish Distillers.*

**Midleton Very Rare 1995 (90)** n23 big pot still with fleeting honey; t24 enormous! Bitter, sweet and tart all together for a chewable battle of apple and barley. Brilliant; b21 some caramel calms proceedings, but Java coffee goes a little way to restoring complexity; b22 they don't come much bigger than this. Prepare a knife and fork to battle through this one. Fabulous. **40%.** *Irish Distillers.*

**Midleton Very Rare 1996 (82)** n21 t22 f19 b20. The grains lead a soft course, hardened by subtle pot still. Just missing a beat on the finish, though. **40%**

**Midleton Very Rare 1997 (83)** n22 t21 f19 b21. The piercing pot still fruitiness of the nose is met by a countering grain of rare softness on the palate. Just dies on the finish when you want it to make a little speech. Very drinkable. **40%.** *Irish Distillers.*

**Midleton Very Rare 1999 (89)** n21 malt and toffee: as sleepy as a nighttime drink; t23 stupendous grain, soft enough to absorb some pounding malt; f22 spices arrive as the blend hardens and some pot still finally battles its way through the swampy grain; b23 one of the maltiest Midletons of all time: a superb blend. **40%.** *Irish Distillers.*

**Midleton Very Rare 2000 (85)** n22 t21 f21 b21. An extraordinary departure even by Midleton's eclectic standards. The pot still is like a distant church spire in an hypnotic Fen landscape. **40%.** *Irish Distillers.*

**Midleton Very Rare 2001 (79)** n21 t20 f18 b20. Extremely light but the finish is slightly on the bitter side. **40%.** *Irish Distillers.*

**Midleton Very Rare 2002 (79)** n20 t22 f18 b19. The nose is rather subdued and the finish is likewise toffee-quiet and shy. There are some fabulous middle moments, some of flashing genius, when the pot still and grain combine for a spicy kick, but the finish really is lacklustre and disappointing. **40%**. *Irish Distillers*

**Midleton Very Rare 2003 (84)** n22 t22 f19 b21. Beautifully fruity on both nose and palate (even some orange blossom on aroma). But the delicious spicy richness that is in mid launch on the tastebuds is cut short by caramel on the middle and finish. A crying shame, but the best Midleton for a year or two. **40%**.

**Midleton Very Rare 2004 (82)** n21 t21 f19 b21. Yet again caramel is the dominant feature, though some quite wonderful citrus and spice escape the toffeed blitz. **40%**.

⠿ **Midleton Very Rare 2005 (??)** n23 t24 f22 b23. OK, you can take this one only as a rough translation. The sample I have worked from here is from the Irish Distillers blending lab, reduced to 40% in mine but without caramel added. And, as Midleton Very Rares always are at this stage, it's an absolute treat. Never has such a great blend suffered so in the hands of colouring and here the chirpiness of the pot still and élan of the honey (very Jameson Gold Label in part) show just what could be on offer given half the chance. Has wonderful natural colour and surely it is a matter of time before we see this great whiskey in its natural state. **40%**

⠿ **Midleton Very Rare 2006 (92)** n22 real punch to the grain, which is there in force and offering a bourbony match for the pot still; t24 stupendously crisp, then a welter of spices nip and sting ferociously around the palate; the oaky coffee arrives early and with clarity while the barley helps solidify the rock-hard barley; f23 usually by now caramel intervenes and spoils, but not this time and again it's the grain which really stars; b23 the best Midleton for some time: as raw as a Dublin rough-house and for once not overly swamped with caramel. An uncut diamond. **40%**. *Irish Distillers.*

**Millars Special Reserve** bott code L5047 **(80)** n20 t21 f18 b21. A big, grainkicking blend which has lost some of its old spicy perzazz and suffers from a harsh finale. Some odd juniper notes here and there. **40%**. A. Millar & Co. Ltd.

**Wm Morrison** (*see* Clancey's)

**O'Briens** bott code L4118 **(78)** n19 t20 f19 b20. Fractionally cleaner than of old; very firm and crisp. **40%**. *Cooley for P.J. O'Brien & Sons.*

**O'Hara** bott code L5043 **(74)** n19 t19 f17 b19. Caramel dominated and showing all the subtlety of Graham Norton. **40%**. *Cooley for Millar Products Ltd.*

**Old Dublin (73)** n17 t20 f17 b19. A clean blend that rarely troubles the inner tastebuds. Sweet with no pretensions of grandeur whatsoever. **40%**. *Irish Distillers.*

**Old Kilkenny (86)** n21 t22 f21 b22. A real shock to the system. Traditional pot still character in an own-label product, and real quality stuff to boot. However, gather up as many of the labels as you can that tell you it's triple distilled. Cooley are likely to take over the blend from Irish Distillers later in 2003 so the biting barley character will be lost for a softer malt-based blend. In this form a collectable one for Irish whiskey lovers worldwide. **40%**. *Asda UK.*

**Old Midleton Distillery Blended Whiskey 1967 35 Years Old (92)** n24 t23 f22 b23. This is a real one-off bottling of a quite unique Irish whiskey (actually coming from the old Midleton distillery, surely that should be "whisky"?). Apparently this one cask was filled in 1967 from a mixture of Midleton pure pot still and Midleton grain. After all this time, no-one knows why. But it was rescued by enthusiasts David Radcliffe and Sukhinder Singh and bottled for their respective businesses. I'm delighted to report (unlike Sukhinder's soon-to-become legendary Dunglass) that this is a little stunner. **41.1%**. *www.potstill.com*

**Paddy (68)** n16 t19 f16 b17. Good old Paddy: I knew it wouldn't let me down. While other lesser Irish whiskies have improved, Paddy has steadfastly refused to budge: dusty, cloyingly sweet and shapeless. Like an ugly duckling, I'm almost becoming fond of it. Hang on a minute, I'll have another taste: no, actually I'm not. Unclassicallly Irish. **40%**. *Irish Distillers.*

**Powers (91)** n23 rugged pot still and beefed up by some pretty nippy grain; t24 brilliant mouth arrival, one of the best in all Ireland: the pot still shrieks and attacks every available tastebud; f22 pulsing spices and mouthwatering, rock-hard pot still. The sweetness is a bit unusual but you can just chew that barley; b22 is it any coincidence that in this bottling the influence of the caramel has been significantly reduced and the whiskey is getting back to its old, brilliant self? I think not. Classic stuff. **40%**. *Irish Distillers.*

**Powers 12 Years Old (77)** n21 t20 f18 b18. Disappointing: surely should be seeing more out of this baby? **40%**. *Irish Distillers.*

**Redbreast Blend (88)** n23 some genuinely telling pot-still hardness sparks like a flint off the no less unyielding grain. Just love this; t23 very sweet and soft, the grain carrying a massive amount of vanilla. Barley offers some riches, as does spice; f20 a climbdown from the confrontational beginnings, but pretty delicious all the same; b22 really impressed with this one-off bottling for Dillons the Irish wine merchants. Must try and get another bottle before they all vanish. **40%**. *Irish Distillers for Dillone IR (not to be confused with Redbreast 12-y-o Pure Pot Still).*

**Sainsbury's Blended Irish Whiskey (79)** n19 t21 f19 b20. A lush, mouthwatering charge of malt towards the very middle. **40%**

**Shamrock (78)** n19 t21 f19 b19. A standard Cooley blend, but the promising complexity is lost under a welter of caramel. **40%**. *Cooley.*

⸬ **Strangford Gold (81)** n20 t21 f20 b20. A simplistic, exceptionally easy drinking blend with high quality grain offering silk to the countering spice but caramel flattens any malt involvement. **40%**. *The Feckin Drinks Co.*

**Tesco Special Reserve Irish Whiskey** bott code L5053 **(87)** n21 belligerent malt, young but well directed, spices the more docile grain; t23 the malts are stupendously juicy and have no problems punching their way entirely through the rich, clean grain; f21 really it's the grains that have the day here, but such is their superb quality, no problem; b22 underlines the fact that Cooley produces one of the world's best grain whiskies and a very sharp, decent malt. **40%**.

**Tir No Nog (78)** n20 t21 f18 b19. Lots of overactive toffee. **40%**. *Cooley.*

**Tullamore Dew (75)** n18 t20 f18 b19. Less than inspiring, maybe. But it has picked up on the pot still in recent years. Less throat-ripping, more balance. There is hope yet. **40%**. *Irish Distillers for Campbell and Cochrane.*

**Tullamore Dew 12 Years Old (81)** n21 t21 f20 b19. Enjoyable citrussy, pot-still tones criss-cross from the nose to the toffeed, Canadian finale. **40%**. *Irish Distillers for Campbell & Cochrane.*

**Tullamore Dew Heritage (79)** n20 t22 f19 b18. Fat and lush, the mouthwatering action is upfront on the tastebuds before the long toffeed, mildly spiced finale. **40%**. *Irish Distillers for Campbell & Cochrane.*

**Waitrose Irish Whiskey (77)** n20 t19 f20 b18. Very sweet but the grain is stupendous. **40%**. *UK.*

**Walker & Scott Irish Whiskey "Copper Pot Distilled" (83)** n20 t22 f20 b21. A collectors' item. This charming, if slightly fudgy-finished blend was made by Cooley as the house Irish for one of Britain's finest breweries. Sadly, someone put "Copper Pot Distilled" on the label, which, as it's a blend, can hardly be the case. And even if it wasn't a blend, would still be confusing in terms of Irish whiskey, there not being any traditional Irish Pot Still, that mixture of malted and unmalted barley. So Sam's, being one of the most traditional brewers in Britain, with the next bottling changed the label by dropping all mention of pot still. Top marks, chaps! The next bottling can be seen below. **40%**. *Sam Smith's.*

**Walker & Scott Irish Whiskey (85)** n21 t22 f21 b21. Oddly, sharper grain has helped give his some extra edge through the toffee. A very decent blend. **40%**.

**The Wild Geese (79)** n20 t22 f18 b19. Easy drinking and pleasant late spice but not enough gravity for the caramel. **40%**. *Cooley for Avalon.*

# American Whiskey

**N**ot that long ago American whiskey meant Bourbon. Or perhaps a very close relation called Tennessee. And sometimes it meant rye. Though nothing like often as it did prior to prohibition. Very, very rarely, though, did it ever get called single malt, because virtually none was made on the entire North American continent. That was a specialist - and very expensive - type left to the Scots and, to a lesser extent, the Irish. Or even the Japanese if a soldier or businessman was flying back from Tokyo.

I say "virtually" none was made because, actually, there was the odd batch of malt produced in America and, in my library, I still have some distilled at a rye distillery in Maryland in the early 1970s. But it was hardly a serious commercial concern and the American public were never made greatly aware of it.

Just how many know about the malt whiskey revolution presently hitting the States is open to debate, but I guess very few. Those I have spoken to about it seem surprised when I tell them the standard of the quality is exceptionally high. I'm not too convinced they believe me. But the healthy state of malt whiskey making was brought home to me just as I was completing this book, when a bottle of Strahan's Colorado Whiskey arrived in my sample room. This is America's latest distillery to bottle and these Denver guys were using, like their Kentucky colleagues, virgin oak casks in which to mature their spirit. So although only two years old the wood impact with the barley was profound: indeed, there were more bourbony notes than barley. But yet again I have been left almost speechless by the sheer excellence of the malt I poured. It may not have eclipsed the stupendous Clear Creek of Oregon - again the Whiskey Bible's Best Small Batch Distillery Whisky of the Year - but it certainly helped underline that the USA has a malt whiskey industry that, though tiny, has now to be taken seriously in terms of quality alone.

Meanwhile back in Kentucky distilleries continued to operate at a fair lick to try and up stocks of both bourbon and rye. Things haven't been right in that department since the Heaven Hill fire and since then interest in and demand for bourbon has grown internationally.

As ever, new brands hit the market place with Buffalo Trace, Heaven Hill and Woodford Reserve being particularly busy. Two entirely new styles of bourbon both carried off awards in this year's Bible. Brown-Forman at last got round to launching the Labrot and Graham's Woodford Reserve Four Grain they had been threatening to for the last two or three years. And it was impossible not to be wowed by the complexity of this idiosyncratic pot still creation. Displaying extra oils and weight - perhaps even a degree of feints - it made the most of every last grain of rye present in the mashbill. However, it was the Buffalo Trace's Experimental Collection Twice Barrelled that really sent me into raptures. For me, it was within touching distance of the world's finest whisky in 2006.

But it was on the rye front that 2006 has to go down as a truly vintage year. Heaven Hill released the Ritterhouse Rye 21 Years old, a single barrel whiskey spread over 31 casks. Tasting notes to all of them can be found on pages 302 and 303, but it was barrel 28 that blew me away. It even outpointed another memorable rye to hit the shelves for the first time, Old Potrero's Hotaling's, an 11 Year Old of astonishing depth and quite unique character. The fact that both actually outgunned the Fall 2006 release of Sazarac 18 gives some indication of the enormity of quality to be found in the rye market today.

The next year for me, though, will be in hoovering up Elijah Craig 12 and Evan Williams 12, the last made at Bardstown. Friends who will be deeply missed.

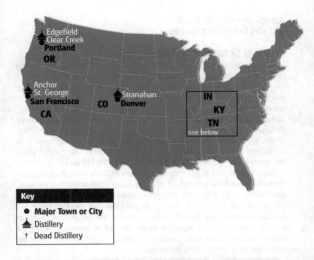

## Key

- ● **Major Town or City**
- ▲ **Distillery**
- † **Dead Distillery**

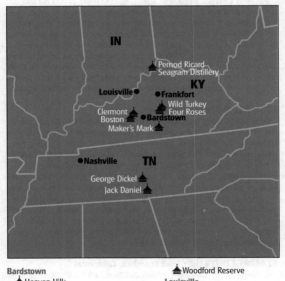

**Bardstown**
- ▲ Heaven Hill†
- ▲ Barton

**Frankfort**
- ▲ Buffalo Trace

- ▲ Woodford Reserve

**Louisville**
- ▲ Early Times
- ▲ Bernheim
- ▲ Stitzel Weller

## American Single Malt
### ANCHOR DISTILLERY (see Rye)

### CLEAR CREEK DISTILLERY (Portland, Oregon)
**McCarthy's Aged 3 Years** bott 05 **(96) n**24 the deepest, most toe-curling peat-reek outside Islay. And better, even, than one or two distilleries on the island...; **t**24 is it the demerara-molassed sweetness or that stunning gristy barley that hits the palate first and stops you in your tracks? It is impossible to determine, though the smoke, which starts as a whisper, builds up to something profound and beautiful; **f**24 the works: demerara sugared Jamaican coffee; dry cocoa and , of course, that distinctly iodiney, gristy peatiness. And a touch of late vanilla; **b**24 it's a straight shoot out between this and a Tasmanian single malt for the best small distiller of the year. I thought the Taz guys had it...until I tasted this. But how can you fault the near faultless....??? **40% (80 proof).**

**McCarthy's Oregon Single Malt Aged 3 Years (92) n**24 smoked kippers, very lightly oiled; old-fashioned Ardbeg; **t**23 very sweet initial arrival that dampens down with a surge of soft oak then sparks again as pressed-cane juice carries with it a rip-tide of peat; **f**22 soft, gentle, pulsating malt and light spice; **b**23 another excellent effort from McCarthy, but the sweetness and oil have just taken a fraction from the normal brilliance. I'm looking forward to when the distillery do finally start batch-marking their bottles, which they will do by the time of the 2007 edition. **40% (80 proof).**

**McCarthy's Oregon Single Malt Aged 3 Years (95) n**23 kippery but also soft grist and spices and a hint of slightly overdone brown toast; **t**24 jackpot hit as the sweetness is controlled and instead we have lush waves of ultra-clean smoke; the oiliness is there but defused enough to allow only a perfect coating of the palate; **f**24 not far off the perfect finale. The oak adds a drier element but really it is the Port Ellen-style fresh gristiness that keeps your tongue working overtime as the finish refuses to fade; **b**24 this is, unquestionably, the finest bottled whiskey I have tasted anywhere in the world from a small-batch distiller. Only Islay's very finest can out-complex this not so little chap. **40% (80 proof).**

### EDGEFIELD DISTILLERY (Portland, Oregon)
**Edgefield Distillery Hogshead** db bott 4 Sep 03 **(93) n**24 **t**24 **f**22 **b**23. It really takes some believing that a distillery, at its third attempt, has come up with something quite this brilliant. I'm not sure where the caramel is coming from: either natural or added, but without it, it would be phenomenal. **46% (92 proof).**

**Edgefield Hogshead (89) n**22 big, big malt and ripe banana; **t**23 silky, tastebud soothing yet intense. The clarity of the barley and total lack of smoke allow the vanilla of the oak full early entry; **f**21 sweetish, with the oak juices mingling happily with the intense barley. Very attractively spiced; **b**23 there have been no fewer than six bottlings of this small-batch malt since the 2005 edition was written. Unfortunately the bottles aren't batch-marked, so the public are denied the fun of comparing differences. Here I went to the distillery in Oregon to try their latest, from 21 March 05. **46%**

### ST GEORGE DISTILLERY (San Francisco, California)
**St George Single Malt Aged 3 Years** db **(75) n**17 **t**19 **f**20 **b**19. Without doubt the fruitiest whisk(e)y I have tasted in nearly 30 years of sampling the stuff. The nose in particular is some kind of raspberry or similar fruit, more eau de vie than whiskey. That said, this is beautifully distilled and clean with a wonderful bite near the finish: it is just that the malt has been lost along the way. **43%**

**St George Single Malt Aged 3 Years Lot 2** db **(82) n**19 **t**21 **f**21 **b**21. Much better. The fruit still clings to the nose, but this time malt rings loud and clear round the tastebuds and there is superb interaction with the oak. Once more, supremely made and, once that fruit is lost, we will have an absolutely toprank malt on our hands. **43%**

**St George Lot 3** db **(82) n**20 **t**20 **f**21 **b**21. Another fruitfest from St George that again shows excellent clarity, but has wandered off the malty path. Quite pithy in places and always enjoyable. **43%**

**St George Lot 4** db **(87) n**23 for some reason there is a beguiling drift of rye, apple and cinnamon, but – at last!!! – it is the richness of the malt that really takes off; **t**20 drier than any other St George, with a slow evolution of malt against some flakey, oaky tones; **f**22 remains dry but the slight bitterness is perfectly received by barley and busy spices; **b**22 Eureka! Them thar pesky Californians have gone and struck themselves malt. Not fool's malt, but the pure stuff, yessiree!!! Just took four years of copper panning. **43%**

## STRANAHAN DISTILLERY (Denver, Colorado)

∴ **Stranahan's Colorado Whiskey Batch No 5** dist 9 Sep 04 **(90) n**23 pretty bourbony as manuka honey and soft liquorice pulse their way through the firm, gently spiced oak. Big stuff!; **t**24 wonderful, bourbon-style honey-sweetness to the delivery and the spice promised on the nose arrives in droves; superb texture and weight and rounded beautifully with touch of oil; **f**21 perhaps slightly over-oaked and thins quickly; **b**22 if the Rockies is where east meets west, then this first-ever Colorado whiskey is where bourbon meets single malt. The quality of the distilling is beyond reproach and this 3,608th, and final, whiskey to go into this 2007 Bible really is the perfect way to end six months' solid tasting. But if the whiskey does have a fault it is the enormity of the oak: for a two-year-old only Indian malt whisky matures faster. My instincts tell me that distillers Jake and Jess will benefit in future years from using a mixture of virgin and used casks to maximise the complexity lurking in the obvious riches found in this gold strike. But hey, this is Colorado. Where you don't mess with a man's woman...or his whiskey... **47% (94 proof).**

# Bourbon Distilleries

Bourbon confuses people. Often they don't even realise it is a whiskey, a situation not helped by leading British pub chains, such as Wetherspoon, whose bar menus list "whiskey" and "bourbon" in separate sections. And if I see the liqueur Southern Comfort listed as a bourbon one more time I may not be responsible for my actions.

Bourbon is a whiskey. It is made from grain and matured in oak, so really it can't be much else. To be legally called bourbon it must have been made with a minimum of 51% corn and matured in virgin oak casks for at least two years. Oh, and no colouring can be added other than that which comes naturally from the barrel.

Where it does differ, from, say Scotch, is that the straight whiskey from the distillery may be called by something other than that distillery name. Indeed, the distillery may change its name which has happened to two this year already and two others in the last three or four. So, to make things easy and reference as quick as possible, I shall list the Kentucky-based distilleries first and then their products in alphabetical order along with their owners and operational status.

## BARTON
Bardstown. Barton Brands. Operating.

## BUFFALO TRACE
Leestown, Frankfort. Sazerac. Operating.

## BROWN-FORMAN
Shively, Louisville. Brown-Forman. Operating.

## FOUR ROSES
Lawrenceburg. Kirin. Operating

## HEAVEN HILL BERNHEIM DISTILLERY
Louisville. Heaven Hill Distillers. Operating.

**JIM BEAM**
Boston and Clermont. Fortune Brands. Operating.
**WOODFORD RESERVE (formely Labrot & Graham)**
Near Millville. Brown-Forman. Operating.
**MAKER'S MARK**
Loretto. Fortune Brands. Operating.
**WILD TURKEY**
Lawrenceburg. Pernod Ricard. Operating.

## Bourbon

**1492 Bourbon** (see Heaven Hill 80 Proof)

**A H Hirsch Reserve 16 Years Old (91) n**23 waxy honeycomb embedded in marzipan and dark chocolate; **t**24 again the honey is at the centre of things with a soft, corny development; more Lubek marzipan, this time with a soft, sweet lemon centre. The mouth-feel is exceptional; **f**21 smaller grains here and developing firmer, drier oak; **b**23 not until November did I discover that this bourbon, the last surviving to be made in Pennsylvania, was still doing the rounds. The distillery closed way back in 1988 and much of its maturing stock was destroyed by court order. I last tasted the 16-y-o back in the 90s and in Jim Murray's Complete Book of Whisky (1997) I described it as "big, confident, highclass whiskey". Says it all. Michter's Distillery, Pennsylvania.

**American Star (86) n**21 **t**22 **f**21 **b**22. A seriously good rye-recipe bourbon with enormous full-bodied and fruity character. Sweet and lingering. **40% (80 proof).** *Bernkasteler Germany.*

**Ancient Age (75) n**18 **t**19 **f**19 **b**19. Light, pleasant but half cooked. **40% (80 proof).**

**Ancient Ancient Age 10 Star (89) n**22 lavender and soft rye amid the rich corn; **t**23 complex small grain, centring around the rye, but also slightly nutty with some raisiny fruits; **f**22 oak comes steaming in to gently dry the broadening corn. Spices begin to bite; **b**22 what we have here is a bourbon that knows how to offer complexity: a thinking man's bourbon. Much better than it once was. **45% (90 proof).** *Buffalo Trace.*

**Ancient Ancient Age 10 Years Old (81) n**20 **t**20 **f**21 **b**20. Drat and blast! One of my favourite whiskeys way off form, here showing its normal complexity only in patches and, by its own massive standards, just all round too plain and flat. **43% (86 proof).** *Buffalo Trace.*

**Ancient Age Preferred (76) n**17 **t**19 **f**20 **b**20. Sweet, thin but with excellent spice build-up. **40% (80 proof).** *Buffalo Trace.*

**Anderson Club** (*see* Heaven Hill Aged 6 Years 90 Proof)

**Aristocrat** (*see* Heaven Hill 80 Proof)

**Austin Nichols Wild Turkey** (*see* Wild Turkey)

**Baker's Aged 7 Years** batch B-90-001 **(85) n**21 **t**22 **f**21 **b**21. Not quite in the same league as the bigger batch 85, but pretty timeless, enjoyable stuff. **53.5%.** *Jim Beam.*

**Barclay's Bourbon (79) n**20 **t**21 **f**18 **b**20. Economical in development, there is still enough rye and nutty oiliness to keep the tastebuds amused. Little sparkle on the finish. **40% (80 proof)**

**Basil Hayden's (77) n**21 **t**19 **f**18 **b**19. Some attractive rye riches, but overall disappointingly thin and lacking in depth. **40% (80 proof).** *Jim Beam.*

**Benchmark** (*see* McAfee's Benchmark)

**Black Jack (86) n**23 **t**22 **f**20 **b**21. What starts as a ryefest loses power dramatically, though the outcome remains tasty. **37%.** *Australia.*

**Blanton's Gold Edition** barrel no 12 w/house H rick 35 dumped 16 Oct 03 **(91) n**22 a fraction closed for Blanton's but spice enough to show it's ticking; **t**24 a velvety coating of sweetcorn with a tingling layer of rye and leathery liquorice; the elan is spellbinding; **f**22 remains sweet with lashings of natural toffee; **b**23 seamless. **51.5% (103 proof).** *Buffalo Trace.*

⁘ **Blanton's Single Barrel Green Label** barrel 139 dumped 10-1-05 **(89) n**23 kumquats and blood orange abound; **t**23 a big rye presence on delivery which shows some delicate touches amid the odd punch; **f**21 drier vanilla; **b**22 deliciously fruity and rye proud. **40%**

**Blanton's Red (91) n**24 an essay in delicate form and complexity; **t**22 your tastebuds are kissed by soft tannins; **f**22 blackberries and cocoa; **b**23 the nose is simply to buy for...this is one of the most delicate Blanton's of all time. **40%**

**Blanton's Silver Edition** barrel no 118 w/house H rick 27 dumped 12 Jun 03 **(83) n**20 **t**22 **f**20 **b**21. Genteel and refined with the accent on corn and some waspish rye spice. **49% (98 proof).** *Buffalo Trace.*

⁘ **Blanton's Single Barrel 7 Years Old (86) n**22 **t**22 **f**21 **b**21. Enjoyable, but not exactly what I expected. The bourbon and oak haven't quite gelled: a teen beauty with a few unsightly spots. **51.5%.** *Buffalo Trace. This is one of the single barrels used to make up 1500 bottles for readers of the Suddeutsche Zeitung Magazin, Germany.*

**Blanton's Single Barrel** barrel no 69 w/house H rick 55 dumped 19 Jan 04 **(91) n**23 a riot of small grains with distant marmalade; sweet ripe plums, too; **t**22 simmering bitter-sweet corn-rye battle with rich banana and custard middle; **f**23 quite intense with a liquorice, bitter coffee surge; **b**23 goes down a treat: one to swallow and never spit. **46.5% (93 proof).** *Buffalo Trace.*

**Blanton's Uncut/Unfiltered (84) n**21 **t**22 **f**20 **b**21. For all its strength this one proves to be on the light, enormously sweet and shy side. **65.9% (131.8 proof).**

**Blue Grass State (77) n**19 **t**19 **f**20 **b**19. Clean, good toast and vanilla. **40% (80 proof).** *Somerfield UK.*

**Bowman's Bourbon (81) n**20 **t**20 **f**21 **b**20. A very decent, well-balanced, softly spiced and rich young-to-medium-age bourbon originating from Heaven Hill. A fine everyday shot. **40% (80 proof).** *A Smith Bowman.*

**Booker's 8 Years 8 Months** batch no. C87-D-21 **(86) n**22 **t**23 **f**20 **b**21. A rich bourbon that varies in style from batch to batch. This one has a better than average middle with no shortage of rye, but is let down in the final stages. **62.45% (124.9 proof).** *Jim Beam.*

**Bourbon Falls** (*see* Heaven Hill 86 Proof)

**Bourbon Royal** (*see* Heaven Hill 80 Proof)

**Buffalo Trace (94) n**24 sharp rye screams above the complex corn, citrus and oak: seriously absorbing; **t**23 stupendous, softly oiled mouthfeel with the corn absorbing some prickly rye and spice; **f**23 sweet, remains oily with some cream toffee. The small grains re-emerge for a last battle with the corn; **b**24 I simply adore this whiskey: the weight is just about perfect as is the corn-oak, bittersweet harmony. The small grains add great colour and complexity. A whiskey gem of the world. **45%. (90 proof).**

⁘ **Buffalo Trace Experimental Collection Fire Pot Barrel Aged 10 Years** dist 6 Feb 96, bott 24 Feb 06 **(92) n**24 an essay in subtlety with caressing fingers of vanilla and kumquat plus gently molassed, Jamaica Blue Mountain light roast; **t**23 gentle oils help mould liquorice and heavy roast raisin to the roof of the mouth; **f**22 long, remaining on that roasty theme; **b**23 the great thing about experiments in bourbon is that the whisky is not under threat from hideous sulphur-stained casks or dreadful European wines. This experiment is a success. **45% (90 proof).**

⁘ **Buffalo Trace Experimental Collection French Oak Aged 10 Years** dist 6 Apr 95, bott 24 Feb 06 **(86) n**23 **t**23 **f**19 **b**21. Unusual, polarized whiskey that is seriously bitter-sweet and though a great experience, it is possible to spot the odd flaw. **45%**

⁘ **Buffalo Trace Experimental Collection Twice Barrelled (96) n**24 big, big age yet an astonishing, fruity freshness piles on the citrus, rye and spice. Just gets better as it sits in the glass and the complexity bedazzles; **t**25 talk about a gentle giant: this really does radiate enormous depth yet without becoming too stuffed on sweet sugars or thumping oak. There is a laid-back, acceptance of pure brilliance in the natural harmonization here that I cannot remember finding in any other bourbon I have ever tasted: and we are talking thousands!! All the usual leathery, liquoricy, honeycombed suspects are there, but the restraint and control is awesome; **f23** long with a gradual increase in vanillas and caramels and a small touch of sugar to ward off encroaching, more bitter oak; **b24** perhaps the ultimate bourbon. Would prefer to have seen this at 50.5 and unchillfiltered – but that's being greedy... **45% (90 proof).**

**Bulleit Bourbon Frontier Whiskey (88) n22** light and teasing: mallows roasting on an open fire plus pine nuts and vanilla. Honest, folks; **t22** the faintest dry oak start vanishes within seconds for a rich follow-through of sweet chestnut, a busy complexity of malted barley and rye and then spice; **f22** mildly oily, softly honeycombed and chocolatey for a chewy, bitter-sweet finale. Like all that's gone before, exceptionally well balanced and satisfying; **b22** absolutely excellent from first to last, an essay in balance and control: I doubt if any frontier whiskey of Boone's day was half as good as this. **45% (90 proof).**

**Cabin Hill** (*see* Heaven Hill 80 Proof)

**Cadenhead's Heaven Hill Aged 8 Years** bott Feb-05 **(88) n21** some polite liquorice and hints of rye; **t22** the corn comes out to play with a sweet, oily rush; **f23** much more complexity here as the small grains and oak really go head to head; some zesty tartness completes a busy finale; **b22** big, complex whiskey. **62%.**

⋰ **Cadenhead's Heaven Hill Aged 14 Years** bott May 06 **(89) n23** polished leather, oranges...the whole nine yards; **t23** glossy coffee-sugar and liquorice; searing spices keep the vanillins in check; **f21** deft mollassed vanillas; **b22** a wonderful bourbon, but just on the way down with the oak showing big control. Still a corker, though. **56.9%**

**Champion** (*see* Heaven Hill 80 Proof)

**Chapin & Gore** (*see* Heaven Hill 80 Proof)

**Chapin & Gore 86 Proof** (*see* Heaven Hill 86 Proof)

**Chesapeake** (*see* Heaven Hill 80 Proof)

**Chillie Gone Crazy** (*see* Heaven Hill 80 Proof)

**Colonel Lee (69) n17 t17 f18 b17.** Should be shot at dawn. **40%.** *Barton.*

**Colonel's Pride** (*see* Heaven Hill 80 Proof)

**Corner Creek Reserve Aged 8 Years (93) n24** one of the fruitiest and frankly most attractive noses on the bourbon shelves: massive orangey citrus lead, wonderful small grain follow-on; **t24** hits a hollow on entry and a few seconds later erupts into a fruity free-for-all with the rye really packing a punch; **f22** a bitter marmalade tartness to the sour dough finale; **b23** hard to find but the unique tune played on this is so worth searching for. **44% (88 proof).** *Corner Creek Distilling Co., Bardstown.*

**Cougar (93) n24** biting, rip-roaring, rabid rye offering astonishing crispness and finesse on the corn. One of the all-time great rye-rich bourbon aromas; **t23** massive rye makes for a crisp, fruity and mouth-watering arrival. The corn eventually softens the impact and ensures sweetness; **f23** much more well-behaved with vanilla and corn now leading the way but the rye just continues to salivate the palate; **b23** one of the most characterful, purposeful bourbons you could imagine. This Illinois cracker is one of the best-kept secrets in the bourbon world. **37%.** *Australia.*

**Daniel Stewart Aged 8 Years (88) n22** rich, leathery and pipe-tobacco sweet but underneath a second stratum of young grain: unusual; **t22** brilliantly spiced yet sweet corn forms an oily-textured middle; **f22** lots of blistering small grain and spice; **b22** very sweet yet complex bourbon of light-to-medium weight. **45%** *Heaven Hill.*

**Daniel Stewart Aged 12 Years (95) n24** floral, honey and outstanding clean oak and corn: a classy act; **t24** heather, honey, hints of citrus and then some serious oak, but always sweetened by the rich corn. The rye offers a spicy and even more complex background; **f23** such a delicate fade: the sweetness falls over aeons, the oak gathering density at the same rate. But the rye continues its merry tune; **b**24 it is pretty obvious that the original old Heaven Hill peaks at 12: it always has in the time I have known it. Awesome, spellbinding bottlings like this place it amongst the world's elite. **53.5% (107 proof).** *Heaven Hill.*

**Dierberg's** (*see* Heaven Hill 80 Proof)

**Distiller's Pride** (*see* Heaven Hill 80 Proof)

**Don & Ben's** (*see* Evan Williams Aged 7 Years 86 Proof)

**Dowling De Luxe 8 Years Old 100 Proof (93) n**23 salty, big-oaked, a touch minty but enough small grain to see it through; **t**23 big burnt oak arrival then the middle is awash with ultra-ripe fruit, especially dates and even over-ripe banana; **f**23 calms down for more oaky strands on which the small grains and soft spices flourish; **b**24 this wasn't a whiskey you would always associate with complexity – until now. Forget the age statement. A very similar proposition to the stunning Virgin 7, but with a little extra fruit. **50% (100 proof).** *Heaven Hill.*

⋙ **Eagle Rare Aged 10 Years Single Barrel Mac Y 10th Anniversary (93) n**23 unmistakable Buffalo Trace whiskey with the vanilla revealed in so many textured layers; **t**23 surging oaks on delivery. Then a backing off to allow a more measured, mildly molassed sweetness to interlink with some orangey citrus; **f**23 slow spice arrival, a brushing of hickory and some developing rye fruitiness; **b**24 beautiful bourbon from the school of complex shades and inferences. **45%.** *Denmark.*

**Eagle Rare Single Barrel Bourbon 10 Years (94) n**23 leathery and honied; astonishingly soft and delicate; **t**23 at first sweet-corn, then a gradual build-up of spices, though the sweetness refuses to fade while a vague murmur of fruit can be found; **f**24 long, lots of vanilla threading through, while the small grains and late rye are a treasure; **b**24 just one of those effortlessly brilliant whiskeys that seem to get it right without trying. The best ERSBB I've come across as yet. **45%**

**Eagle Rare Kentucky Straight Bourbon 17 Years Old 90 Proof** bott Fall 06 **(93) n**23 maple syrup; rye-liquorice mix; **t**23 sweet and delicate arrival; the silky delivery intensifies as the natural oak sugars begin to take hold; **f**24 long, burnt fudge and mocha. Just so beautifully weighted and elegant; **b**23 one of the steadiest ships on the bourbon shelves. **45% (90 Proof).** *Buffalo Trace.* ☺ ☺

**Early Times Kentucky Straight Bourbon (brown label) (80) n**21 **t**20 **f**19 **b**20. Not quite as fruity a profile but the clarity is unblemished. Very corny. **40% (80 proof).**

**Early Times (yellow label) (83) n**20 **t**21 **f**21 **b**21. A heavier, more vanilla rich bourbon that offers a consistent, delicate, sweet theme throughout with butterscotch on the finish. **40% (80 proof).**

**Echo Spring** (*see* Heaven Hill 80 Proof)

**Elijah Craig 12 Years Old (96) n**24 honey-roast nuts with the usual HH kumquaty citrus character. Quite smoky with wonderful bitter-sweet alignment; **t**23 deft, articulate oak offers sweet vanilla and distant honeycomb; fruity with figs and raisin; **f**24 eternally mouthwatering despite the gathering of drier vanilla-oak and spices. Take an evening out to wait for this to end; **b**25 you cannot but sit on the chair, chew on near perfection and be simply amazed. And a couple of bottlings I tried this year were, if anything a tad richer. Grab now: with the loss of the origianl HH distillery, soon they will be gone forever. **47% (94 proof).** ☺ ☺

**Elijah Craig Aged 18 Years Single Barrel** barrel no. 1226, barrelled on 8 Sep 81 **(93) n**23 concentrated tangerine on the turn, but when mixed with rye like this works well. Like disappearing into an old Gentlemen's club leather armchair on which pipes have been smoked. Massive esters. Massive full stop; **t**24 hold on to your armchairs: just so confrontational with screeching rye and malt smashing head-first into the citrussy oak without stopping in time. A collision of flavours and styles that leaves you reeling; **f**22 big tangerine finale with spice and rye: the fade is even and almost infinitely long; **b**24 give anyone who regards bourbon as an inferior species a dose of this and they will be cured: astonishing and truly beautiful. **45% (90 proof).**

**Elmer T Lee Single Barrel (88) n**22 distinct citrus and light corn-rich notes; **t**23 sweet corn again with hints of banana and rye; **f**21 a very settled, toffeed finale with a hint of spicy rebellion; **b**22 a more delicate and less rye-infested bottling than some. Really delicious. **45% (90 proof).** *Buffalo Trace.*

**Elmer T Lee (85) n**22 **t**22 **f**20 **b**21. A tad muted and not quite up to the usual ETL brilliance. **43%**

**Evan Williams** (*see* Heaven Hill 80 Proof)

**Evan Williams 100 Proof** (*see* Heaven Hill 100 Proof)

**Evan Williams Aged 7 Years (83) n**22 **t**21 **f**20 **b**20. Sweet, corn-rich with caramel on the middle and a dry, oaky finish. **43% (86 proof).** *Heaven Hill.*

**Evan Williams 10 Years Old (84) n**22 **t**22 **f**19 **b**21. Fabulous start but loses map towards the finish. **43% (86 proof).**

**Evan Williams 12 Years (96) n**24 how can something so big be so well-mannered and controlled? Expensive suede prickled by rye and small grain. A hint of hickory smoke; **t**24 busy spices attack the tongue from the off, then waves of liquorice and gentle rye wash against the tastebuds. The sweetness is unbelievably exact and refined, balancing against the chunkier roasty notes; **f**24 more corn oil here than other HH oldies, but as well as upping the sweetness exactly when it's needed, it also helps paint broad rye and creosotey stripes across the palate. The very finish has an exotic fruit salad, mainly of the papaya variety – not unknown for this distillery; **b**24 it must be some ten years ago I first came across this in Japan and fell under its spell. This is the first time I have officially tasted it for the Bible, having somehow failed to get up-to-date bottlings. The quality hasn't dropped one iota. Quite simply: one of the greatest whiskey experiences you will ever have. **50.5% (101 proof).**

**Evan Williams 15 Years (95) n**24 rye-induced lavender, black peppers, jack fruit and sweet liquorice: just so busy; **t**24 surprising sweetness to the arrival with corn up front followed by big rye and fruit procession; a wonderful unripened fruit sharpness offers supreme balance; **f**23 recedes so slowly you can barely notice: just enough sweetened spice to see off any oaky counter at this good age; an unusual papaya bitterness at the death completes the exotic festival; **b**24 just such brilliantly balanced and entertaining bourbon that loses out to its younger brother only on account of subtlety. **50.5% (101 proof).**

**Evan Williams 23 Years Old (91) n**23 one of the spiciest noses in all Kentucky! Allow to oxodise after 23 years in barrel and you will see sharp rhubarb battling it out against the oaky polished floors. Just this side of oblivion...; **t**23 the spices leave you spellbound and gasping; bitter yet somehow controlled, with the oak staying the right side of the white line as a burnt Demerara sugar, hickory and toasted raisins assault the tastebuds. No shortage of sweetness as rye and marzipan balance the books; **f**23 little can follow the big assault other than intense vanilla and burnt custard...and bitter marmalade; **b**23 a far greater event than the previous EW23 simply because the oak has never taken control and the complexity refuses to surrender. One for the collection. **53.5% (107 proof).**

**Evan Williams 1783** (*see* Heaven Hill 10 Years 86 Proof)

**Evan Williams Old** (*see* Heaven Hill 100 Proof)

⌁ **Evan Williams Single Barrel 1997** Barrel no. 1, barreled 20 Feb 97, bott 10 Oct 06 **(87) n**22 dense, mildy syrupy but not rye-edged as is the old house style; **t**24 beautifully exotic with massive delivery of varying sugars, mostly brown and molassed. The flavours all arrive in a fury with a burnt liquorice also having a big say. The tastebuds are almost run over in the rush. but what a way to go; **f**20 a surge of oaky bitterness controls the shape: short, thin and limited by EW standards; **b**21 all the wondrous sugary, toasty notes arrive early on, leaving behind a thinner, more bitter finish. For those of you wondering why this is so removed from the usual EW Single barrel we have come to know and love over the last decade, the answer, of course, is that it was made at a different distillery following the Great Heaven Hill fire of 1996: in this case the Clermont Distillery of Jim Beam. The recipe may be identical. But the difference is in the glass for all to taste. **43.3%**

⸭ **Evan Williams Single Barrel Vintage 1996** Barrel no. 1, bott 4 Oct 05 db **(92)** n24 classic nose full of usual fruitcake but beefed up by additional liquorice and molasses; t23 drier than the norm as the oak gets in early but maple syrup and a dash of rye do the biz; f22 lots of natural caramels leached from the oak; b23 up to the usual superb standards. **43.3% (86.6 proof).**

**Evan Williams Vintage 1993 Single Barrel (89)** n22 busy citrus battling with fresh and fruity rye; t22 delicate small grains dominate at first, then a wave of oak followed by sweet corn; f22 pretty long and quite dry with some chalky oak enlivened by returning rye and liquorice; b23 a steady, sexy, delicate bourbon that is a lot more complex than it initially seems. **43.3% (86.6 proof).**

**Evan Williams Vintage 1994 Single Barrel Vintage** barrelled on 28 Oct 94, barrel no. 394, bott 8.12.04 **(89)** n23 carrot cake, red liquorice and honey; t22 enormously sweet: an outpouring of sugar-cane juice and corn; f22 some tingling oak add chocolatey dryness; b22 a shade too sweet for perfection, but one for the ladies. **43.3% (86.6 proof).**

**Evan Williams Vintage 1995 Single Barrel Vintage** barrelled on 1 May 95, barrel no. 308. bott 5 May 05 **(94)** n23 exceptional balance between honeycomb and liquorice; t23 that honey and honeycomb thread is insistent through the brilliance of the vanilla-rye domination; f23 wonderful spices play out as a soft apple and custard sweetness is topped with vanilla; b24 the back label is a must to find: brilliant and just about flawless. **43.3% (86.6 proof).**

**Evan Williams Vintage 1995 Single Barrel Vintage** barrelled on 18 Aug 95, barrel no. 01, bott 13 Oct.04 **(92)** n23 deep cinnamon and fruitcake; t24 sublime oak scaffolding on which the corn and late, fruity rye hang; f22 wonderful small grain spices gain ground; b23 beautifully complex and well weighted. **43.3% (86.6 proof).**

**Ezra Brooks (79)** n19 t20 f20 b20. A light-to-medium weight bourbon with a standard nose but offering good sweet liquorice on the rich finish. **45%**

**Fighting Cock Aged 6 Years (84)** n22 t22 f20 b20. Brilliant nose of old, waxy wooden floors and a really battling palate arrival of almost fruity corn. Quite hot. **51.5% (103 proof).** *Heaven Hill.*

**Four Roses (84)** n22 t21 f20 b21. A sweet and charming bourbon that is light and sophisticated but always pulls up short of being a world beater. Now that the distillery is on its own I expect this perennial under-achiever to go through the roof quality-wise. The stocks are there, as the single-barrel expressions illustrate, and as I have seen over the years when inspecting the warehouses. Keep your eyes peeled and tastebuds at the ready. Four Roses is likely to become a thorn in their competitors' sides. **40% (80 proof).**

**Four Roses Black Label (89)** n21 lazy at first, but gentle handwarming encourages an oaky confrontation with soft rye; t22 thicker, weightier, more intense than the standard bottling, it again leans on the rye to do battle with the tastebuds; sweetening corn adds fine balance; f23 drier, sharper, with a touch of late honeycomb; b23 takes time to get started, but once rolling won't stop. **40% (80 proof).**

**Four Roses Platinum (87)** n24 burnt caramel fudge with diced nuts and dried dates: one of the most integrated and classy little FR noses I've ever come across, especially when the rye delivers a fruity edge; t23 serious weight and early spice to this: only a big influx of sweet-corn and flat caramel buries the gathering complexity; f20 a degree of rye-induced bitterness and spice, but the leaden corn and caramel really is powering; b20 something odd here: you think you have a world-beater on your hands but an avalanche of caramel arrests all further development. A bit of tinkering here and you might have something extra special. **43% (86 proof).**

**Four Roses Single Barrel (90) n**22 unusual port cask-style fruitiness as rye-spices nip at the nose; **t**23 really fresh, full, clean and fruity. Just so mouthwatering; **f**22 the trademark caramel digs in, but some spices keep it alive; **b**23 faultless, refreshing bourbon that underlines this distillery's latent excellence. **43% (86 proof).** *Four Roses Distillery.*

**Four Roses Single Barrel** warehouse no. AS, barrel no. 23-5A **(83) n**23 **t**21 **f**19 **b**20. Great nose of formidable complexity, but what follows is on the dull side with too much sweet-corn and caramel. **50% (100 proof).** *Four Roses Distillery.*

**Four Roses Super Premium (83) n**22 **t**21 **f**20 **b**20. Corn oil dominates, caramel hovers, lazy spices buzz: business as usual. **43% (86 proof).** *Four Roses Distillery.*

**Gentleman Earl** (*see* Heaven Hill 80 Proof)

⋰⋰ **George T. Stagg (94) n**23 vanillin dominates slightly over the small grain, which is unusual, and although there are some citric segments the oak dominates; **t**24 back on course with wondrous verve and vigour, fruity rye tones leading the way followed by big liquorice; **f**23 toasty, hints of hickory; **b**24 another thundering glass of genius and so complex despite the massive strength. Perhaps a shade oakier, though, than some of its predecessors. **70.6% (141.2 proof).** *Buffalo Trace.*

**George T Stagg (97) n**24 for all its enormity in strength, this is a pussycat on the nose with playful yet elegant brushstrokes of cough sweet (Fishermen's Friends!), dried dates and camp coffee. Busy and beautiful; **t**24 wonderful delivery of confident tannins, bolstered by a double whammy of fruit and corn which dissolve in the mouth to quite stunning effect. Enormous, yet so wonderful: perhaps this is what sex is like for masochists; **f**25 again, the alcoholic strength is defied by the deftness of the lapping flavours that break upon the tastebuds: more coffee and also cocoa notes with slightly sweetened citrus zest; **b**24 whisky of the year? Probably has to be. The tasting of whiskies for this year's Bible has been so difficult because the quality has jumped so high. But nothing has quite reached these heights.... **64.5% (129 proof).**

**George T Stagg (97) n**25 **t**24 **f**23 **b**25. I have tried this with water at varying strengths, but to get the best out of this bourbon you must be brave. Take at full strength, but only in very small amounts. Such is the enormity of this whiskey it will soon spread around the palate offering its full service. Along with a certain Ardbeg, this George T Stagg is without any shadow of a doubt one of the two best whiskies it has ever been my luck and privilege to taste in nearly 30 years. **68.8% (137.6 proof).** *Buffalo Trace.*

⋰⋰ **George T. Stagg (96) n**25 can something this delicate really be 140 proof?? An aroma that drifts like butterflies with no shortage of nectar to feed on; the strands of honey are both deft and deep and balance well with the honeycomb; dulcet rye tones soar on the spirity thermals and oak offers a soft, vanilla-rich cladding. Simply the stuff of whiskey dreams...; **t**22 begins sweet but nosedives into something surprisingly dry, mildly compromising the balance for a while until it rediscovers its equilibrium with a wave or ten of Belgian chocolate; **f**25 returns to its brilliance once more with those cocoa notes now harmonising with the returning rye; just so long and the late arrival of an orangey, citrus thread doesn't hurt at all; in fact the finish is near perfection; **b**24 just one moment or two's madness, where the plot is lost may have cost this one World Whisky of the Year. Another staggering Stagg, a serious improvement on the previous bottling and a collector's must-have. **70.3% (140.6 Proof). ncf.**

**George T. Stagg Spring 2005 Release (92) n**22 lazy, depending on heaps of natural caramel; **t**24 big, blustery start and then a massive delivery of spice on top of the coffee-tannin; lashings of sweet corn; **f**23 a long finish, as can be expected, but much more corn than usual and less complexity; **b**23 truly great whiskey, but slightly lacking in style by Stagg's almost untenably high standards. **65.5% (130.9 proof).** *Buffalo Trace.*

**George T Stagg Spring 2005 Release (97)** n24 pulsing corn and rye; more small grain involvement than usual – fabulous complexity and grace; t24 the rye delivers the first bite, then come several waves of rich tannin; lots of Demerara richness in there, too; f24 long, gradually sweetening, soft waxiness helps the burnt honeycomb stick to the roof of the mouth and keep the fun lasting longer; with the Fishermen's Friends cough sweets (on the nose of the 129 version) appearing at the death here; b25 just what is it about George T Stagg? Three bottlings in the last year, and two are in the short-list of six for Whisky of the Year. The quality defies belief...!! **65.9% (131.8 proof)**. *Buffalo Trace.*

**Gold Country Aged 8 Years (88)** n22 marzipan and marmalade; t22 the most teasing criss-crossing soft, sweet vanilla and firmer grains; never more than a gentle caress; f21 soft as a marshmallow and as roasted at the end as a toasted one; b23 exceptionally delicate for its age and colour. Take your time to discover this most subtle of bourbons. **40% (80 proof)**. *France, Denmark.*

**Gold Label** (*see* Heaven Hill 80 Proof)

**Hancock's Reserve Single Barrel (83)** n21 t22 f20 b20. Cream caramel... with a dose of rye to liven things up. **44.45% (88.9 proof)**. *Buffalo Trace.*

**Heaven Hill Old Style Bourbon (77)** n18 t20 f19 b20. Young, yet a sweeter, weightier, mildly oilier expression than a couple of years back, with better balance and depth to finish. **40%**

**Heaven Hill 86 Proof (83)** n20 t22 f20 b21. Probably the maltiest bourbon I have tasted in 29 years of savouring the stuff: barley springs out at you from all directions. Fresh, juicy and mouthwatering: delicious and a real surprise package. **43% (86 proof)**.

**Heaven Hill 100 Proof (78)** n19 t20 f19 b20. Lots of rye and toffee. **50%**

**Heaven Hill 6 Years Old (83)** n19 t21 f22 b2. Quite a change from previous bottlings, with more youth here, less evident rye domination but lashings of mouthwatering grains nonetheless. Some late liquorice hinting age at the finish. **40% (80 proof)**.

**Heaven Hill Old Style Bourbon 6 Years Old 90 Proof (85)** n20 t21 f22 b22. Very well made whiskey on permanant cruise control. **45% (90 proof)**.

**Heaven Hill Old Style Bourbon 6 Years Old 100 Proof (93)** n23 big rye fizz nibbles at the nose while some orangey oakiness adds brilliant balance; t23 massive arrival of small grains, perfectly presented. Demerara sugar gently coats the thickening oak and the spiced fruitiness really takes off as the rye dominates; f23 long, with those soft sugars still keeping the oak under control. The spices pulsate and some deliciously bitter, tangy marmalade completes the mind-blowing complexity; b24 I've been drinking HH at six years for a long, long time. And this is easily the best expression I ever happened across. A firecracker! **50% (100 proof)**.

**Heaven Hill Aged 10 Years 86 Proof (86)** n21 t21 f22 b22. Takes a little time to get going but a sophisticated number in some ways showing greater age than expected with the whole being better than the parts. **43% (86 proof)**.

**Heaven Hill Ultra Deluxe (89)** n22 no shortage of pounding rye lessens an oaky grip; t22 again the rye wants to lead the way, but a custardy, corny sweetness keeps it in check; f22 wonderful small grain interplay lightens the developing big oak liquorice; b23 no age statement on label, so presumably a 4-y-o. The thing is, it's taken off from the old standard bottling which was once the same recipe and age, leaving it standing. Much sturdier, oakier and and just so deliciously bourbony!! Just great stuff and one of the biggest improvements on the Kentucky stage. **40% (80 proof)**.

**Heaven Hill Ultra Deluxe 5 Years (76)** n20 t19 f18 b19. In a bit of a toffeed trough here, halfway between the juicy, lively 4-y-o and the more, smallgrain pounding, oak-heavy 6-y-o. **40% (80 proof)**.

**Heaven Hill Ultra DeLuxe 6 Years** (*see* Heaven Hill Aged 6 Years 90 Proof)

**Henry McKenna** (*see* Heaven Hill Aged 6 Years 80 Proof)

**Henry McKenna Single Barrel Aged 10 Years** barrel 278, barrelled on 21 Jun 94 **(86) n**20 **t**23 **f**21 **b**22. This guy looks as though he's lived most his life in the rafters. Great stuff, but the more complex notes are lost under the oak. **50% (100 proof).**

**Henry Mason Bourbon (83) n**19 **t**21 **f**22 **b**21. Light and playful with a delicious citrus edge to the liquorice. **40% (80 proof).**

**Jacob's Well** batch B-0230-JW459 **(84) n**22 **t**20 **f**21 **b**21. Still seen around from time to time (though pretty rarely), this small-batch bourbon concentrates on a lavender delicacy and subtle sweetness. **42% (84 proof).** *Jim Beam.*

**Jefferson's Reserve 15 Year Old** batch no. 2 **(94) n**24 this is to die for: gently oiled, which means the rye and corn stick to the nose, the sweetness and sharp fruit in equal measure; **t**24 brilliant corn/rye entry on the palate then a shimmering honey. Great age, but always elegant and refined while the complexity dazzles; **f**22 very soft landing with vanilla and rye to the fore. The complexity remains superb; **b**24 a great whiskey: simple as that. **45.1% (90.2 proof).**

**Jim Beam (85) n**21 **t**21 **f**22 **b**21. This whiskey has improved enormously in recent years. Still light and easy going, there appears to be an element of extra age, weight and complexity. **40% (80 proof).**

**Jim Beam Black (91) n**23 big and bruising, there is weighty oil and liquorice; **t**23 beautifully sweet, manuka honey and then liquorice, candy and rich rye; **f**22 soft vanilla and liquorice; **b**23 I just so love this bourbon. The closest in style to a Jack Daniel's because of a mildly lumbering gait. Any time, any day whiskey of the very top order. **43% (86 proof).**

∺ **Jim Beam Premium Aged 7 Seven Years Old** (White Label) db **(82) n**21 **t**21 **f**20 **b**20. Hard, uncompromising and showing little of what is to come with a stunning 8-years-old. Young in character even to the point of the Old Taylor from the same stable entirely outflanking this for complexity and riches. That said, good crispness and a lovely – and unexpectedly – malty tail- off in middle. Decent but disappointing. **40% (80 proof).**

**Jim Beam's Choice Aged 5 Years (86) n**21 **t**21 **f**22 **b**22. Soft and impressive in places with the emphasis on natural caramel. A slightly different Beam style. **40% (80 proof).**

**Jim Porter** (*see* Heaven Hill 80 Proof)
**John Hamilton** (*see* Heaven Hill 80 Proof)
**J T S Brown** (*see* Heaven Hill 80 Proof)
**J T S Brown 86 Proof** (*see* Heaven Hill 86 Proof)
**J T S Brown 100 Proof** (*see* Heaven Hill 100 Proof)
**J T S Brown 6 Years 80 Proof** (*see* Heaven Hill Aged 6 Years 80 Proof)
**J T S Brown 6 Years 100 Proof** (*see* Heaven Hill Aged 6 Years 100 Proof)
**J T S Brown 8 Years** (*see* Old Heaven Hill Very Rare Aged 8 Years 86 Proof)
**J T S Brown 10 Years** (*see* Heaven Hill 10 Years 86 Proof)
**J W Dant 80 proof** (*see* Heaven Hill 80 Proof)
**J W Dant 100 proof** (*see* Heaven Hill 100 Proof)
**J W Kent** (*see* Heaven Hill 80 Proof)
**Kentucky Beau** (*see* Heaven Hill 80 Proof)

**Kentucky Crown Aged 8 Years (88) n**22 pipe-tobacco-sweet, sensual; **t**22 there is a layer of oily, sweet corn before spices arrive; **f**22 sweet vanilla and corn; **b**22 a charmingly sweet yet spicy bourbon. **45% (90 proof).** *Germany.*

**Kentucky Crown Very Rare Aged 16 Years (87) n**22 distinct kumquat and over-ripe pears, really excellent oak; **t**23 sweet, oily corn followed by liquorice and citrus: big, threatening yet mouthwatering; **f**20 levels out with a tad too much natural caramel; **b**22 a mildly abrupt toffeed end just when it was getting good. **53.5% (107 proof).** *Germany.*

**Kentucky deLuxe** (*see* Heaven Hill 80 Proof)
**Kentucky deLuxe 86 Proof** (*see* Heaven Hill 86 Proof)

**Kentucky Gentleman (89) n**23 improbable small-grains complexity for a whiskey so young; **t**23 lots of rye charging around the palate and malt adds something sweet and weighty. The corn imposes itself gently; **f**21 quietens and becomes a little bitter; **b**22 this was always a little belter for its age, but this is the best I have tasted yet. The small-grain quality is unimpeachable. Delicious. **40% (80 proof).** *Barton.*

**Kentucky Gold** (*see* Heaven Hill 80 Proof)

**Kentucky Spirit Single Barrel** (*see* Wild Turkey)

**Kentucky Supreme Aged 8 Years (78) n**20 **t**21 **f**18 **b**19. Flinty, a little rawer, more awkward and younger than it should be for its age, and has changed track from the Old Heaven Hill 8-y-o it used to tread. **40%.** *Heaven Hill.*

**Kentucky Tavern (86) n**22 **t**22 **f**21 **b**21. Typical fare from Barton distillery: for Scotch drinkers, their whiskey is the equivalent of young Speyside malt, refreshing and mouthwatering. This is no exception. **40% (80 proof).** *Barton.*

**Knob Creek Aged 9 Years (90) n**24 marmalade on slightly burnt toast, beautiful, sweet fruit, mainly pears, and then a dash of soft rye and an edge of saltiness, some honey as a side-dish; **t**22 softly spiced, oaky, busy start; then a powerful delivery of natural toffee. A playfully biting, tastebud-nipping character tries to add momentum; **f**22 chocolate toffee balances out the vanilla and ensures a dry, slightly oily and long finish; **b**22 the best aroma from the JBB Small Batch selection; softer on the tastebuds than previous bottlings, but still a power player. **50% (100 proof).** *Jim Beam.*

**Labrot & Graham Woodford Reserve** (see Woodford Reserve)

**Lone Oak Aged 12 Long Years (89) n**23 **t**24 **f**20 **b**22. The short, simple finish is a bit of a surprise package in one of the silkiest bourbons on the market shelf. **50.5% (101 proof).** *Germany.*

**McAfee's Benchmark (79) n**20 **t**21 **f**19 **b**19. Light, young, corn-rich with big caramel. **40% (80 proof).** *Buffalo Trace.*

**McAfee's Benchmark 8 Years Old (83) n**21 **t**21 **f**20 **b**21. Fruity, mouthwatering and refreshing. **40% (80 proof).** *Buffalo Trace.*

**McScrooge's** (*see* Heaven Hill 80 Proof)

**Maker's Mark (Black Wax Seal)** (gold on black label) **(93) n**23 thick, charred notes, deep, mildly waxy, hints of cordite; **t**24 oily and immediately mouthfilling with a quite stupendous soft honey, grainy sweetness that balances almost to perfection with the toasty, liquorice-caramel, burnt sugar deeper tones. A pepperiness is on a wavelength almost too subtle to be heard. This is cerebral drinking; **f**22 much less taxing on the tastebuds with a more toffeed departure. Vanilla and other well-ordered oaky tones are also present and correct; **b**24 simply outstanding bourbon with the most clever weight ratio. A whiskey that demands solitude and the ability to listen. The story it tells is worth hearing again and again. **47.5% (95 proof).**

**Maker's Mark (Gold Wax) Limited Edition (89) n**22 distinctly fruity, nutty and dense; **t**23 full-bodied and full-throttle corn carrying a lovely liquorice sweetness; **f**21 thins out to allow a waxy oakiness to develop; quite flinty at the death; **b**22 majestic and a meal in itself. **50.5% (101 proof).**

**Maker's Mark (Red Wax Seal)** (black on buff label) **(89) n**23 wispy aroma with delightful strands of exotic fruit and honey. The old fruitcake is still there, but these days the complexity and balance are nothing short of stunning. Beguiling oak adds to the overall feeling of class; **t**23 lush, pleasingly deep and quite malty. A firm nuttiness adds extra oily, chewability to the toffee and liquorice; **f**21 perhaps drier than of old with signs of a little extra age. Caramel toffee continues its interplay with the oak to guarantee a bitter-sweet edge; **b**22 an old faithful of a bourbon. Never lets you down and being from the wheaty school always shows good oak balance. **45% (90 proof).** *Fortune Brands.*

**Mark Twain** (*see* Heaven Hill 80 Proof)

**Mark Twain Aged 12 Years 100 Proof (88)** n22 the obvious oak remains light and corny; t22 hard rye and fruity, the sweetness is well camouflaged; f22 slightly burnt toast, very roasty; b22 a well-disciplined bourbon that looks at one point as though the oak has taken too firm a grip but the complexity never ends. **50% (100 proof).** *Heaven Hill.*

**Martin Mills** (*see* Heaven Hill 80 Proof)

**Mattingly & Moore** (*see* Heaven Hill 80 Proof)

**May's** (*see* Heaven Hill 80 Proof)

**Medley (85)** n18 t23 f22 b22. Intimate small grains make this an unusual and sophisticated experience. **40% (80 proof).**

**Mellow Bourbon** (*see* Heaven Hill 80 Proof)

**Military Special** (*see* Heaven Hill 80 Proof)

**Mound City** (*see* Heaven Hill 80 Proof)

**Noah's Mill** batch 02-71, dist 2 Jul 87, bott 1 Nov 02 **(91)** n23 t23 f21 b24. This is one of Kentucky's most complex whiskies by far. Small grains, big heart. **57.15% (114.3 proof).**

**No Face** (*see* Heaven Hill 80 Proof)

**No Face 86 Proof** (*see* Heaven Hill 86 Proof)

**Old 1889** (*see* Heaven Hill 80 Proof)

**Old 1889 Aged 10 Years 86 Proof (85)** n22 t20 f22 b21. Really quite different HH from what I usually see. This is much more light and delicate with less of the usual richness those old big copper stills guaranteed. A real one-off. **43% (86 proof).** *Heaven Hill.*

**Old 1889 Royal Aged 12 Years (79)** n22 t20 f18 b19. Like a heavier, older version of Sam Clay 12 with a unique style based on small grain, but the balance isn't quite there. **43% (46 proof).** *Heaven Hill.*

**Old Bardstown Aged 6 Years (83)** n19 t21 f22 b21. A thin nose compensated for by decent rye-based small grain on entertaining finale. **40% (80 proof).**

**Old Bardstown Aged 10 Years Estate Bottled (95)** n24 syrup; heavyduty molten liquoricel lovely rye sub-strata with even a hint of lavender. Some kumquats and burnt raisin complete the dreamy ultra-complex intro; t24 sit down and take a thumping: like chewing chocolate fudge except each and every tasebud is caked in a beautifully oiled, all-consuming liquor from heaven (hill?); f23 lighter oils allow the small grains to display their soft, surprisingly mouthwatering charms; some surprising late oranges; b24 this is what great bourbon is all about. An absolute masterpiece from the old school and, tragically, also probably from a now lost distillery. Go get!! **50.5% (101 proof).**

**Old Charter 8 Years Old (77)** n19 t19 f20 b19. A simple, sweet, toffeed bourbon with limited complexity. On this evidence, not quite what it once was. **40% (80 proof).**

**Old Charter 10 Years Old (93)** n24 busy, beautifully balanced and ball-busting. Brilliant! t23 so much zipping spice from the off, it's like Talisker has come to Kentucky; f22 sweetens out to its old corn-fest...eventually. Chewy and lip-smacking, being mouthwatering from first to last; b24 whoa! What's happened here? A real candy Charter that has eschewed its old plodding style for something, for all its sweetness, that exudes a touch of dynamite. **43% (86 proof).** *Buffalo Trace.*

**Old Charter 12 Years Old (87)** n22 some dazzling oak but always enough room for the small grains to flourish; t23 small-grain arrival on palate; genuinely complex with a spicy kick all the way; f20 surprising amount of natural toffee flattens it a little; b22 until that toffee arrives this is a deliciously complex dram. Well worth an investigation. **45% (90 proof).**

**Old Charter Proprietor Reserve 13 Years Old (89)** n23 kumquats and lemon peel, marmalade on light toast; t22 fruity from the word go then a wave of corn and very soft rye; f21 gentle vanillas; b23 what an enormously delicate bourbon for such great age. Graceful and charming. **45% (90 proof).**

**Old Crow (79)** n19 t20 f21 b19. Young, sweet, oddly minty, reasonably chewy, and with recent bottlings improving deliciously on some flat offerings of a year or two back. Pretty impressive for a self-declared 3-y-o. **40% (80 proof).** *Jim Beam.*

**Old Fitzgerald (79)** n18 t20 f21 b20. One of the sweetest bourbons around: the nose does it no favours but a chewy toffee fightback. **43% (86 proof).**

**Old Fitzgerald Very Special 12 Years Old (80)** n18 t23 f20 b19. Warming spice paves the way for a crashing wave of corn and oak. But that excellent middle apart, something is curiously lacking. **45% (90 proof).**

**Old Fitzgerald's 1849 8 Years (90)** n21 ethereal corn and wheat; t23 lush and sweet arrival with a mixture of sugar and honey on the corn: the wheat fizzes around the roof of the mouth; f23 remains sweet with a late citrus surge and then drier vanilla tones; b23 light yet big. The sweetness is enormous but avoids going OTT thanks to excellent oak balance. A delight and the best of the Old Fitz range by a country mile. **45% (90 proof).**

**Old Forester (89)** n22 an explosion of small grains pepper the nose, hints of marmalade; t23 chunky and deep with liquorice-toffee but it's the softly spiced apple and pear juiciness that wins the day; f22 the liqorice factor increases as oak makes a stand; b22 if anyone asks me to show them a classic rye-rich bourbon where the small grains really count, as often as not I'll show them this. **43%**

**Old Forester Birthday Bourbon Vintage 1990 (90)** n23 t23 f22 b22. Seriously delicate and sophisticated bourbon. **44.5% (89 proof).** *Brown-Forman.*

**Old Forester Birthday Bourbon Vintage 1990 95 Proof (91)** n22 t23 f23 b23. Not for the squeamish: there is enormous complexity, but laid on with a trowel. **47.5%**

⠿ **Old Forester Birthday Bourbon Distilled Spring 2005 Bottled 2005 (94)** n24 intense, almost concentrated form of a bury-fruited rye-rich Forester. Absolutely massive, yet strokes the nose rather than biffs it; t23 silky from the moment of delivery on the tastebuds to the final fade, that intensity encountered on the nose is no less complete here. There is rye enough to make you swoon, packaged in an oaky cloak; f23 first, great corn oil seeps through the oak-rye dominance to offer a sweeter edge and the most gentle of landings; b24 one of the most rye-studded stars in the bourbon firmament and wholly in keeping with the fabulous quality for which this brand has now become a byword. **40%**

**Old Forester Birthday Bourbon 1995** dist Fall 95, bott 04 **(94)** n23 ultra-ripe apples and sultanas, a sprinkling of black pepper and a firm rye skeleton on which for it to hold; t24 the corn is friendly and yielding, the oak is controlled yet profound with some toasty, burnt raisiny qualities; the rye offers sensuous fruit; f23 sultry, juicy fruits and then a blossoming of gingery spice; b24 just so wonderfully fruity and full: the stuff of traditional British fruitcake. Yet it doesn't come more American than this.... **47% (94 proof).** *Brown-Forman.*

**Old Forester 100 Proof (89)** n23 beautifully weighted clementine, hickory and coffee: a real nose full; t22 cream toffee sweetens out with fat corn and a sprinkling of molassed sugar. The rye thuds in alongside some glittering spice; f22 the spice just continues its tingling journey around the palate, soft toffee and vanilla offering a softer finish than predicted; b22 as ever, very high quality bourbon from one of Kentucky's most consistent distilleries. **50% (100 proof).**

**Old Grand-Dad 100 Proof (89)** n23 excellent hickory and charcoal signature. Excellent weight and gentle fruit input; t23 rugged silky; bites as rye hits home; f21 just loses it here slightly as the oak seems to caramelise out the fun; b22 still has beef and guts, packs a punch and delights. But even so, just not in the same league as the original masterpiece from the lost Frankfort distillery. **50%**

**Old Heaven Hill** (*see* Heaven Hill 80 Proof)

**Old Heaven Hill 100 Proof** *(see* Heaven Hill 100 Proof)

**Old Heaven Hill Very Rare Aged 8 Years 80 Proof (82)** n20 t21 f21 b20. Unusually citrussy for this distillery: lemon and lime knitting with green corn. Amazingly youthful for its age. **40% (80 proof).**

**Old Heaven Hill Very Rare Aged 8 Years 86 Proof (86)** n22 t22 f21 b21. Intriguing bourbon with greater maturity than the 80 proof version: delightful in its own right, but just on the edge of something significant, you feel. **43%**

**Old Heaven Hill Very Rare Old Aged 10 Years (86)** n22 t21 f21 b22. An improvement thanks to some subtle extra rye activity. **40% (80 proof).**

**Old Heaven Hill Very Rare Aged 10 Years 86 Proof** (see Heaven Hill 10 Years 86 Proof)

**Old Heaven Hill Very Rare Aged 10 Years 100 Proof (93)** n23 heavier and rich, fruitcake style. Really beautiful and subtle but telling rye involvement; t24 weighty and just so spectacularly rich. Really is prize-winning heavy British fruitcake with raisins and cherries to chew on before a lovely walnut oiliness arrives, followed by corn concentrate; f23 the lull after the storm, but the birds sing sweetly because the rye re-appears for a gentle but wonderfully complex finale; b23 this is astonishing bourbon, the type that makes you glad to be in the know. Brilliant. **50% (100 proof).**

**Old Heaven Hill Aged 15 Years 100 Proof (86)** n21 t22 f22 b21. For all the whiskey's colour, this doesn't have much of a 15-years-old's normal belligerent attitude. This is sweet and flighty and a little oily, too. Most un-Heaven Hill. **50%**

**Old Joe Aged 12 Years Bottled in Bond** (distilled at DSP KY 39) **(91)** n21 perhaps sluggish at first but some biting corn and oak make amends before the rye really takes off; t24 beautiful radiance of sweet, rich corn backed by deep rye. Lots of copper influence here: amazingly rich yet firm and solid; f23 still bites deep but the rye/oak/coffee/burnt raisin union is strong and long; b24 an absolutely top-notch bourbon, beyond the nose, of the very old school that just exudes class and charisma. **50% (100 proof).**

**Old Kentucky Amber Aged 10 Years (87)** n22 t21 f22 b22. A chilled-out, relaxed bourbon at first finally gets the rye to talk. **45% (90 proof).** Germany.

**Old Kentucky No. 88 Brand Aged 13 Years (92)** n22 t24 f23 b23. Stunning: classic proportions: hard to find, but grab a bottle if you can. **47%** Germany.

**Old Rip 12 Years Old (93)** n22 heavily molassed, kumquats and grapes; t24 shimmering over-ripe tomatoes with red liquorice candy; lots of rye spice prickles about; f23 much more sensual now with sweet corn mash fading out with some vanilla and bitter-sweet chocolate; b24 for a 12-y-o the colour is sensationally dark: must have spent a lifetime in the highest ricks: textbook bittersweet balance. **52.5% (105 proof).**

···· **Old Rip Van Winkle Bourbon Aged 10 Years (91)** n23 bigger than its ten years: must have lived in a warehouse roof. German-style caramelized biscuit and hint of molasses; t22 honeycomb from the off, drying towards middle; again a touch of molasses and rye-rich fruitiness; f23 big, long, slightly fat and some lovely and lively liquorice and Java/Kenya blend medium roast coffee at the very death; b23 big stuff: a bourbon not for the faint hearted. **53.3%.** Buffalo Trace.

**Old Rip Van Winkle 10 Years Old 90 Proof (88)** n23 chocolate marzipan and corn; t22 sweet, slightly oily and demerara sugar; f21 spicy vanilla; b22 really well balanced and weighty whiskey. **45% (90 proof).**

**Old Rip Van Winkle 10 Years Old (92)** n22 tangerine and oak dust; t24 improbable oak arrival for a 10-y-o offset by the mouth luxurious delivery of wonderful rye and asociated fruitiness. The depth of sweetness for balance has been calculated to the nth degree; f22 calms towards vanilla; b24 some 10-y-o! Must have come from the top of the warehouse or thereabouts. A real big mouthful of chunky excellence. **53.5% (107 proof).** Buffalo Trace.

**Old Rip Van Winkle 12 Years Old (89)** n21 light and fruity, figs and distant liquorice; t23 juicy, a hint of malt at first, grass and grapes and then harder rye and soft corn: deliciously complex; f22 liquorice and some gritty rye; b23 wonderful balance and drive to this bourbon: for something so outwardly light, the flavours just keep on coming. **45.2% (90.4 proof).**

᪲ **Old Rip Van Winkle Bourbon Aged 13 Years (87) n**22 so astonishingly spiced and big, this could easily be read as a Swedish aquavit; **t**22 yes, I must be in Stockholm: those extraordinary battles between soft sugars and spice; **f**21 chewy vanilla and caramel; some major age at the death; **b**22 very different: in fact I have never seen a Buffalo Trace whiskey like it. There are restaurants in Stockholm's Old Town whose owners would offer major favours to have a house aquavit like this. **53.3%.** *Buffalo Trace.*

**Old Rip Van Winkle 15 Years Old (95) n**24 intense honey-nut and corn, like breakfast cereal in which you could happily bury your nose; **t**24 biting corn forms the bitter-sweet, slightly oily background with some oak arriving early, but adds only depth and something else to chew on; **f**23 enormously complex: again the corn leads the way but the honey returns with some cocoa and a bit of mouth prickle keeps the tastebuds occupied further; **b**24 this is a cracker. It always was and it appears to have gone up a notch in intensity all along the line. For weight, texture and complexity, this is a superstar whiskey. **53.5% (107 proof).** *Buffalo Trace.*

᪲ **Old Taylor Aged 6 Years** (present bottling) **(89) n**23 marzipan and Seville orange offer a delightful lightness of touch and teasing complexity; **t**23 almost a hint of single malt about the lightness of touch to the honey here; the arrival is sweet and busy with just enough oaky depth to add ballast; **f**21 almost vanishes off the palate though the rye and spice stick around to impress; **b**22 the curiously thin finish is in telling contrast to the superbly honeyed middle that simple dances with small-grain charm. So much lighter than the original Old Taylor (see below) of McCracken Pike. But certainly has enough weight and fruit punch to make this better than the cheap brand it is perceived to be. **40%**

᪲ **Old Taylor Aged 6 Years** (old bottling) **(94) n**24 there is a beautiful affinity between the deep vanilla and the orange and rye fruitiness. Textbook harmonization and bourbon, though I suspect whiskeys old than six are in this; **t**23 comforting oils help propel that distinct rye note to deep areas of the palate; rich and mildly mollassed; **f**21 long, lots more vanilla but you can't escape the twist of rye and a soft honeycomb and spice flourish; **b**24 just a mile from my home in Kentucky stands, or perhaps I should say stood, the Old Taylor distillery. It may not still be there because the widow of my close and dearly missed friend, Cecil Withrow, finally sold it and the old place where Cecil once worked and, until his untimely death, harboured dreams of distilling again, faces the almost certain prospect of the demolition ball. I thought it fitting, then, that for my 1,000th whiskey tasted from this 2007 edition of the Bible it should be an original Old Taylor six-years-old which I found this year in a back street liquor store in Verona, Italy. In fact there are still many bottles of this truly classic bourbon to be found in that country and if visiting Italy for its architecture and food isn't enticing enough, then here must be the ultimate reason. And just to put a strange and fitting twist to this tale, how about this: as I was tasting and writing these notes a delivery van turned up. Nothing unusual there: we get four or five deliveries of samples every day. This, though, was a special shipment from Peru: the very first copy of a special edition of the Whisky Bible I produced for the 2006 US Christmas market. And the book had been specially dedicated to... the memory of Cecil Withrow... **40%.** *Old Taylor & Co.*

᪲ **Old Virginia Aged 8 Years** L434401A **(85) n**22 **t**21 **f**21 **b**21. Vanilla-rich and never quite lives up to the bold nose. **40%.** *La Martiniquaise, France.*

**Old Weller Antique 107 7 Years in Wood (89) n**21 a bit of a young scrapper; **t**22 nitro on a bed of TNT with some unstable plutonium thrown in for good measure; **f**23 at last reveals some sanity as a soft corn base offers some sweet goodies. Long and just so soothing...; **b**22 to think I once called this lethargic...!! Bloody hell...!!! **52.5% (107 proof).** *Buffalo Trace. See also Weller and WL Weller for other members of the same "family".*

**Original Barrel Bourbon Aged 12 Years** (*see* Daniel Stewart Aged 12 Years)

**Pappy Van Winkle 20 Years Old (79)** n19 t22 f19 b19. Just so weird how this whiskey refuses to play ball at this age. It's won awards left, right and centre, got marks fom judges that leave you gasping...yet for me, as ever, it just falls all over the place with an over-sweet, total inability to find its story. That said, one or two wonderful phrases along the way and far less oak than before. **45.2% (90.4 proof)**. *Buffalo Trace.*

**Pappy Van Winkle 23 Years Old (88)** n22 forests of oak somehow tempered by the likes of green peppers and sprawling rye; t23 explosive arrival of salty, tangy, black peppered oak which dovetails with at first soft corn and then a bigger hickory smoke kick; f21 the oak really bites at first, but there is a surprising small grain revival...and then burnt toast; b22 where the 20-y-o fails, the 23-y-o somehow succeeds despite the big oak. Flawed, but defies logic and your tastebuds. **47.8% (95.6 proof)**. *Buffalo Trace.*

**Pennypacker (87)** n22 rye-rich small grains bury themselves deeply into the fruit and oak; t22 a firm, brittle mouthfeel, again with the rye showing brightly; f21 lots of honeyed vanilla and hazelnuts amid the vanilla; b22 the PR blurb from the importers that came with this bottle said the whiskey is three years old. It's a lot older than that, I can assure you. **40% (80 proof)**. *Borco Hamburg.*

**Real McCoy (82)** n21 t20 f21 b20. Some early rye and liquorice fails to give this oily bourbon the firm backbone it needs or a conclusive direction. Attractive and mildly spiced but a little frustrating. **37%**. *Australia.*

**Rebecca** (*see* Heaven Hill 10 Years 86 Proof)

**Rebel Yell (86)** n22 t21 f21 b22. My word: this brand has moved on some. The fiery, spicy peppery attack has vanished entirely and the citrus notes have been replaced by softer strawberries, but stays true to its fruity style. Lovely wheated stuff. **40% (80 proof)**.

**Red Eye Aged 6 Years (86)** n21 t22 f21 b22. A bourbon of attractive complexity and weight. **45% (90 proof)**. *Bardstown.*

**Ridgemont Reserve 1792 (90)** n22 small grains abound with rye and vanilla passionately embraced; a lovely waft of acacia honey offers the balance; t23 subtle delivery of rich small grains again, this time on a bed of Muscovado sugar; f22 a gathering of oaky spices with weighty honeycomb, liquorice and hickory confirming the age; b23 quality bourbon from a distillery that rarely allows its spirit to age this far. The result is a sophisticated bourbon exuding a rye-rich charisma and the most subtle of sweet themes. **46.85% (93.7 proof)**. *Barton Brands.*

**Rock Hill Farms (89)** n21 thin, but honeyed; t22 slightly hot at first with developing sweet corn; f24 slowly awakens and the small grains go wild: the rye kicks in to give a hard fruit edge, a hint of malt but the sweet corn and oak combining is superb; b22 rock by name, rock by nature: a very hard whiskey which rewards patient study handsomely. **50% (100 proof)**. *Buffalo Trace.*

**Rowan's Creek** batch 02-72, dist 26 Feb 85, bott 5 Nov 02 **(78)** n21 t20 f18 b19. Loads of honey and liquorice, but way too heavily oaked. **50% (100 proof)**

**Russell's Reserve 10** (*see* Wild Turkey Russell's Reserve 10 Aged 10 Years)

**Sainsbury's Kentucky Bourbon Three Years Old (71)** n18 t18 f17 b18. Pleasant, sweet but too young to have gathered a personality. The bland, caramel finish is rather odd. **40% (80 proof)**. *Sainsbury's, UK.*

**Sam Clay** (*see* Heaven Hill Aged 6 Years 80 Proof)

**Sam Clay 8 Years** (*see* Old Heaven Hill Very Rare Aged 8 Years 80 Proof)

**Sam Clay Aged 12 Years (87)** n24 it is all about small grain plus a carrot juice and vanilla flourish. Unique...; t22 an uneven arrival of fruit and rye with the corn having varying depth: at once big and small; f20 so light it almost flutters off without noticing, save for a gentle sugar juice layer; b21 really don't know how to describe this, other than different. Suspect more than one distillery's bourbon has gone into this, because it refuses to follow any known route or style. **40% (80 proof)**. *Heaven Hill.*

**Sam Sykes** (*see* Heaven Hill 80 Proof)

**Samuels 1844** (*see* Heaven Hill Aged 6 Years 101 Proof)

**Seven Hills** (*see* Evan Williams Aged 7 Years 86 Proof)

**Smokey Jim's (85) n**21 excellent small-grain complexity; **t**22 rich, full arrival on the palate; brilliant mouthfeel; **f**21 back to a dark, juicy, fruity rye character towards the end; **b**21 genuinely complex and satisfying everyday bourbon. Excellent. **40% (80 proof).**

**Stars & Stripes (79) n**19 **t**20 **f**21 **b**19. Curious whiskey: good colour yet seems young and unfulfilled in many ways. Competent and enjoyable. **40%**

**Ten High (70) n**17 **t**18 **f**17 **b**18. Light, clean and untaxing. Good for mixing. **40% (80 proof).** *Barton.*

**Tesco Old Kentucky (78) n**19 **t**20 **f**19 **b**20. Young, sweet, very clean with a hint of hickory. **40% (80 proof).**

**Thedford Colonial Style** Batch No 001 **(93) n**24 whoa boy!!! Enormous and gratifying. Big age with coffee and vanilla thumping home, but kept in check by old orangey fruitiness. Immense; **t**22 back to normality after the big alcohol bite, bringing in softer vanilla and small grains; **f**24 feather-soft finish with lovely oils and deep, dark mocca; an absolute joy; **b**23 not an easy whiskey to find, but find it you must. It is a tame monster. Last seen at The Vintage House, Soho, London. **46.3% (92.6 proof).** *Josiah Thedford and Sons, Louisville.*

**Tom Moore (83) n**21 **t**20 **f**22 **b**20. The rye on the nose pops up at regular intervals on the palate, but overall this is a really deft, undemanding whiskey yet offering above-average complexity. **40% (80 proof).** *Barton.*

**Tom Sims** (*see* Heaven Hill Aged 6 Years 80 Proof)

**T W Samuels** (*see* Heaven Hill 80, 86 and 100 Proof)

**T W Samuels 6 Years 90 Proof** (*see* Heaven Hill Aged 6 Years 90 Proof)

**Van Winkle Lot B 12 Years Old (80) n**18 **t**21 **f**20 **b**21. Competent, with required chewability, spice and sweetness, but loses out on a slightly suspect nose and too much natural caramel. **47.2% (94.4 proof).** *Buffalo Trace.*

**Van Winkle Special Reserve (82) n**19 **t**22 **f**20 **b**21. Subdued nose, then a sweet, almost molassed explosion before a quick fade. Good early oak, though. **45.2% (90.4 proof).**

**Very Old Barton Aged 6 Years (90) n**22 green and lively with the rye really getting in amongst the powering corn. Green tea is also about; **t**22 brittle small grains melt into the sweetening corn: a touch oily and a tad spicier than of old **f**24 the sharpness to the grain is stunningly accentuated in the late middle and the finish; ends like no other bourbon and offers a freshness that totally batters the tastebuds; **b**22 it's a bit like sweetened green tea in alcohol with a strong rye kick-back. Unique as a style amongst bourbons and wholly enjoyable. More mouth-watering than any other bourbon known to mankind! **40% (80 proof).** *Barton.* ☉ ☉

**Virgin Bourbon 7 Years Old 101 Proof (92) n**23 pungent yet surprisingly deft oak, with chunky kumquats and hickory. Seven years old...?? **t**23 terrific bittersweet arrival like honey and jam on burnt toast; slicks out surprisingly with corn oil. Soft rye noises are everywhere; **f**22 foot off the gas to a degree, but the building of spice ends all hope of corn domination; **b**24 if this is a 7-y-o, then every single barrel must have been drapped down from the top rick. [Allo Allo?] Deep amber and looking three times its stated age. Big stuff, as usual: in some ways even bigger than of old. **50.5% (101 proof).** *Heaven Hill (Meadowlawn Distilling Co.).*

**Virgin Bourbon 15 Years Old 101 Proof (94) n**23 nutty, with small grains drifting in an oaky, saline sea; **t**24 Jeez! The nose doesn't quite prepare you for this Demerara-infested perfection of copper-topped small grain and the most mountainous and brilliantly balanced meltdown of oak and corn. A wizard has been at work here; **f**23 calms slowly, with the oak always showing perfect manners. Traces of liquorice amid some flinty rye and that amazingly gentle corn; **b**24 enjoy these last days of the original Heaven Hill, offering us almost heartbreaking vistas of what we are about to lose for ever. This is a classic bottling that has so improved on the last version. No lot number on this, sadly. It is unlikely you will ever forget the extraordinary bitter-sweet balance on this. A world heritage whiskey. **50.5% (101 proof)**. *Heaven Hill (Meadowlawn Distilling Co.).*

**Vom Fass Kentucky Straight Bourbon (83)** n20 t20 f22 b21. Young, sweet, unchallenging, well-made bourbon with a hint of Fisherman's Friend cough sweet. **40%**. *Austria.*

**Walker & Scott Bourbon (84)** n23 t20 f20 b21. A delightful pub bourbon of good age and impressive complexity. The nose in particular is an orgy of superb small grain. **40%**. *Samuel Smith UK.*

⦂⦂⦂ **Walker's DeLuxe 3 Years Old (86)** n22 t22 f21 b21 excellent by 3-y-o standards. **40% (80 proof).**

**Weller Centennial 10 Years Old (90)** n23 soft fruit, citrus and freshly shelled peas: a delight; t22 very dry start with a soft oak kick and spices: very warming; f22 the small grains are now pounding at the tastebuds relentlessly; b23 what a massive step upwards in a year or two. Once as gentle as a cruise on the Kentucky, now more a bungee off Natural Bridge. **50%**. *Buffalo Trace.*

**Weller 12 Years Old (90)** n23 oak is the star here, and at several levels, offering heavier liquorice notes and soft vanilla. Mint and apple also get in on the act; t23 sublime corn attack but the oak gives it a bitter edge: this is enormously intense stuff; f21 back to that toffee again: sweet and creamy and seeing off the oak; b23 immensely deep and satisfying with a magnificent chewability. **45%**

**W L Weller Special Reserve 7 Years Old (84)** n21 t22 f20 b21 A bigger whiskey than of old with lots of orangey tones on the nose and a lush, sweet and peppery body. **45% (90 proof)**. *For other members of the Weller "family" see also Old Weller and Weller.*

**Westridge** (*see* Heaven Hill 80 Proof)

**Wild Turkey 80 Proof (76)** n18 t19 f20 b19. Reverted to type with the corn not been quite happy either with itself or the half-cocked degree of oak penetration. Improves on palate, but shows little of the genius to follow in later ages. **40% (80 proof)**.

**Wild Turkey 86.8 Proof (87)** n20 attractive traces of walnut oil amid the soft corn and firmer rye; t22 an immediate impact of massive, oak-laden, liquoriced corn and firmer, more mouthwatering grains; f22 sweetens with a slight stirring of honey; b23 it's not just the extra strength that takes this into a different class from the 80 proof. Much better barrel selection, underlined by some surprising liquorice notes. Easily the best non-age-stated standard Wild Turkey I've ever come across. **43.4% (86.8 proof)**.

**Wild Turkey 101 Proof (85)** n19 t21 f23 b22 needs a bit of a kick start and then clucks and gobbles along beautifully. **50.5% (101 proof)**.

**Wild Turkey 8 Years Old (88)** n22 bingo! The real Wild Turkey is standing up with extra spices on the orange field; t22 massive spice infusion from the start with the sweet, oily corn softening things down slightly; f22 more rye to be seen and the oak really does make a gracious exit; b22 quality whiskey showing effortless grace and deceptive weight. **50.5% (101 proof)**.

**Wild Turkey Russell's Reserve Aged 10 Years 101 Proof (96)** n23 stunning rye-citrus combo pans out to reveal a mint and oak-encrusted, leathery corn sweetness; t24 seriously mega for its age, not so much in the firm cocoa-oak but the utter enormity of the small-grain depth. Once more all paths lead to clean and chewy corn; f24 gentle, minty spices cool the mouth; b25 this is dream-time whiskey, entirely befitting the name of my close friend and mentor Jimmy Russell. This is a controlled explosion of complexity, the constant light sweetness overseeing those darker, brooding passages. Only Yoichi in Japan offers a stated 10-y-o whisky which can stand shoulder to shoulder with this, though not always. Entirely flawless whiskey. **50.5% (101 proof)**.

**Wild Turkey Russell's Reserve Aged 10 Years 90 proof (91)** n23 citrussy orange and kumquats play beautifully with the prominent rye; t24 brilliantly subtle and silky mouth arrival with a sweet-corn and acacia honey counter to the darker rye and oak tones; f21 trails off much faster than you might expect for an aged Wild Turkey, allowing the oak-caramel just a little too much depth, though the citrus returns as a pleasant afterthought; b23 I knew there was something quite different here from last year's Russell's Reserve, to which I gave the 10 and Under Bourbon of the Year award: that was élan, real Kentucky dynamite. Don't get me wrong. Remains brilliant to the last drop, but has lost that all-conquering controlled enormity, that touch of genius, that's helping convert people to bourbon the world over. Then I spotted the strength. To my astonishment it has been dumbed down from a 101 to a 90. Bizarre. Absolutely mind-boggling. Especially when you consider that Jimmy Russell himself has told me for the last decade and more that he knows Wild Turkey is at its very best as a 101. This makes it, with no little irony, the weakest of Wild Turkey's top agerange bourbons. Someone has goofed here. Big time. Just keep hunting the original bottling until this is re-instated as one of the absolute world-class top 20 whiskies, as it so recently was. **45%**

**Wild Turkey Aged 12 Years (90)** n22 peaches and cream, topped with demerara sugar, beautiful nutty fruitcake; t22 pretty sweet on the uptake with that sugary quality bursting forward, and estery like an old Jamaican rum; f23 liquorice and corn interweave beautifully; b23 this is great whiskey, perhaps not the most complex from this stable but the effect is uplifting. **50.5% (101 proof)**.

**Wild Turkey Kentucky Spirit Single Barrel** bott 1 Mar 05, barrel 15, warehouse E, rick no. 25 **(89)** n23 crushed black pepper over well-oiled corn and the usual penetrating rye; soft fruits in there, too; t23 goes in rye first, with lovely mouthwatering, tingling riches and liquorice. Chewy and very true to the distillery; f21 flattens out surprisingly as the caramel takes hold; b22 doesn't quite live up to the nose and mouth arrival, but I defy you to say no to a second. **50.5%**.

**Wild Turkey Rare Breed** batch no. WT-03RB **(95)** n25 mesmeric and almost too complex for human analysis. The degree and ratio of honey, mixed spices, vanilla-wielding oak, tart stewed apple (probably from the rye) and softening corn are the stuff of legend and an hour of anyone's time; there is something of the fermenting vessel about this. It is whiskey in all its Kentucky guises; t24 the translation on to the palate is close if incomplete. Liquorice-coated Demerarah honeycomb trailblazes and then a bickering feud follows between the rye and corn; the oak is always around and adds a slightly drier, sawdusty element; f22 only medium length but with a cola-style sharpness and groaning, mildly bitter rye. The corn and oak semed pretty wrapped up and cancel each other out; b24 bourbon at its most complex, and this reminds me very much of some of the very first expresions of this stunning whiskey. An absolute must have. **54.1% (108.2 proof)**.

⟿ **William Larue Weller (92)** n22 doughy, spiced but a tad lazy; t23 hard as nails delivery with as much liquoricey oak as there is small grain; slowly the middle conjures up a much richer backbone and a touch of oil to soften things up. Spices offer a delicate detour; f24 now goes into overdrive as the right degree of sweetness balances the oak; shades of Demerara here though the threatening spice avalanche never arrive; b23 lovely and quite different whiskey here – takes about four or five mouthfuls before you start getting the picture - with a clever build up of sugars. Relatively spiceless for a wheated bourbon but its all about structure and form. Even straight, the strength never overwhelms. **60.95%. (121.9 proof)**. nf

⟿ **William Larue Weller Kentucky Straight Bourbon Barrel Proof Limited Edition (91)** n22 the usual wheated traditional of over-emphasizing the oak and spice. And it is big...; t22 too much oak to begin, splinters all over the tongue; a soft-oiled compensation of gathering liquorice and hickory strides down the middle; f24 goes into super-complexity mode as the full gamut of coffee, hickory and cocoa goes on for ever and a day. Magnificent; b23 it always takes time to adjust to wheated whiskey. And outside of a warehouse it's pretty rare to encounter one such as this. But take your time; don't judge on first tasting and only on your fourth of fifth glass should you begin truly to appreciate all that is on offer. And, for interest, compare the two Larue tasting notes up to the end of the last sentence: sampled about a month apart and without the other's notes to hand. Strikingly similar, or what? **64.95% (129.9 Proof). ncf.** *Second Bottling 2006. Buffalo Trace.*

**Woodford Reserve Distiller's Select batch 19 (88) n**23 pure Forester with the soft molasses oak pitted by firm, fruity rye; **t**22 the rye again is at the vanguard followed by some dry, nipping oak; **f**21 relatively silent with layers of vanilla; **b**22 big, at times broody, but also a bit of a mouse. **45.2%.** *Brown-Forman.*

**Woodford Reserve Distiller's Select batch 20 (87) n**22 burnt raisin, nuts and caramel; **t**23 wonderful acceleration of Demerara and spice that simply exudes harmony and class; **f**20 dry dates and caramel: falls a bit flat; **b**22 the finish is a disappointment but the mouth arrival is a treat. **45.2%.** *Brown- Forman.*

⋙ **Woodford Reserve Master's Collection Four Grain (95) n**24 highly unusual with a different nose from any other bourbon I know: very light liquorice, kind of Old Forester but with souped up intensity, and extraordinary floral tones; **t**24 big and rambling with a quite massive flavour and spice explosion. The small grains are working overtime to provide a deep spicy-fruit texture to the oak. The liquorice comes through, but so does the rye by the spadeful and much softer, oily corn notes. Sensational; **f**23 calms down, though it takes its time: very rarely have I experienced the small grains in a bourbon working with such complexity; the oak drives up the intensity as the story unfolds; **b**24 Sod's law would have it that the moment we removed this from the 2006 Bible, having appeared in the previous two editions without it ever making the shelves, it should at last be belatedly released. But a whiskey worth waiting for, or what? The tasting notes are not a million miles from the original. But this is better bourbon, one that appears to have received a significant polish in the intervening years. Nothing short of magnificent. **46.2%**

**Wm Morrison Old Kentucky Special No. 1 Brand (76) n**18 **t**20 **f**19 **b**19. A very decent cooking bourbon with some weight, spice and natural toffee. A genuine chewing bourbon. **40% (80 proof)**. *Wm Morrison UK. Ignore the back label nattering on about three years and blended and all that rubbish. This is a straight bourbon.*

**Woodstock (86) n**23 **t**22 **f**21 **b**20. A lazy bourbon towards the very end that does its best not to impress despite the early sharp rye presence. Still a charmer, though. **37%.** *Australia.*

**Yellow Rose of Texas** (*see* Heaven Hill 80 Proof)

**Yellow Rose of Texas 8 Years** (*see* Old Heaven Hill Very Rare 8 Years 86 proof)

# Tennessee Whiskey
## GEORGE DICKEL

⋙ **George Dickel Superior No 12 Brand (90) n**21 so floral and perfumy that I actually sneezed! Otherwise a bit lazy and over-relaxed; **t**22 varying intensity throughout; sweetened by a barley-sugar richness unusual in American whiskey. However, resonating rye refreshes the palate and steers it back on course; **f**24 goes into overdrive with astonishing length and stupendous oak: the complexity has earned its corn, so to speak, with the drying oak offering a get-out clause for the developing sugars; **b**23 like watching a sea eagle take to flight after catching a larger fish than anticipated: a lumbering take off that at times looks doomed to failure but finally lift off is achieved with spell-binding grace and beauty. Welcome back to a great whisky after years in the doldrums! **45%**

## JACK DANIEL

**Gentleman Jack Rare Tennessee Whiskey (79)** n19 t21 f20 b19. One of America's cleanest whiskeys, sweet and improbably light. An affront to hardened Jack drinkers, a blessing for those with a sweet tooth. **40%**. *Brown-Forman.*

**Jack Daniel's (Green Label) (84)** n20 t21 f22 b21. A light but lively little gem of a whiskey. Starts as a shrinking violet, finishes as a roaring lion with nimble spices ripping into the developing liquorice. A superb session whiskey. **40% (80 proof)**. *Brown-Forman.*

**Jack Daniel's Old No. 7 Brand (Black Label) (87)** n21 thick, oily, smoky, dense, corn syrupy ... it's Jack Daniel; t23 sweet, fat, chewy, various types of burnt notes: tofffee, toast etc. etc; f21 quite a sweet, fat and toffeed finale; b22 a quite unique whiskey at which many American whiskey connoisseurs turn up their noses. I always think it's worth the occasional visit; you can't beat roughing it a little. **40% (80 proof)**. *Brown-Forman.*

**Jack Daniel's Single Barrel (88)** n22 more fruit on this than most Jacks, still plenty of liquorice and burnt toast; t22 spicy and immediately warming: some real kick to this with the blows softened by the sweetness of the corn and the surrounding thick oils; f22 very consistent with the sweetness fading, despite some rye input, then oak starting to make a stand; b22 a characterful, rich whiskey, with plenty of corn sweetness and some excellent spice. **40% (80 proof)**. *Brown-Forman.*

**Jack Daniel's Single Barrel (90)** n22 JD in concentrate: oily, full, phenolic and a touch sweet; t23 wonderful delivery with the intense corn oil making the liquoricey oak rock. Great depth and harmony and with relatively subdued spices; f22 trails off with a hint of Demerara; b23 just from time to time a real honey pops up with these single barrels, and this sample is one of those. **47% (94 proof)**.

## VIRGINIA BOURBON

**Virginia Gentleman 80** (cream, sepia and red label) **(84)** n20 t22 f21 b21. A very light bourbon with a distinctive, easy-going sweet corn effect then spicy, mildly bitter oak and cocoa. **40% (80 proof)**. *A Smith Bowman.*

**Virginia Gentleman 90** (coloured label) **(89)** n21 the leathery oak has much more to say than the corn, but it's all done in whispers; t23 charming entry onto the palate with, first, chewy oak then more teasing rye and a dash of honey here and there; f22 the small grains really come out to play, accompanied by spices, superb mouthfeel with excellent drying towards the very end; b23 you know, forget about this being the only Virginia whiskey. Romance apart, this is one hell of a whiskey where complexity is the foundation stone. Marvellous stuff. **45% (90 proof)**. *A Smith Bowman.*

## Corn Whiskey

**Dixie Dew Kentucky Straight Corn Whiskey (89)** n22 Very decent oak and vanilla adds to dryish corn; complex by corn whiskey standards; t22 wonderfully balanced, starting dry and oaky then the corn building up with the sweetness; f22 long with even a dash of spice – much improved than in recent years; b23 brilliant whiskey that should have a far wider market. **50%** *Heaven Hill.*

⋰ **Georgia Moon Corn Whiskey** Aged less than thirty days **(84)** n20 t22 f21 b21. Agreeable, sweet, mildly syrupy white dog. Would love to see this at full strength. **40%**. *Heaven Hill.*

**J W Corn 100 Straight Corn Whiskey (87)** n21 oily and rich with some much drier oak present; t22 thumping early oak offsets the sweet corn which fails to quite take off; f22 really spicy and big; b22 this has the biggest oak character on the market at the moment, which means a drier style and no shortage of spice. **50% (100 proof)**. *Heaven Hill.*

**Mellow Corn (85)** n21 t22 f21 b21. I first drank this brand back in 1974 and I can safely say that I've never encountered it, or any other whisk(e)y, with an oilier texture: if you don't like the whiskey, you could always fry your eggs in it. Seriously delicious, though! **50%** *Medley Company. (Heaven Hill).*

## Single Malt Rye
### ANCHOR DISTILLERY

⁘ **Old Potrero 18th Century Style Whiskey Essay 10-RW-ARM-3-C (90)** n20 distinctly 18th century with a cut the size of the Grand Canyon. Or should that be the San Andreas fault....?; t23 Good grief...!!! Where do I start? I won't even bother. Find about an hour and a very quiet room. Don't sip. Take a serious mouthful. Tilt the head back. Chew, allowing every cell in your mouth to be washed by this rye. Then swallow. There are all kinds of oils that should have been re-distilled. But they weren't, so make the most of them, because, frankly, they are fabulous and may never be seen again...; f24 the purists' nightmare continues as praline bites deep into the ultra-rich rye; it's oily tsunamis all the way; b23 always remember something about wide cuts. The nose will be off beam. But the flavours hitting the tastebuds will be off the Richter scale. After tasting this I need to lie down somewhere and rest. Because so few whiskeys in the world are half as big as this, or more fun. Forget about descriptors: this one writes its own book... **62.55% (125.1 proof).**

⁘ **Old Potrero Single Malt Hotaling's Whiskey Aged 11 Years Essay MCMVI-MMVI (96)** n24 aged Geneva with juniper latching onto the rock-hard rye; t25 San Francisco meets Belgium: again that Geneva kick-start with juniper, spices and orange peel. But, like Geneva, there is a rye base and that begins to completely dominate – until the oak-led top quality cocoa arrives as domination is never allowed in greatness. We just weren't given enough tastebuds for this one...; f23 despite some soft oils, thins out quicker than expected with vanilla and rye vying for top dog. The spices also play a quiet but rather beautiful tune; b24 this may sound coarse (and I apologise, but it is relevant), but I belched (twice) whilst tasting this. Oddly enough, that never happens when I taste whisky...only gin...And I was spitting. I think gin lovers will be converted and whiskey drinkers truly amazed. Let's make no bones here: this is one of the world's true great whiskies, which just shows the quality of Ritttenhouse barrel 28. Even so, rarely have I encountered complexity like it. I admit rye whiskey is my favourite genre. And no rye in the world offers anything like this. A must have bottling: there is nothing even close in style. **50% (100 proof).**

**Old Potrero Single Malt Straight Rye Whiskey Aged Three Years Essay 5-RW-ARM-2-A (93)** n24 textbook stuff: liquorice-embossed rye, hard as nails, but caresses the senses. You beauty! t24 big, uncompromising, bold and fruity. Just so sweet with hints of honey and demerara, but the firmness of the rye is the spine to it all and cocoa provides a perfect counterweight; f22 slightly toffeed with rich oaky-vanilla but all the time the rye peppers the tastebuds; b23 this is what makes rye whiskey, for me, the most enjoyable style in the world. Brazen and bedazzling. **62.6% (125.2 proof).** *1880 bottles.*

**Old Potrero Single Malt Straight Rye Essay 10-SRW-ARM-A** db **(93)** n22 despite the lower strength there is no shortage of he-man aromas; the slight feintiness takes a tad longer to burn off but it's a harmless, earthy flaw compensated by a bewildering array of overmatured fruity notes seasoned by soft linseed, a vague herbal note and a dollop of manuka honey. One of the heaviest OP noses yet; t24 you need about five minutes to sort your way through this one: the rye is the first note apparent and then it breaks off into three or four different directions, each with a varied flavour code: part of the rye contains cocoa and is dry and deliciously chocolaty while another faction takes the route to Demerara with a softly estered rum beat to it. As a compliment to this a rye and honeyed thread weaves its way around the palate. Finally the rye also links up with a sawdusty vanilla effect, which passes for oak; **f**23 impossible to tell where the middle ends and the finish starts: this is top shelf whiskey for adults and ones who know how to make the most of the finish of their mouthful: just sit back, eyes closed and listen to spellbinding, bitter-sweet tales of rye and honey; **b**24 I know some of you will be beating your breasts and wailing: OP's down from teeth dissolving barrel proof to a sissified 45% abv. The reason, I have been told, is that barmen have a big problem when trying to mix at cask strength. I understand the problem, but it is one easily overcome: drink it straight ... **45% (90 proof)**.

⋅⋅⋅ **Old Potrero Single Malt Straight Rye Whiskey Essay 10-SRW-ARM-E (94)** **n**24 roasting chestnuts and salted yam; all closely bound by essence of kumquat and rye. Give this time and oxygen and it will undergo countless, giddy transformations. Unique and astonishing...; **t**23 exceptionally fruity and salivating from the off; the rye starts slow and builds up a chewy head of steam; **f**24 delicate spice, layers of bitter-sweet cocoa. Oh..and rye...; **b**23 the whiskey from this distillery never fails to amaze. **45% (90 proof)**.

## Straight Rye

**Fleischmann's Straight Rye (93) n**23 a wonderful confusion of rock hard rye and softer, fruitier notes: uncluttered by too great age, it is unambiguously rye; **t**24 clean arrival, soft fruits and then gradual scaling up of the firmness of the rye: just so magically mouth watering and warming at the same time; **f**22 hard, chunky rye softened by vanilla and orange marmalade; **b**24 it is hard to believe that a whisky as classically simple and elegant as this, and so true to its genre, comes in a plastic bottle. You don't have to pay through the nose for magnificent whisky. **40%**. *Fleischmann Distilling Co (Barton)*.

**Jim Beam Rye (93) n**24 lemon zest, mint and lavender: a stunning bag of tricks; **t**24 early rye broadside followed by some tender fruit and oak. This battle between rock-hard rigidity and gentle fruit is astonishing; **f**22 long and flinty with cocoa rounding things off; **b**23 almost certainly the most entertaining and consistent whiskey in the entire Jim Beam armoury. A classic without doubt. How much longer will it be before they start releasing this worldwide? **40%**

**Old Overholt Four Years Old (86) n**23 **t**21 **f**21 **b**21. A very decent score for a decent whiskey. But it used to be so much more in your face and full of character. Maybe just a blip. **40% (80 proof)**. *Jim Beam*.

**Old Rip Van Winkle 12 Years Old Time Rye (90) n**23 **t**23 **f**22 **b**22. A profound, fruity, refreshing and old-fashioned rye that's hard to find. 45% **(90 proof)**.

**Old Rip Van Winkle 15 Years Old (1985) Family Reserve Rye (91) n**22 **t**23 **f**23 **b**23. A supremely improbable rye that has managed to retain a zesty freshness over 15 summers. Brilliant. **50% (100 proof)**.

**Pikesville Supreme Straight Rye (87) n**23 a curious and delicious mixture of traditional British scrumpy cider and new car interior: this is straight rye at its freshest and fruitiest; **t**21 much lighter arrival than nose suggests, even a hint of corn in there. The fruit slowly starts to return, but only after a sprinkling of brown sugar then a thumping measure of rye; **f**21 that usual Heaven Hill rye bitterness on the ending plus some caramel-vanilla to sweeten things a little; **b**22 not quite as in your face with the rye as was once the case. **40% (80 proof)**. *Heaven Hill*.

**Rittenhouse Straight Rye (85) n**21 **t**21 **f**21 **b**22. This is the only rye in America I'm aware of spelt "Whisky" rather than "whiskey." And has always been the least rye-pronounced. But this bottling makes a virtue of it. 40% **(80 proof)**. *Heaven Hill*.

**Rittenhouse Straight Rye 100 Proof Bottled in Bond (86) n**21 **t**22 **f**21 **b**22. A weighty guy. **50% (100 proof)**. *Heaven Hill*.

⟨⟩ **Rittenhouse Very Rare Single Barrel 21 Years Old (91)** n25 Incredible. Intriguing. Unique. Such is the punch to the super-ripe fruit, so intense is the oak that has fused into it, that it takes literally hours to try and make sense of what is happening here. There is no other aroma in the whisky or whiskey world that matches, the closest relation being ancient pot still whiskey from Ireland for reasons I will explain later. It perhaps needs a whisky lover with the mind of an archaeologist to understand this one, because the nose is a series of layers built up over time. The key is to dig deeper than the surface spices and burnt honeycomb. In there, in varying strata, are diffused mint and lemon zest and a fruity intensity to the rye grain normally found only when malted. Astonishing and almost too beautiful for words; t23 impatient oak rampages through the early, oily arrival of rye concentrate. Then waves of spice, of steadily increasing intensity crash lip-smackingly into the tastebuds. But such is the magnitude of the rye it absorbs the oak without too much early damage and only towards the middle does it begin to lose the battle; f21 a dry finale as the come-of-age oak demands the last say; b22 I may be wrong, but I would wager quite a large amount that no-one living has tasted more rye from around the world than I. So trust me when I tell you this is different, a genuine one-off in style. By rights such telling oak involvement should have killed the whisky stone dead: this is like someone being struck by lightning and then walking off slightly singed and with a limp, but otherwise OK. The closest style of whisky to rye is Irish pot still, a unique type where unmalted barley is used. And the closest whiskey I have tasted to this has been 35 to 50-year-old pot still Irish. What they have in common is a massive fruit base, so big that it can absorb and adapt to the oak input over many years. This has not escaped unscathed. But it has to be said that the nose alone makes this worthy of discovery, as does the glory of the rye as it first melts into the tastebuds. The term flawed genius could have been coined for this whisky alone. Yet, for all its excellence, I can so easily imagine someone, somewhere, claiming to be an expert on whiskey, bleating about the price tag of $150 a bottle. If they do, ignore them. Because, frankly, rye has been sold far too cheaply for far too long and that very cheapness has sculpted a false perception in people's minds about the quality and standing of the spirit. Well, 21 years in Kentucky equates to about 40 years in Scotland. And you try and find a 40-year-old Scotch for £75. If anything, they are giving this stuff away. The quality of the whiskey does vary from barrel to barrel and therefore bottle to bottle. So below I have given a summary of each individual bottling (averaging (91.1). The two with the highest scores show the least oak interference...yet are quite different in style. That's great whiskey for you. **50% (100 proof). ncf.** *Heaven Hill.*

⟨⟩ **Barrel no.  1 (91)** n25 t23 f21 b22. As above. **50%**
⟨⟩ **Barrel no.  2 (89)** n24 t23 f20 b22. Dryer, oakier. **50%**
⟨⟩ **Barrel no.  3  (91)** n24 t23 f22 b22. Fruity, soft. **50%**
⟨⟩ **Barrel no.  4 (90)** n25 t22 f21 b22. Enormous. **50%**
⟨⟩ **Barrel no.  5 (93)** n25 t23 f22 b23. Early rye surge. **50%**
⟨⟩ **Barrel no.  6 (87)** n23 t22 f20 b22. Juicy, vanilla. **50%**
⟨⟩ **Barrel no.  7 (90)** n23 t23 f22 b22. Even, soft, honeyed. **50%**
⟨⟩ **Barrel no.  8 (95)** n25 t24 f23 b23. The works: massive rye. **50%**
⟨⟩ **Barrel no.  9 (91)** n24 t23 f22 b22. Sharp rye, salivating. **50%**
⟨⟩ **Barrel no.10 (93)** n25 t24 f22 b22. Complex, sweet. **50%**
⟨⟩ **Barrel no.11 (93)** n24 t24 f22 b23. Rich, juicy, spicy. **50%**
⟨⟩ **Barrel no.12 (91)** n25 t23 f21 b22. Near identical to no.1. **50%**
⟨⟩ **Barrel no.13 (91)** n24 t24 f21 b22. Citrus and toasty. **50%**
⟨⟩ **Barrel no.14 (94)** n25 t24 f22 b23. Big rye and marzipan. **50%**
⟨⟩ **Barrel no.15 (88)** n23 t22 f21 b22. Major oak influence. **50%**
⟨⟩ **Barrel no.16 (90)** n24 t23 f21 b22. Spicy and toffeed. **50%**
⟨⟩ **Barrel no.17 (90)** n23 t23 f22 b22. Flinty, firm, late rye kick. **50%**

- **Barrel no.18 (91)** n24 t24 f21 b22. Big rye delivery. **50%**
- **Barrel no.19 (87)** n23 t22 f21 b21. Major coffee input. **50%**
- **Barrel no.20 (91)** n23 t24 f22 b22. Spicy sugar candy. **50%**
- **Barrel no.21 (94)** n24 t23 f24 b23. Subtle, fruity. **50%**
- **Barrel no.22 (89)** n23 t22 f22 b22. Mollased rye. **50%**
- **Barrel no.23 (94)** n24 t23 f24 b23. Soft fruit, massive rye. **50%**
- **Barrel no.24 (88)** n23 t22 f21 b22. Intense oak and caramel. **50%**
- **Barrel no.25 (93)** n25 t22 f23 b23. Heavy rye and spice. **50%**
- **Barrel no.26 (92)** n23 t23 f23 b23. Subtle, delicate rye. **50%**
- **Barrel no.27 (94)** n25 t23 f23 b23. Delicate rye throughout. **50%**
- **Barrel no.28 (96)** n25 t24 f23 b24. Salivating, roasty, major. **50%**
- **Barrel no.29 (88)** n23 t22 f21 b22. Hot, fruity. **50%**
- **Barrel no.30 (91)** n24 t23 f22 b22. Warming cough sweets. **50%**
- **Barrel no.31 (90)** n25 t22 f21 b22. Aggressive rye. **50%**

**Sazerac Rye 6 Years Old (91)** n24 the rye is firm, gripping and clean; the fruitiness never diminishes thanks to a low oak profile; t22 clean, fresh rye with a toffee-apple fruitiness; f22 only as the oak arrives does the grain really begin to gather momentum and display complexity; b23 a fascinating rye which seems to change pace and intensity at different points. Great stuff! **45% (90 proof)**.

**Sazerac 6 Years Old (95)** n24 just hold your arms up and surrender to this granite-soft beast; t23 the clarity of the rye could not be sharper: the fruitiness is matched only by the sweetness; f24 the length of the finish leaves you salivating. Just so wonderfully structured and succinct in part, then so unbelievably expansive; b24 this appears to have a very big rye percentage and the freshness of the fruit and grain is spellbinding. Even I suggest the odd drop of water with this one...eventually...!!! **65.4% (130.8 proof)**. *Buffalo Trace.*

⠂ **Sazerac Kentucky Straight Rye 18 Years Old 90 Proof** bott Fall 06 **(94)** n24 the fruit theme of the rye simply pulses from the glass with some countering toasty dryness. It's the honey-demerara with a smidgen of mint that stars, though; t23 as ever, an astonishingly soft façade to something so blisteringly firm as the rye; fruity and so salivating; f24 long, and now firms up entirely with wonderful shafts of oak being drilled into sweeter fruity-rye; b23 one of those whiskeys with a truly unique signature: nothing else like it and the quality entirely uncompromised. Terrific stuff! **45% (90 Proof)**. *Buffalo Trace.*

**Sazerac Rye 18 Years Old Rye** Autumn 2004 release **(96)** n25 trad straight rye doesn't come more complex, confident or clean than this: there's a hard grainy edge,    softened by over-ripe juicy cherry and blackberries. Subtle and sophisticated; t24 the brittle quality of the rye shows to full effect here, but there is a yield – a tad oily – which also beguiles. Fruity and improbably flavoursome: close your eyes and wallow; f23 takes a little rest as the toffee makes a mark, but such is the intensity of the rye and oak that waves of spices and fruit continue to break against the tastebuds; b24 I remember being given my first sample of this: it was in the lab at Buffalo Trace before it went into bottle and a legendary brand was born. I wondered what it would be like to sample away from the romance of the beautiful distillery where the casks were laying ... well, now you know. I was presented with the first-ever bottle of Sazerac Rye as a token of thanks for my help in identifying its qualities and (some hope) weaknesses. I trust the person who stole it out of my bag while I was giving a tasting in New York appreciated. If he/she still has it, I would be grateful if it is returned, no questions asked. And for those who prefer to look at their whiskeys Sideways, the joint hardness and mouth-dousing fruitiness – plus the overall scarcity – makes this the Pinot Noir of the rye world. **45%** *Buffalo Trace.*

⠂ **Thomas H. Handy Sazerac Straight Rye Barrel Proof Limited Edition (93)** n24 boiled fruit candy. Just so mouth-wateringly firm and sexy; t21 takes its time to find a rhythm as neither the oak nor rye are sure whether to lead. Settles towards the middle as the salivating rye takes control; a few hickory notes add further depth; **f25** faultless and mesmeric. The tongue is left to wander the mouth involuntarily investigating myriad flavour trails. Early doubts are erased by the majesty of small grain and the perfection of the bittersweet harmony which unravels. Even the late-arriving spices deliver something almost too teasing to be true. One of the greatest finishes in world whiskey, and no mistake; **b23** what a box of tricks! Early on it's as mad a bag of snakes but the finish is something to inspire you to get in the chimney sweep, clean out the hearth and get the ol' log fire going for the first time in 20 years. A fabulous addition to the ever-growing rye family. **66.35% (132.7 Proof). ncf.** *First-ever bottling.*

**Van Winkle Family Reserve Rye 13 Years Old (91) n23** big and belligerent, the rye forms a fruity, rock-hard crust; **t24** vroom ... !! Off she goes on a massive ryefest. Brilliant bitter-sweet grain stomps with hob-nailed boots around the palate, both fresh yet well aged. Everything is a contradiction – so complex; **f21** quietens down alarmingly as the caramel kicks in which sweetens it a little while some bitter coffee/rye notes still chatter in the background; **b23** an alarmingly complex whiskey that seems to make the rules up as it goes along. Anarchic and adorable. **47.8% (95.6 proof).**

**Wild Turkey Real Kentucky Straight Rye (88) n23** the firmest, fruitiest WT rye nose I've come across in bottled form: clean and compelling; **t23** fabulous micro explosions of juicy, fruity rye; **f20** unusual softening and blunting by caramel. Little of the old spice kick; **b22** still continues to change character from previous bottlings, in some ways for the better, in others worse. But you can't help thinking that this has another gear or two to use. **50.5% (101 proof).**

## MICHTERS DISTILLERY

**Overholt "1810" Sour Mash Straight Rye Whiskey (91) n23** allow a minute or two to oxidize then breath in sweet rye, primroses and ginger bread, and a fair chunk of oak, too; **t23** just fabulously explosive: the oak is pretty big but cannot undermine the intensity of the rye. The spice sizzles and spits at you like a Cumberland sausage; **f22** very hard rye chisels at the taste buds; some cocoa for good, bitter yet balanced effect; **b23** I have been hearing reports that this truly classic Old Timer, complete in 4/5 quart bottles, can still be dug up in back-wood liquor stores. This, the very last of the true Pennsylvanian rye, is Klondike stuff. **46.5% abv (93 proof).** *A Overholt & Co, Pennsylvania.*

## Straight Wheat Whiskey

**Bernheim Original Straight Wheat Whiskey (90) n23** biscuity and crisp, yet sweet, grainy and a little spicy: exceptionally clean and carrying the freshness of newly bound straw; **t23** outstanding mouth arrival with a sharp, salty tang that coats the roof and teases the tastebuds; then melts into a full, slightly oily body, and again the biscuity quality appears. The spices, though, are controlled and even refuse to disappear. Salivating and juicy throughout; **f21** soft vanilla against rock-hard grain. The lightness of the wheat doesn't allow for enormous depth, but the bitterness is seen off by a delicious delivery of sugar cane juice; **b23** great stuff: a superb addition to the American whiskey lexicon. Firm, consumer friendly yet at times fluffy. The complexity comes in broad, sweeping waves rather than small grain intricacy, but the spicy undercurrent guarantees a healthy degree of busy playfulness. A must for those with a sweet tooth, this new style takes until about the third tasting before you begin to fully understand its charm and refreshing richness. An immediate classic. **45% (90 proof).** *Heaven Hill.*

## Kentucky Whiskey

**Early Times Kentucky Whisky (74) n19 t19 f18 b18.** Slightly improved with some extra beefing up, but still light and over sweet. **40% (80 proof).** *Brown-Forman*

# American/Kentucky Whiskey Blends

**Beam's Eight Star Kentucky Whiskey A Blend** 75% grain neutral spirits 25% straight whiskey **(67) n**16 **t**17 **f**17 **b**17. Just the odd wisp of something chewable. **40% (80 proof)**.

**Broker's Reserve American Blended Whiskey 36 Months Old** 80% grain spirits **(61) n**14 **t**16 **f**16 **b**15. A fruity, spicy, synthetic, entirely avoidable little non-whiskey-more-brandy-type number. **40% (80 proof)**.

**Monarch Kentucky Bourbon Whiskey A Blend (69) n**18 **t**17 **f**17 **b**17. Half-decent body with touches of oak and spice. **40% (80 proof)**.

**Potter's Whiskey** 20% straight whiskey 80 grain neutral spirits **(64) n**15 **t**18 **f**16 **b**15. Sweet, clean, caramelised at finish and entirely featureless. **40%**

**Seagram's 7 Crown (89) n**23 rich with heavy vanilla and rye; **t**22 complex grain and oak battle: the softness of the neutral grain acts as the perfect foil for the crisper rye; **f**22 silky, sweet, soft corn and vanilla; **b**22 this is beautiful whiskey, but on this evidence not a patch on the rye-infested giant it has been for the last couple of decades. The rye level seems to have been reduced and I trust that this is just a rogue batch. Still a little mouthwatering stunner for sure, but it was much better the way it was: semi-wild and flavour-explosive. Like that it was an American institution – something too rare and precious to be tampered with ... **40% (80 proof)**.

# Other American Whiskey

**Jackpot (81) n**18 **t**22 **f**21 **b**20. For a label with all four card suits displayed, it's fitting that the nose is a pair of deuces. However, a powering and impressively complex bourbon thrust on mouth arrival comes up trumps. **40%**

**Old Virginia Extra Rare American Whiskey Aged 12 Years** L530133A **(90) n**22 molten honeycomb and dark chocolate; almost a Jamaican rummy ester sweetness; **t**23 imagine a nubile body contouring a silk gown: that's the shape and texture here as excellent vanillas integrate with honey; **f**22 back to the honeycomb again with marmalade as a delightful bitterness creeps in; **b**23 Good grief: this is damn good stuff. The most honeyed and high-class non-bourbon on the market. **40%**. *La Martiniquaise, France.*

**Wild Turkey Sherry Signature** "Made with 10 Years Old Kentucky Straight Bourbon Whiskey finished in sherry casks enhanced with Oloroso Sherry" **(81) n**19 **t**21 **f**20 **b**21. They kind of don't get much stranger than this: bourbon meets Speyside meets Canadian...I suppose the adding of pure oloroso to the mix precludes this from being whiskey at all, but it seems a bit churlish not to have it in the Bible, seeing how the Canadians can add 9.09% of anything and the remainder of the world add caramel. To treat it at face value, an enjoyable, pleasantly honied experience where the oloroso gets out of control, momentarily, only towards the finale. Otherwise, a silky, quite skilfully steered ride. **43%**

# Canadian Whisky

It is becoming hard to believe that Canadian was once a giant among the world whisky nations. Dotted all over its enormous land large distilleries pumped out thousands upon thousands of gallons of spirit that after years in barrel became a clean, gentle whisky.

It was cool to be seen drinking Canadian in cocktail bars on both sides of the pond. Now, sadly, Canadian whisky barely raises a beat on the pulse of the average whisky lover. It would not be beyond argument to now call Canadian the forgotten whisky empire with column inches devoted to it measured now in millimetres. It is an entirely sad, almost heartbreaking, state of affairs though hopefully not an irreversible one. The finest Canadian, for me, is still whisky to be cherished and admired. But outside North America it can be painfully hard to find.

BRITISH COLUMBIA

ALBERTA

MANITOBA

Alberta
Calgary
●Vancouver
Winchester
Cellars
Okanagan †
Palliser
Gimli

**Key**
- ● **Major Town or City**
- ▲ Distillery
- † Dead Distillery

Especially seeing how whiskies containing the permitted 9.09% of non-Canadian whisky (or whisky at all) had been barred from the European market. So just before the completion of last year's Jim Murray's Whisky Bible I went to Canada to taste every Canadian whisky I could find on the market. The result was illuminating. In the two years since I last blitzed Canadian there was now a clear divergence of styles between tradionalist whisky like Alberta Premium and a more creamy textured, fruit-enhanced product once confined to the USA but now found in Canada itself. It has made for a re-evaluation of Canadian and a few surprises. And I returned again three or four times in 2007, not only to continue my search for Canadian but to spend more time with some of the people who make it, blend it, sell it. And, most vitally perhaps, drink it.

There is no doubt that we are seeing a change in the perception of Canadian by drinkers who had previously confined themselves to top quality Scotch malt. Following my award of Jim Murray's Whisky Bible Canadian Whisky of the Year 2006 to Alberta Premium, I had the chance to spend time in televison and radio stations around the country talking about the exceptionally high quality of top Canadian whiskies. It has led to a string of emails from readers telling me they had since tasted Alberta and been somewhat shocked to find a world classic whisky lurking so unobtrusively - and cheaply - on their shelves. For many, this had led to further exploring of Canadian, and uncovering of further gems. The 2007 award goes to Alberta again, this time for their newly launched 25-year-old. It makes the heart pound to see the industry take such confidence in their own whisky, though perhaps they could have been a bit more confident with the price: Canadians have been handed the best bargain in the world whisky right now! There is an entire nation, indeed world, waiting for Canada to show what it can do: in 20 years I have never known such interest. Now I look forward to other Canadian distillers moving away from fruit juice thinking and putting the rye back into good old Canadian Rye.

QUEBEC

ONTARIO

Glenora

NOVA SCOTIA

Valleyfield ● Quebec ● Montreal

Canada Mist ● Toronto
Kittling Ridge
Walkerville

## Canadian Single Malt
### GLENORA

**Glen Breton** db **(81)** n19 t21 f20 **b**21. Enormously sweet malt, in almost concentrated form with a tantalising whiff of smoke hanging around; mildly spiced and slightly oily, soapy finale. **43%**

**Glen Breton Rare** db **(73)** n14 t21 f19 **b**19. This is a version – probably a very early one – I had not seen and it makes for exceptionally grim nosing. However, after that very unpleasant, feinty experience, it comes back to life on the palate with remarkable honey and copper input. A right mixed bag. **40%**

**Glen Breton Rare** db **(80)** n18 t21 f20 **b**21. Caramel nose a bit soapy but the buttery, sweet malt, with its vanilla fizz, makes for a pleasant experience. **43%**

**Glenora 1990 Aged 14 Years Single Cask** db **(89)** n22 firm malt but with a distinctive bourbony (or very old Canadian) weight and some attractive natural toffee; t23 massive malt arrival on the palate buoyed with that dense fudge-caramel; f22 the oak is distinctive and almost Kentuckian; the malt is profound and the chewy weight is excellent; **b**22 by far and away the best Glenora yet bottled. And good to see the distillery use its actual name. **43%**

### OKANAGAN

**Long Wood 8 Years Old Malt** db **(74)** n19 t20 f17 **b**18. There are no discernable off notes and a pleasant liquorice-spice prevails. But the true life has been strangled out if it by caramel. A tragedy, in whisky terms, as this is very rare malt from a lost distillery. **40%**. *Germany.*

## Canadian Grain Single Barrel

**Century Reserve 13 Years Old Single Cask Unblended (92)** n22 massive vanilla and toffee but delicately handled and delivered; some very soft prickle helps balance the sweetening grain; t23 big corn kick from the start with an immediate movement towards sweetness that is stopped in its tracks by developing oak; just so silky despite the natural oak bite; f23 long, lush in part, with the corn really getting stuck into the oak; **b**24 surely "Bush Pilot" by any other name. Those with an affinity with old Scottish grain would recognise this style of corn-led whisky. Very tasty. **40%**. *Century Distilling Co.*

**Century Reserve 15 Years Old 1985 Limited Edition (89)** n20 dry oak; mildly burnt toast and red liquorice; t23 a delicious corn-oil lushness helps keep at bay some bourbony overtures; the degree of Demerara sweetness against the oak is exemplary; f23 cream toffee that you can chew and chew until subtle spices arrive; **b**23 the nose ("smoky, reminiscent of single malt", according to cask selector Nick Bennett; "oaky, reminiscent of Okanagan grain", according to Jim Murray...) reveals little of the joys that are to follow. **40%**. *Century Distilling Co.* Century Reserve 21 Years Old (see Blended Canadian)

**Forty Creek Single Barrel (93)** n23 clean, uncluttered sherry and cherry; t23 more cherry flanked by gentle spice and silky, mildly oily grain: genuinely complex and classy; f24 loses balance towards the end, although the sweetness, combined with the bitter cocoa finale, is not entirely unlike a Belgium cherry chocolate; **b**23 there are so many things about this whisky that infuriate me...yet I adore it. Perhaps I am a sucker for premier quality liquor chocolates; maybe I get turned on by very clean yet complex distillate. So much of this goes against the purists' grain. Yet it has to be said: this is bloody delicious whisky of the highest magnitude!! **40%**. *Kittling Ridge.*

## Canadian Blended Whisky

**Alberta Premium (95)** n24 remains as hard and impenetrable as the Rockies that overlook the distillery from afar; the rye is brittle and rigid, but just gracious enough to allow a sweet fruitiness to develop: classic stuff; t25 one of the great deliveries of world whisky: the rye is both intense and yielding, enveloping and rigidly distant; lovely rye-oriented fruit and then an intrusion of irritating toffee; **f**22 just a fraction too caramel-rich but a distant spice does try to break it up a bit; some late oak also present; **b**24 one of the great, most wonderfully consistent whiskies of the world that is genuinely a Canadian rye and a must have for those searching for the real thing. **40%**. *Alberta Distillers*. ⊙

⋅⋅⋅ **Alberta Premium 25 Years Old (95) n**24 a fabulously weighted nose: diamond couched in silk. It is the vivid hardness which is first to show, with the firmness the rye can muster. Then that softness makes itself felt; a rolling, juicy fruitiness (not dissimilar to an almost lost form of most exquisite Cognac) that has dissolved into it a drier vaguely bourbon-esque oakiness. For complexity few, if any, Canadians are this subtle or sublime. Masterful; **t**23 again we have a bipolar story. On one hand the rye takes a rigid course as a hard edge cuts through all else to dominate. Then it fails as it is swamped by that same soft fruit as on the nose and also a crescendo of cocoa. Soft-hard. Sweet-dry. Velvety caresses-playful nips. Whatever you concentrate on dominates: put the tastebuds into neutral and you have a wonderful battle, not fought by fist but wit; **f**23 my word: if you are into chocolate you'll love this. Gently sweetened cocoa spreads around the palate, first as a hint then as a full-blown plain chocolate dessert sweetened only by a sprinkling of muscovado. Very long. Improbably gentle; **b**25 faultless. Absolutely nothing dominates. Yet every aspect has its moment of conquest and glory. It is neither bitter nor sweet, yet both. It is neither soft nor hard on the palate yet both elements are there. Because of the 100% rye used, this is an entirely new style of whisky to hit the market. No Canadian I know has ever had this uncompromising brilliance, this trueness to style and form. And, frightening to think, it could be improved further by bottling at least 46% and un-chillfiltered. For any whisky lover who ever thought Canadian was incapable of hitting the heights among the world's greats, I have previously recommended Alberta Premium. I still do. But if they want to taste something that will amaze then they can do worse than this. The question will now rage: which is the better of the two? For me, perhaps the Premium, because it also has bite as well as guile and slakes thirsts as well as outrageously entertains. Having made love to a young vixen this, though, is perhaps closer to spending a night in the arms of a sultry lady of greater experience. Passion or elegance? We are back to whisky being a mood thing. And if this doesn't get you in the mood, nothing will. **40%**. *Alberta Distillers*.

**Alberta Springs Aged 10 Years** bott lot no. 04327 **(89) n**24 absolute classic delivery of both intense rye and oak: crisp, weighty and wonderful; **t**23 massive rye again on early delivery, then a succession of waves of vanilla, each reducing the grain input; the delicate Demerara sweetness is a charming constant; **f**20 very short for its age and not helped by a toffee caramel trail-off; **b**22 compared to the way many Canadian whiskies are shaping these days, this, along with Alberta Premium, is becoming something of a port in a storm. Wonderfully traditional in style, this is Canadian at its most rip-ryeing and definitely a degree better than when I last tasted it a couple of years back. Fabulous stuff. **40%**. *Alberta Distillers*.

**Barton's Canadian 36 Months Old (78) n**19 **t**20 **f**19 **b**20. Sweet, toffeed, easy-going. **40%**. *Barton*.

**Black Velvet (80) n**20 **t**20 **f**20 **b**20. Consistent, clean, toffeed Canadian with rich body and decent fizz on the finish. **40%**. *Hiram Walker*.

**Canadian Club Premium (78) n**19 **t**20 **f**19 **b**20. Lovely nip and pinch on the nose and some bite on the finish. Enlivening and, in parts, lush. The most visible Canadian whisky in the world, and pretty consistent, too. **40%**. *Hiram Walker*.

**Canadian Club Sherry Cask Aged Eight Years (76) n**22 **t**17 **f**19 **b**18. The problem with putting Canadian whisky into what here appears to be a very high-quality sherry fresh-fill cask or two is that the spirit is naturally too light to withstand the grapey onslaught. The result is less whisky but more high-proof sherry. I admire the effort; the nose is quite lovely and the late finish also has some delightful fruit-spice moments. But the middle is just too one-dimensional. I'd keep the faith, but some tinkering is needed here. If you don't like it first time round, give it a year and see what happens. **41.3%**. *Hiram Walker*.

**Canadian Club Reserve 10 Years of Age (93) n**23 fizzing, busy grain weaves into and thins a distinctively clean, grapey heart; cinnamon and apples complete the gentle fruit theme; **t**23 soft grains, especially lush corn, surrounded by rich, oily vanilla; **f**24 comes into its own with a return of the fruit and spice; a big, juicy grape impact with a sublime bitter-sweet backbone; some late medium roast Java helps get oak back into circulation; distant honeycomb helps with the bitter-sweet balance; **b**23 what a stunning whisky this has developed into over recent years. More sherry involvement, which can so often result in a disastrous finish. Here the opposite is true: the complexity appears to know no bounds. Quality blending, and remains an everyday whisky of distinction. **40%**. *Hiram Walker*.

**Canadian Club Classic Aged 12 Years (79) n**21 **t**21 **f**18 **b**19. Pleasant at first, but has crossed that fine line where the fruit and caramel interfere to the detriment of the blend. Good spice, though. **40%**. *Hiram Walker*.

**Canadian Club 100 Proof (89) n**21 an odd biryani note gives an exotic feel to the firm grains which course through this; **t**23 one of the sweetest Canadians around with a light Demerara lilt to the intense corn; massive grain assault; **f**22 fruit dives in to break up the cornfest; **b**23 if you are expecting this to be a high-octane version of the standard CC Premium, you'll be in for a shock. This is a much fruitier dram with an oilier body to absorb the extra strength. An entertaining blend. **50%**. *Hiram Walker*.

**Canadian Host (74) n**19 **t**18 **f**19 **b**18. Sweet, light, weirdly fruity. **40%**. *Barton*.

**Canadian Mist (74) n**19 **t**18 **f**19 **b**18. One of those helium-light blends with lots of sweet fruitiness. Lots of vanilla. **40%**. *Brown-Forman*.

**Canadian Pure Gold (81) n**20 **t**20 **f**21 **b**20. Well-made, tastebudattacking whisky full of lush, rich fruit – especially raisins. Molten fruitcake. **40%**. *Kittling Ridge*.

**Canadian Spirit (78) n**20 **t**20 **f**19 **b**19. A real toffee-fest with a touch of hard grain around the edges. **40%**. *Carrington Distillers (Alberta Distillers)*.

**Canadian Supreme (74) n**18 **t**19 **f**19 **b**18. A light, banana-ry blend that is young but extremely fruity. **40%**

**Centennial 10 Years Limited Edition (84) n**20 **t**22 **f**21 **b**21. One of the cleanest, most non-committal noses in Canada, save for the caramel and cherries; the mouth arrival is excellent with caramel and a honied grain thread running through it. But then you are left with one of the cleanest, most noncommittal finishes in Canada...save for the caramel and cherries. Very drinkable and one to appeal to those whose preferred tipple is brandy or fruit spirit. But for corn lovers, not one to wheat your appetite... **40%**. *Highwood Distillers*.

⋯ **Century Reserve 8 Years Old Premium (82) n**20 **t**21 **f**20 **b**21. Clean vanilla and caramel. **40%**. *Century Distillery*.

**Century Reserve 15 Years Old** (*see* Canadian Grain Single Barrel)

**Century Reserve 21 Years Old** (*see* Canadian Grain Single Barrel)

**Century Reserve 21 Years Old (83) n**21 **t**21 **f**20 **b**21. Refreshing, fruity and sweet, it somehow refuses to be its age. Highly drinkable. **40%**. *Century Distilling Co*.

**Corby's Canadian 36 Months Old (85) n**20 **t**21 **f**22 **b**22. Always attractive with fine bitter-sweet balance and I love the late spice kick-back. **40%** *Barton*. *Interesting label: as a keen ornithologist, I had no idea there were parrots in Canada. Must be related to the Norwegian Blue.*

**Crown Royal** bottling lot no. L4110 (Crown Royal on back label printed in red) **(93) n**23 seriously big rye offers a hard and fruity edge to the soft corn and oak; **t**24 rock-hard and crisp mouth arrival thanks to the early rye, softens for the corn and then the rye sends some fruity shockwaves around the palate; **f**22 bitter and booming: big controlled oak finale on gentle oil; **b**24 this has definitely changed in the last seven or eight years, as all blends must. It has a slightly larger rye dependency than of old but the mouthwatering effect is sublime. An international great. **40%**

**Crown Royal** bottling lot no. L4307 (Crown Royal on back label printed in royal blue) **(88)** n23 t21 f22 **b**22. Still plenty of rye to go around, with the complexity really taking off towards the finish, but lacking the overall depth of L4110 and with fruit at a minimum. **40%**

**Crown Royal** bottling lot no. L5035 (Crown Royal on back label printed in royal blue) **(83)** n19 waiting for the trademark rye – it's not there! Instead a light, papery dustiness settles over flattening grape; **t**23 fresh fruitiness, with an attractive intermingling of clean corn and juicy, grapey apple; **f**20 spices dance around to help lighten the developing oaky dryness, but it's all disappointingly and irritatingly flat and overly sweet; **b**21 this is one of my regular drinking whiskies, and I thought I had spotted a massive sea change in recent months. So whilst in Vancouver in May, with the help of my dear friend Mike Smith, I was able to compare this once hallmark whisky with three previously unopened Crown Royals: a wonderful (and par for course) 2004 bottling, a corn-laced, beautifully balanced 1979 vintage, and one from 1968 (youngest whisky 10, oldest 30), an absolute stunner of rye-infused complexity that would have given it a 96 in this Bible had it been on the market today...and very close to how I first tasted it in 1974. The results were staggering, and confirmed my suspicions: someone has decided to up the colour and do away with rye. "The Legendary Whisky" says, rightly, the back label. But not like this was it made legendary: whatever agent is being used to increase the colour (and it isn't age), please drop it and reinstate the rye. This, so recently one of the great whiskies of the world, has followed the fruity trend sweeping Canadian whisky and has become an also ran. So bloody frustrating, considering the marked improvements in its sister blends of Limited Edition and Special Reserve. Oi! Mister!! Please can we have our Crown Royal back...!!! **40%**

**Crown Royal Limited Edition** bott lot no L4315 **(95)** n24 floral tones to the fore as the rye shows its hand with a wonderful and perfectly matched hint of citrus, too; **t**24 thumping rye makes for a mouthwatering, crisp, slightly stark arrival, all this on an oily bed of corn. Some glazed cherries dive in for a sweetening edge; **f**23 layer upon layer of alternating corn and rye; the cherry effect still hangs in there; **b**24 the complexity is awesome with the rye offering a delicate fruitiness and disarming charm to the more succulent cherry and softening corn. This has not so much overtaken Crown Royal, as lapped it...!! **40%**

**Crown Royal Special Reserve** bott lot no: L4350 **(93)** n23 great subtlety: various small grains – you could swear barley was in there somewhere – gang together to offer a nose worth five minutes of anyone's time; **t**23 firm rye impact and then a rich development of sweet corn; **f**23 the fruitiness of the rye positively pulsates with some hickory and vanilla, helping to add some oaky age to the event. Fabulous! **b**24 "re-introduce some life back into the finish and you'd have a classic on your hands," I wrote in last year's Bible. Ladies and gentleman, we have a classic on our hands.... **40%**

**Forty Creek Barrel Select (84)** n22 t21 f22 **b**19. A prime example of where less would be so much more. Of all the world's distillers, there are few I hold in higher esteem than KR's John Hall. But if he reduced the percentage involvement of the sherry here, we would have one of Canada's finest on our hands. Instead he has a really velvety, massively fruited Canadian that would be one basking in its own brilliance...but balance is never achieved, despite the stupendous nose and mouthwatering edges. Because of the massively high quality of the distillate I really think we have a classic whisky in the making...but only if the sherry is tamed in future bottlings: watch this space.... **40%**. *Kittling Ridge*.

**Forty Creek Three Grain (89) n**21 a real, massive amalgam of ripe fruit, including figs, dates and blueberry and grape juice; **t**22 big fruit arrival from the start: slightly bitter and dry, then a rich and unusual delivery of plums and rye; **f**23 drier finale as some small grain complexity make spicy overtures but are overwhelmed by the late dominance of greengages and soft liquorice; **b**23 I am confused: this is fabulous whisky, real late night, dim lights, crackling log fire stuff that improves on the palate with time and perception. Yet, with all that said, why call this Three Grain? The grains are, for the most part, entirely lost under the charming delights of massive fruit. This should surely be called something else entirely, while a whisky made to such extraordinarily high standards in which small grains are blended with maize should be a bourbon-barrel, fruit-free classic in its own right. **40%.** *Kittling Ridge.*

⋯ **Gibson's Bourbon Cask (79) n**20 **t**20 **f**20 **b**19. Silky-sweet; liqueur-ish; limited scope. **40%**

**Gibson's Finest Aged 12 Years (93) n**24 enormously busy with fresh fruit, but it's very light, leaving oak, corn and a touch of rye in the ascendency: in many ways, Canadian whisky nutshelled; **t**23 mouthwatering, fat without being oily, with a lovely Demerara sugar coating to the corn without being particularly sweet; **f**22 soft spices dig in to bolster the already big and chewy finish. Excellent shape and curvature to this, even at the death; **b**24 great to see a wonderful whisky back on tip-top form after a year or two in the doldrums. Great Canadian whisky that balances out with rare depth. **40%**.

**Gibson's Finest Rare Aged 18 Years (92) n**23 bold oak, soft white peppers and befriending corn; **t**23 just such a yielding delivery with hints of ripe banana and raisin amid the melting corn; **f**22 soft vanilla, lazy spice, a hint of fruit and very, very late honey; **b**24 just wonderful whisky in which you can lose yourself. Not quite as honied as before, or as rye-rich as some of the earlier bottlings. But remains a true beaut, though the 12-y-o currently has the greater finesse. Interestingly the back label claims the whisky will "add a new dimension to your drinking enjoyment". While the Bible for the last couple of years has been telling you: "It takes Canadian whisky into a new dimension." Where's my agent when I need her.... **40%**

**Gibson's Finest Sterling Edition (79) n**21 **t**20 **f**19 **b**19. Big disappointment here: this has softened up, gone fruity and lost so much shape. Drinkable in a crowd, but nothing like up to the great Gibson name. **40%**

⋯ **Gibson's New Oak (88) n**22 decent smattering of spice interrupts the sweet fanfare; **t**21 this would be one sensationally lush, almost syrupy, Canadian were it not for sub-strata of light grain and gathering oak; **f**23 this is where that new oak does its business with the casks ensuring a delicious counter dryness and spice; **b**22 distinctly different from any other Canadian doing the rounds: the oak influence makes a wonderful and clever impact. **40%**

**Golden Wedding** (*see* Schenley Golden Wedding)

**Gooderham & Worts Ltd (90) n**23 excellent trilogy of fresh corn, soft rye and something fruity; **t**23 a supremely weighted and deliciously sweet start bursts from the off. Not as much rye as I remember, though, as I was involved in the blending development of this brand; **f**22 lots of rich corn and deep oaky vanilla. Pure Canadian on a golden platter; **b**22 sensational Canadian, though on this bottling the rye input has been taken down a peg or two, which is a shame. Even so, a real stunner for its genre. **45%**

**Hamilton (77) n**18 **t**20 **f**20 **b**19. Young grains are kept on the leash to offer very sweet toffee. Very well made and easy-going. **40%**

**Highwood Pure Canadian (73) n**20 **t**19 **f**17 **b**17. When they say "Pure" Canadian they're not joking: the cleanest nose in Canada, from a wheated distillate brought to the edge of pure alcohol. The rest, I'm afraid, is a tale of caramel. **40%**

**Hiram Walker Special Old (92) n**22 rock-solid nose that is hard as nails yet reveals a soft belly on which corn gently floats and citrus notes flutter; **t**23 brittle, flinty mouth arrival that hints at dryness and then is outmanoeuvred by stunning, well controlled sweet-corn and rye; **f**24 complex, long, with fabulous grain structure and only an echo of caramel as a tangerine, citrus note cuts through any developing weight. Absolutely brilliant rye and oak involvement and the faintest wisps of honey and cocoa complete a brilliant experience; **b**23 anyone wanting to taste good, honest, old-fashioned Canadian at its most understated and complex should give this one a shot. It's always been one I've enjoyed, but in the last couple of years it has really taken on an extra degree of panache. Almost has a touch of the Irish pot still about it. **40%**

**Lot No. 40 (93) n**24 **t**24 **f**23 **b**23. This is great whisky, irrespective of whichever country it came from. As for a Canadian, this is true rye whisky, one with which I was very proud to be associated in the early blending days. Elegant stuff. **43%**

**McGuinness Silk Tassell (79) n**21 **t**20 **f**19 **b**19. Silk by name and nature: softer and silkier than of old, but way too caramel dependent and needs a rye injection. **40%.** *Corby.*

**McMaster's (80) n**19 **t**20 **f**21 **b**20. Velvet-textured and buttered sweet corn. Dangerously easy-to-drink session whisky. **40%.** *Barton.*

**Monarch Canadian Aged Thirty-six Months (84) n**20 **t**22 **f**20 **b**22. An attractive, entirely refreshing Canadian that goes surprisingly easy on the caramel. Sweet and with good grain-oak ratio. Really good fun for the cut-price sector. **40%.** *Monarch Import Company.*

⠿ **Mountain Rock (89) n**22 soft grains and gentle, reserved fruits in the bourbony toffee; **t**22 beautifully mouth-enveloping; faintly lush and never less than juicy; **f**23 simmers down into a more complex, finely-layered beauty and wonderfully deft oak on the long finish; **b**22 an oxymoron of a whisky: for a Mountain Rock, it's just a big - and beautiful - softie! **40%.** *Kittling Ridge.*

**Wm Morrison Imported Canadian Rye (89) n**23 there is actually a touch of rye on the nose here (unusual in Canadian these days) and the fruity depth is compelling; **t**23 more mouthwatering grains with an excellent oaky balance; **f**21 leans too heavily on caramel; **b**22 a top-notch Canadian for a supermarket brand. **40%**

**Northern Light (82) n**20 **t**21 **f**20 **b**21. A young, natural, unpretentious Canadian grain blend with a good, clean character and first-class bite. Very attractive. **40%.** *Barton.*

**Pendleton Let'er Buck Aged 10 Years (81) n**21 **t**22 **f**19 **b**19. A sweet, corny romp. Brought in from Canada. Probably the caramel as well. **40%.** *Hood River Distillers, Oregon.*

**Pike Creek** finished in port barrels **(87) n**21 curious amalgam of corn and fresh wine; **t**23 soft, silky mouthfeel and then a whoosh of sweetness; **f**21 some spices prosper as the port makes a stand, genuinely fruity at first then becoming a little more bitter as the oak arrives; **b**22 much more complexity now than from the first bottlings. A Canadian of genuine style and character. **40%.** *Allied.*

**Potter's Crown (70) n**19 **t**18 **f**16 **b**17. Ferociously fruity and showing little backbone. Pleasant in part. **40%.** *Potter Brands, San José.*

**Potter's Special Old (90) n**22 the clarity of the grain is profound and unambiguous: this is Canadian whisky! **t**23 a natural translation on to the palate with a delicate toffee input, possibly from caramel, but the corn can be heard loud and clear, and those with a penchant for a walnut whip will understand why I find an oily, candy link...; **f**22 chewy with decent oaky vanilla; **b**23 after the strangulation of Canadian whisky in recent times by fruit, have you any idea how refreshing and heart-warming it is to come across such a wonderfully honest and traditional whisky as this? Very limited fruit input, high quality grain all the way. It may come in a plastic bottle. It may be cheap. But it's Canadian whisky as it has been known for the last 100 years and the mark reflects that fact. **40%**

**Pure Gold** (*see* Canadian Pure Gold)

**Royal Reserve (85) n**21 **t**21 **f**22 **b**21. A lovely Canadian which doesn't suffer from too much fruit interference and actually appears to have some discernible rye in the blend. **40%**. *Corby*.

⋗ **Sam Barton Aged 5 Years** L617802A **(83) n**20 **t**21 **f**21 **b**21. Entirely acceptable and mildly juicy Canadian with an attractive honey and vanilla strand. **40%**. *La Martiniquaise, France*.

**Seagram's 83 Canadian Whisky (68) n**18 **t**17 **f**16 **b**17. Caramel-dominated these days. **40%**. *The "83" refers to 1883, not a 1983 vintage, and certainly not its rating...*

**Seagram's Five Star (75) n**18 **t**20 **f**18 **b**19. Doesn't make you physically shudder like the "83" but hasn't improved in time. The middle does still show some admirable graininess despite the cloying sweetness. **40%**

**Seagram's VO** bottling lot no. L5054 **(85) n**20 **t**23 **f**21 **b**21. For all its early charm on the palate, another 2005 bottling of a Canadian great that has lost both its distinctive rye character and its claim to greatness. Is this the start of an extremely worrying trend, or just a one-off blip...? What is going on? **40%**

**Schenley Golden Wedding** bottling lot no. L5018 **(83) n**20 **t**21 **f**21 **b**21. Beautifully silky textured and rich. Great distillate used here which is both prickly and luxurious. Lovely stuff. **40%**.

**Schenley OFC Aged 8 Years (93) n**24 brilliant nose: awesome complexity here as the grains tease around the vanilla. Perfectly weighted; **t**23 again, outstanding balance on the sweetness as you chew at the grain and lick at the thin sugary coating; **f**23 soft spices, vanilla and traces of late honey; **b**23 some re-writing of history here: the label says "Original Fine Canadian" under OFC. Actually, I'm pretty convinced it originally meant Old Fire Copper. I can think of other things OFC stand for, perhaps not suitable for this book, but I will settle instead for Outstandingly Flavoured Creation, for this remains one of Canada's top three finest traditional blends, one which comes back at you with each mouthful with greater and greater complexity. **40%**

**Silk Tassel** (*see* McGuinness Silk Tassel)

**Tangle Ridge Aged 10 Years (67) n**17 **t**17 **f**16 **b**17. One of the worst Canadians I have tasted in years: something sweet and unpleasant has been added. The mouthfeel and effect are dreadful, the nose isn't much better. Considering this is based on rye whisky, you could almost cry. Still see it in specialist outlets from time to time: one to avoid. **40%**

**Tesco Canadian Whisky (75) n**18 **t**18 **f**20 **b**19. A reasonable sweet, clean if uninspiring Canadian. **40%**. *UK*.

**Windsor (91) n**21 kind of typical Canadian – its atypicality packed full of bizarre little nuances that don't quite fit, yet work: perhaps eclectic is the best term here; **t**24 wonderful, and entirely unexpected rye arrival really sets the tastebuds at fever pitch; very clean and grainy all the way; **f**22 some soft fruit and caramel drop in to say farewell; **b**24 an inexpensive, charming, honest and true Canadian that is worth discovering. **40%**

**Wiser's 10 Years Old** (*see* Wiser's De Luxe)

**Wiser's 18 Years Old (88) n**23 of all Canada's whiskies this probably has the most deceptive and delicate nose. There is gentle toffee, but lurking below that apples, leather, oloroso sherry and black pepper; **t**23 some blending brinkmanship going on here, with the oak and corn being pushed to the limit by fruit. The underlying crispness of the grain punches through to plant the Canadian flag; **f**20 here it loses control after taking one bend too many. Crashes into the fruit and oak and comes to a bitter end; **b**22 I spent a couple of days tasting and deliberating over this one, as it is quite an odd fish, and on the first run marked it low. My initial thoughts were that the caramel had perhaps taken too many prisoners and the fruit was out of sync. But over time I found greater shape and complexity. If you fancy yourself as a doctor of whisky, here's one to give a thorough examination to...and then a second opinion! **40%**. *Hiram Walker*.

**Wiser's De Luxe (89) n**23 beefy with sharpening touches of rye and other slightly fruity, citrus notes; **t**23 very busy mouth arrival with a complex array of corn on the cob and then much cleaner, small grain notes. Good weight to the oiliness which never goes OTT; a brief spice fly-past and an early vanilla-oak attack. Absolutely superb! **f**20 a mark or two dropped for the uncharacteristically bitter finale, though not of a rye-based character; slightly more toffee and fruit character, yet against all this soft corn sifts through pleasantly on the unbelievably silky fade-out; **b**23 this is mysterious and magical stuff. They tell me at Hiram Walker that nothing has changed. Yet I have been drinking Wiser's regularly for a decade and I can assure you it has. Far more non-specific fruit now, with the subtle grainy complexity overshadowed by a heavier, richer backdrop. Still genuinely attractive, chewy and fabulously complex whisky, but it seems to have darkened up both in looks and character. This is marketed as Wiser's 10 outside Canada. And remains a classic, if a slightly different one.... **40%**. *Hiram Walker.*

**Wiser's Reserve (90) n**22 rock-firm and almost austere; **t**23 the slow build-up of intensity is almost mesmerising: like watching a train coming at you from a distance. The sweetness is controlled superbly with oaky-spice darting in and adding balancing dryness; **f**22 excellent oak with a really grainy sunset radiating late but weak sweetness, but it's those spices that really make an imprint; **b**23 just a little bit of attitude here goes a long, long way. Impressive. **43%**

**Wiser's Special Blend (76) n**17 **t**21 **f**19 **b**19. A marginally improved, far more silky blend, but still never quite gets over the over-enthusiastic fruit nose or toffeed finish. Still, the middle does have a new shape with the spice kick and firm grain. By no means unpleasant. **40%**. *Hiram Walker.*

# Japanese Whisky

**S**adly, if you want to discover Japanese whisky you must still go to Japan. Of the 181 Japanese whiskies I have tasted for this book, only a handful are available in markets outside the nation in which they were distilled or blended. This is very frustrating when you see that many of the distilleries are nowhere near on full production and some are either silent or closed.

Part of the problem has been the Japanese custom of refusing to trade with their rivals. Therefore a Japanese whisky, if not made completely from home-distilled spirit, will instead contain a percentage of Scotch rather than whisky from fellow Japanese distillers.

This, ultimately, is doing the industry no favours at all. The practice is partly down to the traditional work ethics of company loyalty and an inherent, and these days false, belief that Scotch whisky is automatically better than Japanese. Back in the late 1990s I planted the first seeds in trying to get rival distillers to discuss with each other the possibility of exchanging whiskies to ensure that their distilleries worked more economically.

In the meantime word is getting round that Japanese whisky is worth finding. Indeed, there is so much interest in these little-known brands (outside Japan that is) that I have even given an all-Japanese whisky tasting in Holland.

Two leading lights are getting whisky drinkers switched on to just what oriental delights we are missing: the malts of Yoichi and Hakushu. Both make whiskies that rank unquestionably among the very finest in the world, though Yoichi – the brilliance of which I'm proud to have first brought to the world's attention in 1997 – these days has to be a little more careful with their use of sherry. Less than a handful of Scotch distilleries, though, can match their and Hakushu's supremely complex makes.

As if stirred by the recent success and fame of Yoichi, other distillers in Japan have begun bringing out vintage single cask bottlings. So slowly, as if by degree, interest in Japanese whiskies is being raised. One place this can clearly be seen is at whsiky festivals. Five years ago a bottle or two on Japanese on a table full of scotch would last a long time. Now it is often the first to go.

Word, then, is clearly getting around that Japanese whiskies, in whatever form, are worth finding. Even as I completed the writing of this Bible, I was interviewed by a British national newspaper who were intrigued by the claims of Britain's

Yamazaki ⚫Osaka

⚫Fukuoka

**Key**
- ⚫ **Major Town or City**
- ⚑ Distillery

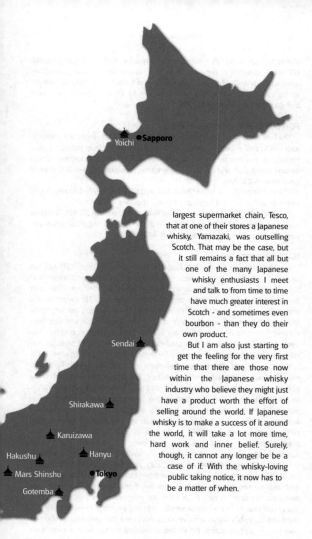

largest supermarket chain, Tesco, that at one of their stores a Japanese whisky, Yamazaki, was outselling Scotch. That may be the case, but it still remains a fact that all but one of the many Japanese whisky enthusiasts I meet and talk to from time to time have much greater interest in Scotch - and sometimes even bourbon - than they do their own product.

But I am also just starting to get the feeling for the very first time that there are those now within the Japanese whisky industry who believe they might just have a product worth the effort of selling around the world. If Japanese whisky is to make a success of it around the world, it will take a lot more time, hard work and inner belief. Surely, though, it cannot any longer be be a case of if. With the whisky-loving public taking notice, it now has to be a matter of when.

## Single Malts
### CHICHIBU

**Golden Horse Chichibu** db **(80) n**19 **t**21 **f**20 **b**20. Light, toasty and delicate yet the oak is prominent throughout. Good balancing sweet malt, though. **43%.** *Toa.*

**Golden Horse Chichibu 10 Years Old Single Malt** db **(82) n**19 **t**22 **f**21 **b**20. Developing citrus notes lighten the weight as the oak and sweet malt go head to head. **43%.** *Toa.*

**Chichibu 14 Years Old Single Malt** db **(89) n**20 tangerine peel and rice: two years older than the 12-y-o, that hint of bourbon has now become a statement; **t**23 brilliantly eclectic arrival on the palate with no organisation at all to the flurry of malt and bourbony oak and tangerine-fruity spices that are whizzing around; **f**23 pretty long with firm vanilla and a distinctive oiliness. Something approaching a whiff of smoke adds some extra ballast to the oak; **b**23 we are talking mega, in-your-face taste explosions here. A malt with a bourbony attitude that is unquestionably superb. **57%**. *Toa*.

## FUJI GOTEMBA, 1973. Kirin Distillers.

The Fuji Gotemba 15 Years Old db **(92) n**21 diced nuts, especially pistachio with vanilla and a sprinkling of sugar; **t**23 mouth watering from the start with a sensational development of sweet malt; **f**24 plateaus out with textbook spices binding sweet malt and dry oak. The length is exemplary; **b**24 quality malt of great poise. **43%**. *Kirin*.

The Fuji Gotemba 18 Years Old db **(81) n**20 t**19 f**21 **b**21. Jelly-baby fruitiness, complete with powdered sugar. Big, big age apparent. **43%**. *Kirin*.

Fuji Gotemba 20th Anniversary Pure Malt db **(84) n**21 t**20 f**22 **b**21. The nose is a lovely mixture of fruit and mixed oak; the body has a delightful sheen and more fruit with the malt. Handsome stuff. **40%**. *Kirin*.

## HAKUSHU, 1973. Suntory.

⠿ The Hakushu Single Malt Aged 18 Years No. 005039 db **(93) n**23 not dissimilar to medium ester Jamaican pot still rum with a squeeze of lemon and a bowl of barley juice thrown in for good measure; **t**23 delicate, ultra-clean barley which intensifies by the second into gristy sweetness; **f**23 toasted vanilla and mallows; then a burst of malt-(milk)chocolate candy; **b**24 this distillery never fails to delight me. The high grade malt is no shock: I realised just how extraordinary their whisky was on my last trip there. Another is overdue. The depth to the intensity of the malt reaches new peaks for this, or probably any other distillery I can think of. A whisky for Malteser lovers the world over... **43%**

Hakushu 1984 db **(95) n**22 delicate banana and malt with a gentle fly-past of peat. The oak is unbowed but sympathetic; **t**25 staggeringly beautiful: wave upon wave of astonishing complexity crashes against the tastebuds. The malt is intense but there is plenty of room for oak in varying guises to arrive, make eloquent speeches and retire. The intensity of spice is spot on – perfect; **f**24 long, more spice and greater malt intensity as the oak fades. Only the softest hints of smoke; mouthwatering to the last as mild coffee appears; **b**24 a masterpiece malt of quite sublime complexity and balance. The sort of experience that gives a meaning to life, the universe and everything ... **61%**

Hakushu 1988 db **(92) n**21 overtly peaty and dense, pleasant but lacking usual Hakushu complexity; **t**24 mouthwatering start with massively lively malt and fresh peating hanging on to its coat-tails. Some amazing heather–honey moments that have no right to be there; the peat intensifies then lightens; **f**23 lots of rich peat and then intense vanilla; crisp and abrupt at the finale with late bitter chocolate; **b**24 like all great whiskies this is one that gangs up on you in a way you are not expecting: the limited complexity on the nose is more than compensated for elsewhere. Superb. If this were an Islay malt the world would be drooling over it. **61%**

Hakushu Vintage Malt 1990 db **(89) n**22 firm barley and firmer oak; **t**23 serious intensity on delivery, this time with all the action being enjoyed by the concentrated, grassy barley; **f**22 layers of vanilla add balance to the fade; **b**22 warming in places with the tastebuds never getting a single moment's peace. **56%**. *Suntory*.

Hakushu Vintage Malt 1981 bott 04 **(90) n**22 biting sherry gnaws at the nosebuds; **t**22 mouthwatering despite the sherry influence and a wonderful chocolate-barley interlude ensures complexity; **f**23 spices that arrive at the middle continue their course towards the finale where more fruit arrives in the form of sultanas and cherries; **b**23 a beautifully clean sherried malt but, fabulous as it may be, the gap between this and the '89 Cask of Hakushu is never less than a chasm. **56%**. *Suntory.*

**Hakushu Vintage Malt 1985** bott 04 **(88)** **n**21 egg yolk; vanilla omelette; **t**22 perky malt edges towards a grassy theme; **f**23 excellent layers of oak and barley with a late fruity development; **b**22 clean, bourbon-matured malt that is younger than normal Japanese whisky of this age and reveals delightful deftness of touch. **56%**. *Suntory.*

**The Cask of Hakushu 1989** Sherry Butt cask 9W50004, dist Nov 89, bott Apr 05 **(96)** **n**25 where the hell can you begin?? OK, in no particular order: high roast Java with whipped cream; a mixing of pot and column still Dememara rum (of at least 8 years matured in Guyana); cocoa oil; liquorice-stained ryerecipe 12-y-o bourbon; some corn-stained 10-y-o rye; playful barley with a dash of very distant smoke. Oh, and some Oloroso sherry. The greatest Japanese nose of all time? Very possibly; **t**23 extraordinary eruption of spices and then a delightful delivery of Walnut Whip, strawberry jam and juicy barley; **f**24 the oloroso returns with myriad layers of oak and barley that pan out towards a cherry pie fruitiness and so much else. The spice continues to nip and bite; the sherry kisses and caresses; **b**24 f*** me!!! I needed about five to ten minutes to recover from this...Now, I don't often mention colour. But this is like an ancient Tawny Port and looks either wonderful or terrifying – because so often sulphur can be detected. Here, there is not a single trace of a trace. This is from an extraordinary butt, the purest imaginable, most probably the best I have seen the in the last decade. In the same league as (if not better than) those great Chivas Speyside casks of the mid to late 70s. What we have here is a whisky that catapults Japan on to the superstar map. Yoichi has done it for years, and Hakushu has given close support, but any whisky lover not yet convinced that Japanese is worth the effort must find a bottle of this. It will change their perception – even their lives – for ever.... **63%**. *Suntory.*

**The Cask of Hakushu 1994** Bourbon cask 4E05405, dist May 94, bott Apr 05 **(92)** **n**24 a wonderful, unbelievable, soft aroma offering hazelnut oil, and barley against very dry oak: absolute harmony; **t**23 sweeter than nose with an early honied, orangey development; **f**22 dries towards vanilla but still the intense barley holds ground; very late spice adds a fighting spirit; **b**23 a wonderful cask that is bursting at the seems with depth and committal but somehow remains in harness. **58%**. *Suntory.*

**Suntory Pure Malt Hakushu Aged 10 Years** db **(89)** **n**23 exemplary grassiness, fresh malt: mouthwatering and refreshes the senses; **t**24 spot-on, top-of-the-range malt. The freshness and integrity of the barley is beyond belief: thirst-quenching whisky of the highest order; **f**20 becomes rather toffeed and less well defined. A subtle display of spice compensates; **b**22 beautifully crafted whisky that's fresh and rewarding. **40%**. *The name Hakushu appears in small writing on the front label.*

**Suntory Pure Malt Aged 12 Years** (no bottling date) db **(84)** **n**20 **t**23 **f**20 **b**21. Deliciously malty with no little fruit, but the finish is disappointingly flat save for some welcome spices. **43%**

**Suntory Pure Malt Hakushu 15 Years Old Cask Strength** db **(92)** **n**21 curiously muted: one assumes it is a fruit-oak influence that is keeping the higher barley notes at bay; **t**24 gets back into the old Hakushu groove with a truly stunning display of mouthwatering malt in all its regalia: honeycomb too. Somehow manages to be big and chewy and light and flighty all at the same time; **f**23 good length, toasted honey, marmalade and spices; **b**24 if only the nose had been right, this would have been one of the truly great whiskies. The enormity on the palate is something you are unlikely to forget for a long time while the balance between barley, honey and oak is extraordinary. **56%**

**Suntory Pure Malt Hakushu Aged 20 Years** db **(94) n**23 fresh, mildly grapey fruit combined with subtle waves of peat; **t**24 the peat is now less subtle: wave upon wave of it bringing with it flotsam of drifting oak and then a very sharp malt tang; **f**23 long, sweet spice but the oak forms a chunky alliance with the firm peat. The bitter-sweet compexity almost defies belief; **b**24 a hard-to-find malt, but find it you must. Yet another huge nail in the coffin of those who purport Japanese whisky to be automatically inferior to Scotch. **56%**

## KARUIZAWA, 1955. Mercian.

**Karuizawa 1972 Aged 31 Years** cask 5530 db **(78) n**19 **t**18 **f**21 **b**20. Oaky and hot with just a bit too much age.

**Karuizawa 1973 Aged 30 Years** cask 6249 db **(84) n**20 **t**21 **f**22 **b**21. Sweet barley and very silky oaky vanilla. Plucked from the cask just in time.

**Karuizawa 1974 Aged 29 Years** cask 6115 db **(91) n**23 brilliant complexity: juicy dates and figs wrapped around a theme of richly oaked barley; **t**22 much sweeter arrival on the nose with burnt fudge and toast arriving for the middle; **f**23 slightly salty, the barley seems both sweet and roasty. Soft liquorice makes this one you can chew for hours; **b**23 an exhibition of bitter-sweet enormity.

**Karuizawa 1975 Aged 28 Years** cask 4066 db **(85) n**20 **t**21 **f**23. Much more relaxed late middle and finish with they honey thread soothing the singed taste buds; **b**21 loud at first, it sings sweet lullabies at the death. Always complex.

**Karuizawa 1976 Aged 27 Years** cask 6949 db **(83) n**19 **t**20 **f**23 **b**21. Big, mouthfilling but just a touch too much oak among the honey.

**Karuizawa 1977 Aged 26 Years** cask 7614 db **(74) n**17 **t**20 **f**19 **b**18. Some decent sweetness but doesn't quite work.

**Karuizawa 1978 Aged 25 Years** cask 2368 db **(87) n**21 seaweedy and shoreline, but without the peat; **t**20 almost violent arrival of searing sherry and vicious oak: hang on to your chair; **f**23 calms down stupendously with soft smoky peat to be found in the many strata of clean fruit and barley; **b**23 extra dry sherry, biting, salty and with a big coastal tang.

**Karuizawa 1979 Aged 24 Years** cask 8835 db **(94) n**23 much more fruit than is usual for this distillery with apples and fresh pear; lots of barley survives despite the age; **t**23 the barley is drinking in gentle honey and cocoa-enriched oak; **f**24 marvellously long with teasing, toasted caramelised oak adding a glorious repost to the rich, Demerara-sweetened barley; **b**24 one of those rare casks that appears to have had a magic wand waved at it and stardust sprinkled liberally.

**Karuizawa 1980 Aged 23 Years** cask 7614 db **(89) n**22 solid age but the softness of the toffee-apple and barley sugar is first class; attractive bourbony notes develop; **t**21 gripping, wild and hot at first, then a series of soothing waves of malt and liquorice; **f**24 peppery and estery; the honey-malt mouthfeel is long, lush and fabulous; **b**22 a classy Japanese malt that relishes the battle against advancing oak.

**Karuizawa 1981 Aged 22 Years** cask 8280 db **(73) n**17 **t**19 **f**19 **b**18. Sharp redcurrants but too obvious off-notes abound.

**Karuizawa 1982 Aged 21 Years** cask 8527 db **(85) n**21 a forest full of honey bees; **t**21 deep honey and toasted fudge; the middle erupts with strangely enjoyable sap; **f**22 gentle malt with a pinch of moscavado sugar and liquorice; **b**21 a mature whisky showing some sag but just hanging onto its sexy, alluring figure.

**Karuizawa 1983 Aged 20 Years** cask 8609 db **(88) n**20 slightly estery; chocolate honeycomb and a slice of pine; **t**24 estery, rich enormous copper presence; **f**22 medium length with elegant wisps of honey and toffee; **b**22 tasted blind you would bet your own grandmother that this was pot still Jamaican rum. And one probably older than your gran ...

**Karuizawa 1984 Aged 19 Years** cask 2563 db **(78) n**17 **t**20 **f**21 **b**20. Some quality touches of grape against smoky grist, and the mild peat is a redeeming and unexpected surprise, but what a shame that minor sulphury blemish.

**Karuizawa 1985 Aged 18 Years** cask 6885 db **(90) n**22 honey as a side dish on butterscotch tart; **t**22 mouth filling, oilier than usual with sumptuous malt and oak; **f**23 wonderful tones of butterscotch sweetened over the broadening oak. Just a slight sprinkling of cocoa; **b**23 whisky that celebrates its middle age with a show of complex intensity.

**Karuizawa 1986 Aged 17 Years** cask 8170 db **(94) n**23 full-frontal, naked sherry. And spicy, too; **t**23 massive, almost uncontrollable sherry-malt explosion; dried dates and vanilla concentrate form an unlikely but delicious alliance; **f**24 long, fruity with hidden spices; the malt ducks in and out playfully; **b**24 find a faultless sherry butt and place in it a whisky of the very finest quality and complexity. This is the result.

**Karuizawa 1987 Aged 16 Years** cask 8694 db **(93) n**23 amazingly soft malt with just a touch of far-away, background smoke; **t**23 brilliant malt arrival: the barley sings from every direction; **f**24 surprising lack of development as the oak remains shy and the barley rules unhindered; just the faintest wisp of smoke here and there; **b**23 almost like a malt-shake in its barley intensity. No complaints here, though.

**Karuizawa 1988 Aged 15 Years** cask 691 db **(88) n**20 malty banana and custard; **t**22 drying oak at first and then the most teasing build-up of honey imaginable; **f**23 this creeping effect continues with a crescendo of acacia honey and green-grassy barley in total control of the oak; **b**23 quite fabulous whisky that exudes confidence and charisma.

**Karuizawa 1989 Aged 14 Years** cask 2941 db **(91) n**22 soaring fruity notes interlock beautifully with soft bourbon; **t**23 hard, metallic arrival at first then a fabulous deployment of sugared fruits on a bed of chewy oak; **f**23 big vanilla, subtle spices and a very late waft of smoke; **b**23 there would be quite a number of Scottish distilleries who would pray to produce a malt this simplistically stylish.

**Karuizawa 1990 Aged 13 Years** cask 7905 db **(85) n**19 **t**21 **f**23 **b**22. Deliciously mouth-watering yet firm and unyielding barley is stand-offish towards the oak. The finish is awesomely rich. The texture is excellent.

**Karuizawa 1991 Aged 12 Years** cask 8294 db **(87) n**22 beautifully fresh and gristy; **t**22 big delivery of clean malt which sweetens; **f**22 a simple barley vanilla tail with some soft brown sugar; **b**21 charming, well proportioned but not overly taxing.

**Karuizawa Pure Malt 15 Years (76) n**17 **t**21 **f**20 **b**18. Some vague sulphur notes on the sherry do no favours for what appears to be an otherwise top-quality malt. (Earlier bottlings have been around the 87–88 mark, with the fruit, though clean, not being quite in balance but made up for by an astonishing silkiness with roast chestnut puree and malt). **40%**

**Karuizawa Pure Malt Aged 17 Years (90) n**20 bourbony, big oak and pounding fruit; **t**24 enormous stuff: the link between malt and fruit is almost without definition; **f**23 amazingly long and silky. Natural vanilla melts in with the almost concentrated malt; **b**23 brilliant whisky beautifully made and majestically matured. Neither sweetness nor dryness dominates, always the mark of a quality dram. **40%**

## KOMAGATAKE

**Komagatake 10 Years Old Single Malt** db **(78) n**19 **t**20 **f**19 **b**20. A very simple, malty whisky that's chewy and clean with a slight hint of toffee. **40%**. *Mars*.

## MIYAGIKYO (see Sendai)

## SENDAI, 1969. Nikka.

**Miyagikyou 10 Years Old** batch 18C10D db **(88) n**22 **t**20 **f**23 **b**23.0 By far and away the most deftly smoked and complex Sendai seen on the market. **45%**

⋰ **Miyagikyou 10 Years Old** Batch 20C44D db **(85) n**19 **t**22 **f**22 **b**22. The nose offers little to encourage, but the sweetened softness of delivery is delicious; there is even a swirl of smoke on the finish to add weight. **45%**

⋰ **Miyagikyou 10 Years Old** Batch 08F20C db **(83) n**20 **t**21 **f**21 **b**21. Light and amazingly even throughout with the accent very much on the barley. **45%**

⋰ **Miyagikyou 12 Years Old** Batch 12F30C db **(88) n**22 gooseberries, oak and barley; **t**21 some Japanese oak bites hard and kicks the big barley off balance; **f**23 recovers sensationally, with soft oils allowing the fruit-barley complexity to really take hold; **b**22 classy and complex. **45%**

⋰ **Miyagikyou 12 Years Old** Batch 24C38A db **(78) n**21 **t**19 **f**19 **b**19. Some pleasant barley-rich moments, but doesn't quite come together. **45%**

⋰ **Miyagikyou 15 Years Old** Batch 02F60B db **(92) n**22 a fruitcake density (and a distant sulphurous something) but big barley, too; **t**24 spiced and lush, a marmalade sharpness bites playfully; amid the sublime integration marzipan offers sweetness; **f**23 long oaky strands of liquorice and vanilla cut through the re-grouping barley; **b**23 the fruit/spice influence has "sherry" written all over it. And, if you are being picky, the odd fault can be found with it. But taking the thing as a whole: wow!!! **45%**

⋰ **Miyagikyou 1990** cask no. 27216, dist 8 Nov 90, bott 26 July 06 db **(91) n**22 pear drops, apples: light and fruity; **t**24 barley sugar melts into the delicate oak. Delicious intensity; **f**22 clean and elegant; **b**23 a mouth-watering, high quality experience. This distillery has definitely improved in recent years. **54%**. *France*.

**Miyagiko Single Malt 12 Years Old 70th Anniversary (93) n**23 any hint of sulphur is extinguished by light smoke and intense barley amid the crushed raisin; **t**24 mouthwatering, mouth-shattering barley that is so brittle that it fragments in a thousand pieces. Gathering spice sits well with the soft honey and liquorice; **f**23 continuous layers of molassed barley and burnt oak. You need teeth to get through this one...; **b**23 Amazing stuff: if it was an earthquake it would fly off the Richter scale. This is big and body-rocking. **58%**. *Nikka*.

**Miyagiko Key Malt Aged 12 Years "Fruity & Rich"** db **(90) n**22 fruit biscuits with burnt raisin and sugar; **t**23 wonderful lift-off of sultana and burnt raisin on a sea of chewy barley. Towards the middle, a brief expression of oak and then much sweeter – and oilier – barley. Fruity; **f**22 rich! **b**23 a very comfortable whisky, much at home with itself. **55%**. *Nikka*.

**Miyagiko Key Malt Aged 12 Years "Soft & Dry"** db **(85) n**22 **t**21 **f**21 **b**21. Perhaps needs a degree of sweetness.... **55%**. *Nikka*.

**Miyagikyou 15 Years Old** batch 20C44C db **(84) n**20 **t**21 **f**22 **b**21. Very typically Sendai: light body and limited weight even with all the fruit. Clean and gathers in overall enjoyability, though. **45%**

**Sendai 12 Years Old** (code 06C40C) db **(83) n**17 **t**22 **f**23 **b**21. To put it politely, the nose is pretty ordinary; but what goes on afterwards is relative bliss with a wonderful, oily, fruity resonance. For those thinking in Scotch terms, this is very Speysidey with the malt intense and chewy. **45%**. *Nikka*.

**Sendai Miyagikyou Nikka Single Cask Malt Whisky 1986** dist 16 May 86 bott, 5 Dec 03 db **(88) n**22 stewed prunes and oranges; the first rumbles of bourbon and smoke wafting around for extra weight; **t**20 big fruit kick but a little out of sync; **f**24 a super nova of a kick back with peat appearing as if from nowhere and the big, booming, bourbony notes and sweetness at the end offering dozens of waves of complexity. A touch of cocoa rounds it off magnificently; **b**22 little to do with balance, everything about effect. **63.2%**

**Sendai Miyagikyou Nikka Single Cask Malt Whisky 1992** dist 22 Apr 92, bott 5 Dec 03 db **(84) n**19 **t**20 **f**24 **b**21. Very strange whisky: I would never have recognised this as Sendai. I don't know if they have used local oak on this but the fruity, off-balance nose and early taste is compensated by an orgy of mouth-watering, softly smoked barley that sends the taste buds into ecstasy. A distinct, at times erratic, whisky that may horrify the purists but really has some perzaz and simply cannot be ignored. **55.3%**

## SHIRAKAWA

**Shirakawa 32 Years Old Single Malt (94) n**23 ripe mango meets a riper, rye-encrusted bourbon. We are talking a major aroma here; **t**24 the most intense malt you'll ever find explodes and drools all over your tastebuds. To make the flavour bigger still, the oak adds a punchy bourbon quality. Beautiful oils coat the roof of the mouth to amplify the performance; **f**23 long, sweet and malty. Some fruitiness does arrive but it is the oak-malt combination that just knocks you out; **b**24 just how big can an unpeated malt whisky get? The kind of malt that leaves you in awe, even when you thought you had seen and tasted them all. **55%**. *Takara.*

## YAMAZAKI, 1923. Suntory.

**Yamazaki Vintage 1979** db **(78) n**20 **t**21 **f**18 **b**19. Spicy and thick malt. But this has plenty of wrinkles and a stoop, too. **56%**. *Suntory.*

**Yamazaki Vintage Malt 1980** db **(75) n**19 **t**19 **f**18 **b**19. Some lovely blood oranges, but no whisky can survive this amount of oak unscathed. **56%**

**Yamazaki Vintage 1982** db **(84) n**20 **t**22 **f**21 **b**21. Big, muscly malt with some sexy spices. **56%**. *Suntory.*

**Yamazaki Sherry Wood Vintage 1986** db **(93) n**24 a sherry butt found in heaven: clean, absolutely dripping in grapejuice yet light enough to allow further complexity from bright malt and a touch of smoke; **t**23 mouthwatering fruit clings, thanks to the estery malt, to every crevice in the mouth; **f**23 exceptionally long fade with a chocolate and sultana finale, topped with a puff of smoke; **b**23 something here for everyone; one of the most outstanding "new" sherry casks of the year. **45%**. *Suntory Whisky.*

**Yamazaki Vintage 1991** db **(88) n**23 a curious mixture of peat reek and Golden Graham breakfast cereal; **t**23 soft smoke at first and then the grain hardens and takes a stranglehold; **f**21 honied yet remaining firm; **b**21 hard and tough as nails towards the finish: a surprising conclusion after such a yielding start. **56%**. *Suntory.*

**Yamazaki 1991** db **(88) n**21 bourbony and light with a substratum of soft malt; **t**23 astonishing unfurling of mouthwatering malt tones that spreads over the mouth revealing a subtle hint of smoke and beautifully graceful oak; **f**22 long, lashings of cocoa powder and again soft barley hand-in-hand with gentle oak; **b**22 closed when cold, improves dramatically when warmed on the hand. But the mouth arrival really does deserve a medal. **61%**

**Yamazaki 1993** db **(87) n**23 smoky and clean; gristy and Port Ellen-ish with a bit of extra exotic oak; **t**23 sweet, spicy, vaguely Islay-ish start with the peats developing but not at the expense of dense malt. The oak is refined and there is something unusually coastal for a non-Scottish peated malt; **f**20 earth hard, closed and brittle. Metallic malt scrapes against rock-like peat; **b**21 a real surprise package. At times quite Islay-ish in style – Port Ellen in particular – but the finish is more realistic. A really delicious experience nonetheless.

**Yamazaki Vintage 1994** db **(91) n**23 butterscotch and cedarwood; **t**24 ultra-clean malt and honey; soft oak and spice add balance; **f**22 drier, toasty with residual malt; **b**22 very high quality whisky without a single blemish. **56%**. *Suntory.*

**Yamazaki Vintage Malt 1983** bott 04 db **(89) n**20 the malt is tired and oak is threatening to pounce despite a hint of smoke; **t**21 uncompromisingly warming and a little thin; **f**25 whoomph!!! Earth to Tokyo...we have whisky!!! Having taken off like a rocket, it now circles the tastebuds sending back unbelievable messages. The first is one of unruined barley, that is both refreshing and refined; next comes a spicy subtext with a Demerara sweetness lightening things. The finale is fabulous, with succulent fruits including greengages and dried dates teaming up with the persisting massive malt; **b**23 slightly hot at first but then goes into overdrive: the finish is something to be etched on to the memory for life. **56%**. *Suntory.*

**Yamazaki Vintage Malt 1989** bott 04 db **(90)** **n**22 seasoned oak with the saltiness adding a piquancy to the malt, too; **t**23 big, unremitting malt with that salty tang transferring to the taste; **f**22 sweetened vanilla and dry cocoa enlivened by a dose of Lukec's finest! **b**23 this is quite enormous whisky that may not seem like too much at first, but on second or third mouthful leaves you in no doubt about its stupendous depth. **56%**. *Suntory.*

**Yamazaki Vintage Malt 1992** bott 04 db **(85)** **n**19 dry parchment; distilled nut kernel; oak; **t**23 gushing, concentrated malt makes for a salivating experience, especially with the fruit of barley juiciness; **f**22 long, well layered malt with some developing cocoa; **b**21 fruity and fractionally fundamental. **56%**. *Suntory.*

**Yamazaki Aged 18 Years** db **(93)** **n**25 one of the most sophisticated Yamazaki noses of them all, somehow combining an ancient Kentucky bourbon, oaky depth with rich plumb pudding, an element of old pot still Port Morant Demerara rum and the most distant smoke. There is no dominance and no beginning nor end: just perfect harmony; **t**22 succulent and chewy, the build-up and middle is one of ever-increasing sugared oak; **f**23 hints of liquorice and burnt raisin balance beautifully with the thick oak and powering malt; **b**23 indisputably brilliant whisky for all its obvious age. **43%**. *Suntory.*

**The Cask of Yamazaki 1990** Hogshead cask 0W70223, dist Nov 90, bott Apr 05 **(89)** **n**21 dried fruits and dry in general; **t**23 a thousand battles for supremacy between insurgent oak and the controlling barley: the barley holds the fort; **f**22 the oak begins to win more and more of the skirmishes and a waft of smoke hangs over the battle scene; some lovely roast Santos completes the job; **b**23 not too many elements involved here, but the effect on the tastebuds is wonderful: pure sophistication...for warriors! **55%**. *Suntory.*

**The Cask of Yamazaki 1993** Hogshead cask 3P70277, dist Apr 93, bott Apr 05 **(91)** **n**24 attractive, light smoke and citrus; the oak well developed yet adding only a required dryness; **t**22 mouthwatering malt and then a relaxed development of something smoky; **f**23 wonderful waves of spice and thickening peat balanced perfectly by fresh barley. The oak, again, adds just the right amount of dryness; **b**22 a fascinating bottling showing Yamazaki at its most stylishly demure despite all the peat. **54%**. *Suntory.*

**Suntory Pure Malt Yamazaki 10 Years Old** db **(79)** **n**20 **t**21 **f**19 **b**19. Almost unnatural fruitiness, as though wild fruit yeast spores have been at work. **40%**

**Suntory Pure Malt Yamazaki 25 Years Old** db **(91)** **n**23 quite intoxicating marriage between grapey fruitiness and rich oak: supremely spiced and balanced with a wave of pure bourbon following through; **t**23 big, big oloroso character then an entrancing molassed, burnt raisin, malty richness; **f**22 subtle spices, poppy seed with some late bitter oak; **b**23 being matured in Japan, the 25 years doesn't have quite the same value as Scotland. So perhaps in some ways this can lay claim to be one of the most enormously aged, oak-laden whiskies that has somehow kept its grace and star quality. **43%**

**Suntory Pure Malt Yamazaki Cask Strength** db **(88)** **n**22 very light, flimsy weight but the malty grassiness impresses; **t**23 absolutely pure Yamazaki in concentrate: refreshing malt that sweetens and fattens; **f**21 a light, toffeed finale without the complexity of either the nose or early palate; **b**22 a malt of indisputably high quality. **56%**

## YOICHI, 1934. Nikka.

**Hokkaido 12 Years Old** db **(87)** **n**23 **t**22 **f**21 **b**21. Full-flavoured malt with absolutely zero yield. Just ricochets around the palate. **43%**. *Nikka.*

**Yoichi 10 Years Old** batch 14116A db **(75)** **n**19 **t**19 **f**18 **b**19. Proof that sulphur can detract even from a great like Yoichi. **45%**

**Yoichi 10 Years Old** (code 14B22 new "Yoichi" distillery label) db **(88)** n18 t23 f23 b24. Typical Yoichi. Even when it shows a flaw it recovers to an unbelievable degree: like a champion ice skater who falls at the first leap and then dances on as if nothing happened. Keeps you guessing to the very last about what is to happen next. Fabulous verve and complexity. **45%**. *Nikka.*

⋅⊱⋅ **Yoichi Single Malt 10 Years Old** Batch 12F04C db **(89)** n21 vague echo of oak sappiness rescued by top-notch, weighty barley; t24 the tongue is forced to inspect the roof of the mouth countless times as wave upon wave of complex barley-honey notes rocket around the palate; f21 long with a tangy, coppery richness that counters perfectly the barley, golden syrup and toffee; b23 mildly dodgy nose, overly toffeed finish... and still it's a lightweight treat! **45%**

**Yoichi 10 Years Old** (code 12I32 old Hokkaido "Yoichi" distillery label) db **(91)** n22 the peat brushes the nose like a feather over skin: just so delicate; t23 immediate flinty malt, amazingly hard and tooth-cracking then softened slowly by a salty, peaty edge; f23 peaty, delicate and now as soft, thanks to vanilla, as it was previously uncompromisingly hard. Some toffee and coffee aid the finale; b23 yet another teasing, unpredictable dram from Yoichi. **43%**. *Nikka.*

**Yoichi 10 Years Old** (code 14H62A old Hokkaido "Yoichi" distillery label) db **(91)** n23 big malt but it is the delicate quality of the peat that is most remarkable. Oak is present, but this is almost too clean to be true; t23 sweet and soft, then that Yoichi trademark gradual build-up of peat; f22 hard and brittle despite the softness of the peat, long and chewy with a hint of liquorice and honey; b23 makes the crispness and bite of this whisky makes it almost blend-like in style – which goes to underline the complexity. **43%**. *Nikka.*

**Yoichi 10 Years Old** (code 14H62B old Hokkaido "Yoichi" distillery label) db **(89)** n23 t21 f22 b23. Soft and delicate with beautifully chewy peat throughout. **43%**. *Nikka.*

**Yoichi 10 Years Old** (code 24G48C old Hokkaido "Yoichi" distillery label) db **(93)** n23 for an aroma carrying smoke this is almost austere: but this is an illusion. Some crisp malty, softly peated notes give it a delicate depth and massive sophistication; t23 enormous malt, absolutely brimming with lusty barley. Refreshing and mouthwatering, yet all the time that soft peat is present; f24 a quite brilliant marriage between rich barley and soft oak. No more than the slightest hint of very distant smoke; b23 a Yoichi in its "Old Speyside" phase, with just a waft of peat-reek to add some ballast to the enormous, clean malt. The fade is nothing short of fabulous. A Japanese version of Ardmore: whisky for grown-ups. **43%**. *Nikka.*

**Yoichi 10 Years Old** (code 24H18C old Hokkaido "Yoichi" distillery label) db **(89)** n20 t23 f23 b23. Another bottle of understated genius. **43%**. *Nikka.*

**Yoichi 12 Years Old** (code 06C14 new Yoichi label with distillery drawing) db **(91)** n21 spicy fresh oloroso; t24 big, clean sultana-fruit with a gathering intensity of ripe dates and sweet, gently smoked malt; f22 dies slightly, but the dates remain, as does the smoke. The oak kicks in with a late bitter finale; b24 absolutely magnificent malt with a no-holds-barred intensity of fruit and malt. **45%**. *Nikka.*

⋅⊱⋅ **Yoichi Single Malt 12 Years Old** Batch 14F36A db **(91)** n22 soft smoke and under-ripe fruit; t23 profound, chewy barley; lots of small still coppery sharpness and then a gentle awakening of peat; f23 sweet peats dusted with demerara; it takes some time for the chalky oak to finally have a say; b23 best when left in the glass for 10-15 minutes: only then does the true story emerge. **45%**

**Yoichi 12 Years Old** (code 16J32 new Yoichi label with distillery drawing) db **(87)** n20 t22 f23 b22. A pretty light Yoichi almost devoid of peat. After getting over a toffee-led lull the malt comes to life with impressive results. **45%**. *Yoichi.*

**Yoichi Key Malt Aged 12 Years** "Peaty & Salty" lott 12D50B db **(95)** n23 the peat rumbles like distant thunder, difficult to pinpoint but letting you know that it is there. The oaky tones suggest a mixing of Kentucky and something local; soft fruits make an almost apologetic appearance; t25 there is perfect distribution of peat. It rumbles around the palate offering bitter-sweet depth, and a salty, coastal tang emphasises the richness of the malt; f23 waves of vanilla begin to outflank the soft peat: the finish is long and there is no victor between the sweet malt and the more bitter, salty oak; b24 of all the peated whiskies of the world, only Ardbeg can stand shoulder to shoulder with Yoichi when it comes to sheer complexity. Here is an astonishing example of why I rate Yoichi in the best five whiskies in the world. Forget the odd sulphur-tarnished bottling. Get Yoichi in its natural state with perfect balance between oak and malt and it delivers something approaching perfection. And this is just such a bottling. **55%**. *Nikka.*

**Yoichi Key Malt Aged 12 Years "Sherry & Sweet"** lott 12D48C db **(80)** n19 t22 f19 b20. Sad to report that this should be called "Very Slight Sulphur and Sweet". A real pity because it is obvious that had the Spaniards not molested these butts, they would have been absolutely top-of-the-range. And probably would have scored in the low to mid 90s. I could weap. **55%**. *Nikka.*

**Yoichi Key Malt Aged 12 Years "Woody & Vanillic"** lott 12D50C db **(83)** n21 t22 f20 b20. Pretty decent whisky. Not sure about creating one that sets out to be woody: that means balance has been sacrificed to concentrate on a particular essence to the whisky that should be used only as a component of complexity. Still, there is enough sweet malt on arrival to make this a dram to be enjoyed. **55%**

**Yoichi 12 Years Old 70th Anniversary** db **(96)** n24 what a tease! The most gentle of smokes creeps around playfully but adding telling, near perfect weight to the lighter, orange-flecked malt. Again, showing extraordinary balance, the fruit-oak harmonisation is practically faultless. Meanwhile the earthiness is not entirely like the animal house at the zoo. Sounds awful: it's not. It's wonderful. Wow!! t24 salivating young barley offers an unusual gristy feel, and then the smoke arrives, keeping in check the drier, slightly bitter-chocolate oak; f24 long, with wave upon wave of smoky oak. A late tangerine tartness lightens the load. But then it would, wouldn't it? b25 just incredible. Had they chosen this selection of casks but from two or three years earlier, so the oak was not quite such a force, I think the record books regarding the Bible would have to be re-written. Confirmation, not that it is ever needed, that Yoichi can offer something that just about no other distillery can. **58%**. *Nikka.*

∴ **Yoichi Single Malt 15 Years Old** Batch 04F44D db **(86)** n22 t22 f20 b22. Zesty and tangy; most peculiar by Yoichi standards. But still big, rich and lip-smacking. **45%**

**Yoichi 15 Years Old** (code 10J44 old green back label) db **(94)** n23 roast chestnuts plus salty, soft peat and dried dates: awesome complexity; t24 the dates have moistened, the peat positively glows, having been seasoned with salt, the fruitiness is full but in perfect proportion; f23 for the enormity of the nose and mouth arrival, the soft peated spices offer a charming sophistication to the intense barley. The fruit remains yielding and the oak no less soft and accommodating; b24 the kind of whisky that propels a distillery into super league status. A classic. **45%**. *Nikka.*

**Yoichi 15 Years Old** (code 06C10 new buff-coloured back label) db **(90)** n22 nutty, intense clean malt with just a light dusting of peat. The fruits are light and plummy; t22 very clean malt, almost gristy in its delicate nature. The peat no more than tickles the tastebuds. A weak grapejuice sweetness offers further complexity; f23 amazingly delicate, a beautiful combination of barley and vanilla. The peat remains playful and wonderfully balanced; b23 this is a succulent malt of enormous complexity. Typical Yoichi. **45%**. *Nikka.*

**Yoichi 20 Years Old** db **(95)** n23 magnificently intense oloroso (a tiny fleck of sulphur burns off in about 10 minutes when warmed), the background malt oak-laden; t23 again it's oloroso that leads the way, apparently too intensely at first but quickly settling to allow some stupendous spices to unravel and create balance. Fabulous bitter-sweet harmony; f25 Okay, guys, help me out here. Spot the fault. I can't. The fruit is now spotlessly clean and displaying a grapey complexity, the spices are warming but not entirely engulfing, the oak is firm and adds no more than a hint of dryness and at last the malt comes into full play to offer both mouthwatering barley and something slightly smoky. If you can pick a defect, let me know; **b**24 I don't know how much they charge for this stuff but either alone or with mates get some for one hell of an experience. What makes it all the more remarkable is that there is a slight sulphury note on the nose: once you taste the stuff that becomes of little consequence. **52%**. *Nikka*.

⋰ **Yoichi 1987** cask no. 113200, dist 19.7.87, bott 27 Jul 06 db **(87)** n20 heavy duty, orangey but slightly flawed sherry; **t**24 juicy grape, concentrated barley then, slowly, the peat delivers by degree; **f**21 dries significantly as the sulphur takes a grip; **b**22 dense and desirable at times: just so easily could have been a great dram but undone by a poor butt. **63%**. *France*.

**Yoichi Single Cask 1987** No. 3 dist 27 Apr 87, bott 1 Feb 05 db **(87)** n22 throbbing oak; marmalade on toast; **t**23 the malt is just so intense, offering at first a charismatic, mouthwatering depth and then something more deeply oaky; **f**20 dry, tannin heavy and chewy; **b**22 hints here of old age and over-exposure to oak. But the overall thrust remains delightfully rich. **52%**. *Nikka*.

**Yoichi Single Cask 1988** No. 29 dist 7 May 88, bott 3 Feb 05 db **(89)** n21 a distinct bourbony style to this, with citrus abounding; **t**23 light and bourbony at first, then intensifies as a fruity maltiness digs deep into the tastebuds; **f**22 spices and vanilla; **b**23 effortless to the point of arrogantly beautiful. **60%**. *Nikka*.

**Yoichi Nikka Single Cask Malt Whisky 1990** db dist 4 Aug 90, bott 17 Oct 03 **(84)** n21 t20 f22 b21. Most probably a dry sherry cask set the tone for this: astringent by Yoichi standards and although the finish offers a complex vanilla and liquorice counter, this isn't an Hokkaido great. **60.8%**

**Yoichi Nikka Single Cask Malt Whisky 1991** db dist 25 Feb 91, bott 12 Dec 03 **(95)** n24 t24 f23 b24. It was because I managed to taste many casks like this while tramping through Yoichi's warehouses over the years that I declared the distillery in the world's top six. Taste this, then e-mail me to disagree. **64.5%**

# Unspecified Malts

**"Hokuto" Suntory Pure Malt Aged 12 Years (93)** n22 trademark delicate lightness; fleeting barley chased by soft vanilla; **t**24 melt-in-the-mouth malt arrival; hints of honey work well with the loftier barley and earthier oak; **f**23 honey on toast with just a little toffee; **b**24 another example of Suntory at its most feminine: just so seductive and beautiful. Although a malt, think Lawson's 12-y-o of a decade ago and you have the picture. **40%**

**Nikka Whisky From the Barrel (89)** n20 carries some weight; good age and subtle malty sugars; **t**23 exemplary mouthfeel: delightful oils and nipping spices but the malt remains clean and very sweet; **f**22 some dryer oakiness but the malt keeps its balancing sweetness; **b**24 a whisky that requires a bit of time and concentration to get the best out of. You will discover something big and exceptionally well balanced. **51.4%.** *Nikka*.

⋰ **Nikka Whisky From the Barrel** Batch 02F26A **(82)** n20 t22 f20 b20. Some attractive honey notes and caramel, but a bit laboured. **51.4%**

⋰ **Nikka Whisky From the Barrel** Batch 12F32C db **(91)** n22 date and brazil cake; **t**24 monumental delivery with soft smoke melting into the most glorious honeycomb known to man; tingly spices and toffee-apple, too; **f**22 caramel kicks in slightly but some butterscotch rounds it off wonderfully; **b**23 truly great whisky that mostly overcomes the present Japanese curse of big caramel finishes. **51.4%**

# Vatted Malts

**All Malt (86)** n22 t21 f21 b22. The best example by a mile of an almost unique style of vatted whisky: both malt and "grain" are distilled from entirely malted barley, identical to Kasauli malt whisky in India. Stupendous grace and balance. **40%**. *Nikka*.

**All Malt "Pure & Rich" (89) n**22 honeycomb and liquorice with some thumping oak; **t**24 beautifully mouthfilling, and "rich" is an understatement. Barley sugar and molten brown sugar combine and then there is a soft gristiness. Big...; **f**21 vanilla and caramel with some residual malt; **b**22 my word, this has changed! Not unlike some bottlings of Highland Park with its emphasis on honey. If they could tone down the caramel it'd really be up there. **40%.** *Nikka.*

◈ **All Malt Pure & Rich** Batch 14F24A **(77) n**19 **t**20 **f**19 **b**19. My former long term Japanese girlfriend, Makie (hope you enjoyed your 30th birthday in April, by the way), used to have a favourite saying, namely: "I am shocked!" Well, I am shocked by this whisky because it is much blander than the previous bottling (04E16D), with all that ultra-delicate and complex honeycomb lost and lovely gristiness removed. For me, one of the biggest surprises – and disappointments - of the 2007 Bible. But proof that, when using something so potentially dangerous as caramel, it is too easy to accidentally cross that fine line between brilliance and blandness. Because, had they gone the other way, we might have had a challenger for World Whisky of the Year. **40%.** *Nikka.*

**Hokuto Pure Malt Aged 12 Years (86) n**20 **t**22 **f**22 **b**22. An oaky threat never materialises: excellent mixing. **40%.** *Suntory.*

**Malt Club "Pure & Clear" (83) n**21 **t**22 **f**20 **b**20. Another improved vatting, much heavier and older than before with bigger spice. **40%.** *Nikka.*

**Mars Maltage Pure Malt 8 Years Old (84) n**20 **t**21 **f**21 **b**22. A very level, intense, clean malt with no peaks or troughs, just a steady variance in the degree of sweetness and oak input. Impossible not to have a second glass of. **43%.** *Mars.*

**Nikka Malt 100 The Anniversary Aged 12 Years (73) n**18 **t**19 **f**18 **b**18. The depressing and deadly fingerprint of sulphur is all over this. Shame, as the spices excel. **40%**

**Pure Malt Black** batch 02C58A **(95) n**24 an exquisitely crafted nose: studied peat in luxuriant yet deft proportions nestling amid some honeyed malt and oak. The balance between sweet and dry is faultless. There is neither a single off-note nor a ripple of disharmony. The kind of nose you can sink your head into and simply disappear; **t**23 for all the evident peat, this is medium-weighted, the subtlety encased in a gentle cloak of oil; **f**23 long, silky, fabulously weighted peat running a sweet course through some surging malt and liquorice tones with a bit of salt in there for zip; **b**25 well, if anyone can show me a better-balanced whisky than this you know where to get hold of me. You open a bottle of this at your peril: best to do so in the company of friends. Either way, it will be empty before the night is over. **43%.** *Nikka.*

◈ **Pure Malt Black** Batch 06F54B **(92) n**24 great balance to the nose with a careful sprinkling of barley, honey, peat and oak – but never too much of any; **t**24 massive, ultra-intense sweet malt with a delicate sub-stratum of smoke; a spiced fruitiness also cranks up the weight and depth; **f**21 vanilla kicks in as it thins surprisingly fast; **b**23 not the finish of old, but everything else is present and correct for a cracker! **43%.** *Nikka.*

**Pure Malt Red** batch 02C30B **(86) n**21 **t**21 **f**22 **b**22. A light malt that appears heavier than it actually is with an almost imperceptible oiliness. **43%.** *Nikka.*

◈ **Pure Malt Red** Batch 06F54C **(84) n**21 **t**22 **f**20 **b**21. Oak is the pathfinder here, but the oily vanilla-clad barley is light and mouth-watering. **43%.** *Nikka.*

**Pure Malt White** batch 02C30C **(92) n**23 massive, Islay-style peat with a fresh sea kick thanks to brine amid the barley; **t**24 again, the peat-reek hangs firmly on the tastebuds from the word go, the sweetness of the barley tempered by some drying oaky notes suggesting reasonable age. Lots of subtle oils bind the complexity; **f**22 liquorice and salt combine to create a powerful malty-oak combo. An oily, kippery smokiness continues to the very end; **b**23 a big peaty number displaying the most subtle of hands. **43%.** *Nikka.*

**Pure Malt White** batch 06J26 **(91) n**22 soft peat interrupted by gentle oak; **t**23 biting, nippy malt offering a degree of orangey-citrus fruit amid the building smoke; **f**22 sweet vanilla and light smoke that dries towards a salty, tangy, liquorice finish; **b**24 a sweet malt, but one with such deft use of peat and oak that one never really notices. Real class. **43%**. *Nikka*.

‹∰› **Pure Malt White** Batch 10F46C **(90) n**23 the quality of the delicate peat is beyond reproach; some attractive kumquat juices it up nicely; **t**23 wonderful balance between silky-soft and nail-hard malts with some tasty local oak getting in on the act; **f**22 the smoke lessens to allow vanilla and toffee dominance; a sawdusty dryness brings down the curtain; **b**22 there is a peculiarly Japanese feel to this delicately peated delight. **43%**

**Southern Alps Pure Malt (93) n**24 bananas and freshly peeled lemon skin: one of the world's most refreshing and exhilarating whisky noses; **t**23 crisp youngish malts, as one might suspect from the nose, mouthwatering and as a clean as an Alpine stream; **f**22 some vanilla development and a late slightly creamy flourish but finished with a substantial and startling malty rally boasting a very discreet sweetness; **b**24 this is a bottle I have only to look at to start salivating. Sadly, though, I drink sparingly from it as it is a hard whisky to find, even in Japan. Fresh, clean and totally stunning, the term "pure malt" could not be more apposite. Fabulous whisky: a very personal favourite. **40%**. *Nikka*.

**Super Nikka Vatted Pure Malt (76) n**20 **t**19 **f**19 **b**18. Decent and chewy but something doesn't quite click with this one. **55.5%**. *Nikka*.

**Taketsuru Pure Malt 12 Years Old (80) n**19 **t**22 **f**19 **b**20. For its age, heavier than a sumo wrestler. But perhaps a little more agile over the tastebuds. Lovely silkiness impresses, but lots of toffee. **40%**. *Nikka*.

**Taketsuru Pure Malt 17 Years Old (89) n**21 firm oak, but compromises sufficiently to allow several layers of malt to battle through with a touch of peat-coffee; **t**22 massive: a toasted, honeyed front gives way to really intense and complex malt notes; **f**23 superb. Some late marmalade arrives from somewhere: the toast is slightly burnt but the waves of malty complexity are endless; **b**23 not a whisky for the squeamish. This is big stuff – about as big as it gets without peat or rye. No bar shelf or whisky club should be without one. **43%**. *Nikka*.

**Taketsuru Pure Malt 21 Years Old (88) n**22 middle-aged bourbon with a heavy, vaguely honeyed malt presence; **t**21 the oak remains quite fresh and chewy. Again, the malt is massive; **f**22 sweet, oily and more honey arrives; **b**23 a much more civilised and gracious offering than the 17-y-o: there is certainly nothing linear about the character development from Taketsuru 12 to 21 inclusive. Serious whisky for the serious whisky drinker. **43%**. *Nikka*.

**Zen (84) n**19 **t**22 **f**22 **b**21. Sweet, gristy malt; light and clean. **40%**. *Suntory*.

## Japanese Single Grain

**Nikka Single Cask Coffey Grain Whisky Aged 12 Years "Woody & Mellow" (93) n**22 delicate vanalins and tannins; **t**24 sweet and yielding (probably corn) with layers of drying spices. Stupendous; **f**23 long, with subtle oils lengthening the grain effect and spice; more vanilla at the very death...eventually. Vague bourbony tones towards the finale; **b**24 exceptional grain whisky by any standards – and helps explain why Japanese blends are so damn good!! **55%**. *Nikka*.

**Nikka Single Cask Coffey Grain 12 Years Old 70th Anniversary (85) n**20 biting, nose, tingling oak; **t**22 massive oak delivery sweetened and soothed by the rich grain; lush and brilliantly weighted throughout; **f**22 long liquorice and cocoa tones are met by some bitter, zesty, oaky notes; **b**21 more woody than the "woody and mellow". **58%**. *Nikka*.

‹∰› **Nikka Single Cask Coffey Grain Aged Over 13 Years** Batch 20 116399, dist 31.1.92, bott 30.5.05 db **(85) n**22 **t**23 **f**20 **b**20. Distinctly subdued by this brand's normal high standards, though the early bourbon riches are mesmerizing. The finish, though attractive, is too simplistic. **62%. sc.**

**Nikka Single Cask Coffey Grain Whisky 1991** dist 1 Oct 91, bott 12 May 03 db **(93) n**22 **t**24 **f**23 **b**24. I have tasted much Japanese straight grain over the years but this is the first time in bottled form for public consumption. And Nikka have exceeded themselves. Forget the word "grain" and its inferior connotations. This is a monster whisky from the bourbon family you are unlikely ever to forget. Use the first couple of mouthfuls for a marker: once you get the idea, life will never quite be the same again. Track down...and be consumed. **61.9%**

⟜ **Nikka Single Cask Coffey Grain 1992** dist 31.2.92, bott 25.706 db **(95) n**24 a curious mixture with hints of Japanese oak (from the cask heads?) and a bourbony, hickory edge. Rich and rousing; **t**24 sweet, flushed with maize and a silky body, almost verging on demerara. Honeyed and revelling in its bourbon theme; **f**23 vanilla layers, again with a deep, delicious touch of molasses; **b**24 make no mistake: this grain is as entertaining as any malt. Those loving high-class bourbon will be thrilled. **57%**. *France*.

## Blends

**Ajiwai Kakubin** (*see* Kakubin Ajiwai)

**Amber (75) n**18 **t**20 **f**18 **b**19. Similar in style to "Old" but with more toffee caramel. A silky experience. **40%**. *Mars*.

**Black Nikka (72) n**17 **t**20 **f**17 **b**18. Big grain presence and decent middle; carries a caramel tang. **37%**. *Nikka*.

**Black Nikka Special (70) n**16 **t**20 **f**17 **b**17. Simliar to ordinary Black Nikka, except weighed down by extra caramel **42%**. *Nikka*.

**Black Nikka Aged 8 Years (82) n**20 **t**21 **f**21 **b**20. Beautifully bourbony, especially on the nose. Lush, silky and great fun. Love it! **40%**. *Nikka*.

**The Blend of Nikka (90) n**21 a dry, oaky buzz infiltrates some firm grain and sweeter malt; **t**23 brilliant! Absolutely outstanding explosion of clean grassy malts thudding into the tastebuds with confidence and precision: mouthwatering and breath-catching; **f**22 delightful grain bite to follow the malt; **b**24 an adorable blend that makes you sit up and take notice of every enormous mouthful. Classy, complex, charismatic and brilliantly balanced. **45%**. *Nikka*.

**Boston Club** (Brown Label) **(73) n**17 **t**20 **f**18 **b**18. "More Boston Strangler than Boston Club", I wrote somewhere on tasting this some years back. They have sorted out the dreadful finish on the old bottling. Pleasant enough, but devoid of any challenge thanks possibly to caramel although the spice does. **40%**. *Kirin*.

**Boston Club (70) n**16 **t**19 **f**18 **b**17. Less opaque than the Brown Label, lighter in body with a fraction less toffee-caramel **37%**. *Kirin*.

**Crescent (82) n**19 **t**22 **f**20 **b**21. Fresh, grassy, lightweight malt dominates. A spot of the old caramel toffee, perhaps? Without it, this would be a stunner. **43%**. Kirin.

**Diamond Whisky (73) n**17 **t**20 **f**18 **b**18. Another blend where complexity takes second place to caramel though it does have some sweet, attractive moments. **43%**. *Nikka*.

**Emblem (76) n**18 **t**20 **f**18 **b**20. Richly textured bend with a deliciously clean and salivating malt character. **40%**. *Kirin*.

**Evermore (90) n**22 big age, salt and outstanding malt riches to counter the oak; **t**23 more massive oak wrapped in a bourbony sweetness with glorious malts and a salty, spicy tang; **f**22 long, sweet malt and crisp grains: plenty to chew on and savour; **b**23 top-grade, well-aged blended whisky with fabulous depth and complexity that never loses its sweet edge despite the oak. **40%**. *Kirin*.

**Gold & Gold (83) n**21 **t**22 **f**20 **b**20. Some lovely, crisp malty moments set against firm grain and softened by honey. Something to get your teeth into, but perhaps a touch too much toffee. **43%**. *Nikka*.

**Golden Horse Bosyuu (80) n**20 **t**21 **f**19 **b**20. Soft grain melts beautifully in the mouth. **40%**. *Toa*.

**Golden Horse Busyuu Deluxe (93)** n22 some decent signs of age with some classy oak alongside smoke: sexy stuff; t24 enormous flavour profile simply because it is so fresh: massive malt presence, some of it peaty, bananas and under-ripe grapes; f23 clean malt and some sharpish grain with a touch of bite, continuing to tantalise the tastebuds for a long time; b24 whoever blended this has a genuine feel for whisky: a classic in its own right and one of astonishing complexity and textbook balance. **43%**. *Toa. To celebrate the year 2000.*

**Golden Horse Grand (78)** n19 t21 f19 b19. Decent malt, sweet and a little chalky. **39%**. *Toa.*

**Hibiki (82)** n20 t19 f23 b20. The grains here are fresh, forceful and merciless, the malts bouncing off them meekly. Lovely cocoa finale. A blend that brings a tear to the eye. Hard stuff – perfect after a hard day! Love it! **43%**. *Suntory.*

**Hibiki 17 Years Old** 50.5 **(89)** n22 light and complex; egg-plant and stewed celery with an oaky-bourbony half-thrust against the hiding peat; t24 much fuller bodied on the palate with an enormous malt theme. The oak is dense but fails to indent into the richness of the barley; the grain offers a threading of delicious bourbony tones; f21 the honey of old has been replaced by toffee: much flatter and a disappointing end to a grand dram; b22 Suntory blends tend to be light and clean – usually their greatest strength. This, though, has taken a different route, being full-bodied to the point of enormity. However, the most recent bottling is even bigger still, though has lost out on the finish with some extra caramel digging in and flattening out the complexity that sets it apart not only from many of its Japanese rivals, but from Scotch whiskies, too. That said, it's still a whisky you could never say no to... **50.5%. ncf.** *Suntory.* ☺ ☺

**Hibiki 21 Years Old (93)** n24 fruitier notes of cherry and sherry with a triumphal triumvirate of intense malt, the subtlest of peat smoke and leathery oak combining for maximum, stupendous complexity, also a dash of kumquats; t22 fat and oily, like the nose hinting slightly at bourbon but the grains thin the middle out sufficiently to let the malt, mildly peaty and otherwise, through; f23 long and intense with more lightly orchestrated smoke and lashings of late, grapey fruit and a build-up of, first, sweet malts, then a drier, spicier oak; b24 when people refer to Yoichi as the exception that proves the rule about Japanese whisky, I tend to point them in the direction of this. If I close my eyes and taste this, cherry blossom really does form in my mind's eye. **43%**. *Suntory.*

**Hibiki 30 Years Old (87)** n21 curious mix of peat and bourbon; t22 sweet, fat oak: bourbon all the way; f22 the glorious rich-textured sweetness continues forever; b22 Kentuckians would really go for this one: the smoke might confuse them a little, though. Pretty unique the world over. **43%**. *Suntory.*

**Hi Nikka Whisky (68)** n16 t18 f17 b17. Very light but lots of caramel character. A good mixer. **39%**. *Nikka.*

꘎ **Hokuto (86)** n22 t24 f19 b21 a bemusing blend. At its peak, this is quite superb, cleverly blended whisky. The finish, though, suggests a big caramel input. If the caramel is natural, it should be tempered. If it is added for colouring purposes, then I don't see the point of having the whisky non-chillfiltered in the first place. **50.5%. ncf.** *Suntory.*

**Imperial (81)** n20 t22 f19 b20. Flinty, hard grain softened by malt and vanilla but toffee dulled. **43%**. *Suntory.*

**Kakubin (80)** n19 t21 f20 b20. A beautifully constructed, fresh, bright and mouthwatering blend. Refreshing and so dangerously moreish! **40%**. *Suntory.*

**Kakubin Ajiwai (82)** n20 t21 f20 b21. Usual Kakubin hard grain and mouthwatering malt, with this time a hint of warming stem ginger. **40%**. *Suntory.*

**Kakubin New (90)** n21 gritty grain with very hard malt to accompany it; t24 stunning mouth arrival with heaps of mouthwatering young malt and then soft grain and oil. Brilliant stuff; f21 some beautiful cocoa notes round off the blend perfectly; b24 seriously divine blending: a refreshing dram of the top order. **40%**. *Suntory.*

**Kingsland (81)** n21 t22 f17 b21. An ultra-lively and mouthwatering blend with a short, dry finish. Overall, quite impressive, refreshing and moreish. *Nikka*.

**Master's Blend Aged 10 Years (87)** n21 t23 f22 b21 chewy, big and satisfying. **40%**. *Mercian/Karuizawa*.

**New Kakubin Suntory** (*see* Kakubin New)

**New Shirokaku (74)** n18 t19 f19 b18. Grain-heavy, hard and toffeed. **40%**. *Suntory*.

**Nikka Master Blend Blended Whisky 12 Years Old 70th Anniversary (94)** n24 nothing shy or retiring here: big oak, big sherry. A little nervousness with the smoke, maybe; t23 lush, silky grain arrives and then carries intensely sweet malt and weightier grape; f24 dries as the oak takes centre stage. But the peripheral fruit malt, gentle smoke and grain combine to offer something not dissimilar to fruit and nut chocolate; b23 an awesome blend swimming in top quality sherry. Perhaps a fraction too much sweetness on the arrival, but I am nit-picking. A blend for those who like their whiskies to have something to say. And this one just won't shut up. **58%**. *Nikka*.

**The Nikka Whisky Aged 34 Years** blended and bottled in 99 **(93)** n23 t23 f24 b23. A Japanese whisky of antiquity that has not only survived many passing years, but has actually achieved something of stature and sophistication. Over time I have come to appreciate this whisky immensely. It is among the world's greatest blends, no question. **43%**. *Nikka*.

**Oak Master (78)** n19 t20 f19 b20. Foraging malts on nose and palate counter big grain surge. Silky whisky, if a little on the bitter side. **37%**. *Mercian*.

**Ocean Luckey (70)** n17 t18 f17 b18. Grainy, chalky, weightless. **37% Merc.**

**Ocean Whisky Special Old (83)** n20 t21 f21 b21. Deliciously rich malt is absorbed effortlessly into melt-in-the-mouth grain. Good blending. **40%**

**Old (77)** n18 t20 f20 b19. Sweet, chewy, clean session whisky. **43%**. *Mars.*

**Old Halley (71)** n18 t19 f17 b17. Flat, pleasant but toffee-reliant. **37%**. Toa

**Red (75)** n17 t19 f20 b19. On the thin side: the grains are to the fore and aft but there is good late spicy bite amid the toffee. **39%**. *Suntory*.

**Robert Brown (74)** n19 t20 f17 b18. What a pity! Too much toffee has overshadowed some lovely spice. **40%**. *Kirin.*

**Royal 12 Years Old** (89) n22 chalky and dry, but malt and oranges add character; t23 fabulously complex arrival on the palate with some grainy nip countered by sparkling malt and a hint of smoke; f21 the grains and oak carry on as the spice builds; b23 a splendidly blended whisky with complexity being the main theme. Beautiful stuff. **43%**. *Suntory*.

**Royal 15 Years Old (91)** n23 kumquats and lime give a fruity start to an immensely malty aroma; t23 the grain kicks off early bringing with it some oak, then an immediate malt explosion with a spicy drop-out, lashings of clean, juicy fruit; f22 the grain rules OK. But the oaky vanilla is a joy; b23 this is outstanding blended whisky. **43%**. *Suntory*.

**Special Reserve 10 Years Old (94)** n23 magnificent approach of rich fruit buttressed by firm, clear grain. Some further fruity spices reveal some age is evident; t24 complex from the off with a tidal tsunami of malt crashing over the tastebuds. The grain holds firm and supports some budding fruit; f23 a touch of something peaty and pliable begins to take shape with some wonderful malty spices coating the mouth; b24 a beguiling whisky of near faultless complexity. Blending at its peak. **43%**. *Suntory*.

⋅❖⋅ **Special Reserve Aged 12 Years (89)** n21 peaches and cream with a dollop of caramel; t24 luxurious delivery of perfect weight and softness to body; the barley sweetness works beautifully with the buzz of oak and yielding grains; f21 caramel-coffee crème from a box of chocs; b23 a tactile, voluptuous malt that wraps itself like a sated lover around the tastebuds, though the complexity is compromised very slightly by bigger caramel than the 10-y-o. **40%**. *Suntory*.

**Suntory Hibiki 17 Years Old (88) n**20 a weighty, lumbering assembly of big, almost bourbony oak and macho malt. Sumo stuff; **t**22 the grains absolutely go into overdrive on immediate mouth arrival before a wonderful gathering of eclectic barley notes take off into every direction; grain tries to get involved but is shoe-horned out; **f**23 beautiful spices and some impressive grain-inspired coffee notes dovetail with the thick malt; **b**23 this is a massive whisky, but not just because of the strength. The crescendo is glass-shattering, only elements of toffee towards the late middle and finish prevents the explosion. **50.5%. ncf.**

**Suntory Old (87) n**19 dusty and fruity. Attractive nip and balance; **t**24 mouthwatering from the off with a rich array of chewy, clean fresh malt: textbook standard, complete with bite; **f**22 thins out far quicker than it once did leaving the vanilla to battle it out with toffee; **b**22 a delicate and comfortable blend that just appears to have over-simplified itself on the finale. Delicious, but can be much better than this. **40%**

**Suntory Old Mild and Smooth (84) n**19 **t**22 **f**21 **b**22. Chirpy and lively around the palate, the grains soften the crisp malts wonderfully. **40%**

**Suntory Old Rich and Mellow (89) n**20 very lightly smoked with healthy maltiness; **t**23 complex, fat and chewy, no shortage of deep malty tones, including a touch of smoke; **f**23 sweeter malts see off the grain, excellent spices; **b**23 a pretty malt-rich blend with the grains offering a fat base. Impressive blending. **43%**

**Super Nikka (93) n**23 excellent crisp, grassy malt base bounces off firm grain. A distant hint of peat, maybe, offers a little weighty extra; **t**23 an immediate starburst of rich, mouthwatering and entirely uncompromising malt that almost over-runs the tastebuds; **f**23 soft, fabulously intrinsic peaty notes from the Yoichi School give brilliant length and depth. But the cocoa notes from the oak-wrapped grain also offer untold riches; **b**24 a very, very fine blend which makes no apology whatsoever for the peaty complexity of Yoichi malt. Now, with less caramel, it's pretty classy stuff. However, Nikka being Nikka you might find the occasional bottling that is entirely devoid of peat, more honeyed and lighter in style (21-22-23-23 Total 89 – no less a quality turn, obviously). Either way, an absolutely brilliant day-to-day, anytime, any place dram. One of the true 24-carat, super nova commonplace blends not just in Japan, but in the world. **43%**. *Nikka.*

**Torys (77) n**19 **t**20 **f**19 **b**19. Lots of toffee in the middle and at the end of this one. The grain used is top class and chewy. **37%**. *Suntory.*

**Torys Whisky Square (80) n**19 **t**20 **f**21 **b**20. At first glance very similar to Torys, but very close scrutiny reveals slightly more "new loaf" nose and a better, spicier and less toffeed finale. **37%**. *Suntory.*

**Tsuru (93) n**23 apples, cedar, crushed pine nuts, blood oranges and soft malt, all rather chalky and soft – and unusually peatless for Nikka; **t**24 fantastic grain bite bringing with it a mouthwateringly clean and fresh attack of sweet and lip-smacking malt; **f**22 a continuation of untaxing soft malts and gathering oak, a slight "Malteser" candy quality to it, and then some late sultana fruitiness; **b**24 gentle and beautifully structured, genuinely mouthwatering, more-ish and effortlessly noble. If they had the confidence to cut the caramel, this would be even higher up the charts as one of the great blends of the world. As it is, in my house we pass the ceramic Tsuru bottle as one does the ship's decanter. And it empties very quickly. **43%**. *Nikka.*

**The Whisky (88) n**22 **t**22 **f**21 **b**23. A really rich, confident and well-balanced dram. **43%** *Suntory.*

**White (75) n**20 **t**19 **f**18 **b**18. After a classically nippy nose, proves disappointingly bland. **40%**. *Suntory.*

**Za (79) n**19 **t**21 **f**19 **b**20. Some lively boisterous grain offers a suet-pudding chewiness. A little bitter on the finish. **40%**. *Suntory.*

# European Whisky

**E**urope is getting bigger and more diverse ... and I don't just mean thanks the recent enlargement of the EU. In whisky terms distilling has not only expanded and embraced new cultures, but to a degree has become a little more refined.

It is a continent where distillers appear impressed by single malt and other whisky traditions, but are determined to go about things in their own, idiosyncratic way. In previous Bibles I have told you about the quite brilliant, and entirely unique oat whisky from Austria's Oswald Weidenauer; from France Eddu Silver, a massively flavoured dram made from buckwheat – or Black Wheat as they call it there.; from Germany Hessicher whisky made from 56% corn and the remainder split equally between barley and rye; in Switzerland Eddie Pierri has been perfecting the making of malt whisky in stills on wheels. Each year I wonder what was coming next. Last year was a wheat whisky. Whilst Heaven Hill were launching theirs with a fanfare, back in Austria the ever resourceful Oswald Weidenauer was quietly unleashing the world's first Spelt whisky - another form of wheat distillate.

This year it is Swedish. The launching of the malts from Mackmyra was the highlight on the world's new whisky front simply because we have a distillery determined to make no "me too" malt. Mackmyra's is as individualistic as they come. The fact that they saw off the Swiss to land Jim Murray's Whisky Bible 2007 European Whisky of the Year reveals that quality plays a part every bit as important as style.

Naturally, the biggest Eurosceptics come from the UK, where I have listened to arguments among people in the trade there that these whiskies are a poor relation to Scotch. And certain critics' marks I have seen given for these whiskies tend also to treat them as if by the same rules as, say, a Speyside malt.

Of course they could not be any more different. It is like comparing Pure Irish Pot Still to an Irish single malt or straight rye to a straight bourbon. Comparisons are pointless: they are a different species of whisky and should be enjoyed and treated that way. Therefore, in the marks I give the points are dropped only if they are poorly made or matured, or suffer by comparison to previous bottlings from the same distillery or region, or if vital balance is lacking. It is not because they don't taste like Scotch ... In the same way, it would be pointless comparing a Buffalo Trace against the Hessicher Whisky from Germany.

Again Switzerland, as a nation, have provided the best quality malts when spread as an average amongst their distilleries. Topping the bill yet again was Eddie Pierri's Swissky who was pipped to a gong only by Mackmyra's bravery and star quality, though I am increasingly finding myself drawn to Swissky as an every day drinking malt: there are very few where the barley plays such a convincing role. Castle Hill's new bottling also took this intense barley route and it was wonderful to see the husband and wife team at Zurcher prove their one previous bottling of some years back was not beginners' luck.

The Welsh whisky of Penderyn has continued to blaze the most impressive international marketing trail, finding itself being sold extensively in North America and has kept up its early high quality and promise. Other European malts, with much smaller stills, will have to settle for now to sell to their own localised markets and whisky clubs.

And this year I tasted the promising new make of a brand new distillery in Denmark while distilling begins at the first purpose-built distillery in England for over a century. European whisky is not just getting better in quality year by year, it is expanding at a heart-warming rate. Continue to watch this space...!!

# AUSTRIA
## HAIDER (see Waldviertler Roggenhof)

## REISETBAUER
Reisetbauer Single Malt Whisky 7 Years db **(76)** n18 t19 f20 **b**19. No great nose, but the nuttiness on the palate is attractive. **43%**

Reisetbauer Single Malt Whisky 1996 Destilliert db **(71)** n16 t18 f18 **b**18. Some sound maltiness, but the stale tobacco and nuttiness are a problem **56%**

Reisetbauer Single Malt Whisky 1997 Destilliert db **(73)** n17 t19 f18 **b**19. Some mouthwatering malt, but struggles with a belligerent degree of feintiness. **56%**

## WALDVIERTLER ROGGENHOF
Roggenraith. Working.

## Single Malt
J H Gersten-Malzwhisky L10/99 db **(80)** n19 t21 f19 **b**21. Slightly chalky with a tad more oak interference than it needs. That said, the malt is gristy, chewy and clean with a slight buzz of spice. Impressive. **41%**

J H Gersten-Malzwhisky L10/99 Fassstärke db **(83)** n20 t21 f21 **b**21. Holds together better on the nose at a fuller strength plus an extra hint of honey on the finish. More compact and not far off delicious. **54%**

J H Gersten-Malzwhisky Karamell L66/98 db **(74)** n16 t19 f20 **b**19. An off-beam nose – well it was a very early barrel – is rescued to a degree by a sweet malt surge towards the death. **41%**

J H Gersten-Malzwhisky Karamell L66/98 Fassstärke db **(77)** n16 t21 f20 **b**20. Much more early intense malt offers a sugared coating at the start and a hint of liquorice on the finale. A big difference. **55%**

J H Gersten-Malzwhisky Nougat L3/99 Fassstärke db **(78)** n17 t20 f21 **b**20. The rye sparkles much more here than at the lower strength, especially on the long finish. **50%**

Waldviertler Gersten-Malzwhisky Fassstärke (single malt) L10/99 db **(90)** n22 thick malt with equally weighty oak; t22 first the malt comes through loud and clear. Then liquorice kicks in as the oak really goes into overdrive. Lovely oils coat the palate; f23 huge finale with the emphasis very much on dark – though not bitter – chocolate; **b**23 this is right back up there with some of those great casks I nosed some years back. Massive and the stuff of stars. **54%**

⁙ Waldviertler J H Single Malt L18/00 db **(85)** n21 t22 f21 **b**21. Eminently drinkable stuff; the tobacco edge to the nose doesn't translate onto the thick, barley-sugared tinted delivery and follow through. Big stuff. **41%**

⁙ Waldviertler J H Fassstärke Single Malt L10/01 db **(91)** n23 chunky, intense with good oak distribution; t22 excellent early spice-barley fruit balance; a short burst of sweetness, mouth-watering and increasingly lush and oily; f23 settles for some serious complexity with layers of cocoa and it dries with supreme elegance; **b**23 a similar beauty to last year's bottling. If they can maintain this brand, it will become an Austrian institution. **54.5%**

⁙ Waldviertler J H Single Malt Karamell L22/00 db **(80)** n18 t19 f22 **b**21. Saved by the long chocolate-caramel (also powerful hints of chocolate Swiss roll) on the finish after a less than glorious opening. **41%**

## Pure Rye Malt
J H Roggen-Malzwhisky Reserve Nougat L17/99 db **(75)** n18 t18 f20 **b**19. Sharp, hot and hard as nails. **43%**

J H Roggen-Malzwhisky L20/98 db **(90)** n22 intense, sweet rye and clean, spicy, fruit; t23 outstanding clarity of crisp, hard rye that sweetens by the second, quite plummy and juicy; f22 the bitterness returns – and then some – and dry pounding oaky tones add a late chalkiness. Hints of honey lurk in the background; **b**23 simply excellent and quite classic rye whisky. Congratulations to all concerned for a delicious job well done. **41%**

**J H Roggen-Malzwhisky Fassstärke L6/98** db **(88) n**20 surprisingly closed nose; **t**25 high octane, faultlessly clean rye that completely hammers the palate with a welter of fruity, cherry-laden punches. Clean, chewy and breathtaking: man, this is rye whisky!!!! **f**21 just like the nose, flattens alarmingly; **b**22 if it could be like the arrival on the palate from nose to finish, we'd have a world classic! **55%**

**J H Roggen-Malzwhisky Nougat L3/99** db **(74) n**17 **t**19 **f**19 **b**19. The rye has been flattened into submission. **41%**

⸰⸙⸰ **Waldviertler J H Pure Rye Malt L3/01** db **(92) n**22 crunchingly hard rye; elements of the house tobacco diced with clove; **t**23 soft delivery, at first sweet and almost gristy; hardens as the rye takes command; **f**24 astonishingly long finish for its strength; the degree of complexity amazes as the vanillins begin to make their play; **b**23 just so delicate and elegant. **41%**

⸰⸙⸰ **Waldviertler J H Pure Rye Malt Nougat L9/00** db **(77) n**17 **t**21 **f**19 **b**20. Still something of an acquired taste (or should that be nose?), though this has kinder and more complex elements than previous bottlings. New-found spices impress. **41%**

**Waldviertler Roggen-Malzwhisky** (pure rye malt) L6/99 db **(91) n**21 hard to get beyond the rye, though when fully warmed there is a hint of cloves; **t**24 absolutely hard as nails: the rye dominates and chisels and drills into the tastebuds like a demented dentist. Mouthwatering and sharp; **f**23 no yield or give at all: it's rye all the way, with the oak trying to get the odd word in but usually failing. Some very late honey does ease the tension; **b**23 this is uncompromising and wonderful whisky of a style so different from those other rye malt makers at Old Potrero. Here the flintiness is of a unique race. **41%**

# Rye

**J H Feinster Roggenwhisky L4/00** db **(88) n**22 fabulously pungent in that unique Haider style: both floral and fruity at the same time and in equal measure with a dollop of manuka honey for extra kerpow; **t**23 soft mouth arrival, a quiet punch-up between spices and then an oily smattering of rye; **f**21 quite hard but always chewy rye and oak; **b**22 this is a highly unusual, in your face, whisky which takes some acclimatising to: once you get the picture it's fun all the way. **41%**

**J H Feinster Roggenwhisky Fassstärke L4/99** db **(88) n**21 a distinctively herbal rye style with minimum fruit; **t**22 mouthfilling and sweetened by almost molassed rye; **f**23 the rye hangs round but only to keep the oak development under control; unrefined sugar softens the final blows; **b**22 something of a bruising whisky where the aggressive rye fist-fights all comers ... and wins. **54%**

**J H Feinster Roggenwhisky L21/98 (81) n**18 **t**20 **f**22 **b**21. Very sweet with excellent oak weight and even rye distribution. Lovely spice v demerara at the finale. **41%**

**J H Feinster Roggenwhisky Fassstärke L42/97 (91) n**20 sharp, hard and flinty. The grains really kick hard here; **t**24 brilliant weight on the mouth and then a series of slow spicy explosions, each unleashing clear, chewy rye on the palate: a pyrotechnical display of rye at near enough perfection; **f**24 superb chocolate adds sublime balance to the fruity rye and bitter oranges; **b**23 look at this from any angle and you have a minor masterpiece on your hands: quite sublime. **54%**

**Waldviertler Feinster Roggenwhisky** (rye whisky) L19/98 db **(83) n**19 **t**20 **f**23 **b**21. Slight tobacco on the nose, but the enormity of the rye cannot be suppressed, especially for the excellent finish. **41%**

⸰⸙⸰ **Waldviertler J H Fassstärke Rye Whisky L11/01** db **(89) n**20 rye impeded by closed oak; **t**23 another story entirely as the rye first melts into the mouth, then explodes to colossal effect. Classic fruit and spice kick as you would expect; f23 a beautiful molassed sheen to the grain guarantees a stunning bitter-sweet play; not only big rye kick but cloves oil, too; b23 forget the nose. With this one it's all about what happens on the palate. And what happens is brilliance! **54.4%**

## WEIDENAUER DISTILLERY
**Kottes. Working.**
### Oat whisky

Waldviertler Hafer Whisky 1998 db **(79)** n20 t21 f18 b20. An oily, assertive whisky that, while sweet, shows signs of a bitterness and imbalance despite the enormous fruitiness on the nose. That said, the oats do come through loud and clear and make quite a porridge, if a slightly salted one. **42%**

Waldviertler Hafer Whisky 1999 db **(89)** n23 oat-crunchies breakfast cereal combined with soft honey and a sprinkling of sugar: amazingly clean yet so much going on; t21 initially hard on the palate then it softens as a grainy sweetness spreads across the roof of the mouth, excellent texture; f22 pure oats: just so pure and clean, you could almost chew it: remarkable; b23 this is unique whisky and as such deserves time in the glass to oxidise and warm. Once you become accustomed to the taste, the complexity is spellbinding. **42%**

Waldviertler Hafer Whisky 2000 db **(94)** n23 some delicate spices link beautifully with oak 'n' oats; t24 sumptuous, just about perfectly weighted with the most sublime oil involvement, then that unique oaty quality that is sweetish, but softly so, yet with a drying mealiness; f24 long, really intense oat character which dries in the most delicious manner of any whisky I have ever encountered! b23 this was the best new whisky worldwide of 2002. Totally unique in character, flawless in distillation and awesome in subtlety. **42%**

Waldviertler Hafer Whisky (with 2004 silber medaille sticker on neck) db **(89)** n21 sharp and punchy nose; a salted porridge character; t23 so much sweeter than the nose with the most astonishing take-off of tart oat, with a countering subtle, milky sweetness that fills the palate; f22 still sharp and bitters slightly; a vaguely rye-like fruitiness hovers around a bit; b23 brilliant, though not quite the all-round grace of the last uniquely oaty bottling; but still your taste buds know they've been hafered ... **42%**. *Bottled Nov 03, though not stated.*

### Spelt whisky

Waldviertler Dinkel-Whisky (marked with 2005 golden label on neck) db **(88)** n21 a touch smoky, like very lightly cured bacon. A kind of feint overture, but never quite reaches the second bar; t23 big, mouthwatering grain notes that seem to gather in intensity; the mildly m???sugar is a delightful touch making for very subtle complexity. Very big indeed; f22 big vanilla and more layered grain; b22 the distiller here has taken the widest cut he can and got away with it – just! The result is a throbbing, full-flavoured beast that keeps the tastebuds on maximum alert. **40%**

## WOLFRAM ORTNER DESTILLERIE
Nock-Land Pure Malt 2000 db **(77)** n18 t20 f19 b20. Intense, sweet malt and spices combine with a mild tobacco effect for a curious, distinctive but decent dram. **48%**

## BELGIUM
### DISTILLERIE LAMBICOOL

Belgium Pure Malt db **(81)** n19 t19 f22 b21. This is a new make and therefore not strictly whisky. The distillers are marketing this in order to fund their whisky-making venture, a wise move not least because the rich, superbly textured finish overcomes the hesitant tobacco-smoke start for a rewarding and impressive finale; and there is even lavender on the nose of the empty glass. Well worth finding a bottle to help support a promising cause. **40%**

# BULGARIA

**12 Years Finest Bulgarian** db **(81)** n19 t21 f21 b20. Some whisky! Takes no prisoners with an onslaught of what appears to be fresh European oak: more like a 35–40-year-old Scotch. Chewy, sweet with a big liquorice finish. Some decent malt does makes it through and shows at the end. Beautifully textured, clean and obviously well made. Very drinkable whisky indeed, but not for the lilylivered. **43%**

# FRANCE
## Single Malt
### DISTILLERIE DES MENHIRS

⋇ **Eddu Gold (93)** n22 greater harmonization than the silver; still a hint of tobacco but now a richer, honeyed tone compensates and flourishes; t23 big, bulging arrival. There is a real pulse to the grain, a sturdiness which helps intensify the controlled Demerara sweetness. Big yet elegant; f24 now goes into overdrive as the oak adds further weight and spices. Yet the satin effect remains intact; b24 rarely do whiskies turn up in the glass so rich in character to the point of idiosyncrasy. Some purists will recoil from the more assertive elements. I simply rejoice. This is so proud to be different. And exceptionally good, to boot!! **43%**

**Eddu Grey Rock Special Blend (89)** n21 pleasantly grainy and clean, though flat and unprepossessing; t23 soft, lilting, melt-in-the-mouth with an enormous surge of juicy, grassy barley; f22 exceptionally clean, with little oak interfering with the grassy grains; b22 a classy, chic blend that sates the tastebuds. **40%**

**Eddu Silver** db **(91)** n21 slight tobacco yet clean enough to allow the grain a big fruity entrance; t24 an outstanding arrival of something sweet and simmering; a unique mouthwatering character appears half rye half barley yet something deliciously different again; the salivating sweetness that builds is surprising and has a distinct Demerara sugar feel to it; f22 quite a deep and lengthy final chapter with the clean, boiled apple fruitiness balancing comfortably with subtle oak. Some bitterness digs in but is dealt with by pulsating grain; b24 once, the best whisky to come out of France by some considerable distance. This is distilled from Buckwheat, the kind of thing the Japanese are tempted to work with on their own indigenous spirits. The massive flavour profile will win appreciation from anyone who enjoys a no-holds-barred rye. **40%**

### DISTILLERIE GLANN AR MOR

⋇ **Taol Esa 1999** dist Dec 99, bott May 04 db **(94)** n24 perhaps the best marriage yet of malt and French wine: the high quality Bordeaux is so easy to detect (and even a touch of vinegar), but it's the effortless integration with the rich barley and resultant mildly salty, spicy complexity that really sets the pulses racing. It's the best of both worlds. Magnifique!; t24 salivating and sensuous, again we have complete harmony between the pulsing grape and the vivid, mildly honeyed barley. The trick, though, is that it never becomes too sweet or dry; f22 quite long and shows just a little too much bitter oak b24 Taol Esa means "The Essay" in traditional Breton language. And this really is an essay in finely distilled whisky matured in sympathetic casks. A genuine joy. And honour, due to its scarcity. Because not only are there just 99 bottles of this, the still with which it was made is now redundant. I sincerely hope they bring it back into service for one special distillation a year. **46%. nc ncf.** *99 bottles.*

### DISTILLERIE WARENGHEM

**Armorik** db **(63)** n15 t18 f14 b16. Too feinty and what appears to be caramel dependent. Some of the fat, oiliness is pleasant for a while, but a long way to go on the learning curve here. **40%**

## DOMAINE MAVELA DISTILLERIE ARTISANALE

⇝ **P&M Pure Malt Whisky** bott 05 db **(91) n**23 an extraordinary injection of kumquats makes for a pleasing – and individualistic – aroma; **t**23 amazingly sharp and mouth-watering. There are flavours new to me here – and that doesn't happen often; **f**22 almost bitter at times; **b**23 an outstanding whisky which, being French, seems to offer a style that is entirely different from anything else around. I have been told there is chestnut within the grist which, strictly speaking, means this is not whisky as we know it. My French is not good enough to discover the truth of this. Between now and the 2008 Bible I shall travel to the distillery in Corsica to get to the bottom of this. In the meantime, though, I shall occasionally enjoy this delicious dram! **42%**

## Blends

⇝ **P&M Blend Supérieur (82) n**21 **t**21 **f**20 **b**20. Bitter and botanical, though no shortage of complexity. **40%.** *Mavela Distillerie.*

⇝ **P&M Whisky (89) n**22 light, lemony, mildly Canadian wheated in style; **t**23 beautiful, sharpish citrus ensures a salivating experience; **f**22 soft oak lowers the sweetness levels; **b**22 no mistaking this is from a fruit distillery. Still quite North American, though. **40%.** *Mavela Distillerie.*

**Whisky Breton (80) n**19 **t**20 **f**21 **b**20. An altogether better effort; malty and assertively drinkable with attractive, firm, chewy grains and a late, lingering sweetness. A lively, characterful and creditable blend. **40%**

## GERMANY
### BLAUE MAUS
#### Eggolsheim-Neuses. Working.

**Blaue Maus Single Malt** Fass Nr 2, dist 8/92, bott 3/04 db **(83) n**20 **t**21 **f**22 **b**20. The nose offers childhood memories of damp washing through a mangler. **40%**

**Blaue Maus Single Malt Whisky** Fassstärke 2, dist 8/93, bott 9/02 db **(84) n**19 **t**22 **f**21 **b**22. This is more of a man than a maus: big, oily, heavyweighted deep molassed sweetness. Lovely spices, too. Really well balanced and a better nose would catapult it into the top bracket. **40%**

**Blaue Maus Single Malt** Fass Nr 1, dist Jun 94, bott Apr 05 db **(85) n**22 **t**19 **f**23 **b**21. Bitter delivery apart, this is getting better and better. **40%**

**Blaue Maus Single Malt** Munhner Whiskyfestival 4-6 Februar 2005 Fass Nr 1, dist Jul 90 db **(93) n**23 minty, lavender, faintly herbal; **t**24 dry and toasty at first, there is a mad rush of malt before the soft liquorice, oaky notes begin to arrive in numbers, as does the deep honey; **f**22 cream toffee and wonderful honeycomb; **b**24 tasted blind this could so easily be mistaken for a bourbon. The oldest European mainland whisky I have ever come across. **40%**

**Gruner Hund Single Malt** Fass Nr 3, dist Sep 92, bott Apr 05, db **(84) n**22 **t**21 **f**20 **b**21. Chewy, silky, spicey: cream toffee has edged out usual complexity. **40%**

**Krottentaler Single Malt Whisky** Fassstärke 1, dist 6/94, bott 7/02 db **(77) n**16 **t**21 **f**21 **b**19. On the feinty side but, as ever, the result is a big whisky with chewy sweet oils and intense malt. Once over the nose, it's a lovely journey. **40%**

**Krottentaler Single Malt** Fass Nr 2 dist 7/94, bott 3/04 db **(87) n**21 freshbaked fruitcake; **t**23 quite an impressive arrival of legions of burnt raisins sweetened with toffee; **f**22 sweet with lingering oak and barley; **b**21 caramel cuts out some complexity but also the bitterness: a very big whisky. **40%**

**Krottentaler Single Malt** Fass Nr 1 dist Jul 95, bott Jan 05 db **(90) n**23 wonderfully confident honey with surging bourbony tones. Rich and beautiful; **t**21 the usual Blaue Maus bitterness is calmed down here by silky, sweetening malt. Strands of liquorice continue the soft bourbon theme; **f**22 toasty and delicate with receding vanilla; **b**23 a little gem of a whisky. **40%**

**Mouse** db **(92)** **n**22 rich, big vanilla and thick malt: a touch of distant honey to a nose more akin to bourbon than malt; **t**24 sensational: the mouthfeel is near perfect with just the right amount of subtle sweetness leaking into the big oak; **f**23 more bitter as the tannins mount, roast Java coffee; **b**23 this is an outstanding whisky that any bourbon lover will cross a few countries for. And you will have to: this is malt kept in a small barrel at the distillery bar at Egolsheim/Neuses. You cannot get it anywhere else. *Strength unknown.*

**Piraten Pur Malt Whisky** Fass Nr 1 dist 8/95, bott 1/04 db **(84)** **n**20 **t**21 **f**22 **b**21. As chewy as a mouth of tobacco and Bristol-fashion on the superbly honeyed if somewhat toffeed finale. Whimsically, the first-ever whisky I know of to come with its own leather eye-patch: just as well you don't need your sight to enjoy this. Do ye all knock it back at once ... **40%**

**Schwarzer Pirat Single Malt** Fass Nr 1 dist 7/94, bott 3/04 db **(86)** **n**19 **t**22 **f**23 **b**22. Similar in many ways to Krottentaler (bott 04) except that there is less toffee and the complexity has risen accordingly. **40%**

**Schwarzer Pirat Single Malt Whisky** Fassstärke 3, dist 7/94, bott 9/02 db **(77)** **n**17 **t**20 **f**20 **b**20. Again the nose is hard going but this is compensated for by a sweet, spicy, charismatic malt on the palate. **40%**

**Schwarzer Pirat Single Malt** Fass Nr 2 dist Aug 95, bott May 05 **(87)** **n**21 bourbon and honeycomb; **t**22 sweet liquorice and toasted raisins; **f**22 excellent depth to the finish: like an of bourbon with leathery liquorice and burnt honeycomb; **b**22 delightfully complex and engaging. **40%**

**Spinnaker Single Malt** Fass nr 2 dist 7/93, bott 1/04 db **(85)** **n**19 **t**22 **f**22 **b**22. Seriously enjoyable, intense malt whisky. **40%**

**Spinnaker Single Malt Whisky** Fassstärke 3, dist 9/93, bott 9/02 db **(82)** **n**19 **t**22 **f**21 **b**20. Superbly made malt, delicate in its weight and possessing a light muscovado sugar sweetness the entire voyage. Just a little heavy on the nose to be a ship-shape great whisky, but I could drink this one any time any place. Especially Germany ... **40%**

**Spinnaker Single Malt** Fass 1, dist May 92, bott May 05 db **(89)** **n**23 comfortable signs of age with the oak melting into a treacle cake and intense malt sweetness; **t**23 bitter coffee and then sweetening molasses; **f**21 tons of natural oak-stained caramel; **b**22 the consistency from this small distillery is getting impressive. **40%**

## GRUELS

**Schwabischer Whisky Single Grain** db **(80)** **n**19 **t**21 **f**19 **b**21. Full credit for an excellent first attempt. The nose is good if a tad off-key and the dying embers a little bitter. But the intense oily, rich, sweet, buttery middle is a delight. Familiarity breeds anything but contempt with this characterful whisky. **43%**

**Schwabischer Whisky Single Grain 1991** db dist Feb 91 **(84)** **n**20 **t**22 **f**21 **b**21. Nutty-toffee nose translates into a firm, mouth watering whisky of some finesse that loses out at the finish with that toffee again. **43%**

## BRENNEREI HOEHLER

**Hessicher Whiskey** db dist 17 Feb 01 bott 17 Feb 04 **(91)** **n**23 A diamond hard nose, the sparkle offered by a clever malt-oaky sweetness, the rigidity by the unforgiving rye: lovely stuff; **t**22 stunning arrival of rye that does a comprehensive hatchet job on the tastebuds as it gets into stride. The corn offers a more neutral sweetness; **f**23 remains hard at the core but there is a toffee sweetness lurking and some latent spice; **b**23 one of the real perks of the job is the sheer diversity: here we have a superbly made bourbon style German whiskey with roughly 56/22/22 recipe of corn/rye/malted barley. And it has been distilled to a very high standard. It doesn't taste exactly like bourbon, nor is it like malt. But it is entirely delicious. Go and find it. **42%**

## OBST-KORN BRENNERIE
### Köngen. Working.

**Schwäbischer Whisky (76) n**18 **t**20 **f**19 **b**19. Digestive biscuit and enormously intense malt. Sharp and slightly out of alignment. **40%**.

## BRENNEREI RABEL

**Brennerei Rabel Single Grain (81) n**19 **t**21 **f**20 **b**21. Quite light and very gently oiled, but the integration with oak makes for an impressive depth. **40%**

## SLYRS

**Slyrs Bavarian Single Malt 1999** db **(84) n**20 **t**21 **f**22 **b**21. Competently made malt whisky that celebrates its clean simplicity. Nose is vanilla-bound but on the palate it takes off slowly, first clearing a soft oak hurdle and then really letting the malt go into overdrive. Thoroughly enjoyable, high-quality quaffing whisky that will need to be made in greater amounts if they keep up this standard. **43%**

**Slyrs Bavarian Single Malt 2001** db **(79) n**18 **t**19 **f**22 **b**20. Different fingerprints from previous bottlings with the nose offering curious bacon pizza and the palate shimmering with distant honey on the excellent malty finish. **43%**

**Slyrs Bavarian Single Malt 2002 (84) n**20 **t**21 **f**22 **b**21. The 1999 version may well have been a blip, as this is so much closer to the '99 in style (I have this very moment noticed that I have marked them identically!), though this one has a touch extra sweetness and attitude coursing through it. **43%**

···: **Slyrs Bavarian Single Malt 2003** L14413 **(88) n**21 docile honey and marzipan; **t**22 lush barley with a tiny dash of golden syrup; **f**23 now this is classy with fabulous length and glorious cocoa, complete with oils, to aid the dull barley throb; vaguely bourbony at times; **b**22 a distinct improvement on all previous bottlings: this young distillery is finding its feet with style. **43%**

## SONNEN SCHEIN

**Sonnen Schein Sherry Wood Finish 1989** db bott 00 **(57) n**14 **t**17 **f**12 **b**14. Oddly enough, the sherry appears to accentuate the dreadful tobacco smoke character to this. The finish really does hurt. **43%**

**Sonnen Schein Single Malt Whisky 1989** bott 00 db **(69) n**17 **t**17 **f**18 **b**17. Very unusual stale tobacco aroma and possibly (I am guessing as a lifelong non-smoker) taste. A whisky that tastes slightly better second time round, though not by much. Room for improvement here, I think. **43%**

## STEIGERWALD

**Whisky aus dem Steigerwald 1988 Single Grain 13 Years Old (88) n**21 just wonderful sugared vanilla; **t**23 the tastebuds are brushed with spices and golden syrup. Some of the oak is perhaps a little too old, but such is the delicate nature of the sugars present it works stupendously well; firm and probing throughout; **f**22 long, gentle vanilla with oak now tamed; **b**22 highly unusual malt that at times reminded me of OTT over-aged pot still Irish. But this has a deftness to the sweetness that makes for a lovely dram. **43%**. *Celtic Spirit Whisky Jounal.*

## BRENNEREI VOLKER THEURER
### Tübingen-Unterjesingen. Working.

**Black Horse Ammertal Whisky Malt & Grain (88) n**20 **t**23 **f**23 **b**23 a busy, beautifully punctuated whisky that gets past the indifferent nose to unleash a welter of complex tone poems. Hardly surprising, considering this 7-year-old is made up from 70% malted barley and 30% wheat and rye and has been aged in three different types of cask ranging from sherry refill to new German oak...whew!!! **40%**

⁘ **Black Horse Ammertal Whisky Malt & Grain** BL 2005 **(91) n**22 a shade cleaner perhaps; a touch of celery and bourbon to the nougat and nuts but it's the warm haystacks that star; **t**23 soft barley layers arrive early before a delivery of something more profound and tasty - the rye; **f**23 a wonderfully rich continuation on a theme, though now some Java coffee and demerara-sweetened cocoa have become embroiled with the juicier grains; **b**23 less immediate impact, mouth-watering or rye-rich. Or so it at first seems. Then the gradual realisation that the complexity levels have risen significantly, as have the distilling skills. Quite excellent. **40%**

## UNIVERSITÄT HOHENHEIM

**Hohenheim Universität Single Malt (82) n**21 **t**20 **f**20 **b**21. The aroma is atractively nutty, marzipan even, and clean; the taste offers gentle oak, adding some weight to an otherwise light, refreshing maltiness. Pleasant if unspectacular. **40%.** *Made at the university as an experiment. Later sold!*

## LATVIA

**L B Lavijas Belzams (83) n**20 **t**22 **f**20 **b**21. Soft and yielding on the palate, this is said to be made from Latvian rye, though of all the world's rye whiskies this really does have to be the softest and least fruity. I'll be astonished if there isn't a fair degree of thinning grain in there, too. **40%**

## POLAND
### LIEBONA GIORA

**Dark Whisky (77) n**19 **t**19 **f**20 **b**19. Lots of grain character with perhaps a tad too much toffee, but the texture is alluring and appealing and finishes well with decent oak and lustre. **40%**

## SPAIN
### Blends

**DYC (81) n**20 **t**21 **f**19 **b**21. Thin and grainy in parts but the bite is attractive and assertive while the malt comfortably holds its own. **40%**

## SWEDEN

⁘ **Mackmyra Preludium 01 Svensk Single Malt Whisky** bott 07 Feb 06 db **(91) n**23 gentle aniseed and Swedish oak combine for a weighty heralding to Sweden's first malt. The sweet malty edge ensures balance and helps cushion the impact. Once you acclimatise, it makes for gently honeyed, surprisingly soft nosing; **t**24 exceptional body weight and near perfect oil ratio. The barley purrs over the tastebuds, leaving a manuka honey trail in its wake; **f**21 slightly bitter as the oaks gain a foothold; spices I had expected to see earlier arrive with burnt toast; **b**23 So here it is: a new dawn (from a country that has far fewer than most), a new distillery, a new whisky, a new distilling nation. We'll draw a discreet veil over Mackmyra's claims that this is the first ever Scandinavian single malt (actually, chaps, you were beaten to it by a decade or two by the Finns and Danes) and instead concentrate on a whisky I have been watching mature since the end of the last century. Or was it the beginning of this one? Well, whenever, I was the first whisky guy to visit the place...and predicted stardom. So I have left this to last while writing The Bible 2007, as I regard this the most vital and exciting addition to the whisky world this year and wanted to leave on a high. Or low, depending on the final product. Well it is certainly different, something it always promised to be from the evidence of my past visits. The input of European oak (or should I say Scandinavian?) has been vital as it has shaped the nose in a direction some whisky lovers may find strange. But you will also find a similar tint to the aromas of whiskies made in Germany, Austria, the Czech Republic and elsewhere. This is one whisky I had to swallow: no matter how professional, there is nothing like a touch of romance to make you do things that perhaps you shouldn't...I can't say it's faultless: the finish might have been improved. But is it good whisky? Indubitably. Is it excellent whisky? Undoubtedly. Is it a true great? Not yet. But it unquestionably has the potential. **55.6%**

⟐ **Mackmyra Preludium 02 Svensk Single Malt Whisky** bott 14.7.06 db **(91)** **n**23 a dense, tight nose with better control of the oak and some welcome citrus to thin and integrate with the barley. Intriguingly, there is something of the Alpine meadow about this with a delightful floral lilt; **t**23 oily delivery with the citrus again digging deep into the oak; the barley is more shielded here and appears towards the very middle as some whacky vanillins also take position; **f**22 a curiously smoky finish – probably something local – but I wish they'd get a handle on that trailing bitterness; **b**23 a roller-coaster of a malt, at times superbly integrated, at others heading off in any direction at will. Oh, if only Sven had been this unpredictable and exciting... **54.2%**

⟐ **Mackmyra Preludium 03 Svensk Single Malt Whisky** bott 13 Oct 06 db **(95)** **n**24 Mackmyra!!! That unique half kipper, half smoky bacon, half Rupp (and there's nothing more unique than three halves) that comes from malting from local wood and peat. I've only ever found the style at this distillery, and couldn't wait until I saw it in bottle. I am not disappointed. Subtle? Superb? Not half...!!!; **t**24 for the first time it is the barley that really springs forward, sweet, gristy and young. As it should be. The oak has backed off allowing the malt full rein. There is also an unexpected fruity element to this, almost like powering Melton Hunt Cake, with a orange peel and sultana; **f**23 still evidence of that damn bitterness. But now there is so much to counter it, especially those long, glorious, silky waves of smoked barley; **b**24 this was the one I had been waiting for – especially the nose. If the first two bottlings were the distillery clearing its throat, here is the speech that clearly marks Mackmyra's intentions to be a complete one off. This is the Great Whisky I had been hoping for: full of unique aromas, flavours and shapes on the palate and more delicate than I could possibly have predicted.. Some of you, I suspect, will taste this and wonder what all the fuss is about. All I ask is that you forget Scotch, Japanese and all the other malts for a while. Clear your mind and start afresh. Others will already be booking tickets for Stockholm. Abba Dabba Doo...!!! **52.2%**

# SWITZERLAND
## HAGEN DISTILLERY
### Huettwilen. 1919. Working.

**HR Distillery** Lott no.10099, dist Dec 99, bott Jan 05 db **(88)** **n**21 clean, fine malt. Crisp with a degree of fruit, especially freshly bitten green apple. Some soft dough adds the extra depth; **t**22 mouthwatering and deft, this offers a butterfly delivery of sweet young malt backed again by that apple-fresh fruitiness; **f**22 lovely delivery of vanilla which balances just so well with the barley; **b**22 again we have an enormously impressive whisky from Switzerland. Here we have a classic case of a whisky that has matured for a few years side by side with fruit spirit (probably apple) and has breathed in some of those delicate elements. **42%**

## BRAUEREI LOCHER
### Appenzell. Working.

**Santis Swiss Highlander Single Malt** db **(86)** **n**22 **t**22 **f**20 **b**22. Lovely stuff from a whisky that shows more than a degree of sophistication. Apparently the whisky has been matured in 60-year-old oak beer barrels and despite the age makes a telling and slightly unusual contribution. **40%**

## BRENNEREI SCHWAB
### Oberwil. Working.
**Buechibaegger Singelmalt** db **(84) n**23 **t**21 **f**20 **b**20. The nose is immaculate with essence of praline running with the malt. But the intensity of the European oak just tips the balance away from the excellence the whisky threatens. Lovely whisky, but could do with a little extra youth, though the innate sweetness does enough to see off the oaky excesses. **42%**

## MAISON LES VIGNETTES
**Glen Vignettes "Abred" Peated Swhisky Pur Malt** db **(89) n**22 delicate peat; beautifully gristy nose and the background noise is easily ignored; **t**23 awesome delivery with top-rate bittersweet edge as the peat yodels without an off-note in the background; **f**22 dryish vanilla and sweet peat; **b**22 fabulous whisky from a distillery that finds peat to its liking and suiting its style: no coastal notes here – hardly surprising ...! – but just great virtuosity with the smoke. **45%**

**Glen Vignettes "Annouim" Initial Swhisky Pur Malt** db **(85) n**19 **t**22 **f**22 **b**22. The odd distilling anomaly cannot disguise a top-grade malt of easy drinking. **45%**

**Glen Vignettes "Gwenwed" Syrah Cask Swhisky Pur Malt** db **(74) n**17 **t**20 **f**18 **b**19. A lush, big-impact malt weighed down by caramel and that distinctive celery-spicy distilling character. **45%**

## WHISKY CASTLE
### Elfingen. Working.
**8820 Whisky** 1378 Tage im Fass (days in cask) db **(87) n**20 vaguely piny and herbal; **t**22 massive malt that sweetens with each crashing wave. The opening is typically European, threatens to turn nasty but in seconds changes direction and goes into malty overdrive; **f**23 fabulous oak interaction as vanilla and very dry walnut and date cake; **b**22 one of those whiskies that grow on you once you understand that it has a different viewpoint. Hugely entertaining. **55%**. *For Wadi Brau Wadenswil.*

**Castle Hill Whisky** unfiltiert Nummer1 1125 Tage im Fass (days in cask) db **(84) n**20 **t**21 **f**22 **b**21. Big, chewy malt. The oaky bitterness is easily matched by the sweet, grassy barley. **43%**

⋆ **Castle Hill Whisky** Nummer 4, 1125 Tage im Fass **(93) n**22 big barley from a small still. There is a copperish element to this, plus a nutty intonation. Something to really get the nose into; **t**24 near perfect delivery: the full mouthfeel is stunning. Perfectly weighted, just the right degree of natural sweetness and the most glorious barley development; **f**23 a light finale yet the waves of sweet peat and vanilla are almost endless. Long, charming and a magic wand waved over the degree of gristy sweetness; **b**24 has someone moved Cardhu to Switzerland??? I am truly astonished. I have missed out on nummers 2&3 (but I'm hunting!), but this is so far removed from nummer 1 that they are hardly worth comparison. One of the cleanest, most malt intense and unerringly delightful whiskies you will find in Europe and would be a title contender but for the slightly more elegant Swissky. Reaffirmation, that Switzerland is the finest producer of malt whisky on mainland Europe. **40%**

## BRENNEREI-ZENTRUM BAUERNHOF
### Zug. Working.
**Swissky** db **(91) n**23 young, clean, fresh malt which sparkles with a hint of apple: one of the best noses on the European scene; **t**23 stunningly clean arrival and then the most delicate of malty displays that all hinges around a juicy youth to the barley. The sweetness is controlled, refined and evenly distributed; a soft oiliness helps to lubricate the tastebuds; **f**22 no less soft

and simple with the oak offering the kind of weight that can barely be detected; **b**23 while retaining a distinct character, this is the cleanest, most refreshing malt yet to come from mainland Europe. Hats off to Edi Bieri for this work of art. Moving stuff. **42%**

**Swissky** (label shows boxed drawing of pot still) db **(84) n**19 t22 f21 b22. Only the most distant hint of feintiness takes away from the beauty of this rich malt. The oils are sublime, as usual from this distillery, and the malt is sweet and chewy. If anything, I am marking down. **42%**

**Swissky** (label shows man working a pot still) db **(83) n**20 t21 f21 b21. A thinnish, clean malt at first with some decent oak depth to bolster the copper-rich finale. **42%**

**Swissky Exklusiv Abfüllung** db **(93) n**23 just so clean: absolutely flawless. Despite the clarity the malt has a Cardhueque richness and purpose that is spellbinding; **t**23 intensity of the malt is stupifying: again a Cardhu character except this probably has a bit of extra vanilla spice early on; **f**23 layers of ultraclean barley; **b**24 every year every new bottling of Eddie's just gets better and better. Only the sheer brilliance and depth of McCarthy's keeps this off small batch whisky of the year. But of the entirely non-peated or smoked variety this has no peer: there will many a distiller in Scotland who would wish their maturing spirit possessed such élan. Swiss it may be, but there is absolutely nothing neutral about this! **40%**

⋅❖⋅ **Swissky Exklusiv Abfüllung** L3365 **(94) n**23 more intrinsic barley than previous years; the oak offers the perfect frame for the diced, slightly spiced apples and pears; **t**23 mouth-watering, beautifully clean barley in Swissky's classic style; **f**24 drier, vanilla-led but the waves of rich barley and delicate oak seem endless; **b**24 a supremely distilled whisky with the most subtle oak involvement yet. Year after year this distillery bottles truly great single malt, a benchmark for Europe's growing band of small whisky distillers. **40%**

## SPEZIALITÄTENBRENNEREI ZURCHER
### Port. Working.

**Zurcher Single Lakeland Malt Whisky 3 Years Old** (dist 10 Jul 00, bott 10 Sep 03. Not stated on bottle) db **(94) n**23 t24 f23 b24. A one-off bottling from a highly respected Swiss distiller. On this evidence whisky should be a regular part of their life: for first attempt nothing short of spectacular. Had I received it when launched, would have been a certain award winner. If you happen to be in Switzerland and see one in a shop somewhere, rip the seller's arm off.... **42%**

⋅❖⋅ **Zurcher Single Lakeland 3 Years Old** dist Jul 03, bott Jul 06 db **(93) n**22 the house style of mesmerising intensity has been continued: less smoke, more spiced honey, but a hint of feints; **t**24 a real small pot still feel to this, with the richness of it all almost making you swoon; the stupendously spiced middle really does offer a fabulous counter to those sweeter, persistent honey tones and the vague fruity sub-text; the weight is sheer perfection; **f**23 the intensity dissipates slightly to allow a more relaxed vanilla-oak unfolding. The spices becoming ever more frenzied before suddenly vanishing; **b**24 the label claims smoke, but I can't find any though there's no shortage of spice. The distillery's second bottling: the first was sensational, this is Highland Park on steroids. A wonderful follow up, depite the extra width to the cut. And as for a three-year-old...well, even I'm agog...!!! Let's now hope that this will become an annual offering, rather than once every three years. We need more! **42%**

## TURKEY

**Ankara Turk Viskisi (80) n**20 t20 f19 b21. Soft and gentle despite the clear grain with soft delicate oak on the finish. Quite beautifully balanced: a genuinely charming whisky to be taken seriously. **43%**

# WALES

**Penderyn** cask nos 5–99 db **(91) n**23 raisins on the nose, light playful malt and then a backdrop of sweet wine; **t**23 absolutely staggering arrival on the palate of malt landing with almost snowflake delicateness. Immediately a second movement, this time of bitter-sweet fruit, blood orange included, sweeps down over the startled tastebuds. Astonishing stuff; **f**22 slightly bitter and tart towards the finish and two variants of oak begin to dive into the melee; **b**23 it was my pleasure and privilege to be the first person from outside the company to discuss and analyse the beauty of this whisky at its spectacular official launch on St David's Day 2004. I told them they were tasting not just an historic malt whisky, but one that deserved the highest praise in its own right. Re-tasting it again for the Bible, I stand by every word. **46%**

**Penderyn** bott code 04/02 db **(89) n**22 **t**22 **f**22 **b**23 exceptional balance and charisma for a whisky so young. **46%**

**Penderyn** bott code 04/03 db **(86) n**21 **t**21 **f**22 **b**22. Not quite so well integrated as the previous bottlings, though cask choice was probably limited by now. Even so, still a gentle joy, especially for its tender years. **46%**

**Penderyn** bott code 04/04 db **(90) n**23 **t**23 **f**21 **b**23 the old Welsh magic has returned. Brilliant! **46%**

**Penderyn** bott code 05-04 db **(91) n**22 big oak input; **t**24 salivating stuff that wallows in the sweetest young malt while combining with an ethereal oak presence; just so wonderfully lip-smacking; **f**22 dries quite forcefully towards the finish as the delicate fruit fades; **b**23 they've done it again! Another outrageously fine whisky for one so young. **46%. ncf.**

**Penderyn** bott code 08-04 db **(86) n**20 **t**23 **f**21 **b**22. There appears to be an extra intensity of fruit that works well on the palate but is too much for the nose: proving what a delicate flower this is. **46%. ncf.**

**Penderyn** bott code Sep 04 db **(81) n**19 **t**21 **f**20 **b**21. A fraction warming and relatively off-key early on, and after an attractive recovery vanishes off the radar again except for un-Penderynesque bitterness. Good, but not up to the usual very high standards. **46%. ncf.**

**Penderyn** bott code Oct 04 db **(93) n**22 lithe, almost organic in its shape and freshness; **t**24 what a quite astonishing display of ultra-ripe grape sitting so comfortably with a gristy malt: the tastebuds are worked overtime to cope; **f**23 beautiful oaky spice but with wave upon wave of fresh, crushed, moist sultana; **b**24 a brilliant recovery from the previous month's expression, this absolutely oozes fresh fruit and beautifully textured malt. Go find! **46%. ncf.**

**Penderyn** bott code Nov 04 db **(89) n**21 unsalted butter on spotted dog; **t**24 fabulous combination of malt concentrate and fruitcake; **f**22 the oak hits back with a late bitter edge; **b**22 the mouth arrival is to Di [Dai?] for.... **46%. ncf.**

**Penderyn** bott code Dec 04 db **(83) n**19 **t**22 **f**22 **b**20. Assertive and warming, but struggles slightly against a big oak imbalance. **46%. ncf.**

**Penderyn** bott code Jan 05 db **(91) n**20 this really takes the biscuit: hints of crushed gingernuts amid the fruit shortbread and digestive; **t**24 mind-blowing malt delivery underpinned by a sensational wave of voluptuous grape: the balance could have been calculated with a slide rule; **f**23 first-rate spice adds extra length; **b**24 what a little jewel! The malt somehow finds the legs to pierce through the powerful Madeira shell. **46%. ncf.**

**Penderyn** bott code Feb 05 db **(82) n**18 **t**22 **f**21 **b**21. After the disappointingly soapy nose the fruit integrates with the malt superbly to save the day and deliver a decent malt. **46%. ncf.**

⦂ **Penderyn** bott code Jun 05, casks 55-165 db **(89) n**23 an impressive collision between candy store grape and thumping oak; **t**22 soft and sultana-led; **f**22 drier as the vanillas arrive, but tantalizing fruit to the last; **b**22 for those of you wondering what happened to the March, April and May 2005 bottlings, fear not: they don't exist. The whiskies which would have supplied them were instead harnessed to create the special "Grand Slam" edition, to celebrate the country's rare success in the Six Nations Rugby championship. But service is resumed as normal here with a delicately fruity number. **46%. ncf.**

⬤ **Penderyn** bott code July 05, casks 160-270 db **(91) n**23 molten vanilla ice-cream topped with breadfruit ad sultanas. Very different and curiously attractive; **t**22 mouth-watering barley, lots of oak buzz but calmed by lush fruit; **f**23 just so delicate and complex, with more of what went before except in tantalizing, shadowy form; **b**23 a complex, thinking man's whisky. **46%. ncf.**

⬤ **Penderyn** bott code Aug 05, casks 160-270 db **(79) n**21 **t**21 **f**18 **b**19. Mouth-watering and juicy as usual but a bitter bite to the finish has crept in. **46%. ncf.**

⬤ **Penderyn** bott code Sep 05 db **(87) n**22 loads of soft oaky vanillins of varying hues **t**22 big, clean barley kick-off and then becomes oily and little spiced; **f**21 crème caramel; **b**22 lots of natural caramels (and for those of you who write in to me, no, Penderyn doesn't add colouring to their whisky, though they don't yet state the fact) make this an charming and unusual ride. Oh, and the sharp-eyed collectors amongst you may, also, have noticed that there are no barrel references to this bottling. That is because they kind of lost track back in Wales (see the confusing numbers above)...and just gave up...!! **46%. ncf.**

⬤ **Penderyn** 750ml bottle USA batch db **(93) n**23 injection of extra oak, light hints of young bourbon and sultana pudding; **t**24 big oak-fruit statement from the off with spices abounding and some zesty, refreshing barley filling in elsewhere. A mouth-filler with no shortage of bourbon notes; **f**23 pretty lengthy with the accent on chalky vanilla; **b**23 quite weighty affair compared to other bottlings so far and the chewability goes off the scales: the mouth arrival is classic. Or at least as classic as a distillery this young can get... **46% (92 proof). ncf.** *(bott 01 Sept 05 but not stated).*

⬤ **Penderyn** bott code Oct 05 db **(92) n**22 wonderful, half-praline/half-Lubeck-style dry marzipan wrapped in soft, European oak; **t**24 pure silk: the yielding grape carries with it in equal measures delicate barley and firm oak. A myriad of textures; **f**23 lovely spices tingle and sultanas and spotted dick make for a lovely finale; **b**23 sumptuous and highly complex, a malt that takes some time to unravel. And it's worth every second. **46%. ncf.**

⬤ **Penderyn** bott code Nov 05, casks 160-270 db **(84) n**20 **t**21 **f**22 **b**21. Nose suggests a bitter-ish, almost fruit-stone brandy style borne out by the early delivery. Gentle, fruity somewhat sweet and simplistic delivery. **46%. ncf.**

⬤ **Penderyn** bott code Dec 05 db **(88) n**21 dried grapeskin and vanilla; **t**23 lush, fat; some very serious Madeira influence; **f**22 creamy-textured vanilla and toasted raisin; **b**22 one of the fruitier expressions. **46%. ncf.**

⬤ **Penderyn** bott code B266 - Jan 06 db **(89) n**21 weak orangey-citrus, vanilla; **t**23 the tastebuds are nuked by big spice parade; **f**22 butterscotch and vanilla; late juicy barley; **b**23 wonderfully lively and bracing. **46% (92 proof). ncf.**

⬤ **Penderyn** bott code Feb 06 db **(92) n**22 spotted dog, sultanas and custard; **t**23 the spicy spearhead is swamped with some salivating grape and barley; **f**24 long, multi-layered and continues of the clean fruit theme. Perhaps the softest Penderyn landing yet; **b**23 starts off similarly to the Jan bottling, but then fruits out. **46%. ncf.**

⬤ **Penderyn** bott code Mar 06 db **(83) n**20 **t**21 **f**21 **b**21. Busy vanilla with some spicy oak and young bourbon notes. **46%. ncf.**

⬤ **Penderyn** bott code Apr 06 db **(85) n**20 **t**22 **f**22 **b**21. Soft, supple and opens out to offer a fruity sheen. **46%. ncf.**

⬤ **Penderyn** bott code May 06 db **(91) n**22 an unusual salty tang complements the barley; **t**23 soft delivery yet very busy with a mottled barley and oak effect; **f**23 the usual vanilla, but a lovely gristy cameo; **b**23 the first bottling for a couple of months to accentuate the barley. **46%. ncf.**

⋆ **Penderyn** bott code Jun 06 db **(88)** n21 in your face pubescent bourbon; t22 lovely early wine delivery, refreshing and vaguely tart. Soft vanilla and barley bring up the second act; f23 long and astonishingly well defined and cultured. The mildest spice buzz accentuates the oak and the fruit-barley core goes on forever; b22 in many ways, this is a pretty average Penderyn. Which says much... **46%.**

⋆ **Penderyn** bott code Jul 06 db **(90)** n21 slightly disproportionate oak; t23 pure silk as the plummy, greengagey fruit takes hold and mouth-watering barley makes a sweet counter attack; f23 back to the oak which is again heading down a honeycomb-bourbon path; b23 another big whisky from this small distillery. **46%. ncf.**

⋆ **Penderyn** bott code Aug 06 db **(88)** n20 hmmm, slightly sweaty armpit. Misbalance between fruit and some of the oak extract; t23 no problem here as the palate is swamped with a glorious marriage of astonishingly fit grape and ultra-intense barley. There is a teasing spice rift towards the middle; f23 more grapey glory on the finale which is long, warming and just so wonderfully delicate; b22 ignore the nose and just get on to the tasting bit! **46%. ncf.**

**Penderyn Cask Strength First Release** db **(86)** n21 t21 f22 b22. A very different Penderyn that should seduce the gin and tonic merchants: oddly delicious. **61.8%**

⋆ **Penderyn Grand Slam Edition 2005** Madeira finish db **(89)** n22 light grape, spiced oak; t23 soothing juicy fruit then a delivery of spice and chewy oak: very much the nose in liquid form, except more intense; f21 a movement toward bitterness is checked by honeycomb; b23 chunky and chewy: a good try, some Welsh might say... **46%. ncf.** *Limited Bottling.*

**The Penderyn Millenium Cask 2000** db **(90)** n22 delicate soft-bourbon oaky tones, which is not what you expect from a three-year-old whisky; the fruit is soft yet somehow champions the clean malt; t22 warming, massively malt at first and then big vanilla and a mouthwatering grape and lychee fruit cocktail; f23 just so long with loads of natural toffee vanilla perfectly at home with the concentrated malt and layered fruitiness; b23 this is one very complex whisky offering style and first-class integrity. A dilemma for those who own this historic whisky: luckily you can taste the miniature while keeping the full bottle for posterity. Or should that be the other way round? **61.6%**

**Penderyn Oloroso Edition** db **(76)** n17 t20 f21 b18. By no means showing Penderyn at its best: the nose is poor and imbalanced (it needs a good half-hour in the glass to find some clean fruit) but there is a degree of compensation on the sweet depth of the finish, especially once the influence of the grape has lessened. A reminder of what a delicate creature this Welsh whisky is and just how steep the learning curve can be.... **50%**

**Penderyn Peated Edition** db **(92)** n22 just so delicate and gristy: the smoke almost makes an apology on its aromatic arrival; t24 subtle, mouthwatering and quite stunningly crafted; the malt works on two levels in that the barley is clear and clean, yet the smoke gives much to chew on. The middle, in which some spicy oak interaction takes place, is almost the stuff of erotic dreams; f22 not too long, with a gentle, pulsing smokiness; b24 this low level of peating absolutely fits the shape of the whisky like a glove: inspired stuff! You would never in a million years believe its youth. **50%**

⋆ **Penderyn Welsh Rugby Union 125th Anniversary Edition** Madeira finish db **(95)** n23 dripping in lightly spiced grape, the vanilla-barley sub-plot adds just the right weight; t24 My word! There'll be a few people in Madeira surprised that their fortified wine can be quite this good...the spice-fruit balance is now the stuff of Welsh legend; f24 the accent falls on the oak but so many layers of grape and barley and black-peppered spice wash over it that you wonder if it will ever end. Even a tendency towards bitterness works in its favour as that honeycomb arrives to absorb it. Stunning; b24 lamb apart, the best thing from Wales I have ever got my lips round... (!) And I say that with full apologies to a young lady from Maesteg, but it's true, you see... **50%.** *1250 bottles.*

# World Whiskies

I have long said that whisky can be made just about anywhere in the world; that it is not writ large in stone that it is the inalienable right for just Scotland, Ireland, Kentucky and Canada to have it all to themselves. And so, it seems, it is increasingly being proved. Perhaps only sandy deserts and fields of ironstone can prevent its make physically and Islam culturally, though even that has not been a barrier to malt whisky being distilled in both Pakistan and Turkey. While not even the world's highest mountains or jungle can prevent the spread of barley and copper pot.

Outside of North America and Europe, whisky's traditional nesting sites, you can head in any direction and find it being made. South America may be well known for its rum, but in the south of Brazil, an area populated by Italian and German settlers many generations back, malt whisky is thriving. In even more lush and tropical climes it can now also be found, with Thailand leading the way.

Japan has long represented Asia with distinction and whisky-making there is in such an advanced state and to such a high standard Jim Murray's Whisky Bible has given it its own section. But while neighbouring South Korea has ended its malt distilling venture, further east, and at a very unlikely altitude, Nepal has forged a small industry to team up, geographically, with fellow malt distillers India and Pakistan. The one malt whisky from this region making inroads in world markets is India's Amrut single malt. The tasting notes included here are from the first bottling, but for the 2007 edition I included two extraordinary single casks, too. Both reveal that the quality really can raise eyebrows: this is a much better balanced affair, quite excellent in places, and it appears the distillers are beginning to learn how to make the most of their fast-maturing stocks.

And Africa is also represented. There has long been a tradition of blending Scotch malt with South African grain but now there is single malt there, as well. Two malt distilleries, to be precise, with a second being opened this year at the Drayman's Brewery in Pretoria

One relatively new whisky-making region is due immediate study: Australia. From a distance of 12,000 miles, the waters around Australia's distilleries appear to be muddied. Quality appears to range from the very good to extremely poor. And during the back end of 2004 I managed to discover this first hand when I visited three Tasmanian distilleries and Bakery Hill in Melbourne which perhaps leads the way regarding quality malt whisky made south of the Equator.

Certainly green shoots are beginning to sprout at the Tasmania Distillery which has now moved its operation away from its Hobart harbour site to an out of town one close to the airport. The first bottlings of that had been so bad that it will take some time and convincing for those who have already tasted it to go back to it again. However, having been to the warehouse — and having tasted samples from every single cask they have on site — I reported in previous Bibles that it was only a matter of time before those first offerings would be little more than distant — though horrific — memories. Well, as predicted, it is now safe to put your head above the parapet. Their latest bottling was a bloody beaut.

It may still be a year or two before Whisky Tasmania's malt is ripe enough for bottling, though they have now made some heavily peated spirit which will give them vatting options in three or four years time. Away from Tasmania there is malt distilling — and further plans to distil — all over Australia. On that has already made it into the shops is from Booie Range, which like Sullivan's Cove suffers from a frighteningly unattractive nose, but unlike early bottlings of the Hobart whisky regroups and recovers significantly on the palate. Meanwhile, the remaining casks of Wilson's malt from New Zealand are disappearing fast and when in New Zealand I discovered the stills from there were not just making rum in Fiji but whisky as well. We are all aware of the delights of island whisky ... just what a Pacific Island whisky will be like though? I can feel another journey coming on .... Which leaves Antarctica as the only continent not making whisky, though what some of those scientists get up to for months on end no one knows. Still, effluent might be a problem there, though it should make the perfect whisky with ice ...

# ARGENTINA

**Breeders Choice (84) n**21 **t**22 **f**21 **b**20. A sweet blend using Scottish malt and, at the helm, an unusually lush Argentinian grain. **40%**

# AUSTRALIA

## BAKERY HILL DISTILLERY, 1999. Operating.

∴ **Bakery Hill Classic Malt** barrel 2606, bott 06 db **(93) n**23 enough citrus to start a Vitamin C factory; beautifully refreshing with pulsing malts; **t**23 salivating and fresh with continuous waves of young, clean barley with not all the new make element completely lost; **f**24 major complexity here as the oak inches itself in with a vanilla sheen, but malt refuses to fade; **b**23 just so beautiful..!!! **46%. ncf.**

∴ **Bakery Hill Classic Malt** db **(83) n**19 **t**22 **f**21 **b**21. Lots of serious attitude and gristy sweetness, but a tad feinty. **46%**

**Bakery Hill Classic Malt** cask no. 08, bott 04 db **(91) n**22 florid, highly intense malt with a speckle of feint and peat; **t**23 beautifully salivating and rich with the intensity of the sweet malt leaping off the scales; **f**23 mega cocoa, long and wonderfully structured wind-down; **b**23 this has moved on massively from the first test bottlings of a year ago. The slight feints burn off on the nose quickly and we are left with something copper and malt rich and very special from Australia's finest distillery. **46%**

**Bakery Hill Classic Malt Cask Strength** db **(87) n**22 astonishingly clean with young gooseberries attached to the malt; **t**22 young malt rips through the tastebuds and settles comfortably with an oily landing; **f**22 big cocoa thrust seems to be the hallmark of the distillery; **b**21 relatively youthful and for all its malty razzmatazz would benefit with a touch more oak. **65%**

∴ **Bakery Hill Classic Malt Cask Strength** barrel 2606, bott 06 db **(94) n**23 a distinct Speyside style with fresh grasses and citric fruits linking with delicate vanilla for a beaut of an aroma; **t**24 almost unbelievable barley intensity, but wonderful cocoa background (curiously cocoa can arrive as an effect of new make, slightly under-matured malt, or later from the oak: here it is possibly from all of these); **f**24 that wonderful cocoa theme continues but again the barley is spot on; **b**23 there are about 20 distilleries in Speyside that would die to be able to make a whisky this stunningly integrated. Young, barely pubescent but sheer, unadulterated, class... **60.1%**

∴ **Bakery Hill Classic Malt Cask Strength** db **(86) n**20 **t**22 **f**23 **b**21. A shadow of something feinty, but nothing like the 46% version. The result, though, is about as big a whisky as you'll get for something theoretically unsmoked...! **60.1%**

**Bakery Hill Double Wood** cask no. 0508, bott 04, db **(80) n**19 **t**19 **f**21 **b**21. The introduction of the French oak serves only to add a certain fruity astringency to an otherwise clean and attractive dram. **46%**

∴ **Bakery Hill Double Wood** db **(84) n**21 **t**22 **f**20 **b**21. Attractively chewy, juicy in places but ultimately heavy duty and a tad fey on the finish. **46%**

∴ **Bakery Hill Double Wood** cask no. 2621, bott 06 db **(91) n**23 juicy; incredible clarity to the barley; **t**23 decent spice peppers the fruity barley; a lovely bitter-sweet tale; **f**22 long, lush and light; **b**23 does whisky come any more refreshing than this? **46%**

**Bakery Hill Peated Malt** cask no. 12, bott 04 db **(90)** n22 soft peat harmonises with intense malt, deftly weighted and oozing class; t23 there is teasing gentleness to the smoke that borders on eroticism, the sweetness is refined and layered with oak piling in the riches; f22 thins out a little towards the dry finale; b23 for sureness of touch at such young age, this is quite an amazing malt. For those who prefer their peat brushed on rather than glued. **46%**

⠿ **Bakery Hill Peated Malt** cask n. 2006, bott 06 db **(93)** n23 "dry" iodine: nothing coastal, just a tangy, clean peatiness lightened by soft citrus; t23 sweet, fresh young and then a big bursting out of grassy barley amid the smoke and spices; f23 pretty long with lashings of late vanilla and butterscotch; remains salivating; b24 seriously well-made malt with genuine complexity. Textbook balance. **46%**

⠿ **Bakery Hill Peated Malt** db **(89)** n21 ultra delicate: the very lightest smoke and vanilla; t22 delightful barley sugar lead with peat tagging along as a faint shadow; f23 the peats begin to gather and some spices arrive; b23 restrained and delicate from first to last. **46%**

**Bakery Hill Peated Malt Cask Strength** cask no. 14, bott 04 (aged 4 years) db **(94)** n24 kippery aroma with a dash of lemon on the side; t23 a real mouthful of subtle, pulsating peats which have to battle through the sweet malt; young but has such extraordinary depth and charisma; f24 goes into overdrive, fabulously long with layer upon layer of encrusted peat that clings limpet-like to the roof of the mouth; b23 show this to anyone and tell them it not an Islay: they will never believe you. The phenol levels here are quite stunning, but so too is the excellence of distillation. I found this cask in Bakery Hill's warehouse last year and swooned, even queried its origins – so distillery Dave Baker bottled it! The good news is that I have tasted a cask or two similar to this at the distillery: there is more of this kind of brilliance to come over the years! **65%**

⠿ **Bakery Hill Peated Malt Cask Strength** cask no. 2006, bott 06 db **(91)** n22 disorganised and wild; a three-day cold peat fire and citrus; t23 sma' still copperiness, a touch of honeycomb 'n' apple to the metallic sheen; f23 long, remaining on that coppery theme but now the peats gather for a rich finale; b23 you get the feeling that this is made in an ancient still. Lush and rich all the way. How long before we see it in the Scarlet Bar? **60.1%**

⠿ **Bakery Hill Peated Malt Cask Strength** db **(89)** n23 clean, the usual citrus house-style; the peats are a bit laid-back but charming; t23 stunningly refreshing with superb soft oils for the sweet peat to melt into; f21 a minor vanilla fest and some coppery sharpness; b22 another really lovely malt from this outstanding distillery. **60.1%**

## BOOIE RANGE DISTILLERY

**Booie Range Single Malt** db **(72)** n14 t20 f19 b19. Mounts the hurdle of the wildly off-key nose impressively with a distinct, mouth watering barley richness to the palate that really does blossom even on the finish. **40%**

## TASMAN DISTILLERY

**Great Outback Rare Old Australian Single Malt** **(92)** n24 I could stick my nose in a glass of this all day. This is sensational: more a question of what we don't have here! The malt is clean, beautifully defined and dovetails with refined, orangey-citrus notes. The oak is near perfection adding only a degree of tempered weight. I don't detect peat, but there is some compensating Blue Mountain coffee; t24 just so beautifully textured with countless waves of clean, rich malt neither too sweet nor too dry. This is faultless distillate; f21 lightens considerably with the oak vanilla dominating; b23 What can you say? An Australian whisky distillery makes a malt to grace the world's stage. But you can't find it outside of Australia. This will have to be rectified. *Strength not known.*

## LARK DISTILLERY

**Lark Distillery Single Malt Single Cask Bottled April 01** db **(88) n**22 apples and cinnamon: other peppery spices dig in to the oily malt; **t**22 massively malty, clean and fruity with a powdery oak offering further complexity; oily and fat; **f**22 beautifully spiced and delicate with fluttering malty tones caressing the palate; **b**22 this is lovely whisky, superbly made and offering both guile and charisma. Congratulations: Australia has entered the ranks of serious whisky distilling nations. **40%**

**Lark Distillery Single Malt Single Cask Bottled Jan 03** db **(83) n**19 **t**21 **f**22 **b**21. Again big malt intensity but the body is thinner, the finish, as the malts begin to show their complexity, is brilliant. A superb dram with a slight nose blemish. **40%**

**Lark Distillery Single Malt Whisky** Sept 03 db **(79) n**18 **t**21 **f**20 **b**20 this has to be the Jekyll and Hyde of malt whisky. Taste it direct from the bottle and the feints trouble you. Allow it to breath in the glass for an hour and burn off the oils and you are left with a superbly peated malt of great character. Patience is certainly a virtue with this one. *(My marks are an average between the two)*.

## SMALL CONCERN DISTILLERY

**Cradle Mountain Pure Tasmanian Malt (87) n**21 curiously vivid bourbon character; sweet vanilla with hints of tangerine and hazelnut. Really very, very attractive; **t**22 an almost perfect translation onto the palate: gloriously sweet and gently nutty. The mouthfeel and body is firm and oily at the same time, the barley sparkles as the oak fades. Exceptionally subtle, clean and well made; **f**21 pretty long with some cocoa offering a praline effect; **b**23 a knock-out malt from a sadly now lost distillery in Tasmania. Faultlessly clean stuff with lots of new oak character but sufficient body to guarantee complexity. **43%**

⋰ **Cadenhead's World Whiskies Cradle Mountain Aged 10 Years** Ex Cabernet Sauvignon barrel, bott Sept 06 **(71) n**14 **t**19 **f**20 **b**18. Entirely baffling whisky. The Cab Sauv cask is horrendous and not helped by some feints, but what happens next is bemusing: it has every hallmark of rum. Had this not been sent to me as a whisky, I'd have never guessed. That said, some decent notes beyond the nose. **57.9%**. *270 bottles.*

## TASMANIA DISTILLERY

**Old Hobart** db **(69) n**16 **t**19 **f**17 **b**17. The nose still has some way to go before it can be accepted as a mainstream malt, though there is something more than a little coastal about it this time. However, the arrival on the palate is another matter and I must say I kind of enjoyed its big, oily and increasingly sweet maltiness and crushed sunflower seed nuttiness towards the end. Green (and yellow) shoots are growing. The whisky is unquestionably getting better. **40%**

**Old Hobart** db **(78) n**18 **t**20 **f**21 **b**19. Ground-breaking stuff. The first-ever truly drinkable whisky from the Tasmania Distillery. An impressive double whammy of virgin oak and fresh Australian port wood manages to overpower the usual ugly aroma that offers little more than a minor blemish. Some bite and spice on the finish guarantees complexity to a fruity procession. **60%**. *(2003 bottling)*.

**Sullivan's Cove** db **(61) n**13 **t**15 **f**17 **b**16. Some malt but typically grim, oily and dirty; awesomely weird. **40%**. *(2003 bottling). Australia.*

**Sullivan's Cove Classic** (capped with a black seal) db **(64) n**15 **t**16 **f**17 **b**16. A feinty dram, off-key and in need of a good tidy-up, though much better and cleaner than the gold seal. As this is a distillery's first attempt, I would rather encourage than fire off shells at a soft target. My advice is always to buy a bottle and see how a new distillery evolves. Again, the whisky can be improved dramatically by heating the glass in your hand to burn off the excess oils. **40%**

**Sullivan's Cove Classic** (capped with a gold seal) db **(58) n**12 **t**15 **f**16 **b**15. Feinty with a weird aroma of rotting vegetables on top. Some malt gurgles through, but it's not a pleasant experience. The gold cap and seal at the top was used only by the founders of the distillery and therefore represents the first-ever bottlings from Sullivan's Cove. **40%**

⫶ **Sullivans Cove Single Malt Whisky 6 Years Old** Bourbon maturation cask no. HH0274 db **(95) n**23 rich and intense, there is a lovely jammy fruitiness attached to the big barley; **t**24 barley concentrate with a dab of golden syrup and raspberry jam towards the middle. The body and weight are nigh perfect. Sensational!!; **f**24 lovely strands of vanilla interplay with the barley and then cocoa to see out the lightly oiled finish; **b**24 great on these guys. This must be the biggest Australian comeback since Larwood and Voce taught them how to bowl. A distillery once understandably a byword for less than brilliant whisky has come up with something that is truly beautiful. When I was in their warehouse a few years back, I detected the odd cracking cask, so knew their future could be bright. But perhaps not quite this brilliant...! **60%**

⫶ **Sullivans Cove Single Malt Whisky 6 Years Old** Port maturation cask no. HH0571 db **(90) n**23 so much grape but enough room for lots of natural caramel and vanilla; **t**23 lush, grapey delivery, which is no surprise. Excellent spice burst in the middle; **f**22 those caramels begin to spread; **b**22 high quality whisky helped by some pretty top dog casks. **60%**

⫶ **Sullivans Cove Single Malt Whisky 6 Years Old** Matured in French Oak Port and American Oak Bourbon casks db **(88) n**22 butterscotch tart, grape juice and barley in just-so portions; **t**23 oak-led and dry with just enough clean barley to sweeten the edge; **f**21 vanilla and toast breeze through to the finish; **b**22 subtle and sensuous. A bit like your average Tasmanian... **40%**

# BRAZIL
## HEUBLEIN DISTILLERY
**Durfee Hall Malt Whisky (81) n**18 **t**22 **f**20 **b**21. Superbly made whisky; the intensity of the malt is beautifully layered without ever becoming too sweet. Very light bodied and immaculately clean. Good whisky by any standards. **43%**

## UNION DISTILLERY
**Barrilete (72) n**18 **t**19 **f**18 **b**17. Nothing particularly wrong with it technically; it just lacks vitality. Thin but extremely malt intense. **39.1%**

## Blends
**Cockland Gold Blended Whisky (73) n**18 **t**18 **f**19 **b**18. Silky caramel. Traces of malt there, but never quite gets it up. **38%**. *Fante.*

**Green Valley Special Reserve** batch 07/01 **(70) n**16 **t**19 **f**17 **b**18. A softly oiled, gently bitter-sweet blend with a half meaty, half boiled sweet nose. An unusual whisky experience. **38.1%**. *Muraro & Cia.*

**Natu Nobilis** batch 277929A **(81) n**19 **t**21 **f**20 **b**21. The grain is sympathetic and soft; the malt is shy but makes telling, complex interceptions. Very easy and enjoyable dramming. **39%**. *Seagram do Brasil.*

**Malte Barrilete Blended Whisky** batch 001/03 **(76) n**18 **t**20 **f**19 **b**19. This brand has picked up a distinctive apple-fruitiness in recent years and some extra oak, too. **39.1%**. *Union Distillery.*

**O Monge** batch 02/02 **(69) n**17 **t**18 **f**17 **b**17. Poor nose but it recovers with a malty mouth arrival but the thinness of the grain does few favours. **38.5%**. *Union Distillery.*

**Old Eight (83) n**22 **t**20 **f**20 **b**21. A decent, very lightly peated blend with no shortage of grain. **39%**

**Pitt's (84) n**21 **t**20 **f**22 **b**21. The pits it certainly aint!! A beautifully malted blend where the barley tries to dominate the exceptionally flinty grain whenever possible. Due to be launched later in 2004, this will be the best Brazil has to offer – though some fine tuning can probably improve the nose and middle even further and up the complexity significantly. I hope, when I visit the distillery early in 2005, I will be able to persuade them to offer a single malt: on this evidence it should, like Pitt's, be an enjoyable experience and perfect company for any World Cup finals. **40%**. *Busnello Distillery*.

# INDIA
## AMRUT DISTILLERY

**Amrut Single Malt** B.No.01 25-2-04 db**(82)** n20 t22 f19 **b**21. A very decent quality single malt easily mistaken for a Speysider at about 35 or 36 years. That, usually, isn't always good. However, the sweet richness of the malt on the palate is a joy, with a boundless energy that pulses through to the prickly, oaky finish. Solid, honest whisky (with a non-scotch flourish at the finish) that would, after a black coffee, follow the finest Chicken Korma. (If you want to know more about Indian whisky, find the chapter on the distilleries I visited there in Jim Murray's Complete Book of Whisky). **40%. ncf.**

⋙ **Amrut Cask Strength** dist 6 May 01, bott May 06 db **(94)** n24 vibrant blood oranges with a sugar-coated vanilla topping. Clean and classy; t23 early arrival of rich, bourbony oak offers a momentarily dry start but sweet barley is not far behind. Bitter-ish honeycomb which sweetens in layers until the middle: a sumptuous battle between oak and barley with no winners..or losers; f23 an essay in chewability: wave upon wave of contradictory sweet and dry notes forged by the enormous confidence of high quality oak and intense malt; **b**24 From the moment you take in the aroma, stunningly structured with the citrus overture teasingly overtaken by the near near-perfect harmonization of vanilla and barley, you know you are if for a rare treat. Certainly the best non-peated Indian single malt to hit the international market. **62.8%**

⋙ **Amrut Cask Strength** dist 6 May 02, bott May 06 db **(92)** n23 chunky, dry, forests of fresh oak – even an unmistakable, and delightful, degree of bourbon which provides the required sweetness. And with an additional touch of seaweed and sea salt we have India's first coastal aroma; t23 lush, slightly viscous with spices clutching the palate and punctuating the soft barley; f22 oak arrives, but at a slower rate than the nose suggests but retains balance at all stages with the sweet, rich barley; **b**24 it is impossible not to be impressed with a sub-continental showstopper like this. Broad brushes here rather than delicate pastels but the balance is awesome. **62.6%**

## PONDA DISTILLERY

⋙ **Stillman's Dram Single Malt Whisky Limited Edition** Bourbon cask ref. 11186-90 **(94)** n23 beautifully soft peats fuse with lime-led citrus notes. At once delicate and enormous; t23 softly smoked malts dissolve into honeyed pools on the palate. Sexier and more relaxing than a Goan foot massage; f24 the way the delicate oak washes gently against the palate, the manner in which the soft peats build to a crescendo - and yet still refuse to overpower – the entrancing waves of muscovado-sweetened coffee, all make for a sublime finale; **b**24 well, I thought I had tasted it all with the Amrut cask strength. And then this arrived at my lab...!! I predicted many years back that India would dish out some top grade malt before too long. But I'd be stretching the truth if I said I thought it would ever be this good... **42.8%**. *McDowell & Co Ltd, India*.

# Blends

⋙ **Antiquity** Blend of Rare Scotch and matured Indian malts, bott 14.2.06 **(79)** n20 t21 f19 **b**19. Uncluttered but clever in places with a silky and distinctly malty delivery on the palate; the oak – not noticeable on the nose - dominates the finish intertwined with toffee-caramel. Attractive, but never quite works out which direction it is going. **42.8%**. *Shaw Wallace Distilleries, India. No added flavours.*

⋙ **Antiquity Blue** bott Oct 05 **(85)** n19 t23 f21 **b**22. A deliciously subtle smoky edge to this guarantees excellent weight and chewability throughout. Hugely enjoyable. **42.8%.** *Shaw Wallace Distilleries, India. No added flavours.*

⠿ **Blenders Pride** Blend of imported Scotch malts and select Indian grain spirits, bott Sept 05 **(74) n**19 **t**20 **f**17 **b**18. The rich mouth arrival descends into dullness: don't know too many blenders who would be proud of that! **42.8%.** *Seagram Distilleries, India.*

⠿ **Peter Scot Malt Whisky (84) n**20 **t**21 **f**22 **b**21. Enjoyable balance between sweetness and oak and entertainingly enlivened by what appears to be some young, juicy malt. **42.8%.** *Khoday India Limited.*

⠿ **Royal Challenge** A blend of rare Scotch and Matured Indian Malt Whiskies, batch no. 350, bott 29 Dec 05 **(78) n**21 **t**20 **f**18 **b**19. A clean, exceptionally firm blend that could do with a little lift on the finish. **42.8%.** *Shaw Wallace Distilleries, India.*

⠿ **Royal Stag** A blend of imported Scotch malts and select Indian grain spirits, batch no. 068, 27 Feb 06 **(90) n**20 firm, clean good oak and barley presence; **t**23 crisp, refreshing Speyside-style malt dominates early; **f**24 attractive drying cocoa and spice prickle; gathering sweetness and even a touch of something very vaguely smoky; **b**23 thoroughly attractive, well-balanced and rewarding whisky by any standards: the finish is fabulous. Average nose part, just love it! **42.8%.** *Seagram's/Gemini Distilleries, India.*

⠿ **Signature** Batch no. 01, bott Dec 05 **(87) n**20 very young, Bowmore-esque tint that needs an extra dimension; **t**23 superb mouth arrival that luxuriates in an softly oiled and delicate peatiness. Other grassy malts also abound and makes for a mouth-watering experience; **f**22 plenty of vanilla and a curious bitter cherry sharpness amid the smoke and cocoa; **b**22 there is an appealing youthfulness to this whisky and no little complexity, nose apart. An enjoyable and rewarding journey. **42.8%.** *McDowell & Co Ltd, India.*

# NEW ZEALAND
## WILSON DISTILLERY

⠿ **Milford Aged 10 Years** Batch 321M42, dist 93, bott 04 db **(89) n**20 less than impressive with a touch of soap; **t**23 fresh, grassy barley with a mildly metallic hardness; **f**23 waves of vanilla, soft spices and that continuing grassy, metallic theme; **b**23 what a shame that the Wilson distillery is not still extant and rich new make was being filled into some high quality bourbon casks. **43%.** *4780 bottles.*

**Milford Aged 10 Years Limited Edition** dist 91 bott Aug 02 batch no. F9/0/08 **(89) n**22 mildly minty, dry oak suppressing slightly the barley-sugar sweetness; gentle peat adds lovely depth; **t**23 rich, clean malt then that superb, trademark Wilson distillery fizz accompanying that delicate smoke; **f**21 softer oaky notes but some brittle peat offers some length to an otherwise abrupt finish; **b**23 charming yet always busy on the palate. **43%** *New Zealand Malt Whisky Co. 5573 bottles.*

**Milford Aged 12 Years Limited Edition** dist 90 bott Oct 02 batch no. E50/0 **(88) n**22 firm, crisp barley; the oak is dry despite a faint burbony character; a slight shake of black pepper; **t**24 beautifully mouth-watering and rich, the malt is stunningly intense and its usual ultra-clean self. A little bite and fizz towards the middle; **f**20 quite light, short and a touch thin; **b**22 the mouth arrival and barley lift-off is the stuff of New Zealand whisky legend; only the closed finish prevents this being a major classic. Excellent whisky. **43%.** *New Zealand Malt Whisky Co. 2840 bottles.*

⠿ **Milford Aged 15 Years** Batch 89M414, dist 88, bott 04 db **(91) n**21 battling, lively vanilla with the barley. Even the most distant hint of coal smoke; **t**24 beautiful barley delivery that shows remarkable freshness and zest. Lubeck marzipan offers a mild nutty sweetness, bringing with it some soft oaks which cranks up the complexity towards the middle; **f**23 light with strands of vanilla and a touch of citrus; **b**23 quality whisky though slightly flattened by age but shows enough early on to confirm its class. **43%.** *1878 bottles.*

**Lammerlaw Aged 12 Years Peated Malt Sherry Cask Finishing (85)** n22 t19 f23 b21. Gets over the hurdle of the rough start to finish how it began on the nose: wonderfully! **50%. nc ncf.** *From Wilson Distillery, though it says Willowbank on the label.*

**Cadenhead's Lammerlaw 10 Years Old (88)** n22 big, fresh malt with a drying, chalky oak influence; t23 mouthwatering, clean, juicy malt. A touch of salt seasons it; complexity is further aided by warming spices and the most subtle hints of citrus; f21 back to that drying, chalky oak; b22 seriously sensuous and complex malt from a tragically lost distillery. Pure New Zealand, but Speyside in style, and its complexity puts a good number of Speysiders to shame. **48.2%**

⁂ **Cadenhead's World Whiskies Lammerlaw Aged 10 Years** bott May 06 **(90)** n 21 very slightly soapy; fabulous citrus tries to lift it; t22 rich, juicy barley overcomes that soap; f24 beautiful orangey notes link heavenly with the barley; b23 not even a sub-standard bourbon cask can ruin this beautiful malt. **47.3%.**

⁂ **Cadenhead's World Whiskies Lammerlaw Aged 10 Years** Bourbon, bott Sept 06 **(90)** n22 dry oak forms an elegant structure on which the crisp barley hangs; t23 sensuous and mouth-watering dovetailing of crystal-clear, fruity malt and balancing oak; f22 as dry as the nose with the usual cocoa-oak suspects; b23 one could almost weep for the loss of this unique distillery. The malt, in this classy and delicate form, is comparable with Speyside's finest. **47.7%.** *222 bottles.*

**Meenan's Lammerlaw 12 Years Old (90)** n23 beautifully honeyed, with lavender and a very distant rumble of peat: the oak suggests something older; t23 an outstanding delivery of soft, fruity malts, a layer of sweet honey and some oak and distant smoke; f23 heaps of vanilla and soft spice and a gradual build-up of something peaty; b23 this is a genuinely complex, beautifully made malt where the oak makes a wonderful divergence. A classic from any continent. **50%.** *Available only in New Zealand.*

## Blends

**Kiwi Whisky (37)** n2 t12 f11 b12. Strewth! I mean, what can you say? Perhaps the first whisky containing single malt offering virtually no nose at all and the flavour appears to be grain neutral spirit plus lashings of caramel and (so I am told) some Lammerlaw single malt. The word bland has been redefined. As has whisky. **40%.** *Ever-Rising Enterprises, NZ, for the Asian market.*

**Wilson's Superior Blend (89)** n22 stupendously clean and malt rich. Imperiously mouthwatering and enticing; t23 brilliant, almost dazzling clean malt arrival sharpened even further with mildly though distant crisp grain. One of the world's maltiest, most salivating blends, perhaps a touch simplistic but the charm of the malt endures while the ultra-delicate oak offers a teasing weight; f21 loses marks only because of a caramel-induced toffee arrival, but still the malt and grain are in perfect sync while the drying oak offers balance; b23 apparently has a mixed reception in its native New Zealand but I fail to see why: this is unambiguously outstanding blended whisky. On the nose you expect a mouthwatering mouthful and it delivers with aplomb. Despite this being a lower priced blend it is, intriguingly, a marriage of 60% original bottled 10-y-o Lammerlaw and 40% old Wilson's blend, explaining the high malt apparent. Dangerous and delicious and would be better still at a fuller strength...and with less caramel. **37.5%.** *Continental Wines and Spirits, NZ.*

## SOUTH AFRICA
### Single malt
#### JAMES SEDGWICK DISTILLERY

**Three Ships 10 Years Old** db **(83)** n21 t21 f20 b21. Seems to have changed character, with more emphasis on sherry and natural toffee. The oak offers a thrusting undercurrent. **43%**

## Blends

**Harrier (87) n**20 bit of a culture clash but is pretty tactile; **t**22 sweet and silky with a wonderful spice development; **f**23 more cotton and silk but with stunning smoke guaranteeing length, weight and style; **b**22 this guy is getting better and better. An extra dose of smoke has given it great poise and body. Harrier is taking off. **43%.** *South African/Scotch Whisky.* ⊙ ⊙

**Knights (77) n**19 **t**20 **f**19 **b**19. Sweet, pleasant, but a little flat. **43%.** *South African/Scotch Whisky.* ⊙

**Three Ships Bourbon Cask Finish** db **(91) n**22 sweet, biscuity malt and the mildest glazed ginger; **t**23 the best arrival of any South African whisky: the softness and sheen is exemplary, and the follow-through is of wonderfully gentle malt-oak complexity; **f**23 just so many layers of delicate oak, yet never over-dries or appears too old; **b**23 a minor classic here, with the emphasis being on a mouthwatering lushness. **43%** ⊙

**Three Ships 5 Years Old (89) n**22 sweet gristy peat and a unique hint of mildly roasted Colombian (coffee...!); **t**22 young, chewy, sweet peat of a Bowmore variety, softened and thinned by the trademark velvet grain; **f**23 long, spiced and elegant; **b**22 first-rate blending: it is as if they are beginning to understand the balancing values of their own whiskies. **43%.** *South African/Scotch Whisky.* ⊙

∴ **Three Ships Original (82) n**19 **t**22 **f**21 **b**20. Not sure if this is meant to be the 3-yo. Certainly has different character, being smokeless save perhaps some late, late spice. Great grains, though. **43%**

## MISCELLANEOUS

**Jaburn & Co Pure Grain & Malt Spirit (53) n**14 **t**13 **f**13 **b**13. Tastes like neutral grain and caramel to me. Some shop keepers, I hear, are selling it as whisky though this is not claimed on the label. Trust me: it isn't. **37.5%.** *Jaburn & Co, Denmark.*

**House of Westend Blended Whisky (67) n**17 **t**18 **f**16 **b**16. No more than OK if you are being generous; some tobacco-dirty notes around. Doesn't mention country of origin anywhere on the label. **40%.** *Bernkasteler Burghof, Germany.*

**Prince of Wales Welsh Whisky (69) n**17 **t**18 **f**17 **b**17. A syrupy aroma is compounded by an almost liqueurish body. Thin in true Scotch substance, probably because it claims to be Welsh but is really Scotch with herbs diffused in a process that took place in Wales. Interestingly, my "liqueur" tasting notes were written before I knew exactly what it was I was tasting, thus proving the point and confirming that, with these additives, this really isn't whisky at all. **40%**

**Shepherd's Export Finest Blend (46) n**5 **t**16 **f**12 **b**13. A dreadful, illdefined grain-spirit nose is softened on the palate by an early mega-sweet kick. The finish is thin and eventually bitter. Feeble stuff. **37.2%.** *"A superb blend of Imported Scotch Malt whiskies and Distilled N.Z. grain spirit", claims the label which originally gives the strength as 40%, but has been over-written. Also, the grain, I was told, was from the USA. Southern Grain Spirit, NZ.*

## CROSS-COUNTRY VATTED MALT

**Cradle Mountain** db **(77) n**19 **t**21 **f**18 **b**19. Doesn't quite gel for me, though it has some delicious malty moments. **46%.** *This is a vatting of Aussie malt from Cradle Mountain and Springbank single malt scotch.*

**Cradle Mountain Double** db **(88) n**20 no shortage of fruit with tangerines and diced green apples to the fore; **t**23 in your face malt of almost awesome intensity. Lashings of clean barley, grassy notes showing both age and youth; **f**23 lingers at first, then the Cradle Mountain signature of fruit and nuts descends. Also the cocoa is back with some serious oak present but always in control; **b**22 this appears to be a different vatting to the 46% with greater Tasmanian whisky evident – although it isn't! Much more poise and zest and no shortage of charisma. Brilliant stuff. **54.4%.** *This is a vatting of Aussie malt from Cradle Mountain and single malt scotch from Springbank.*

⸫ **Jon, Mark and Robbo's The Smooth Sweeter One** a vatting of Scottish and Irish malt **(92) n**24 a real citrus and grassy kick to this with soft vanilla offering only a background noise. So delicate, you feel it might shatter if you nose too hard; **t**22 fresh and fruity; **f**23 long with some genuine complexity in the gently-spiced waves;controlled barley sweetness but drier vanillas dominate with those spices at the end; **b**23 a beautiful whisky. Intriguing as it may be, claims I have heard of this being the first such whisky of its type are way off mark – not to mention Jon and Robbo. A hundred years ago and more it was not uncommon to find bottled malt whisky being a combination of Scotch and Irish. It would have come under the general title "whisky" and brought together by merchants procuring whiskies at the best prices they could get. In my library somewhere I have old labels of these forebears. That said, those whiskies of a century ago would have been hard pushed to better it. **40%.** *Edrington.*

⸫ **Premium Bottler Vatted Malt Whisky Aged 10 Years** ACHN 102 (99% Auchentoshan Scotch, 1% Glenora Canadian) **(84) n**21 **t**22 **f**20 **b**21. Very young, enormously citrussy effort with all the usual Auchtoshan foibles. Coming from a third fill makes for interesting dramming. **46%. nc ncf.**

⸫ **Premium Bottler Vatted Malt Whisky Aged 12 Years** GLLS 101 (99% Glen Lossie Scotch, 1% Glenora Canadian) **(86) n**21 **t**22 **f**22 **b**21. Very drinkable, pre-pubescent Lossie. Beware the false finale: it appears to vanish for a short finish and then reappears even more intensely than before. **46%. nc ncf.**

⸫ **Premium Bottler Vatted Malt Whisky Aged 12 Years** MRTL 101 (99% Mortlach Scotch, 1% Glenora Canadian) **(83) n**21 **t**20 **f**21 **b**21. Very decent heavyweight despite the lack of oak involvement. Excellent natural oils. **46%. nc ncf**

⸫ **Premium Bottler Vatted Malt Whisky Aged 10 Years** SCAP 101 (99% Scapa Scotch, 1% Glenora Canadian) **(90) n**23 stewing apples form the centre ground of this astonishingly young, new make-coated aroma. As refreshing as a face full of driven rain; **t**23 that glorious freshness now turns into something so salivating you'll have to drink a pint of water ahead of time to survive. Rarely is barley this concentrated; **f**22 layering of intense barley continues, with just a drying coffee to offer the required balance; **b**22 absolutely amazing malt. This Scapa, from a third-fill bourbon cask one assumes, appears half its age and simply glories in its natural brilliance. If this doesn't prove what world-great whisky this distillery conjures up in its most simple form, nothing will. **46%. nc ncf.**

⸫ **Premium Bottler Vatted Malt Whisky Aged 10 Years** STRT 101 (99% Strathisla Scotch, 1% Glenora Canadian) **(86) n**20 **t**22 **f**23 **b**21. Early evidence, on the nose particularly, of an over-tired cask but the natural exuberance and lustre of the distillate carries it through. Wonderfully chewy in part. **46%. nc ncf.**